Lecture Notes in Computer Science   16515

Founding Editors

Gerhard Goos
Juris Hartmanis

Editorial Board Members

Elisa Bertino, *Purdue University, West Lafayette, IN, USA*
Wen Gao, *Peking University, Beijing, China*
Bernhard Steffen, *TU Dortmund University, Dortmund, Germany*
Moti Yung, *Columbia University, New York, NY, USA*

The series Lecture Notes in Computer Science (LNCS), including its subseries Lecture Notes in Artificial Intelligence (LNAI) and Lecture Notes in Bioinformatics (LNBI), has established itself as a medium for the publication of new developments in computer science and information technology research, teaching, and education.

LNCS enjoys close cooperation with the computer science R & D community, the series counts many renowned academics among its volume editors and paper authors, and collaborates with prestigious societies. Its mission is to serve this international community by providing an invaluable service, mainly focused on the publication of conference and workshop proceedings and postproceedings. LNCS commenced publication in 1973.

Roderich Groß · Aaron T. Becker ·
Gianni A. Di Caro · Bahar Haghighat ·
M. Ani Hsieh · Razanne Abu-Aisheh ·
Mohamed S. Talamali · Marco Dorigo
Editors

Swarm Intelligence

15th International Conference, ANTS 2026
Darmstadt, Germany, June 8–10, 2026
Proceedings

 Springer

Editors
Roderich Groß
Technical University of Darmstadt
Darmstadt, Germany

Gianni A. Di Caro
Carnegie Mellon University in Qatar
Doha, Qatar

M. Ani Hsieh
University of Pennsylvania
Philadelphia, PA, USA

Mohamed S. Talamali
University of Sheffield
Sheffield, UK

Aaron T. Becker
University of Houston
Houston, TX, USA

Bahar Haghighat
University of Groningen
Groningen, The Netherlands

Razanne Abu-Aisheh
University of Bristol
Bristol, UK

Marco Dorigo
Université libre de Bruxelles
Bruxelles, Belgium

ISSN 0302-9743   ISSN 1611-3349 (electronic)
Lecture Notes in Computer Science
ISBN 978-3-032-26122-9   ISBN 978-3-032-26123-6 (eBook)
https://doi.org/10.1007/978-3-032-26123-6

This Springer imprint is published by the registered company Springer Nature Switzerland AG
The registered company address is: Gewerbestrasse 11, 6330 Cham, Switzerland

If disposing of this product, please recycle the paper.

Preface

These proceedings contain the papers presented at ANTS 2026, the 15th International Conference on Swarm Intelligence, held from June 8–10, 2026 in Darmstadt, Germany.

The ANTS conference series began in 1998 with the First International Workshop on Ant Colony Optimization (ANTS'98), held in Brussels and organized by Marco Dorigo. Since then, ANTS has been held biennially and has evolved into a leading international forum for researchers in the broader field of swarm intelligence. In 2004, this evolution was acknowledged by the inclusion of the term *Swarm Intelligence* alongside *Ant Colony Optimization* in the conference title. From 2010 onward, the conference has been officially devoted to the field of swarm intelligence as a whole, without bias toward specific methodologies or research directions. This is reflected in its current title: *International Conference on Swarm Intelligence.*

This volume contains 55 papers selected from 93 submissions. Of these, 21 were accepted as full-length papers and 21 as short papers, resulting in an overall acceptance rate of approximately 45%. Also included in this volume are 13 extended abstracts. Submissions received an average of four single-blind reviews. All accepted contributions were presented either in plenary oral sessions or in poster sessions.

The theme of the 2026 edition, "Reaching beyond—swarm intelligence across systems, disciplines, and communities", encouraged new perspectives, helping to bridge traditional boundaries and enabling open debate on what could be ambitious, exploratory, and groundbreaking endeavors to embark on. In addition to the regular call for papers, the conference also invited lightning talks and poster presentations from researchers studying self-organizing systems across the sciences and the humanities, thereby fostering a fruitful interdisciplinary exchange.

We gratefully acknowledge the many individuals and organizations who contributed to the success of ANTS 2026. We thank the authors for submitting their work, the members of the International Program Committee, and the additional referees for their thorough and insightful reviews. We thank Guido de Croon (Delft University of Technology), Sharon Glotzer (University of Michigan), and Jesús Gómez-Gardeñes (University of Zaragoza) for their invited plenary talks and Meeyoung Cha (Max Planck Institute for Security and Privacy and Korea Advanced Institute of Science and Technology), Thomas Watteyne (Analog Devices) and Liam Young (SCI Arc) for their invited perspective talks. Finally, we gratefully acknowledge the support of the conference sponsors, including emergenCITY (platinum sponsor), fictionlab, NOKOV, and Siemens (silver sponsors), and the Robotics Institute Germany (technical co-sponsor).

We hope that this collection of papers serves both as a valuable reference documenting current advances in swarm intelligence and as a source of inspiration for future research in swarm intelligence and related fields.

June 2026

Roderich Groß
Aaron T. Becker
Gianni A. Di Caro
Bahar Haghighat
M. Ani Hsieh
Razanne Abu-Aisheh
Mohamed S. Talamali
Marco Dorigo

Organization

General Chair

Roderich Groß   Technical University of Darmstadt, Germany

Honorary Chair

Marco Dorigo   Université libre de Bruxelles, Belgium

Technical Program Chairs

Aaron T. Becker   University of Houston, USA
Gianni Di Caro   Carnegie Mellon University, Qatar
Bahar Haghighat   University of Groningen, The Netherlands
M. Ani Hsieh   University of Pennsylvania, USA

Conference Theme and Publicity Chair

Razanne Abu-Aisheh   University of Bristol, UK

Finance Chair

Grace McFassel   Technical University of Darmstadt, Germany

Publication Chair

Mohamed S. Talamali   University of Sheffield, UK

Paper Submission Chair

Julian Rau	Technical University of Darmstadt, Germany

Local Organization Committee

Usama Ali	Technical University of Darmstadt, Germany
Uta Drews	Technical University of Darmstadt, Germany
Ecem Isildar	Technical University of Darmstadt, Germany
Suet Lee	Technical University of Darmstadt, Germany
Jenny von Trzebiatowski	Technical University of Darmstadt, Germany

Steering Committee

Marco Dorigo	Université libre de Bruxelles, Belgium
Andries Engelbrecht	Stellenbosch University, South Africa
Heiko Hamann	University of Konstanz, Germany
Alcherio Martinoli	École polytechnique fédérale de Lausanne, Switzerland
Radhika Nagpal	Princeton University, USA
Thomas Stützle	Université libre de Bruxelles, Belgium
Guy Theraulaz	CNRS CRCA, France

Program Committee

Aigul Adamova	Astana IT University, Kazakhstan
Julie Adams	Oregon State University, USA
Saurav Agarwal	University of Pennsylvania, USA
Dario Albani	Technology Innovation Institute, UAE
Hande Alemdar	Middle East Technical University, Türkiye
Merihan Alhafnawi	Princeton University, USA
Khulud Alharthi	University of Bristol, UK
Christine Allen-Blanchette	Princeton University, USA
Francesco Amigoni	Politecnico di Milano, Italy
Martyn Amos	Northumbria University, UK
Rosario Aragüés	Universidad de Zaragoza, Spain
Farshad Arvin	Durham University, UK
Anna Bakenecker	Technical University of Darmstadt, Germany
Jagdish Chand Bansal	South Asian University, India
Palina Bartashevich	Humboldt University of Berlin, Germany
Jacob Beal	Raytheon BBN, USA

Giovanni Beltrame	Polytechnique Montréal, Canada
Spring Berman	Arizona State University, USA
Christian Bettstetter	University of Klagenfurt, Austria
Anastasia Bizyaeva	Cornell University, USA
Johanna Blee	University of Bristol, UK
Christian Blum	Artificial Intelligence Research Institute, Spain
Roland Bouffanais	University of Geneva, Switzerland
Nicolas Bredèche	Sorbonne Université, France
Daniel Brown	University of Utah, USA
Alfred Bruckstein	Technion – Israel Institute of Technology, Israel
David C. Burnett	Villanova University, USA
Christian Camacho	Université libre de Bruxelles, Belgium
Timoteo Carletti	University of Namur, Belgium
Marco Castellani	University of Birmingham, UK
Davis Catherman	Worcester Polytechnic Institute, USA
Stephen Chen	York University, Canada
Anders Lyhne Christensen	University of Southern Denmark, Denmark
Mela Coffey	Boston University, USA
Óscar Cordón	Universidad de Granada, Spain
Michael Crosscombe	University of Tokyo, Japan
Philip Dames	Temple University, USA
Sanjoy Das	Kansas State University, USA
Guido de Croon	Delft University of Technology, The Netherlands
Gonzalo De Polavieja	Champalimaud Foundation, Portugal
Alessandro Di Stefano	Teesside University, UK
Karl Doerner	University of Vienna, Austria
Marco Dorigo	Université libre de Bruxelles, Belgium
Qiqi Duan	Southern University of Science and Technology, China
Victoria Edwards	University of Pennsylvania, USA
Mohammed El-Abd	American University of Kuwait, Kuwait
Ali Emre Turgut	Middle East Technical University, Türkiye
Andries Engelbrecht	University of Stellenbosch, South Africa
Chuchu Fan	Massachusetts Institute of Technology, USA
Sandor Fekete	Technische Universität Braunschweig, Germany
Eliseo Ferrante	Vrije Universiteit Amsterdam, The Netherlands
Manon Flageat	University of Cambridge, UK
Ryusuke Fujisawa	University of Kitakyushu, Japan
Hector Garcia de Marina	Universidad de Granada, Spain
José García-Nieto	University of Málaga, Spain
Simon Garnier	New Jersey Institute of Technology, USA
David Garzón Ramos	University College Dublin, Ireland

Ebi George	University of Lausanne, Switzerland
Debasish Ghose	Indian Institute of Science, India
Maria Gini	University of Minnesota, USA
Dan Goldman	Georgia Institute of Technology, USA
Heiko Hamann	University of Konstanz, Germany
Julia Handl	University of Manchester, UK
Negin Harandi	Ghent University, Belgium
Helen Harman	University of Lincoln, UK
Ken Hasselmann	Royal Military Academy, Belgium
Kiyohiko Hattori	University of Electro-Communications, Japan
Sabine Hauert	University of Bristol, UK
Tomohiro Hayakawa	Shizuoka University, Japan
Mary Katherine Heinrich	Université libre de Bruxelles, Belgium
Ayah Helal	Manchester Metropolitan University, UK
Mardé Helbig	Griffith University, Australia
Motoaki Hiraga	Kyoto Institute of Technology, Japan
Wolfgang Hönig	Technical University of Berlin, Germany
Junyan Hu	Durham University, UK
Danny Hughes	KU Leuven, Belgium
Edmund Hunt	University of Bristol, UK
Takashi Ikegami	University of Tokyo, Japan
Kaushik Jayaram	University of Colorado Boulder, USA
Yongnan Jia	University of Science and Technology Beijing, China
Simon Jones	University of Bristol, UK
Tanja K. Kaiser	University of Technology Nuremberg, Germany
Kathryn Kasmarik	University of New South Wales, Australia
Yuri Kaszubowski Lopes	Santa Catarina State University, Brazil
Yara Khaluf	Vrije Universiteit Amsterdam, The Netherlands
Solmaz Kia	University of California Irvine, USA
Andrew J. King	Swansea University, UK
Andreas Kolling	Amazon Robotics, USA
Tomas Krajnik	Czech Technical University in Prague, Czech Republic
Jonas Kuckling	University of Konstanz, Germany
Sandeep Ameet Kumar	University of the South Pacific, Fiji
Daisuke Kurabayashi	Tokyo Institute of Technology, Japan
Tin Lun Lam	Chinese University of Hong Kong, China
Suet Lee	Technical University of Darmstadt, Germany
Liang Li	University of Konstanz, Germany
Mengguang Li	Technical University of Darmstadt, Germany
Jing Liang	Zhengzhou University, China

Simone Ludwig	North Dakota State University, USA
Danna Ma	Cornell University, USA
Vittorio Maniezzo	University of Bologna, Italy
Alcherio Martinoli	École polytechnique fédérale de Lausanne, Switzerland
Bernd Meyer	Monash University, Australia
Genki Miyauchi	University of Sheffield, UK
Nicolas Monmarché	Université de Tours, France
Radhika Nagpal	Princeton University, USA
Changjoo Nam	Sogang University, South Korea
Arouna Ndam Njoya	Institut Universitaire de Technologie de Ngaoundéré, Cameroon
Frank Neumann	University of Adelaide, Australia
Tri-Hai Nguyen	Van Lang University, Vietnam
Geoff Nitschke	University of Cape Town, South Africa
Gennaro Notomista	University of Waterloo, Canada
Jason O'Kane	Texas A&M University, USA
Kazuhiro Ohkura	Hiroshima University, Japan
Ana Carolina Olivera	National Scientific and Technical Research Council, Argentina
Beatrice Ombuki-Berman	Brock University, Canada
Mahamed Omran	Abdullah Al Salem University, Kuwait
Jun Ota	University of Tokyo, Japan
Michael Otte	University of Maryland, College Park, USA
Sujit P. Baliyarasimhuni	Indian Institute of Science and Research Bhopal, India
Jacopo Panerati	Polytechnique Montréal, Canada
Shinkyu Park	King Abdullah University of Science and Technology, Saudi Arabia
Konstantinos Parsopoulos	University of Ioannina, Greece
Paola Pellegrini	Université Gustave Eiffel, France
Gilbert Peterson	US Air Force Institute of Technology, USA
Tatjana Petrov	University of Trieste, Italy
Carlo Pinciroli	Worcester Polytechnic Institute, USA
Benoît Piranda	FEMTO-ST Institute, CNRS, France
Leslie Pérez Cáceres	Pontificia Universidad Católica de Valparaíso, Chile
Alberto Quattrini Li	Dartmouth College, USA
Günther Raidl	Vienna University of Technology, Austria
Sneha Ramshanker	Princeton University, USA
Andreagiovanni Reina	Max Planck Institute of Animal Behavior, Germany
Andreas Reinhardt	Clausthal University of Technology, Germany

Rui P. Rocha	University of Coimbra, Portugal
Nicolás Rojas	Universidad Técnica Federico Santa María, Chile
Andrea Roli	University of Bologna, Italy
Pawel Romanczuk	Humboldt University of Berlin, Germany
Michael Rubenstein	Northwestern University, USA
Lorenzo Sabattini	University of Modena and Reggio Emilia, Italy
Brian Sadler	University of Texas at Austin, USA
Erol Sahin	Middle East Technical University, Türkiye
Mohammad Salahshour	Max Planck Institute of Animal Behavior, Germany
Guillaume Sartoretti	National University of Singapore, Singapore
Thomas Schmickl	University of Graz, Austria
Melanie Schranz	Lakeside Labs GmbH, Austria
Roman Senkerik	Tomas Bata University in Zlín, Czech Republic
Dylan Shell	Texas A&M University, USA
John W. Sheppard	Montana State University, USA
Masashi Shiraishi	Hiroshima City University, Japan
Himani Sinhmar	Princeton University, USA
Rebeca Solis-Ortega	Instituto Tecnológico de Costa Rica, Costa Rica
Karthik Soma	Polytechnique Montréal, Canada
Mohammad Soorati	University of Southampton, UK
Martin Stefanec	University of Graz, Austria
Kasper Stoy	IT University of Copenhagen, Denmark
Volker Strobel	Université libre de Bruxelles, Belgium
Daniel Stroembom	Lafayette College, USA
Thomas Stützle	Université libre de Bruxelles, Belgium
Dirk Sudholt	University of Passau, Germany
Petras Swissler	New Jersey Institute of Technology, USA
Katia Sycara	Carnegie Mellon University, USA
Kenneth Sörensen	University of Antwerp, Belgium
Mohamed S. Talamali	University of Sheffield, UK
Herbert Tanner	University of Delaware, USA
Danesh Tarapore	University of Southampton, UK
Guy Theraulaz	CNRS CRCA, France
Joseph Thomas	Google Cloud, USA
Ljiljana Trajkovic	Simon Fraser University, Canada
Vito Trianni	Istituto di Scienze e Tecnologie della Cognizione – Consiglio Nazionale delle Ricerche, Italy
Elio Tuci	Université de Namur, Belgium
Vivek Shankar Varadharajan	Polytechnique Montréal, Canada
Andrew Vardy	Memorial University of Newfoundland, Canada

Sebastian von Mammen	University of Würzburg, Germany
Vojtech Vonasek	Czech Technical University in Prague, Czech Republic
Mostafa Wahby	University of Lübeck, Germany
Rolf Wanka	Friedrich-Alexander-Universität Erlangen-Nürnberg, Germany
Thomas Watteyne	Analog Devices, USA
Tomer Weiss	New Jersey Institute of Technology, USA
Justin Werfel	Harvard University, USA
Malte Wirkus	DFKI, Germany
Carsten Witt	Technical University of Denmark, Denmark
Cheng Xu	University of Science and Technology Beijing, China
Shengxiang Yang	De Montfort University, UK
Toshiyuki Yasuda	University of Toyama, Japan
Raina Zakir	Université libre de Bruxelles, Belgium
Yating Zheng	Humboldt University of Berlin, Germany
Tamara Zhukabayeva	Eurasian National University, Kazakhstan

Additional Reviewers

Usama Ali
Nemanja Antonic
Burak Aslan
Simay Atasoy Bingol
Chanaka Bandara
Jesús Bautista Villar
Atakan Botasun
Sandip Chakraborty
Fei Chen
Yacine Derder
Tanishq Duhan
Wenke E.
Kagan Erunsal
Kunal Garg
Melvin Gauci
Jaskaran Grover
Jose Hinojosa
Paolo Leopardi
Jeric Lew

Ruochen Li
Chek-Manh Loi
Enric Morella
Honghao Pan
Guillem Rodríguez Corominas
Matthias Rössler
Udo Schilcher
Marcus Schref
Yu-Hsiang Su
Aymeric Vellinger
Tobias Wallner
Yusi Wei
Di Wu
Yang Xu
Khalil Youssefi
Mohsen Zahmatkesh
Songyuan Zhang
Panpan Zhou

Sponsoring Organizations

emergenCITY (Platinum Sponsor)
    www.emergencity.de

fictionlab (Silver Sponsor)
    www.fictionlab.pl

NOKOV (Silver Sponsor)
    www.nokov.com

Siemens (Silver Sponsor)
    www.siemens.com

SIEMENS

Springer Nature (Bronze Sponsor)
    www.springernature.com

SPRINGER NATURE

Technical University of Darmstadt (Bronze Sponsor)
    www.tu-darmstadt.de

Robotics Institute Germany (Technical Co-sponsor)
    www.robotics-institute-germany.de

Contents

Short Papers

Full Papers

A Fast Distributed Algorithm for Breakage Detection in Modular Robots

Ikrame Yazidi[1], Lucas Berthome[2], Morvan Ouisse[2] (ID),
and Benoit Piranda[1]([envelope]) (ID)

[1] Marie and Louis Pasteur University, FEMTO-ST Institute, CNRS, Monbéliard,
France
`benoit.piranda@umlp.fr`

[2] Marie and Louis Pasteur University, SUPMICROTECH, FEMTO-ST Institute,
CNRS, Besançon, France
`morvan.ouisse@umlp.fr`

Abstract. In this paper, we present a fully distributed method that allows a group of magnetically connected modular robots to assess the mechanical stability of their structure. Stability is verified based on four mechanical phenomena: vertical and rotational sliding and rotational debonding for vertical and lateral connectors. We present a mechanical model applicable to the *Blinky Blocks* robot system. We also propose an efficient, fully distributed algorithm that runs simultaneously on all robots, enabling them to check global stability and detect the type and the breakage positions. Our algorithmic solution avoids the global resolution of the system and is effective for both free-loop and complex loop or multi-loop configurations; for the latter, it systematically enumerates all possible spanning trees and traverses each one to assess the stability of the modular structure. The approach was validated both in simulation with *VisibleSim* and on real *Blinky Blocks* hardware. Experiments demonstrate accurate and robust detection of all four breakage types in a wide variety of configurations, with low computational overhead and excellent scalability. These results confirm that distributed spanning-tree-based analysis provides an effective alternative to solving global equilibrium equations in modular robotics, enabling reliable structural integrity assessment even in large and highly connected assemblies.

1 Introduction

Over the past 20 years, many studies have introduced the concept of programmable matter [1,3] as a solution for creating materials with new properties, such as changing color or shape on command from an integrated program. They have proposed hardware techniques and software solutions for creating the first self-reconfigurable robot systems [5,6,8–10].

Programmable matter consists of small, reconfigurable modular robots attached to one another in a regular grid. The concept of modular robots is

Supplementary Information The online version contains supplementary material available at https://doi.org/10.1007/978-3-032-26123-6_1.

important because it introduces the concept of autonomy: it is the elements that make up the material itself that modify an attribute such as their color or reorganize themselves to change the overall shape they construct. The first challenge proposed by Programmable matter is its requirement for small robots as they define the resolution of the objects they construct.

This brings us to the second major challenge raised by the concept of programmable matter, which is the issue of distributed programming. In order to establish consistent emergent behaviors among all robots, they must communicate and synchronize their actions. This large group of robots will therefore build a network and an associated graph that executes its processes within its nodes: the robots. The solution is provided by distributed programming algorithms, often carried out by distributed agents.

Despite their promising potential, a challenge remains: creating robust systems and algorithms that can respond to unforeseen situations caused by communication delays, missed travel deadlines, or module failures. Mechanical stability is a major concern for system robustness. Even if the robots are perfectly functional and the reconfiguration algorithm perfectly organizes their movements, the robots are subject to the mechanical stability of the system they build. Consequences of instability can include breaking an attachment link between modules, cutting the network between two modules due to excessive deformation of the link, or the system falling and deteriorating, which jeopardizes any future movement.

The majority of algorithms for planning and controlling the self-reconfiguration of modular robots assume that all motions verify stability criteria. Early work [7] proposed precise but iterative solutions that required excessive computation time and message counts for a system to use them in an auto-reconfiguration process. In [2], Bray and Groß used a distributed control strategy to reconfigure self-assembled structures that fill a void, while incorporating local force measurements to build structures that do not disintegrate under their own weight. However, autonomous reconfiguration planning that considers mechanical constraints remains an open and complex problem. A more recent work [12,13] has proposed dealing only with the validation of the balance of a configuration placed on the ground. This decision is made quickly by running through all the modules once. Three static mechanical phenomena will be addressed: slippage, tearing, and detachment. Our goal is to incorporate this tool into our auto-reconfiguration algorithms to verify structural stability before moving a module. Therefore, this process must be fast enough to evaluate multiple potential movements.

To illustrate the effectiveness of our approach, we will present several experiments using different numbers of modules. The verification is carried out in a dedicated simulator *VisibleSim* [11], as well as experimentally on real robotic modules *Blinky Blocks* [4].

2   Context

Blinky Blocks are centimeter-sized modular robots that are attached via permanent magnets (cf. Fig. 1(a)). Each block, approximately a 41 mm large cube,

Table 1. Quantities used in the paper.

Quantity	Parameter	Value	Variable	Expression	Value
Blinky Block width	a	$41\,\mathrm{mm}$	T_a	$\dfrac{f\,F_{magL}}{mg}$	14.5
Mass	m	$61.2\,\mathrm{g}$	T_b	$\dfrac{A f F_{\mathrm{magL}}}{6mg}$	4.77
Gravity	g	$9.81\,\mathrm{ms}^{-2}$	T_c	$\dfrac{h F_{\mathrm{magL}}}{mga}$	13.4
Friction coefficient	f	0.5	T_d	$\dfrac{F_{\mathrm{magV}}}{2mg} - \dfrac{1}{2}$	9.47
Rotation center height	h	$2.15\,\mathrm{cm}$			
Magnetic force (side)	F_{magL}	$15.0\,\mathrm{N}$			
Magnetic force (top)	F_{magV}	$12.0\,\mathrm{N}$			

has computing power, sensors, actuators and inter-block communication capabilities. All blocks execute the same program and communicate via a neighbor-to-neighbor model. The embedded program can detect neighborhood evolutions in a robot, enabling real-time adaptations based on new physical arrangements. For the purpose of detecting breakage, we consider that the *Blinky Block* placed on the ground is fixed to it, and that they are all subject only to the vertical force of gravity, magnetic and contact forces between *Blinky Blocks*. The magnetic forces produced by the magnets on the lateral and vertical faces, as well as the friction forces, were measured experimentally. All the data used in this article are specified in Table 1.

Our mechanical study is based on the use of the fundamental law of static. A mechanical system is in static equilibrium if and only if the sum of the forces and the sum of the moments acting on it are equal to zero. This can be expressed mathematically as:

$$\sum \vec{F_i} = 0 \tag{1}$$

where $\vec{F_i}$ represents the forces applied to the body. Additionally, for rotational equilibrium, the sum of the moments must also be zero:

$$\sum \vec{M_i} = \sum \vec{r_i} \times \vec{F_i} = 0 \tag{2}$$

Here, $\vec{M_i}$ represents the moments to which the body is subjected, about a point. The forces at play are gravity, contact and magnetic forces that hold the cubes together. We present here the four types of breakage phenomena addressed in this paper:

a) The vertical sliding is produced by the vertical motion of the group H in green in Fig. 1(b).a along the vertical plane P_a and following the vertical axis $-\vec{z}$.

b) The rotational sliding is the rotation of the group H around the interface face between G and H.

c, d) The rotational debounding can appear in a vertical interface plane (Fig. 1(b).c) or in an horizontal interface plane (Fig. 1(b).d), the H group turns around the red axis.

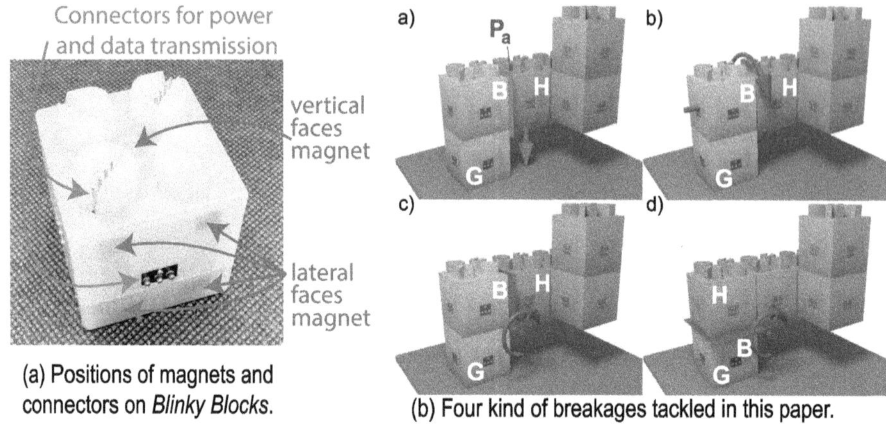

(a) Positions of magnets and connectors on *Blinky Blocks*.

(b) Four kind of breakages tackled in this paper.

Fig. 1. *Blinky Block* Hardware and possible brackages. (Color figure online)

For all these phenomena, we consider a fixed G part attached to the ground represented by gray *Blinky Blocks* in Fig. 1(b) and the group of *Blinky Blocks* H that can be separated to G due to external forces. We call B the *Blinky Block* of G whose one face forms the interface between G and H.

To establish the vertical sliding criterion for a lateral connection, we consider the system in static equilibrium at the sliding limit. According to Eq. 1 we can write the static resultant, along to z axis (cf. Fig. 2(b)):

$$- n_H \, mg + T = 0 \tag{3}$$

where n_H is the number of blocks of H and T is the tangential friction force. At the sliding limit, $T = fN$ with f the coefficient of friction and N the force normal to the faces at the link. In the case of a loop-free structure, $N = F_{\mathrm{magL}}$ is the magnetic force on one side of a cube. Therefore, for sliding to occur, the weight of the cantilever cubes must be greater than the tangent friction force, which means that:

$$n_H > \frac{f F_{\mathrm{magL}}}{mg} \tag{4}$$

Considering our *Blinky Blocks*, $T_a = \frac{f \, F_{magL}}{mg} \approx 14.5$, then we have to check if N_H, the number of connected modules in H, is greater than 14.

About rotational sliding criterion (lateral detachment), the focus is not on vertical sliding, but on rotational sliding around the axis normal to the link faces and passing through their center A, as illustrated in Fig. 2(b). The total moment of friction $\overrightarrow{M_A}$, is the sum of the components of all the points M, which are defined by the $\overrightarrow{AM}$ polar coordinates (r, θ) of the face:

$$\overrightarrow{M_A} = \iint_{\mathrm{face}} \overrightarrow{AM} \wedge \mathrm{d}\overrightarrow{T}(r, \theta) \tag{5}$$

Using a symbolic method to simplify this equation, we get: $M_A = \frac{BfaF_{\mathrm{magL}}}{6}$.
The static moment theorem yields:

$$mga \left| \sum_{i \in H} (y_i - y_A) \right| = \overrightarrow{M_A} . \overrightarrow{e_x} \Rightarrow \left| \sum_{i \in H} (y_i - y_A) \right| = \frac{BfF_{\mathrm{magL}}}{6\,mg} \tag{6}$$

With y_i the non-dimensional y coordinate of the center of gravity of *Blinky Block* i and y_A the non-dimensional y coordinate of the center of reference face A (i.e. (x_i, y_i) are the cell coordinates in the grid). The physical coordinates write $Y_i = ay_i$. Setting $T_b = \frac{BfF_{\mathrm{magL}}}{6mg}$, we deduce that rotational sliding occurs if:

$$\left| \sum_{i \in H} (y_i - y_A) \right| > T_b \text{ or } \left| \sum_{i \in H} (x_i - x_A) \right| > T_b \tag{7}$$

Considering the rotational debonding criterion on a lateral face $(0, \overrightarrow{z}, \overrightarrow{x})$ with normal vector $+\overrightarrow{x}$, Eq. 8 holds when the system is such that the contact force cancels.

$$- mga \left| \sum_{i \in H} (x_i - x_A) \right| + hF_{\mathrm{magL}} = 0 \tag{8}$$

With x_A the non-dimensional positions of the center of face A. Setting $T_c = \frac{hF_{\mathrm{magL}}}{mga}$, with $h = \frac{a}{2}$ we can deduce that a rotational debonding occurs if:

$$\left| \sum_{i \in H} (x_i - x_A) \right| < T_c \text{ or } \left| \sum_{i \in H} (y_i - y_A) \right| < T_c. \tag{9}$$

Similar conditions can be derived for rotational debonding criterion relatively to the vertical interface for a face with normal vector $+\overrightarrow{z}$: We define $T_d = \frac{F_{magV}}{2mg} - \frac{1}{2}$. Considering a connection to a top or a bottom interface, the integrity is not ensured if:

$$\left| \sum_{i \in H} x_i - x_A \right| < T_d \quad \text{or} \quad \left| \sum_{i \in H} y_i - y_A \right| < T_d. \tag{10}$$

Creating only loop-free structures is restrictive, particularly in terms of mechanical integrity. For the generalization to 3D looped configuration, we consider p a point placed anywhere along the rotation axis. For example, in the Fig. 2(b), p can be placed anywhere on the red axis x since the breakage condition around this axis does not depend on x coordinates. This figure also shows the parameters used in the following stability-condition equations, F^{bj} is the magnetic force apply to the face b of block j.
The breakage condition around the x-axis is expressed as:

$$s_p \left[M_{bpx} + \sum_{j=1}^{n} \left[(y_{bj} - y_p) F_z^{bj} - (z_{bj} - z_p) F_y^{bj} \right] \right] < 0 \tag{11}$$

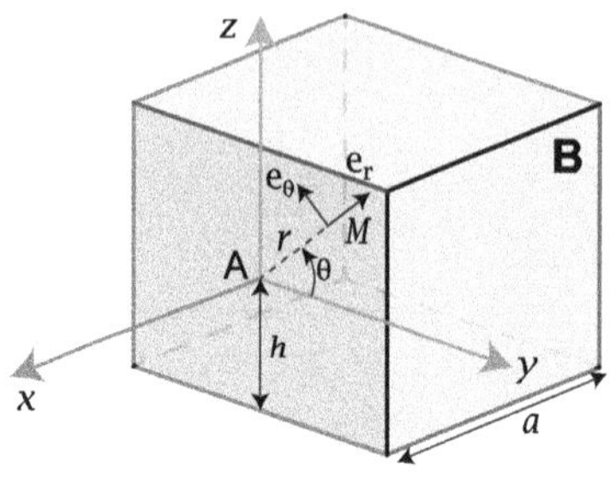

(a) Coordinate system centered at the face of the lateral interface.

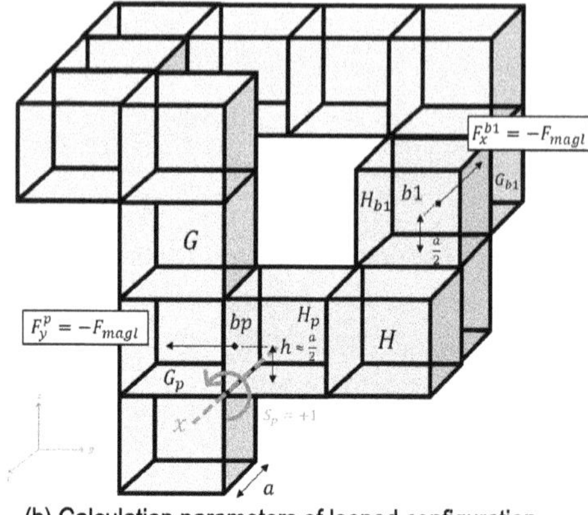

Fig. 2. Geometrical parameters for the mechanical expressions.

Similary, for a y-axis:

$$s_p \left[M_{bpy} + \sum_{j=1}^{n} \left[(z_{bj} - z_p)F_x^{bj} - (x_{bj} - x_p)F_z^{bj} \right] \right] < 0 \qquad (12)$$

With M_{bp} represents the moment of gravity.

When the pivot joint is mounted on a lateral face, sliding conditions and potential rotation must be checked by:

$$|N_H mg| > f \left(|F_{magL}| + \sum_{j=1}^{n} |F_x^{bj}| + \sum_{j=1}^{n} |F_y^{bj}| \right) \qquad (13)$$

The conditions for a rotational debonding around the axis normal to the face:

- For a normal x face:

$$\left| -mga \sum_{i \in H} (y_i - y_{bp}) + \sum_{j=1}^{n} \left[(y_{bj} - y_{bp})F_z^{bj} - (z_{bj} - z_{bp})F_y^{bj} \right] \right| > |M_A| \quad (14)$$

- For a normal y face:

$$\left| -mga \sum_{i \in H} (x_i - x_{bp}) + \sum_{j=1}^{n} \left[(z_{bj} - z_{bp})F_x^{bj} - (x_{bj} - x_{bp})F_z^{bj} \right] \right| < |M_A| \quad (15)$$

To sum up, for each G-H separation, we must check whether the pivot joint is vertical or lateral. If it is **vertical**, we need to verify Eqs. 11 and 12. If it is **lateral**, we must also verify Eqs. 13, 14 and 15. Therefore, for each cut, the pivot orientation must be changed, and the necessary checks must be repeated. **Vertically**, there are **four possible rotation axes**: two along the x-axis and two along the y-axis. **Laterally**, there are only **two possible pivot** along the z-axis.

3 Algorithmic Contribution

The proposed algorithms are a fully distributed, tree-based partitioning algorithms designed to efficiently handle a substantial number of modules. they provide scalability by handling communication between neighbouring modules efficiently, meaning that modular robots can interact and collaborate autonomously to solve the stability problem.

If we study the models associated with the four breakage phenomena (Eqs. 4, 7, 9, and 10), we notice that they can be written as Boolean functions that only depend on $\sum x$, $\sum y$ and N_H. This property allows us to define the break detection algorithm in two steps: we construct a spanning tree from the *Blinky Block* fixed to the ground by performing a BFS from this block and then traversing the tree from the leaves, we determine the values $\sum x$, $\sum y$ and N_H for each module. Once these quantities are defined, the above conditions are applied to validate the stability of the subtree with respect to each internal node. Once the root is reached, the stability of the entire configuration can be concluded.

Considering a reference frame centered on the interface module B, we define S_x^c as the sum of the distances along the axis $\vec{x}$ between the centers of the modules of H and the center of module B:

$$S_x^c = \sum_{i \in H} x_i - x_B = \sum_{i \in H} x_i - N_H \times x_B \tag{16}$$

But if we now consider a reference point centered on the normal face $\vec{x}$ at the interface between B and H (as in Fig. 2(b)), we define the distance S_X^f:

$$S_x^f = \sum_{i \in H} x_i - x_O = \sum_{i \in H} x_i - N_H \times (x_B + 0.5) \tag{17}$$

and if the normal is $-\vec{x}$, we get:

$$S_{-x}^f = \sum_{i \in H} x_i - x_O = \sum_{i \in H} x_i - N_H \times (x_B - 0.5) \tag{18}$$

Using these tools, we define the four boolean functions that are true if a breakage occurs. We also use the quantities shown in Table 1 to verify these functions:

$$F_a = (N_H > T_a)$$
$$F_b = \left((face_{+\vec{x}} \vee face_{-\vec{x}}) \wedge \left(\left| S_y^f \right| > T_b \right) \vee \left((face_{+\vec{y}} \vee face_{-\vec{y}}) \wedge \left(\left| S_x^f \right| > T_b \right) \right) \right)$$
$$F_c = \left((face_{+\vec{x}} \vee face_{-\vec{x}}) \wedge \left(\left| S_y^f \right| < T_c \right) \vee \left((face_{+\vec{y}} \vee face_{-\vec{y}}) \wedge \left(\left| S_x^f \right| < T_c \right) \right) \right)$$
$$F_d = \left(\left(\left| S_x^f \right| < T_d \right) \vee \left(\left| S_y^f \right| < T_d \right) \right)$$
$$\tag{19}$$

Algorithm 1: Enumeration of Spanning Trees

---

1 **Function** enumerateSpanningTrees(T_0 , A_p):
2   Push initial tree T_0 onto stack S
3   Add T_0 to list of visited trees
4   **while** $S! = \emptyset$ **do**
5 $T \leftarrow \text{pop}(S)$
6   **foreach** *edge* $a \in A_p$ **do**
7   **if** $a \notin T$ **then**
8 $T_a \leftarrow T \cup \{a\}$
9 $cycle \leftarrow \text{findCycle}(T_a, a)$
10   **foreach** *edge* $f \in cycle \mid f \neq a$ **do**
11 $T_{new} \leftarrow T \cup \{a\} \setminus \{f\}$
12   **if** *reverse(f)* $\in T_{new}$ **then**
13   Remove reverse(f) from T_{new}
14   **if** $T_{new} \notin visited$ **then**
15   Add T_{new} to *visited*
16   push T_{new} into S

Our algorithm is based on the propagation of messages between modules via a dynamically built spanning tree from a leader. At startup, the leader triggers the propagation of a "Request" message to all its neighbors, initiating the construction of a spanning tree. When a module receives a "Request" message for the first time, it designates the sender as its parent. Then, it sends "Requests" to all its own neighbors. If this module is a leaf in the tree, so it sends a "Result" message directly to its parent. A handler is called when a module receives a "Result" response from one of its child modules.

The module checks for rotational, lateral, or vertical breakage, as well as slippage, using the data sent by its child. The module sums up the positions and number of nodes of its children. Once all the expected responses have been received, the module adds its own position to the sum and returns the "Result" message to its parent, continuing the propagation of results to the tree root. This continues the propagation of results to the tree root.

The proposed algorithm for looped configurations is an algorithm in which each module collaborates with its neighbors to build and explore all possible spanning trees of a graph representing the network of connected modules. In looped configurations, there are several possible spanning trees. The aim is to build and explore them one by one. The first step is to build the basic spanning tree the same way as the free-loop algorithm. The leader initiates the propagation of a broadcast message. When a module receives this message for the very first time, it considers the sender to be its parent. At this point, it adds the edge linking it to its parent to a list called $T0$. This $T0$ list will contain all the edges of the basic spanning tree. It is built up progressively as modules connect to each other through the propagation of the initial message. When a module receives other broadcast messages after the first one, the module doesn't change parent, but takes note that other connections are possible. The edge between the module and these other senders is added to another list called Ap. This Ap list

---

Algorithm 2: Traversal from leaf to root and stability checking

---

1 Function `traverseToRoot`(*start, adj, position, parents*)**:**
2 $visited \leftarrow \emptyset$
3 $sumH \leftarrow (0, 0, 0)$
4   push *start* in q_1
5 $nh \leftarrow 0$
6   **while** $q_1 ! = \emptyset$ **do**
7 $node \leftarrow \text{pop}(q_1)$
8   **if** *node* $\notin$ *visited* **then**
9 $visited \leftarrow visited \cup node$
10 $nh \leftarrow nh + 1$
11 $sumH \leftarrow sumH + position[node]$
12   **if** *node has a parent in parents* **then**
13 $parent \leftarrow parents[node]$
14 $Fp \leftarrow \text{computeMagneticForce}(position[node], position[parent])$
15   check breakage for different cases
16   **if** *parent* $\notin$ *visiteds* **then**
17   push *parent* into q_1

---

contains all the edges that are part of the basic tree, as well as those that represent valid connections between modules. These are known as additional edges and are useful for generating other spanning trees. If the module configuration contains no cycles, each module has only one path to reach from the leader. Consequently, only one spanning tree is possible. In this case, the *Ap* list is the same as the base tree $T0$, which is the only spanning tree for the entire structure. No further variants are generated. If the configuration includes cycles, then the *Ap* list contains additional edges. This brings us to the second step, where these edges can be added to the base tree to create a temporary cycle. Then, another edge of this cycle is removed to produce a new spanning tree different from the previous one. The code explores all possible combinations of this type. Each tree is temporarily stored in a stack and then processed one by one.

After the enumeration of all valid spanning trees (Algorithm 1), the final stage consists in traversing each of these trees to perform the mechanical verification of every inter-module bond as shown in Algorithm 2. This phase aims to identify potential rupture points under the hypotheses defined by the moment-based stability criteria.

4   Experiments and Results

The experiments on Free-loop configurations were conducted on two types of platforms: the *VisibleSim* simulator and *Blinky Block* hardware. The algorithm presented has been implemented in the *VisibleSim* simulator and tested on many different robot configurations. In particular, we tested different topologies with 2- and 3-dimensional configurations with and without loops. The four types of breaks are handled by our implementation and appear in different colors on the blocks that detected them as displayed Fig. 3 (Red for vertical detachment, blue for rotational breakage and purple for lateral detachment and orange for the sliding breakage).

The algorithm has been implemented in *Blinky Block* hardware as well. The embedded program checks the stability of the configuration when powering on. A supply block is connected to the *Blinky Block* fixed on the floor, which is also the root of the spanning tree. *Blinky Blocks* that detect a breakage with their children light up in color: orange for case A, blue for case B, red for case C and purple for case D. The picture of Fig. 4(a) shows an the experiment with multiple breakage detection. The supplementary video shows how the program works using several experiments with *Blinky Blocks* highlighting each of the breakage cases studied in this paper.

For Multi-Loop Configurations, the experiments were conducted using the *VisibleSim* simulator. The results presented in Figs. 4(b) highlight the ability of the proposed method to comprehensively verify the stability of inter-modular connections for different types of configurations. A red leader indicates that instability was detected, while a green leader indicates no instability. Our tests applied to a large set of reconfigurations shows that the method is robust. We test it to simulated modules with a different number of connection as well.

Complexity: We can now express the complexity of this distributed algorithm. Since processing time is primarily due to message delays, time complexity is related to the number of messages transferred to perform the computation. The complexity of the first algorithm can be expressed as: $O(k_t d)$ where d is the diameter of our configuration and the height of our equilibrated spanning tree, and k_t is a constant representing the message transmission delay. Tackling loops problem, the processing complexity of a loop is $O(N_{loop}^2)$. When multiple loops

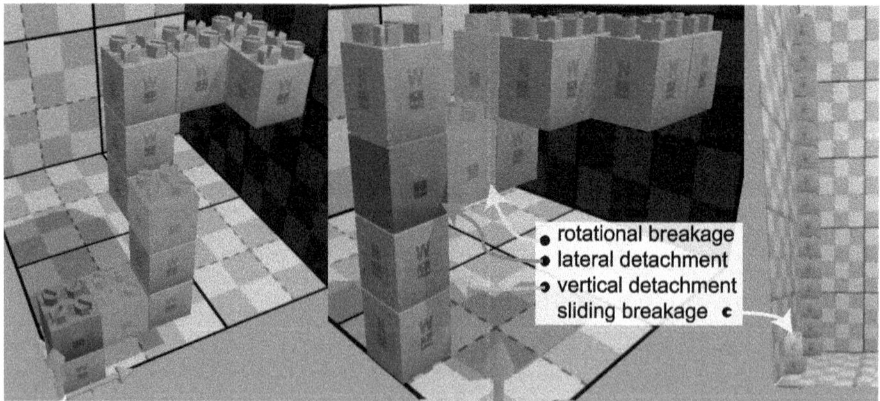

Fig. 3. Example of breakage detection, each colored block detects a kind of breakage on the face connected to the free part of the structure. (Color figure online)

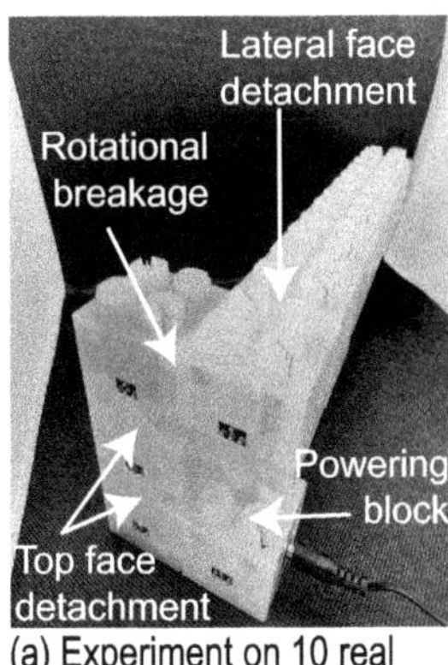

(a) Experiment on 10 real *Blinky Blocks*.

(b) Left: single-loop configuration showing stability. Right: multi-loop configuration showing instability.

Fig. 4. Several experiment on *Blinky Block* Hardware and *VisibleSim* simulator.

are present, only the cuts on the common modules require combining both module sets. If m modules are common: $O((1 + m)(N_1^2 \times N_2^2))$.

5   Conclusion

The subject addressed in this article aims to deal quickly and effectively with the mechanical stability of a configuration for programmable matter.

The proposed algorithms implement hierarchical communication between the network's modules, initiated by the leader and enabling dynamic, progressive verification of system breakages. In the case of free-loop configurations, each module participates in the collection of information, progressively aggregating it and transmitting it to its parent, thus verifying the breakages likely to occur at all these interfaces. Finally, the leader gathers all the data to display the modules in which one or more breakages have been detected.

However, in the case of single or multi-loop configurations, rather than solving a global system of coupled equilibrium equations, which would require intensive message exchange and long convergence times in a distributed context, the proposed solution relied on an innovative decomposition strategy. By enumerating all possible spanning trees and systematically analyzing their stability, the algorithm effectively transformed the complex looped problem into a set of simpler, acyclic cases.

The experimental results confirmed that the proposed algorithms of both cases, accurately identified rupture interfaces, with reasonable computational cost even for large-scale assemblies.

Acknowledgments. This work has been supported by the EIPHI Graduate School and the SELF-CONTROL Project "ANR-17-EURE-0002".

Disclosure of Interests. The authors have no competing interests to declare.

References

1. Bourgeois, J., et al.: Programmable matter as a cyber-physical conjugation. In: International Conference on Systems, Man, and Cybernetics, Budapest, Hungary (2016). https://doi.org/10.1109/SMC.2016.7844687
2. Bray, E., Groß, R.: Distributed optimisation and deconstruction of bridges by self-assembling robots (2022). https://eprints.whiterose.ac.uk/187863/
3. Goldstein, S.C., Campbell, J.D., Mowry, T.C.: Programmable matter. IEEE Comput. **38**(6), 99–101 (2005). http://www.cs.cmu.edu/~claytronics/papers/goldstein-computer05.pdf
4. Kirby, B., et al.: Catoms: moving robots without moving parts. In: Proceedings of the National Conference on Artificial Intelligence, vol. 20/4, p. 1730. AAAI Press, Menlo Park; MIT Press, Cambridge (2005)
5. Piranda, B., Bourgeois, J.: Designing a quasi-spherical module for a huge modular robot to create programmable matter. Auton. Rob. **42**(8), 1619–1633 (2018). https://doi.org/10.1007/s10514-018-9710-0
6. Piranda, B., Bourgeois, J.: Datom: a deformable modular robot for building self-reconfigurable programmable matter. In: 15th International Symposium on Distributed Autonomous Robotic Systems (DARS 2021), Kyoto, Japan (2021). https://publiweb.femto-st.fr/tntnet/entries/17404/documents/author/data
7. Piranda, B., Chodkiewicz, P., Hołobut, P., Bordas, S.P.A., Bourgeois, J., Lengiewicz, J.: Distributed prediction of unsafe reconfiguration scenarios of modular robotic programmable matter. IEEE Trans. Robot. **37**(6), 2226–2233 (2021). https://doi.org/10.1109/TRO.2021.3074085
8. Romanishin, J., Gilpin, K., Rus, D.: M-blocks: Momentum-driven, magnetic modular robots. In: IROS, pp. 4288–4295 (2013)
9. Spröwitz, A., et al.: Roombots—towards decentralized reconfiguration with self-reconfiguring modular robotic metamodules. In: 2010 IEEE/RSJ International Conference on Intelligent Robots and Systems (IROS) (2010). https://doi.org/10.1109/IROS.2010.5649504
10. Swissler, P., Rubenstein, M.: FireAnt: A modular robot with full-body continuous docks. In: Proceedings of the 2018 IEEE International Conference on Robotics and Automation (2018)
11. Thalamy, P., Piranda, B., Naz, A., Bourgeois, J.: VisibleSim: a behavioral simulation framework for lattice modular robots. Robot. Auton. Syst. 103913 (2021). https://doi.org/10.1016/j.robot.2021.103913, https://www.sciencedirect.com/science/article/pii/S0921889021001986
12. Yazidi, I., Piranda, B., Ouisse, M., Bourgeois, J.: Balance-driven self-reconfiguration algorithm for programmable matter. In: 17th International Symposium on Distributed Autonomous Robotic Systems (DARS 2024). Springer, New-York (2024)
13. Yazidi, I., Piranda, B., Ouisse, M., Bourgeois, J.: Efficient balance detection for modular robots. In: 2024 IEEE/RSJ International Conference on Intelligent Robots and Systems (IROS), pp. 14119–14124 (2024). https://doi.org/10.1109/IROS58592.2024.10802149

A Micro-Macro Model
of Encounter-Driven Information Diffusion
in Robot Swarms

Davis S. Catherman$^{(\boxtimes)}$ and Carlo Pinciroli

Robotics Engineering, Worcester Polytechnic Institute, Worcester, MA, USA
{dscatherman,cpinciroli}@wpi.edu

Abstract. In this paper, we propose the problem of *Encounter-Driven Information Diffusion (EDID)*. In EDID, robots are allowed to exchange information only upon meeting. Crucially, EDID assumes that the robots *are not allowed to schedule their meetings*. As such, the robots have no means to anticipate when, where, and who they will meet. As a step towards the design of storage and routing algorithms for EDID, in this paper we propose a model of information diffusion that captures the essential dynamics of EDID. The model is derived from first principles and is composed of two levels: a *micro* model, based on a generalization of the concept of 'mean free path'; and a *macro* model, which captures the global dynamics of information diffusion. We validate the model through extensive robot simulations, in which we consider swarm size, communication range, environment size, and different random motion regimes. We conclude the paper with a discussion of the implications of this model on the algorithms that best support information diffusion according to the parameters of interest.

1 Introduction

Effective communication is an essential mechanism to facilitate multi-robot coordination and cooperation [13]. Multi-robot applications in which communication plays a pivotal role are diverse and include warehouse logistics [18], agriculture [1], climate monitoring [14], firefighting [29], space exploration [37], and underground mining [32]. Extensive work exists on the constraints communication imposes on robot swarms, including maintaining connectivity [12], dealing with bandwidth [26] and power [41] limitations, and designing robust countermeasures to message loss [24].

This paper focuses on *Encounter-Driven Information Diffusion (EDID)*, a peculiar form of communication defined by two distinctive conditions. First, the robots are assumed to have a short communication range relative to the size of the environment. Thus, they can exchange messages only upon meeting each other. Second, robot motion is dictated by factors that act *independently* from

DISTRIBUTION STATEMENT A. Approved for public release; distribution is unlimited. OPSEC#10389.

communication needs. Consequently, robots cannot necessarily predict who and when they will meet in the future. The latter condition sets EDID apart from prior work on sparse swarms [33] and opportunistic communication [4,5,25], in which the robots maintain agency in their motion patterns.

Compared to other types of constrained communication, research on EDID has received little attention. Yet, EDID appears in many robotics engineering applications (e.g., underwater operations [3], planetary exploration [6]), and in the study of natural collective behavior through wearable devices [15,27,28].

Ultimately, the goal of this work is to produce a model for information diffusion that will inform the design of a new class of algorithms for information management that target EDID. EDID is different from typical scenarios that involve message loss, bandwidth limitations, and sparsity. At its most fundamental level, the fact that robot motion is not a controllable variable means that information diffusion cannot rely on algorithms that optimize network topology [19,22,23,36] or adapt information routing [5,25]. Stochastic aspects dominate the dynamics, such as when, how long, and which robots meet during a mission. Local encounter rates do not map linearly to global information diffusion, making it necessary to develop models that combine microscopic (robot-level) and macroscopic (swarm-level) factors.

In this paper, we propose the first model of EDID. Our model links the microscopic aspects of individual robot motion with the macroscopic dynamics of information diffusion. At the microscopic level, we identify the concept of *mean free path* [11] as an informative model component. At the macroscopic level, our model reveals that the dynamics of information diffusion presents a bifurcation driven by parameters such as robot density and motion patterns. We derive the model from first principles and validate it in an extensive campaign of physics-accurate simulated experiments, exploring the role of swarm size, communication range, environment size, and various types of random motion.

2   The Microscopic Model

Our model is composed of two parts: a *microscopic* model that captures the dynamics of individual encounters, and a *macroscopic* one that characterizes aggregate behavior.

Encounters and Mean Free Path. Consider a swarm of N robots capable of communication within a range C. The robots are distributed in a square area of side L and move according to some form of random walk (we will specify this aspect in Sect. 4). An *encounter* occurs when two or more robots are within communication range, making it possible for messages to be exchanged.

Our microscopic model originates from the concept of *mean free path* [11], i.e., the distance a robot covers between two encounters on average. The mean free path models the microscopic dynamics of colliding gas particles. The use of mean-free-path and kinetic-gas-theoryâĂŞinspired reasoning to model inter-robot encounters is not new in swarm robotics. For example, Wahby et al. [38]

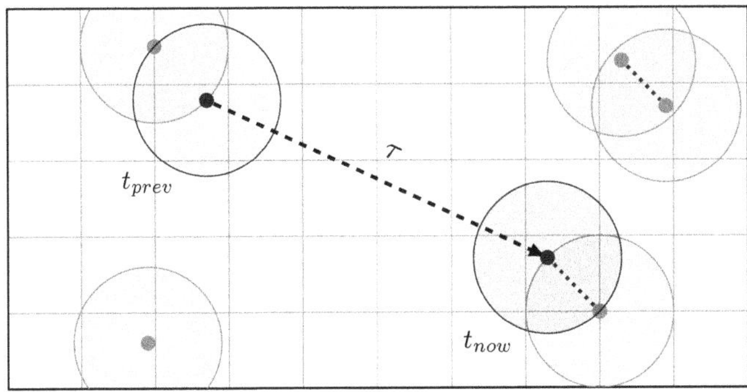

Fig. 1. A representation of the mean free path τ as the average time between subsequent interactions between an agent (depicted in red) and surrounding agents (in blue). (Color figure online)

employ encounter statistics derived from this physical intuition to adapt aggregation behavior to dynamic swarm densities and environmental conditions.

In our scenario, encounters occur when two robots cross each others' communication range; notably, an encounter does not necessarily imply a change in direction, i.e., a physical collision. Thus, our microscopic model will include a corrective term. A diagram depicting the mean free path is reported in Fig. 1.

Deriving the Ideal Mean Free Path. We first derive the expression of the 'ideal' mean free path, l_{ideal}, which corresponds to the definition found in gas particle modeling. To derive l_{ideal}, we resort to a probabilistic argument:

- The probability that a robot encounters another along the mean free path is $P(\text{encounter}) = dx/l_{\text{ideal}}$ where $dx < l_{\text{ideal}}$ is the distance covered by the robot in a time dt.
- Another approach to calculate $P(\text{encounter})$ involves considering when two robots intersect each others' communication range. The average number of robots that can be encountered per unit of area is $(N-1)/L^2$; along a path of length dx, we expect to encounter $(N-1)/L^2 \cdot dx$ robots. As the robot moves in the 2D environment, it communicates with all the robots within a range C, so $P(\text{encounter}) = C \cdot (N-1) \cdot dx/L^2$.

Putting the two expressions together yields:

$$P(\text{encounter}) = \frac{dx}{l_{\text{ideal}}} = \frac{C \cdot (N-1)}{L^2}dx \Rightarrow l_{\text{ideal}} = \frac{L^2}{C \cdot (N-1)}.$$

Because our macroscopic model will capture the time dynamics of information diffusion, we will need the microscopic model to be time-based. To achieve this, we consider the mean time between two encounters, denoted by τ_{ideal}. If the robots move at a constant speed V, then we simply have

$$\tau_{\text{ideal}} = \frac{l_{\text{ideal}}}{V} = \frac{L^2}{C \cdot (N-1) \cdot V} \tag{1}$$

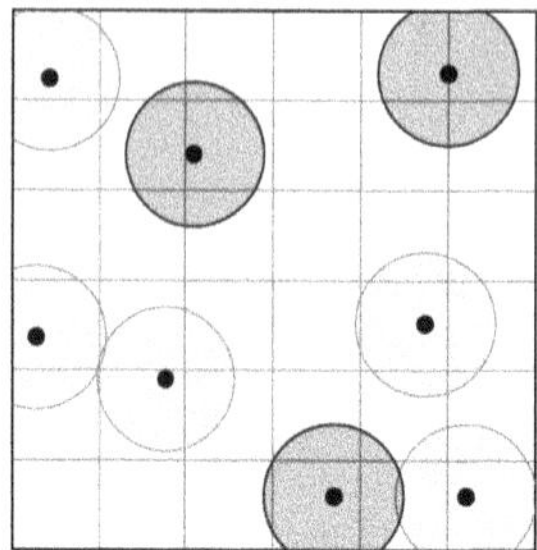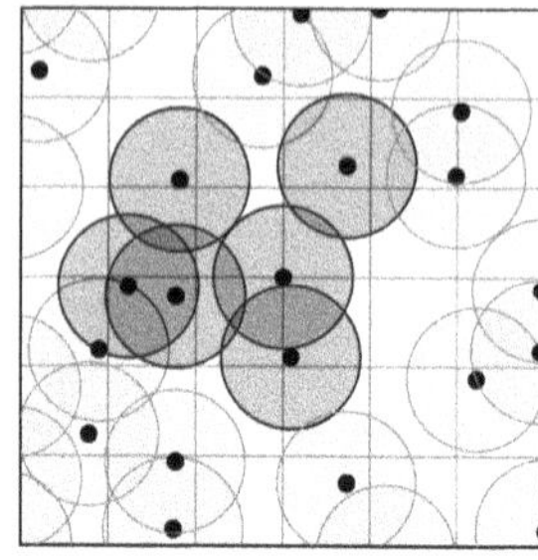

Fig. 2. Our macro model identifies two possible regimes: low-density, well mixed (left) and high-density, not-mixed (right).

The effect of the parameters of interest $\langle L, N, C, V \rangle$ are not surprising. As the environment side L increases, the mean time between interactions increases super-linearly. Conversely, as the swarm size N increases, τ drops. Analogously, a larger communication range C facilitates more frequent encounters. These effects are related to robot density—the higher the density, the shorter the times between robot encounters. The role of the speed V is to promote mixing: Higher speeds result in lower τ_{ideal}.

The Generalized Mean Free Path. While τ_{ideal} is derived from the kinetic theory of gases, it assumes point-mass particles and instantaneous collisions. Real robotic encounters differ in two critical ways: they have a finite duration (determined by C/V) during which the robots remain in range, and they occur within a bounded environment where boundary effects influence density. To bridge the gap between the idealized gas model and physical reality, we treat Eq. (1) as a semi-empirical formulation. We introduce a factor $\beta = \tau/\tau_{\text{ideal}}$ as a phenomenological parameter derived via regression from the experimental data in Fig. 3. This additional parameter serves as a corrective term that accounts for the non-zero duration of communication and the geometric constraints of the arena. In our macroscopic model, we will use $\tau = \beta \cdot \tau_{\text{ideal}}$.

3   The Macroscopic Model

We now derive the macroscopic model from first principles. Let us call $P_n(t)$ the probability that exactly n robots are informed at time t, $\sum_{n=0}^{N} P_n(t) = 1$. The evolution of $P_n(t)$ is determined by robot encounters. We call $W_{n \to n+1}$ the transition rate (probability per unit time) that the swarm jumps from n to $n+1$ informed robots. Given these quantities, we can write the master equation

$$\frac{dP_n}{dt} = P(\text{gain}) - P(\text{loss}) = W_{n-1 \to n} P_{n-1} - W_{n \to n+1} P_n.$$

In the above equation, we consider each state with n informed robots as a 'bin', with probabilities that flow from one bin to another (i.e., gain and loss) as robots become informed. The master equation allows us to calculate the dynamics of the expected number of informed robots $\langle n \rangle = \sum_{n=0}^{N} n P_n$:

$$\frac{d\langle n \rangle}{dt} = \sum_{n=0}^{N} n \frac{dP_n}{dt} = \underbrace{\sum_{n=0}^{N} n W_{n-1 \to n} P_{n-1} - \sum_{n=0}^{N} n W_{n \to n+1} P_n}_{(*)}. \tag{2}$$

We modify term $(*)$ by introducing the change of variable $m = n - 1$:

$$\sum_{m=-1}^{N-1} (m+1) W_{m \to m+1} P_m = \sum_{m=0}^{N} (m+1) W_{m \to m+1} P_m = \sum_{n=0}^{N} (n+1) W_{n \to n+1} P_n,$$

where: $a)$ the second step exploits the facts that $P_m = 0$ for $m = -1$ and that $W_{N \to N+1} = 0$; and $b)$ the third step simply relabels m as n. Plugging the resulting expression into Eq. (2) yields

$$\frac{d\langle n \rangle}{dt} = \sum_{n=0}^{N} (n+1) W_{n \to n+1} P_n - \sum_{n=0}^{N} n W_{n \to n+1} P_n = \sum_{n=0}^{N} W_{n \to n+1} P_n \tag{3}$$

This equation depends on the specific form of $W_{n \to n+1}$. Intuitively, we can identify two potential dynamics acting as 'extremes' (see Fig. 2): $a)$ A low-density, well-mixed regime; and $b)$ A high-density, not-mixed regime. We hypothesize that most real deployments will display dynamics that blend elements of these extremes. Next, we study these extreme scenarios individually. In both cases, we consider the rate of change of the fraction of informed robots $I = \langle n \rangle / N$ over time, i.e., $dI/dt = d\langle n \rangle / dt$.

Low-Density, Well-Mixed Regime. In a low-density regime, the robots rarely meet each other. Thus, every meeting is important to diffuse information across the swarm. If the robots are also well-mixed, when a meeting occurs, it is likely to involve two robots who rarely (or never) met before. This phenomenon can be captured by considering a meeting between an informed robot and an uninformed one. The informed robot meets other robots at a rate $1/\tau$; due to well-mixedness, the uninformed robot can be chosen uniformly at random, i.e., with a probability $(N - n)/N$. Thus, the rate of change of informed robots follows the law:

$$\frac{d\langle n \rangle}{dt} = \sum_{n=0}^{N} n \cdot \underbrace{\frac{1}{\tau} \cdot \frac{N-n}{N}}_{W_{n \to n+1}} \cdot P_n = \frac{1}{\tau} \left[\langle n \rangle - \frac{\langle n^2 \rangle}{N} \right].$$

In the mean field limit, i.e., for $N \to \infty$, $\mathrm{Var}(n) = \langle n^2 \rangle - \langle n \rangle^2 \sim O(\sqrt{N})$—fluctuations become negligible—and $\langle n^2 \rangle \sim \langle n \rangle^2$. We can approximate

$$\frac{d\langle n \rangle}{dt} \approx \frac{1}{\tau} \left[\langle n \rangle - \frac{\langle n \rangle^2}{N} \right] = \frac{\langle n \rangle}{\tau} \left[1 - \frac{\langle n \rangle}{N} \right]$$

which, using $I = \langle n \rangle / N$, becomes the well-known logistic law [10]:

$$\frac{dI}{dt} = \frac{I(1-I)}{\tau}.$$

(4)

High-Density, Not-Mixed Regime. In a high-density, not-mixed regime, information propagates in waves and is conveyed redundantly by several robots. An uninformed robot is likely to receive several copies of the same message, making the average amount of information exchanged per-meeting much lower than in the logistic case. In this regime, the limiting factor is not the number of uninformed robots, as in the logistic case, which produced the term $(N-n)/N$. Rather, it is how *surprising* a message is. To model this phenomenon, we need a factor $\eta(n/N)$ to express how surprising a message is for a robot. The new factor must satisfy two basic constraints: *a)* $\eta(n/N)$ is continuous and monotonically decreasing; and *b)* $\eta(n/N) \to 0$ as $n/N \to 1$. There are infinite possible choices for $\eta(n/N)$. Drawing inspiration from information theory, we propose the ansatz $\eta = -\ln(n/N)$, which expresses the Shannon self-information [42] of having n informed robots. Self-information indeed quantifies how surprising an event is. When n/N is small, receiving a message from an informed robot is surprising (high η); when $n/N \to 1$, it is completely predictable ($\eta \to 0$). Now we can derive our model for this regime:

$$\frac{d\langle n \rangle}{dt} = \sum_{n=0}^{N} n \cdot \underbrace{\frac{1}{\tau} \cdot \left(-\ln \frac{n}{N} \right)}_{W_{n \to n+1}} \cdot P_n.$$

Using $I = \langle n \rangle / N$, the final form of this equation is a Gompertz law [40]:

$$\frac{dI}{dt} = \frac{1}{\tau} I \ln \frac{1}{I}.$$

(5)

Combined Model. The next step is linearly combining Eq. (4) and Eq. (5) through a weight $\lambda \in [0, 1]$ that governs the mixture of the two regimes:

$$\frac{dI}{dt} = \lambda \frac{I}{\tau} \ln \frac{1}{I} + (1 - \lambda) \frac{I(1-I)}{\tau}.$$

(6)

This combined model cannot, in general, be integrated into a closed-form solution. The only two closed-form solutions exist for $\lambda = 0$ (pure logistic) and $\lambda = 1$ (pure Gompertz):

$$I(t)_{\lambda=0} = \frac{I_0}{I_0 + (1 - I_0) \cdot e^{-(t-t_0)/\tau}} \qquad \text{(LGSTC)}$$

$$I(t)_{\lambda=1} = \exp\left(-\ln I_0 \cdot e^{-(t-t_0)/\tau} \right) \qquad \text{(GMPRZ)}$$

Table 1. For CRW, LW, and Hybrid walks, the parameters were studied across a range specified by $(start, stop, step)$.

Parameter	Default	Parameter Study
N	20	$\{6, 10, 14, 18, 22, 26, 30, 34, 38, 42, 46, 50\}$
C (m)	10	$\{6, 10, 14, 18, 22, 26, 30, 34, 38, 42, 46, 50\}$
L (m)	200	$\{40, 60, 80, 100, 120, 140, 160, 180, 200, 220\}$
V (m/s)	0.05	$\{0.05\}$
Walk	CRW $(\rho = 0.7)$	$\{CRW(\rho = (0.1, 0.9, 0.1)),$ $LW(\alpha = (1.4, 2.8, 0.1)),$ $Hybrid(\rho = (0.2, 0.8, 0.2), \alpha = (1.4, 2.4, 0.2))\}$

where $I_0 = 1/N$ is the number of informed robots at the start of an experiment. Because Eq. (6) is a nonlinear differential equation, its solution is not, in general, the weighted sum of the individual logistic and Gompertz solutions. Nevertheless, both limiting curves are smooth sigmoids that differ only slightly in shape under the parameter ranges we observed, making a linear-combination approximation practically accurate for our data (the typical root-mean-square error is $\approx 10^{-2}$). For this reason, it is practically acceptable to approximate the solution of Eq. (6) as a linear combination of (LGSTC) and (GMPRZ). This is our final model:

$$\boxed{\begin{aligned} I(t) &\approx \lambda \exp\left(-\ln I_0 \cdot e^{-(t-t_0)/\tau}\right) + \\ &+ (1 - \lambda)\frac{I_0}{I_0 + (1 - I_0) \cdot e^{-(t-t_0)/\tau}}. \end{aligned}} \quad \text{(MDL)}$$

4 Experimental Evaluation

To validate our model, we ran an extensive set of simulated experiments in the ARGoS multi-robot simulator [30]. It is worth highlighting that our simulations are physically accurate with respect to real-world dynamics, as opposed to simple numerical simulations of mass-less particles. We opted for this approach to fully evaluate the correspondence between our model and realistic mobility dynamics.

Experimental Setup. The parameters we analyzed are summarized in Table 1. For each configuration, we adjusted a single parameter while keeping the other parameters at the reported default value. We ran 40 repetitions for each parameter configuration, for a total of 3,160 simulations. The duration of each simulation was 100 simulated hours with a step resolution of 1 s. At the start of each simulation, the robots are uniformly distributed in an empty arena of size L. Any pair of robots experience an encounter with each other while the separation distance is less than the communication range. To study information diffusion during a simulation, we examine a single robot that generates a new message every hour for the first $50\,h$ and record the duration for each peer to receive the message. We utilize the standard definitions of Correlated Random Walks (CRW) and Levy Walks (LW) as described in Dimidov $et\ al.$ [7]. We vary the direction correlation parameter $\rho \in [0, 1]$ for CRW and the step length distribution exponent $\alpha \in [1, 2]$ for LW. As $\rho \to 0$, the motion is increasingly brownian, meanwhile the LW step distribution is characterized by long relocations as $\alpha \to 0$. The hybrid walk then combines the two components in one random motion.

Microscopic Model. We performed experiments to validate our microscopic model (τ) across the parameters of interest listed in Table 1. The results are plotted in Fig. 3. The model shows a good match between predicted values and experimentally derived ones. For brevity, we omitted the plots in which we varied the random walks, because we observed negligible effects.

Macroscopic Model: Parameter Fit. We fit the parameters of the macroscopic model to the data we collected. The results show a remarkable accuracy across the experiment conditions. We present the fits across the swarm and environment parameters in Fig. 4a and across the random walks in Fig. 4b. These plots demonstrate that our model captures well a wide span of experimental conditions. The blending parameter λ offers a physical interpretation of the swarm's 'informational viscosity.' As shown in Fig. 5, λ acts as a sliding scale between the well-mixed regime (Logistic, $\lambda \approx 0$) and the redundant, wave-propagation regime (Gompertz, $\lambda \approx 1$). We observe that λ increases sharply with communication range C. Physically, a larger communication radius increases local network density, causing robots to receive redundant transmissions from neighbors they have already met; this saturation of local information mirrors the 'surprisal' decay modeled by the Gompertz function. Conversely, as the environment size L increases or the motion becomes more directed (higher ρ), λ trends toward 0. In these high-mobility or sparse scenarios, the swarm approaches the 'well-mixed' ideal: encounters are rare events between agents who are unlikely to share immediate neighbors, making the Logistic model the dominant driver of diffusion.

Macroscopic Model: Propagation Time. We studied the effect of the parameters of interest on the propagation time of the messages. The results for $\langle N, C, L \rangle$ are reported in Fig. 4a. Not surprisingly, as the density of the robots increases, the propagation time decreases. As for random walks, the results are reported in Fig. 4b. The propagation time varied notably across different random walks. LWs provided long propagation times with multiple messages not having fully propagated when the experiment ended. For increasing ρ there is a noticeable decrease in wall time. Additionally, for decreasing α, which is related to having a heavier tail for step length, there appears to be decreasing wall time. For both walks, a generally more straight path movement related to lower propagation times. These latter results are obtained with $\rho = 0.7$, helping to account for

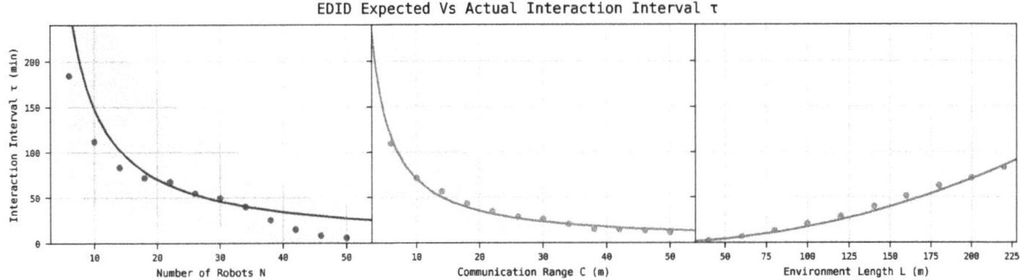

Fig. 3. Interaction interval for swarm configurations considering the number of robots (N), communication range (C) and the square-environment length (L) given the robot velocity (v). The plot reports means and inter-quartile ranges.

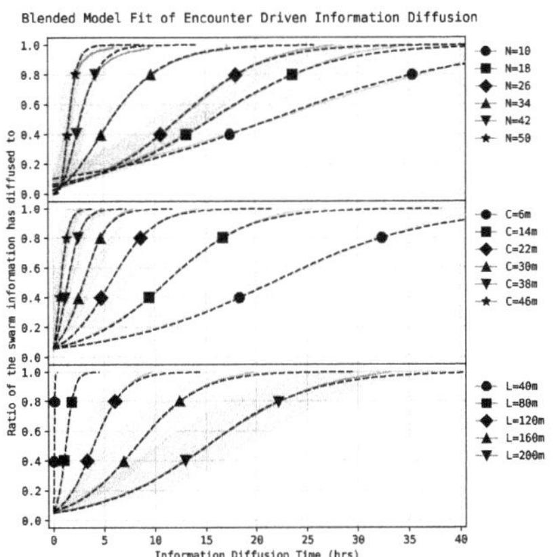

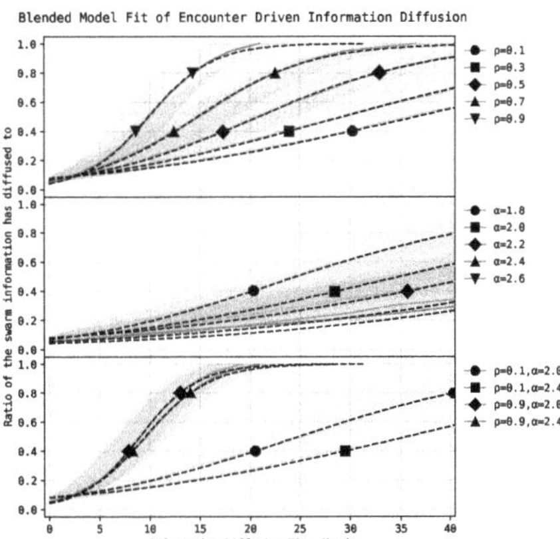

(a) The message propagation over time for multiple experimental configurations with varying parameters N (red), C (blue), and L (green). The dashed line represents the output of the fitted blended model for each curve.

(b) The message propagation over time for multiple experimental configurations with varying random walk parameters: $CRW(\rho)$ (red), $LW(\alpha)$ (blue), and $Hybrid(\rho, \alpha)$ (green). The dashed line represents the output of the fitted blended model for each curve.

Fig. 4. Message propagation over time for a subset of the various experimental conditions. (Color figure online)

likely path deviations or obstacle avoidance. This reaffirms that motion dynamics, and not just communication density, is relevant to understanding the lifespan of a message.

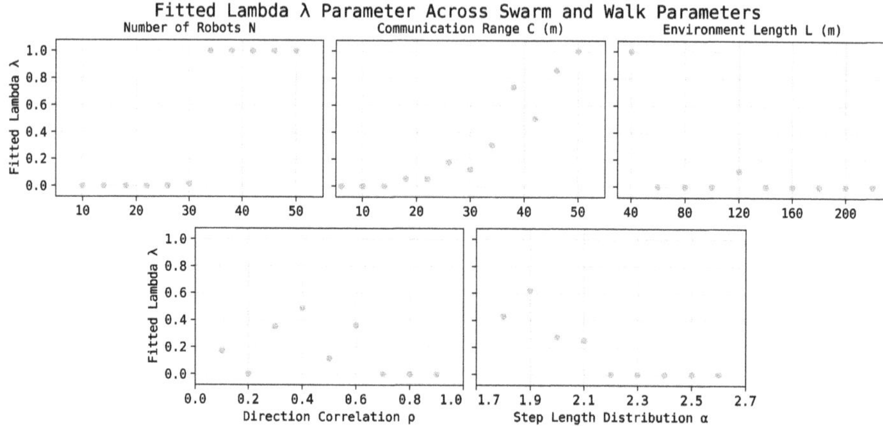

Fig. 5. Parameter λ for blending the Logistic and Gompertz as fit across all IVs.

5   Conclusion

In this paper, we proposed a novel micro-macro model for Encounter-Driven Information Diffusion (EDID) in robot swarms. The model is composed of two parts: a microscopic model, based on the concept of *mean free path*, that estimates the expected rate of encounters among robots. The macroscopic model, on the other hand, targets swarm-level information diffusion. The main insight in our macroscopic model is the identification of two regimes that dominate the diffusion dynamics as a consequence of robot density. For high communication density, our model follows the Gompertz curve, which captures the diminishing returns of information transfer due to message replication. For low communication density, the logistic model proves accurate. Our final model blends these two extremes and provides excellent fit to the experimental data we collected.

This model, while simple, sheds light on the design of algorithms for information diffusion in robot swarms. Specifically, if the goal is to achieve fast and uniform diffusion, uncorrelated random walks produce Gompertz-like dynamics. If, conversely, the goal is to diffuse in a hierarchical, controllable manner, correlated motion provides better results due to the logistic dynamics it produces.

Our model contributes to the broader literature on population dynamics in swarm robotics and ecology by establishing a novel connection between density-driven regimes and functional forms of macroscopic diffusion. While prior work has extensively applied logistic dynamics to robot swarms under well-mixed assumptions [16,31,35], and the Gompertz equation has been used to model tumor growth [2,21] and epidemic spreading on networks [9], no existing work applies Gompertz dynamics to robot swarm information diffusion or models a continuous bifurcation between these regimes. The blending parameter λ in our model addresses this gap by capturing how communication density drives a transition from well-mixed logistic spreading to redundant Gompertz-like propagation [34]. Our micro-macro derivation extends kinetic-theory-based encounter models [20,39] beyond timing predictions to reveal the specific functional form of growth curves, connecting mean free path not merely to diffusion rates but to the qualitative character (logistic versus Gompertz) of the macroscopic dynamics [8,17].

In the context of EDID, our model provides a way to characterize the expected diffusion behavior given measurable parameters, such as the size of the environment, the number of robots involved, and the communication range. We plan to use our model as a component in a new class of storage-and-routing algorithms for EDID scenarios.

Acknowledgments. This work was supported by the Automotive Research Center (ARC), a US Army Center of Excellence for modeling and simulation of ground vehicles, under Cooperative Agreement W56HZV-24-2-0001 with the US Army DEVCOM Ground Vehicle Systems Center (GVSC).

Disclosure of Interests. The authors have no competing interests to declare.

References

1. Albiero, D., Garcia, A.P., Umezu, C.K., de Paulo, R.L.: Swarm robots in agriculture. arXiv preprint arXiv:2103.06732 (2021)
2. Benzekry, S., Sentis, C., Coze, C., Tessonnier, L., André, N.: Population modeling of tumor growth curves and the reduced Gompertz model improve prediction of the age of experimental tumors. PLoS Comput. Biol. **16**(2), e1007178 (2020). https://doi.org/10.1371/journal.pcbi.1007178
3. Champion, B.T., Joordens, M.A.: Underwater swarm robotics review. In: 2015 10th System of Systems Engineering Conference (SoSE), pp. 111–116. IEEE (2015)
4. Cheraghi, A.R., Zenz, J., Graffi, K.: Opportunistic network behavior in a swarm: passing messages to destination. In: 2020 5th Asia-Pacific Conference on Intelligent Robot Systems (ACIRS), pp. 138–144. IEEE (2020)
5. Cladera, F., Ravichandran, Z., Miller, I.D., Hsieh, M.A., Taylor, C.J., Kumar, V.: Enabling large-scale heterogeneous collaboration with opportunistic communications. In: 2024 IEEE International Conference on Robotics and Automation (ICRA), pp. 2610–2616. IEEE (2024)
6. de la Croix, J.P., et al.: Multi-agent autonomy for space exploration on the CADRE lunar technology demonstration. In: 2024 IEEE Aerospace Conference, pp. 1–14 (2024)
7. Dimidov, C., Oriolo, G., Trianni, V.: Random walks in swarm robotics: an experiment with kilobots. In: International Conference on Swarm Intelligence (ANTS), pp. 185–196 (9 2016)
8. Elamvazhuthi, K., Berman, S.: Mean-field models in swarm robotics: a survey. Bioinspir. Biomimet. **15**(1), 015001 (2020). https://doi.org/10.1088/1748-3190/ab49a4
9. Estrada, E., Bartesaghi, P.: From networked SIS model to the Gompertz function. Appl. Math. Comput. **419**, 126882 (2022). https://doi.org/10.1016/j.amc.2021.126882

10. Feller, W.: On the logistic law of growth and its empirical verifications in biology. Acta. Biotheor. **5**(2), 51–66 (1940)
11. Feynman, R.P., Leighton, R.B., Sands, M.: The Feynman Lectures on Physics, vol. 1, chap. 43. Basic Books (2011). New millennium edition
12. Garzón, M., Valente, J., Roldán, J.J., Cancar, L., Barrientos, A., Del Cerro, J.: A multirobot system for distributed area coverage and signal searching in large outdoor scenarios. J. Field Robot. **33**(8), 1087–1106 (2016)
13. Gielis, J., Shankar, A., Prorok, A.: A critical review of communications in multi-robot systems. Curr. Robot. Rep. **3**, 213–225 (2022)
14. Hafid, A., Hocine, R., Guezouli, L.: Analyzing swarm robotics approaches in natural disaster scenarios: a comparative study. In: 2024 1st International Conference on Innovative and Intelligent Information Technologies (IC3IT), pp. 1–6. IEEE (2024)
15. Hałgas, E.A., van Eijndhoven, K.H.J., Gevers, J.M.P., Wiltshire, T.J., Westerink, J.H.D.M., Rispens, S.: A review of using wearable technology to assess team functioning and performance. Small Group Res. **54**(1), 41–76 (2023)
16. Hamann, H., Valentini, G., Khaluf, Y., Dorigo, M.: Derivation of a micro-macro link for collective decision-making systems. In: Bartz-Beielstein, T., Branke, J., Filipič, B., Smith, J. (eds.) PPSN 2014. LNCS, vol. 8672, pp. 181–190. Springer, Cham (2014). https://doi.org/10.1007/978-3-319-10762-2_18
17. Hamann, H., Wörn, H.: A framework of space-time continuous models for algorithm design in swarm robotics. Swarm Intell. **2**(2), 209–239 (2008). https://doi.org/10.1007/s11721-008-0015-3
18. Hönig, W., Kiesel, S., Tinka, A., Durham, J.W., Ayanian, N.: Persistent and robust execution of MAPF schedules in warehouses. IEEE Robot. Autom. Lett. **4**, 1125–1131 (2019). https://api.semanticscholar.org/CorpusID:61807902
19. Kantaros, Y., Zavlanos, M.M.: Distributed intermittent connectivity control of mobile robot networks. IEEE Trans. Autom. Control **62**(7), 3109–3121 (2016)
20. Kernbach, S.: Diffusion of information in robot swarms. arXiv preprint arXiv:1110.5183 (2011)
21. Laird, A.K.: Dynamics of tumour growth. Br. J. Cancer **18**(3), 490–502 (1964). https://doi.org/10.1038/bjc.1964.55
22. Luo, W., Sycara, K.: Minimum k-connectivity maintenance for robust multi-robot systems. In: 2019 IEEE/RSJ International Conference on Intelligent Robots and Systems (IROS), pp. 7370–7377. IEEE (2019)
23. Majcherczyk, N., Jayabalan, A., Beltrame, G., Pinciroli, C.: Decentralized connectivity-preserving deployment of large-scale robot swarms. In: 2018 IEEE/RSJ International Conference on Intelligent Robots and Systems (IROS), pp. 4295–4302. IEEE (2018)
24. Manfredi, S., Natalizio, E., Pascariello, C., Zema, N.R.: Stability and convergence of a message-loss-tolerant rendezvous algorithm for wireless networked robot systems. IEEE Trans. Control Netw. Syst. **7**(3), 1103–1114 (2020). https://doi.org/10.1109/TCNS.2019.2963470
25. Mox, D., Garg, K., Ribeiro, A., Kumar, V.: Opportunistic communication in robot teams. In: 2024 IEEE International Conference on Robotics and Automation (ICRA), pp. 12090–12096. IEEE (2024)
26. Nunnally, S., et al.: Human influence of robotic swarms with bandwidth and localization issues. In: 2012 IEEE International Conference on Systems, Man, and Cybernetics (SMC), pp. 333–338. IEEE (2012)

27. Olguın, D.O., Gloor, P.A., Pentland, A.S.: Capturing individual and group behavior with wearable sensors. In: Proceedings of the 2009 AAAI Spring Symposium on Human Behavior Modeling, SSS, vol. 9 (2009)
28. Olguın Olguın, D.: Sociometric badges: Wearable technology for measuring human behavior. Master's thesis, Massachusetts Institute of Technology, Cambridge, MA (2007)
29. Penders, J., et al.: A robot swarm assisting a human fire-fighter. Adv. Robot. **25**(1–2), 93–117 (2011)
30. Pinciroli, C., et al.: ARGoS: a modular, parallel, multi-engine simulator for multi-robot systems. Swarm Intell. **6**(4), 271–295 (2012)
31. Reina, A., Valentini, G., Fernández-Oto, C., Dorigo, M., Trianni, V.: A design pattern for decentralised decision making. PLoS ONE **10**(10), e0140950 (2015). https://doi.org/10.1371/journal.pone.0140950
32. Tan, J., Melkoumian, N., Harvey, D., Akmeliawati, R.: Evaluating swarm robotics for mining environments: insights into model performance and application. Appl. Sci. **14**(19), 8876 (2024)
33. Tarapore, D., Groß, R., Zauner, K.P.: Sparse robot swarms: moving swarms to real-world applications. Front. Robot. AI **7** (2020)
34. Tjørve, K.M.C., Tjørve, E.: The use of Gompertz models in growth analyses, and new Gompertz-model approach: an addition to the unified-Richards family. PLoS ONE **12**(6), e0178691 (2017). https://doi.org/10.1371/journal.pone.0178691
35. Valentini, G., Ferrante, E., Hamann, H., Dorigo, M.: Collective decision with 100 Kilobots: speed versus accuracy in binary discrimination problems. Auton. Agent. Multi-Agent Syst. **30**(3), 553–580 (2015). https://doi.org/10.1007/s10458-015-9323-3
36. Vandermeulen, I., Groß, R., Kolling, A.: Re-establishing communication in teams of mobile robots. In: 2018 IEEE/RSJ International Conference on Intelligent Robots and Systems (IROS), pp. 7947–7954. IEEE (2018)
37. Varadharajan, V.S., Beltrame, G.: A multi-robot exploration planner for space applications. IEEE Robot. Autom. Lett. **10**(3), 2446–2453 (2025). https://doi.org/10.1109/LRA.2025.3532158
38. Wahby, M., Petzold, J., Eschke, C., Schmickl, T., Hamann, H.: Collective change detection: Adaptivity to dynamic swarm densities and light conditions in robot swarms. In: Artificial life Conference Proceedings, pp. 642–649. MIT Press (2019)
39. Wilson, S., Buffin, A., Pratt, S.C., Berman, S.: Closed-loop task allocation in robot swarms using inter-robot encounters. Swarm Intell. **14**(1), 57–85 (2020). https://doi.org/10.1007/s11721-019-00166-x
40. Winsor, C.P.: The Gompertz curve as a growth curve. Proc. Natl. Acad. Sci. **18**(1), 1–8 (1932)
41. Zhang, F., Bertozzi, A., Elamvazhuthi, K., Berman, S.: Performance bounds on spatial coverage tasks by stochastic robotic swarms. IEEE Trans. Autom. Control **63**, 1473–1488 (2018)
42. Zheng, Z.: Shannon theory. In: Zheng, Z. (ed.) Modern Cryptography Volume 1. Financial Mathematics and Fintech, pp. 91–151. Springer, Singapore (2022). https://doi.org/10.1007/978-981-19-0920-7_3

A Social Interaction Model for Forager Task Allocation in Honey Bees

Atakan Botasun[1](✉) (iD), Babür Erdem[1](✉) (iD), Elvin Gültekinoğlu[1,2] (iD),
Ali Emre Turgut[1,2] (iD), and Erol Şahin[1,3] (iD)

[1] Center for Robotics and Artificial Intelligence (ROMER), Middle East Technical
University, Ankara, Turkey
{abotasun,ebabur}@metu.edu.tr
[2] Department of Mechanical Engineering, Middle East Technical University, Ankara,
Turkey
[3] Department of Computer Engineering, Middle East Technical University, Ankara,
Turkey

Abstract. Foraging is essential for honey bee survival and colony repro-
duction, underpinning the pollination services that support agriculture,
plant biodiversity, and ecosystem health. Using an agent-based model,
we address how colonies allocate foraging effort across multiple resource
sites under changing environmental conditions. Contrary to existing task
allocation models of honey bee foraging, we introduce a holistic approach
to dissect foraging by incorporating positive and negative drivers identified in the literature. To this end, we utilize a Finite-State Machine
framework to simulate task allocation for varying food source qualities, predator stress on foragers, and unloading constraints. The model
holistically integrates waggle dancing (recruitment), tremble dancing
(unloading-limitation feedback), and stop signaling (predation-risk inhibition) within explicit behavioral states, using parameters grounded in
empirical field experiments for biological realism. In simulations, the
colony self-organizes into stable distributions of retrieval, recruitment,
and inhibition behaviors, reallocating effort in response to dynamic
changes in food quality, predator risk, and receiver availability. These
results support the model as a compact, behaviorally grounded platform
for ecological analysis of foraging dynamics and as a basis for future
extensions toward richer environmental drivers and predictive colony-
level monitoring.

Foraging is a vital activity for honey bees (*Apis mellifera*) survival and reproduc-
tion, as well as for agriculture, plant biodiversity, and ecosystem health [4]. For
many plants, the production of seeds and fruit is tightly coupled with honey bee
foraging activities, establishing honey bees as a keystone species for agricultural
efficiency and ecosystem stability [1]. Internal to the colony, this activity is the
primary driver of survival. Honey bees gather nectar, pollen, and water during foraging, which are essential resources for energy, larval development, and
thermoregulation [12,30].

© The Author(s), under exclusive license to Springer Nature Switzerland AG 2026
R. Groß et al. (Eds.): ANTS 2026, LNCS 16515, pp. 28–40, 2026.
https://doi.org/10.1007/978-3-032-26123-6_3

Honey bees, as a eusocial species with a division of labor and foraging strategies, are highly suitable for researching foraging behavior and task allocation. Honey bees exhibit age-based division of labor (temporal polyethism): younger bees carry out in-hive tasks such as *receiving* food and depositing it in the comb. Conversely, older bees become foragers and *retrieve* food as nectar or pollen [24]. A forager departs the hive when weather conditions are favorable [29], and collects food. If it returns from a food-abundant area, it performs the waggle dance to inform other foragers of its location [10]. The bees performing the waggle dance can be described as "*disseminators*", while the dance followers are "*naive*" foragers who are ready to receive information. If a forager that has brought food fails to unload the nectar to the *receivers* within a certain timeframe, the forager exhibits a different behavior called the *tremble dance* [25]. The tremble dance informs other foragers to take over the nectar loading task instead of foraging. Bees performing the tremble dance also signal other dancing bees (waggle or tremble) to stop [19]. Upon encountering a predator on a visited flower, a forager starts *stop signaling* in the hive, thus suppressing dissemination and subsequent foraging activity for a limited time [20]. We provide a biological flowchart of task allocation in honey bee foraging in Fig. 1.

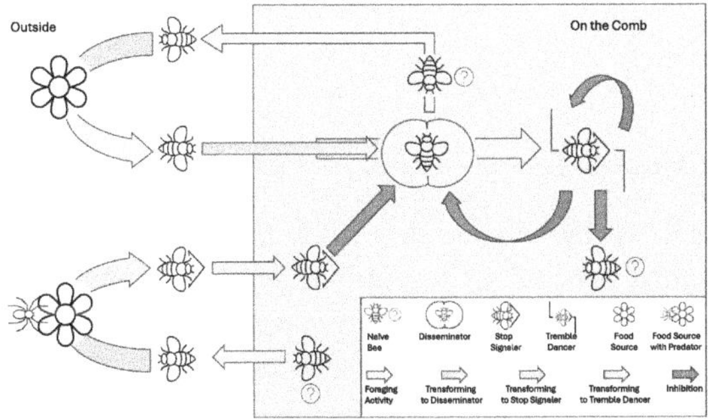

Fig. 1. Behavioral ontogeny of forager bees and the social interactions between them. The flowchart shows transitions and influence among states.

Like foraging in honey bees, collective decision-making is often framed as the best-of-n problem in swarm intelligence [28]. Eusociality also inspires models of swarm consensus that remain robust against malicious actors [2]. Quality-sensitive foraging has been implemented in robotic swarms using augmented-reality food sources [18]. An earlier work in task allocation enables resource discrimination for aggregating robots through ad-hoc strategies [8]. An adaptive collective decision-making solution highlights the need for exploration and task non-commitment in dynamic environments [3]. The constraints of communication and time found in search-and-rescue problems [15] mirror the environmental pressures faced by foraging honey bees. Task allocation can also be optimized for energy consumption [17], which is critical for both robots and animals.

Previous models have captured the social interactions driving honey bee task allocation through agent-based modeling; however, most focus on isolated mechanisms. Specifically, the waggle dance is often prioritized, excluding negative feedback effects on task allocation [7,11,23]. The benefits of incorporating both negative and positive feedback mechanisms on task allocation have been investigated in a model, albeit without the explicit description of how honey bees engage in such behaviors [22].

In this paper, we propose an agent-based Finite-State Machine model to demonstrate how forager honey bees allocate tasks based on food quality, predation risk, and receiver bee availability. We implement this framework by incorporating waggle and tremble dancing, as well as stop signals within the states, to simulate the social interactions of foragers. For biological realism, we use model parameters grounded in empirical data sourced from established field experiments [9,21,23–27]. Our key contribution is the holistic application of these well-known social interactions, whereas previous studies have generally examined their effects separately [7,11,23], or examine such effects in an abstract manner that do not directly relate to honey bees [22]. This application enables us to analyze the foraging behavior of honey bees, allowing us to predict how the foraging behavior of bees, the colony's breaking points, and its sustainability are affected by changing environmental conditions.

1 Methods

1.1 Modeling Social Interactions of Foragers

Our model primarily focuses on two bee roles: foragers and receivers. Foragers are tasked with searching for, collecting, and transporting nectar from food sources to the colony (*retriever*). Foragers are also tasked with communicating information regarding food quality (*disseminator*), receiver availability (*tremble dancer*), and predator risks (*stop signaler*) to other foragers waiting to depart from the hive (*naive*). *Receivers* remain inside the hive, accept nectar from returning foragers, process it, and store it within the comb. We only model tasks allocated to forager or receiver bees, and ignore other in-hive roles.

The behavior of each bee is dictated by parameters that govern its state transitions. These parameters, along with the forager count, food quality, and acquisition duration, define the simulation environment. For simplicity, we maintain constant parameter values throughout the simulation, ignoring the effect of the time of day and other environmental effects on behavior. The specific parameters and expressions used in this model, derived from Seeley's work and related literature, are summarized in Table 1. Where biological data were insufficient, we introduced supplementary parameters. Our Finite-State Machine closely follows the biological flowchart given in Fig. 1. We provide the overall pseudocode governing the behavior in Algorithm 1.

Table 1. Experiment parameters, expressions, and their references from the literature.

Description	Symbol	Value	Reference
Distance to hive	d	400 m	[27]
Number of feeders	n	$\{1, 2\}$	
Forager count		2000	
Receiver count		75	
Quality values	q_k	0.75 M, 2.5 M, 1.0 M	[27]
Total duration		8 h	[27]
Timestep length	Δt	0.5 min	
Memory retained per timestep	ρ	0.99	
Heuristic mixing weight	b	0.6	
Random choice rate	γ	0.05	
Predator encounter rate	P_S	0.85	
Visited forage site	k	$k \in \{1, ..., n\}$	
Heuristics of given bee at k	h_k^{bee}		
Last saved timestamp	t_i^{bee}		
Food unloading time	T_U	$-1.142857 q_k + 3.857143$ minutes	[27]
Tremble dance duration	T_T	27.3 ± 24.3 min	[27]
Energy gain from food	q_t	$q_k + 0.97082941$	[23]
Waggle dance probability	P_D	$0.956937(1 + e^{\frac{0.2721966 - q_t}{0.2624014}})$	[23]
Naive bee pause duration	T_N	2 min	[27]
Dissemination duration	T_D	$3.1635 \cdot q_t$ minutes	[21]
Foraging trip duration	T_R	82 ± 42 minutes (all sites)	[26]
Stop signaling duration	T_S	10 min	[9]
Stop signal count	n_S	3.2 ± 2.4	[9]
Tremble dance probability	P_T	$(1 + e^{(0.11(100 - 19.2 q_k - t_W))})^{-1}$	[25]

Algorithm 1. Forager

1: **start** as retriever on foraging trip (R), Algorithm 2, $t_i^{bee} \leftarrow 0, t \leftarrow 0$
2: **if** retriever on foraging trip (R) **then go to** Algorithm 2
3: **else if** retriever waiting for receiver (W) **then go to** Algorithm 3
4: **else if** retriever unloading food (U) **then go to** Algorithm 4
5: **else if** disseminator (D) **then go to** Algorithm 6
6: **else if** tremble dancer (T) **then go to** Algorithm 8
7: **else if** stop signaling (S) **then go to** Algorithm 7
8: **else if** naive bee (N) **then go to** Algorithm 9
9: **end if**

A *retriever*'s foraging action is abstracted within the model as a forage trip duration, food quality, and a potential encounter with a predator. When the retriever returns to the hive, it *waits* for a receiver and then *unloads* food. According to the quality of the acquired food and the present environmental hazards, the retriever may transition to dissemination, stop signaling, or enter a naive state. If receiver availability is low, the retriever may initiate a tremble dance. We initialize foragers at this state at different initialization times. The logic for these states is detailed in Algorithms 2, 3, and 4.

Algorithm 2. Retriever on Foraging Trip (R)

1: **if** $t - t_i^{bee} < T_R^k$ **then** *bee* still retrieving food at site k
2: **else** start waiting for receiver (W), $t_i^{bee} \leftarrow t, h_k^{bee} \leftarrow q_k, q^{bee} \leftarrow q_k$
3: **end if**

Algorithm 3. Retriever Waiting for Receiver (W)

1: **if** receiver found **then** unload to receiver (U)
2: **else**
3:     **with** $p = (1 + e^{(0.11(100 - 19.2q_k - t_i^{bee} + t))})^{-1}$: become a tremble dancer (T)
4:     **otherwise** keep waiting for receiver
5: **end if**

Algorithm 4. Retriever Unloading Food (U)

1: **if** $t - t_i^{bee} < -1.142857q_k + 3.857143$ **then** still unloading food
2: **else** unloading complete, $T_N^{bee} \leftarrow 0$
3:     **if** no predator encountered **then**
4:         **with** $p = 0.956937(1 + e^{\frac{-0.69863281 - q_k}{0.2624014}})$:
5:             become a disseminator (D), $T_D^{bee} \leftarrow 3.1635q_k + 3.07121884$
6:         **otherwise** become a naive bee (N)
7:     **else** become a stop signaler (S), restrict food site k
8:     **end if**
9: **end if**

While *receiver* bees do not forage directly, they act as a critical constraint on the foraging process; specifically, their availability to receive food has a significant effect on *tremble dancing*. We incorporate two distinct receiver states: *idle* or *working*. Idle receivers will receive food from waiting retrievers, prioritizing those with the highest food quality. This assignment is determined by a probability mass function weighted by the retrieved food quality. The logic for these states is detailed in Algorithm 5.

Algorithm 5. Receiver

1: **if** idle **then**
2:     **if** $W \neq \emptyset$ **then with** $p \propto q^{bee}, bee \in W$: bee finds this receiver, start working
3:     **else** wait for retrievers
4:     **end if**
5: **else if** working **then**
6:     **if** unloading complete **then** become idle
7:     **end if**
8: **end if**

A *disseminator* promotes a food source by sharing its perceived quality with naive bees. These heuristics are shared with all naive bees currently attending the dance. The duration of dissemination is directly proportional to the perceived quality value. Each bee maintains a memory of heuristics associated with visited food sources. Over time, this memory decays to remove outdated information. The logic for this state is detailed in Algorithm 6.

$$h^{bee}_{t+1} \leftarrow \rho h^{bee}_t$$

Algorithm 6. Disseminator (D)

1: **if** $t - t^{bee}_i < T^{bee}_D$ **then**
2:     **if** stop signal **then** become a naive bee (N), $t^{bee}_i \leftarrow t$
3:     **end if**
4: **else** become a naive bee (N), $t^{bee}_i \leftarrow t$
5: **end if**

Algorithm 7. Stop Signaler (S)

1: **if** $t - t^{bee}_i < T^{bee}_S$ **then**
2:     **if** $D \neq \emptyset$ **then**
3:         $bee' \leftarrow sample(D)$
4:         bee' gets stop signal at $t + 1$
5:     **end if**
6: **else** become a naive bee (N), $t^{bee}_i \leftarrow t$
7: **end if**

Algorithm 8. Tremble Dancer (T)

1: **if** stop signal **then**
2:     become a naive bee (N), $t^{bee}_i \leftarrow t$
3: **else if** $t - t^{bee}_i < T_T$ **then**
4:     $bee' \leftarrow sample(N, D, S, T)$
5:     **if** $bee' \in D \cup T$ **then**
6:         bee' gets stop signal at $t + 1$
7:     **end if**
8: **else** become a naive bee (N), $t^{bee}_i \leftarrow t$
9: **end if**

Stop signaling is initiated to inhibit the dancing activity of disseminators after predator encounters. *Tremble dancers* inhibit the dancing activity of all dancing bees following a shortage of receivers. Both stop signaling and tremble dancing last for a set duration. The logic for these behaviors is detailed in Algorithms 7 and 8.

Algorithm 9. Naive (N)

1: **if** $t - t_i^{bee} > T_N^{bee}$ **then**
2:     **if** $D \cup T \neq \emptyset$ **then with** $p = \gamma$:
3:         $d \leftarrow sample(D, T)$
4:         **if** $d \in T$ **then** $t_i^{bee} \leftarrow t, T_N^{bee} \leftarrow 2$
5:         **else**
6:             $h \leftarrow bh_{k_d}^{bee} + (1-b)h_{k_d}^d$, select $k', P(h_{k'}^{bee}|\boldsymbol{h}^{bee})$, $h' \leftarrow h_{k'}^{bee}$
7:             $h \leftarrow \max(h, h'), k \leftarrow \mathrm{argmax}(h, h')$
8:         **end if**
9:     **else**
10:         **if** $D \cup T \neq \emptyset$ **or** $\sum_{k=1}^{n} h_k^{bee} \approx 0$ **then** $k \leftarrow random(\{1, ..., n\})$
11:         **else** select $k, P(h_k^{bee}|\boldsymbol{h}^{bee})$
12:         **end if**
13:         $h \leftarrow h_k^{bee}$
14:     **end if**
15:     **if** $h > 0$ and k not restricted **then** retrieve (R) from food source k, $t_i^{bee} \leftarrow t$
16:     **else** stay naive
17:     **end if**
18: **else** stay naive
19: **end if**

In the *naive* state, the bee randomly selects a disseminator or tremble dancer to follow. Selecting a tremble dancer causes the bee to pause all actions for a set period. We have set this period to the average unloading time in Seeley's experiments [27]. If a disseminator is selected, it shares its heuristics with the naive bee, which informs the bee's selection of a suitable site. Afterwards, the bee will choose between its known best site and the site informed by the disseminator. In the absence of disseminators or tremble dancers, the naive bee solely relies on its internal memory. Generally, naive bees depart for a sortie as retrievers unless they encounter a tremble dancer or have previously encountered a predator at the given site, in which case they may decide to stay in the hive. Specifically, if the naive bee itself has had an encounter with a predator at the selected site, it will not leave on a sortie at this site for the rest of the day [9]. We also introduce a small probability γ of a naive bee disregarding all information and selecting a safe food source at random, to encourage exploration and robustness in decision-making. We provide a pseudocode for this state in Algorithm 9.

2 Experiments

We investigate the effects of allocated tasks on the foraging process in four different settings. All experiments are conducted in 10 seeded random trials. The foragers start their first task as a retriever at different times.

2.1 One Food Source with Constant Food Quality

Our first set of experiments consists of a single food source with a constant quality. Bees can transform the information about the position of an abundant nectar source to promote foraging from it with the waggle dance [10]. When receiver bee availability is insufficient, returning retrievers tremble dance to suppress recruitment until receiver availability recovers, at which point disseminators resume recruiting naive bees. This regulatory cycle, illustrated in Fig. 2, continues until the system reaches an optimal task distribution that maximizes retrieval without overwhelming the receiver population.

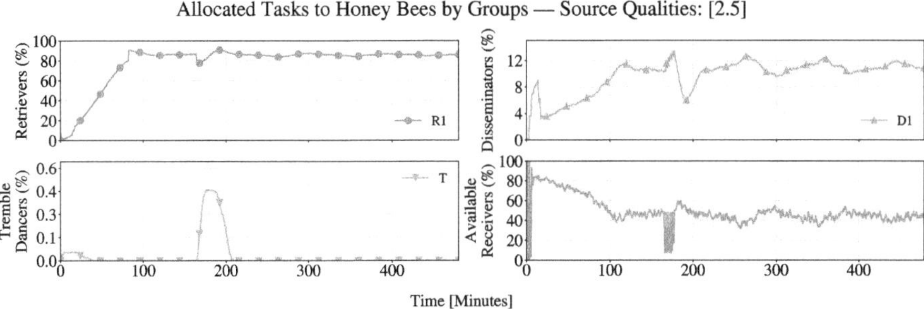

Fig. 2. One food source at constant quality. Receiver availability is limited. Disseminators promote retriever allocation, and tremble dancing counteracts retriever allocation when receiver availability is low. **Top left:** Retriever distribution over time. **Top right:** Disseminator distribution over time. **Bottom left:** Tremble dancer distribution over time. **Bottom right:** Receiver availability over time.

2.2   One Food Source with Sudden Predation

Honey bees reduce visitation when a sit-and-wait predator is present. Experiments with crab spiders on inflorescences showed that bees strongly avoided flower clusters [14]. Thus, bees can learn to avoid locations associated with unsuccessful predation attempts or predator cues. Also, when a forager is bitten or attacked at a food source, it often returns to the nest and produces vibrational stop signals on waggle dancers [20]. Here, we demonstrate the effect of predation attempts, where bees leave a profitable area when a predator appears. The results are given in Fig. 3.

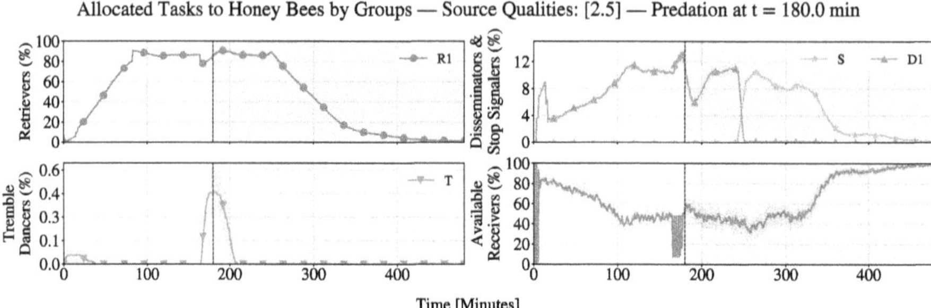

Fig. 3. A dynamic simulation with one food source, where a predator appears at $t = 180$ min. The bees react by stop signaling to suppress retriever recruitment by disseminators. After directly encountering the predator, bees stop visiting the source for the rest of the day. **Top left:** Retriever distribution over time. **Top right:** Distribution of stop signalers and disseminators over time. **Bottom left:** Tremble dancer distribution over time. **Bottom right:** Receiver availability over time.

2.3   Two Food Sources with a Sudden Change in Food Qualities

The classic feeder experiments with living bees showed that forager honey bees can learn multiple daily times of food reward (typically sugar syrup) and associate each specific time with a specific feeder location [5,10,16]. In these experiments, bees learned to arrive at a given feeder at specific times of day [16]. In natural systems, this temporal switching is also documented at the plant–community level. Early field work and later experiments show that honey bees can reallocate nectar-collecting sites within a day, matching specific flower patches to specific time windows. Von Buttel-Reepen's classic observations around 1900 showed that honey bees visited buckwheat fields only in the morning hours, leaving the crop once nectar secretion ceased. This implies that foragers track the daily secretion schedule of a plant and then shift elsewhere when it is no longer profitable [6]. Here, we simulate two areas covered with different plant species whose inflorescences offer temporally differing rewards. Consequently, the bees visit the first plant in the beginning and then shift to the second species later. The results are given in Fig. 4.

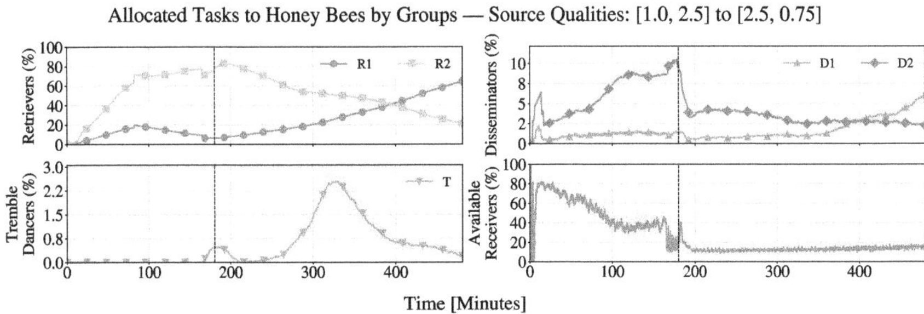

Fig. 4. A dynamic simulation with two food sources. Food source qualities are changed at $t = 180$ min. Retrieval tasks shift to the source with a higher quality, similar to results seen in Seeley's experiments [27]. **Top left:** Retriever distribution over time. **Top right:** Disseminator distribution over time. **Bottom left:** Tremble dancer distribution over time. **Bottom right:** Receiver availability over time.

2.4 Two Food Sources with Sudden Predation at One Food Source

Following the results from our previous experiments, we provide two equally profitable food sources to our model, then introduce a sit-and-wait predator in the vicinity of one of these food sources. We observe the effects of tremble dancing and dissemination on recruitment promotion and suppression until the appearance of the predator triggers stop signaling and increases suppression of recruitment, until foragers switch to the safer food source option. The results are given in Fig. 5.

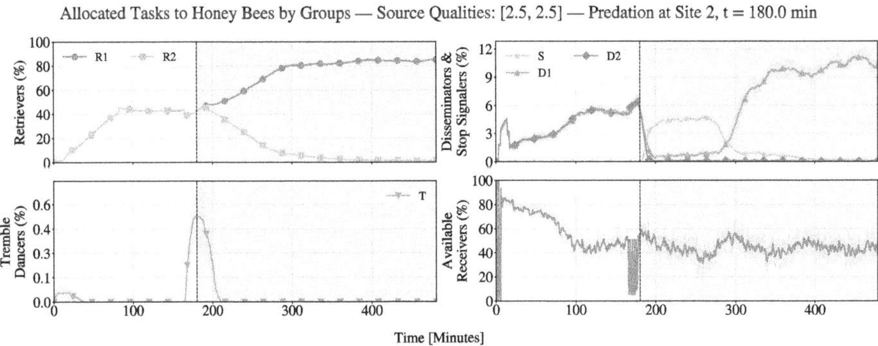

Fig. 5. A dynamic simulation with two identical food sources, where a sit-and-wait predator appears at one food source at $t = 180$ min. Stop signalers suppress recruitment until the bees shift retrieval tasks to the source that is safer. **Top left:** Retriever distribution over time. **Top right:** Disseminator distribution over time. **Bottom left:** Tremble dancer distribution over time. **Bottom right:** Receiver availability over time.

3   Conclusion

This study aims to provide a biologically realistic model of honey bee behavior for ecological research, which predicts how foraging responds to changing environmental conditions and forecasts colony and sustainability trajectories under environmental change. To this end, we present a Finite-State Machine model of social interactions to study how colonies allocate effort across food sources under varying food quality, predator risk, and the availability of receiver bees. While developing the model, we used empirical data from the literature to create a realistic background for the model. The model combines waggle dancing, tremble dancing, and stop signaling to simulate the self-organized task allocation of honey bees into a stable distribution of retrieval, recruitment, and inhibition behaviors.

Our experiments demonstrate these mechanisms in action. Single-source scenarios show that tremble dancing effectively reduces recruitment when receivers become a limiting factor, maintaining a balance between recruitment and inhibition. Two-source scenarios illustrate rapid switching toward higher-quality options, supported by quality-sensitive allocation and heuristic-based dissemination. Furthermore, the inclusion of memory decay and random exploration enables flexible reallocation under dynamic conditions. Finally, the introduction of predation risk demonstrates the suppression of foraging via stop signaling, prompting a shift toward safer resource locations or staying in the hive if no safe option is available.

While the model addresses some changing environmental conditions, it does not yet account for meteorological variables or internal drivers like circadian rhythms. Future iterations will incorporate these factors into the model. In addition, field experiments will be conducted with artificial flowers [13] to further refine our understanding of predator stress on honey bee foraging behavior. Collectively, these efforts will provide a robust foundation for a digital twin that accurately reflects complex foraging dynamics and enable swarm robotics applications of similar social interactions.

Acknowledgments. We thank the Middle East Technical University, Scientific Research Projects Directorate (BAP) [grant number: ADEP-302-2024-11468]; and the European Union [RoboRoyale, grant number: 964492] for their support in the project.

Disclosure of Interests. The authors have no competing interests to declare.

References

1. Aizen, M.A., Garibaldi, L.A., Cunningham, S.A., Klein, A.M.: How much does agriculture depend on pollinators? Lessons from long-term trends in crop production. Ann. Botany **103**, 1579 (2009). https://doi.org/10.1093/AOB/MCP076, https://pmc.ncbi.nlm.nih.gov/articles/PMC2701761/
2. Antonic, N., Zakir, R., Dorigo, M., Reina, A.: Collective robustness of heterogeneous decision-makers against stubborn individuals. In: Proceedings of the

23rd International Conference on Autonomous Agents and Multiagent Systems, AAMAS 2024, pp. 68–77. International Foundation for Autonomous Agents and Multiagent Systems, Richland (2024). https://dl.acm.org/doi/10.5555/3635637.3662853

3. Arvin, F., Turgut, A.E., Bazyari, F., Arikan, K.B., Bellotto, N., Yue, S.: Cue-based aggregation with a mobile robot swarm: a novel fuzzy-based method. Adapt. Behav. **22**, 189–206 (2014). https://doi.org/10.1177/1059712314528009

4. Atanasov, A.Z., Koleva, M.N., Vulkov, L.G.: Inverse problem numerical analysis of forager bee losses in spatial environment without contamination. Symmetry **15**(12) (2023). https://doi.org/10.3390/sym15122099, https://www.mdpi.com/2073-8994/15/12/2099

5. Bloch, G., Bar-Shai, N., Cytter, Y., Green, R.: Time is honey: circadian clocks of bees and flowers and how their interactions may influence ecological communities. Philos. Trans. Roy. Soc. B: Biol. Sci. **372** (2017). https://doi.org/10.1098/RSTB.2016.0256, https://royalsocietypublishing.org/doi/10.1098/rstb.2016.0256

6. Buttel-Reepen, H.: Sind die bienen reflexmaschinen?: Experiementelle beiträge zur biologie der honigbiene. Erweiterter ... Abdr. aus dem "Biologischen Centralblatt", Bd 20, 1900, Arthur Georgi (1900). https://books.google.com.tr/books?id=DkQ6AAAAQAAJ

7. Camazine, S., Sneyd, J.: A model of collective nectar source selection by honey bees: self-organization through simple rules. J. Theor. Biol. **149**, 547–571 (1991). https://doi.org/10.1016/S0022-5193(05)80098-0

8. Campo, A., Garnier, S., Dédriche, O., Zekkri, M., Dorigo, M.: Self-organized discrimination of resources. PLoS ONE **6** (2011). https://doi.org/10.1371/journal.pone.0019888

9. Dong, S., et al.: An inhibitory signal associated with danger reduces honeybee dopamine levels. Curr. Biol. **33**, 2081–2087.e4 (2023). https://doi.org/10.1016/j.cub.2023.03.072, https://www.cell.com/action/showFullText?pii=S0960982223003925

10. von Frisch, K.: The Dance Language and Orientation of Bees. Harvard University Press, Cambridge and London (1993). https://doi.org/10.4159/harvard.9780674418776

11. George, E.A., Brockmann, A.: Social modulation of individual differences in dance communication in honey bees. Behav. Ecol. Sociobiol. **73**, 41 (2019). https://doi.org/10.1007/S00265-019-2649-0, https://link.springer.com/article/10.1007/s00265-019-2649-0

12. Ghosh, S., Jeon, H., Jung, C.: Foraging behaviour and preference of pollen sources by honey bee (APIs mellifera) relative to protein contents. J. Ecol. Environ. **44**, 4 (2020). https://doi.org/10.1186/S41610-020-0149-9

13. Gültekinoğlu, E., et al.: Flobuzz: a modular feeder system for automated aversive conditioning in bees. bioRxiv, p. 2026.02.08.704633 (2026). https://doi.org/10.64898/2026.02.08.704633, https://www.biorxiv.org/content/10.64898/2026.02.08.704633v1

14. Huey, S., Nieh, J.C.: Foraging at a safe distance: crab spider effects on pollinators. Ecol. Entomol. **42**, 469–476 (2017). https://doi.org/10.1111/EEN.12406, https://onlinelibrary.wiley.com/doi/full/10.1111/een.12406

15. Kang, W., Jeong, E.J., Shim, S., Ha, S.: Optimization of task allocation for resource-constrained swarm robots. IEEE Trans. Autom. Sci. Eng. (2024). https://doi.org/10.1109/TASE.2024.3389013

16. Koltermann, R.: 24-std-periodik in der langzeiterinnerung an duft- und farbsignale bei der honigbiene. Z. Vgl. Physiol. **75**, 49–68 (1971). https://doi.org/10.1007/BF00335137
17. Liu, W., Winfield, A.F., Sa, J., Chen, J., Dou, L.: Towards energy optimization: emergent task allocation in a swarm of foraging robots. Adapt. Behav. **15**, 289–305 (2007). https://doi.org/10.1177/1059712307082088
18. Font Llenas, A., Talamali, M.S., Xu, X., Marshall, J.A.R., Reina, A.: Quality-sensitive foraging by a robot swarm through virtual pheromone trails. In: Dorigo, M., Birattari, M., Blum, C., Christensen, A.L., Reina, A., Trianni, V. (eds.) ANTS 2018. LNCS, vol. 11172, pp. 135–149. Springer, Cham (2018). https://doi.org/10.1007/978-3-030-00533-7_11
19. Nieh, J.C.: The stop signal of honey bees: reconsidering its message. Behav. Ecol. Sociobiol. **33**, 51–56 (1993). https://doi.org/10.1007/BF00164346
20. Nieh, J.C.: A negative feedback signal that is triggered by peril curbs honey bee recruitment. Curr. Biol. **20**, 310–315 (2010). https://doi.org/10.1016/J.CUB.2009.12.060
21. Rajagopal, S., Brockmann, A., George, E.A.: Environment-dependent benefits of interindividual variation in honey bee recruitment. Anim. Behav. **192**, 9–26 (2022). https://doi.org/10.1016/J.ANBEHAV.2022.07.011
22. Reina, A., Marshall, J.A.R.: Negative feedback may suppress variation to improve collective foraging performance. PLoS Comput. Biol. **18**(5), 1–11 (2022). https://doi.org/10.1371/journal.pcbi.1010090
23. Schürch, R., Grüter, C.: Dancing bees improve colony foraging success as long-term benefits outweigh short-term costs. PLOS ONE **9**, e104660 (2014). https://doi.org/10.1371/JOURNAL.PONE.0104660, https://journals.plos.org/plosone/article?id=10.1371/journal.pone.0104660
24. Seeley, T.D.: Adaptive significance of the age polyethism schedule in honeybee colonies. Behav. Ecol. Sociobiol. **11**, 287–293 (1982). https://doi.org/10.1007/BF00299306
25. Seeley, T.D.: The tremble dance of the honey bee: message and meanings. Behav. Ecol. Sociobiol. **31**, 375–383 (1992). https://doi.org/10.1007/BF00170604
26. Seeley, T.D., Visscher, P.K.: Assessing the benefits of cooperation in honeybee foraging: search costs, forage quality, and competitive ability. Behav. Ecol. Sociobiol. **22**, 229–237 (1988). https://doi.org/10.1007/BF00299837
27. Seeley, T., Camazine, S., Sneyd, J.: Collective decision-making in honey bees: how colonies choose among nectar sources. Behav. Ecol. Sociobiol. **28** (1991). https://doi.org/10.1007/BF00175101
28. Valentini, G., Ferrante, E., Dorigo, M.: The best-of-n problem in robot swarms: formalization, state of the art, and novel perspectives. Front. Robot. AI **4** (2017). https://doi.org/10.3389/frobt.2017.00009
29. Vincze, C., Leelőssy, Á., Zajácz, E., Mészáros, R.: A review of short-term weather impacts on honey production. Int. J. Biometeorol. **69**, 303 (2024). https://doi.org/10.1007/S00484-024-02824-0, https://pmc.ncbi.nlm.nih.gov/articles/PMC11785677/
30. Winston, M.L., Punnett, E.N.: Factors determining temporal division of labor in honeybees. **60**, 2947–2952 (1982). https://doi.org/10.1139/Z82-372, https://cdnsciencepub.com/doi/10.1139/z82-372

AID: Agent Intent from Diffusion
for Multi-agent Informative Path Planning

Jeric Lew$^{(\boxtimes)}$, Yuhong Cao, Derek Ming Siang Tan,
and Guillaume Sartoretti$^{(\boxtimes)}$

Department of Mechanical Engineering, National University of Singapore, Singapore,
Singapore
{jericlew,caoyuhong,derektan}@u.nus.edu, mpegas@nus.edu.sg

Abstract. Information gathering in large-scale or time-critical scenarios (e.g., environmental monitoring, search and rescue) requires broad coverage within limited time budgets, motivating the use of multi-agent systems. These scenarios are commonly formulated as multi-agent informative path planning (MAIPP), where multiple agents must coordinate to maximize information gain while operating under budget constraints. A central challenge in MAIPP is ensuring effective coordination while the belief over the environment evolves with incoming measurements. Recent learning-based approaches address this by using distributions over future positions as "intent" to support coordination. However, these autoregressive intent predictors are computationally expensive and prone to compounding errors. Inspired by the effectiveness of diffusion models as expressive, long-horizon policies, we propose *AID*, a fully decentralized MAIPP framework that leverages diffusion models to generate long-term trajectories in a non-autoregressive manner. *AID* first performs behavior cloning on trajectories produced by existing MAIPP planners and then fine-tunes the policy using reinforcement learning via Diffusion Policy Policy Optimization (DPPO). This two-stage pipeline enables the policy to inherit expert behavior while learning improved coordination through online reward feedback. Experiments demonstrate that *AID* consistently improves upon the MAIPP planners it is trained from, achieving **4×** **faster** execution and up to **17% increased information gain**, while scaling effectively to larger numbers of agents. Our implementation is publicly available at github.com/marmotlab/AID.

1 Introduction

Information gathering tasks, such as inspections of large-scale structures [35], environmental monitoring [17], or search and rescue operations [1], are often laborious, time-consuming, and potentially hazardous for humans. Autonomous robotic systems offer a safer and more efficient alternative that can operate in complex and dangerous environments with minimal human supervision. The difficulty in such scenarios lies in determining how robots should travel to efficiently collect information with minimal *a priori* information, which has motivated extensive research in adaptive *Informative Path Planning* (IPP) [15,19].

© The Author(s), under exclusive license to Springer Nature Switzerland AG 2026
R. Groß et al. (Eds.): ANTS 2026, LNCS 16515, pp. 41–54, 2026.
https://doi.org/10.1007/978-3-032-26123-6_4

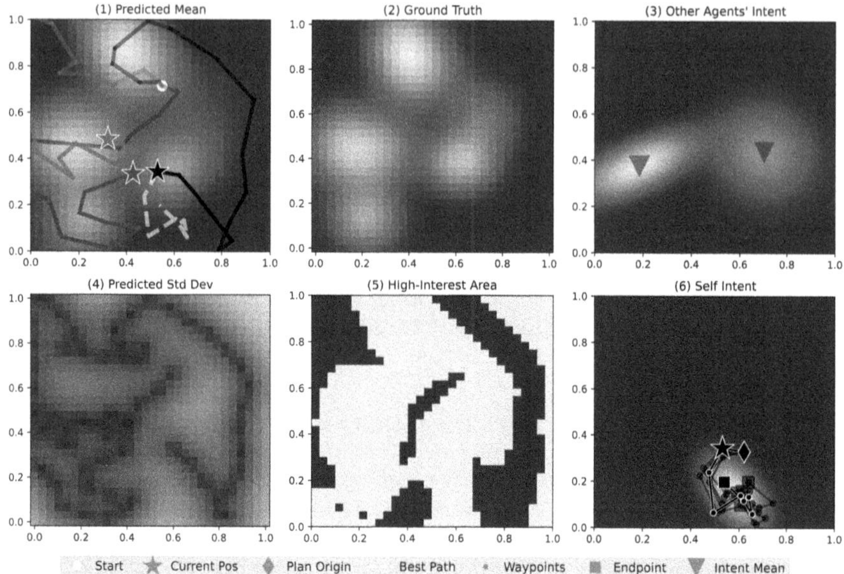

Fig. 1. Example run of *AID* with 3 agents. (1) shows agent trajectories (colored lines) with the best planned path of the black agent. **(1)** and **(4)** depict the GP-predicted mean and standard deviation of the information distribution (Sect. 3.1). **(2)** shows the ground-truth information distribution, and **(5)** highlights the current high-interest area (Sect. 3.2). **(6)** visualizes the black agent's intent distribution, while **(3)** shows the fused intent distribution of the other agents (Sect. 4.2).

In adaptive IPP, an autonomous agent must plan a path that maximizes information gain about an environment while satisfying constraints such as distance or time. The environment is typically modeled as a continuous spatial field inferred from sparse, noisy measurements, with Gaussian Processes commonly used to maintain both predictions and uncertainty [4,8,19,34]. As the agent begins with little prior knowledge, each new measurement reshapes the estimated information distribution and shifts which regions are most informative, requiring frequent replanning and real-time computation. As IPP is NP-hard [14], existing solutions, ranging from meta-heuristics to deep reinforcement learning [4,8,19,22], aim to balance solution quality with computational efficiency.

Expanding upon single-agent IPP, *multi-agent informative path planning* (MAIPP) aims to accelerate information gathering and expand coverage [12,32], which is particularly valuable in time-critical scenarios like post-disaster search and rescue. MAIPP has added challenges as agents must coordinate to maximize collective information gain, avoid redundant coverage, and adapt to a dynamically changing belief, making decentralized cooperation a difficult open problem.

MAIPP methods can rely on *Sequential Greedy Assignment* (SGA) [6], where agents plan one after another using single-agent IPP solvers while considering previously assigned paths to maintain coordination. Recent works, such as IntentMAIPP [34], adopt deep reinforcement learning (DRL) and models each agent's future trajectory as "intent" to promote cooperative behavior. However, IntentMAIPP generates trajectories autoregressively which is computationally costly and results in noisy intent predictions when prediction horizon increases.

To address the challenges of MAIPP, the limitations of autoregressive methods and the need for long-horizon intent predictions, we propose *AID* (**A**gent **I**ntent from **D**iffusion), a diffusion-based framework for MAIPP. Diffusion models, are well suited for planning and control because they can represent complex, multi-modal action distributions and naturally support long-term trajectory generation [3,5,13]. *AID* leverages these properties by first cloning the behavior of existing MAIPP solvers and then fine-tuning via online reinforcement learning to produce faster and less noisy intent predictions. This approach improves multi-agent coordination and information gathering while maintaining computational efficiency. We demonstrate the flexibility and scalability of *AID* by applying it to both sampling-based planners such as RIGTree [10] and DRL-based planners such as IntentMAIPP [34], showing consistent improvements, robust performance with increasing team size, and up to a 4× speedup. Our results indicate that diffusion-based policies are an effective tool for MAIPP, facilitating long-horizon planning and decentralized cooperation through fine-tuning.

2   Related Works

Single-Agent IPP: Single-agent IPP has been addressed through a variety of traditional planners, including sampling-based [8,10] methods and viewpoint-selection approaches [2,16]. Among these, RIGTree [10] is a RRT-style sampling-based solver that select high information-gain branches efficiently, making it suitable for iterative replanning in adaptive IPP. More recently, deep reinforcement learning [18,28,31] has emerged as strong alternative. CAtNIPP [4] captures information of the environment through a probabilistic roadmap and uses a graph attention network to embed global belief information for local decision making. This attention mechanism enables fast, context-aware action selection, improving both solution quality and inference efficiency.

Multi-agent IPP: MAIPP remains relatively underexplored. An effective baseline is Sequential Greedy Assignment (SGA) [6], where agents plan one after another while accounting for other agent's planned paths. SGA is simple, scalable, and compatible with any single-agent IPP planner, but frequent updates to the shared belief map often require repeated replanning, which can hinder coordinated behavior. As in single-agent IPP, reinforcement learning has similarly proven to be an effective alternative in MAIPP [29,32,33]. IntentMAIPP [34], building on CAtNIPP, plans using the global belief and an intent map that encodes other agents' future positions as Gaussian distributions. This compact representation allows easy combination of multiple agents' intents, but as more future nodes are sampled, compounding errors can accumulate, degrading long-term planning performance.

Diffusion for Multi-agent Systems: Diffusion models [9,26] are a class of generative models that have achieved state-of-the-art performance in image synthesis. Their ability to capture multi-modal action distributions and suitability for high-dimensional output spaces have driven growing interest in robotics applications. Recent works have demonstrated the effectiveness of diffusion models in generating robot behaviors for manipulation [5], legged locomotion [11], and visual navigation [24,27], among others. In multi-agent settings, however, the use of diffusion remains limited. Some existing approaches rely on offline datasets to learn trajectory distributions that ensure coordination or collision avoidance in multi-agent path finding [25]. MADIFF [36] introduces a multi-agent diffusion framework but incorporates centralized elements by performing attention across all agents at every decoder layer, which may limit scalability and decentralization. In contrast, our method extends the use of diffusion models toward decentralized multi-agent coordination by leveraging their long-horizon trajectory generation capabilities to model intent. The use of behavior cloning further aligns with a promising direction of distilling optimal solutions into scalable decentralized policies [20].

3   Background

3.1   Gaussian Processes (GPs)

In IPP, an agent's objective is to collect information from an environment where the underlying information is modeled as a continuous function over a 2D space, $\zeta : \mathcal{E} \to \mathbb{R}$, with $\mathcal{E} \subset \mathbb{R}^2$ representing the environment. However, this function is unknown to the agent(s) and must be inferred from limited measurements. Following previous works [4,8,19,34], Gaussian Processes (GPs) provide a way to estimate this unknown function by interpolating between sparse observations.

A GP defines a distribution over functions and enables us to approximate the true function ζ using a probabilistic model, $\zeta \approx GP(\mu, P)$, where μ and P represent the mean and covariance functions of the GP, respectively. Given a set of n measurement locations $X \subset \mathcal{E}$ and corresponding observations Y, along with a set of query locations $X^* \subset \mathcal{E}$ where the agent seeks to infer values, the GP posterior mean $\mu(X^*)$ and covariance $P(X^*)$ are given by:

$$\mu(X^*) = \mu(X^*) + K(X^*, X)[K(X, X) + \sigma_n^2 I]^{-1}(Y - \mu(X)), \tag{1}$$

$$P(X^*) = K(X^*, X^*) - K(X^*, X)[K(X, X) + \sigma_n^2 I]^{-1}K(X^*, X)^T, \tag{2}$$

where $K(\cdot, \cdot)$ is a kernel function defining the spatial correlation, σ_n^2 represents the measurement noise, and I is the identity matrix. In this work, we utilize the Matérn 3/2 kernel, commonly used in IPP literature [4,8,19,34].

3.2   Multi-agent Informative Path Planning

In MAIPP, the objective is to determine an optimal set of trajectories $\psi^* = \{\psi_1, \ldots, \psi_m\}$ for m agents, such that the collective information gain is maximized while ensuring that each agent adheres to its individual budget constraint. The problem is formulated as:

$$\psi^* = \arg\max_{\psi \in \Psi} \sum_{i=1}^{m} I(\psi_i), \quad \text{s.t.} \quad C(\psi_i) \leq B, \quad 1 \leq i \leq m, \tag{3}$$

where $I(\psi_i)$ represents the information gain from trajectory ψ_i, $C(\psi_i)$ denotes the trajectory cost, and B is the allocated budget (path length) for each agent.

Following prior works [4,34], the information gain $I(\psi_i)$ is defined as the reduction in uncertainty over high-interest areas: $I(\psi_i) = \text{Tr}(P_I^-) - \text{Tr}(P_I^+)$, where $\text{Tr}(\cdot)$ denotes the trace of a matrix, and P_I^- and P_I^+ represent the prior and posterior covariance matrices of the high-interest areas, respectively. These high-interest areas are determined using an upper confidence bound, $X_I = \{x_i \in X^* \mid \mu_i^- + \beta P_{i,i}^- \geq \mu_{th}\}$, where μ_i^- and $P_{i,i}^-$ correspond to the mean and variance of the GP at location x_i, while μ_{th} and β control the threshold and confidence interval, respectively.

Thus, the planner must adapt to new measurements, as they continuously update the agent's belief and redefine high-interest areas. This necessitates online replanning to maximize information gain and ensure efficient exploration. Figure 1 illustrates the MAIPP problem, the use of GPs to estimate the information in the environment and an example run of *AID*.

4   Method

To leverage diffusion models for MAIPP, our proposed *AID* framework adopts a fully decentralized two-stage approach. In the first stage, we pre-train a diffusion policy via behavior cloning on a dataset of trajectories generated by existing MAIPP planners. This follows prior work on diffusion-based policies [5,13].

To go beyond behavior cloning and further enhance agent coordination, we employ *Diffusion Policy Policy Optimization* (DPPO) [21], a recent reinforcement learning approach that fine-tunes pre-trained diffusion policies online to improve performance. By combining supervised pre-training with online fine-tuning, *AID* achieves both improved sample efficiency and stronger policy performance in contrast to training a diffusion policy from scratch with DPPO.

This two-stage training pipeline allows *AID* to fully exploit the advantages of diffusion models: representing complex action distributions and generating long-horizon trajectories in a single forward pass. Unlike autoregressive policies such as those used in IntentMAIPP [34], which require costly iterative updates and can accumulate compounding errors, *AID* outputs temporally consistent plans, enabling more effective long-term planning and coordination across multiple agents. The overall pipeline of our framework is illustrated in Fig. 2.

4.1   Sequential Decision-Making Problem

We formulate MAIPP as a sequential decision-making problem in continuous space, providing greater flexibility compared to previous works that employ DRL

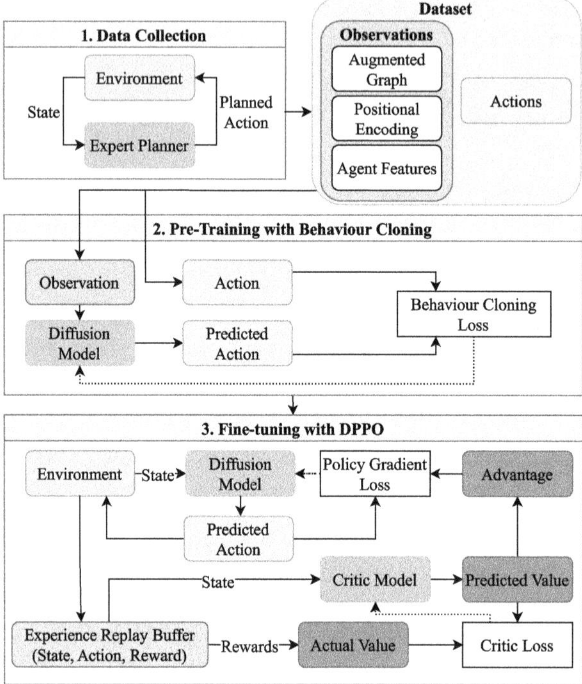

Fig. 2. Pipeline for *AID*.

on a graph [4,34]. We assume an obstacle-free environment, but obstacle handling can be incorporated by adding standard collision-checking and avoidance.

Each agent i starts from the same initial position and moves asynchronously to their next position which can be of different distance for each agent. Thus, the time steps, t, each agent can take before exhausting their budget might be different. Agents iteratively plan and execute their paths in a receding horizon manner until their budget is exhausted. At that point, the final trajectory of agent i is given by: $\psi_i = \{\psi_1^i, \ldots, \psi_t^i\}$, $\forall \psi_n^i \in \mathbb{R}^2$ with trajectory length $C(\psi_i) = \sum_{j=1}^{n_i-1} L_2(\psi_j^i, \psi_{j+1}^i)$, where $L_2(\cdot, \cdot)$ denotes the Euclidean distance.

4.2 Modeling Agent's Intent

To facilitate coordination among agents, we represent each agent's planned future positions as a probabilistic distribution, termed as *intent* [34]. Each agent updates and shares its intent when it plans a new trajectory, allowing others to incorporate this information into their decision-making.

An agent's intent is modeled as a Gaussian distribution $GD(\mu^i(t), \Sigma^i(t))$, where $\mu^i(t)$ and $\Sigma^i(t)$ are the mean and covariance matrix fitted to the planned trajectory of agent i at time step t. This distribution provides a probabilistic estimate of where the agent is likely to move.

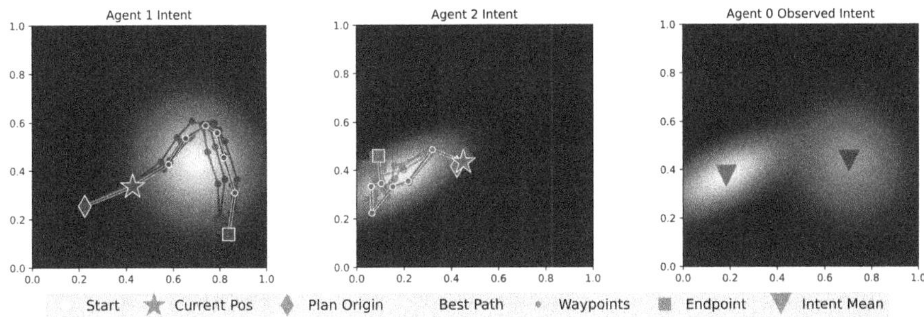

Fig. 3. Agent intent generated by diffusion model. 5 trajectory predictions were generated per agent with a planning horizon $T_p = 8$ (Sect. 4.3). Elements with white borders denote the chosen path that is executed. The fused intent visualization shows the normalized distribution of positions from other agents' sampled trajectories.

To ensure effective coordination, each agent aggregates the intent of all other $m - 1$ agents to form a fused intent map. This is achieved by summing the Gaussian distributions of the other agents' intents and normalizing the result. The fused intent map, shown in Fig. 3, serves as an additional input to the agent's decision-making process, allowing it to make more informed path-planning decisions while adapting to the predicted movements of its teammates.

4.3   Pre-training with Behavior Cloning

In the first stage of *AID*, we pre-train a diffusion policy using behavior cloning. This stage aims to initialize the diffusion model with behaviors from existing MAIPP planners before fine-tuning it through reinforcement learning. To achieve this, we construct a dataset of trajectories generated by existing MAIPP planners. Each agent's state-action pairs are recorded independently at every time step, following the same inputâ€“output structure used by the diffusion policy. The collected dataset thus consists of pairs of *observations* and corresponding *actions*, defined as follows:

Observation: The input (observation) to the diffusion model for agent i at time step t is $s_t^i = \{V'^i, Q^i, A^i\}$. The augmented graph nodes, V'^i, represents information in the environment and is derived from a probabilistic roadmap (PRM), where there are n nodes which are connected to their k nearest neighbors, forming $G^i = (V^i, E^i)$, $i \in \{1, ..., m\}$, where $V^i = \{v_1^i, ..., v_n^i\}$ represents the nodes and E^i the edges. The PRM graph is then augmented with additional information such that each node $v_j'^i = (\hat{x}_j^i, \hat{y}_j^i, \mu(v_j^i), P(v_j^i), f(v_j^i)) \in V'^i$, $j \in \{1, ..., n\}$, where $(\hat{x}, \hat{y})$ is the relative position from the agent's current location, $\mu(v_j^i), P(v_j^i)$ are the mean and variance of the predicted information from the GP, and $f(v_j^i)$ is the intent information of the other $m - 1$ agents at the current node's position. The positional encoding of the graph, Q^i, is computed based on graph connectivity using eigenvalues [7], resulting in a 32-dimensional representation per node.

Lastly, the agent-specific input A^i is defined as $A^i = (v^i_t, B^i_t, \mu_{th})$, where v^i_t is the agent's current position, $B^i_t = B - C(\psi^i)$ represents the remaining budget, and μ_{th} is the threshold for defining high-interest areas.

Action: At each time step t, agent i processes its updated observation s^i_t through a diffusion model, which outputs a sequence of delta x and y positions $\Delta^i_t = \{\delta^i_t, \delta^i_{t+1}, ..., \delta^i_{t+T_p-1}\}$ over a horizon of length T_p. This sequence of delta positions are then cumulatively summed to yield a sequence of future way-points $\psi^i_{t+1:t+T_p} = \{\psi^i_{t+1}, \psi^i_{t+2}, ..., \psi^i_{t+T_p}\}$, $\psi^i_j \in \mathbb{R}^2$. This represents the predicted path, which is executed in a receding horizon manner over T_a steps to maintain adaptability in response to new information from updated observations.

As the data is collected offline, we have access to complete trajectories, providing flexibility in defining how intent information is derived. If intent is available from the existing MAIPP planner (e.g. in sampling-based methods where a planned path is provided), we use it directly. Otherwise, intent can be retroactively assigned based on the agent's actual future positions. The same approach is applied when collecting the actions from offline trajectories. With the collected trajectories, we pre-train the diffusion policy following Chi et al. [5] using a behavior cloning objective. Specifically, for each agent i at time step t, Gaussian noise $\varepsilon_k \sim \mathcal{N}(0, I)$ is added to the ground-truth delta action sequence $\Delta^{0,i}_t$, and the diffusion model ε_θ is trained to predict this noise conditioned on the agent's observation s^i_t and the noisy action sequence at diffusion step k. The resulting mean squared error loss is:

$$\mathcal{L}_{\text{BC}} = \text{MSE}\Big(\varepsilon_k, \ \varepsilon_\theta(s^i_t, \ \Delta^{0,i}_t + \varepsilon_k, \ k)\Big), \tag{4}$$

4.4 Fine-Tuning with DPPO

After pre-training the diffusion policy via behavior cloning, we fine-tune it online using reinforcement learning. The policy interacts with the environment to collect rollout trajectories containing observations, actions, rewards, and value estimates, which are then used for optimization.

DPPO (Diffusion Proximal Policy Optimization) [21] extends PPO to diffusion policies by treating each denoising step as an action within a *Diffusion MDP*. This allows reward signals to propagate through the entire denoising process, enabling end-to-end policy improvement. As in PPO, DPPO stabilizes training using a clipped surrogate objective.

A critic network is trained alongside the policy to predict state values, which are used to compute advantage estimates via Generalized Advantage Estimation (GAE) [23]. These advantage estimates guide the policy to favor denoising actions that yield higher cumulative rewards. The critic itself is optimized using a MSE loss between predicted state values and the returns computed with GAE, ensuring accurate value estimation and improving the quality of policy updates during fine-tuning.

Reward: When an agent depletes its budget, it receives a negative reward:

$$r_f = -\alpha \left(\frac{\mathrm{Tr}(P^f)}{\mathrm{Tr}(P^i)} \right)^{\beta}, \tag{5}$$

where $\mathrm{Tr}(P^i)$ and $\mathrm{Tr}(P^f)$ denote the initial and final covariance traces over high-interest regions, α is a scaling factor, and $\beta \in [0,1]$ controls the concavity of the penalty ($\alpha = 5$, $\beta = 0.5$ in practice). A concave function is chosen because reducing uncertainty becomes increasingly difficult as the covariance trace approaches zero. With $\beta < 1$, the reward structure reflects this by assigning relatively greater incentive to small but harder reductions at low uncertainty, compared to easy reductions of the same magnitude when uncertainty is high. This sparse reward directly encourages agents to minimize final uncertainty [34], promoting cooperative information gathering during fine-tuning.

4.5 Neural Network Architecture

Graph Attention Encoder: Given input observation s_t^i, each feature in s_t^i, namely $\{V'^i, Q^i, A^i\}$, is projected into a d-dimensional embedding, $\{\hat{V}'^i, \hat{Q}^i, \hat{A}^i\}$. The embedded node features, $\hat{V}'^i$, are summed with the corresponding embedded positional encoding, $\hat{Q}^i$, and passed through a *multi-head self-attention* [30] layer, following the approach in [4,34], to capture relational dependencies between different nodes in the environment. The output is a set of enhanced node features, which are then passed through a *multi-head cross-attention* layer, where the enhanced node features serve as the key and value, while the agent's embedded features, $\hat{A}^i$, serve as the query. This cross-attention mechanism allows the encoder to focus on the most relevant parts of the environment, taking into account the agent's current state, such as its location and remaining budget. The final output is a d-dimensional encoded state representation, $\hat{s}_t^i$, which encapsulates agent i's perception of the environment. This representation is then used as the input for the diffusion model and critic model, with each network having its own graph attention encoder.

Diffusion Model: Conditioned on $\hat{s}_t^i$, a U-Net-based diffusion model [5] iteratively denoises a randomly sampled action sequence of length T_p, producing a refined planned action sequence $\Delta_t^i = \{\delta_t^i, \delta_{t+1}^i, ..., \delta_{t+T_p-1}^i\}$.

Critic Model: The critic takes $\hat{s}_t^i$ as input and passes it through a three-layer multi-layer perceptron (MLP) to predict the state value, $V(s_t^i)$, providing the necessary estimates for advantage computation during DPPO training.

4.6 Implementation Details

Environment Setup: Training environments are generated by sampling between 8–12 Gaussian functions to produce diverse, multimodal belief landscapes. Each environment contains three agents ($m = 3$). A Probabilistic

Table 1. Comparison of coverage and planning across 100 environments.

Method	3 Agents		5 Agents		10 Agents	
	Cov. Trace	Time (s)	Cov. Trace	Time (s)	Cov. Trace	Time (s)
RIGTreeSGA	68.4 ± 22.0	47.1 ± 1.1	22.7 ± 10.5	86.1 ± 1.2	4.5 ± 2.6	177.0 ± 4.0
AID (PT RIGTreeSGA)	89.7 ± 27.4	9.5 ± 0.8	47.6 ± 23.3	16.9 ± 1.0	22.5 ± 12.8	32.2 ± 0.8
AID (PT RIGTreeSGA + FT)	56.5 ± 15.2	11.0 ± 0.9	20.9 ± 8.9	19.6 ± 1.3	5.9 ± 4.0	38.2 ± 2.8
IntentMAIPP	28.5 ± 10.7	38.6 ± 2.0	8.7 ± 3.1	96.0 ± 5.2	3.4 ± 1.5	312.2 ± 2.8
AID (PT IntentMAIPP)	33.5 ± 10.5	7.8 ± 0.9	12.0 ± 4.0	14.8 ± 1.3	5.0 ± 3.0	30.9 ± 1.5
AID (PT IntentMAIPP + FT)	27.5 ± 6.6	13.0 ± 1.3	8.7 ± 3.6	27.3 ± 2.3	2.6 ± 0.9	67.3 ± 5.3

Roadmap (PRM) with 200 nodes and $k = 20$ nearest neighbors is used. The high-interest threshold is set to $\mu_{th} = 0.4$, and the confidence parameter is $\beta = 1$. Each agent is allocated a budget of $B = 3$ steps per episode.

Diffusion Policy: The diffusion model uses 20 denoising steps, with only the last 10 denoising steps fine-tuned with DPPO. The graph-attention encoder has an embedding dimension of $d = 64$ and processes two consecutive states from time steps t and $t-1$. The planning horizon is $T_p = 8$ and the action horizon is $T_a = 2$. During fine-tuning and execution, the policy generates 5 candidate paths per step and executes the trajectory that yields the greatest reduction in covariance trace. These generated trajectories are also used to construct agent intent during multi-agent planning. Model training was done on an NVIDIA GeForce RTX 4080 SUPER. Diffusion policies were pre-trained for 1,000 epochs (9 h), with the best-performing model selected via evaluation. Fine-tuning with DPPO was performed for up to 500 epochs or until performance plateaued. Total training time varied between 15âĂŞ30 h depending on the base planner and DPPO parameters. Additional details and code are available at github.com/marmotlab/AID.

5   Experiments

To assess the effectiveness of *AID*, we evaluate it on two representative MAIPP baselines. The first is RIGTreeSGA, an extension of RIGTree [10], an RRT-based single-agent IPP planner, augmented with SGA [6] to enable multi-agent coordination. The second is IntentMAIPP [34], an attention-based reinforcement learning approach that autoregressively samples future intent trajectories.

All methods are evaluated on a fixed set of 100 unseen environments. Performance is measured using (i) the remaining covariance trace within high-interest regions which reflects the residual uncertainty over the environment's underlying information, as defined in Sect. 3.2, and (ii) the overall planning time, defined as the total time required for a planner to expend its budget, which captures computational efficiency. **PT** denotes diffusion models trained solely by behavior cloning their respective baseline planner, whereas **FT** denotes the same models after additional online fine-tuning.

As shown in Table 1, diffusion-based policies consistently reduce planning time across all baselines and team sizes. *AID* achieves approximately a **4×** **speedup** over sampling-based RIGTreeSGA and autoregressive IntentMAIPP, with the advantage increasing as the number of agents grows, highlighting its computational scalability.

In terms of information-gathering performance (covariance trace), the improvements are more nuanced. Pure behavior cloning (PT) variants exhibit higher variance and reduced performance compared to their experts, consistent with prior observations that diffusion policies are unable to fully match long-horizon expert behavior [5, 21]. However, after fine-tuning, performance becomes more competitive. With 3 agents, *AID* (PT RIGTreeSGA + FT) improves covariance trace by approximately **17%** over RIGTreeSGA while maintaining a significant runtime reduction. For IntentMAIPP, gains from fine-tuning are more modest, likely because the expert is already near-optimal, but comparable performance is achieved with substantially reduced runtime.

Finally, scaling to 5 and 10 agents shows similar trends: diffusion-based policies match or improve baseline performance within variance while planning significantly faster. These results suggest that AID primarily offers a favorable trade-off between information gain and computational efficiency, making it a scalable and practical approach for larger multi-agent teams.

6   Conclusion

In this work, we introduced *AID*, a decentralized framework that integrates diffusion models into multi-agent informative path planning. Instead of relying on autoregressive policy sampling, diffusion models allow direct generation of long-horizon trajectories in a single forward pass, which supports coherent planning and provides a stable intent signal for coordination.

Through experiments on both sampling-based and learning-based MAIPP solvers, we showed that *AID* improves multi-agent cooperation, increases information gain, and planning time when compared to existing methods. These results highlight the benefits of combining behavior cloning with online fine-tuning through DPPO to obtain robust diffusion policies for multi-agent planning.

Future work include scaling this algorithm to hundreds or even thousands of agents and applying *AID* to 3D IPP environments with real robot experiments. We are also interested in extending *AID* to other multi-agent tasks that require coordinated actions, like multi-drone cooperative manipulation.

Acknowledgments. This work was supported by NUS under grant TL/FS/2025/01.

Disclosure of Interests. The authors have no competing interests to declare.

References

1. Baxter, J.L., Burke, E.K., Garibaldi, J.M., Norman, M.: Multi-robot search and rescue: a potential field based approach. In: Mukhopadhyay, S.C., Gupta, G.S. (eds.) Autonomous Robots and Agents. Studies in Computational Intelligence, vol. 76, pp. 9–16. Springer, Heidelberg (2007). https://doi.org/10.1007/978-3-540-73424-6_2
2. Binney, J., Sukhatme, G.S.: Branch and bound for informative path planning. In: 2012 IEEE International Conference on Robotics and Automation, pp. 2147–2154 (2012). https://doi.org/10.1109/ICRA.2012.6224902
3. Cao, Y., Lew, J., Liang, J., Cheng, J., Sartoretti, G.: DARE: diffusion policy for autonomous robot exploration. In: 2025 IEEE International Conference on Robotics and Automation (ICRA), pp. 11987–11993 (2025). https://doi.org/10.1109/ICRA55743.2025.11128196
4. Cao, Y., Wang, Y., Vashisth, A., Fan, H., Sartoretti, G.A.: CAtNIPP: context-aware attention-based network for informative path planning. In: Conference on Robot Learning, pp. 1928–1937. PMLR (2023)
5. Chi, C., et al.: Diffusion policy: visuomotor policy learning via action diffusion. Int. J. Robot. Res. (2024)
6. Corah, M., Michael, N.: Efficient online multi-robot exploration via distributed sequential greedy assignment. In: Robotics: Science and Systems, Cambridge, MA, vol. 13 (2017)
7. Dwivedi, V.P., Bresson, X.: A generalization of transformer networks to graphs. In: AAAI Workshop on Deep Learning on Graphs: Methods and Applications (2021)
8. Hitz, G., Galceran, E., Garneau, M.É., Pomerleau, F., Siegwart, R.: Adaptive continuous-space informative path planning for online environmental monitoring. J. Field Robot. **34**(8), 1427–1449 (2017). https://doi.org/10.1002/rob.21722, https://onlinelibrary.wiley.com/doi/abs/10.1002/rob.21722
9. Ho, J., Jain, A., Abbeel, P.: Denoising diffusion probabilistic models. In: Larochelle, H., Ranzato, M., Hadsell, R., Balcan, M., Lin, H. (eds.) Advances in Neural Information Processing Systems, vol. 33, pp. 6840–6851. Curran Associates, Inc. (2020). https://proceedings.neurips.cc/paper_files/paper/2020/file/4c5bcfec8584af0d967f1ab10179ca4b-Paper.pdf
10. Hollinger, G.A., Sukhatme, G.S.: Sampling-based robotic information gathering algorithms. Int. J. Robot. Res. **33**(9), 1271–1287 (2014). https://doi.org/10.1177/0278364914533443, https://doi.org/10.1177/0278364914533443
11. Huang, X., et al.: Diffuseloco: real-time legged locomotion control with diffusion from offline datasets (2024). https://arxiv.org/abs/2404.19264
12. Jakkala, K., Akella, S.: Multi-robot informative path planning from regression with sparse gaussian processes. In: 2024 IEEE International Conference on Robotics and Automation (ICRA), pp. 12382–12388 (2024). https://doi.org/10.1109/ICRA57147.2024.10610484
13. Janner, M., Du, Y., Tenenbaum, J., Levine, S.: Planning with diffusion for flexible behavior synthesis. In: International Conference on Machine Learning (2022)
14. Krause, A.: Optimizing sensing: theory and applications. Carnegie Mellon University (2008)
15. Lim, Z.W., Hsu, D., Lee, W.S.: Adaptive informative path planning in metric spaces. In: Akin, H.L., Amato, N.M., Isler, V., van der Stappen, A.F. (eds.) Algorithmic Foundations of Robotics XI. STAR, vol. 107, pp. 283–300. Springer, Cham (2015). https://doi.org/10.1007/978-3-319-16595-0_17

16. Meliou, A., Krause, A., Guestrin, C., Hellerstein, J.M.: Nonmyopic informative path planning in spatio-temporal models. In: AAAI, vol. 10, pp. 16–7 (2007)
17. Mishra, R., Chitre, M., Swarup, S.: Online informative path planning using sparse gaussian processes. In: 2018 OCEANS - MTS/IEEE Kobe Techno-Oceans (OTO), pp. 1–5 (2018). https://doi.org/10.1109/OCEANSKOBE.2018.8559183
18. Popović, M., Ott, J., Rückin, J., Kochenderfer, M.J.: Learning-based methods for adaptive informative path planning. Robot. Auton. Syst. **179**, 104727 (2024)
19. Popović, M., Vidal-Calleja, T., Hitz, G., Chung, J.J., Sa, I., Siegwart, R., Nieto, J.: An informative path planning framework for UAV-based terrain monitoring. Auton. Robot. **44**(6), 889–911 (2020). https://doi.org/10.1007/s10514-020-09903-2, http://link.springer.com/10.1007/s10514-020-09903-2
20. Prorok, A., Blumenkamp, J., Li, Q., Kortvelesy, R., Liu, Z., Stump, E.: The holy grail of multi-robot planning: Learning to generate online-scalable solutions from offline-optimal experts. In: Proceedings of the 21st International Conference on Autonomous Agents and Multiagent Systems, AAMAS 2022, pp. 1804–1808. International Foundation for Autonomous Agents and Multiagent Systems, Richland (2022)
21. Ren, A.Z., et al.: Diffusion policy policy optimization. arXiv preprint arXiv:2409.00588 (2024)
22. Rückin, J., Jin, L., Popović, M.: Adaptive informative path planning using deep reinforcement learning for UAV-based active sensing. In: 2022 International Conference on Robotics and Automation (ICRA), pp. 4473–4479 (2022). https://doi.org/10.1109/ICRA46639.2022.9812025
23. Schulman, J., Moritz, P., Levine, S., Jordan, M.I., Abbeel, P.: High-dimensional continuous control using generalized advantage estimation. In: Bengio, Y., LeCun, Y. (eds.) 4th International Conference on Learning Representations, ICLR 2016, San Juan, Puerto Rico, 2–4 May 2016, Conference Track Proceedings (2016). http://arxiv.org/abs/1506.02438
24. Shah, D., et al.: ViNT: a foundation model for visual navigation. In: 7th Annual Conference on Robot Learning (2023). https://arxiv.org/abs/2306.14846
25. Shaoul, Y., Mishani, I., Vats, S., Li, J., Likhachev, M.: Multi-robot motion planning with diffusion models. In: The Thirteenth International Conference on Learning Representations (ICLR), also at AAAI 2025 Workshop on Multi-Agent Path Finding (2025)
26. Sohl-Dickstein, J., Weiss, E., Maheswaranathan, N., Ganguli, S.: Deep unsupervised learning using nonequilibrium thermodynamics. In: International conference on machine learning, pp. 2256–2265. PMLR (2015)
27. Sridhar, A., Shah, D., Glossop, C., Levine, S.: NoMaD: goal masked diffusion policies for navigation and exploration. In: 2024 IEEE International Conference on Robotics and Automation (ICRA), pp. 63–70 (2024). https://doi.org/10.1109/ICRA57147.2024.10610665
28. Tan, D.M.S., et al.: Search-TTA: a multi-modal test-time adaptation framework for visual search in the wild. In: Proceedings of The 9th Conference on Robot Learning, vol. 305, pp. 2093–2120. PMLR (2025)
29. Vashisth, A., Kulshrestha, M., Conover, D., Bera, A.: Scalable multi-robot informative path planning for target mapping via deep reinforcement learning (2025). https://arxiv.org/abs/2409.16967
30. Vaswani, A., et al.: Attention is all you need. In: Advances in Neural Information Processing Systems, vol. 30 (2017)

31. Wei, Y., Zheng, R.: Informative path planning for mobile sensing with reinforcement learning. In: IEEE INFOCOM 2020 - IEEE Conference on Computer Communications, pp. 864–873 (2020). https://doi.org/10.1109/INFOCOM41043.2020.9155528

32. Westheider, J., Rückin, J., Popović, M.: Multi-UAV adaptive path planning using deep reinforcement learning. In: 2023 IEEE/RSJ International Conference on Intelligent Robots and Systems (IROS), pp. 649–656 (2023). https://doi.org/10.1109/IROS55552.2023.10342516

33. Yanes Luis, S., Perales Esteve, M., Gutiérrez Reina, D., Toral Marín, S.: Deep Reinforcement learning applied to multi-agent informative path planning in environmental missions. In: Azar, A.T., Kasim Ibraheem, I., Jaleel Humaidi, A. (eds.) Mobile Robot: Motion Control and Path Planning. Studies in Computational Intelligence, vol. 1090, pp. 31–61. Springer, Cham (2023). https://doi.org/10.1007/978-3-031-26564-8_2

34. Yang, T., Cao, Y., Sartoretti, G.: Intent-based deep reinforcement learning for multi-agent informative path planning. In: 2023 International Symposium on Multi-Robot and Multi-Agent Systems (MRS), pp. 71–77 (2023). https://doi.org/10.1109/MRS60187.2023.10416797

35. Zhu, H., Chung, J.J., Lawrance, N.R., Siegwart, R., Alonso-Mora, J.: Online informative path planning for active information gathering of a 3D surface. In: 2021 IEEE International Conference on Robotics and Automation (ICRA), pp. 1488–1494 (2021). https://doi.org/10.1109/ICRA48506.2021.9561963

36. Zhu, Z., et al.: MaDiff: offline multi-agent learning with diffusion models. arXiv preprint arXiv:2305.17330 (2023)

Bigraphical Model Checking
for Coordinated Drone Landings
on Vertiports

Dominik Grzelak[✉][ID], Tianxiong Zhang[ID], and Uwe Aßmann[ID]

Software Technology Group, Technische Universität Dresden, Dresden, Germany
{dominik.grzelak,tianxiong.zhang,uwe.assmann}@tu-dresden.de

Abstract. Coordinating multiple drones for landing on *vertiport*-like infrastructures constitutes a general safety-critical swarm intelligence problem that combines discrete decision-making with domain-specific spatial occupancy constraints. Existing scheduling and control approaches often lack formal, executable correctness guarantees and remain loosely coupled to low-level control logic, making cyber-physical inconsistencies likely, especially when the number of drones increases. This work presents a formal and executable model for flight operation management of multiple tiny drones on multiple simplified vertiports based on *bigraphical reactive systems*. The proposed model captures both the spatial layout and the interactions among drones and the infrastructure, providing a unified understanding of a complex coordination problem. Compositionality enables the reconfiguration of takeoff and landing pad topologies, as well as fleet sizes, without altering the underlying rules. We employ model checking to generate the full state space from a set of initial states and verify safety invariants for 4 drones on a 3×7 grid, and 3 drones on a 4×5 grid. Landing success is formalized as a reachability condition. The compositional design of the specification facilitates reusability and modular verification, and the rule-based specification allows for execution of the traces of the proof.

1 Introduction

Managing multiple drones on a ground infrastructure containing multiple vertiports (drone-tailored takeoff and landing pads) requires careful coordination to ensure safety and efficiency [9,33]. However, as the number of simultaneous drone operations grows, the complexity of preventing accidents and delays increases [32]. This challenge is central to domains in Innovative Air Mobility (IAM) including drone logistics, last-mile delivery, and infrastructure inspection. In fact, among the key technical concerns in drone swarm vertiport operations are communication, scheduling, and collision avoidance. This paper focuses on the latter. Sequential operations are the safest by design but limit throughput. In contrast, parallel operations improve efficiency but require rigorous safety guarantees. Designing collision-free procedures using formal methods is therefore a central problem for flight operation management of multiple drones.

R. Groß et al. (Eds.): ANTS 2026, LNCS 16515, pp. 55–68, 2026.
https://doi.org/10.1007/978-3-032-26123-6_5

Despite a growing body of work on scheduling algorithms, structured designs, or intelligent control schemes for vertiports (refer to [9,33]), many existing approaches do not produce machine-executable models whose correctness can be formally verified. Moreover, they are often decoupled from low-level drone control logic, resulting in potential inconsistencies at runtime. Formal methods (e.g., model checking) have been proposed to rigorously verify swarm coordination [2,14,18,21]. Typically, analysis is limited to small-scale instances involving only a few agents (between two and six), due to the combinatorial growth of the underlying state space.[1] This exponential blow-up has historically limited the applicability of exhaustive model checking in larger or dynamic swarm scenarios, motivating the development of alternative approaches (see [8,10,13]). Further, many modeling languages lack spatial compositionality, making it difficult to reuse and scale already verified behaviors across different infrastructure layouts or swarm sizes (cf. [25]).

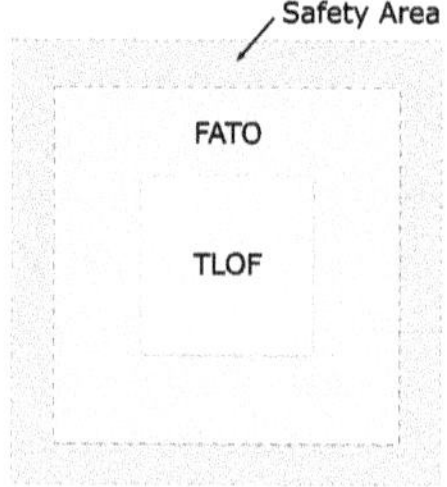

Fig. 1. Two exemplary vertiport infrastructure scenarios. Crazyflie tiny drones approach and land on a grid of pads while maintaining collision-freeness.

Fig. 2. Hierarchical structure of a drone-tailored takeoff and landing pad following PTS-VPT-DSN.

Scenario. Our use case centers on the coordinated landing of multiple drones within a vertiport infrastructure composed of modular landing pads. This scenario is representative of next-generation drone delivery within IAM infrastructures, where airspace traffic and ground resource constraints necessitate safe, and formally certifiable coordination strategies. Figure 1 illustrates two scenarios in which a potential drone swarm approaches the vertiport infrastructure from different directions. Each drone must approach the vertiport and land on an available pad without colliding with other drones, violating no-fly zones, or entering already-occupied pads. According to PTS-VPT-DSN, which possess regulatory character, a single vertiport pad is structured into three hierarchical zones: the Touchdown and Lift-Off area (TLOF), the Final Approach and Take-Off area (FATO), and the Safety Area. Refer to Fig. 2 for a schematic representation.

---

[1] For example, modeling the positions of r robots on an $n \times n$ grid, each with four directions and two movement modes, yields a state space of size $(n \cdot n \cdot 4 \cdot 2)^r$ [16].

Contributions. This paper makes the following contributions: (i) We apply a formal and executable model based on *bigraphical reactive systems* (BRSs) [30] to the problem of flight operation management of multiple tiny drones on multiple simplified takeoff and landing pads, capturing both spatial layout and rule-based agent behavior within a unified formalism. (ii) We demonstrate how the European Union Aviation Safety Agency's (EASA) Prototype Technical Specifications for Vertiport Design (PTS-VPT-DSN) [19] can be formalized within our framework.[2] (iii) We define collision-free landing as a reachability problem and perform full state-space model checking for two scenario configurations, varying in grid size, drone count, and vertiport layout. While not detailed in this paper, the model has been deployed on a physical testbed using the Crazyflie platform, demonstrating trace-driven execution consistent with the verified state-spaces.

2 Abstract Syntax for Space

This work builds on a spatial, graph-based syntax specified by a set of custom "bigraphical axioms" (Fig. 3), hereafter termed *bi-spatial structures*. These constitute elementary building blocks, which can be composed under laws of category theory in the context of BRS. Refer to [3,30], for a practical introduction to the essential definitions. For now, it suffices to think of bigraphs as ordinary graphs with more than one edge type and interface nodes for operations.[3]

Here, we practically instantiate the bigraph theory by devising a dedicated topological semantic layer that explicitly models discrete physical space, going beyond the abstract containment semantics intrinsic to bigraphs. *Bi-spatial structures* form a new class of"location-aware" bigraphs, constructed from reusable building blocks that define spatial adjacency of discrete spaces.[4] Here, we only give a lightweight introduction, serving as an accessible complement to the formal and practical treatment in the initial works [24–27]. For completeness, Fig. 3 presents the current axiomatic landscape in diagrammatic form, as specified by the definitions in [27]. We first introduce a simplified bigraph language used in this paper, followed by our model and illustrative examples.

Bigraph Term Language. Bigraphs form a process algebra and are therefore equipped with an algebraic term notation. For this work, we employ a *sugared form* to reduce categorical overhead (Fig. 3). The syntax of this language is defined by the following grammar using the Extended Backus-Naur Form (EBNF): $p ::= \mathsf{c}_{n_1,\ldots,n_{ar(\mathsf{c})}} \cdot p \mid p \mid p \mid p \parallel p \mid \boxed{i}$. The grammar constitutes the static semantics of a generic bigraphical language $\varXi$ comprised of a fixed set of elementary bigraphs and operators. The precedence of operators is determined by the utilization of parentheses. The first operator is *nesting* ".", meaning that a

---

[2] The Federal Aviation Administration (FAA, Eng. Brief 105 [20]) and the EASA are developing technical specifications for safe, drone-tailored takeoff and landing pads.

[3] For example, compared to a *scene graph*, which primarily represents static scene structure, a BRS equips such a graph with rules that define scene evolution.

[4] Alternative location-aware bigraph models have been explored, for example, in [1,7].

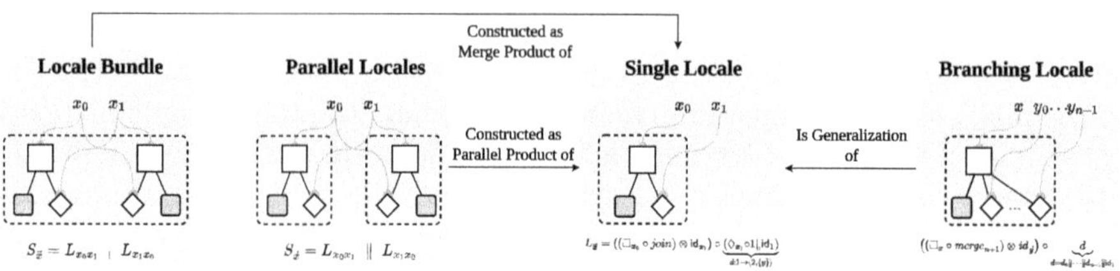

Fig. 3. Overview of bi-spatial axioms that define a dedicated spatial syntax for BRSs. These axioms provide modular building blocks for specifying spatial structure, aiming to simplify both modeling and verification.

bigraphical term p can be put under a node assigned type $\mathsf{c} \in \Sigma_\Xi$ (the signature of Ξ). To make a term explicit, we annotate the type with a node identifier by placing v_i above the symbol, e.g., $\overset{v_i}{\mathsf{c}}$. The ports of that node are indexed by n_k, $(k \in arity(\mathsf{c}))^5$ and are named to denote attachment to open links $n_k \in \{\boldsymbol{y}\}$. The operators"$|$" and "$\parallel$" denote the merge and parallel product, respectively, that is, placing terms under a shared root or under separate roots. The placeholder $\boxed{i}$ is also called a *site*, where $i \geq 0$ and unique over all p terms of the language.

Bi-grids. A particular subclass of bi-spatial structures, which we term *bi-grids*, models grid-like topologies. Example configurations are shown visually in Fig. 4, and their bigraph-algebraic counterpart in Fig. 1. A bi-grid is our modular, topological structure that represents the connectivity between abstract realms (e.g., discrete points, dimensionless regions, or other domain-specific locales). Its primary components include: Locale ($\square$), representing spatial regions; Route ($\lozenge$), representing paths within a locale that can connect to other locales; and *sites*, serving as placeholders to represent potential entities within a locale, such as drones or obstacles. It may capture additional properties such as direction and orientation (by the usage of $\lozenge$-typed nodes), and resolution (by varying the amount of $\square$-typed nodes). Two locales can be connected unidirectionally, either from the left region to the right or vice versa (see [27], Example 3). Bi-grids further support coordinates, as introduced for the cyber-physical game in [6] and subsequently applied to the multi-drone path planning problem in [27].[6]

Example 1 (Four bi-grid constructions). The bi-grids (a)–(d) shown in Fig. 4 represent basic spatial configurations and are specified using the bigraph term language as follows:

(a) $\overset{v_0}{\square}_{y_0} \overset{v_1}{\lozenge}_{y_1} \mid \overset{v_2}{\square}_{y_1}$

(b) $\overset{v_0}{\square}_{y_0} . \overset{v_1}{\lozenge}_{y_1} \mid \overset{v_2}{\square}_{y_1} . \overset{v_3}{\lozenge}_{y_0}$

(c) $\overset{v_0}{\square}_{y_0} . (\overset{v_1}{\lozenge}_{y_1} \mid \overset{}{\lozenge}_{y_2}) \mid \overset{v_3}{\square}_{y_1} . (\overset{}{\lozenge}_{y_0} \mid \overset{}{\lozenge}_{y_3}) \mid \overset{v_6}{\square}_{y_2} . (\overset{}{\lozenge}_{y_0} \mid \overset{}{\lozenge}_{y_3}) \mid \overset{v_9}{\square}_{y_3} . (\overset{}{\lozenge}_{y_1} \mid \overset{}{\lozenge}_{y_2})$

---

[5] The arity of a node type determines how many ports a node has in the final bigraph.

[6] In our experiments, explicit coordinate representations are not required, as the physical coordinates are provided by an external system.

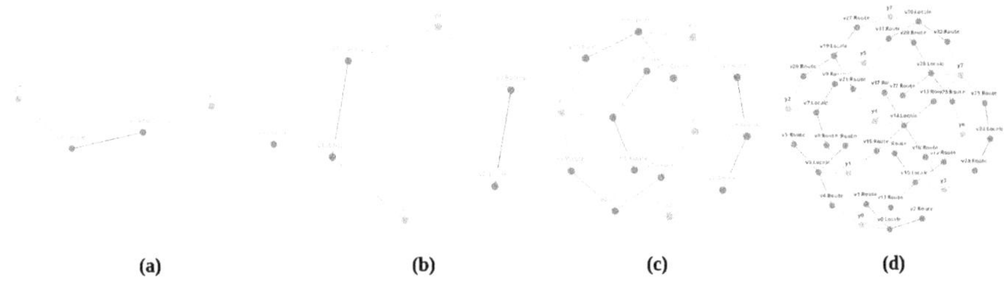

Fig. 4. Examples of bi-grids illustrating different forms of *connectedness* (green nodes and edges) between neighboring *locales* (red nodes and black edges). Roots and sites are omitted: (a) (1×2)-bi-grid, unidirectional. (b) (1×2)-bi-grid, bidirectional. (c) (2×2)-bi-grid, bi. (d) (3×3)-bi-grid, bi. (Color figure online)

$$(d) \quad \overset{v_0}{\square}_{y_0} \cdot (\Diamond_{y_1} \mid \Diamond_{y_3}) \mid \overset{v_3}{\square}_{y_1} \cdot (\Diamond_{y_0} \mid \Diamond_{y_2} \mid \Diamond_{y_4}) \mid \overset{v_7}{\square}_{y_2} \cdot (\Diamond_{y_1} \mid \Diamond_{y_5}) \mid$$
$$\overset{v_{10}}{\square}_{y_3} \cdot (\Diamond_{y_0} \mid \Diamond_{y_4} \mid \Diamond_{y_6}) \mid \overset{v_{14}}{\square}_{y_4} \cdot (\Diamond_{y_1} \mid \Diamond_{y_3} \mid \Diamond_{y_5} \mid \Diamond_{y_7}) \mid \overset{v_{19}}{\square}_{y_5} \cdot (\Diamond_{y_2} \mid \Diamond_{y_4} \mid \Diamond_{y_8}) \mid$$
$$\overset{v_{23}}{\square}_{y_6} \cdot (\Diamond_{y_3} \mid \Diamond_{y_7}) \mid \overset{v_{26}}{\square}_{y_7} \cdot (\Diamond_{y_4} \mid \Diamond_{y_6} \mid \Diamond_{y_8}) \mid \overset{v_{30}}{\square}_{y_8} \cdot (\Diamond_{y_5} \mid \Diamond_{y_7})$$

3 Formal Specification

Figure 5 exemplifies the graphical conventions applied to node types: Drone is depicted as a drone symbol, Route as a diamond, and OccupiedBy as a rounded rectangle.

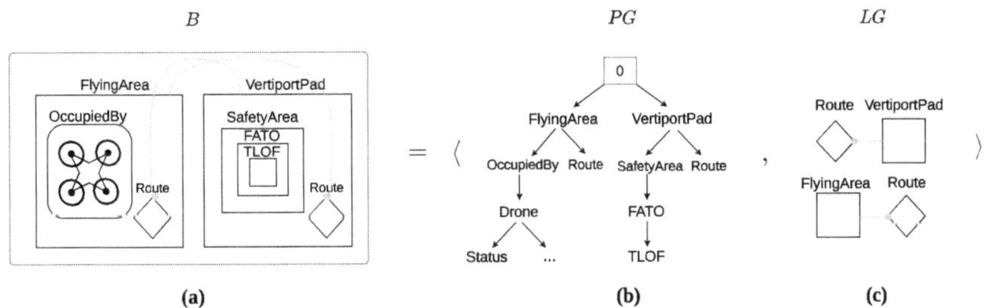

Fig. 5. Bigraph example of a drone-vertiport scenario: (a) the complete bigraph $B = \langle PG, LG \rangle$; (b) its place graph PG, illustrating the hierarchical structure (drone details omitted); and (c) its link graph LG, illustrating connectivity relations. Note that (b) and (c) show the two components that jointly constitute the bigraph in (a).

Refinement. Building on the spatial syntax in Sect. 2, we introduce a domain-specific refinement to reduce the model and rule size. In the original setting, entities are nested into placeholders of □-typed nodes. Here, we re-label the type □ by assigning more specific types, such as FlyingArea and VertiportPad. Spatial adjacency between FlyingArea and VertiportPad instances is made explicit through ◇-typed nodes, which define neighborhood relations between regions.

3.1 Complete Model

We follow the compositional bigraph-based modeling structure introduced in [27, Eq. (1)], which provides a general template for discrete multi-agent path planning models. In this work, we specialize that structure to the composition $w \stackrel{\text{def}}{=} V \circ D^\star$, where V denotes the vertiport infrastructure model (Sect. 3.2) and $D^\star$ represents the parallel composition of drone instances forming a swarm (Sect. 3.3). Thus, the state w is captured as a bigraph obtained by composing the topology and agent parts. An instance of this composite model is illustrated in Fig. 7. The sites $s_0, \ldots, s_9$ in the *empty* bi-grid (Fig. 6) are populated either with drone instances (Drone.$\boxed{\text{o}}$) or the safety infrastructure for vertiports (SafetyArea.FATO.TLOF) to form the entire (simplified) vertiport infrastructure.

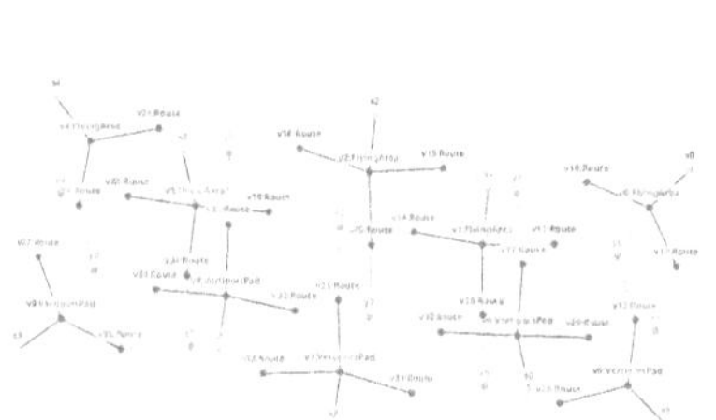

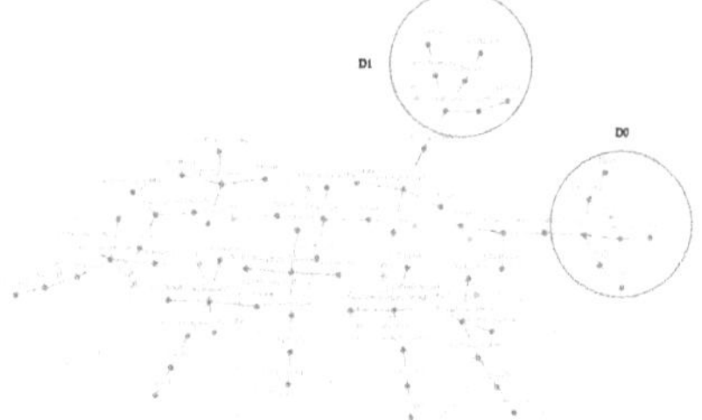

Fig. 6. A 2 × 5-bi-grid model (orthogonal movement); gray nodes indicate indexed placeholders.

Fig. 7. The complete bi-grid with 2 drones (solid circles) and 5 vertiports (dotted circles).

3.2 Vertiport Infrastructure Model

Vertiport Design. Since the bigraph structure abstracts away metric distances, we only model the hierarchical relationships of the vertiport following PTS-VPT-DSN. In the place graph, each virtual vertiport pad is represented as a locale containing three nested layers, from outermost to innermost: SafetyArea, FATO, and TLOF, corresponding to their respective ranges. By default, drones landing on the vertiport are expected to dock within the TLOF.

Example 2 (Infrastructure Model). The bigraph shown in Fig. 5 (a) encodes a minimal drone-vertiport configuration and can be expressed in bigraph algebra as $V = $ FlyingArea$_x$.(OccupiedBy.Drone $|$ $\Diamond_y$) $|$ VertiportPad$_y$.(SafetyArea. FATO.TLOF $|$ $\Diamond_x$). In this structure, the FlyingArea node represents a top-level spatial region containing two key components: an OccupiedBy node, which hosts a drone instance, and a $\Diamond$ (Route-typed) node representing navigational connectivity. The Drone node may contain additional attributes such as ID or Status. The VertiportPad node encodes a landing zone and includes nested sub-regions SafetyArea, FATO, and TLOF, capturing the standard containment hierarchy used in vertiport design. Green edges connect VertiportPad and FlyingArea via $\Diamond$-nodes, encoding bidirectional logical connectivity and enabling drone traversal between regions. $\Diamond$-typed nodes may connect multiple FlyingArea and VertiportPad instances, to represent flexible traffic corridors.

3.3 Multi-drone Model

For drone modeling, we adopt the drone template introduced in [27, Def. 13]. In this representation, each drone is conceptually modeled as a pointlike mass, and bigraphically as a *record*-like datatype (refer to [30]). That is, a term called Drone, extended with a set of child nodes encoding its properties. These property nodes may represent discrete, categorical, or Boolean attributes.

In the present model, we define three core properties for each drone: ID, Status, and Battery. The ID node specifies a unique identifier for each drone instance. The Status node encodes the current operational mode, holding either a Flying or Landed value. The Battery node contains one or more Pow subnodes, representing discrete energy levels. An example instance of such a drone model is illustrated in Fig. 7 (solid circles).

The collection of all drones is defined as the parallel composition of multiple $D^{(i)}$ (i.e., drone instances): $D^\star = D^{(0)} \parallel D^{(1)} \parallel \cdots \parallel D^{(n)}$, where each term $D^{(i)}$ corresponds to a specific *site* s_i in the infrastructure bi-grid model (Fig. 6).

3.4 Rule-Based Operational Semantics

We define reaction rules to endow bigraphs with dynamic behavior for representing drone mobility. The state-space of the model is derived from a given set of initial states and reaction rules. Specifically, we formalize the problem of managing multiple drones across multiple takeoff and landing pads using a multi-agent pathfinding framework based on BRS, as introduced in [27]. This framework enables explicit modeling of both spatial structure and dynamic agent behavior, and supports state-space exploration via model checking. Time in our approach is modeled as discrete logical progression of a bigraph, where each time step corresponds to the application of a reaction rule rather than physical or wall-clock time (cf. also [31,35]). This is consistent with the general notion in graph rewriting and process algebra: $w^{(t)} \longrightarrow_\mathsf{R} w^{(t+1)}$. Here, $w^{(t)}$ denotes the state at logical time t, and R is the reaction rule applied, also written R $\overset{\text{def}}{=} LHS \longrightarrow RHS$.

The resulting state $w^{(t+1)}$ reflects a valid transition in the BRS induced by R. In our model, spatial constraints are incorporated *without* additional modeling overhead by means of bi-spatial structures (cf. Sect. 2) and [4].

Landing Rule. Equation 1 defines a reaction rule for safe landing. It captures the transition of a drone from a FlyingArea into the TLOF zone of an available VertiportPad. On the LHS, the drone "D1" (this identifier represents a unique drone instance) is located in a FlyingArea with status Flying. The VertiportPad is unoccupied and reachable via a $\diamondsuit$. On the RHS, the drone has moved into the TLOF area of the pad, and its status is updated to Landed. The original FlyingArea becomes available for reuse. This rule enforces spatial safety by construction: only one Drone may occupy a VertiportPad at any time. The SafetyArea and nested containment structure ensure exclusive access to landing zones, thereby preventing collisions. The reverse operation (takeoff) is symmetric. For additional drones (e.g., D2, D3), further reaction rules must be instantiated. This drone-specific rule is expressed as:

$$
\begin{aligned}
\mathsf{R}_{Landing} = {} & \mathsf{VertiportPad}_{arrival}.(\boxed{0} \mid \mathsf{SafetyArea.FATO.TLOF}) \mid \\
& \mathsf{FlyingArea}_{departure}.(\boxed{1} \mid \diamondsuit_{arrival} \mid \mathsf{OccupiedBy.Drone}_{d1}.(\mathsf{ID.D1} \mid \\
& \mathsf{Status.Flying} \mid \boxed{2})) \\
& \longrightarrow \\
& \mathsf{FlyingArea}_{departure}.(\boxed{0} \mid \diamondsuit_{arrival} \mid \mathsf{OccupiedBy}) \mid \\
& \mathsf{VertiportPad}_{arrival}.(\boxed{1} \mid \mathsf{SafetyArea.FATO.TLOF}. \\
& \mathsf{Drone}_{d1}.(\mathsf{ID.D1} \mid \mathsf{Status.Landed} \mid \boxed{2}))
\end{aligned}
\tag{1}
$$

Additional Rules. The full set of parameterized reaction rules is available in the BiGGer [22] repository.[7] These include, for instance, $\mathsf{R}_{ApproachInit}$ (initial link to a reachable pad), $\mathsf{R}_{ApproachOccupied}$ (approaching an occupied pad), $\mathsf{R}_{EnterEmpty}$ (entering a free pad), and $\mathsf{R}_{HopBetweenPads}$ (reallocation between pads).

4 Verification

4.1 Approach

Model Checking. For the two test cases in this paper we perform full state-space exploration of the formal model using a model checker (solving a reachability problem). During this exploration, predicates defining mission success are evaluated at the level of individual states (after [11, Def. 1]). Specifically, the goal state is defined as $B_\alpha = P_0 \mid P_1 \mid \cdots \mid P_{n-1}$, where each term $P_i \overset{\mathrm{def}}{=}$ $\mathsf{VertiportPad}_{yi}.(\boxed{0} \mid \mathsf{SafetyArea.FATO.TLOF.Drone}_{di}.(\boxed{1} \mid \mathsf{Status.Landed}))$. Each P_i represents a VertiportPad whose TLOF region contains a drone node. The overall goal state B_α is the merge product of one such term per drone, requiring all drones ($n \leq$ number of vertiports) to have successfully landed in distinct pads.

---

[7] https://github.com/bigraph-toolkit-suite/bigraphs.grgen-bigraphs.

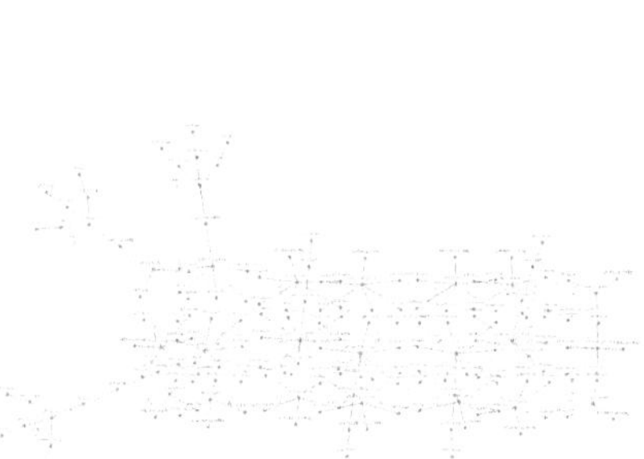

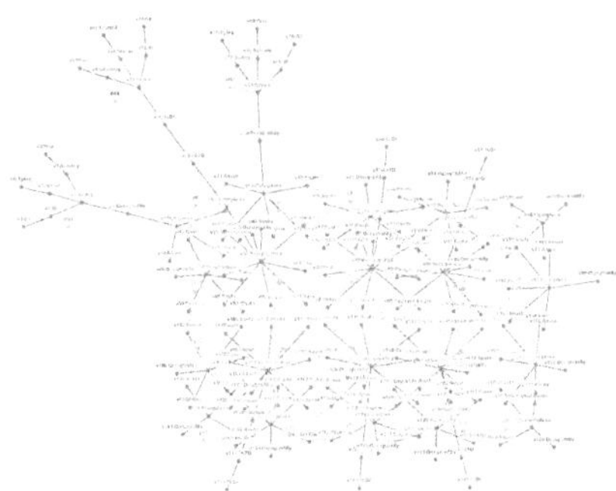

Fig. 8. Scenario A: 3×7 bi-grid (diagonal movements) with $n = 3$ drones and 5 vertiports.

Fig. 9. Scenario B: 4×5 bi-grid (diagonal movements) with $n = 3$ drones and 6 vertiports.

Test Cases. We evaluate our approach across two vertiport layouts. Two representative examples of initial states in Fig. 8 and 9. **Scenario A** uses a 3×7 bi-grid with $n = 4$ drones and 5 vertiports arranged in a centered 1×5 layout, surrounded by empty or occupied FlyingArea nodes (Fig. 1, right-hand side). The layout allows diagonal movement between adjacent □-like nodes. **Scenario B** uses a 4×5 bi-grid with $n = 3$ drones and 6 vertiports arranged in a 2×3 layout across two rows, also with diagonal movement allowed (Fig. 1, left-hand side). Each scenario is parameterized by two variables: n (total number of drones) and m (number of drones already landed). Thus, $n - m$ indicates the number of drones still airborne. We only vary m and keep n. Then, for each scenario, we randomly select one configuration from the set of all admissible initial states, considered here as spatial permutations of drone placements (landed or flying) across the vertiport layout. This is sufficient for a brief analysis, since most of these configurations are structurally symmetric and yield similar behavioral properties, thus, transition systems.

Table 1. Model checking results for the two test scenarios.

Scenario	Drones Landed	Edges	Total States	Final States	Time (s)
A(3×7, $n = 4$)					
	$m = 1$	239	108	12	253.57
	$m = 2$	54	27	4	49.33
	$m = 3$	13	7	2	10.12
B(4×5, $n = 3$)					
	$m = 1$	175	77	18	89.83
	$m = 2$	21	11	4	11.34

4.2   Results

For all test cases using our rule set, no collision was observed, and landing was successful for all variations. Table 1 shows the number of final states, and the total number of states and edges for different m. An exemplary transition system for each scenario generated by our model checker is depicted in Fig. 10 and 11 (blue nodes indicate initial states; green marked nodes represent goal states).[8]

Fig. 10. Scenario A: 5 vertiports, $n = 4$ drones, of which $m = 1$ is initially landed. (Color figure online)

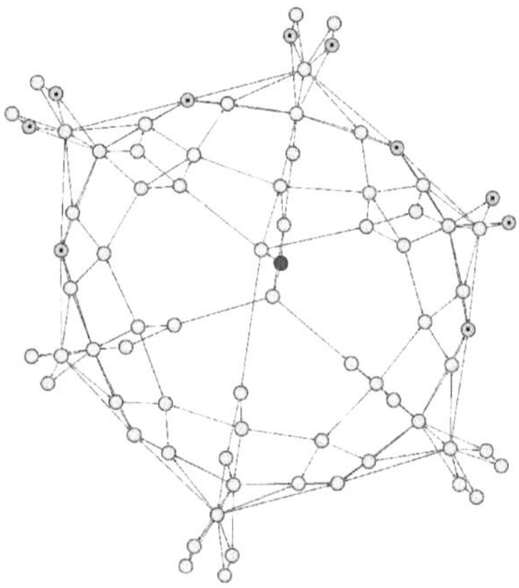

Fig. 11. Scenario B: 6 vertiports, $n = 3$ drones, of which $m = 1$ is initially landed. (Color figure online)

Collision-Freeness. This property emerges as an invariant of the system specification. It is guaranteed by construction through the use of location-aware reaction rules (Sect. 3.4) and the underlying structure (i.e., the *bi-grid* enforces spatial separation and occupancy exclusivity of the vertiports at the structural-semantic level). No two drones can occupy the same spatial region simultaneously. A general proof of non-interference and spatial exclusivity was shown in [27] and instantiated in several subsequent works [24–26], including the present.

Complexity. From a formal perspective, the complexity of our approach is dominated by the size of the generated state space, which grows combinatorially with the number of agents and the grid size of the environment. This is a well-known limitation of exhaustive state-space exploration in swarm and multi-agent verification (see, e.g., [2,14,16–18,21,26,29,34]). For instance, [18] reports analyses limited to two robots on grids of size 5×5 to 8×8, and three robots

---

[8] The formal specification was written and executed using Bigraph Framework [23], which uses [12] as model checker. The transition system was visualized using Gephi.

on grids up to 6×6, due to state-space explosion. In addition to exploration cost, modeling effort itself can become expensive as system size increases, particularly in the absence of compositional structure. Compositional modeling approaches [5,15,28,29], including bigraph-based frameworks [25–27], mitigate this issue by enabling modular construction and analysis of spatially distributed systems.

Modeling Assumptions. The framework adopts an abstract perspective that favors analytical tractability over physical realism. While spatial constraints are modeled structurally, uncertainty is not explicitly represented but could be incorporated through probabilistic rule extensions. In our case study, compositional specification only hints at modular verification, whose efficiency benefits would be more pronounced for larger swarms ($n \gg 4$).

5   Conclusion

This work presented a formal BRS-based framework for coordinating multiple drones operating within a simplified vertiport infrastructure. Collision-free landing was formulated as a reachability problem in model checking, with spatial constraints and agent behaviors encoded through location-aware reaction rules. The resulting bigraph model captures both environmental structure and multi-drone interactions, preserving safety invariants by construction.

A key strength of the approach is its compositional design: vertiport layouts and swarm sizes can be reconfigured without modifying the underlying rules, preserving prior verification results and enabling modular reasoning. Compared to related work, this study does not address optimization objectives or scheduling strategies. Instead, our focus lies on formally proving the existence of valid, collision-free landing "paths" (i.e., *traces*) for any infrastructure configuration.

As a next step, we find it promising to benchmark the verification performance using the BiGGer model checker [22], which has demonstrated efficient evaluation of similar bi-spatial models such as self-sorting robots [26].[9] In addition, we aim to further exploit parallelism by using rule composition [27, Prop. 6] and modular model checking to increase the throughput of the vertiport infrastructure (i.e., allowing concurrent multi-drone landing).

Acknowledgments. This research was funded by the German Research Foundation (DFG, Deutsche Forschungsgemeinschaft) as part of RTG-AirMetro, grant number GRK 2947/1, 508591287.

Disclosure of Interests. The authors have no competing interests to declare.

---

[9] Refer also to https://github.com/bigraph-toolkit-suite/BiggerBenchmarkSolution.

References

1. Ang, K.R.R.: Building bigraphs of the real world (2025). https://doi.org/10.48550/arXiv.2508.00003
2. Antuña, L., Araiza-Illan, D., Campos, S., Eder, K.: Symmetry reduction enables model checking of more complex emergent behaviours of swarm navigation algorithms. In: Dixon, C., Tuyls, K. (eds.) TAROS 2015. LNCS (LNAI), vol. 9287, pp. 26–37. Springer, Cham (2015). https://doi.org/10.1007/978-3-319-22416-9_4
3. Archibald, B., Calder, M., Sevegnani, M.: Practical modelling with bigraphs. Form. Asp. Comput. **37**(3), 20:1–20:36 (2025). https://doi.org/10.1145/3721142
4. Bacci, G., Miculan, M., Rizzi, R.: Finding a forest in a tree. In: Maffei, M., Tuosto, E. (eds.) TGC 2014. LNCS, vol. 8902, pp. 17–33. Springer, Heidelberg (2014). https://doi.org/10.1007/978-3-662-45917-1_2
5. Bakirtzis, G., Vasilakopoulou, C., Fleming, C.H.: Compositional cyber-physical systems modeling. Electron. Proc. Theor. Comput. Sci. **333**, 125–138 (2021). https://doi.org/10.4204/EPTCS.333.9
6. Benford, S., Calder, M., Rodden, T., Sevegnani, M.: On lions, impala, and bigraphs: modelling interactions in physical/virtual spaces. ACM Trans. Comput.-Hum. Interact. **23**(2), 9:1–9:56 (2016). https://doi.org/10.1145/2882784
7. Birkedal, L., Debois, S., Elsborg, E., Hildebrandt, T., Niss, H.: Bigraphical models of context-aware systems. In: Aceto, L., Ingólfsdóttir, A. (eds.) FoSSaCS 2006. LNCS, vol. 3921, pp. 187–201. Springer, Heidelberg (2006). https://doi.org/10.1007/11690634_13
8. Bradley, A.R.: SAT-based model checking without unrolling. In: Jhala, R., Schmidt, D. (eds.) VMCAI 2011. LNCS, vol. 6538, pp. 70–87. Springer, Heidelberg (2011). https://doi.org/10.1007/978-3-642-18275-4_7
9. Brunelli, M., Ditta, C.C., Postorino, M.N.: New infrastructures for Urban air mobility systems: a systematic review on vertiport location and capacity. J. Air Transp. Manage. **112**, 102460 (2023). https://doi.org/10.1016/j.jairtraman.2023.102460
10. Burch, J.R., Clarke, E.M., McMillan, K.L., Dill, D.L., Hwang, L.J.: Symbolic model checking: 1020 states and beyond. Inf. Comput. **98**(2), 142–170 (1992). https://doi.org/10.1016/0890-5401(92)90017-A
11. Calder, M., Koliousis, A., Sevegnani, M., Sventek, J.: Real-time verification of wireless home networks using bigraphs with sharing. Sci. Comput. Program. **80**, 288–310 (2014). https://doi.org/10.1016/j.scico.2013.08.004
12. Chiapperini, A., Miculan, M., Peressotti, M.: Computing (optimal) embeddings of directed bigraphs. Sci. Comput. Program. **221**, 102842 (2022). https://doi.org/10.1016/j.scico.2022.102842
13. Clarke, E., Biere, A., Raimi, R., Zhu, Y.: Bounded model checking using satisfiability solving. Formal Methods Syst. Design **19**(1), 7–34 (2001). https://doi.org/10.1023/A:1011276507260
14. De Nicola, R., Di Stefano, L., Inverso, O.: Multi-agent systems with virtual stigmergy. Sci. Comput. Program. **187**, 102345 (2020). https://doi.org/10.1016/j.scico.2019.102345
15. Di Stefano, L., Lang, F.: Compositional verification of stigmergic collective systems. In: Dragoi, C., Emmi, M., Wang, J. (eds.) VMCAI 2023. LNCS, vol. 13881, pp. 155–176. Springer, Cham (2023). https://doi.org/10.1007/978-3-031-24950-1_8
16. Dixon, C., Winfield, A., Fisher, M.: Towards temporal verification of emergent behaviours in swarm robotic systems. In: Groß, R., Alboul, L., Melhuish, C., Witkowski, M., Prescott, T.J., Penders, J. (eds.) TAROS 2011. LNCS (LNAI),

vol. 6856, pp. 336–347. Springer, Heidelberg (2011). https://doi.org/10.1007/978-3-642-23232-9_30

17. Dixon, C., Winfield, A.F., Fisher, M.: Verification of swarm robots: the alpha algorithm. In: Proceedings of the Automated Reasoning Workshop (ARW), Westminster, UK, pp. 10–11 (2010)

18. Dixon, C., Winfield, A.F.T., Fisher, M., Zeng, C.: Towards temporal verification of swarm robotic systems. Robot. Auton. Syst. **60**(11), 1429–1441 (2012). https://doi.org/10.1016/j.robot.2012.03.003

19. EASA, E.U.A.S.A.: Prototype technical design specifications for vertiports | EASA (2022). https://www.easa.europa.eu/en/document-library/general-publications/prototype-technical-design-specifications-vertiports

20. Federal Aviation Administration (FAA): Engineering Brief No. 105A: Vertiports, U.S. Department of Transportation (2024). https://www.faa.gov/airports/engineering/engineering_briefs/eb_105a_vertiports

21. Ghaffari Saadat, M., Dixon, C., Fisher, M.: Specification and verification of the alpha swarm algorithm using NuXMV and GROOVE. Form. Asp. Comput. (2025). https://doi.org/10.1145/3736689

22. Grzelak, D.: BiGGer: a model transformation tool written in java for bigraph rewriting in grgen.net. J. Open Sour. Softw. **9**(98), 6491 (2024). https://doi.org/10.21105/joss.06491

23. Grzelak, D.: Model-oriented programming with bigraphical reactive systems: theory and implementation. Ph.D. thesis, Technische Universität Dresden (2024). https://nbn-resolving.org/urn:nbn:de:bsz:14-qucosa2-910504

24. Grzelak, D.: Programming drone collectives: towards safe plug-and-play modularity. In: 1st German Robotics Conference (GRC). Robotics Institute Germany, Nürnberg, Germany (2025). Standalone video contribution, Abstract, Poster

25. Grzelak, D.: Proof everything everywhere but not all at once. Presentation. Technische Universität Dresden. CC BY 4.0. (2025). https://doi.org/10.25368/2025.369

26. Grzelak, D., Hamann, M.: Improving bigraph rewriting with GrGen.NET to enable efficient system simulation. Form. Asp. Comput. (2025). https://doi.org/10.1145/3736704

27. Grzelak, D., Lindner, M., Belov, M., Aßmann, U., Husak, O., Fricke, H.: A bigraphical framework for modeling and simulation of uav-based inspection scenarios. Preprint (revised). Technische Universität Dresden (2024). https://nbn-resolving.org/urn:nbn:de:bsz:14-qucosa2-908655

28. Heckel, R.: Compositional verification of reactive systems specified by graph transformation. In: Astesiano, E. (ed.) FASE 1998. LNCS, vol. 1382, pp. 138–153. Springer, Heidelberg (1998). https://doi.org/10.1007/BFb0053588

29. Lion, B., Arbab, F., Talcott, C.: Runtime composition of systems of interacting cyber-physical components. In: Madeira, A., Martins, M.A. (eds.) WADT 2022. LNCS, vol. 13710, pp. 141–162. Springer, Cham (2023). https://doi.org/10.1007/978-3-031-43345-0_7

30. Milner, R.: The Space and Motion of Communicating Agents, 1st edn. Cambridge University Press, New York (2009)

31. Rosas, F.E., et al.: Software in the natural world: a computational approach to hierarchical emergence (2024). https://doi.org/10.48550/arXiv.2402.09090

32. Sastre, C., Wubben, J., Calafate, C.T., Cano, J.C., Manzoni, P.: Safe and efficient take-off of VTOL UAV swarms. Electronics **11**(7), 1128 (2022). https://doi.org/10.3390/electronics11071128

33. Schweiger, K., Preis, L.: Urban air mobility: systematic review of scientific publications and regulations for vertiport design and operations. Drones **6**(7), 179 (2022). https://doi.org/10.3390/drones6070179
34. Winfield, A.F.T., Liu, W., Nembrini, J., Martinoli, A.: Modelling a wireless connected swarm of mobile robots. Swarm Intell. **2**(2), 241–266 (2008). https://doi.org/10.1007/s11721-008-0018-0
35. Wolfram, S.: A class of models with the potential to represent fundamental physics. Complex Syst. **29**(2), 107–536 (2020). https://doi.org/10.25088/ComplexSystems.29.2.107

Closing the Loop Between BEECLUST and Honeybee Thermotaxis

Martin Stefanec[1]([✉]) [iD], Alexander Herlitz[1] [iD], Daniel Reisinger[1] [iD],
Johannes Diebold[1] [iD], Daniel Nicolas Hofstadler[1] [iD], Anna Reichenpfader[1] [iD],
Laurenz Alexander Fedotoff[1] [iD], Farshad Arvin[2] [iD], Ronald Thenius[1] [iD],
and Thomas Schmickl[1] [iD]

[1] Artificial Life Lab, Institute of Biology, University of Graz, Graz, Austria
`martin.stefanec@uni-graz.at`
[2] Department of Computer Science, Durham University, Durham, UK

Abstract. Swarm intelligence describes collective problem-solving that emerges from adaptive group behavior and decentralized control. This concept has led to a variety of bio-inspired optimization algorithms, many of which require further systematic experimental validation. In this study, we reexamine the biological validity of the BEECLUST algorithm by applying the experimental conditions and performance metrics of swarm robotics to a biological context. We find that real honeybees achieve aggregation at the thermal optimum even in relatively small groups. This indicates that the behavioral transition from individual to collective dynamics already emerges at low group sizes, suggesting that the most informative regime may occur at lower densities than reported in robotic implementations of the BEECLUST algorithm. We discuss possible explanations for this discrepancy and propose directions for future refinement.

1 Introduction

Swarm-intelligent systems rely on local interactions among individuals, through which coordinated and adaptive group behavior can emerge without centralized control [4]. It is often employed as an engineering paradigm in artificial systems, reflecting analogous processes in natural systems [11,19,21,25,26]. Historically, the flow of inspiration between biology and engineering has been largely unidirectional: Naturally occurring forms of swarm intelligence have provided the conceptual foundation for many control algorithms in swarm robotics, optimization, and artificial life [4]. In this work, we invert the direction of inspiration. Instead of deriving algorithms from biological observations, we use the well-established field of swarm robotics as our framework. We adopt its models, experimental paradigms, and quantitative performance to directly compare robotic experiments with biological experiments.

One prominent example of control algorithms widely used in swarm robotics is the honeybee-inspired BEECLUST, derived from behavioral observations of

© The Author(s), under exclusive license to Springer Nature Switzerland AG 2026
R. Groß et al. (Eds.): ANTS 2026, LNCS 16515, pp. 69–81, 2026.
https://doi.org/10.1007/978-3-032-26123-6_6

young honeybees aggregating in temperature gradients [16,18]. It represents a minimal model of swarm intelligence in which collective decision-making emerges from simple local interactions without communication. In brief, BEECLUST can be described as follows: (i) agents move randomly, (ii) when two agents collide, both stop moving, and (iii) the higher the local environmental quality at the collision site, the longer they remain stationary. In the idealized BEECLUST model, simple local rules are sufficient to produce self-organized aggregation at a global optimum, even without global information or explicit gradient sensing. This emergent mechanism allows the collective to differentiate between local and global optima and adapt to changing conditions, solving an optimization problem that a single individual cannot. Over the past fifteen years, BEECLUST has evolved from a biologically grounded proof of concept into a widely used model for swarm coordination, especially in the field of swarm robotics [2,6,10,13,14,27]. It has been implemented on numerous robotic platforms [3,9,12,15], used to study processes such as aggregation [1], collective decision making [5], adaptive response [14], and examined in both physical experiments [27] and theoretical analyses [7,8]. However, the engineering success of BEECLUST has largely proceeded by decoupling the model from the organism. In this study, we analyze both within the same framework, examining how closely swarm algorithms reflect the collective dynamics observed in real honeybees. In particular, we apply the experimental setups and quantitative performance metrics from [2] and [27] to real honeybees in order to evaluate and quantify the performance of honeybees from a swarm robotics perspective.

2   Methodology

We conducted experiments under three experimental conditions (Fig. 1), adapted from [2,27]: (**A**) a thermal gradient with a single global optimum to assess swarm-level aggregation and influence of group size; (**B**) the same gradient with a U-shaped barrier generating a local optimum to test whether bees become trapped or collectively escape suboptimal regions; and (**C**) a uniform thermal field serving as a control for spontaneous aggregation in the absence of gradients.

In [2], aggregation driven by the BEECLUST algorithm was described using a power-law function, $D(t) = \alpha \cdot t^k$, where $D(t)$ denotes the number of robots at time t at a defined aggregation zone, α the scaling coefficient, and k the rate of aggregation. By fitting this model to empirically observed data, [2] derived quantitative measures of collective convergence to benchmark swarm-robotic performance.

Similarly, in [27], a complementary swarm-robotic performance metric was proposed to evaluate how a swarm exploits favorable environmental conditions. Rather than quantifying aggregation rate directly, the performance metric of [27], denoted by Ω, captures the mean environmental quality experienced by all robots over time, thereby measuring how efficiently a swarm positions itself within regions of high reward (e.g., temperature, light intensity, or resource abundance).

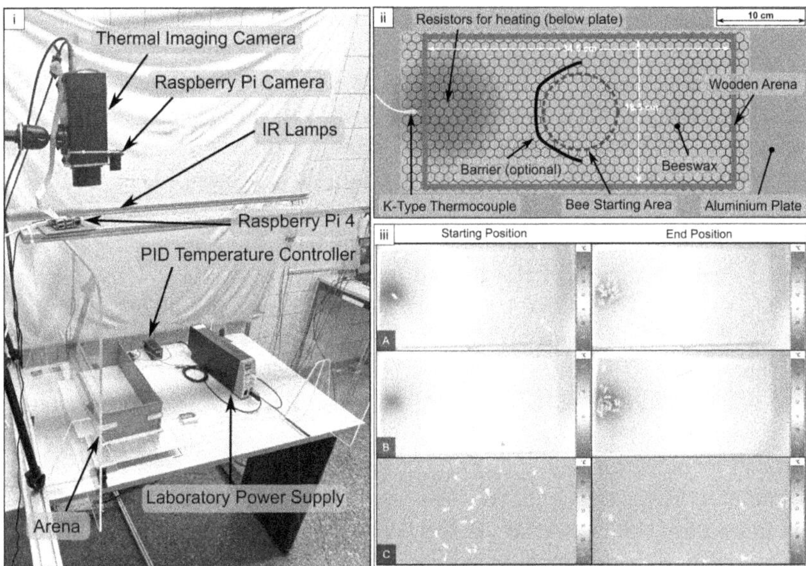

Fig. 1. Experimental setup. **(i)** Photograph of the recording apparatus. **(ii)** Top-down schematic of the arena, heated region (red), beeswax surface (yellow), and the optional U-shaped barrier for Condition B (black). **(iii)** Thermal camera images without the barrier (top row, A), with the barrier (middle row, B), and a control trial without heating (bottom row, C), showing bee distributions at the start (left) and end (right) of a 15-min run.

It is defined as $\Omega = (\sum_{t=t_{\min}}^{t_{\max}} \sum_{i=1}^{N_{\text{robots}}} \lambda(i,t))/(N_{\text{robots}} \cdot (t_{\max} - t_{\min}))$, where $\lambda(i,t)$ denotes the local environmental quality sensed by robot i at time t, and N_{robots} is the swarm size. By definition, $\lambda(i,t) \in [0,1]$, such that Ω is normalized, with higher values indicating better exploitation of the environment's optimum.

Experiments were conducted with groups of *Apis mellifera carnica* honeybees. All individuals were newly emerged ($<$36 h old), a developmental stage during which honeybees cannot fly or sting and naturally remain within the brood area of the hive [17,18,24]. Experiments were conducted in a specially constructed arena (345 × 185 mm) consisting of a 1 mm thick aluminum base plate covered with beeswax (Zander base). This configuration aligns with the experimental design of [2], having been adapted to yield analogous densities in the bee experiments as in the robot experiments. This results in a density that is considerably lower than the highly congested conditions of a natural brood nest. The temperature optimum was achieved using four parallel-connected 6.2 Ω resistors controlled via a PID regulator (Inkbird ITC-100VL) linked to a PT-800 K-type thermocouple. This maintained a stable thermal spot at $36 \pm 1°$C, simulating an optimal brood-nest temperature. A thermal imaging camera continuously monitored the temperature field. The arena was enclosed in a PTFE-coated wooden frame treated with silicone oil to prevent escape. The same silicone oil was also used to coat the 24-mm-high barrier from condition B, to prevent bees from climbing over it, forcing them to maneuver around. Illumination was provided solely by infrared LEDs, outside the visual spectrum of honeybees, enabling recordings under dark conditions using an IR-sensitive Raspberry Pi HQ camera. Before each trial, the beeswax sheet was replaced to prevent potential pheromonal or chemical bias, and the thermocouple was repositioned between the aluminum base and the wax layer. The system was allowed to equilibrate until the heated spot reached the target temperature of $36 \pm 1°C$, verified by both the PID controller and thermal imaging. The required number of bees for each group size was then counted and released at the center of the arena, after which recording commenced. Ambient temperature and time of day were documented for each trial. Experiments were conducted in an actively temperature-controlled dark room. Each recording lasted 15 min, during which bee behavior was simultaneously captured using thermal and infrared video cameras. After each run, the bees were removed, and the arena was cleaned and prepared for the next trial. The three experimental conditions (**A–C**) were implemented under identical environmental and recording settings.

Experiment A comprised ten repetitions for group sizes of 1, 6, 12, and 18 bees. Experiment B comprised ten repetitions for the group size of 18 bees. Order of trials was randomized. In A1 (single bee), one repetition was discarded due to the escape of one honeybee. The control condition C comprised five repetitions with 18 bees. Experiments were performed between August 18 and 22, 2025. Following data acquisition, the recorded trajectories were analyzed using the power-law aggregation model of [2] and the Ω-metric of [27]. **Thermal field modeling:**

To quantify collective thermotactic performance, we applied the previously defined performance metric Ω from [27].

Calculating this metric requires a continuous model of the arena's thermal field $T(x, y)$, because the temperature value beneath the bee's exact position must be estimated and cannot be directly captured with top down thermal imaging (see thermal bee spots in Fig. 1, iii). We modeled this field using a 9-parameter, single-center, double-Gaussian field as defined in Eq. 1 (see Table 1 for fitted values).

$$T(x, y) = T_{offset} + \underbrace{A_{sharp}e^{-\left(\frac{(x-x_0)^2}{2\sigma_{x,sharp}^2} + \frac{(y-y_0)^2}{2\sigma_{y,sharp}^2}\right)}}_{\text{Heating Element}} + \underbrace{A_{wide}e^{-\left(\frac{(x-x_0)^2}{2\sigma_{x,wide}^2} + \frac{(y-y_0)^2}{2\sigma_{y,wide}^2}\right)}}_{\text{Conductive Glow}}$$

$$(1)$$

This model represents the physics of the single heat source as two components: (1) a sharp, narrow Gaussian for the local heat of the element, and (2) a wide, asymmetric Gaussian representing the conductive "glow" across the arena, shaped by the plate's conductive properties and finite geometry. All components share a common center (x_0, y_0) and rest on a global temperature offset T_{offset}. To validate this model and derive its parameters, we performed a constrained optimization (`scipy.optimize.curve_fit`) on an averaged, high-resolution thermal image (590×320 px, InfraTec VarioCAM HD) from a representative trial. This fit (Table 1, "Value" column) provided an excellent match to the empirical data ($R^2 = 0.961$). For the final analysis, these physical parameters were transformed into the (0–1) normalized coordinate system used for our analyses (Table 1, "Normalized" column). This normalized, static model was used to find the temperature T_i for each bee's coordinates at each time step. These values were normalized to the quality λ_i (0=min, 1=max field temperature), and $\Omega(t)$ was computed as the mean λ_i of all N bees.

Table 1. Parameters for the single-center double-Gaussian thermal model. The "Value" column shows the parameters derived from a constrained fit (mean ± standard error) to the 590×320 px thermal image. The "Normalized" column shows the corresponding parameters used for the performance metric computation. $^{+}$Indicates the pixel-fit parameter converged to its *upper* bound. $^{-}$Indicates convergence to the *lower* bound.

Component	Parameter	Value ± SE	Normalized
Shared Center	Center (x_0) [px]	41.50 ± 0.08	0.1383
	Center (y_0) [px]	139.91 ± 0.07	0.4664
Sharp Peak	Amplitude (A_{sharp}) [° C]	4.94 ± 0.01	0.45572
	Sigma ($\sigma_{x,sharp}$) [px]	31.19 ± 0.11	0.10397
	Sigma ($\sigma_{y,sharp}$) [px]	$31.00 \pm 0.09^{+}$	0.10333
Wide Glow	Amplitude (A_{wide}) [° C]	5.90 ± 0.01	0.54428
	Sigma ($\sigma_{x,wide}$) [px]	$150.00 \pm 0.14^{+}$	0.5
	Sigma ($\sigma_{y,wide}$) [px]	$200.00 \pm 0.51^{-}$	0.66667
Global Offset	Offset (λ_{offset}) [° C]	28.79 ± 0.00	0.0

Temporal Aggregation Dynamics: To gain insight into the formation of bee aggregates in cases where the heat source or target zone is absent, we employ the network theoretical concept of connected components. Specifically, we construct a proximity network based on pairwise Euclidean distances between individual bees where an edge is formed between two bees if their Euclidean distance is below a threshold of $S^* = 15\,\text{mm}$ (typical length of a Western honeybee). We then determine the number of connected components, denoted as M, or aggregates of bees, that arise under this criterion. A lower number of M connected components indicates stronger aggregation.

3   Results

Figure 2 shows the temporal evolution of aggregation across experimental conditions, with the median aggregate size fitted using the nonlinear power-law $D(t)$, following the approach of [2]. Aggregation was considered complete when 70%

of the bees were located within the aggregation zone, defined as a circle with a radius of one third of the arena length ($D = 116.7\,\text{mm}$) around the center of the global optimum. The corresponding fit parameters are listed in Table 2 alongside the values reported for the robotic BEECLUST swarm [2]. In experimental conditions A and B, aggregate size increased rapidly during the first 100–150 s, reaching a stable state between 200 and 350 s depending on group size. In condition C, we observe no aggregation. The fitted exponent k was of comparable magnitude to that reported for robotic swarms, but in contrast to [2], it increased from small to larger groups ($N = 6$ to 18). Extending the fit beyond 70% reveals the limitations of the power law, which cannot model the system's saturation behavior due to its inherently non-saturating nature.

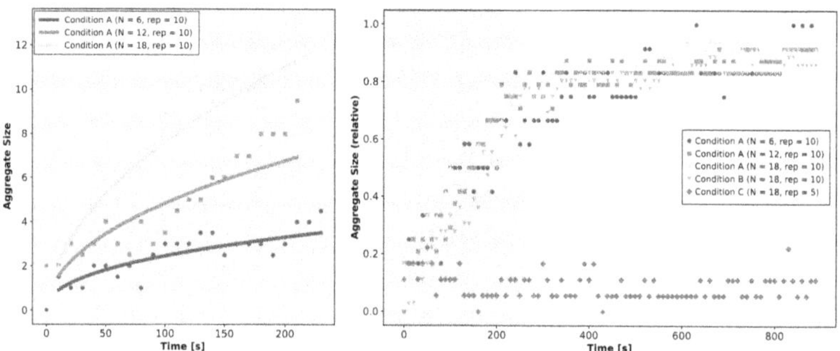

Fig. 2. Temporal dynamics of honeybee aggregation under different experimental conditions. Each point represents the median aggregate size across repetitions, with fitted power-laws shown as solid lines; fitted parameters are listed in Table 2. The aggregation zone was defined as a circle with a radius of one third of the arena length around the center of the global optimum, following [2]. Aggregation was considered complete when 70% of bees were within this zone. **Left**: Absolute aggregate size (number of bees) over time for experimental condition A with varying group sizes ($N = 6, 12, 18$). **Right**: Relative aggregate size (normalized by group size) including condition B (barrier) and condition C (control).

Table 2. Comparison of fitting properties between bees and robots (70% in the aggregation zone). Comparative data are derived exclusively from the "Gradient light" model parameters in Table 2 of Ref. [2]; the visualization in Fig. 5 of the same study was excluded as it lacks explanation to reproduce. "Population" refers to group size.

Population	Present work			Arvin et al. [2]		
	α	k	R^2	α	k	R^2
6	0.078	0.431	0.691	0.134	0.576	0.95
12	0.096	0.489	0.767	0.811	0.460	0.98
18	0.106	0.534	0.854	4.555	0.253	0.99

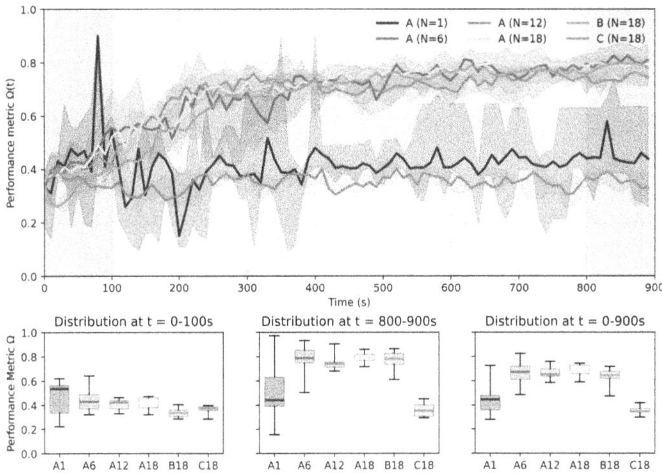

Fig. 3. Collective thermotactic performance metric Ω for all experimental conditions and group sizes. Solid lines show the median Ω across all repetitions for each group size in condition A ($N = 1, 6, 12, 18$) and for $N = 18$ in conditions B and C. Shaded regions indicate the interquartile range (IQR). Gray vertical bands mark the temporal windows analyzed below. **Bottom:** Boxplots of Ω values for the initial (0–100 s), final (800–900 s), and full (0–900 s) time windows. Boxes show the IQR, whiskers span the full data range (minimum–maximum). Control data (C18) were evaluated against a virtual thermal field at an equivalent location to the heat source in the gradient conditions. (Color figure online)

Figure 3 summarizes the thermotactic clustering performance of the honeybees across all conditions, as well as its temporal evolution and variability. We utilized the performance metric Ω [27], which quantifies how effectively individuals occupy high-quality regions of an area they are confined in. Ω increased within the first 300 s for experimental conditions A and B for all group sizes > 1 and reached a stable plateau thereafter, indicating successful aggregation near the heat source. Larger groups ($N = 12, 18$) exhibited narrower variability ranges (compared to $N = 1, 6$), suggesting more robust clustering. In contrast, solitary individuals ($N = 1$) showed strong fluctuations and a low overall performance, reflecting the instability of individual thermotaxis without social interactions. The barrier condition (B) produced good performance levels with a slightly higher variability range (compared to A, $N = 18$), while the control group (C) maintained low Ω values throughout. Control data were evaluated against a virtual thermal field. The Ω analysis thus integrates temporal and spatial information into a single measure of thermotactic efficiency.

To further characterize how bee aggregation evolves independently of thermal heating, we also examined clustering dynamics based on direct bee–bee proximity (Fig. 4). For $N = 18$ bees, experimental conditions A and B form aggregates at a similar rate and end up stagnant at the same value of around $M = 4$ connected components (aggregates). Condition C starts out at a similar rate, but stops aggregating at around $M = 10$. This shows the applicability of the BEECLUST algorithm to honeybees, indicating that the presence of the thermal cue (conditions A and B) induces aggregation behavior distinct from random clustering aggregation. Comparing different group sizes N by using the metric of M connected components (or aggregates), it is clear that each starts at different absolute values of M. Note that N is the upper limit of M aggregates that can form. However, all three values of N tested (except for $N = 1$ that is only included as reference), lead to similar final M, revealing that the aggregating performance for the highest N is the greatest, as should be expected with a swarm algorithm that works well.

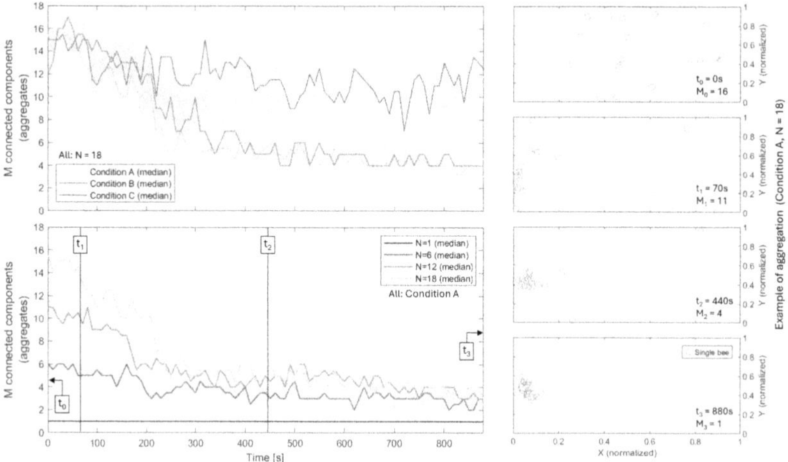

Fig. 4. Aggregation performance for all experimental conditions and group sizes. Shaded areas represent the interquartile range. **Top left:** Comparison between different experimental conditions (medians for each condition at $N = 18$). **Bottom left:** Aggregation in condition A (medians for each N) with different numbers of bees. **Right column:** Example of aggregation for a single experiment. Circles represent bees, lines connecting the circles indicate that a cluster has been identified.

While the fitted dynamics capture how rapidly the collective reaches its stable configuration, they provide little insight into how bees navigate the spatial temperature field during this process. We therefore analyzed the spatio-temporal trajectories of the colonies' collective centers of mass across experiments (Fig. 5).

Figure 5 shows the spatio-temporal evolution of honeybees and their collective center of mass across experiments. In A, where a thermal optimum was placed on the left side, the collective center of mass moved directly along the gradient toward this optimum, showing efficient thermal alignment. In B, an additional U-shaped barrier created a local thermal optimum. The swarm's center of mass did not remain trapped within this local optimum. Instead, it initially moved against the gradient before turning and proceeding toward the global optimum, passing

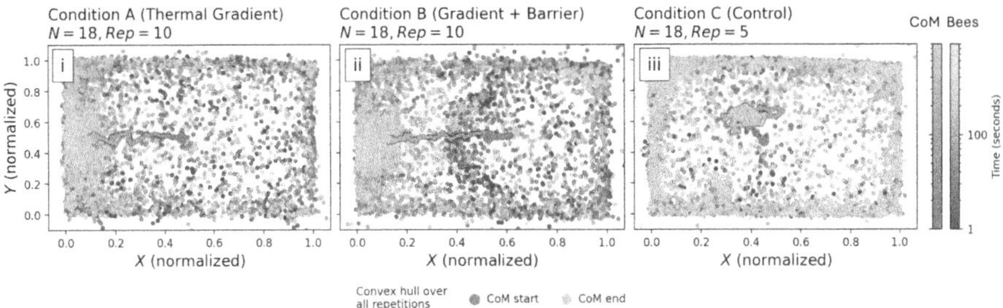

Fig. 5. Spatio-temporal evolution of bees (blue to green dots) and their collective center of mass (pink to orange trajectory). The figure shows the aggregated center of mass (CoM) in experimental conditions A (thermal gradient, i), B (thermal gradient + U-shaped barrier, ii), and C (control, iii). The convex hull represents the area in which the center-of-mass trajectories were confined during all experimental repetitions. (Color figure online)

the barrier through its midpoint–indicating a group split when escaping local traps. Thus, what would constitute a local optimum for gradient-following agents does not seem to constrain honeybee swarms, consistent with BEECLUST-based swarm-robotics results [27]. In C, without a thermal optimum or barrier, the center of mass showed no directional trend; movement was exploratory, with individuals mainly along arena edges and corners.

4   Discussion

Our results confirm that honeybee groups reliably aggregate near a global environmental optimum within a shallow thermal gradient [22,24], as shown in Figs. 2, 3, and 5. This robust collective performance is comparable to that of robotic swarms. The introduction of a U-shaped barrier, which created a local thermal optimum, had little effect on the overall aggregation performance. Bees navigated around the barrier as individuals, but still collectively converged on the global optimum, as shown in Fig. 5. During the experiments, we have never observed bees climbing the barrier. Individual bees, by contrast, move largely randomly under these conditions and show little targeted response to the global optimum, as shown in Fig. 3 and 4.

As shown in Fig. 2, the temporal dynamics of aggregation in our experiments did not follow a power-law model very well as described for robotic BEECLUST swarms [2]. Following the procedure of [2], we fitted the model only until 70% of the bees had entered the aggregation zone; however, the power-law model did not adequately fit the data (Table 2, note low R^2-values), indicating that the dynamics of real bees might deviate from the idealized formulation used in robotic BEECLUST implementations in this aspect. However, for both biological and robotic clustering behavior, the aggregation curves must approach a saturation limit due to the finite number of individuals, which cannot be expressed by a power law. In real honeybees, unlike the robotic experiments by [2], aggregation rates differed only marginally between group sizes of six, twelve, and eighteen bees, suggesting that even relatively small groups can achieve efficient collective aggregation at the environmental cue optimum under these specific experimental settings. This lack of divergence could have several causes: despite replicating the arena size and densities of [2], adjusted to honeybees, our data suggest a behavioral transition between individual honeybees and groups as small as six individuals, implying that the most informative regime may already occur at lower densities. This is particularly striking given that these experimental densities are already far below natural hive conditions. It suggests that biological social feedback does not scale linearly; instead, the "swarm effect" appears to saturate rapidly, kicking in at densities significantly lower than those typically required for BEECLUST controlled robotic swarms. A deeper investigation into this non-linear scaling is warranted, as incorporating such saturation limits could significantly improve the biological fidelity of future swarm-robotic algorithms. Alternatively, the thermal gradient in our setup may have been sufficiently steep to minimize gradual differences in aggregation rate, effectively saturating collective performance across the tested group sizes. With increasing group size, the variance in aggregation dynamics decreased markedly, indicating greater stability and robustness of the collective process (Fig. 3). This contrast becomes most evident when comparing solitary individuals ($N = 1$) with groups ($N > 1$): single bees moved towards the thermal optimum mostly by chance, whereas groups reliably located and maintained the optimal zone—an emergent property absent at the individual level. However, toward the second half of the experiment, the median performance metric of individual bees exceeded that of the control group, which was evaluated against a virtual thermal gradient in the absence of any real temperature cue. This slightly higher median performance may suggest a weak bias of individual bees toward warmer regions, indicating that the thermal gradient in our setup, while relatively shallow, might still have been detectable by single bees to a limited extent. Using an additional, environment-independent aggregation measure, we further demonstrated that bees exhibit a weak but measurable tendency to cluster even under homogeneous temperature conditions (see Fig. 4). This spontaneous clustering may reflect intrinsic social attraction mechanisms or, alternatively, arise as a statistical consequence of random encounters between moving individuals [20]. During the initial phase (approximately 50–200 s), the aggregation dynamics of conditions A, B, and C overlapped almost completely, suggesting that early clustering might be driven by unspecific social interactions or random encounter effects before environmental cues begin to dominate collective organization. In the barrier condition (Experiment B), a U-shaped obstacle was introduced to create a local thermal optimum that would trap any agent strictly following a gradient-ascent rule. However, the honeybees showed no great difficulty navigating this structure: in all repetitions, the group's center of mass crossed the barrier region and reached the global thermal optimum, see Fig. 5. This apparent "collective passage" did not occur as a coordinated group movement but rather as the result of individuals circumventing the barrier from both sides before re-aggregating at the global optimum. Despite this structural constraint, the overall aggregation dynamics between conditions A and B differed only marginally, with a short initial collective motion against the thermal gradient in condition B. This suggests that local optima may have little effect on swarm-level thermotactic organization. In contrast, the control condition (Experiment C) revealed pronounced wall-following behavior, with individuals spending a large proportion of time along the arena edges. This tendency likely reflects boundary effects under homogeneous temperature conditions and may depend strongly on ambient temperature, as suggested by [23], which predicts that clustering behavior in non-gradient environments is modulated by thermal background conditions.

In this study, we closed the loop between swarm robotics and biology by inverting the traditional biomimetic trajectory. Rather than using bees to validate robots, we used the rigorous metrics of swarm robotics to interrogate the biological validity of the BEECLUST algorithm. Originally derived from animal behavior, swarm-robotic systems have evolved into a standard framework for studying collective decision-making, parameter sweeps, and environmental interactions under highly controlled conditions. Here, we reversed this process by using experimental insights from the robotic implementations to re-examine the biological system that inspired them. Our goal was to test whether the simplified abstractions developed for swarm robots still capture the essential dynamics of the original honeybee behavior. Certain concepts–such as the performance metric Ω–translate remarkably well and provide a robust means to quantify swarm-level efficiency in biological collectives, provided that the environmental gradient is well characterized. Other aspects, such as the assumed power-law scaling of aggregation dynamics, do not generalize straightforwardly to the bees' behavior. Moreover, while robotic implementations typically explore minimal agent groups under sparse conditions, honeybee colonies operate at vastly higher densities and within complex sensory and social contexts that cannot be easily replicated in artificial swarms. Our results nonetheless demonstrate that even small groups of bees can exhibit robust, self-organized thermotactic performance consistent with the principles underlying swarm-robotic control. By reintroducing bio-inspired algorithms into their original biological context, we can potentially both validate and refine the models that were once derived from them. Such reciprocal testing not only strengthens the theoretical foundations of swarm intelligence but also offers a powerful methodological bridge, with swarm robotics inspiring biological validation.

Acknowledgments. This article is supported by the Field of Excellence COLIBRI (Complexity of Life in Basic Research and Innovation), University of Graz.

Disclosure of Interests. The authors have no competing interests to declare.

References

1. Acevedo, O., Rios, Y.Y., García, L., Narvaez, D.: A study of the beeclust algorithm for robot swarm aggregation. In: 2022 IEEE International Conference on Machine Learning and Applied Network Technologies (ICMLANT), pp. 1–6. IEEE (2022)
2. Arvin, F., Attar, A., Turgut, A.E., Yue, S.: Power-law distribution of long-term experimental data in swarm robotics. In: Tan, Y., Shi, Y., Buarque, F., Gelbukh, A., Das, S., Engelbrecht, A. (eds.) Advances in Swarm and Computational Intelligence. ICSI 2015. LNCS, vol. 9140, pp. 551–559. Springer, Cham (2015). https://doi.org/10.1007/978-3-319-20466-6_58
3. Bodi, M., Thenius, R., Szopek, M., Schmickl, T., Crailsheim, K.: Interaction of robot swarms using the honeybee-inspired control algorithm beeclust. Math. Comput. Model. Dyn. Syst. 18(1), 87–100 (2012)
4. Bonabeau, E., Dorigo, M., Theraulaz, G.: Swarm Intelligence from Natural to Artificial Systems. Santa Fe Institute Studies in the Sciences of Complexity, Oxford University Press (1999)
5. Hamann, H., Schmickl, T., Wörn, H., Crailsheim, K.: Analysis of emergent symmetry breaking in collective decision making. Neural Comput. Appl. 21(2), 207–218 (2012)
6. He, S., et al.: drone orchestration via predictive optimization. In: Proceedings of the 18th International Conference on Mobile Systems, Applications, and Services, pp. 299–311 (2020)
7. Hereford, J.: Analysis of beeclust swarm algorithm. In: 2011 IEEE Symposium on Swarm Intelligence, pp. 1–7. IEEE (2011)
8. Hereford, J.: Beeclust swarm algorithm: analysis and implementation using a markov chain model. Int. J. Innov. Comput. Appl. 5(2), 115–124 (2013)
9. Kengyel, D., Zahadat, P., Kunzfeld, T., Schmickl, T.: Collective decision making in a swarm of robots: how robust the beeclust algorithm performs in various conditions. In: Proceedings of the 9th EAI International Conference on Bio-inspired Information and Communications Technologies (formerly BIONETICS), pp. 264–271 (2016)
10. Kiszli, Z., Na, S., Arvin, F.: Toward a myriad robot swarm aggregation. In: 2022 7th International Conference on Control and Robotics Engineering (ICCRE), pp. 1–4. IEEE (2022)
11. Palacci, J., Sacanna, S., Kim, S.H., Yi, G.R., Pine, D.J., Chaikin, P.M.: Light-activated self-propelled colloids. Philos. Trans. R. Soc. A Math. Phys. Eng. Sci. 372(2029), 20130372 (2014)
12. Pan, M., Yang, Y., Qin, X., Liu, L.: Self-organized aggregation with physical interaction. In: 2023 IEEE International Conference on Real-time Computing and Robotics (RCAR), pp. 182–187. IEEE (2023)
13. Rios, Y.Y., Acevedo, O., García, L.L.: Robot swarm aggregation using an improved beeclust method. Int. J. Intell. Robot. Appl. 1–11 (2025)
14. Sadeghi Amjadi, A., Raoufi, M., Turgut, A.E.: A self-adaptive landmark-based aggregation method for robot swarms. Adapt. Behav. 30(3), 223–236 (2022)
15. Sadeghi Amjadi, A., Raoufi, M., Turgut, A.E., Broughton, G., Krajník, T., Arvin, F.: Cooperative pollution source exploration and cleanup with a bio-inspired swarm robot aggregation. In: Gao, H., Wang, X., Iqbal, M., Yin, Y., Yin, J., Gu, N. (eds.) Collaborative Computing: Networking, Applications and Worksharing. CollaborateCom 2020. LNICS, Social Informatics and Telecommunications Engineering, vol. 350, pp. 469–481. Springer, Cham (2021). https://doi.org/10.1007/978-3-030-67540-0_30

16. Schmickl, T., Hamann, H.: Beeclust: a swarm algorithm derived from honeybees. In: Bio-inspired Computing and Communication Networks, pp. 95–137. CRC Press, Boca Raton, FL (2011)

17. Schmickl, T., et al.: Assisi: charged hot bees shakin'in the spotlight. In: 2013 IEEE 7th International Conference on Self-Adaptive and Self-Organizing Systems, pp. 259–260. IEEE (2013)

18. Schmickl, T., et al.: Get in touch: cooperative decision making based on robot-to-robot collisions. Auton. Agent. Multi-Agent Syst. **18**(1), 133–155 (2009)

19. Seeley, T.D., Buhrman, S.C.: Group decision making in swarms of honey bees. Behav. Ecol. Sociobiol. **45**(1), 19–31 (1999)

20. Soysal, O., Şahin, E.: A macroscopic model for self-organized aggregation in swarm robotic systems. In: Şahin, E., Spears, W.M., Winfield, A.F.T. (eds) Swarm Robotics. SR 2006. LNCS, vol. 4433, pp. 27–42. Springer, Berlin, Heidelberg (2007). https://doi.org/10.1007/978-3-540-71541-2_3

21. Sumpter, D.J.: The principles of collective animal behaviour. Philos. Trans. R. Soc. B: Biol. Sci. **361**(1465), 5–22 (2006)

22. Szopek, M., Schmickl, T., Thenius, R., Radspieler, G., Crailsheim, K.: Dynamics of collective decision making of honeybees in complex temperature fields. PLoS ONE **8**(10), e76250 (2013)

23. Szopek, M., Stefanec, M., Bodi, M., Radspieler, G., Schmickl, T.: A cellular model of swarm intelligence in bees and robots. In: 10th EAI International Conference on Bio-inspired Information and Communications Technologies (formerly BIONET-ICS), pp. 11–18 (2017)

24. Szopek, M., Stokanic, V., Radspieler, G., Schmickl, T.: Simple physical interactions yield social self-organization in honeybees. Front. Phys. **9**, 670317 (2021)

25. Te Vrugt, M., Jeggle, J., Wittkowski, R.: Jerky active matter: a phase field crystal model with translational and orientational memory. New J. Phys. **23**(6), 063023 (2021)

26. Vicsek, T., Zafeiris, A.: Collective motion. Phys. Rep. **517**(3–4), 71–140 (2012)

27. Vogrin, M., Stefanec, M., Schmickl, T.: Social distancing in robot swarms: modulating exploitation and exploration without signal exchange. In: 2020 IEEE Symposium Series on Computational Intelligence (SSCI), pp. 2233–2240. IEEE (2020)

Convergence and Running Time of Time-Dependent Ant Colony Algorithms

Bodo Manthey[1] , Jesse van Rhijn[1(✉)] , Ashkan Safari[2(✉)] ,
and Tjark Vredeveld[2]

[1] Faculty of Electrical Engineering, Mathematics, and Computer Science, University
of Twente, Enschede, The Netherlands
`{b.manthey,j.vanrhijn}@utwente.nl`
[2] Department of Quantitative Economics, School of Business and Economics,
Maastricht University, Maastricht, The Netherlands
`{a.safari,t.vredeveld}@maastrichtuniversity.nl`

Abstract. We consider two time-dependent adaptations of the n-ANT algorithm: Attiratanusanthron and Fakcharoenphol's (2008) n-ANT algorithm with time-dependent evaporation rate (n-ANT/tdev) and n-ANT with time-dependent lower pheromone bound (n-ANT/tdlb). We analyze the running time of both variants on the single destination shortest path problem (SDSP). We show that n-ANT/tdev has a super-polynomial running time on the SDSP. In contrast, we show that n-ANT/tdlb achieves a polynomial running time on this problem. This demonstrates rigorously how these time-dependent adaptions affect the performance of ACO variants, both positively and negatively. Moreover, we show that Gutjahr's Graph-based Ant System with time-dependent evaporation rate (GBAS/tdev) converges to the optimal solution under a slightly stronger evaporation rate function than was previously known.

1 Introduction

This paper studies the runtime analysis of three time-dependent Ant Colony Optimization (ACO) algorithms. ACO is a nature-inspired metaheuristic [4], and since its inception, many variants have been proposed, implemented, and applied to different problems [1,3,6,11,12,17,19,20,22,24]. ACO algorithms rely on several user-defined parameters, such as the pheromone evaporation rate and the minimum pheromone level, which have a significant impact on the algorithm's performance. In particular, changing the parameters during the algorithm's execution in a time-dependent manner has been shown to be beneficial in some cases [14,23], while degrading the performance in other cases [18].

The main motivation of this paper is to understand the algorithmic consequences of time-dependent parameter adaptation in ACO. Such mechanisms are widely used in practice, particularly for NP-hard combinatorial optimization problems, yet their impact on running time guarantees is poorly understood. By

R. Groß et al. (Eds.): ANTS 2026, LNCS 16515, pp. 82–94, 2026.
https://doi.org/10.1007/978-3-032-26123-6_7

analyzing a time-dependent evaporation rate and lower pheromone bound [9] on an "easy" problem, we aim to isolate their fundamental effects.

Some of the earliest theoretical studies of ACO were performed by Gutjahr [8, 10], on a variant called the *Graph-Based Ant System* (GBAS). Since GBAS is not guaranteed to converge to an optimal solution, Gutjahr later proposed two modified variants [5,8]: one that adjusts the pheromone evaporation rate (*GBAS/tdev*) and another that modifies the pheromone lower bound on each arc (*GBAS/tdlb*). Both variants were proven to converge to an optimal solution with probability one. However, the impact of these modifications on the algorithm's running time was analyzed only for *GBAS/tdlb* on a set of artificial problems [7], leaving open the question of how such adaptations influence the performance of ACO algorithms on more realistic problem instances.

One such more realistic problem is the Single-Destination Shortest Path problem (SDSP), which Attiratanasunthron and Fakcharoenphol [1] considered in the context of ACO by analyzing the running time of the *Max-Min Ant System* (MMAS) [1,11,21,22,24] on directed acyclic graphs (DAGs). They showed that MMAS can require exponential time to converge when each ant starts from the same source vertex. They therefore proposed n-ANT, inspired by 1-ANT [16] and AntNet [2], which places one ant on each node. Each ant independently searches for the target node, and is responsible only for updating the pheromone on the outgoing edges of its source node. For a DAG with n nodes and m edges, they obtain a running time bound of $O\left(\frac{1}{\rho}n^2 m \log n\right)$, which was later improved for general graphs by Sudholt and Thyssen [22].

Although n-ANT is guaranteed to find an optimal solution in polynomial time, its fixed pheromone lower bound means that non-optimal edges are always chosen with positive probability, even as the number of *cycles* $k \to \infty$, where a cycle denotes one complete execution round in which each ant constructs a walk and pheromone values are subsequently updated, following the definition of Gutjahr [8–10]. This theoretical shortcoming is one of the motivations for exploring time-dependent variants, which we analyze in this work.

Our Contribution. In this paper, we analyze the running time of time-dependent variants of ACO. First, we establish a running time bound for GBAS/tdev, and additionally improve the evaporation rate function required for convergence (Theorem 1). Next, we build on the prior works by Attiratanasunthron and Fakcharoenphol [1], and Sudholt and Thyssen [22] by analyzing *n-ANT/tdev*. We establish an exponential lower bound for the running time of this variant on the SDSP (Theorem 2). On the positive side, we show that by introducing a decreasing pheromone lower bound in the n-ANT algorithm, resulting in the variant *n-ANT/tdlb*, we can establish a polynomial upper bound on the expected running time for the SDSP (Theorem 3), while simultaneously guaranteeing that the pheromone on "wrong" edges decreases to 0 as the number of cycles $k \to \infty$. Theorems 2 and 3 together show that, for the n-ANT algorithm, dynamically changing the evaporation rate leads to a poor worst-case running time, while adapting the pheromone lower bound yields polynomial running times. Interestingly, this contrast is in line with mixed results from experimental studies [14,18,23], where some forms of parameter adaptation were found to improve performance, while others worsened it.

2   GBAS/tdev

For completeness, we sketch GBAS/tdev and refer to the full version of this paper [13] for the complete algorithm and proofs. In GBAS, a set S of ants solves an optimization problem by walking on a problem-specific graph with n nodes, called the *construction graph*. Walks on this graph correspond to solutions to the optimization problem. GBAS/tdev extends the original GBAS by introducing a time-dependent evaporation rate that decreases over time, denoted by $\rho(k) = \frac{\alpha}{k}$ in cycle k, with $\alpha < \frac{1}{2L}$, where L is an upper bound to the number of nodes in an optimal walk. This adjustment gradually reduces the influence of pheromone evaporation, allowing the algorithm to emphasize exploitation in later iterations while maintaining exploration in the early phase.

Theorem 1. *Let $\rho(k) = \frac{\alpha}{k}$ be the value of the evaporation rate used by GBAS/tdev in cycle k, where $\alpha < \frac{1}{2L}$. Fix some $\varepsilon > 0$. Then there exists a constant $c > 0$ such that, if $m^{1-2\alpha L} \geq c \cdot \frac{n^{2L}}{|S|} \cdot \ln \frac{1}{\varepsilon}$, the probability that no ant traverses an optimal walk in GBAS/tdev in the first m cycles is bounded from above by ε.*

3 n-ANT Variants

In this section, we explain the two variants of Ant Colony Optimization we consider in this paper, which are based on the n-ANT algorithm [1]: n-ANT/tdev (n-ANT with time-dependent evaporation rate) and n-ANT/tdlb (n-ANT with time-dependent lower pheromone bound). In the n-ANT algorithm [1], we are given a weighted directed graph $\mathcal{G} = (\mathcal{V}, \mathcal{A})$, with $|\mathcal{V}| = n$, as well as one ant a_i assigned to each node $i \in \mathcal{V}$. Each ant a_i is responsible for finding a shortest path from node i to a termination node $t \in \mathcal{V}$. A *cycle* is a time period during which every ant either finds a path to t, or reports that such a path has not been found after at most n iterations, since any shortest path in $\mathcal{G}$ has at most n nodes.

Ant a_h goes from node i to i' in cycle m with probability

$$p_{i,i'}(m) = \frac{\tau_{i,i'}(m)}{\sum_{i'':(i,i'')\in\mathcal{A}} \tau_{i,i''}(m)},$$

where $\tau_{i,i'}(m)$ is the pheromone value of the arc (i, i') in cycle m. At the beginning of cycle 1, we initialize $\tau_{i,i'}(1) = \frac{1}{\deg_o(i)}$, where $\deg_o(i)$ is the out-degree of node i. With this initialization, we ensure that initially the sum of the pheromone values of all the outgoing arcs of node i is equal to 1.

In n-ANT/tdev, we consider a decreasing function $0 < \rho(m) < 1$ for the value of the evaporation rate at cycle m. In n-ANT/tdlb, the evaporation rate has a constant value $0 < \rho < 1$; however, in this variant, the pheromone values of the arcs in $\mathcal{G}$ are constrained by upper and lower bounds, with $\tau_{\max}$ as the maximum possible pheromone value and $\tau_{\min}(m)$ as the minimum possible pheromone value at cycle m.

Let $f_i(m)$ be the length of the path found by ant a_i from i to t in cycle m, and $\hat{f}_i$ be the length of the best path found so far by a_i from i to t. Moreover, let $S_i(m)$ and $\hat{S}_i$ be the set of the corresponding nodes to $f_i(m)$ and $\hat{f}_i$, respectively. At the end of each cycle m, first each ant a_i updates the values of $\hat{f}_i$ and $\hat{S}_i$; i.e., if $f_i(m) < \hat{f}_i$, then we reassign $\hat{f}_i = f_i(m)$ and $\hat{S}_i = S_i(m)$. Then, each ant a_i updates the pheromone values of all outgoing arcs (i, i') from i based on the specific variant of the n-ANT algorithm being applied. The generic time-dependent n-ANT pheromone update rule is

$$\tau_{i,i'}(m+1) = \begin{cases} \min\{(1 - \rho(m)) \cdot \tau_{i,i'}(m) + \rho(m), \tau_{\max}\} & \text{if } i' \in \hat{S}_i, \\ \max\{(1 - \rho(m)) \cdot \tau_{i,i'}(m), \tau_{\min}(m)\} & \text{otherwise.} \end{cases}$$

In n-ANT/tdev, we set $\rho(m) = \alpha_n/m^\beta$ with $\alpha_n, \beta > 0$ and $\tau_{\min} = 0$ and $\tau_{\max} = \infty$. For n-ANT/tdlb we set $\tau_{\min}(m) = c_n/\ln(m+1)$ as recommended by Gutjahr [8], with $c_n \leq \frac{1}{n^2}$, while ρ is constant.

According to these update rules, each ant a_i locally updates the pheromone values of all the outgoing arcs of node i. As any shortest path in $\mathcal{G}$ has at most n nodes, if an ant a_i does not reach t after n iterations in cycle m, we set $f_i(m) = \infty$. We note that the update rule of the n-ANT/tdev has a useful normalization property.

Lemma 1. *The total pheromone value of the outgoing arcs of any node i in n-ANT/tdev is always equal to 1.*

Furthermore, we have the following lemma on the total amount of pheromone values on the outgoing arcs of any node i in n-ANT/tdlb.

Lemma 2. *The total pheromone value of the outgoing arcs of any node i in n-ANT/tdlb is at least equal to 1 when $\tau_{max} \geq 1$.*

We now proceed to analyze the running time of n-ANT/tdev and n-ANT/tdlb on the SDSP. For both of these algorithms, we derive a recurrence relation for the time that an ant a_i takes to find its shortest path, as a function of the time taken for ants "closer" to the target node. In the case of n-ANT/tdev, the recurrence relation yields a lower bound for the running time, while for n-ANT/tdlb we obtain an upper bound. For details of the proof in the analysis, we refer to the full version of this paper [13].

3.1   Running Time Analysis of n-ANT/tdev

In this part, we provide a super-polynomial lower bound on the total number of cycles required for all ants a_i to find a shortest path from their respective starting nodes i to the target node t in n-ANT/tdev. To this end, we consider an instance with a directed path P of $n + 2$ nodes, along with some extra arcs. The last node on this path is the target node t. We call the node preceding the target node the *attractor node*. The remaining n nodes form the *chain C*, and are labeled as $\{1, \ldots, n\}$. Node 1 has two outgoing arcs: one leading to the attractor node, which we call its *incorrect arc*, and one directly to the target node, which we refer to as its *correct arc*. For each subsequent node $i > 1$, there are also two outgoing arcs: one to the attractor node (its *incorrect arc*) and one to node $i - 1$ (its *correct arc*). Every arc in this instance has a weight of 1, except the arc from the attractor node to the target node, which has a weight of $M - 1$, where $M > n$. We call this structure the *series* instance (see Fig. 1). The constructed instance belongs to a class of layered worst-case graphs commonly used in runtime analyses of ACO for shortest path problems [22].

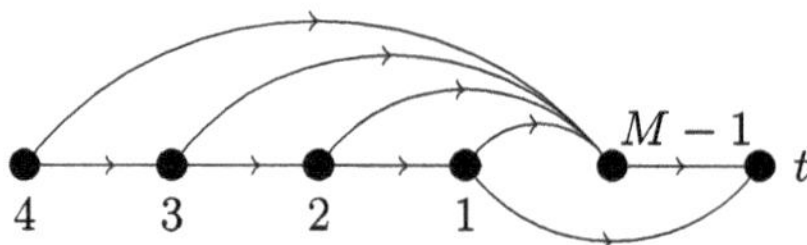

Fig. 1. The series instance for $n = 4$. Arc weights not shown are equal to 1. The first four nodes on the left form the chain C; the remaining unlabeled node is the attractor.

In the series instance, each node i in the chain C is associated with an ant a_i. To find the shortest path, an ant on node i in C must always choose the correct arc of this node. If an ant chooses an incorrect arc at any point, then it finds a strictly longer path due to the final arc from the attractor to the target node.

Our analysis follows a standard approach in the runtime analysis of ACO, where progress is measured by waiting until pheromone values at individual vertices are sufficiently stabilized before bounding the probability of extending shortest paths [1,22]. For the analysis, we assume that $\rho(m) = \alpha_n/m^\beta$ with $\alpha_n < 1$ and $\beta \geq 0$. Here, α_n in general depends on n; however, we assume β is a fixed constant. We choose α_n to be a non-increasing function of n.

The analysis for $\beta > 1$ is essentially trivial: The evaporation rate decreases quickly enough that the quantity of pheromone on the incorrect arcs is bounded from below by a constant. This suffices to ensure that the ant on node n finds the target node with exponentially small probability in each cycle. Hence, we will focus on the case $\beta \leq 1$, which is substantially more difficult. We must now carefully consider the evolution of the pheromone values during the execution of the algorithm, as we cannot assume that there is always a constant probability of any ant making the wrong choice during any iteration in a cycle.

First, we need a few definitions. We say that a node $i \in C$ is *ε-processed* if the incorrect arc of i has a pheromone value of at most $\varepsilon \in (0, 1)$, which is a fixed constant that we leave ambiguous–its precise value is not important. For most of this subsection, we simply say *processed* for brevity, since the value of ε

does not change throughout the analysis. For an ant a_i, we define $L_i(m)$ to be the number of ants with label smaller than i that have *not* processed their node in cycle m. Note that $L_i(m)$ is a random variable.

As each non-processed node has a pheromone value of at most $(1 - \varepsilon)$ on its good arc, the probability that an ant a_i finds its shortest path in cycle m is at most $(1 - \varepsilon)^{L_i(m)}$, since it needs to choose the correct arc on each node with a label smaller than i. This immediately yields the following.

Lemma 3. *The probability that a_i finds its shortest path in cycle m, given that $L_i(m) \geq c\sqrt{n}$ for some constant $c > 0$, is bounded from above by $2^{-\Omega(\sqrt{n})}$.*

This shows that, if $\Omega(\sqrt{n})$ nodes ahead of some ant a_i are not processed, then a_i is unlikely to find its shortest path in $2^{o(\sqrt{n})}$ cycles.

We next divide the ants starting on the chain C into $k = \lceil \sqrt{n} \rceil$ segments S_i, each of size of at least $\lfloor \sqrt{n} \rfloor - 1$. For a fixed constant $\eta \in (0, 1)$, we say that a segment S_i is η-processed if at least $\eta|S_i|$ ants in S_i have processed their nodes. As with ε, we leave the value of η ambiguous, as its precise value is not important. Let T_i be the first cycle in which segment S_i is η-processed. In the following, we write *with high probability* or whp as a shorthand for "with probability at least $1 - 2^{-\Omega(\sqrt{n})}$".

We wish to show that the variables T_i satisfy a certain recurrence inequality with high probability. For this, need to assume that sufficiently many ants only start reinforcing their correct arc after sufficiently many ants ahead of them in the chain have processed their nodes. Lemma 4 ensures that this holds for a constant fraction of ants in each segment S_i whp.

Lemma 4. *With high probability, every segment S_i contains $\Omega(\sqrt{n})$ ants that never reinforce their correct arcs until they first see their shortest paths.*

We are now in a position to derive a generic recurrence inequality satisfied by the variables T_i.

Lemma 5. *Let $a_h \in S_i$ be an ant that has not reinforced its correct arc before first seeing its shortest path. Define the following two events:*

- *$\mathcal{E}(i - 1, m) : S_{i-1}$ is first η-processed in cycle m.*
- *$\mathcal{F}(a_h, m) : a_h$ first sees its shortest path in cycle m.*

Let $F(m)$ denote a whp lower bound for the number of cycles needed for a_h to first see its shortest path, conditioned on $\mathcal{E}(i-1, m)$, and let $G(m)$ denote a whp lower bound for the number of cycles needed for a_h to process its node, conditioned on $\mathcal{F}(a_h, m)$. Then either $T_i = 2^{\Omega(\sqrt{n})}$ for some $i \in [k]$, or T_i satisfies whp the recurrence inequality $T_i \geq T_{i-1} + F(T_{i-1}) + G(T_{i-1} + F(T_{i-1}))$.

Proof. Suppose that $T_i = 2^{o(\sqrt{n})}$ for each $i \in [k]$. Then by Lemma 3, the probability that an ant in S_i finds its shortest path before T_{i-1} is $2^{-\Omega(\sqrt{n})}$, since for any ant $a \in S_i$ starting at node j we have $L_j(m) = \Omega(\sqrt{n})$ for any $m < T_{i-1}$. If we furthermore assume that a has not reinforced its correct arc before seeing its shortest path, then a needs whp $F(T_{i-1})$ cycles after T_{i-1} to find its shortest path. Subsequently, a needs $G(T_{i-1} + F(T_{i-1}))$ cycles to process its node.

If we could guarantee that no ant in $a \in S_i$ reinforces its correct arc before seeing its shortest path, we could immediately say that $T_i \geq T_{i-1} + F(T_{i-1}) + G(T_{i-1} + F(T_{i-1}))$ whp. In reality, some ants may reinforce their correct arcs before T_{i-1}, so we must deal with this event. However, Lemma 4 guarantees that whp every segment contains $\Omega(\sqrt{n})$ ants that never reinforce their correct arc before first finding their shortest paths, which suffices for our purposes. Consequently, every segment contains $\Omega(\sqrt{n})$ ants for which the assumptions on ant a from the lemma statement hold whp, and so the sequence T_i indeed satisfies the claimed recurrence whp. $\qquad\square$

To apply Lemma 5, we need to find expressions for the functions F and G. The latter can be derived from the following lemma.

Lemma 6. *Suppose a_i sees its optimal solution for the first time in cycle $m > 1$, and it has never reinforced its correct arc before cycle m. Then the number of cycles that a_i needs to process node i is at least*

1. $\left(\left(\frac{1}{2\varepsilon} \right)^{\frac{1-\alpha_n}{\alpha_n}} - 1 \right) \cdot m + 1 - \left(\frac{1}{2\varepsilon} \right)^{\frac{1-\alpha_n}{\alpha_n}}$ *cycles, if $\beta = 1$;*

2.
$$\left((m-1)^{1-\beta} + (1-\beta) \cdot \frac{1-\alpha_n}{\alpha_n} \ln \frac{1}{2\varepsilon} \right)^{\frac{1}{1-\beta}} - (m-1) \geq \left((1-\beta) \cdot \frac{1-\alpha_n}{\alpha_n} \ln \frac{1}{2\varepsilon} \right)^{\frac{1}{1-\beta}}$$
cycles, if $\beta < 1$.

It is straightforward to show from Lemma 5 and 6 that for $\beta = 1$ the variables T_i satisfy whp the recurrence inequality $T_i \geq c \cdot T_{i-1}$, for some constant $c > 1$. This immediately yields the desired result for $\beta = 1$.

In case for $\beta = 1$, we can ignore the term in the recurrence inequality that involves $F(\cdot)$, since in this case the function $G(m)$ is proportional to m. However, for $\beta < 1$ we instead have $G(m) \propto m^\beta$, which is not sufficient on its own to guarantee a super-polynomial running time. We thus need to take F into account as well for this case. The following lemma provides an bound for $F(m)$.

Lemma 7. *Suppose $\beta < 1$, and assume S_{i-1} is first processed in cycle m. Then whp, there are $\Omega(\sqrt{n})$ ants in S_i that need at least*

$$\exp\left(\frac{a}{1-\beta} \left(m^{1-\beta} - 1 \right) \right)$$

cycles after m to see their shortest paths for the first time.

We are now in a position to prove our main result on n-ANT/tdev.

Theorem 2. *For all $n \geq 3$, there exists an instance of the SDSP on n vertices such that n-ANT/tdev takes $2^{\Omega(\sqrt{n})}$ cycles until all ants have seen their shortest paths, provided that the evaporation rate function has the form $\rho(m) = \alpha_n/m^\beta$ for $\alpha_n < 1$ and $\beta > 0$, where α_n is a non-increasing function of n and β is a constant.*

Proof. As mentioned above, the case $\beta \geq 1$ is straightforward; thus, we consider only $\beta < 1$. Let $k = \lceil \sqrt{n} \rceil$. We compute a lower bound for $\mathbb{E}[T_{k-1}]$. According to Lemmas 6 to 7 we have for each $2 \leq i \leq k$

$$T_i \geq T_{i-1} + \exp\left(\frac{\alpha_n}{1-\beta}\left((T_{i-1})^{1-\beta} - 1\right)\right)$$

$$+ \left((T_{i-1} - 1)^{1-\beta} + (1-\beta)\cdot\frac{1-\alpha_n}{\alpha_n}\ln\frac{1}{2\varepsilon}\right)^{\frac{1}{1-\beta}} - (T_{i-1} - 1)$$

$$\geq T_{i-1} + \exp\left(\frac{\alpha_n}{1-\beta}\left((T_{i-1})^{1-\beta} - 1\right)\right) + \left(\frac{1-\alpha_n}{\alpha_n}\ln\frac{1}{2\varepsilon}\right)\cdot(T_{i-1} - 1)^\beta, \quad (1)$$

using in the latter inequality that $T_{i-1} \geq 1$ and $\beta < 1$.

According to Lemma 7, we also have $T_1 \geq 1 + (1-\beta)^{\frac{1}{1-\beta}}\left(\frac{1-\alpha_n}{\alpha_n}\ln\frac{1}{2\varepsilon}\right)^{\frac{1}{1-\beta}}$; this holds since whp there are $\Omega(\sqrt{n})$ ants in S_1 that need at least two cycles to find their shortest paths (this follows easily from a simple Chernoff bound [15]), and hence the second part of Lemma 6 applies to these ants.

If we ignore the second term above, then we obtain the simpler recurrence inequality

$$T_i \geq T_{i-1} + \left(\frac{1-\alpha_n}{\alpha_n}\ln\frac{1}{2\varepsilon}\right)\cdot(T_{i-1} - 1)^\beta$$

with initial condition for T_1 as stated above. The solution to this recurrence inequality can be bounded from below; see the full version [13] for a detailed proof. We then have for each $1 \leq i \leq k$,

$$T_i \geq 1 + (1-\beta)^{\frac{1}{1-\beta}}\left(\frac{1-\alpha_n}{\alpha_n}\ln\frac{1}{2\varepsilon}\right)^{\frac{1}{1-\beta}} \cdot [1 + \gamma_\beta\cdot(i-1)]^{\frac{1}{1-\beta}}, \quad (2)$$

where $\gamma_\beta > 0$ depends only on β.

In Eq. (2), let $i = k - 1$. Since each term in this inequality is non-negative, we can take for a lower bound only the second term. Plugging in Eq. (2) and simplifying then yields

$$T_{k-1} \geq \exp\left(-\frac{\alpha_n}{1-\beta}\right)\cdot\exp\left(\gamma_\beta\cdot(1-\alpha_n)\cdot\ln\left(\frac{1}{2\varepsilon}\right)\cdot(k-2)\right).$$

Note that β and ε are both constants. Moreover, we require $\alpha_n < 1$ with α_n non-increasing in n. Thus, we have $1 - \alpha_n = \Omega(1)$. Finally, recalling that $k = \Omega(\sqrt{n})$, we obtain $T_{k-1} = 2^{\Omega(\sqrt{n})}$ whp and in expectation. $\quad\square$

3.2 Running Time Analysis of n-ANT/tdlb

zthe total number of cycles required for all ants a_i to find a shortest path from their respective starting nodes i to the target node t in n-ANT/tdlb. We say an ant a_i *sees* its optimal solution if $\hat{f}_i = f_i^*$, where f_i^* is the length of the shortest path from node i to t. Let S_i^* be the set of the corresponding nodes to f_i^*. For an ant a_i, an arc (i, i') is called *incorrect* if $i' \notin S_i^*$. Moreover, we say that node i is ε-*processed* if $\tau_{i,i'} \leq \varepsilon = 1/n^2$ for all the incorrect arcs (i, i'). Let $1, 2, \ldots, n = t$ be an enumeration of the vertices in $\mathcal{G}$ with $\ell(1) \geq \ell(2) \geq \ldots \geq \ell(n)$ where $\ell(i)$ is the maximum number of arcs on any shortest path from node i to t. With this ordering of the vertices, all the shortest paths from node i to t only use vertices from $\{i+1, i+2, \ldots, n\}$; otherwise, there would exist a shortest path from i to t with more than $\ell(i)$ arcs.

To analyze the total number of cycles, we first derive an upper bound on the number of cycles required for node i to become ε-processed after ant a_i sees its optimal solution for the first time (Lemma 8). Then, assuming that all nodes reachable from i to t have already been ε-processed, we compute the expected number of cycles until ant a_i sees its optimal solution (Lemma 9). To determine this expected value, we first establish a lower bound on the probability that ant a_i sees its optimal solution in any cycle m under the same assumption. Finally, in Theorem 3, we report the total number of cycles for all ants to find their shortest paths to the target node.

Lemma 8. *Suppose ant a_i sees its optimal solution for the first time in cycle m^*. In at most $O\left(\frac{1}{\rho} \ln \frac{\tau_{max}}{\varepsilon}\right)$ cycles after m^*, node i is ε-processed.*

To continue our analysis, we define the following random variables. Let T_k denote the first cycle in which all nodes i with $\ell(i) - \ell(t) \leq k$ are ε-processed. Moreover, let S_k denote the number of cycles *after* T_{k-1} needed for an ant a_i with $\ell(i) - \ell(t) = k$ to see its optimal solution for the first time as a function of T_{k-1}. Furthermore, let Δ_k denote the number of cycles required for a node i with $\ell(i) - \ell(t) = k$ to become ε-processed after ant a_i has seen its optimal solution for the first time. According to Lemma 8, we have $\Delta_k = O\left(\frac{1}{\rho} \ln \frac{\tau_{max}}{\varepsilon}\right)$.

Lemma 9. *The expected number of cycles until ant a_i sees its optimal solution for the first time with $\ell(i) - \ell(t) = k$, given that all the nodes reachable from i to t have already been ε-processed, is $\mathbb{E}[S_k \,|\, T_{k-1}] = O\left(\dfrac{n \cdot \tau_{max}}{c_n} \cdot \ln \dfrac{n \cdot \tau_{max} \cdot T_{k-1}}{c_n}\right)$ when $\tau_{max} \geq 1$ and $\tau_{min}(m) = \frac{c_n}{\ln(m+1)}$, for $0 < c_n \leq \frac{1}{n^2}$.*

Finally, we provide an upper bound on the expected number of cycles to ε-process all the nodes in $\mathcal{G}$. To do so, we will need the following technical lemma.

Lemma 10. *Let M_k be a sequence defined recursively for $k \geq 1$ as*

$$M_k = M_{k-1} + a \cdot \ln M_{k-1} + b,$$

with the initial value $M_1 = b$ for $b \geq a > 0$. Then,

$$M_k = O(b \cdot k + a \cdot k \cdot \ln(a \cdot k)).$$

Now our main result on n-ANT/tdlb follows from Lemmas 8 to 10.

Theorem 3. *Let $\mathcal{G} = (\mathcal{V}, \mathcal{A})$ be an instance of the SDSP on which we run n-ANT/tdlb with $\tau_{min}(m) = c_n / \ln(m+1)$. The expected number of cycles until all ants have found their shortest paths from their respective starting nodes in $\mathcal{G}$ is*

$$O\left(\frac{n^2 \cdot \tau_{max}}{c_n} \cdot \ln\left(\frac{n \cdot \tau_{max}}{c_n}\right) + \frac{n}{\rho}\ln(n \cdot \tau_{max})\right),$$

for $\tau_{max} \geq 1$ and $0 < c_n \leq \frac{1}{n^2}$.

Proof. Let the random variable T denote the smallest number of cycles after which all the nodes in $\mathcal{G}$ are ε-processed. We describe a recurrence relation that allows us to compute $\mathbb{E}[T]$. This recurrence implicitly assumes that ant a_i at node i sees its shortest path before processing its node; hence, $\mathbb{E}[T]$ also yields an upper bound to the number of cycles until all ants have seen their shortest paths.

According to Lemma 8, and since $\ell(1) - \ell(n) \leq n - 1$, we have

$$\mathbb{E}[T] \leq \mathbb{E}[T_{n-2}] + \mathbb{E}[S_{n-1}] + \Delta_{n-1} = \mathbb{E}[T_{n-2}] + \mathbb{E}[S_{n-1}] + O\left(\frac{1}{\rho}\ln\frac{\tau_{max}}{\varepsilon}\right),$$

where the second inequality arises as follows. Consider a node i with $\ell(i) - \ell(t) = k$. For this node to be ε-processed, it suffices for a_i to first see its shortest path and then wait for Δ_k cycles. After T_{k-1}, the ant a_i is guaranteed to see its shortest path in S_k more cycles.

To compute $\mathbb{E}[S_{n-1}]$, we use Lemma 9 to find

$$\mathbb{E}[S_{n-1} \mid T_{n-2}] = O\left(\frac{n \cdot \tau_{max}}{c_n} \cdot \ln\left(\frac{n \cdot \tau_{max}}{c_n} \cdot T_{n-2}\right)\right).$$

On using total expectation, we obtain the desired expectation; however, this requires us to compute $\mathbb{E}[\ln T_{n-2}]$. We therefore use Jensen's inequality, exploiting the concavity of the logarithm to obtain

$$\mathbb{E}[S_{n-1}] - O\left(\frac{n \cdot \tau_{max}}{c_n} \cdot \ln\frac{n \cdot \tau_{max}}{c_n} + \frac{n \cdot \tau_{max}}{c_n} \cdot \ln\mathbb{E}[T_{n-2}]\right).$$

Therefore, we get

$$\mathbb{E}[T_{n-1}] \leq \mathbb{E}[T_{n-2}] + O\left(\frac{n\tau_{max}}{c_n} \cdot \ln\mathbb{E}[T_{n-2}] + \frac{n\tau_{max}}{c_n} \cdot \ln\frac{n\tau_{max}}{c_n} + \frac{1}{\rho}\ln\frac{\tau_{max}}{\varepsilon}\right).$$

From Lemmas 8 and 9, we have $\mathbb{E}[T_1] = O\left(\frac{n \cdot \tau_{max}}{c_n} \cdot \ln\frac{n \cdot \tau_{max}}{c_n} + \frac{1}{\rho}\ln\frac{\tau_{max}}{\varepsilon}\right)$. By solving the recurrence relation for $\mathbb{E}[T_{n-1}]$ based on Lemma 10, we get

$$\mathbb{E}[T] = O\left(\frac{n^2 \cdot \tau_{max}}{c_n} \cdot \ln\left(\frac{n \cdot \tau_{max}}{c_n}\right) + \frac{n}{\rho}\ln\frac{\tau_{max}}{\varepsilon}\right).$$

On simplifying the terms inside the $O(\cdot)$ and replacing ε by $\frac{1}{n^2}$, the result follows.
$\square$

Furthermore, as any shortest path in $\mathcal{G}$ has at most n nodes, the number of iterations in each cycle is upper-bounded by $O(n^2)$.

Corollary 1. *Let $\mathcal{G} = (\mathcal{V}, \mathcal{A})$ be an instance of the SDSP on which we run n-ANT/tdlb with $\tau_{min}(m) = c_n / \ln(m+1)$. The expected number of iterations until all ants have found their shortest paths from their respective starting nodes in $\mathcal{G}$ is*

$$O\left(\frac{n^4 \cdot \tau_{max}}{c_n} \cdot \ln\left(\frac{n \cdot \tau_{max}}{c_n} \right) + \frac{n^3}{\rho} \ln(n \cdot \tau_{max}) \right), \; \textit{for } \tau_{max} \geq 1 \textit{ and } 0 < c_n \leq \tfrac{1}{n^2}.$$

Theorem 3 implies that as the number of cycles $m \to \infty$, the only arcs with positive pheromone are those of an optimal solution of the SDSP instance. This follows since the time until all nodes are ε-processed is finite with probability one (from Theorem 3 and Markov's inequality) and the properties of the pheromone update. To be more precise, once all nodes are ε-processed, then all ants have found some shortest path to the target node. Hence, the pheromone on arcs not on these shortest paths will decrease geometrically to $\tau_{\min}$, which itself decreases to zero. Meanwhile, the pheromone on the remaining arcs is increased by ρ in each subsequent cycle, eventually reaching a value of $\tau_{\max}$. This resolves a theoretical shortcoming of n-ANT as stated in Sect. 1.

4   Discussion

In this paper, we have analyzed three time-dependent variants of Ant Colony Optimization: GBAS/tdev, n-ANT/tdev, and n-ANT/tdlb. For GBAS/tdev, we derived a running-time bound and slightly improved the evaporation rate function that guarantees convergence (Theorem 1) compared to the function used by Gutjahr [9]. For the n-ANT algorithm, our results highlight a clear contrast between the two mechanisms: adapting the evaporation rate over time can lead to poor running-time guarantees (Theorem 2), whereas a time-dependent pheromone lower bound yields a polynomial expected running time on the single-destination shortest path problem and ensures that the probability of choosing non-optimal edges vanishes (Theorem 3). This contrast is in line with mixed results from experimental studies [14, 18, 23].

Although our analysis focuses on the SDSP, it provides insight into the effects of dynamic parameter adjustment in ACO, whose main applications are NP-hard optimization problems. Extending runtime analyses of ACO on harder problems to time-dependent variants remains an interesting direction for future work. In particular, it is an interesting question whether the analyses of MMAS on the Travelling Salesperson Problem [12, 24] can be extended to these time-dependent variants.

Acknowledgments. This research is supported by NWO grant OCENW.KLEIN.176.

Disclosure of Interests. The authors have no competing interests to declare.

References

1. Attiratanasunthron, N., Fakcharoenphol, J.: A running time analysis of an ant colony optimization algorithm for shortest paths in directed acyclic graphs. Inf. Process. Lett. **105**(3), 88–92 (2008)
2. Di Caro, G., Dorigo, M.: Antnet: distributed stigmergetic control for communications networks. J. Artif. Intell. Res. **9**, 317–365 (1998)
3. Dorigo, M., Di Caro, G.: Ant colony optimization: a new meta-heuristic. In: Proceedings of the 1999 congress on evolutionary computation-CEC99 (Cat. No. 99TH8406), vol. 2, pp. 1470–1477. IEEE (1999)
4. Dorigo, M., Maniezzo, V., Colorni, A.: The ant system: an autocatalytic optimization process. Res. Rept. 91–016 (1991)
5. Dorigo, M., Stützle, T.: The ant colony optimization metaheuristic: algorithms, applications, and advances. Handb. Metaheuristics 250–285 (2003)
6. Dorigo, M., Stützle, T.: Ant Colony Optimization. The MIT Press, Massachusetts (2004)
7. Gutjahr, W.: First steps to the runtime complexity analysis of ant colony optimization. Comput. Oper. Res. **35**(9), 2711–2727 (2008). part Special Issue: Bio-inspired Methods in Combinatorial Optimization
8. Gutjahr, W.: A graph-based ant system and its convergence. Futur. Gener. Comput. Syst. **16**(8), 873–888 (2000)
9. Gutjahr, W.: ACO algorithms with guaranteed convergence to the optimal solution. Inf. Process. Lett. **82**(3), 145–153 (2002)
10. Gutjahr, W.: A generalized convergence result for the graph-based ant system metaheuristic. Probab. Eng. Inf. Sci. **17**(4), 545–569 (2003)
11. Kötzing, T., Lehre, P., Neumann, F., Oliveto, P.: Ant colony optimization and the minimum cut problem. In: Proceedings of the 12th Annual Conference on Genetic and Evolutionary Computation (GECCO), pp. 1393–1400 (2010)
12. Kötzing, T., Neumann, F., Röglin, H., Witt, C.: Theoretical analysis of two ACO approaches for the traveling salesman problem. Swarm Intell. **6**(1), 1–21 (2012)
13. Manthey, B., van Rhijn, J., Safari, A., Vredeveld, T.: Convergence and running time of time-dependent ant colony algorithms. arXiv preprint arXiv:2501.10810 (2025)
14. Mavrovouniotis, M., Yang, S.: Adapting the pheromone evaporation rate in dynamic routing problems. In: Esparcia-Alcázar, A.I. (eds.) Applications of Evolutionary Computation. EvoApplications 2013. LNCS, vol. 7835, pp. 606–615. Springer, Berlin, Heidelberg (2013). https://doi.org/10.1007/978-3-642-37192-9_61
15. Mitzenmacher, M., Upfal, E.: Probability and Computing: Randomized Algorithms and Probabilistic Analysis. Cambridge University Press, Cambridge (2005)
16. Neumann, F., Witt, C.: Runtime analysis of a simple ant colony optimization algorithm. Algorithmica **54**(2), 243–255 (2009)
17. Neumann, F., Witt, C.: Ant colony optimization and the minimum spanning tree problem. Theor. Comput. Sci. **411**(25), 2406–2413 (2010)
18. Pellegrini, P., Stützle, T., Birattari, M.: A critical analysis of parameter adaptation in ant colony optimization. Swarm Intell. **6**, 23–48 (2012)
19. Shyu, S., Yin, P., Lin, B.: An ant colony optimization algorithm for the minimum weight vertex cover problem. Ann. Oper. Res. **131**, 283–304 (2004)
20. Stützle, T., Hoos, H.: Max-min ant system and local search for the traveling salesman problem. In: Proceedings of 1997 IEEE International Conference on Evolutionary Computation (ICEC), pp. 309–314. IEEE (1997)

21. Stützle, T., Hoos, H.: Max–min ant system. Futur. Gener. Comput. Syst. **16**(8), 889–914 (2000)
22. Sudholt, D., Thyssen, C.: Running time analysis of ant colony optimization for shortest path problems. J. Discret. Algorithms **10**, 165–180 (2012)
23. Tian, Y., Zhang, J., Wang, Q., Liu, S., Guo, Z., Zhang, H.: Application of hybrid algorithm based on ant colony optimization and sparrow search in UAV path planning. Int. J. Comput. Intell. Syst. **17**(1), 286 (2024)
24. Zhou, Y.: Runtime analysis of an ant colony optimization algorithm for TSP instances. IEEE Trans. Evol. Comput. **13**(5), 1083–1092 (2009)

Decoding Spatial and Temporal Influence in Collective Behavior Using Information Theory

Udoy S. Basak[1,2,3], Sulimon Sattari[4], Iacopo Hachen[1,2], Iain D. Couzin[2,5,6], and Liang Li[2,5,6,7]

[1] Max Planck Institute of Animal Behavior, Konstanz, Germany
`{ubasak,ihachen}@ab.mpg.de`
[2] Department of Biology, University of Konstanz, 78464 Konstanz, Germany
`{udoy.basak,li}@uni-konstanz.de`
[3] Department of Mathematics, Pabna University of Science and Technology, Pabna, Bangladesh
`udoy@pust.ac.bd`
[4] Research Institute for Electronic Science, Hokkaido University, Sapporo, Japan
[5] Department of Collective Behaviour, Max Planck Institute of Animal Behavior, 78464 Konstanz, Germany
`{icouzin,lli}@ab.mpg.de`
[6] Centre for the Advanced Study of Collective Behaviour, University of Konstanz, 78464 Konstanz, Germany
[7] Department of Computer and Information Science, University of Konstanz, 78464 Konstanz, Germany

Abstract. Understanding how neighbors influence each other in space and time is essential for explaining how collective behavior emerges. In this work, we present an information-theoretic approach that uses time-delayed mutual information to extract the optimal temporal influence delay and distance constrained transfer entropy to extract the spatial influence range. We first validate the approach with synthetic data generated by an agent based model with different interaction delays, spatial cutoffs, and noise levels, and we show that the method recovers the true temporal delay and spatial influence range. We then apply the approach to experiments in which a zebrafish follows a virtual fish performing controlled perturbations. The analysis reveals an interaction delay of about 600 milliseconds and a spatial interaction range between 3 and 6 body lengths, depending on how much information flows from the leader to the follower. These results demonstrate that information-theoretic tools can quantify the sensorimotor delays and spatial interaction ranges that shape social responses in animal collectives.

1   Introduction

Collective behavior is one of the most captivating and fundamental phenomena in nature. From the synchronized flight of bird flocks and the coordinated swimming of fish schools to the spontaneous organization of human crowds, collective motion emerges across vastly different biological and physical systems [2,5,8,16,19,27]. Despite the diversity of species and contexts, these systems share remarkable regularities in how simple local interactions can give rise to large-scale coordination [9]. Understanding the principles underlying collective behavior is therefore a central challenge across disciplines. It provides not only key insights into biological organization and evolution but also valuable inspiration for the design of autonomous robotic systems, distributed sensing networks, and swarm intelligence algorithms [14].

Earlier studies have largely relied on mathematical and agent-based modeling to explain these dynamics [10,17,33,35]. While these approaches have provided valuable conceptual insights, few have been able to capture the detailed complexity observed in real biological data. Recent advances in computer science and sensing technologies now allow the collection of large-scale, high-resolution behavioral datasets, opening new opportunities for data-driven modeling to uncover the detailed mechanisms behind collective coordination [18,22,23].

A variety of data-driven approaches have been developed to infer interaction rules within collectives. For example, some studies quantify the social forces between fish as a function of their relative distance, while others use correlation analyses to identify leader–follower relationships[7,15,19,26,31]. Information theory, which provides model-free tools for quantifying statistical dependencies between variables, offers another powerful framework for uncovering potential, information-transfer pathways and for measuring the amount of information exchanged between individuals. For instance, mutual information has been used to infer spatial interaction structures in fish schools [30], while transfer entropy has been applied to quantify dynamic information flows within moving groups [11], to reveal causal relationships in fish–robot interactions [28], and to identify leadership in pairs of zebrafish [6].

In this work, we introduce an information-theoretic framework for estimating the effective interaction range in animal groups. By combining time-delayed mutual information (TDMI) and distance constrained transfer entropy (TE), we quantify directional information flow between individuals and identify the spatiotemporal scales of social interaction. We first validate the framework using synthetic data generated from agent based simulations, and then apply it to experimental data in which a fish follows a virtual leader in a controlled environment. The results reveal an optimal interaction delay of about 600 milliseconds and a spatial interaction range of 3 to 6 body lengths, depending on how much information the leader transfers to the follower. These findings provide new insight into how fish perceive and respond to their neighbors during coordinated motion.

2 Methods and Results

2.1 Spatiotemporal Interaction Inference Based on Information Theory

To quantify interaction ranges in animal collectives using data driven analysis, we introduce a spatiotemporal interaction inference framework based on information theory. The approach first identifies the time lag at which predictive information between individuals is maximized. Using this characteristic lag, we then evaluate transfer entropy across expanding spatial neighborhoods to determine the spatial scale over which information exchange declines.

To identify the delay associated with the maximum information exchange, we consider two discrete-time Markov processes, $X = (\ldots, x_{t-1}, x_t, x_{t+1}, \ldots)$ and $Y = (\ldots, y_{t-1}, y_t, y_{t+1}, \ldots)$, with corresponding probability mass functions $p(x_t)$ and $p(y_t)$. We then employ the time-delayed mutual information (TDMI) with a time lag τ [13], defined as

$$\mathcal{I}(X(t); Y(t + \tau)) = \sum_{x_t} \sum_{y_{t+\tau}} p(x_t, y_{t+\tau}) \log_2 \frac{p(x_t, y_{t+\tau})}{p(x_t)p(y_{t+\tau})}. \tag{1}$$

TDMI quantifies how much knowing the state of process X at time t reduces the uncertainty about process Y at a later time $t + \tau$. The temporal asymmetry of TDMI, $\mathcal{I}(X(t); Y(t+\tau)) \neq \mathcal{I}(Y(t); X(t+\tau))$, enables the identification of the interaction delay. The time lag τ^* that maximizes $\mathcal{I}(X(t); Y(t + \tau))$ represents the characteristic interaction delay:

$$\tau^* = \arg \max_{\tau} \mathcal{I}(X(t); Y(t + \tau)), \tag{2}$$

where $\tau^* > 0$ indicates that the state of X is most predictive of Y after a delay τ^*; if $\tau^* < 0$, the state of Y is most predictive of X after a delay $|\tau^*|$.

While TDMI successfully identifies the presence and timing of an interaction, it does not reliably determine the direction of information flow [4]. To establish directionality, we use transfer entropy (TE) [34]:

$$\begin{aligned}
\mathcal{T}_{X \to Y} &= I(y_{t+\tau}; x_t | y_t), \\
&= H(y_{t+\tau} | y_t) - H(y_{t+\tau} | y_t, x_t), \\
&= \sum_{y_{t+\tau}} \sum_{y_t} \sum_{x_t} p(y_{t+\tau}, y_t, x_t) \log_2 \frac{p(y_{t+\tau} | y_t, x_t)}{p(y_{t+\tau} | y_t)},
\end{aligned} \tag{3}$$

where the conditional entropy terms $H(.|.)$ account explicitly for Y's historical dependence. This definition ensures that only novel information transfer is measured, providing a more robust measure of direct causal influence. When properly estimated with appropriate conditioning, a statistically significant positive $\mathcal{T}_{X \to Y}$ provides strong evidence of directed causal influence from X to Y, as it demonstrates that X carries unique information about Y's future that cannot be derived from Y's past [34].

However, this conventional TE ignores spatial relationships, which can obscure directional coupling in systems where interactions are local, such as fish schools, neural circuits, or proximity based signaling networks [10, 20, 29, 38]. Distance constrained TE, $\mathcal{T}(\lambda)$, addresses this limitation by evaluating information transfer only among events that occur within a specified interaction range λ [3]:

$$\mathcal{T}(\lambda)_{X \to Y} = \sum_{y_{t+\tau}} \sum_{y_t} \sum_{x_t} p(y_{t+\tau}, y_t, x_t | d_t < \lambda) \times$$
$$\log_2 \frac{p(y_{t+\tau}|y_t, x_t, d_t < \lambda)}{p(y_{t+\tau}|y_t, d_t < \lambda)}, \tag{4}$$

where d_t is the inter-agent distance at time t. We use $\mathcal{T}(\lambda)_{X \to Y}$ as a tool to infer the interaction range of a collectively moving group using only the position data of the agents.

3   Method Validation Using Synthetic Data

To validate the proposed spatiotemporal interaction inference, we first generated synthetic data using a modified Vicsek model that incorporates both an interaction delay and graded distance dependent interaction weights within a specified range. We then applied TDMI to infer the interaction delay and the distance constrained TE to determine the effective interaction range from the simulated trajectories.

3.1   Modified Vicsek Model with Interaction Delay and Graded Distance Dependent Coupling

We consider a system of N self-propelled agents moving in a two-dimensional periodic domain of side length L. We extend the standard Vicsek model (VM) [37] by introducing (i) a finite interaction delay and (ii) a distance-dependent interaction weight. Each agent i, located at position $\mathbf{x}_i(t) \in \mathbb{R}^2$, updates its heading at time $t + \kappa$, where κ is the interaction delay capturing the response time between sensing neighbors' orientations and adjusting its own.

At time $t + \kappa$, the heading of agent i is influenced by the orientations of neighbors j whose positions at the earlier time t lie within a maximum interaction radius R. The influence of each neighbor is modulated by a distance-dependent weight function $w_{ji}(t)$, which depends on the Euclidean separation $Z_{ij}(t) = \|\mathbf{x}_j(t) - \mathbf{x}_i(t)\|$, so that nearby neighbors contribute less to alignment, while those closer to the cutoff boundary exert stronger influence. Specifically, the influence weight $w_{ji}(t)$ is defined as:

$$w_{ji}(t) = 1 - \exp\left(-k \frac{Z_{ij}(t)}{R}\right), \tag{5}$$

where $k > 0$ controls the steepness of the distance dependence. This interaction function yields three characteristic regimes:

1. For $Z_{ij} \ll R/k$, $w_{ji}(t) \approx 0$, meaning very close neighbors exert negligible alignment influence, consistent with collision avoidance.
2. For $0 < Z_{ij} < R$, $w_{ji}(t)$ increases monotonically with $Z_{ij}(t)$, being approximately linear for small distances $w_{ji}(t) \approx \frac{k}{R} Z_{ij}(t)$, and gradually saturating as Z_{ij} approaches R.
3. As $Z_{ij} \to R^-$, $w_{ji}(t)$ saturates to $1 - e^{-k}$, approaching uniform alignment in the limit $k \to \infty$.

Heading Update. The orientation of agent i evolves according to

$$\theta_i(t + \kappa) = \arg\left[\sum_{j \in \mathcal{N}_i(t)} w_{ji}(t)\, e^{i\theta_j(t)} \right] + \Delta\theta_i(t), \tag{6}$$

where the interaction neighborhood is

$$\mathcal{N}_i(t) = \{\, j \mid Z_{ij}(t) \le R \,\} \cup \{i\}, \tag{7}$$

and $\Delta\theta_i(t)$ is uniformly distributed angualr noise in $[-\eta/2,\, \eta/2]$.

Position Update. Agents translate at constant speed v_0:

$$\mathbf{x}_i(t + 1) = \mathbf{x}_i(t) + v_0 \begin{bmatrix} \cos\theta_i(t) \\ \sin\theta_i(t) \end{bmatrix} \tag{8}$$

The standard VM is recovered in the limit $\kappa = 1$ and $k \to \infty$, where all neighbors within R contribute equally.

For simplicity and to illustrate the method, we conducted simulations with $N = 2$ agents moving in a periodic domain of size $L = 10$ with a constant speed $v_0 = 0.3$ (arbitrary units), consistent with Ref. [3]. The agents were initialized with random positions and orientations, and each system was evolved for 5×10^4 simulation steps. The values of R and k were set to 2 and 7, respectively. Similar behavior was observed for R values in the range 1–3 and κ values in the range 1–15. Interaction delays of $\kappa = 1, 10, 20$, and 30 steps were examined, while the noise amplitude η was varied from 0.05π to 1.6π in doubling increments. Each simulation condition was repeated $M = 200$ times to enable statistical averaging.

For the computation of both TDMI and TE between agents, agent headings $\theta \in [0, 2\pi)$ were discretized into six equal-width bins to estimate the probability distributions required in Eqs. (1) and (3). Similar patterns were observed when testing bin numbers from 3 to 8. Both TDMI and TE were computed for each realization, but only those values that passed a statistical significance test based on surrogate data were included in the analysis [24], ensuring that the measured information transfer reflects genuine interactions rather than chance.

3.2   Estimating Interaction Delay in the Modified Vicsek Model

To quantify the temporal dependence between agents' headings and estimate the interaction delay κ, we analyzed the simulated trajectories using TDMI defined in Eq. 1. The averaged TDMI, $\langle \mathcal{I}(\tau) \rangle$, is computed over all unique pairs of agents and M independent realizations across a range of time delays τ, and is given by

$$\langle \mathcal{I}(\tau) \rangle = \frac{1}{M} \sum_{m=1}^{M} \frac{1}{N(N-1)} \sum_{i,j\ (i \neq j)} I\left(\theta_i^{(m)}(t); \theta_j^{(m)}(t+\tau)\right), \tag{9}$$

where $I\left(\theta_i^{(m)}(t); \theta_j^{(m)}(t+\tau)\right)$ denotes the TDMI (Eq. 1) between the headings of agents i and j in the m-th independent simulation run.

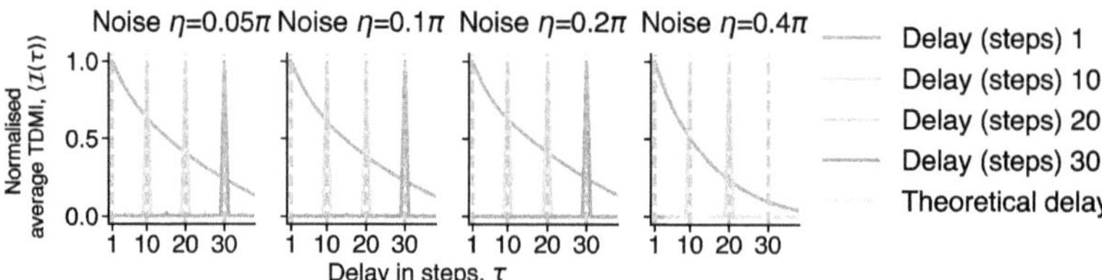

Fig. 1. Normalized average TDMI $\langle \mathcal{I}(\tau) \rangle$ vs. delay τ under varying imposed delays and noise levels.

Figure 1 shows the normalized averaged TDMI, $\langle \mathcal{I}(\tau) \rangle$, between the headings of agent pairs in the modified VM as a function of the time delay τ, for different imposed interaction delays κ. Each of the curves was normalized by its own maximum and minimum values, allowing a clear comparison across delays. The TDMI was found to reliably identify the interaction delay in the system, with the peak of $\langle \mathcal{I}(\tau) \rangle$ occurring at $\tau = \kappa$. This peak arises because TDMI quantifies the shared information between an agent's heading at time t and its neighbor's heading at time $t + \tau$, which is maximized when the lag τ matches the true interaction delay κ. For a given κ, we also observed smaller secondary peaks at $\tau = n\kappa$, with $n \in \mathcal{N}$ denoting the set of natural numbers, and the amplitude of these peaks decreases as n increases. This results from ongoing interaction cycles, whereas noise leads to a gradual decay of correlations.

To examine the performance of the method under different noise levels, we varied the noise amplitude η (Fig. 1). TDMI reliably identified all imposed interaction delays for noise levels up to $\eta \approx 0.4\pi$. Within this range, TDMI successfully detected short delays ($\kappa = 1$–20), whereas longer delays ($\kappa = 30$) produced statistically insignificant TDMI values, causing the method to fail in detecting larger interaction delays.

3.3 Estimating Interaction Range in the Modified Vicsek Model

We further evaluate whether the distance-constrained TE approach (see Eq. 4) can reliably recover the interaction range in the modified VM under different noise levels. $\mathcal{T}(\lambda)_{i \to j}$ was computed using only the time points corresponding to

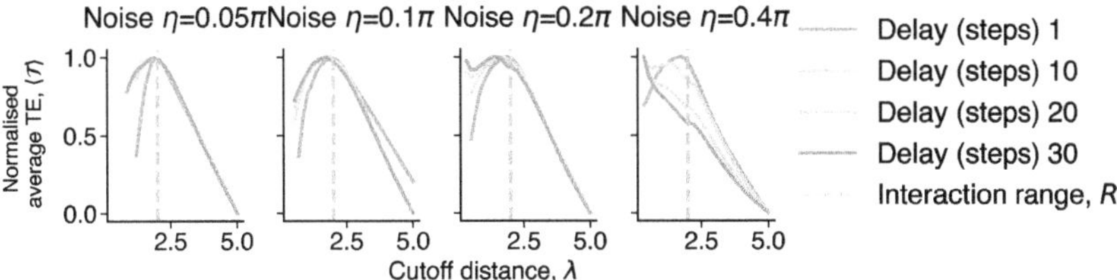

Fig. 2. Verification of the cutoff distance using transfer entropy evaluated at the optimal delay extracted via TDMI.

the delay τ^* estimated by the TDMI method that yields the highest TDMI, and where the inter-individual distance $Z_{ij}(t)$ was below a specified cutoff λ.

Averaging over all agent pairs and $M = 200$ realizations yields the mean information transfer:

$$\langle \mathcal{T}(\lambda) \rangle = \frac{1}{M} \sum_{m=1}^{M} \left[\frac{1}{N(N-1)} \sum_{i} \sum_{j \neq i} \mathcal{T}_{i \to j}^{m}(\lambda) \right], \tag{10}$$

where $\mathcal{T}_{i \to j}^{m}$ for the mth realization is defined in Eq. 4.

Figure 2 shows how the normalized average TE, $\langle \mathcal{T}(\lambda) \rangle$, varies with the cutoff distance λ evaluated at τ^*. For small cutoff distances ($\lambda \ll R$), only a limited number of close-proximity interactions are available, producing short data segments. As a result, TE values computed from these short trajectories typically fail the statistical significance test. Consequently, no significant TE values are obtained, resulting in the empty region at low λ for all noise levels and interaction delays. We find that at low noise levels ($\eta = 0.05\pi$), the averaged TE, $\langle \mathcal{T}(\lambda) \rangle$, exhibits a clear peak at the true interaction range ($R = 2$) for all interaction delays κ used in the simulations. Because the interaction weight w_{ji} increases with distance, very close neighbors (where $w_{ji} \approx 0$) produce negligible information transfer. As λ increases up to R, w_{ji} grows, and the effective coupling strengthens, yielding larger TE values that peak near $\lambda = R$, where the interaction weight saturates. For $\lambda > R$, the additional pairs included no longer interact, so they contribute only noise rather than informative coupling, causing the averaged TE to decrease beyond the true interaction range.

Similarly, to examine how noise affects the accuracy of the method, we find that it performs well up to noise levels of $\eta = 0.4\pi$ (Fig. 2). Within this range, the method reliably detects only short delays, while it fails to recover all longer delays.

4 Application to Biological Data

After validating our information-theoretic framework on the modified VM, we applied it to zebrafish (*Danio rerio*) trajectories recorded in a virtual reality (VR) setup [22,36]. This application aims to infer the interaction delay and interaction range in zebrafish following behavior, which are two key properties underlying collective coordination and decision-making.

4.1   Data Generation and Preprocessing

We controlled a virtual fish, matched in size to the real fish, to swim at an average speed of 4 cm/s in a bowl-shaped arena (water-surface diameter: 0.34 m; water depth: 0.09 m) [22]. The virtual fish swam back and forth near the center of the arena at a depth of 0.03 m below the water surface. When a real fish approached and swam together with the virtual fish for approximately 1 s within a distance of 0.03 m, while the virtual fish was positioned at the center, we applied a perturbation to the virtual fish's heading. The perturbation angles ranged from $-180°$ to $150°$ in increments of $30°$ (Fig. 3). We assessed the real fish's response by comparing its motion 1.5 s before and 2 s after the perturbation across all angles. 56 fish were tested, and a total of 2,667 trials were recorded, with more than 200 repetitions for each condition.

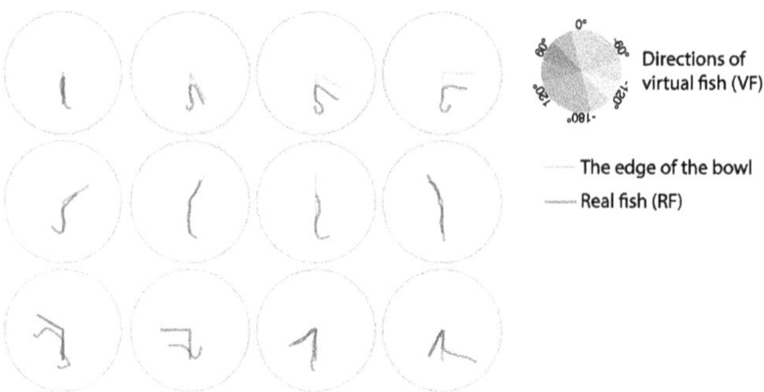

Fig. 3. Example of a real fish following a virtual fish that executes a sudden perturbation turn ranging from -180 to $150°$ after a period of steady following.

4.2   Derivation of Orientation Measures and Information-Theoretic Variables

To apply our method, we converted the trajectories into directional relationships between the real zebrafish and the virtual fish. Because the virtual conspecific (V) moved independently according to predefined trajectories, whereas the real zebrafish (R) could respond to its motion, information flow was expected only from V to R. Therefore, we focused exclusively on $\mathcal{I}_{V \to R}$ and $\mathcal{T}_{V \to R}$ to quantify how the virtual fish influenced the real fish's behavioral dynamics.

To quantify these directional interactions, we first applied a moving average of 21 frames (210 ms) to the real zebrafish position data to smooth and reduce tracking noise. We then defined the orientation of the real zebrafish with respect to the virtual fish, θ_R and vice versa, θ_V, as described in [12]:

$$\theta_R(t) = \cos^{-1}\left(\frac{\mathbf{v}_R(t)\cdot\mathbf{r}_{RV}(t)}{|\mathbf{v}_R(t)||\mathbf{r}_{RV}(t)|}\right), \tag{11}$$

where $\mathbf{v}_R(t)$ is the zebrafish's velocity, and $\mathbf{r}_{RV}(t) = \mathbf{x}_V(t) - \mathbf{x}_R(t)$ is the displacement vector from the zebrafish to the virtual conspecific.

The reciprocal orientation of the virtual agent with respect to the zebrafish was defined as

$$\theta_V(t) = \cos^{-1}\left(\frac{\mathbf{v}_V(t)\cdot\mathbf{r}_{VR}(t)}{|\mathbf{v}_V(t)||\mathbf{r}_{VR}(t)|}\right), \tag{12}$$

with $\mathbf{r}_{VR}(t) = -\mathbf{r}_{RV}(t)$.

Under these definitions, values of θ_R closer to 0 and θ_V closer to π indicate a stronger leader–follower relationship in which the real fish follows the virtual fish [12]. For the information-theoretic analysis, we discretized both θ_R and θ_V into four equal width bins, each assigned a unique symbol.

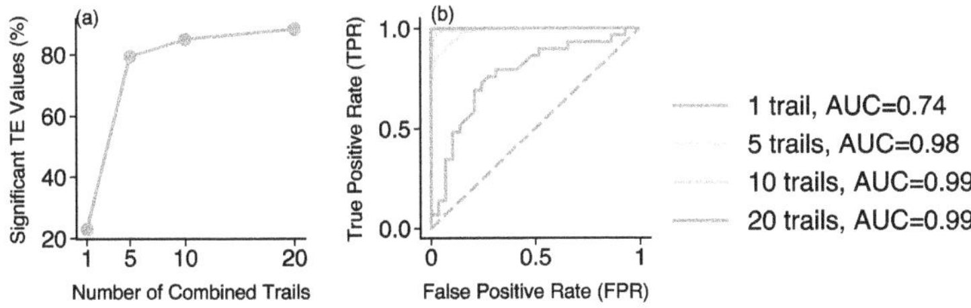

Fig. 4. Effect of trial pooling on Net TE analysis. (a) Proportion of statistically significant Net TE values for perturbation angle –150° as a function of the number of pooled trials, showing improved statistical power with larger pooled datasets. (b) ROC curves for individual and pooled trials, with the 20-trial combination yielding an AUC near 1.0, indicating highly accurate recovery of directional information flow.

Because each trial was short (about 3.5 s) and contained substantial noise, we pooled multiple trials within each perturbation-angle condition to obtain more reliable estimates of the information-theoretic measures [25,32]. To determine how many trials should be combined, we evaluated how pooling affects statistical power by examining the net TE ($\mathcal{T}_{V\to R} - \mathcal{T}_{R\to V}$) and its ability to recover the known direction of influence from the virtual fish to the real fish. As the number of pooled trials increased (1, 5, 10, 20), both the proportion of statistically significant net TE values and the accuracy of direction detection improved. Direction-classification accuracy was quantified using the AUC of ROC curves, where higher AUC values indicate a better ability to distinguish the correct interaction direction. At a perturbation angle of $-150°$, pooling 20 trials resulted in nearly 90% significant net TE values (Fig. 4(a)) and an AUC close to 1 (Fig. 4(b)), indicating near-perfect directional detection.

4.3   Estimating Interaction Delays of Zebrafish

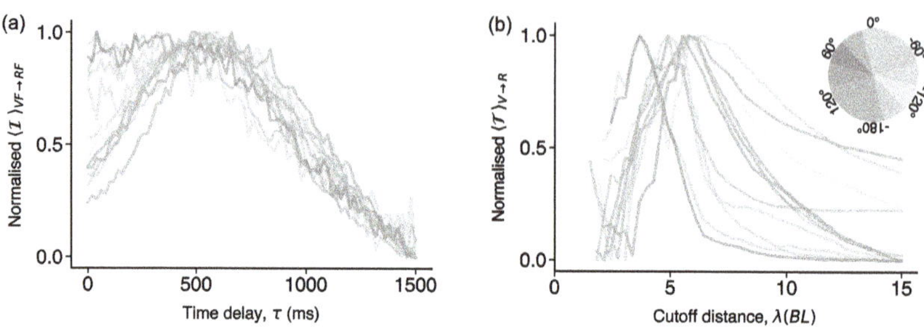

Fig. 5. Normalized average TDMI (a) and normalized average transfer entropy (b) from the virtual fish to the following real zebrafish across different perturbation angles.

Figure 5(a) shows the normalized average TDMI, $\langle\mathcal{I}\rangle_{V\to R}$, as a function of the delay time τ across all perturbation angles. For small perturbation angles (between $-60°$ and $+60°$), $\langle\mathcal{I}\rangle_{V\to R}$ already attains high values at relatively short delays (0–500 ms), indicating that modest heading changes can be accommodated through rapid, low-amplitude adjustments in the follower's motion. In contrast, for larger perturbations (e.g. $\pm120°$, $\pm150°$, and $180°$), $\langle\mathcal{I}\rangle_{V\to R}$ exhibits a pronounced maximum at a delay of approximately 600 ms, reflecting the dominant sensorimotor processing and motor execution timescale associated with substantial reorientation. Only a few extreme cases deviate from this pattern, such as at $0°$, where the virtual fish produces no effective perturbation and, consequently, no measurable predictive signal.

4.4   Inferring the Zebrafish Interaction Range Using Transfer Entropy

Having identified the characteristic interaction delay ($\tau^* \approx 600$ ms) from the TDMI analysis, we next sought to determine the spatial extent of influence between the virtual conspecific and the zebrafish. To this end, we employed the distance-constrained transfer entropy, $\mathcal{T}(\lambda)_{V\to R}$ (Eq. 4). Rather than evaluating all possible delays, we focused on the delay τ^* that maximizes the predictive power of one agent's state over the other, using this value to infer the interaction range.

We computed the average transfer entropy from V to R as a function of the cutoff distance λ, $\langle\mathcal{T}(\lambda)\rangle_{V\to R}$, by averaging across trials for each perturbation angle condition using the concatenated datasets:

$$\langle\mathcal{T}(\lambda)\rangle_{V\to R} = \frac{1}{M}\sum_{m=1}^{M}\mathcal{T}_{V\to R}^{m}(\lambda). \tag{13}$$

Figure 5(b) shows $\langle T(\lambda)\rangle_{V\to R}$ as a function of the cutoff distance λ for different perturbation-angle conditions. We observe a clear peak across conditions, with peak distances ranging from approximately 3 body lengths (BL) when the virtual fish moves continuously (likely providing less informative motion cues) to about 6 BL when the virtual fish performs a sudden backward movement (likely providing stronger information signals).

5 Discussion and Conclusion

This study presents a unified framework combining time-delayed mutual information (TDMI) and distance-constrained transfer entropy (TE) to extract both temporal and spatial interaction ranges from observational trajectory data. We first validated this approach using synthetic data from a modified agent-based model, systematically varying interaction delays, spatial ranges, and noise levels, which confirmed that the framework can reliably extract interaction characteristics across diverse conditions.

Applying the framework to zebrafish interacting with a virtual conspecific, we identified an optimal (majority) interaction delay of approximately 600 ms. This delay is longer than the 300–350 ms lag reported by Amichay et al. [1] for reciprocal burst-to-burst coordination, which may reflect the one-way interaction used in our study. Moreover, we find that the estimated delay depends on the magnitude of information change: smaller angular perturbations yield shorter delays, whereas beyond a threshold (around 60°) the delay converges to around 600 ms, largely independent of perturbation size—even for extreme changes such as a 180° flip.

Using this inferred delay of 600 ms, we estimated a spatial interaction range of approximately 3–6 body lengths. While broadly consistent with previous observational estimates of 5–7 body lengths [7,22], this range is larger than distances shown by force map visualizations, where alignment and attraction peak near 1.5 body lengths [15]. This discrepancy highlights methodological and contextual differences: force-based approaches measure the magnitude of instantaneous responses, whereas distance-constrained TE captures the spatial extent of predictive information transfer, including weak influences that may not produce immediate strong responses. Synthetic validation further shows that noise can bias TE-based estimates toward shorter distances (Fig. 2), suggesting that long-range interactions may be underestimated in naturalistic settings. In contrast, the virtual leader's controlled, noise-free trajectories enhanced signal detection, facilitating the identification of longer-range information transfer. Additional differences may arise from species-specific behavior, group size, and interaction context, as our dyadic setup isolates directional influence compared to freely interacting groups.

Looking forward, this approach opens several directions for future research. To better reflect the complexity of real-world collective behavior, we will extend our framework and experiments to systems with more than two agents. In the current study, we used a histogram binning approach to discretize the data for estimating information-theoretic measures, which can introduce biases and limit resolution. To address this, we plan to adopt continuous estimation methods, such as the Kraskov–Stögbauer–Grassberger (KSG) estimator [21], to achieve more accurate and reliable quantification of information flow.

Acknowledgments. We thank X. L. R. for insightful discussions. U.S.B. acknowledges support from the Alexander von Humboldt Foundation and Pabna University of Science and Technology. I.H. was supported by the EU MSCA postdoctoral fellowship No. 101153670. I.D.C. acknowledges support from the Max Planck Society, the Office of Naval Research (N00014-64019-1-2556), the EU Horizon 2020 MSCA grant 860949, the PathFinder EIC Work Programme 101098722, the SI-BW, DFG Excellence Strategy EXC 2117–422037984, DFG project 462886202, and the DFG Leibniz Prize 584/22. L.L. acknowledges funding from the Sino-German Centre mobility grant M-0541 and the Messmer Foundation Research Award.

Ethical Approval. The authors have no competing interests to declare.

Data Availability. The data that support the findings of this study are available from the corresponding author upon request.

References

1. Amichay, G., Li, L., Nagy, M., Couzin, I.D.: Revealing the mechanism and function underlying pairwise temporal coupling in collective motion. Nat. Commun. **15**(1), 4356 (2024). https://doi.org/10.1038/s41467-024-48458-z
2. Ballerini, M., et al.: Interaction ruling animal collective behavior depends on topological rather than metric distance: evidence from a field study. Proc. Natl. Acad. Sci. U.S.A. **105**(4), 1232–1237 (2008). https://doi.org/10.1073/pnas.0711437105
3. Basak, U.S., Sattari, S., Horikawa, K., Komatsuzaki, T.: Inferring domain of interactions among particles from ensemble of trajectories. Phys. Rev. E **102**(1), 012404 (2020). https://doi.org/10.1103/PhysRevE.102.012404
4. Basak, U.S., Sattari, S., Hossain, M., Horikawa, K., Komatsuzaki, T.: Transfer entropy dependent on distance among agents in quantifying leader-follower relationships. Biophys. Physicobiol. **18**, 131–144 (2021). https://doi.org/10.2142/biophysico.bppb-v18.015
5. Buhl, C., et al.: From disorder to order in marching locusts. Science **312**(5778), 1402–1406 (2006). https://doi.org/10.1126/science.1125142
6. Butail, S., Mwaffo, V., Porfiri, M.: Model-free information-theoretic approach to infer leadership in pairs of zebrafish. Phys. Rev. E **93**(4), 042411 (2016). https://doi.org/10.1103/PhysRevE.93.042411
7. Calovi, D.S., et al.: Disentangling and modeling interactions in fish with burst-and-coast swimming reveal distinct alignment and attraction behaviors. PLoS Comput. Biol. **14**(1), e1005933 (2018). https://doi.org/10.1371/journal.pcbi.1005933
8. Cavagna, A., et al.: Scale-free correlations in starling flocks. Proc. Natl. Acad. Sci. U.S.A. **107**(26), 11865–11870 (2010). https://doi.org/10.1073/pnas.1005766107
9. Couzin, I.D., Krause, J.: Self-organization and collective behavior in vertebrates. In: Advances in the Study of Behavior, vol. 32, pp. 1–75. Elsevier (2003). https://doi.org/10.1016/S0065-3454(03)01001-5

10. Couzin, I.D., Krause, J., James, R., Ruxton, G.D., Franks, N.R.: Collective memory and spatial sorting in animal groups. J. Theor. Biol. **218**(1), 1–11 (2002). https://doi.org/10.1006/jtbi.2002.3065

11. Crosato, E., et al.: Informative and misinformative interactions in a school of fish. Swarm Intell. **12**(4), 283–305 (2018). https://doi.org/10.1007/s11721-018-0157-x

12. Daftari, K., Mayo, M.L., Lemasson, B.H., Biedenbach, J.M., Pilkiewicz, K.R.: Probing asymmetric interactions with time-separated mutual information: a case study using golden shiners. Entropy **26**(9), 775 (2024). https://doi.org/10.3390/e26090775

13. De Lellis, P., Marín, M.R., Porfiri, M.: Inferring directional interactions in collective dynamics: a critique toexploring rare cellular activity in more than one million cells by a transscale scope. J. Phys. Complex **4**(1), 015001 (2022). https://doi.org/10.1088/2632-072X/acace0

14. Dorigo, M., Theraulaz, G., Trianni, V.: Swarm robotics: past, present, and future [point of view]. Proc. IEEE **109**(7), 1152–1165 (2021). https://doi.org/10.1109/JPROC.2021.3072740

15. Escobedo, R., et al.: A data-driven method for reconstructing and modelling social interactions in moving animal groups. Philos. Trans. R. Soc. B **375**(1807), 20190380 (2020). https://doi.org/10.1098/rstb.2019.0380

16. Gallup, A.C., et al.: Visual attention and the acquisition of information in human crowds. Proc. Natl. Acad. Sci. U.S.A. **109**(19), 7245–7250 (2012). https://doi.org/10.1073/pnas.1116141109

17. Heins, C., Millidge, B., Da Costa, L., Mann, R.P., Friston, K.J., Couzin, I.D.: Collective behavior from surprise minimization. Proc. Natl. Acad. Sci. U.S.A. **121**(17), e2320239121 (2024). https://doi.org/10.1073/pnas.2320239121

18. Heras, F.J., Romero-Ferrero, F., Hinz, R.C., de Polavieja, G.G.: Deep attention networks reveal the rules of collective motion in zebrafish. PLoS Comput. Biol. **15**(9), e1007354 (2019). https://doi.org/10.1371/journal.pcbi.1007354

19. Katz, Y., Tunstrøm, K., Ioannou, C.C., Huepe, C., Couzin, I.D.: Inferring the structure and dynamics of interactions in schooling fish. Proc. Natl. Acad. Sci. U.S.A. **108**(46), 18720–18725 (2011). https://doi.org/10.1073/pnas.1107583108

20. Knežević, M., Welker, T., Stark, H.: Collective motion of active particles exhibiting non-reciprocal orientational interactions. Sci. Rep. **12**(1), 19437 (2022). https://doi.org/10.1038/s41598-022-23597-9

21. Kraskov, A., Stögbauer, H., Grassberger, P.: Estimating mutual information. Phys. Rev. E **69**(6), 066138 (2004). https://doi.org/10.1103/PhysRevE.69.066138

22. Li, L., Nagy, M., Amichay, G., Wu, R., Wang, W., Deussen, O., Rus, D., Couzin, I.D.: Reverse engineering the control law for schooling in zebrafish using virtual reality. Sci. Robot. **10**(101), eadq6784 (2025). https://doi.org/10.1126/scirobotics.adq6784

23. Li, L., Ravi, S., Xie, G., Couzin, I.D.: Using a robotic platform to study the influence of relative tailbeat phase on the energetic costs of side-by-side swimming in fish. Proc. R. Soc. A **477**(2249), 20200810 (2021). https://doi.org/10.1098/rspa.2020.0810

24. Mohiuddin, M., Basak, U.S., Hossain, M.M., Sattari, S., Toda, M., Komatsuzaki, T.: Detecting existence of a hidden mediator between a pair of individual time series. Sci. Rep. **15**(1), 21610 (2025). https://doi.org/10.1038/s41598-025-04436-z

25. Montalto, A., Faes, L., Marinazzo, D.: Mute: a matlab toolbox to compare established and novel estimators of the multivariate transfer entropy. PLoS ONE **9**(10), e109462 (2014). https://doi.org/10.1371/journal.pone.0109462

26. Mozzi, G., Comoglio, C., Manes, C.: Flow velocity and boundary effects on fish interaction. Sci. Rep. **15**(1), 31585 (2025). https://doi.org/10.1038/s41598-025-13332-5
27. Nagy, M., Ákos, Z., Biro, D., Vicsek, T.: Hierarchical group dynamics in pigeon flocks. Nature **464**(7290), 890–893 (2010). https://doi.org/10.1038/nature08891
28. Neri, D., Ruberto, T., Cord-Cruz, G., Porfiri, M.: Information theory and robotics meet to study predator-prey interactions. Chaos **27**(7) (2017). https://doi.org/10.1063/1.4990051
29. Nunez, P.L., Srinivasan, R.: Electric fields of the brain: the neurophysics of EEG. Oxford University Press (2006). https://doi.org/10.1093/acprof:oso/9780195050387.001.0001
30. Peterson, A.N., Swanson, N., McHenry, M.J.: Fish communicate with water flow to enhance a school's social network. J. Exp. Biol. **227**(17), jeb247507 (2024). https://doi.org/10.1242/jeb.247507
31. Puy, A., Gimeno, E., Torrents, J., Bartashevich, P., Miguel, M.C., Pastor-Satorras, R., Romanczuk, P.: Selective social interactions and speed-induced leadership in schooling fish. Proc. Natl. Acad. Sci. U.S.A. **121**(18), e2309733121 (2024). https://doi.org/10.1073/pnas.2309733121
32. Ramos, A.M., Macau, E.E.: Minimum sample size for reliable causal inference using transfer entropy. Entropy **19**(4), 150 (2017). https://doi.org/10.3390/e19040150
33. Sattari, S., Basak, U.S., James, R.G., Perrin, L.W., Crutchfield, J.P., Komatsuzaki, T.: Modes of information flow in collective cohesion. Sci. Adv. **8**(6), eabj1720 (2022). https://doi.org/10.1126/sciadv.abj1720
34. Schreiber, T.: Measuring information transfer. Phys. Rev. Lett. **85**(2), 461 (2000). https://doi.org/10.1103/PhysRevLett.85.461
35. Seara, D.S., Colen, J., Fruchart, M., Avni, Y., Martin, D.G., Vitelli, V.: Socio-hydrodynamics: Data-driven modeling of social behavior. Proc. Natl. Acad. Sci. U.S.A. **122**(35), e2508692122 (2025). https://doi.org/10.1073/pnas.2508692122
36. Stowers, J.R., Hofbauer, M., Bastien, R., Griessner, J., Higgins, P., Farooqui, S., Fischer, R.M., Nowikovsky, K., Haubensak, W., Couzin, I.D., et al.: Virtual reality for freely moving animals. Nat. Methods **14**(10), 995–1002 (2017). https://doi.org/10.1038/nmeth.4399
37. Vicsek, T., Czirók, A., Ben-Jacob, E., Cohen, I., Shochet, O.: Novel type of phase transition in a system of self-driven particles. Phys. Rev. Lett. **75**(6), 1226 (1995). https://doi.org/10.1103/PhysRevLett.75.1226
38. Vicsek, T., Zafeiris, A.: Collective motion. Phys. Rep. **517**(3–4), 71–140 (2012). https://doi.org/10.1016/j.physrep.2012.03.004

Distributed MPC
for Connectivity-Constrained Fixed-Wing Aerial Swarms

Yacine Derder[(✉)] [iD], Augustin Desombre, İzzet Kağan Erünsal [iD],
and Alcherio Martinoli [iD]

Distributed Intelligent Systems and Algorithms Laboratory (DISAL), EPFL,
Lausanne, Switzerland
`yacine.derder@epfl.ch`
`https://www.epfl.ch/labs/disal/`

Abstract. This paper addresses the problem of maintaining communication connectivity within a swarm of fixed-wing aerial vehicles operating under dynamic and range constraints. Fixed-wing platforms, while offering superior endurance and coverage capabilities compared to rotary-wing ones, pose additional challenges due to their nonholonomic dynamics and limited maneuverability. To tackle these challenges, we propose both centralized and distributed model predictive control formulations that explicitly integrate the algebraic connectivity of the inter-vehicle communication graph into the control framework. The resulting controllers allow each vehicle to anticipate connectivity degradation and adjust its trajectory proactively while pursuing observation and coverage objectives. The proposed approaches are benchmarked against heuristic and convex optimization-based controllers in a simulated multi-target surveillance scenario. Simulation results demonstrate that the distributed model predictive control scheme achieves comparable mission performance to centralized schemes while maintaining consistent network connectivity and robustness to target switches. These findings highlight the potential of predictive, connectivity-aware control for enabling scalable and resilient coordination of fixed-wing swarms in real-world applications.

1 Introduction

Unmanned Aerial Vehicles (UAVs) have become prevalent across domains such as surveillance [15], fire monitoring [3], and agriculture [26]. When missions require persistent sensing over large areas, fixed-wing platforms provide superior endurance and range compared to rotary-wing drones, but their nonholonomic dynamics and maneuverability constraints make multi-vehicle coordination more challenging and can induce connectivity losses during waypoint transitions. Multi-robot deployment can yield superadditive benefits when supported by appropriate coordination strategies [21], yet robust connectivity remains a

© The Author(s), under exclusive license to Springer Nature Switzerland AG 2026
R. Groß et al. (Eds.): ANTS 2026, LNCS 16515, pp. 109–122, 2026.
https://doi.org/10.1007/978-3-032-26123-6_9

key requirement to enable real-time mission reconfiguration and reliable transmission of sensing streams. Moreover, treating connectivity as a constraint can extend operational range by allowing vehicles to relay communication between the ground station and distant agents. These considerations motivate nonmyopic (multi-step lookahead) controllers that can anticipate connectivity degradation while respecting realistic fixed-wing dynamics.

Connectivity maintenance in mobile robot networks has been widely studied. Early work modeled communication as proximity graphs and designed potential-based or consensus-style controllers that preserve initial connectivity during motion [11,19]. Other decentralized strategies rely on received signal strength [18] or flocking rules [27], and bio-inspired methods pursue similar objectives [1]. Subsequent approaches leveraged algebraic connectivity (the second smallest Laplacian eigenvalue) as a smooth proxy for network connectedness, enabling distributed control laws that explicitly maximize or constrain connectivity via spectral quantities [30,40]. Control Barrier Functions and rigidity maintenance techniques further integrate connectivity with safety constraints [5,36,41], but these methods are typically reactive and often assume simplified agent dynamics and continuous communication.

Model Predictive Control (MPC) [24] provides a principled framework to balance task objectives, safety, and communication requirements over a prediction horizon. Some early studies used predicted trajectories for routing [29], while other MPC-based swarm controllers focus on cooperative tasks without explicitly guaranteeing connectivity [12,13,32,33]. Connectivity-aware MPC has been introduced through mixed-integer constraints [6], penalties on connectivity degradation [20], or pairwise distance constraints [9]; more recently, connectivity has been combined with Lyapunov and barrier-function reasoning in receding-horizon schemes [38]. However, most existing MPC-based methods target holonomic or rotary-wing platforms and do not capture the nonlinear, coupled dynamics and feasibility constraints of fixed-wing UAVs.

Fixed-wing fleets introduce additional challenges due to minimum-speed constraints and limited turn rates. Formation-keeping and cooperative planning methods have been studied through geometric or leader–follower strategies [8,28], but they often assume reliable communication or neglect connectivity constraints. Recent efforts have begun addressing connectivity-aware control for fixed-wing systems [37,39], typically via heuristic range constraints or simplified dynamics. Such approximations may fail under rapid maneuvers or complex mission geometries, underscoring the need for predictive, dynamically feasible connectivity-aware controllers.

In summary, while strong foundations exist for connectivity maintenance and MPC-based coordination, a gap remains in integrating graph-based connectivity constraints within predictive controllers for fixed-wing UAV swarms. This work addresses that gap by developing centralized and distributed MPC formulations that couple fixed-wing dynamics with predictive connectivity maintenance, using a smooth distance-based communication model to capture non-ideal link quality. We evaluate the proposed algorithms in simulation and compare them against heuristic and convex optimization-based baselines in a multi-target surveillance scenario, demonstrating improved connectivity robustness and competitive mission performance.

2   Methodology

The goal we aim to achieve is the observation of several targets simultaneously with a team of UAVs, all starting from a ground station. For our case study, we will assume at all times one target is designated as the main one, g_0. This target will have a priority status with respect to the other ones, which will be reflected in the proposed controllers. This distinction will in turn be expressed in the performance metrics for the algorithms that will be proposed in Sect. 3.6. All drones are assumed to be able to act as a relay in the communication network and they each have a communication model based on their respective physical distance. No explicit sensing range is considered, but it is assumed that sensing is optimal on the target and degrades linearly with distance. We further assume that each UAV has continuous access to absolute localization through GNSS, providing global position estimates throughout the mission. In this model, we denote the total number of drones as M and the total number of targets as N. Figure 1 illustrates a possible surveying mission.

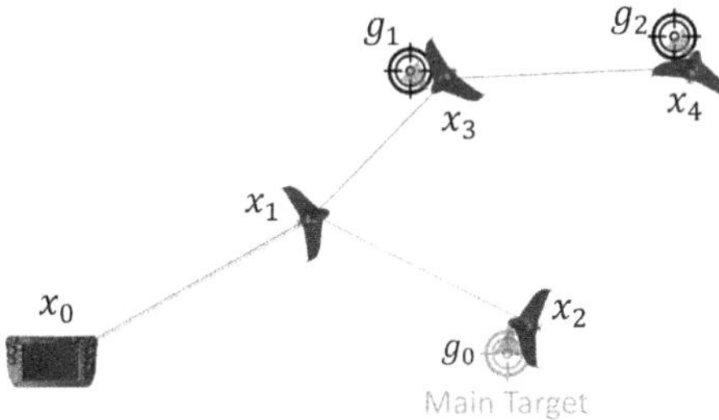

Fig. 1. Example mission situation, with x_i denoting the UAVs and ground station and g_k the targets.

2.1   Fixed-Wing Model

For predictive control, we adopt a reduced coordinated-turn model instead of the full 6-DOF rigid-body aircraft dynamics. In our case study, we consider planar motion and assign each UAV a distinct altitude to avoid inter-vehicle collisions; such altitude assignment can be solved via graph coloring methods such as Dsatur [4].

Each UAV i is described by the state and input vectors

$$\boldsymbol{x}_i = \begin{bmatrix} x_i \; y_i \; \psi_i \; V_{a,i} \end{bmatrix}^T, \qquad \boldsymbol{u}_i = \begin{bmatrix} \mu_i \; a_i \end{bmatrix}^T, \tag{1}$$

where (x_i, y_i) is the planar position, ψ_i the heading angle, $V_{a,i}$ the airspeed, μ_i the bank angle, and a_i the tangential acceleration.

The continuous-time dynamics are

$$\dot{\boldsymbol{x}}_i = \left[V_{a,i} \cos \psi_i \ \ V_{a,i} \sin \psi_i \ \ \frac{g \tan \mu_i}{V_{a,i}} \ \ a_i \right]^T, \tag{2}$$

with turn rate $\omega_i = \frac{g \tan \mu_i}{V_{a,i}}$. Using forward Euler discretization with timestep Δt, the discrete-time model becomes

$$\boldsymbol{x}_{i,t+1} = \boldsymbol{x}_{i,t} + \Delta t \left[V_{a,i,t} \cos \psi_{i,t} \ \ V_{a,i,t} \sin \psi_{i,t} \ \ \omega_{i,t} \ \ a_{i,t} \right]^T. \tag{3}$$

We denote the discrete-time dynamics compactly as $\boldsymbol{x}_{i,t+1} = \boldsymbol{f}(\boldsymbol{x}_{i,t}, \boldsymbol{u}_{i,t})$, which is used in the MPC formulations below. All states and inputs are constrained within admissible sets $\boldsymbol{x}_i \in \mathbb{X}_i$ and $\boldsymbol{u}_i \in \mathbb{U}_i$, explicitly enforcing fixed-wing requirements such as minimum airspeed.

2.2   Communication Model

The inter-UAV communication network is defined as an undirected graph $\mathcal{G} = (\mathcal{V}, \mathcal{E}(k))$ with the set of nodes $\mathcal{V} \in \{1, \ldots, M\}$ representing all the available drones and the set of edges $\mathcal{E}(k) \subset \mathcal{V} \times \mathcal{V}$ connecting the pair of vehicles within communication range at time k. Communication is considered established between a pair of robots $\{i, j\}$, i.e. $\{i, j\} \in \mathcal{E}$, if and only if both nodes are located within the max communication range $\rho_{max} > \rho_{50}$, ρ_{50} being the distance at which the link quality is half of its maximum, and ρ_{max} being the distance beyond which the link is considered nonexistent and therefore $\{i, j\} \notin \mathcal{E}(k)$. In the distributed schemes introduced later, we assume that each UAV has access to the current positions of its neighbors, as allowed by the communication links defined by $\mathcal{E}(k)$. Similarly to [23, 31], we choose the function describing the link quality between two nodes $w_{ij} \in [0, 1]$, to be smooth and dependent on the distance between two UAVs. We model it using the logistic function in Eq. (4)

$$w_{ij}(k) = \begin{cases} \frac{e^{-\alpha(d_{ij} - \rho_{50})}}{1 + e^{-\alpha(d_{ij} - \rho_{50})}}, & \forall (i, j) \in \mathcal{E} \\ 0, & \forall (i, j) \notin \mathcal{E} \end{cases} \tag{4}$$

with d_{ij} the distance between nodes i and j, and α a parameter describing how fast the quality degrades around ρ_{50}. Figure 2 shows a plot of w_{ij} for varying values of α. We select $\alpha = 5.0$ for the simulations.

Given M drones spread out in positions $\boldsymbol{p}_i, i \in \{1, \ldots, M\}$ across the plane, we can now build the symmetric adjacency matrix $\boldsymbol{A}(k) \in \mathbb{R}^{M \times M}$ with zero diagonal entries, as well as its associated diagonal degree matrix $\boldsymbol{D}(k) \in \mathbb{R}^{M \times M}$.

$$a_{ij}(k) = w_{ij}(k) \quad \forall i \neq j \in \{1, \ldots, M\} \tag{5a}$$

$$d_{jj}(k) = \sum_{i=0}^{M-1} a_{ij} \quad \forall j \in \{1, \ldots, M\} \tag{5b}$$

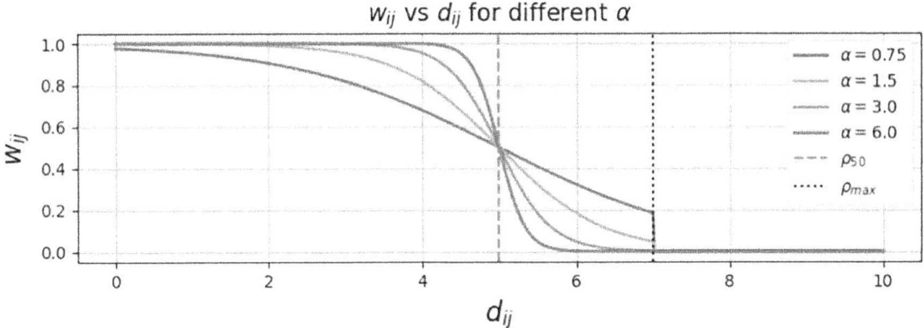

Fig. 2. Quality of the link as a function of inter-node distance, for different tuning factors α, $\rho_{50} = 5.0$ and $\rho_{max} = 7.0$.

The Laplacian matrix is defined in Eq. (6).

$$\boldsymbol{L}(k) = \boldsymbol{D}(k) - \boldsymbol{A}(k) \tag{6}$$

The second smallest eigenvalue of $\boldsymbol{L}(k)$, denoted $\lambda_2(k)$ and known as the Fiedler value [14], satisfies $\lambda_2(k) > 0$ if and only if the graph $\mathcal{G}(k)$ is connected. Larger values correspond to increased connectivity robustness [7,34]. In the proposed controllers, connectivity is enforced by requiring

$$\lambda_2(k) \geq \underline{\lambda_2} > 0. \tag{7}$$

with $\underline{\lambda_2}$ a predefined constant set by the user.

3   Control Algorithms

In this section, five algorithms used to solve the task described in Sect. 2 are introduced. They range from purely heuristic to largely optimization-based. The goal of this experimental approach is to provide a quantitative comparison of the performance and show an enhancement of connectivity in MPC-based approaches. To the best of the authors' knowledge, there are no state-of-the-art methods tailored to this particular case study; therefore, we introduce our own heuristic algorithms as a comparison baseline.

3.1   Heuristic Centralized

The centralized heuristic controller is based on an intuitive approach to the surveillance task: if the main target is out of communication range of the ground station, evenly spaced intermediate goal positions, henceforth refered to as waypoints, are computed on a straight line to the target. Because the task involves the concurrent observation of several distant targets, replicating waypoint chains for each secondary target would result in unnecessary redundancy and inefficiency. For this reason, the remaining targets are clustered using the K-Means algorithm [22] in as many groups as there are remaining available UAVs. Evenly spaced waypoints are then computed to each cluster centroid. If the number of available drones is insufficient to assign all the waypoints, the number of clusters is then iteratively decreased until this condition is satisfied. Once the number of waypoints corresponds to the number of available vehicles, the Munkres algorithm [25] is used for optimal assignment. Figure 3 (top) shows the flowchart of the algorithm.

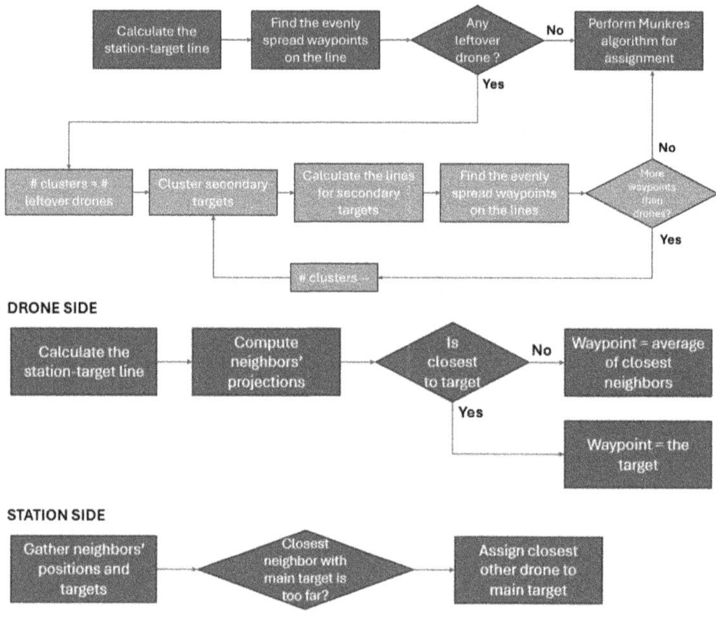

Fig. 3. Both heuristic algorithms (centralized on top, decentralized on the bottom) described as flowcharts.

3.2 Heuristic Distributed

The distributed heuristic controller operates on the same principle as its centralized counterpart, except for the way the waypoints are computed. This version assumes the central station only assigns the targets and clusters to each drone, the waypoints are then computed onboard each UAV through an iterative averaging of the neighbors' positions as described in Fig. 3 (bottom), resulting in a hybrid computing strategy.

3.3 Convex Centralized

As a point of comparison for the performance of optimization-based controllers, a centralized convex optimization-based controller is proposed. Its role is to set the optimal position of the waypoints and assign them to each UAV in a way that minimizes the related cost function $J_{con}(\boldsymbol{p}, \boldsymbol{g}, \boldsymbol{\gamma})$, where $\boldsymbol{p}$ denotes the position of the drones, $\boldsymbol{g}$ the position of the targets and γ_{ij} a boolean variable indicating whether vehicle i is assigned to task j. Unlike the MPC-based approaches introduced later, this convex formulation does not account for the UAV dynamics; it computes a static assignment of waypoints and tasks, which is executed open-loop and recomputed only when the mission objectives (e.g., target positions or priorities) change. This minimization problem is solved by sequentially tackling the three subproblems composing it: the waypoint computation, the graph topology, and the target assignment.

$$\min_{\boldsymbol{z}} \sum_{i=0}^{M-1} c(p_i, \pi(p_i)) + \sum_{i=0}^{M-1}\sum_{j=0}^{N-1} \beta_j \gamma_{ij}\|g_k - p_i\|_2 \tag{8a}$$

$$\text{s.t.} \quad \boldsymbol{z} \in \{\boldsymbol{p}, \pi, \boldsymbol{\gamma}\} \tag{8b}$$

$$\sum_{i=0}^{M-1} \gamma_{ij} = 1, \quad \gamma_{ij} \in \{0,1\} \quad \forall j \in [0,\ldots,N-1] \tag{8c}$$

$$\lambda_2(\boldsymbol{L}(\mathcal{G}_t)) - \underline{\lambda_2} \geq 0 \tag{8d}$$

$J_{con}(\boldsymbol{p}, \boldsymbol{g}, \boldsymbol{\lambda})$ is detailed in Eq. (8a), in which we introduce the function $\pi(v) = u$, which outputs the parent u of node v in the tree graph structure $\mathcal{G}_t$, i.e. the connected node closer to the ground station. Equation (8) describes the problems to solve sequentially, with $\boldsymbol{z}$ taking the value of the variable of interest. The function $c : \mathcal{V} \times \mathcal{V} \rightarrow \mathbb{R}$ is a penalty term for the distance between consecutive communicating waypoints and β_j is the weight (importance) of each target. Possible choices of c can be a linear penalty after the ideal communication range $c(p_i, p_j) = \max(\rho_{50}, \|p_i - p_j\|_2)$, or the inverse of the link quality $c(p_i, p_j) = \frac{1}{w_{ij}}$. Equation (8c) ensures that exactly one vehicle is assigned to each waypoint and Eq. (8d) ensures connectivity through the Fiedler value.

3.4 Centralized MPC

The MPC formulation adopts the same underlying principles as the convex optimization problem, penalizing excessive separation between neighboring nodes and deviations from assigned targets. The graph topology assignment problem is rewritten with the introduction of a boolean variable α_{ij} whose value is 1 if and only if an edge $\mathcal{E}$ exists between nodes $\mathcal{V}_i$ and $\mathcal{V}_j$.

$$\min_{p,\alpha,\gamma} \sum_{t=0}^{T-1} \left(\sum_{i=0}^{M-1} \sum_{k=0}^{M-1} \alpha_{ik,t} c(p_{i,t}, p_{k,t}) + \sum_{i=0}^{M-1} \sum_{j=0}^{N-1} \beta_j \gamma_{ij,t} ||g_j - p_{i,t}|| \right) \tag{9a}$$

$$\text{s.t.} \quad \boldsymbol{x}_{i,t+1} = \boldsymbol{f}(\boldsymbol{x}_{i,t}, \boldsymbol{u}_{i,t}) \tag{9b}$$

$$\boldsymbol{x}_{i,t} \in \mathbb{X}_i, \quad \boldsymbol{u}_{i,t} \in \mathbb{U}_i \tag{9c}$$

$$\lambda_2(\boldsymbol{L}(\mathcal{G}_t)) - \underline{\lambda_2} \geq 0 \qquad \forall t \in [0,\dots,T-1], \forall i \in [0,\dots,M-1] \tag{9d}$$

$$\sum_{i=0}^{M-1} \gamma_{ij,t} = 1 \qquad \forall j \in [0,\dots,N-1] \tag{9e}$$

With the dynamics $\boldsymbol{f}$, the states $\boldsymbol{x}$, inputs $\boldsymbol{u}$ and acceptable sets $\mathbb{X}$ and $\mathbb{U}$ as defined in Sect. 2. T is the chosen number of steps of the time horizon.

3.5 Distributed MPC

As both double sums in Eq. (9a) loop over the M robots, the cost can be rewritten as in Eq. (10b) where each drone locally minimizes the terms related to its own index, as well as its own input and state constraints.

$$\min_{p,\alpha,\gamma} \sum_{i=0}^{M-1} \left[\sum_{t=0}^{T-1} \left(\sum_{k=0}^{M-1} \alpha_{ik,t} c(p_{i,t}, p_{k,t}) + \sum_{j=0}^{N-1} \beta_j \gamma_{ij,t} ||g_j - p_{i,t}|| \right) \right] \tag{10a}$$

$$\text{D-MPC}: \quad \min_{p_i,\alpha_i,\gamma_i} \sum_{t=0}^{T-1} \left(\sum_{k=0}^{M-1} \alpha_{ik,t} c(p_{i,t}, p_{k,t}) + \sum_{j=0}^{N-1} \beta_j \gamma_{ij,t} ||g_j - p_{i,t}|| \right) \tag{10b}$$

The remaining challenge lies in determining the boolean coefficients α_{ik} and γ_{ij}, which represent connectivity and task-assignment decisions, respectively, in a distributed manner. This is achieved by leveraging the properties of the Fiedler vector v_2, which can be computed in a fully distributed fashion as demonstrated by Bertrand et al. [2]. As shown in [35], the derivative of the Fiedler value with respect to any element of the Laplacian matrix L_{ij} equals the product of the corresponding entries of the Fiedler vector, denoted $v_{2,i}$ and $v_{2,k}$ for nodes i and k. From Eq. (6), it therefore follows that:

$$\frac{\partial \lambda_2}{\partial L_{ik}} = v_{2,i} \cdot v_{2,k}, \quad \frac{\partial \lambda_2}{\partial A_{ik}} = -v_{2,i} \cdot v_{2,k} \tag{11}$$

Using Eq. (11), $\boldsymbol{\alpha}_i$ can be determined as the link for which decreasing the adjacency decreases the least connectivity, i.e. the most robust link in the neighborhood $\mathcal{N}$ of vehicle i. The index k of the chosen link is therefore selected according to Eq. (12), with a small example situation illustrated in Fig. 4, and Fig. 5 showing the same method applied to a larger run in the final simulator.

$$k = \arg\min_k -v_{2,i} \cdot v_{2,k} \cdot A_{ik} \tag{12}$$

The γ_{ij} assignments are simply computed based on the current distance between each drone and the target j.

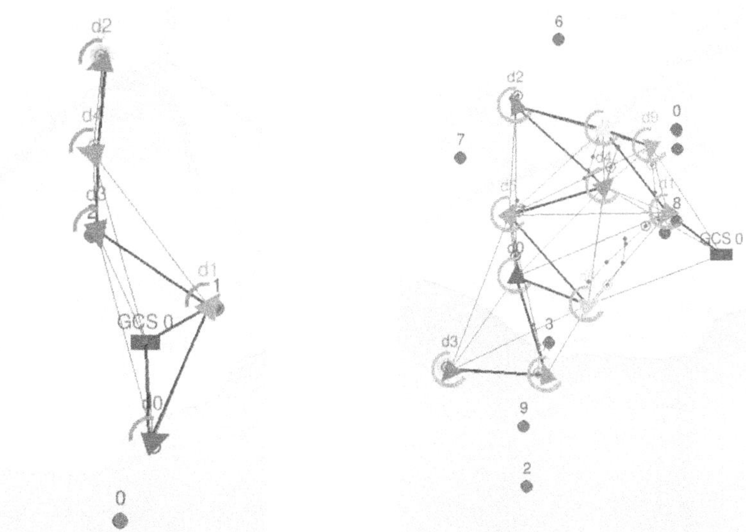

Fig. 4. Examples of the distributed computation of the most important edges. (Left) Simulation with $M = N = 5$. (Right) Simulation with $M = N = 10$. Both figures feature the UAVs (triangles), targets (red circle for secondary, blue for main) and the Ground Control Station (GCS) (rectangle). All valid communication links (i.e., link quality is nonzero) are represented with gray lines, with the computed most important links in red. (Color figure online)

3.6 Metrics

In each test environment, we compare the values of the cost function J as defined in Eq. (13) for each proposed algorithm, as well as the distance to the main target over time $d_{main} = \min_i \|x_i - g_{k_0}\|$ and the algebraic connectivity value λ_2.

$$J(\boldsymbol{p}, \boldsymbol{\alpha}, \boldsymbol{\gamma}) = \sum_{i=0}^{M-1} \sum_{k=0}^{M-1} \alpha_{ik,t} c(p_{i,t}, p_{k,t}) + \sum_{i=0}^{M-1} \sum_{j=0}^{N-1} \beta_j \gamma_{ij,t} \|g_j - p_{i,t}\| \qquad (13)$$

It is worth noting that constraints Eqs. (8d) and (9e) prevent all coefficients α and γ from taking a value of zero, which would result in $J = 0$.

4 Simulations

We evaluate the proposed controllers in a custom Python-based simulator that includes the fixed-wing dynamics and CVXPY-based solvers for optimization methods [10,16,17]. For each run, the simulator places N targets at feasible distances (within $M \cdot \rho_{max}$ m) from the Ground Control Station (GCS) and initializes M fixed-wing UAVs at the origin. Each simulation lasts $T_{sim} = 5400\,\mathrm{s}$

(typical fixed-wing endurance) with a $1\,\mathrm{Hz}$ update rate; the main target switches every $T_{\text{switch}} = 1000\,\mathrm{s}$. We assign $\beta_j = 10$ to the main target and $\beta_j = 1$ to all secondary targets. The inter-vehicle penalty $c(p_{i,t}, p_{k,t})$ grows linearly beyond the ideal range, $c(p_i, p_j) = \max(\rho_{50}, \|p_i - p_j\|_2)$, and the MPC horizon is $T_{\text{MPC}} = 5$. The target speed is set to $16\,\mathrm{m/s}$ and the minimum speed to $12\,\mathrm{m/s}$. We set ideal communication range $\rho_{50} = 4000$ m and $\rho_{max} = 4500$ m. To probe robustness, we repeat each experiment 15 times while injecting zero-mean Gaussian noise into position and heading updates. It should be noted that the tool does not aim to be a realistic flight simulator.

We compare the five controllers presented in Sect. 3: a centralized heuristic (HEUR), a distributed heuristic (D-HEUR), a convex optimizer (CON), a centralized MPC (MPC), and the proposed distributed MPC (D-MPC). Results are reported for two scenarios, $(M, N) = (5, 5)$ and $(10, 10)$. The metrics from Sect. 3.6 are summarized in Fig. 5: cumulative cost J, distance to the main target d_{main}, and the algebraic connectivity λ_2.

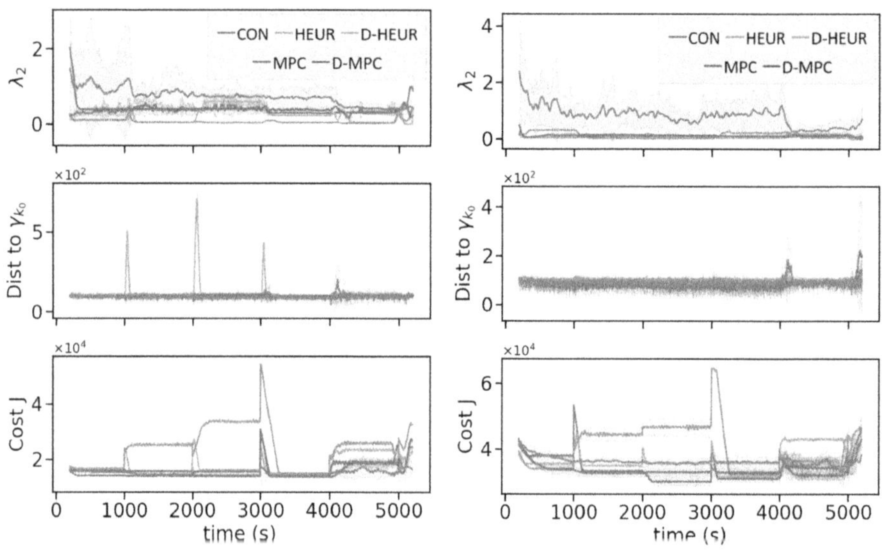

Fig. 5. Metrics from Sect. 3.6 for all controllers: convex (CON), heuristic (HEUR), distributed heuristic (D-HEUR), MPC and distributed MPC (D-MPC). (Left) $M = 5$, $N = 5$. (Right) $M = 10$, $N = 10$.

Across both scenarios, D-HEUR provides no formal connectivity guarantees and intermittently loses contact with the main target and the swarm, increasing cost due to larger inter-vehicle separations. In contrast, MPC, D-MPC, and CON recover quickly after target switches and maintain stable performance. While centralized MPC and CON achieve slightly lower cost in the larger environment, D-MPC exhibits the most stable cost profile across runs and sustains among the highest λ_2 values, indicating improved robustness.

Table 1. Computation times [s] (mean $\pm$ standard deviation)

Env.	CON [s]	HEUR [s]	D-HEUR [s]	MPC [s]	D-MPC [s]
$M = N = 5$	0.012 ± 0.007	0.026 ± 0.012	0.008 ± 0.0044	0.05 ± 0.1	$\mathbf{0.007 \pm 0.0004}$
$M = N = 10$	0.18 ± 0.17	0.036 ± 0.015	$\mathbf{0.011 \pm 0.005}$	0.5 ± 0.9	0.014 ± 0.0006

We also report per-step computation time in Table 1. D-MPC achieves the lowest and most consistent runtimes, comparable to D-HEUR. When doubling (M, N), centralized optimization (CON) and MPC increase by roughly an order of magnitude, where as D-MPC grows only by a factor of ~ 2, suggesting favorable scalability.

5   Conclusions and Future Work

This work presented both centralized and distributed MPC formulations for maintaining connectivity in swarms of fixed-wing UAVs subject to dynamics and communication constraints. By explicitly integrating the algebraic connectivity of the communication graph into the predictive control framework, the proposed approach enables nonmyopic coordination that guarantees continuous network connectivity while achieving mission objectives such as target observation and coverage. Simulation results demonstrated that the distributed MPC achieves comparable mission performance to centralized formulations while offering a computationally cheaper solution and ensuring consistent connectivity and robustness to target switches. In contrast, heuristic controllers exhibited higher variability and occasional network disconnections. Future work will focus on extending the proposed framework by quantifying the computation times with hardware-in-the-loop experiments, as well as demonstrating the results on real hardware.

Acknowledgments. This work leverages the results of the master thesis of Augustin Desombre (Technical Report AGEAGLE-DISAL-MP56), carried out in 2024 at EagleNXT and co-supervised by DISAL members. Yacine Derder and İzzet Kağan Erünsal have been partially supported in this effort by the Swiss National Science Foundation under grant Nr. 10.001.747.

References

1. Beegum, T.R., Idris, M.Y.I., Ayub, M.N.B., Shehadeh, H.A.: Optimized routing of uavs using bio-inspired algorithm in fanet: a systematic review. IEEE Access **11**, 15588–15622 (2023)
2. Bertrand, R., Moonen, M.: Distributed computation of the fiedler vector with application to topology inference in ad hoc networks. Signal Process. **93**(5), 1106–1117 (2013)

3. Bouguettaya, A., Zarzour, H., Taberkit, A.M., Kechida, A.: A review on early wildfire detection from unmanned aerial vehicles using deep learning-based computer vision algorithms. Signal Process. **190** (2022)

4. Brelaz, D.: New methods to color the vertices of a graph. Commun. ACM **22**, 251–256 (1979)

5. Capelli, B., Sabattini, L.: Connectivity maintenance: global and optimized approach through control barrier functions (2020). arXiv:2003.10178

6. Caregnato-Neto, A., Maximo, M., Afonso, A., Rubens, R.: A line of sight constraint based on intermediary points for connectivity maintenance of multiagent systems using mixed-integer programming. Eur. J. Control (2022)

7. Carron, A., Saccani, D., Fagiano, L., Zeilinger, M.N.: Multi-agent distributed model predictive control with connectivity constraint. IFAC-PapersOnLine **56**(2), 3806–3811 (2023)

8. Chen, H., Cong, Y., Wang, X., Xu, X., Shen, L.: Coordinated path-following control of fixed-wing unmanned aerial vehicles. IEEE Trans. Syst. Man Cybern.: Syst. **52**(4), 2540–2554 (2022)

9. Di, B., Zhou, R., Duan, H.: Potential field based receding horizon motion planning for centrality-aware multiple uav cooperative surveillance. Aerosp. Sci. Technol. **46**, 386–397 (2015)

10. Diamond, S., Boyd, S.: Cvxpy: a python-embedded modeling language for convex optimization. J. Mach. Learn. Res. **17**(83), 1–5 (2016)

11. Dimarogonas, D.V., Kyriakopoulos, K.J.: Connectivity preserving distributed swarm aggregation for multiple kinematic agents. In: 46th IEEE Conference on Decision and Control, pp. 2913–2918. New Orleans, LA, USA (2007)

12. Erunsal, I.K., Ventura, R., Martinoli, A.: Nonlinear model predictive control for formations of multi-rotor micro aerial vehicles: an experimental approach. In: Siciliano, B., Laschi, C., Khatib, O. (eds.) Experimental Robotics. ISER 2020. Springer Proceedings in Advanced Robotics, vol. 19, pp. 449–461. Springer, Cham (2021). https://doi.org/10.1007/978-3-030-71151-1_40

13. Erunsal, I.K., Ventura, R., Martinoli, A.: A distributed architecture for onboard tightly-coupled estimation and predictive control of micro aerial vehicle formations. In: Bourgeois, J., et al. (eds.) Distributed Autonomous Robotic Systems. DARS 2022. Springer Proceedings in Advanced Robotics, vol. 28, pp. 156–172. Springer, Cham (2024). https://doi.org/10.1007/978-3-031-51497-5_12

14. Fiedler, M.: A property of eigenvectors of nonnegative symmetric matrices and its application to graph theory. Czechoslov. Math. J. **25**(4), 619–633 (1975)

15. Gohari, A., Ahmad, A.B., Rahim, R.B.A., Supa'at, A.S.M., Razak, S.A., Gismalla, M.S.M.: Involvement of surveillance drones in smart cities: a systematic review. IEEE Access **10**, 56611–56628 (2022)

16. Grant, M., Boyd, S.: Cvx: matlab software for disciplined convex programming, version 2.1 (2014)

17. Grant, M., Boyd, S., Ye, Y.: Disciplined convex programming. In: Liberti, L., Maculan, N. (eds.) Global Optimization. Nonconvex Optimization and Its Applications, vol. 84, pp. 155–210. Springer, Boston, MA (2006) https://doi.org/10.1007/0-387-30528-9_7

18. Hauert, S., Leven, S., Zufferey, J.C., Floreano, D.: Communication-based leashing of real flying robots. In: IEEE International Conference on Robotics and Automation, pp. 15–20 (2010)

19. Jadbabaie, A., Lin, J., Morse, A.S.: Coordination of groups of mobile autonomous agents using nearest neighbor rules. IEEE Trans. Autom. Control **48**(6), 988–1001 (2003)

20. Kandath, H., Dutta, R., Senthilnath, J.: Optimal connectivity during multi-agent consensus dynamics via model predictive control. In: American Control Conference (ACC), pp. 5193–5198. Atlanta, GA, USA (2022)
21. Kuyucu, T., Tanev, I., Shimohara, K.: Superadditive effect of multi-robot coordination in the exploration of unknown environments via stigmergy. Neurocomputing **148**, 83–90 (2015)
22. Mahajan, M., Nimbhorkar, P., Varadarajan, K.: The planar k-means problem is np-hard. Theor. Comput. Sci. **442**, 13–21 (2012)
23. Mikkelsen, J.H., Galeazzi, R., Fumagalli, M.: Optimal multi-robot communication-aware trajectory planning by constraining the fiedler value (2024). arXiv:2406.18452
24. Morari, M., Garcia, C.E., Prett, D.M.: Model predictive control: theory and practice. IFAC Proc. Vol. **21**(4), 1–12 (1988)
25. Munkres, J.: Algorithms for the assignment and transportation problems. J. Soc. Ind. Appl. Math. **5**(1), 32–38 (1957)
26. Rejeb, A., Abdollahi, A., Rejeb, K., Treiblmaier, H.: Drones in agriculture: a review and bibliometric analysis. Comput. Electron. Agric. **198** (2022)
27. Reynolds, C.W.: Flocks, herds, and schools: a distributed behavioral model. In: ACM SIGGRAPH Conference, pp. 25–34 (1987)
28. Richards, A., How, J.P.: Aircraft trajectory planning with collision avoidance using mixed integer linear programming. In: American Control Conference, vol. 3, pp. 1936–1941 (2002)
29. Rosati, S., Kruzelecki, K., Heitz, G., Floreano, D., Rimoldi, B.: Dynamic routing for flying ad hoc networks. IEEE Trans. Veh. Technol. **65**(3), 1690–1700 (2015)
30. Sabattini, L., Secchi, C., Chopra, N.: Decentralized connectivity maintenance for networked lagrangian dynamical systems. In: IEEE International Conference on Robotics and Automation, pp. 2433–2438. Saint Paul, MN, USA (2012)
31. de San Bernabe, A., Martínez-de Dios, J.R., Regoli, C., Ollero, A.: Wireless sensor network connectivity and redundancy repairing with mobile robots. In: Cooperative Robots and Sensor Networks 2014, vol. 554, pp. 185–204 (2014)
32. Scattolini, R.: Architectures for distributed and hierarchical model predictive control-a review. J. Process Control **19**(5), 723–731 (2009)
33. Soria, E., Schiano, F., Floreano, D.: Predictive control of aerial swarms in cluttered environments. Nat. Mach. Intell. **3**(6), 545–554 (2021)
34. Sydney, A., Scoglio, C., Gruenbacher, D.: The impact of optimizing algebraic connectivity in hierarchical communication networks for transmission operations in smart grids. In: IEEE PES Innovative Smart Grid Technologies Conference (ISGT), pp. 1–6 (2013)
35. Tam, E., Dunson, D.: Fiedler regularization: learning neural networks with graph sparsity. In: International Conference on Machine Learning, pp. 9346–9355 (2020)
36. Wang, L., Ames, A.D., Egerstedt, M.: Safety barrier certificates for collisions-free multirobot systems. IEEE Trans. Rob. **33**(3), 661–674 (2017)
37. Wang, M., Zhang, D., Li, C., Zhang, Z.: Multiple fixed-wing uavs collaborative coverage 3d path planning method for complex areas. Defence Technology **47** (2025)
38. Wang, Y., Qu, Y., Wang, T., Pan, L., Ayanian, N.: Distributed connectivity maintenance and recovery for quadrotor motion planning (2025). arXiv:2510.03504
39. Yildiz, A.T., Keskin, K.: Dual-objective model predictive control for longitudinal tracking and connectivity-aware trajectory optimization of fixed-wing uavs. Drones **9**(10) (2025)

40. Zavlanos, M.M., Pappas, G.J.: Distributed connectivity control of mobile networks. IEEE Trans. Rob. **24**(6), 1416–1428 (2008)
41. Zelazo, D., Franchi, A., Bülthoff, H., Robuffo Giordano, P.: Decentralized rigidity maintenance control with range measurements for multi-robot systems. Int. J. Robot. Res. 105–128 (2014)

Distributed Multi-coverage for Robot Swarms

Mariem Guitouni[(✉)] and Aaron T. Becker[(✉)]

University of Houston, Houston, TX 77204, USA
{mguitoun,atbecker}@cougarnet.uh.edu

Abstract. Autonomous drone swarms deployed for surveillance, environmental monitoring, and infrastructure inspection must maintain reliable coverage of critical assets despite robot failures. This requires multi-coverage: each asset must be observed by multiple robots for redundancy, with coverage requirements varying by asset importance. While recent work [3] has solved the centralized problem optimally using integer programming, practical deployments face constraints that demand distributed solutions: robots operate with limited communication ranges, onboard computation restricts global planning, and partial system failures must not cause mission abort. We present a distributed multi-coverage algorithm for robot swarms operating with local sensing, local communication, and no global coordination (Code available at: https://doi.org/10.5281/zenodo.18626854).

1   Introduction

The optimal placement of robots to monitor a set of assets is a fundamental problem in robotics, with applications ranging from environmental monitoring to infrastructure inspection. When robots are subject to failures, single-coverage is insufficient—each asset must be observed by multiple robots. Figure 1 illustrates how multi-coverage provides fault tolerance when robots fail. This leads to the *General Multi-Coverage* problem: given n assets in a workspace and m robots with circular sensing regions, determine positions $\mathbf{y}_i \in \mathbb{R}^2$ and radii $r_i \geq 0$ such that each asset p is covered by at least $\kappa(p)$ robots, while minimizing the total sensing cost $\pi\sum_{i=1}^{m} r_i^2$, which relates directly to energy consumption.

The centralized variant of this problem has recently been solved to provable optimality using Integer Programming [3]. By exploiting geometric properties—that any optimal disk covering a subset of points must have 1, 2, or 3 points on its boundary—a finite candidate set of $O(n^3)$ disk positions can be enumerated. Coverage constraints are then formulated as integer linear constraints, yielding provably optimal solutions via modern IP solvers. However, this approach inherently assumes global knowledge: a central planner must know all asset locations, compute all candidate positions, and communicate the solution to all robots.

This assumption fails in many realistic deployment scenarios. Consider a swarm of $m = 200$ drones monitoring a wildfire with $n = 500$ hotspots [1]. The

R. Groß et al. (Eds.): ANTS 2026, LNCS 16515, pp. 123–134, 2026.
https://doi.org/10.1007/978-3-032-26123-6_10

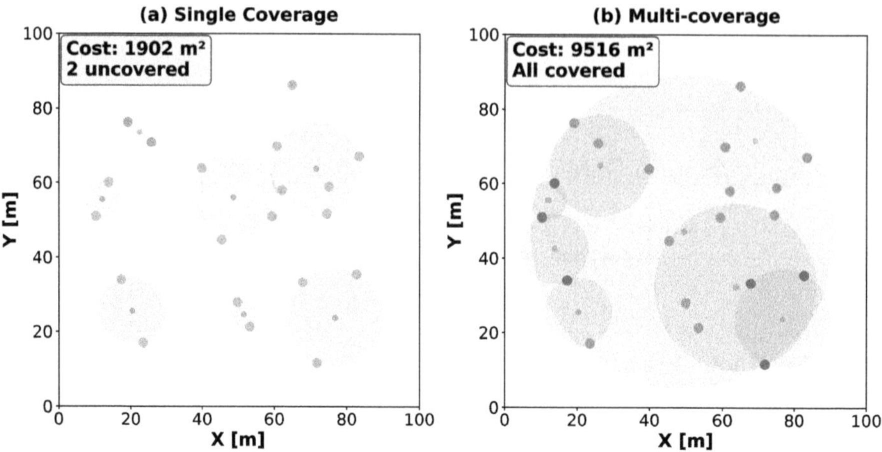

Fig. 1. Multi-coverage enables fault tolerance: (a) single coverage ($\kappa = 1$) fails when a robot is lost, while (b) heterogeneous multi-coverage maintains monitoring of critical assets. Asset coverage requirements: $\kappa = 1$, $\kappa = 2$, $\kappa = 3$, indicates uncovered assets. Robot coverage disks: active robots, failed robots. ($n = 20$ assets, $m = 8$ robots in a 100 m $\times$ 100 m workspace.)

centralized IP formulation generates $O(500^3) \approx 125$ million candidate disks, far exceeding computational tractability. Alternatively, consider a drone swarm inspecting critical structural points—welds, joints, and stress points on a large bridge structure spanning 1.2 km, [12]. With typical WiFi-based communication ranges of approximately 100 m [5], further degraded by metal structural interference from bridge components, and with drones continuously repositioning for inspection, maintaining a global communication topology for centralized coordination becomes impractical.

These motivating scenarios share common constraints: *local sensing* (each robot observes only assets within radius $r_{\max}$), *local communication* (robots exchange information only with neighbors within range r_{comm}), and *distributed computation* (no central processor coordinates the swarm). Under these constraints, centralized algorithms are inapplicable.

We present a distributed algorithm for multi-coverage with an *exploration phase* where robots utilize Lloyd's algorithm initialized from a structured grid to discover all assets through grid-based partitioning, followed by an *optimization phase* where robots ensure coverage requirements $\kappa(p)$ are satisfied using only local information about nearby assets and neighboring robot states and they minimize their coverage costs during *refinement phase*.

Our technical contributions are:

1. A distributed multi-coverage algorithm, operating under local sensing and communication constraints without global coordination.

2. Experimental characterization across static and dynamic scenarios, quantifying fundamental tradeoffs between solution optimality, computational scalability, and adaptability to changing environments.

The remainder of this paper is organized as follows. Section 2 reviews related work on multi-coverage optimization, and distributed control. Section 3 provides formal problem definition. Section 4 presents our distributed algorithm. Section 5 evaluates performance through comprehensive experiments comparing centralized and distributed approaches. Section 6 discusses the obtained results and concludes.

2 Related Work

The distributed multi-coverage problem intersects two major research streams: optimization methods for multi-coverage with quality guarantees, and distributed control algorithms enabling decentralized coordination. We review recent advances in both areas and position our contribution.

2.1 Multi-coverage Optimization

The multi-coverage problem—ensuring each asset is monitored by multiple robots for fault tolerance—has been extensively studied under centralized coordination. Early work by Slijepcevic and Potkonjak [10] introduced power-efficient organization through set covers that achieve k-coverage, where each field is monitored by k robots. Huang and Tseng [4] formalized the coverage problem as a decision problem and presented polynomial-time algorithms to verify whether every region is covered by at least k robots, establishing theoretical foundations for coverage verification. Their work demonstrated applications in fault-tolerant monitoring and energy conservation through redundant sensor scheduling. Our prior work [3] solved the centralized variant optimally using Integer Programming. However, this centralized approach inherently requires global knowledge of all asset positions and computational complexity that grows cubically with problem size, limiting scalability for large deployments. Recent metaheuristic approaches provide practical alternatives when exact methods become intractable. Zhou et al. [14] applied hybrid Genetic Algorithm and Particle Swarm Optimization to visual sensor placement, balancing reconstruction error and coverage quality. More recently, a PSO-based deployment framework [8] achieved 91.4% average coverage with extended operational lifetime for heterogeneous wireless sensor networks. While these methods demonstrate strong empirical performance, they remain centralized and cannot adapt locally to dynamic environmental changes or sensor failures during mission execution.

2.2 Distributed Coverage

Distributed control enables scalability and robustness by allowing agents to make decisions using only local information. Centroidal Voronoi Tessellation (CVT) provides the theoretical foundation for distributed coverage. The seminal work of Cortés et al. [2] introduced distributed control laws that partition the workspace among agents using Voronoi diagrams, with each agent moving toward its cell's centroid weighted by an importance function. Using Lyapunov analysis, they proved convergence to locally optimal configurations that minimize a coverage metric. Recent extensions have addressed CVT limitations. Lee et al. [6] introduced time-varying density functions enabling dynamic adaptation to changing environments. Zhou et al. [13] proposed Buffered Voronoi Cells (BVC) that maintain safety margins between agents, enabling collision-free coordination for dynamic vehicles. While CVT methods excel at continuous positioning optimization, they optimize where agents position themselves to minimize a coverage metric over continuous space, whereas multi-coverage requires ensuring discrete coverage requirements $\kappa(p)$ are satisfied through geometric disk placement with optimized radii.

3   Problem Formulation

We formalize the distributed multi-coverage problem, extending the centralized formulation from [3] with realistic constraints on sensing, communication, and coordination.

3.1   Multi-coverage Problem

Given a set S of n assets (points) in a bounded workspace $\mathcal{W} \subset \mathbb{R}^2$, and m robots indexed by $i \in \{1, \ldots, m\}$, the *General Multi-Coverage (GMC)* problem seeks to assign each robot i a position $\mathbf{y}_i \in \mathcal{W}$ and sensing radius $r_i \geq 0$ such that each asset $p \in S$ is covered by at least $\kappa(p)$ robots, where $\kappa : S \rightarrow \mathbb{N}$ specifies the coverage requirement for each asset based on its importance, while minimizing the total sensing cost $\pi \sum_{i=1}^{m} r_i^2$, which directly relates to energy consumption. Formally, the problem is defined as follows

$$\text{minimize} \quad \pi \sum_{i=1}^{m} r_i^2 \tag{1}$$

$$\text{subject to} \quad \sum_{i=1}^{m} \mathbb{1}[\|\mathbf{y}_i - p\| \leq r_i] \geq \kappa(p), \quad \forall p \in S \tag{2}$$

$$r_i \geq 0, \quad \mathbf{y}_i \in \mathcal{W}, \quad \forall i \in \{1, \ldots, m\}. \tag{3}$$

Here $\mathbb{1}[\cdot]$ is the indicator function. The centralized solution [3] assumes global knowledge: a central planner knows all asset positions, computes all $O(n^3)$ candidate disk positions, and optimally assigns robots using integer programming.

3.2   Distributed Constraints

In practical deployments, robots operate under strict locality constraints that preclude centralized coordination. We introduce three fundamental restrictions:

Local Sensing. Each robot i can only detect assets within a maximum sensing radius $r_{\max} > 0$. While a robot may choose any radius $r_i \in [0, r_{\max}]$, it cannot observe assets beyond this physical limit:

$$r_i \leq r_{\max}, \quad \forall i \in \{1, \ldots, m\}. \tag{4}$$

Local Communication. Robots exchange information only with neighbors within communication range $r_{\mathrm{comm}} > 0$. For robot i at position $\mathbf{y}_i$, the set of neighbors is:

$$\mathcal{N}_i = \{j \in \{1, \ldots, m\} : j \neq i \text{ and } \|\mathbf{y}_i - \mathbf{y}_j\| \leq r_{\mathrm{comm}}\}. \tag{5}$$

Robot i can only access the state $(\mathbf{y}_j, r_j)$ and covered asset list of robots $j \in \mathcal{N}_i$.

No Global Coordination. Robots have no knowledge of the global state. Each robot makes decisions based solely on:

- Its own state $(\mathbf{y}_i, r_i)$ and locally sensed assets $A_i \subseteq S$.
- Neighbor $\mathcal{N}_i$ within communication range and their states $\{(\mathbf{y}_j, r_j, A_j) : j \in \mathcal{N}_i\}$.
- Global parameters: workspace bounds $\mathcal{W} = [x_{\min}, x_{\max}] \times [y_{\min}, y_{\max}]$, coverage requirements $\kappa(\cdot)$, and number of robots m.

4   Method

We present a distributed algorithm for multi-coverage that operates in three phases: (1) *exploration* to discover assets through systematic deployment, (2) *optimization* to satisfy coverage requirements through local coordination, and (3) *refinement* to minimize sensing cost by reducing overcoverage. Throughout all phases, when a robot recomputes its minimum bounding disk using Welzl's algorithm [11], it updates both position $\mathbf{y}_i$ (disk center) and radius r_i (disk radius), physically moving to the new center location.

Phase 1: Exploration. Robots utilize Lloyd's algorithm [7] to distribute themselves optimally across the workspace. Initial centroids are determined by a structured grid partition that minimizes wasted cells:

$$(n_r, n_c) = \underset{\substack{n_r, n_c \in \mathbb{N} \\ n_r \cdot n_c \geq m}}{\arg\min} (n_r \cdot n_c - m) + \lambda |n_r - n_c|, \tag{6}$$

where $\lambda > 0$ favors square grids. Robot i initializes at cell $(r, c) = (\lfloor i/n_c \rfloor, i \bmod n_c)$:

$$\mathbf{y}_i^{(0)} = \begin{pmatrix} x_{\min} + (c + 0.5)\Delta x \\ y_{\min} + (r + 0.5)\Delta y \end{pmatrix}, \tag{7}$$

where $\Delta x = (x_{\max} - x_{\min})/n_c$ and $\Delta y = (y_{\max} - y_{\min})/n_r$.

Lloyd's algorithm iteratively refines positions via Voronoi partitioning. During each iteration, robots sense nearby assets within range $r_{\max}$ and construct Voronoi cells by assigning each sensed asset to the nearest robot position. Each robot then relocates to the centroid of its assigned assets:

$$\mathbf{y}_i^{(t+1)} = \frac{1}{|V_i^{(t)}|} \sum_{j \in V_i^{(t)}} \mathbf{p}_j \,, \tag{8}$$

where $V_i^{(t)} = \{j : \|\mathbf{p}_j - \mathbf{y}_i^{(t)}\| \leq \|\mathbf{p}_j - \mathbf{y}_k^{(t)}\|, \forall k \neq i\}$ is robot i's Voronoi cell. The radius is set to $r_i^{(t+1)} = \min(\max_{j \in V_i^{(t)}} \|\mathbf{p}_j - \mathbf{y}_i^{(t+1)}\|, r_{\max})$. Iteration terminates when $\max_i \|\mathbf{y}_i^{(t+1)} - \mathbf{y}_i^{(t)}\| < tol$, with $tol = 0.01$.

After Lloyd convergence, each robot computes the minimum bounding disk of its covered assets using Welzl's algorithm [11].

Phase 2: Optimization. Robots coordinate through local communication to achieve required coverage levels. Each robot i exchanges its covered assets list with neighbors $\mathcal{N}_i$ to compute local coverage counts:

$$c_i(p) = \mathbb{1}[p \in A_i] + \sum_{j \in \mathcal{N}_i} \mathbb{1}[p \in A_j] \,, \tag{9}$$

where $\mathbb{1}[\cdot]$ is the indicator function. For each undercovered asset p where $c_i(p) < \kappa(p)$ and $p \notin A_i$, robot i computes the marginal cost (area increase) of covering p:

$$\Delta_i(p) = \pi r_i^{\mathrm{new}}(p)^2 - \pi r_i^2 \,, \tag{10}$$

where $r_i^{\mathrm{new}}(p)$ is the radius of the minimum bounding disk covering $A_i \cup \{p\}$. If $r_i^{\mathrm{new}}(p) > r_{\max}$, set $\Delta_i(p) = +\infty$. After exchanging marginal costs with neighbors, robot i selects the minimum-cost robot for each undercovered asset:

$$j^* = \underset{j \in \mathcal{N}_i \cup \{i\}}{\arg\min} \, \Delta_j(p) \,, \tag{11}$$

Ties within relative tolerance $\epsilon - 0.01$ are broken deterministically via hash function $h(\mathrm{iter}, p, j)$ to ensure reproducibility. If $i = j^*$, robot i adds p to A_i and recomputes its minimum bounding disk, repositioning itself to the new disk center and adjusting its radius accordingly. If no progress occurs (all costs infinite), the robot with maximum capacity $r_{\max} - r_i$ covers its nearest undercovered asset. This process iterates until all coverage requirements are satisfied. The algorithm operates in synchronous rounds where all robots simultaneously exchange information with neighbors, compute marginal costs, determine winners via (11), and update their disk configurations before proceeding to the next iteration.

After achieving required coverage, robots perform pairwise asset swaps with neighbors to reduce total sensing cost [9]. For each neighbor pair $(i, j) \in \mathcal{N}_i$ where $i < j$, robot i considers transferring asset $p \in A_i$ to robot j if: (1) $\|\mathbf{x}_p - \mathbf{y}_j\| < \|\mathbf{x}_p - \mathbf{y}_i\|$ (asset closer to receiving robot), (2) $\|\mathbf{x}_p - \mathbf{y}_i\| > 0.9 r_i$ (asset near donor's boundary), and (3) $c_i(p) - \mathbb{1}[p \in A_j] \geq \kappa(p)$ (coverage preserved after swap). Both forward and reverse swaps between each pair are evaluated. The swap is executed if it reduces total area by threshold $\tau = 0.005$: $\pi(r_i^2 + r_j^2) - \pi(r_i'^2 + r_j'^2) > \tau \cdot \pi(r_i^2 + r_j^2)$, where r_i' and r_j' are the radii of minimum bounding disks covering $A_i \setminus \{p\}$ and $A_j \cup \{p\}$ respectively, subject to $r_i', r_j' \leq r_{\max}$. The process iterates until no beneficial swaps exist.

Phase 3: Refinement. To minimize sensing cost, each robot i iteratively removes overcovered assets from A_i where $c_i(p) - 1 \geq \kappa(p)$ (using local coverage $c_i(p)$ from (9)) and recomputes a smaller bounding disk. Before removing asset p, robot i verifies $c_i(p) - 1 - |\{j \in \mathcal{N}_i : j \text{ removing } p\}| \geq \kappa(p)$ to prevent simultaneous removals by neighbors from violating coverage constraints. This continues until no further radius reduction is possible. Because robots use only local neighbor information, the result may retain some overcoverage compared to the globally-optimal solution. A robot cannot determine if an asset is overcovered beyond its communication neighborhood—if additional robots outside r_{comm} also cover the asset, this information is unavailable for local decision-making.

5   Results

Experimental Setup. For performance evaluation, we use benchmark instances from [3]. These instances consist of two configurations: *uni_sm* with variable asset count ($n = 20$ to 200) and fixed robot count ($m = 20$), and *uni_fix_n* with fixed asset count ($n = 250$) and variable robot count ($m = 20$ to 100). Assets are uniformly distributed in a $100\,\text{m} \times 100\,\text{m}$ workspace with coverage requirements $\kappa(p)$ uniformly sampled from $\{1, 2, 3\}$, representing heterogeneous importance levels. We set communication range $r_{\text{comm}} = 55\text{m}$ and maximum sensing radius $r_{\max} = 40\,\text{m}$. All experiments were run on an Intel Core Ultra 7 165H with 32 GB RAM.

Convergence Behavior. Figure 2 illustrates the convergence behavior of the distributed algorithm across its three phases. Phase 1 rapidly deploys robots using Lloyd's algorithm to explore the workspace establishing initial coverage. Phase 2 eliminates all undercovered assets through distributed coordination, achieving full coverage while overcoverage increases to 240 assets and cost rises to $128079.89\,\text{m}^2$. Phase 3 gradually reduces overcoverage to 147 assets while maintaining zero undercovered assets, achieving a cost reduction to $32258.03\,\text{m}^2$.

Performance Evaluation. Figure 3 compares our distributed algorithm against the centralized IP baseline, which computes the global optimum. The distributed algorithm maintains near-constant computation time ($<5\,\text{s}$) regardless of problem size, achieving median time-to-feasibility of $0.05\,\text{s}$ and time-to-final-refinement of $0.61\,\text{s}$ for uni_sm, $0.19\,\text{s}$ and $3.43\,\text{s}$ for uni_fix_n. While

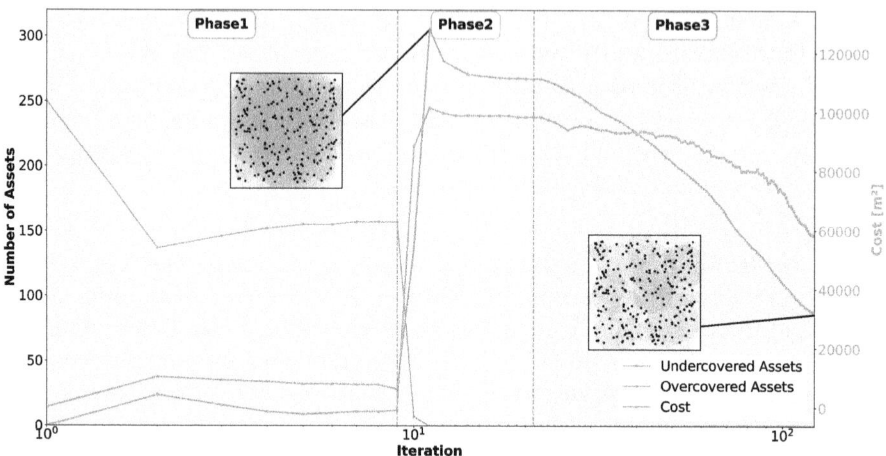

Fig. 2. Convergence behavior of the distributed algorithm showing the number of undercovered/overcovered assets (left axis) and total coverage cost (right axis) across three phases. Inset visualizations show robot coverage disks (blue circles) centered at robot positions, with black dots representing asset locations that robots must cover. Phase 1 explores the workspace, Phase 2 ensures coverage requirements are met, and Phase 3 optimizes cost by reducing overcoverage. Parameters: $n = 250$ assets, $m = 50$ robots, $r_{comm} = 55$ m, $r_{max} = 40$m, in a workspace 100m × 100 m. For all lines, lower is better. (Color figure online)

centralized time grows up to 60 s for *uni_sm* and reaches 2053 s for *uni_fix_n*, yielding speedups of 12× and 410× respectively. As expected, the local optimization approach incurs an optimality gap compared to the global optimum: on average 45.78% for *uni_sm* and 69.41% for *uni_fix_n*. The gap increases with robot count due to increased coordination complexity in local decision-making. Nevertheless, all distributed solutions satisfy coverage requirements $\kappa(p)$. Applications requiring real-time response and operating under local sensing and communication constraints justify accepting higher cost rather than globally optimal solutions, while centralized optimization remains preferable for offline planning with relaxed time constraints and global control possibility.

Centralized Failure Scenario. To demonstrate operational advantages under dynamic conditions, we design an experiment where new assets appear during an active mission. We deploy $m = 20$ robots to cover $n_{init} = 270$ assets forming "ANTS" in a 100 m × 100 m workspace, with coverage requirements $\kappa(p) \in \{1, 2, 3\}$ and sensing parameters $r_{max} = 40$ m, $r_{comm} = 55$ m. After both approaches achieve initial coverage, $n_{new} = 70$ additional assets forming "2026" appear at $T = 0$, simulating scenarios such as wildfire spread or structural damage discovery. The distributed algorithm responds through local adaptation: nearby robots detect new assets, trigger Phase 2 optimization using local communication, and adjust positions/radii via marginal cost bidding while

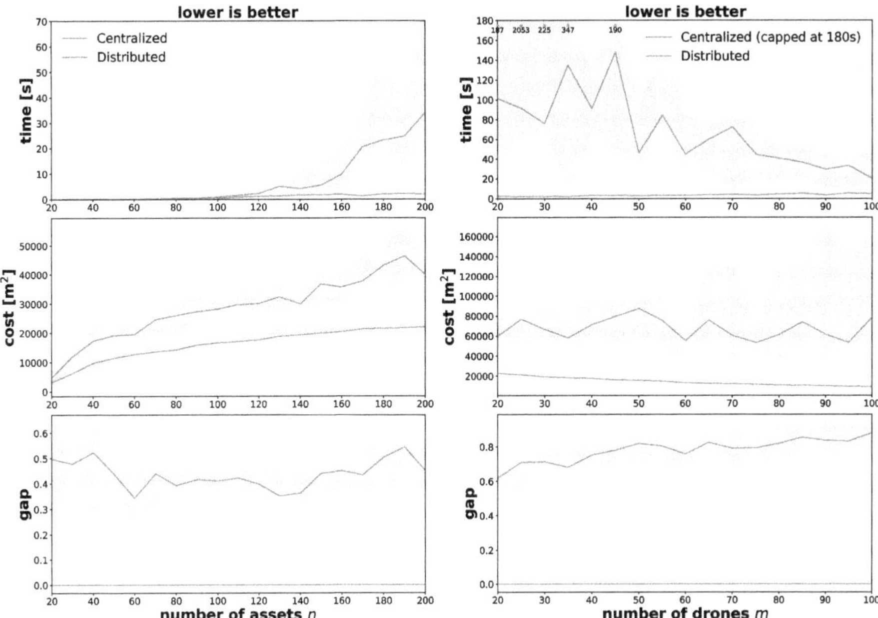

Fig. 3. Comparison of runtime, coverage cost (total area), and optimality gap between the optimal centralized solver [3] and the decentralized algorithm. Lines show median over 5 trials; shaded regions show min-max range. On all plots, lower is better. (Left) *uni_sm*: fixed $m = 20$, variable n (Right) *uni_fix_n*: fixed $n = 250$, variable m. Instance details are provided in the Experimental Setup.

distant robots remain unaffected. The centralized solver must recompute the entire solution, solving a new IP with $O(340^3) \approx 39.3$ million candidate disks and needs 82.34 s. Figure 4 shows both approaches across initial coverage and post-adaptation states for the combined $n_{\text{total}} = 340$ asset system.

Sensitivity Analysis. We analyze the algorithm's sensitivity to communication radius r_{comm} and maximum sensing radius r_{max} in Fig. 5. When varying r_{comm} with fixed $r_{\text{max}} = 40\,\text{m}$ (Fig. 5(b)), the algorithm fails below $r_{\text{comm}} = 15\,\text{m}$ due to insufficient coordination between robots. As r_{comm} increases, total cost decreases as robots gain better knowledge of neighboring coverage, reducing unnecessary disk growth. Conversely, when varying r_{max} with fixed $r_{\text{comm}} = 55\,\text{m}$ (Fig. 5(a)), the algorithm fails below $r_{\text{max}} = 20\,\text{m}$ due to physical infeasibility. Beyond this threshold, cost increases with r_{max} due to a communication-sensing mismatch: robots can sense and cover distant assets up to r_{max} away, but can only communicate within r_{comm}, causing them to perceive already-covered distant assets as undercovered and grow unnecessarily large disks. While r_{comm} and r_{max} are determined by sensor specifications, algorithmic parameters $\epsilon = 0.01$ (tie tolerance), $\tau = 0.005$ (swap threshold), chosen empirically, prove robust

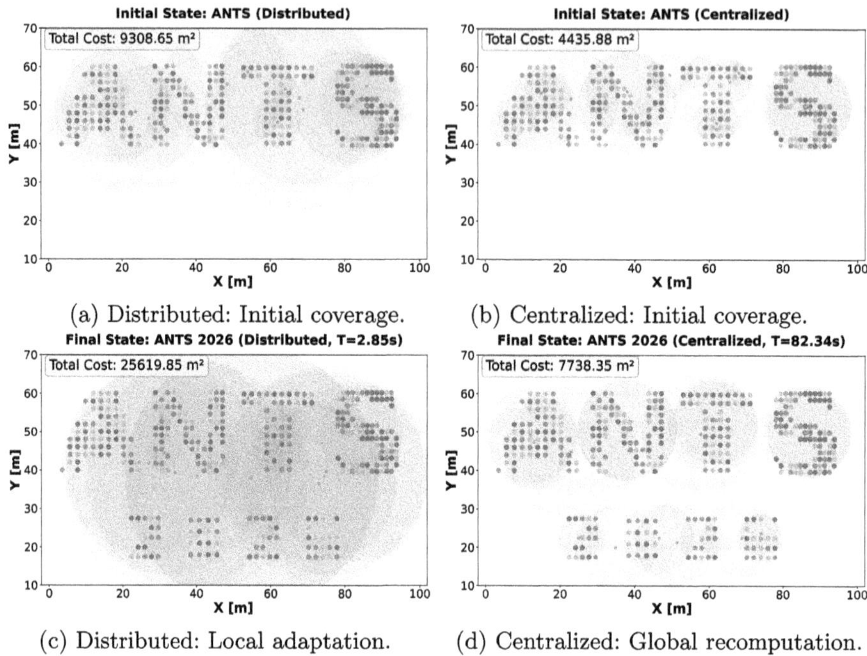

(a) Distributed: Initial coverage.

(b) Centralized: Initial coverage.

(c) Distributed: Local adaptation.

(d) Centralized: Global recomputation.

Fig. 4. Comparison of distributed vs. centralized approaches for dynamic asset appearance. The workspace contains 270 initial ANTS assets and 70 new 2026 assets (340 total), covered by 20 robots. Asset colors indicate coverage requirements: $\kappa = 1$, $\kappa = 2$, $\kappa = 3$. Translucent blue disks show robot coverage regions.

across instances. For new deployments: use hardware values for r_{comm}, r_{max}, and tune ϵ, τ.

6   Discussion and Conclusion

We presented a distributed multi-coverage algorithm for robot swarms operating under local sensing (r_{max}), local communication (r_{comm}), and no global coordination. Through systematic exploration, marginal cost optimization, and iterative refinement, the algorithm satisfies heterogeneous coverage requirements $\kappa(p)$ while maintaining near-constant computation time across problem scales.

Key limitations include: (1) sensitivity to parameter selection—the algorithm fails when $r_{\mathrm{comm}} < 15\,\mathrm{m}$ or $r_{\mathrm{max}} < 20\mathrm{m}$ for our test instances, and requires $r_{\mathrm{comm}} \geq r_{\mathrm{max}}$ to avoid coordination failures; (2) increasing optimality gap with larger swarm sizes due to coordination complexity; and (3) potential for persistent overcoverage in Phase 3 refinement, as local neighbor information cannot eliminate all unnecessary redundancy achievable through global optimization.

Despite these limitations, the 45.78%–69.41% optimality gap is acceptable for applications prioritizing responsiveness (12–410× speedup), operation under

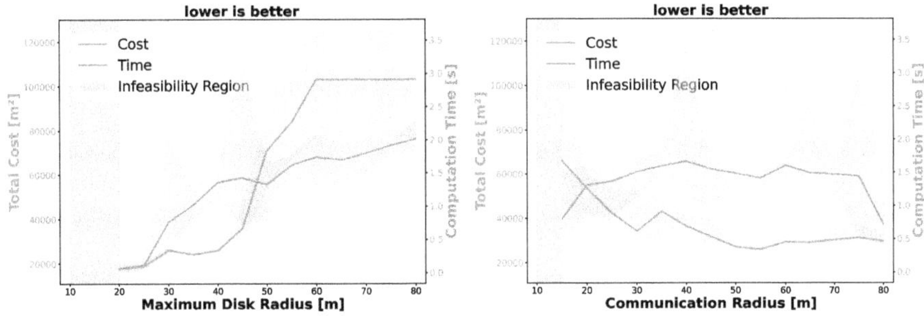

(a) Varying r_{max} with $r_{\mathrm{comm}} = 55\,\mathrm{m}$ fixed. (b) Varying r_{comm} with $r_{\mathrm{max}} = 40\,\mathrm{m}$ fixed.

Fig. 5. Sensitivity analysis showing coverage cost and runtime varying (a) maximum disk radius r_{max} and (b) communication radius r_{comm}. Lines show median over 10 trials on 10 problem instances; shaded regions show min-max range. Red shaded regions indicate parameter ranges where the algorithm fails to achieve coverage requirements ($n = 200$ assets, $m = 50$ robots in a $100\,\mathrm{m} \times 100\,\mathrm{m}$ workspace, coverage requirements $\kappa(p)$ uniformly sampled from $\{1, 2, 3\}$). (Color figure online)

communication constraints ($r_{\mathrm{comm}} <$ workspace), or dynamic adaptation (29× faster in Fig. 4). These tradeoffs make our algorithm suitable for deployments where local constraints preclude centralized control and responsiveness outweighs solution optimality. Centralized methods remain preferable for offline planning with fixed assets, cost-constrained deployments justifying longer computation, or small problems solvable in seconds.

Future work includes theoretical analysis of optimality bounds and hardware experiments with failing robots. Handling infeasible parameter regions could involve graceful degradation strategies that prioritize critical assets while relaxing $\kappa(p)$ for lower-priority assets. Extending the algorithm to asynchronous execution, where robots update at different rates, would require timestamped state exchange and conservative bid validation to maintain correctness, likely increasing iteration counts but enabling deployment on systems without global clock synchronization. Our marginal cost bidding framework generalizes to distributed task allocation and formation control, providing a template for distributed algorithms via conservative coordination.

Acknowledgments. This work was supported by the Army Research Laboratory under Cooperative Agreement Number W911NF-23-2-0014. The views and conclusions contained in this document are those of the authors and should not be interpreted as representing the official policies, either expressed or implied, of the Army Research Laboratory or the U.S. Government. The U.S. Government is authorized to reproduce and distribute reprints for Government purposes notwithstanding any copyright notation herein.

Disclosure of Interests. The authors have no competing interests to declare.

References

1. Chen, X., et al.: Wildland fire detection and monitoring using a drone-collected RGB/IR image dataset. IEEE Access **10**, 121301–121317 (2022). https://doi.org/10.1109/ACCESS.2022.3222805
2. Cortés, J., Martínez, S., Karatas, T., Bullo, F.: Coverage control for mobile sensing networks. IEEE Trans. Robot. Autom. **20**(2), 243–255 (2004). https://doi.org/10.1109/TRA.2004.824698
3. Guitouni, M., Loi, C.M., Fekete, S.P., Perk, M., Becker, A.T.: Multi-covering a point set by m disks with minimum total area. In: 2025 IEEE International Conference on Robotics and Automation (ICRA), Atlanta, GA, USA, pp. 3000–3006 (2025). https://doi.org/10.1109/ICRA55743.2025.11127835
4. Huang, C.F., Tseng, Y.C.: The coverage problem in a wireless sensor network. Mob. Netw. Appl. **10**(4), 519–528 (2005). https://doi.org/10.1007/s11036-005-1564-y
5. Khan, M.A., Qureshi, I.M., Khanzada, F.: A hybrid communication scheme for efficient and low-cost deployment of future flying ad-hoc network (FANET). Drones **3**(1) (2019). https://doi.org/10.3390/drones3010016, https://www.mdpi.com/2504-446X/3/1/16
6. Lee, S.K., Diaz-Mercado, Y., Egerstedt, M.: Multirobot control using time-varying density functions. IEEE Trans. Rob. **31**(2), 489–493 (2015). https://doi.org/10.1109/TRO.2015.2397771
7. Lloyd, S.: Least squares quantization in PCM. IEEE Trans. Inf. Theory **28**(2), 129–137 (1982). https://doi.org/10.1109/TIT.1982.1056489
8. Priyadarshi, R.: Efficient node deployment for enhancing coverage and connectivity in wireless sensor networks. Sci. Rep. **15**(1), 29052 (2025). https://doi.org/10.1038/s41598-025-14252-0
9. Shahsavar, M., Rajasekaran, S., Kabin, R., Yannuzzi, M., Becker, A.T.: Tracking multiple moving assets with a smaller group of drones. In: 2025 IEEE 21st International Conference on Automation Science and Engineering (CASE), pp. 171–178. IEEE, Los Angeles, CA, USA (2025). https://doi.org/10.1109/CASE58245.2025.11164124
10. Slijepcevic, S., Potkonjak, M.: Power efficient organization of wireless sensor networks. In: Proceedings of IEEE International Conference on Communications (ICC), vol. 2, pp. 472–476. IEEE (2001). https://doi.org/10.1109/ICC.2001.936985
11. Welzl, E.: Smallest enclosing disks (balls and ellipsoids). In: Maurer, H. (ed.) New Results and New Trends in Computer Science. LNCS, vol. 555, pp. 359–370. Springer, Heidelberg (1991). https://doi.org/10.1007/BFb0038202
12. Witcher, T.: An icon at 80: the golden gate bridge. Civ. Eng. Mag. **87**(6), 42–45 (2017). https://doi.org/10.1061/ciegag.0001205, https://ascelibrary.org/doi/abs/10.1061/ciegag.0001205
13. Zhou, D., Wang, Z., Bandyopadhyay, S., Schwager, M.: Fast, on-line collision avoidance for dynamic vehicles using buffered voronoi cells. IEEE Robot. Autom. Lett. **2**(2), 1047–1054 (2017). https://doi.org/10.1109/LRA.2017.2656241
14. Zhou, J., Deng, H., Zhao, Z., Zou, Y., Wang, X.: Sensor placement optimization of visual sensor networks for target tracking based on multi-objective constraints. Appl. Sci. **14**(5), 1722 (2024). https://doi.org/10.3390/app14051722

Emergent In-group Bias: Sociality and Individuation in Robotic Swarms

Roman Miletitch[1(✉)] and Limor Raviv[1,2]

[1] Language Evolution and Adaptation in Diverse Situations (LEADS) Group, Max Planck Institute for Psycholinguistics, Nijmegen, The Netherlands
`roman.miletitch@mpi.nl`
[2] Donders Center for Cognition, Radboud University, Nijmegen, The Netherlands

Abstract. The tendency to favour members of one's own group, also known as *in-group bias*, is ubiquitous in social mammals from rats to humans. This preference for in-group members (which often translates into aggression against out-group members) plays a major role in mammalian social life, and governs how individuals and groups perceive and behave toward others. Understanding how such social dynamics emerge, evolve, and impact behaviour is crucial for evolutionary theory and for the design of more mammal-like agents. Yet current swarm robots are typically extremely social and cooperative, and do not differentiate between individual robots. Here, we introduce two cognitive and social layers to a swarm engaged in a foraging task and a communication game: robot individuation (a partner-specific memory) and evolving sociality (a partner-specific tendency to interact based on previous interactions). We test whether social asymmetries such as in-group bias can spontaneously emerge from repeated local interactions without implicit group markers or pre-assigned identity tags, and study its strength and stability over varying conditions: cognitive (memory size and degree of decay), social (group size and innate sociality) and environmental (spread of resources). We show that implementing these two mammal-like features leads to the spontaneous emergence of in-group bias, which is robust across ecologies. These results shed light on the evolution of social asymmetries, and pave the way for modelling the complex social dynamics of mammals.

1 Introduction

Cooperation is widely recognized as a key driver of evolutionary success [37], supporting diverse behaviours such as territorial defence [26], collective foraging [6], and the care of injured or vulnerable group members [28]. A rich body of research [19] has identified multiple mechanisms through which cooperative behaviours arise and are maintained, including kin selection [9], direct and indirect reciprocity [35], network reciprocity, and group selection [33]. In particular, models of group selection highlight that individuals often behave differently toward members of their own group compared to outsiders, yielding intra-group benefits while simultaneously promoting inter-group differentiation and competition

R. Groß et al. (Eds.): ANTS 2026, LNCS 16515, pp. 135–148, 2026.
https://doi.org/10.1007/978-3-032-26123-6_11

[23]. The expression and stability of cooperation are further shaped by ecological conditions [27] such as resource availability, spatial structure, and environmental risk, as well as by the interaction patterns and social mechanisms that govern populations [38].

In-group bias, namely, the tendency to favour and preferentially cooperate with individuals who are perceived as members of one's own group, has been documented across a wide range of species [15], including social insects [10], mammals [14], non-human primates [11], and humans. Although ubiquitous in the animal kingdom, the expression of this bias differs profoundly across taxonomic groups. In social insects such as ants, which constitute one of the primary biological inspirations for swarm robotics models [2], in-group favouritism is largely innate and genetically determined: colony-specific chemical cues allow individuals to identify nestmates [39]. In contrast, in mammals [32] and certainly in primates [36], in-group bias is flexible and acquired, and arises through learning, social experience, and the accumulation of partner-specific histories. These differences raise key evolutionary questions: to what extent is in-group bias an adaptive feature? How, and under which ecological conditions, does it emerge?

In-group bias has been investigated through a wide range of approaches, from naturalistic observations to mathematical models and agent-based simulations (see review in [15]). Although these models can provide valuable insights (e.g., on how the spread of resources impacts food sharing [24]), they are not without problems. The first issue is that many of these models rely on strong assumptions with respect to the target behaviour: most notably, individuals are typically a priori assigned to groups, for example through arbitrary tags [30]. These make group membership a pre-defined input of the system rather than an emergent outcome, and deviate from learned, mammal-like social dynamics. Second, most models rely on abstract agents that lack embodiment, spatial constraints, or physical interaction, even though these factors are known to strongly influence social behaviour and cooperation [12,20,21]. Swarm robotics models are thus particularly well positioned to address these gaps, and have already been used to model complex collective behaviours such as social insects foraging [4,25,31] and to provide insights into language evolution [3,16,34]. Here, we propose swarm robotics as the ideal framework for modelling this complex social layer, and to test whether social asymmetries such as in-group bias can emerge spontaneously, without any implicit group markers or pre-assigned identity tags.

As we are interested in modelling mammal-like social behaviour, an important first step is to create more mammal-like robots, with more complex behavioural and cognitive features. Specifically, swarm robotics typically assumes that robots are insect-like with relatively limited cognitive capabilities, such as minimal memory or restricted local sensors. However, a key difference between insect and mammal social systems is the role of partner-specific memory, which is in itself a cognitive ability: many mammals modulate their behaviour toward others and decide who to cooperate with based on their past interactions and shared history with other individuals, whereas coalition formation in insect societies relies largely on innate or cue-based recognition. As most swarm robotic models follow the insect paradigm, they lack robot-specific memory and omit interaction histories. However, incorporating such histories appears crucial for modelling experience-based in-group bias, as well as mammal-like social dynamics more broadly. To this end, we introduce two novel cognitive and behavioural mechanisms to existing models: *robot individuation*, in which each robot maintains a partner-specific memory of previous encounters, and *dynamic sociality*, whereby robots' tendency to interact with others is based on their particular history rather than on a fixed sociality parameter.

In this article, we study three intertwined dynamics: foraging, communication, and adaptive sociality. The first two are well known in swarm robotics research, with foraging typically used as the classic ecological testbed, and the Minimal Naming Game (MNG) typically used for studying language emergence [1]. The third component, as far as we are aware, is novel to swarm robotics, with robots operationalized as unique individuals who also keep track of their past interactions with other unique individuals, and modulate their behaviour toward them accordingly. Within this integrated framework, we examine whether introducing these more mammal-like social and cognitive layers leads to the spontaneous emergence of in-group bias from repeated local interactions, most notably without predefined group structure besides spatial proximity (or nest origin). Importantly, although nest origin indirectly affects interaction frequencies, robots do not perceive or encode nest membership, and have no way of knowing to which nest other robots belong. We further investigate how emergent social asymmetries are modulated by robots' memory, their baseline sociality (a so-called *innate* tendency to cooperate, a level of cooperation that is typically high for all agents in swarm robotics), as well as other social and ecological conditions previously proposed to impact social dynamics (group size and the spatial distribution of resources).

Our goal is to identify the minimal cognitive and ecological requirements under which such fundamental social dynamics can emerge in embodied collective systems, so that in the future we could leverage these systems to study complex behaviours that are typical of primates and humans.

2   The Model

Robots are distributed across two nests (marked on the floor as grey disks) and engage in a foraging task: each robot explores the environment, aiming to retrieve items from scattered resources.

2.1   Foraging

We implemented a probabilistic finite state machine (PFSM), shown in Fig. 1a, which guides robots' behaviour. This PFSM is composed of three states:

- **Exploring**: robots explore their surroundings by following a random walk.
- **Going to nest**: robots move toward the position of their nest.

– **Going to resource**: robots move toward the position of a known resource.

Robots can learn about new resources by reaching an item (discovery)[1]. When robots find an item, they remember its location as a resource area, later targeted in the *Going to resource* state. Robots return to the nest when they have found an item, are rejected during an interaction with another robot, or with probability $P_{return} = 0.0001$. This latter scenario ensures that exploration is centered around the nests, and allows experiments in an open environment. Once robots reach the nest, they immediately go back to either exploring or moving toward a known resource. If robots encounter an item on their path toward a known resource, they pick it up, bring it back to the nest, and update the location of this resource in memory. If a robot manages to reach a known resource position without interruption and without finding a food item, it forgets the resource position and switches back to the exploring state. Notably, this PFSM requires robots to remember landmark positions. This can be achieved through odometry and social feedback, as robots correct their position estimates by exchanging them with nearby peers [8,17].

2.2   Minimal Naming Game

In parallel to foraging, robots can play a Minimal Naming Game (MNG) [13] with local neighbours (Fig. 1*b*). The MNG is a category of language games modelling the cultural evolution of language in populations of agents [29]. In this context, language is operationalized as an evolving lexicon (a list of words, represented here as an 8-bit unsigned vector), specific to each robot. The MNG ensures that the lexicon of all robots in a *well mixed* swarm will converge on a single word. Note that words do not refer to any physical object, but are rather an abstract representation of robots' linguistic variants. When playing this language game, a robot takes one of two roles: sender (with a small probability $P_{send} = 0.01$) or receiver (decided based on partner-specific social history, as detailed in Sect. 2.3). The sender starts the game by selecting a random word from its lexicon (if the lexicon is empty, it creates a word first) and then broadcasts it within a given range. If the interaction is accepted by the receiver, they check the word against the content of their lexicon. If the word already appears in their lexicon, the game is considered a success, and the receiver keeps only that word in their lexicon, deleting other stored variants. If the word is not already in the lexicon, the game is considered a failure, and the receiver appends the word to their lexicon. Finally, the receiver signals whether the game was a success or a failure to the sender, who in the case of success, also deletes all other words in their lexicon,

---

[1] Since our objective was to first understand how primate-like social dynamics interact with linguistic exchange, we intentionally omitted recruitment and other cooperative foraging mechanisms, as these would create an even stronger group-level structure by design and would mechanically reinforce any in-group bias for reasons unrelated to the social layer considered in this work. As such, current foraging primarily serves to structure the swarm's spatial distribution and interaction patterns in a realistic yet controlled manner.

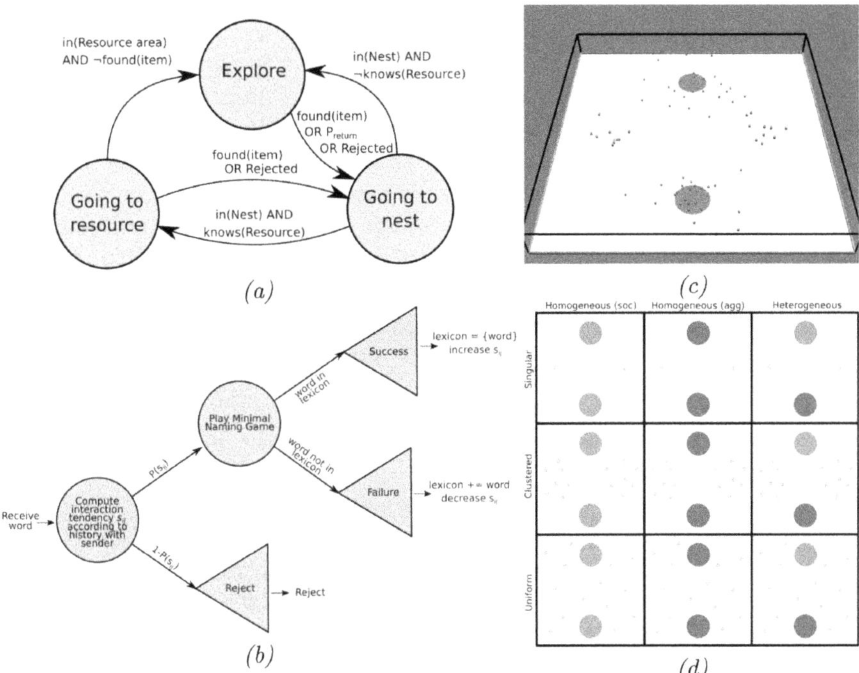

Fig. 1. The behaviour automaton *(a)* guides robots foraging strategy. In any state, a robot can become a *sender* in a Minimal Naming Game (MNG). A nearby robot can then become a *receiver* in this interaction, and decides on its reaction according to the interaction decision-tree *(b)*. The robots are embodied in a simulated world *(c)* with a 2D physics engine, populated by two nests and randomly distributed food items. We observe social and linguistic outcomes in 9 environments *(d)*, with nests inhabited by either aggressive (red) or social (blue) robots, and distributions of items (green). (Color figure online)

keeping only the selected word. In our study, the MNG provides a structured interaction allowing sociality to shape language dynamics.

2.3 Partner-Specific Sociality

The novelty of our approach is in the introduction of two novel cognitive features. The first is robot individuation, whereby robots have a partner-specific memory and keep track of the outcomes of past interactions with other robots. Crucially, robots are not able to tell whether or not another robot comes from the same nest. Let $mng_{ij}^{k} \in \{0, 1\}$ denote the outcome of the k-th validated MNG between robots i and j (1 for a success, 0 for a failure). We define K_{ij} as the total number of interactions between robots i and j, and let robot i maintain a fixed-size memory window $\mathcal{B}_{ij}^{K_{ij}}$ of the last w validated outcomes with robot j:

$$\mathcal{B}_{ij}^{K_{ij}} = \left(mng_{ij}^{K_{ij}}, mng_{ij}^{K_{ij}-1}, \ldots, mng_{ij}^{K_{ij}-w+1} \right) \tag{1}$$

The second feature is flexible (or evolving) sociality: robots' tendency to interact with others (i.e., their willingness to accept the role of receiver in an incoming MNG) is based on the degree of sociality toward the specific sender robot. This robot-specific sociality value is based on prior experience: successful communication between two robots increases their sociality toward each other (and therefore their willingness to communicate again), while a failed communication decreases their sociality toward each other. More specifically, we compute sociality (or the probability of interacting) $s_{ij}(K_{ij}, t)$ as a weighted moving average of the number of successful past interactions between robots i and j:

$$s_{ij}(K_{ij}, t) = \frac{1}{w} \sum_{k=K_{ij}-w+1}^{K_{ij}} \left(d_{ij}^k \times mng_{ij}^k + (1 - d_{ij}^k) \times s_i^0 \right),$$

$$\text{with } d_{ij}^k = e^{-\lambda\,(t - t_{ij}^k)}, \quad mng_{ij}^k \in \{0, 1\} \tag{2}$$

where s_i^0 is the baseline sociality of robot i, t_{ij}^k the time of the k-th interaction between both robots, w the memory window size, and λ the memory decay parameter. The latter controls how quickly the influence of past interactions fades, gradually pulling $s_{ij}(K_{ij}, t)$ back toward the baseline value s_i^0. To stabilize early dynamics, we introduce a prior consisting of a pre-filled backlog of interactions. We make them infinitely old, hence neutral toward the baseline sociality s_i^0 because of decay.

3　Experimental Setup

We set up a swarm of robots allocated to two nests, in a $10\,\mathrm{m} \times 10\,\mathrm{m}$ enclosed arena. The arena was large enough so that robots would (almost) never reach its limits, making it akin to an open environment. At the center of the arena, we placed two nests (above and below the midpoint) and two resources (left and right), creating a symmetrical layout (Fig. 1c). Both nests are $1.2\,\mathrm{m}$ in diameter and $3\,\mathrm{m}$ apart. Resources are equidistant from each nest and $2\,\mathrm{m}$ apart from one another. We examine the emergence, strength, and stability of in-group bias across ecological, cognitive, and social conditions:

- **Ecological Parameters**: items are distributed according to a Gaussian kernel centered on each resource, with standard deviations $\sigma \in \{0.1, 1, 10\}$, corresponding to *singular*, *clustered*, and *uniform* distributions. Each resource holds up to 25 items; when below capacity, new items appear automatically following their respective Gaussian kernel.
- **Cognitive Parameters**: the evolution of robots' sociality depends on two parameters: how well robots remember their past interactions, controlled by the memorydecay rate $\lambda \in \{0.001, 0.0001, 0.00001\}$, and the size of their bounded memory window, $w \in \{10, 30, 60\}$.

- **Social Parameters**: each robot i has a baseline sociality value $s_i^0 \in \{0.1, 0.9\}$, corresponding respectively to initially *aggressive* or *social* robots. We test both homogeneous (aggressiveaggressive, socialsocial) and heterogeneous (aggressivesocial) nest configurations, and vary the number of robots per nest with population size $N \in \{12, 25, 50\}$.

For each experimental setup, we performed 50 runs, carried out with ARGoS3 [22], a physically realistic simulator made for swarm robotics experimentation, with a simulation rate of 10 ticks per second. We simulated e-puck robots [5, 18], a robot that uses a range-and-bearing system to communicate locally [7].

4   Results

4.1   Ecological Conditions

We first evaluate whether the emergence of social asymmetries is impacted by ecology. Although resource topology could in principle shape interaction patterns, our results reveal a surprisingly stable outcome across conditions. Indeed, we find that in-group bias consistently emerges in all ecological configurations (*singular*, *clustered* and *uniform* resource spread). Similarly, none of the resource distributions produced substantial differences in social or linguistic outcomes (see supplementary material). This robustness may stem from the individual nature of the foraging task; without recruitment or coordinated search (which we plan to reintroduce in future work), resource topology minimally affects robots' movement and encounter rates. Given this consistency, we adopt a uniform resource distribution for all subsequent experiments.

4.2   Cognitive Conditions

Next, we examine how sociality varies as a function of the rate of memorydecay and the size of the memory window. In the following experiments, we have $N = 25$ robots per nest, focusing on homogeneous populations where all robots are initialized with the same baseline sociality (Fig. 2).

Memory decay λ and memory window size w shape social dynamics similarly. Smaller memory windows and slower decay make robots update their sociality levels quicker: a lower w gives disproportionate weight to each new interaction, and a slower decay preserves that influence longer. Conversely, large memory windows introduce substantial inertia, and a high memory decay prevents robots from diverging from their baseline sociality. For social robots, sociality slightly increases toward both in-group and out-group members, resulting in minimal preference given their already near-ceiling sociality. On the other hand, aggressive robots, starting from a low sociality baseline, develop a strong and persistent in-group bias, with sociality toward out-group remaining almost null, while sociality toward in-group reaches levels that are nearly as high as social robots.

We see that memory decay has little effect at the beginning of the simulation when past interactions have not yet accumulated. At this stage, each interaction

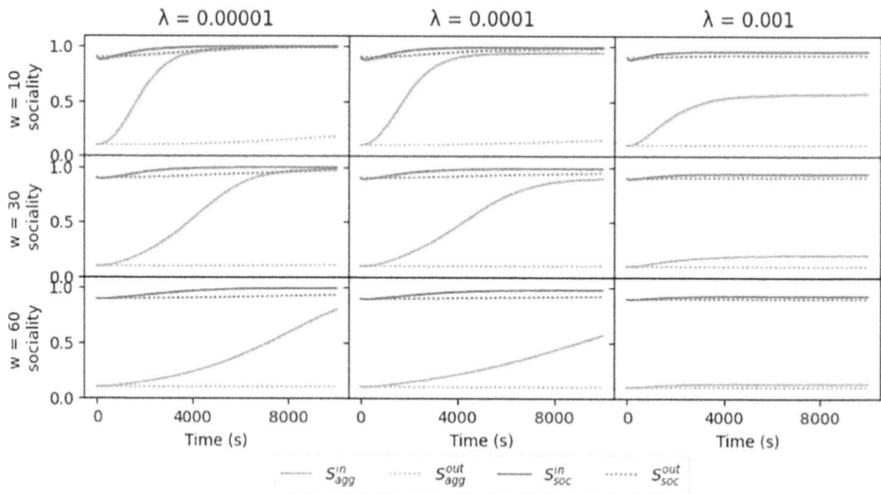

Fig. 2. Evolution of the overall sociality over time in a homogeneous configuration (both sub-swarms have the same baseline sociality s_i^0) for different values of decay λ (columns), memory window size w (rows) and baseline sociality (orange for aggressive robots, blue for social robots). Curves for both sociality conditions (aggressive and social robots) are plotted together in each panel. Solid lines correspond to in-group interactions, and dashed lines to out-group interactions. Overall, initially highly social robots remain equally willing to interact with both in- and out-groups, while robots with initial low sociality gradually become more social toward in-group robots (solid orange) but maintain low sociality toward out-group robots (dashed orange). (Color figure online)

contributes roughly $1/w$ to the sociality estimate. Therefore, smaller memory window sizes produce much stronger early fluctuations, accelerating divergence between in-group and out-group. A higher λ gives an upper bound to the sociality curves, reinforced with a lower w. Intuitively, this happens because after reaching a certain sociality, the rate at which new successes enter the window becomes roughly constant, and counterbalances the continuous decay of older entries, creating a balance between gain and loss that naturally bounds the curve.

Next, we analyse MNG activity, social interaction patterns, and vocabulary convergence, with $\lambda = 0.0001$, $w = 30$ and $N = 25$ (Fig. 3). Social homogeneous swarms show the baseline pattern expected for highly sociable populations (default swarm robotics behaviour). Cross-group interactions gradually increase as robots explore the arena and are not rejected by others (neither in-group nor out-group). As a result, the rate of MNGs played between the two social groups increases. Over time, both swarms grow increasingly similar. Aggressive robots, by contrast, begin with few interactions overall, regardless of group membership. Early rejections frequently interrupt exploration and send robots back to their nest, leading to more in-group interactions. This contributed to a strong in-group bias in both interaction frequency and MNG rate: robots play significantly more

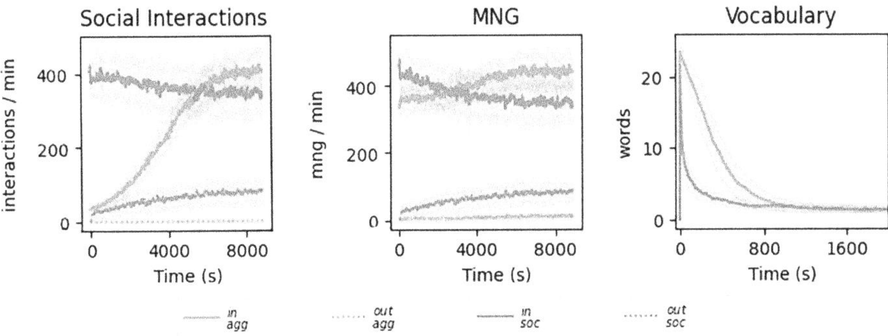

Fig. 3. Evolution, per swarm, of, left to right, the overall rate of social interactions initiated over time, the rate of naming games played over time, and the number of words present in the swarm's lexicon for different baseline sociality values (colors). Curves for both baseline sociality conditions (aggressive and social) are plotted together in each panel. Please note the different time scale used for the vocabulary panel.

MNGs with in-groups and almost none with out-groups. Social robots achieve quick lexical convergence thanks to frequent MNGs played even with out-group robots, whereas aggressive robots interact far less and thus converge more slowly.

4.3   Social Conditions

Group Size. Next, we examine how group size affects swarm social dynamics. In this section, we keep $\lambda = 0.0001$ and $w = 30$ (Fig. 4). Although more robots increase the number of potential interactions, each robot must interact with a larger set of partners. In practice, the rise in interactions does not counterbalance the difficulty of robots reaching one another exhaustively, resulting in slower social dynamics. This is partly driven by physical congestion: with more robots

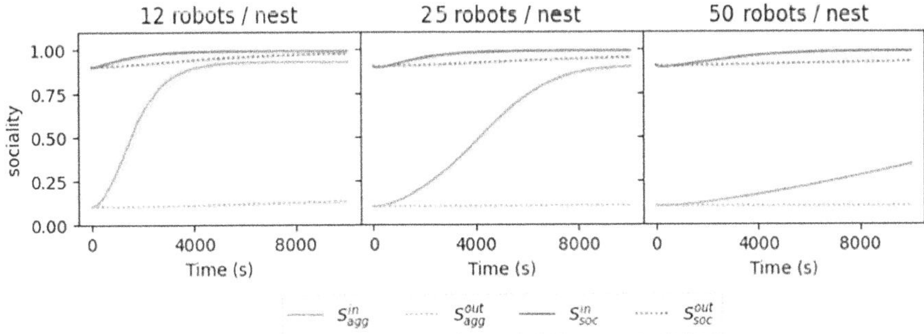

Fig. 4. Evolution of overall swarm sociality in a homogeneous configuration for different number of robots per nest (columns) and baseline sociality (colors). Curves for both sociality conditions (aggressive and social robots) are plotted together in each panel.

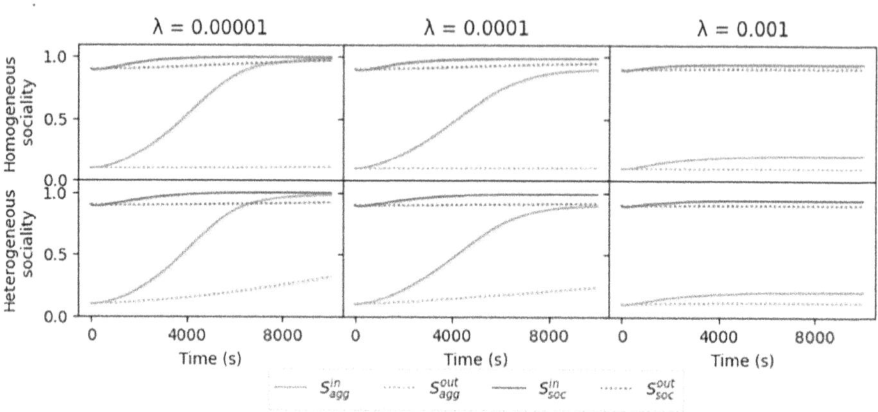

Fig. 5. Evolution of sociality over time in homogeneous configuration (top, both sub-swarms have the same baseline sociality) and heterogeneous configuration (bottom, each sub-swarm has a different baseline sociality value) for different values of decay λ (columns) and memory window size $w = 30$. In heterogeneous contexts, the two colors of curve correspond to each sub-swarm (social or aggressive) of the same experience.

in the arena, collisions and impeded navigation become more frequent, making it harder to reliably reach one another and leaving the swarm less *well mixed*.

Heterogeneous Scenario. Finally, we examine the impact of different baseline sociality. In the following experiments, we keep $\lambda = 0.0001$, $w = 30$ and $N = 25$, focusing on heterogeneous populations where one nest is initialized with a high baseline sociality and the other with a low sociality (see Fig. 5). Introducing heterogeneity does not substantially alter within-group interactions. In-group patterns mirror those in homogeneous settings. Social robots show reduced sociality toward the out-group (aggressive robots), as they are rejected more often. On the other hand, aggressive robots are influenced by social out-group robots: their sociality increases compared to purely out-group aggressive robots, though an in-group bias is still present. High decay rates (or small memory windows) allow sociality to increase so quickly that aggressive robots become more open to out-group interactions, which gradually reduces the in-group bias.

5   Conclusion

Our paper set out to model the spontaneous emergence of a well-documented social asymmetry, namely the in-group bias, which governs animals' social dynamics in the wild. Rather than being innate, in mammals and humans this social bias is acquired over time, and evolves according to prior history and flexible group membership representations. To this end, we created modified swarms with novel cognitive abilities like memory and individual recognition, mimicking some of the complex social dynamics that guide mammalian behaviour. We then tested the minimal conditions that give rise to this bias, and how its strength and stability are affected by various cognitive, social, and ecological variables.

Our results show that an in-group bias can spontaneously emerge in a swarm of embodied agents. With the introduction of mammal-like cognitive features, robots gradually differentiated between individuals they encountered frequently and those they encountered rarely. While highly social robots maintain broad cooperation and show only mild asymmetries (as expected from classic simulations where all robots have a maximal tendency to cooperate), we find that initially aggressive robots develop a strong in-group bias, where robots from their own nest are favoured (i.e., high sociality values), while robots from the other nest are rejected (i.e., low sociality values). Importantly, these effects arise purely from interaction frequencies shaped by spatial structure, and not from any a priori encoded group membership. In other words, cumulative patterns of interaction lead robots to develop strong group membership associations, effectively forming sub-swarms that tend to communicate mostly among themselves.

The emergence of in-group bias appears robust across ecologies, with different resource distributions having little influence on the model outcomes. In contrast, cognitive parameters such as memory size and decay rate strongly affected how quickly social patterns emerged: larger, more stable memories slow down social dynamics for both in-group and out-group, potentially delaying the development of in-group bias while making it more persistent once established. Group size played a role as well, with larger swarms displaying slower and more variable dynamics due to congestion and reduced mixing. In heterogeneous scenarios, social robots could partly pull aggressive robots toward higher sociality, eventually eliminating group bias over time with small memory size and low decay. When memory is robust, a reliable in-group bias emerges over time.

Overall, our work demonstrates that simple social-cognitive extensions allow swarms of robots to reproduce key aspects of mammal-like social dynamics, offering a physically grounded framework to study emergent social structure and cultural divergence in more complex species.

5.1 Future Work

Our broader goal here is to create more primate-like swarms that can help model human behaviour. One natural extension is to reintroduce cooperative foraging, fully integrated with social and linguistic dynamics, rather than as a separate process. Another direction is to explore the relative time scales of foraging, linguistic convergence, and social adaptation, which our results suggest strongly shape group structure. In particular, we plan to study patterns of linguistic convergence (same or different words across sub-swarms) depending on the sociality of the robots. Finally, moving beyond fixed nests and toward naturalistically emergent territories would bring the model closer to mammalian spatial organisation. This would diversify movement patterns beyond simple nestresource exploitation loops. This increased spatial complexity could create favourable conditions for richer, potentially compositional communication systems.

Disclosure of Interests. The authors have no competing interests to declare.

References

1. Baronchelli, A., Felici, M., Loreto, V., Caglioti, E., Steels, L.: Sharp transition towards shared vocabularies in multi-agent systems. J. Stat. Mech: Theory Exp. **2006**(06), P06014 (2006)
2. Brambilla, M., Ferrante, E., Birattari, M., Dorigo, M.: Swarm robotics: a review from the swarm engineering perspective. Swarm Intell. **7**(1), 1–41 (2013)
3. Cambier, N., Miletitch, R., Frémont, V., Dorigo, M., Ferrante, E., Trianni, V.: Language evolution in swarm robotics: a perspective. Front. Robot. AI **7**, 12 (2020)
4. Font Llenas, A., Talamali, M.S., Xu, X., Marshall, J.A., Reina, A.: Quality-sensitive foraging by a robot swarm through virtual pheromone trails. In: International Conference on Swarm Intelligence, pp. 135–149. Springer (2018)
5. Garattoni, L., Francesca, G., Brutschy, A., Pinciroli, C., Birattari, M.: Software infrastructure for e-puck (and TAM). IRIDIA, Institut de Recherches Interdisciplinaires et de Développements en ... (2016)
6. Giraldeau, L.A., Caraco, T.: Social Foraging Theory. Princeton University Press (2018)
7. Gutiérrez, Á., Campo, A., Dorigo, M., Donate, J., Monasterio-Huelin, F., Magdalena, L.: Open e-puck range & bearing miniaturized board for local communication in swarm robotics. In: 2009 IEEE International Conference on Robotics and Automation, pp. 3111–3116. IEEE (2009)
8. Gutiérrez, Á., Campo, A., Santos, F.C., Monasterio-Huelin, F., Dorigo, M.: Social odometry: imitation based odometry in collective robotics. Int. J. Adv. Rob. Syst. **6**(2), 11 (2009)
9. Hamilton, W.D.: The genetical evolution of social behaviour. II. J. Theor. Biol. **7**(1), 17–52 (1964)
10. Keller, L., Ross, K.G.: Selfish genes: a green beard in the red fire ant. Nature **394**(6693), 573–575 (1998)
11. Kutsukake, N., Suetsugu, N., Hasegawa, T.: Pattern, distribution, and function of greeting behavior among black-and-white colobus. Int. J. Primatol. **27**(5), 1271–1291 (2006)
12. Livingstone, D.: The evolution of dialect diversity. In: Simulating the Evolution of Language, pp. 99–117. Springer (2002)
13. Loreto, V., Baronchelli, A., Puglisi, A.: Mathematical modeling of language games. In: Evolution of Communication and Language in Embodied Agents, pp. 263–281. Springer (2010)
14. Madden, J.R., Drewe, J.A., Pearce, G.P., Clutton-Brock, T.H.: The social network structure of a wild meerkat population: 3. position of individuals within networks. Behav. Ecol. Sociobiol. **65**(10), 1857–1871 (2011)
15. Masuda, N., Fu, F.: Evolutionary models of in-group favoritism. F1000prime Rep. **7**, 27 (2015)
16. Miletitch, R., Reina, A., Dorigo, M., Trianni, V.: Emergent naming of resources in a foraging robot swarm. arXiv preprint arXiv:1910.02274 (2019)

17. Miletitch, R., Trianni, V., Campo, A., Dorigo, M.: Information aggregation mechanisms in social odometry. In: Proceedings of the 20th European Conference on Artificial Life (ECAL 2013), pp. 102–109. MIT Press, Cambridge (2013)
18. Mondada, F., et al.: The e-puck, a robot designed for education in engineering. In: Proceedings of the 9th Conference on Autonomous Robot Systems and Competitions, pp. 59–65. No. CONF, IPCB: Instituto Politécnico de Castelo Branco (2009)
19. Nowak, M.A.: Five rules for the evolution of cooperation. Science **314**(5805), 1560–1563 (2006)
20. Nowak, M.A., May, R.M.: Evolutionary games and spatial chaos. Nature **359**(6398), 826–829 (1992)
21. Nowak, M.A., May, R.M.: The spatial dilemmas of evolution. Int. J. Bifurcat. Chaos **3**(01), 35–78 (1993)
22. Pinciroli, C., et al.: Argos: a modular, parallel, multi-engine simulator for multi-robot systems. Swarm Intell. **6**(4), 271–295 (2012)
23. Pisor, A.C., Surbeck, M.: The evolution of intergroup tolerance in nonhuman primates and humans. Evol. Anthropol. Issues News Rev. **28**(4), 210–223 (2019)
24. Premo, L.S.: Exploratory agent-based models: towards an experimental ethnoarchaeology. In: Digital Discovery: Exploring New Frontiers in Human Heritage. CAA, pp. 29–36 (2006)
25. Reina, A., Miletitch, R., Dorigo, M., Trianni, V.: A quantitative micro-macro link for collective decisions: the shortest path discovery/selection example. Swarm Intell. **9**(2), 75–102 (2015)
26. Sinervo, B., et al.: Self-recognition, color signals, and cycles of greenbeard mutualism and altruism. Proc. Natl. Acad. Sci. **103**(19), 7372–7377 (2006)
27. Spikins, P., French, J.C., John-Wood, S., Dytham, C.: Theoretical and methodological approaches to ecological changes, social behaviour and human intergroup tolerance 300,000 to 30,000 bp. J. Archaeol. Method Theory **28**(1), 53–75 (2021)
28. Spikins, P., Needham, A., Wright, B., Dytham, C., Gatta, M., Hitchens, G.: Living to fight another day: the ecological and evolutionary significance of neanderthal healthcare. Quatern. Sci. Rev. **217**, 98–118 (2019)
29. Steels, L.: Modeling the cultural evolution of language. Phys. Life Rev. **8**(4), 339–356 (2011)
30. Tajfel, H.: Social Identity and Intergroup Relations, vol. 7. Cambridge University Press (2010)
31. Talamali, M.S., Bose, T., Haire, M., Xu, X., Marshall, J.A., Reina, A.: Sophisticated collective foraging with minimalist agents: a swarm robotics test. Swarm Intell. **14**(1), 25–56 (2020)
32. Tang-Martinez, Z.: The mechanisms of kin discrimination and the evolution of kin recognition in vertebrates: a critical re-evaluation. Behav. Proc. **53**(1–2), 21–40 (2001)
33. Traulsen, A., Nowak, M.A.: Evolution of cooperation by multilevel selection. Proc. Natl. Acad. Sci. **103**(29), 10952–10955 (2006)
34. Trianni, V., De Simone, D., Reina, A., Baronchelli, A.: Emergence of consensus in a multi-robot network: from abstract models to empirical validation. IEEE Robot. Autom. Lett. **1**(1), 348–353 (2016)
35. Trivers, R.L.: The evolution of reciprocal altruism. Q. Rev. Biol. **46**(1), 35–57 (1971)
36. Van Leeuwen, E.J., et al.: Chimpanzees behave prosocially in a group-specific manner. Sci. Adv. **7**(9), eabc7982 (2021)

37. West, S.A., Cooper, G.A., Ghoul, M.B., Griffin, A.S.: Ten recent insights for our understanding of cooperation. Nat. Ecol. Evol. **5**(4), 419–430 (2021)
38. West, S.A., Griffin, A.S., Gardner, A.: Evolutionary explanations for cooperation. Curr. Biol. **17**(16), R661–R672 (2007)
39. van Zweden, J.S., d'Ettorre, P.: Nestmate recognition in social insects and the role of hydrocarbons. Insect Hydrocarbons Biol. Biochem. Chem. Ecol. **11**, 222–243 (2010)

Energy-Efficient Flocking in Self-organized Robot Swarms

Sina Mahdavi Nasab[1]([✉]) [iD], Dushyant Singh[1] [iD], Peter Klapwijk[1] [iD],
Georges Jetti[1] [iD], Michael Khayyat[1] [iD], Francesco Braghin[1] [iD],
and Eliseo Ferrante[2,3] [iD]

[1] Politecnico di Milano, Milan, Italy
sinamahdavinasab@gmail.com
[2] New York University Abu Dhabi, Abu Dhabi, United Arab Emirates
[3] Vrije Universiteit Amsterdam, Amsterdam, The Netherlands

Abstract. Natural systems such as migratory birds achieve remarkable energy efficiency through self-organization and dynamic formation reconfiguration. We show that fully decentralized, memoryless ground robots can reproduce these effects using only range and bearing sensing, a digital compass, and battery level monitoring. We apply an existing evolutionary framework capable of optimizing Hebbian plasticity parameters of neural networks, giving robots the ability to continuously adapt and learn. In a uniform headwind setting, robots learn to form drag-reducing patterns and exhibit emergent formation reconfiguration that reallocates the energetic load, based on battery levels and without relying on direct communication or any wind sensor. Validation experiments in simulation show that the resulting controller outperforms a traditional flocking baseline method. Our results show that the adaptive controller can lead to the emergence of formation reconfiguration in the presence of very limited local information.

1 Introduction

Multi-robot systems that rely on centralized control or global communication face limited scalability, robustness, and adaptability in resource-constrained (e.g., GNSS-denied) environments. Swarm robotics addresses these issues by coordinating simple agents through local interactions, yielding scalable and cost-effective solutions [5,7,8,11]. It takes inspiration from collective natural systems like bird flocks, fish schools, and insect colonies, which achieve complex, collective behaviours in dynamic conditions through local interactions and no explicit leaders. Many studies have been conducted to explore the mechanisms behind these efficient behaviours [1,2,14,17,24,30].

One of the useful collective behaviours observed in nature is collective motion [29], where individuals move in groups coherently and in an aligned fashion. This offers numerous benefits, such as enhanced foraging [6], predator evasion [25], efficient navigation [6], and improved hydrodynamic and aerodynamic performance [3]. Improved aerodynamic performance is often found to be associated with the ability to dynamically reconfigure positions: the group tries to

R. Groß et al. (Eds.): ANTS 2026, LNCS 16515, pp. 149–161, 2026.
https://doi.org/10.1007/978-3-032-26123-6_12

distribute the energetic load during flight by periodically reassigning energy-demanding positions to different members, thus exchanging positions. Using this strategy, migratory birds save about 11–71% energy depending on their position within the flock, while the flock itself can extend its flight range by up to 44.6%. [2,24,30,35]. Similar mechanisms appear in human cycling pelotons [4].

Although there is evidence in biology that natural systems address energy efficiency through continuously reconfiguring position, the literature in swarm robotics has considered energy efficiency and formation reconfiguration in isolation and not together.

Concerning studies of energy efficiency in swarm robotics, early studies often treated energy as an abstract reward signal rather than a physical, hard constraint [12,15,31]. Subsequently, Wenguo et al. (2007) [21,32] demonstrated that response-threshold policies let agents self-assign to foraging or resting, improving efficiency without centralized control. Complementary strategies cut energy use by optimizing hardware and selectively activating perception and communication, such as eliminating redundant signals and modulating sensing in response to environmental and leader cues [34,36], and by distributing computation across resource-constrained UAVs to enable control through deep neural networks within tight onboard budgets [26]. However, the aforementioned works frequently idealize battery dynamics and only partially capture the energetic cost of motion, reconfiguration, and adverse environmental conditions.

Concerning studies related to pattern formation and dynamic formation reconfiguration, the effort in swarm robotics is limited, and most of the literature focusing on this problem concerns multi-robot systems not necessarily meet the requirements of swarm robotics. For example, several works have attempted to achieve more aerodynamically optimal patterns like the V-shape of birds using different control strategies [10]. Yang et al. (2016) [33] use MPC and achieve V-formation by optimizing over velocity matching between agents, clear view, and upwash benefit, in both centralized and decentralized frameworks. Roy et al. (2020) [27] optimize a similar cost function and propose a learning based framework that combines MPC with DNC as a teacher-learner pair. Although these works were able to achieve the V-shaped flocking pattern using simple local rules, dynamic formation reconfiguration is missing from them. In addition, they required full knowledge of the aerodynamic landscape. Instead, a greedy leading/trailing replacement heuristic was proposed by Mirzaeinia et al. (2019) [23] to achieve dynamic formation reconfiguration using battery thresholds. Then, Liu et al. (2024) [19,20] frame the same issue as an optimization problem but require the energetic cost of the positions as input. However, both works assumed particular fixed patterns, such as the V-formation, and solved dynamic position assignment within the confines of these formations. Also, they took advantage of global communication between members.

In this work, we focus on the problem of energy-efficient collective motion based on battery monitoring for simple memory-less robots. We utilize an existing evolutionary swarm robotics [28] framework first proposed in [9], and we evolve a swarm that has to move in a group while saving battery. The core contribution of this paper is not a new method, but the application of the method proposed in [9] to a novel problem: robots have to move as a group in a common target direction, using standard range and bearing capabilities within the swarm, a battery monitoring sensor, and while exposed to a wind-stressed environment that cannot be sensed by the robots. Importantly, we find that energy-efficient flocking and formation reconfiguration emerge without requiring it in the fitness function.

The remainder of the paper is organized as follows. Section 2 discusses the dynamics and architecture of the robots along with the evolutionary algorithm used. In Sect. 3, we present the simulation environment and equations governing battery drainage. The results of our experiments are discussed in Sect. 4 and finally, in Sect. 5 we consolidate our findings and discuss the scope of future work.

2   Methodology

The methodology is heavily based on the framework presented in [9], whereby robots are equipped with neural controllers whose weights are updated by Hebbian learning rules, and a separate outer-loop evolutionary optimizer is used to learn the Hebbian learning update rules. All evolutionary and validation experiments are performed on a point-mass kinematic simulator with wind implementation in MATLAB. The full workflow is depicted in Fig. 1.

2.1   Individual Robot Neural Controller

We consider differential-drive ground robots, whose locomotion capabilities are regulated by forward velocity v^i and angular velocity ω^i.

The perception capabilities of the robots are as follows: Every robot can perceive neighbours only when they are within a sensing radius R (in our experiments $R = 2.01$). R defines a sensing circle that is divided into 4 equal quadrants $q \in [1, 2, 3, 4]$. In each quadrant, a sensor gives the distance, $d_q \in [0, R]$, and bearing, $\psi_q \in [0, \pi/2]$, of the nearest neighbour in that quadrant (see Fig. 2). The robot is battery-aware, that is, it senses its remaining battery percentage, $B_0 \in [0, 100]$. The last sensor that is added to the robot is a digital compass, $\theta_0 \in (-\pi, \pi]$ that provides an approximate task direction context.

Each robot runs a 10-10-10-2 Multi-Layer Perceptron (MLP) with ReLU hidden layers and tanh outputs. The 10-dimensional inputs to the neural network for agent i will be the 8 local sensory readings of all 4 quadrants (d_q^i, ψ_q^i), the battery of the agent (B_0^i), and the heading of the agent (θ_0^i). The default input (sensory reading) for when there is no neighbour in a quadrant is $d_q^i = R$, and $\psi_q^i = 0$. The ten inputs are rescaled to $[-1, 1]$. The input layer is followed by two hidden layers with 10 neurons each. The output layer contains two neurons: the first outputs the linear velocity v^i and the second one the angular velocity ω^i of the agent, which are then rescaled to $v^i \in [-0.2, 0.2]$ m/s and $\omega^i \in [-\pi/5, \pi/5]$ rad/s. The MLP has 220 weights that are randomly initialized at the beginning

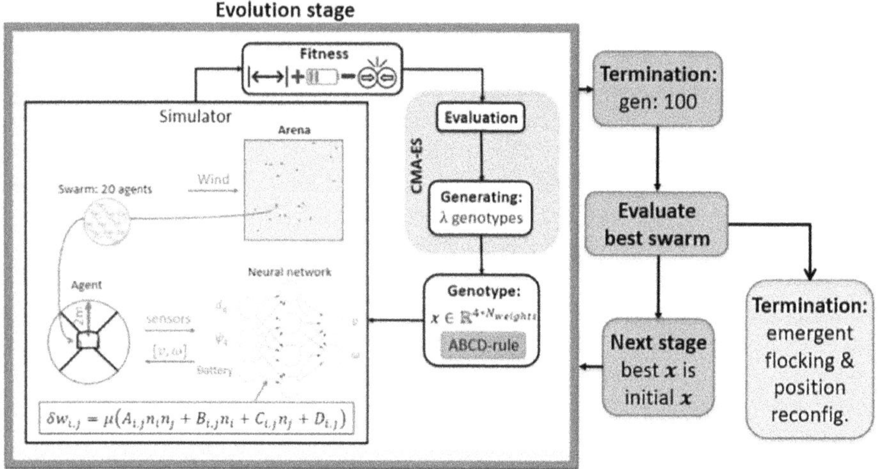

Fig. 1. Overview of the Methodology. Our setup comprises a swarm with robots, each equipped with a neural network controller. Each swarm shares one set of Hebbian learning rules, which are learned by the CMA-ES algorithm through evolution. The robots are simulated in the windy arena for fitness calculation.

of each experiment using a uniform distribution in $[-1, 1]$, and the bias of each weight is set to zero. Each NN weight of every robot is updated during the experiment using a Hebbian learning update rule. As [9], we use the Hebbian learning update in Eq. 1, where $\delta w_{i,j}$, is the weight change corresponding to the connection between pre- and post-synaptic neurons i and j, μ is the constant learning rate, n_i and n_j are the activations of the neurons, and $A_{i,j}, B_{i,j}, C_{i,j}, D_{i,j}$ are the 4 Hebbian learning update rules or genotype which from now on we shall refer to as ABCD-rules for simplicity. Each robot will have a different set of NN weights that will vary under the effect of ABCD-rules during its own experience. We keep normalising the weights to prevent unbounded growth during the simulation [18].

$$\delta w_{i,j} = \mu(A_{i,j}n_in_j + B_{i,j}n_i + C_{i,j}n_j + D_{i,j}) \tag{1}$$

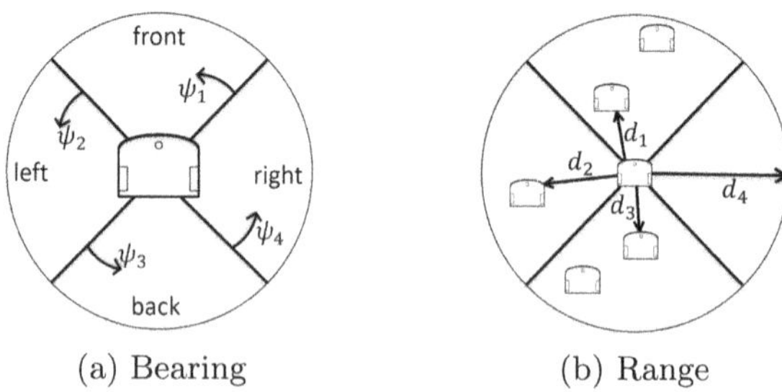

(a) Bearing   (b) Range

Fig. 2. Sensing capabilities of the individual robots.

Table 1. Evolving swarm experiment parameters for every stage.

Parameter	Description	Value
N_{ABCD}	Number of rules	880
λ	Population size	30
N_{gen}	Termination condition	100
σ_0	Initial covariance value	0.3
N_{repeats}	Number of repeats per individual	3
μ	Hebbian learning rate	0.1

The ABCD-rules vary across each weight of the NN, resulting in 880 parameters (4 for each of the 220 weights) that need to be optimized for the entire swarm. In particular, the swarm shares the genotype of these 880 parameters, which allows the evolutionary algorithm to scale independently from the swarm size [9].

2.2 The Evolutionary Algorithms

The Hebbian learning update parameters are optimized using Covariance Matrix Adaptation Evolution Strategy (CMA-ES) [16]. Each generation evaluates a population size λ of 30 candidate solutions, where each candidate solution represents a complete set of 880 ABCD parameters that define the Hebbian learning rules for all agents in a swarm. At the beginning of the evolutionary process, the ABCD-rules are sampled uniformly from $[-5, 5]$. The fitness f of each candidate is evaluated by running 3 simulations (each with a different random seed) of a swarm of 20 agents at full battery until one agent's battery depletes to zero. The fitness f of each candidate is determined as the median of the 3 runs, while the individual fitness of each simulation is calculated as explained in Sect. 2.3.

The evolution strategy then makes a rank-based and elitist selection of the best $\lambda/2 = 15$ candidates. CMA-ES then uses these 15 elites to update the search distribution, and samples 30 new ABCD-rules from the search distribution for the next generation. A summary of other Evolution parameters can be found in Table 1.

2.3 Evolutionary Stages

In this paper, we perform staged evolutionary experiments, meaning that we consider three stages whereby the complexity of the task increases from one stage to the next. This corresponds to a different fitness function in each stage. At the end of each simulation during evolution, the following set of data is recorded that is used to formulate the fitness function: average heading of all the agents θ_{avg}, collision time t_{col}, border collision time t_{wcol}, distance travelled towards the left x_{avg} and remaining battery $B_{\text{avg,end}}$, both averaged over all the agents.

Table 2. Fitness function during each evolution stage

Stage	Goal	Fitness function
1	To walk left	$f = x_{avg}$
2	Save battery and avoid wall collision	$f = x_{\mathrm{avg}} + \dfrac{B_{\mathrm{avg,end}}}{5} - \dfrac{3 \cdot t_{\mathrm{wcol}}}{500}$
3	Save battery and avoid all collision	$f = x_{\mathrm{avg}} + \dfrac{B_{\mathrm{avg,end}}}{5} - \dfrac{t_{\mathrm{col}} + 3 \cdot t_{\mathrm{wcol}}}{250}$

In stage 1, the wind model is disabled, and the fitness encourages agents to learn to move towards a target that is assumed to be on the left. Since in our original scenario, the wind blows left to right, the swarm is eventually required to move against the wind, recalling that they have no sensor to detect the wind direction. This stage is necessary to avoid evolving trivial strategies where agents evolve to move in the same direction as the wind. In stage 2, the wind model is activated, and the fitness combines distance, average remaining battery, and a penalty on wall collisions. The walls are placed to confine agents within a wide horizontal band (in our experiments, defined by coordinates $y = \pm 5$). This stage promotes the emergence of early forms of coordinated motion. In stage 3, the fitness is similar to stage 2 but includes an additional term penalizing inter-robot collisions. We hypothesize that this final stage will promote the emergence of advanced coordinated motion that includes formation reconfiguration. Each of these stages lasts for $G = 100$ generations. Table 2 reports the precise expression of the fitness function used in each stage.

3   Experimental Setup

Our simulation environment is a 10-meter-wide corridor along which the agents can walk. In practice, we have a 10×10 meter frame that is centered on the x-axis and moves horizontally with the agents. This is done to simulate an environment that is unbounded horizontally. The wind is prescribed as a constant and spatially uniform aligned with the x-axis, blowing from left to right. The global position and heading of the robots are updated using a kinematic model. We set $\Delta t = 0.5$s due to computational burden. In addition, v_i and ω_i are sampled every 0.5 s (2 Hz) from the memoryless NN controller.

The main simulation effort of this work has been to model the battery drainage. This is done by considering three components, one that depends on the wind drag P_{wind}, and two that act on the battery independent from the wind: motor consumption P_{mot}, and idle consumption due to onboard electronics P_{idle}. The latter elements are introduced both to capture a complete model of energy consumption, but also to obtain simulations where robots will eventually, no matter what, run out of battery, corresponding to a pragmatic termination condition. To calculate P_{wind}, a modelling effort was performed to capture the wind dynamics and their contribution as drag on each robot.

To determine the effect of wind on the robots, we simulate a two-dimensional wind field using a ray-marching scheme (Fig. 3). The arena is discretised into

$N_x \times N_y$ cells with a free-stream wind speed $U_\infty = 100\%$ (percentage scale) blowing along $+x$. The wind-percentage field $U_{i,j}^{\%} \in [0, 100\%]$ at each cell (i, j) is propagated left-to-right (like a ray) according to five simple rules: when a ray intersects a robot, the local wind percentage decreases and then gradually recovers downstream. The procedure also mimics wake formation behind groups of robots. Two exponential-smoothing windows are convolved over the grid indices i, j. An example wake behind a wall of robots is shown in Fig. 3b.

The resulting $U_{i,j}^{\%}$ provides the local wind speed percentage. If we scale it with the free-stream physical wind speed $V_\infty = 10$ m/s:

$$V_{\text{wind}} = V_\infty \, U_{i,j}^{\%}. \tag{2}$$

The mechanical power drawn by the wind load P_{wind} is modelled as:

$$P_{\text{wind}} = \kappa V_{\text{rel}}^2 \, v \cos \theta. \tag{3}$$

where $\kappa = 10$ is a constant and V_{rel} is the magnitude of the relative speed between the wind and the agent. Using differential-drive kinematics, we can derive the left and right wheel speeds of the robot v_l, v_r from its forward and angular velocities. Battery drainage of the motor is then taken as:

$$P_{\text{mot}} = \gamma(|v_L| + |v_R|), \tag{4}$$

and the total peragent power usage combines both effects accounting for some idle drainage P_{idle} in case robots don't move:

$$P_{\text{use}} = \max\left(P_{\text{idle}}, P_{\text{mot}} - P_{\text{wind}}\right), \qquad P_{\text{idle}} = 0.1 \ \%/\text{s}. \tag{5}$$

Battery state $B \in [0, 100]$ evolves in discrete time with step $\Delta t = 0.5$ s:

$$B(t + \Delta t) = B(t) - P_{\text{use}} \Delta t. \tag{6}$$

This compact phenomenological approximation of aerodynamic disturbances and energy consumption, allows realtime swarmscale simulations without full fluid dynamics. All implementation details and default parameters are provided in our open-source code repository.

4 Experimental Results

The fitness progression of the evolution of the ABCD-rules on a swarm of 20 agents across 300 generations (for the three stages described in Sect. 2.3) is depicted in Fig. 4. After evolution, we evaluate the best controller obtained after each evolutionary stage and compare it with the standard collective motion baseline [13]. The baseline is implemented using only proximal control and goal-seeking terms. The parameters are reported in Table 3.

Each controller is evaluated over 100 simulation runs of a swarm of 20 robots, initialized with random positions and random network weights; each simulation

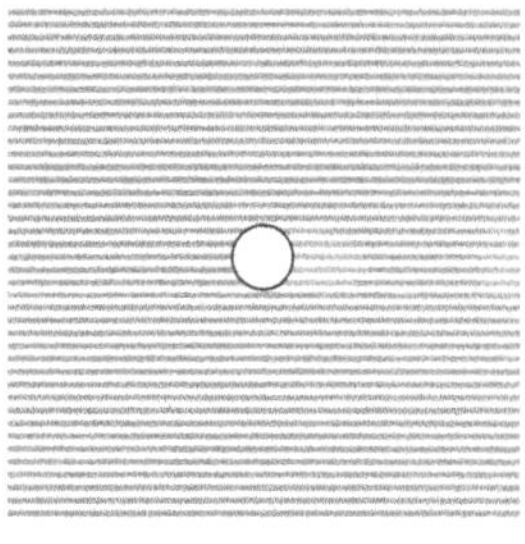

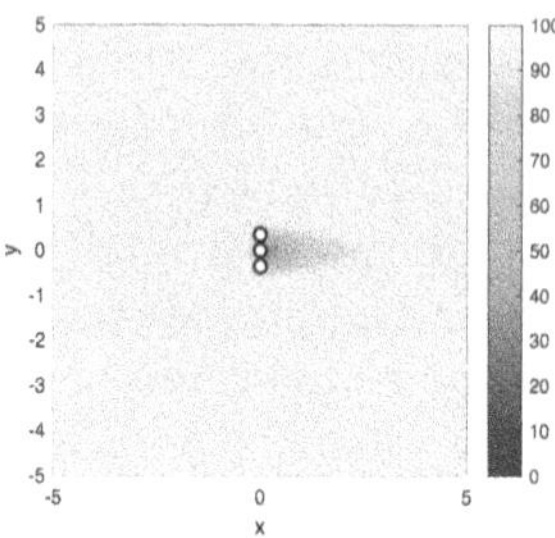

(a) Ray–marching scheme

(b) Wake behind a vertical column of three agents

Fig. 3. Illustrations of the windfield model. (a) Rays propagate left-to-right and lose speed percentage when they intersect a robot. (b) When agents align vertically, a thick low-speed wake forms; the legend shows wind speed as a percentage of free-stream wind speed (0% = navy, 100% = yellow). (Color figure online)

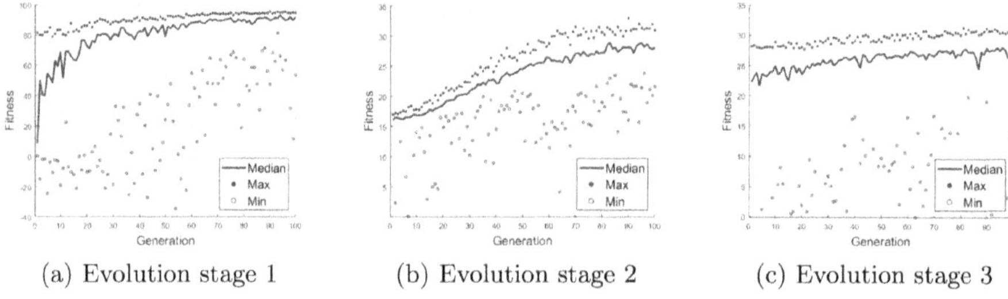

(a) Evolution stage 1   (b) Evolution stage 2   (c) Evolution stage 3

Fig. 4. Fitness evolution during the three evolutionary stages.

terminates when the battery of any robot is depleted. Performance is measured as the distance travelled to the left at termination and the average remaining battery across the swarm.

Figure 5a summarizes the main results. Each point corresponds to one simulation of the best controller from stage 1 (cluster 1), stage 2 (cluster 2), and stage 3 (cluster 3), or the baseline (cluster 4), plotted in terms of distance travelled versus the average battery level of the swarm members at the end of the simulation. In stage 1, as fitness only rewards going towards the target, they swarm evolves to learn to move left whether they are alone or in a group (Figs. 6a and 6c). Accordingly, cluster 1 exhibits the worst performance in terms of both distance travelled and battery savings, because agents deplete the battery faster, and as a result, they travel a relatively short distance. In stage 2, as the wind is introduced and the fitness function considers, among the other components, the battery consumption, it corresponds to cluster 2 that achieves a greater distance and better energy savings than stage 1. In stage 3, we observe that flocking becomes more consistent, and agents learn a formation reconfiguration strategy. Comparing clusters 2 and 3, we observe that this strategy facilitates better load distribution among agents, leading the swarm to trade some better savings for

Table 3. Simulation parameters for the baseline controller.

Parameter	Description	Value
K_1	MDMC linear gain	0.05 m/s
K_2	MDMC angular gain	0.5 rad/s
α	Steepness of potential function	2
ϵ	Strength of potential function	1
d_{des}	Desired interrobot distance	0.7 m
D_{p}	Max. interaction range (proximal control)	3 m
K_{goal}	Goal seeking weight	3

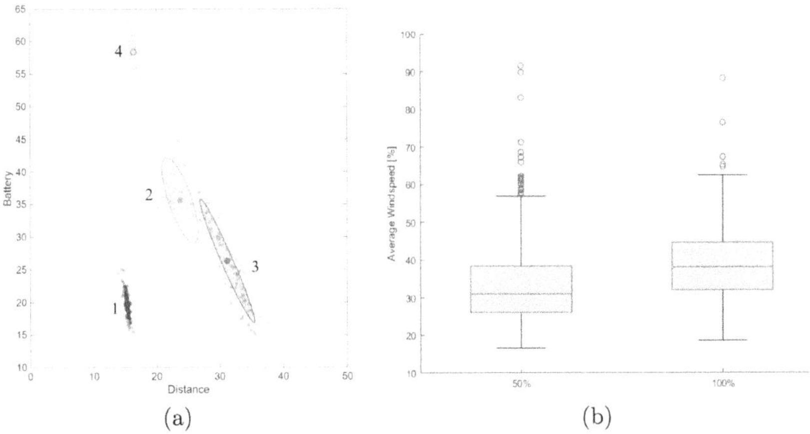

(a)   (b)

Fig. 5. (a) Travelled distance against remaining battery of 100 simulations of the best controller of each evolution stage (1, 2, 3), and the baseline (4). Qualitative comparisons of all stages are provided in the supplementary video [22]. (b) Wind speed experienced by the agents initialized at 50% (left), and 100% (right) over 100 simulations.

a greater achieved distance. This improvement, however, is likely due to longer training rather than the modification of the fitness function.

We argue that the strategies learned in stage 3 rely primarily on local interrobot interactions rather than the compass information. We contrast the controllers of stages 1 and 3 by testing them with 1 and 5 agents. Figures 6a, 6c show the trajectories of agents with the first-stage controller. As pointed out, the robots adopt the same near-linear path toward the target whether in a group or in isolation. In contrast, the agents with the third-stage controller perform new manoeuvrers–rotations associated with the formation reconfiguration phenomena–when inside a group (Fig. 6d). Full rotations do not manifest when the third-stage controller is tested on 1 agent (Fig. 6b), implying that these strategies are collective behaviours arising from local interactions.

Table 4. Results of battery awareness experiment ($p = 2.799e - 9, df = 198$)

Experiment	No. of runs	Mean	Standard deviation
Agent with 100% battery	100	38.7	9.4
Agent with 50% battery	100	33.8	11.2

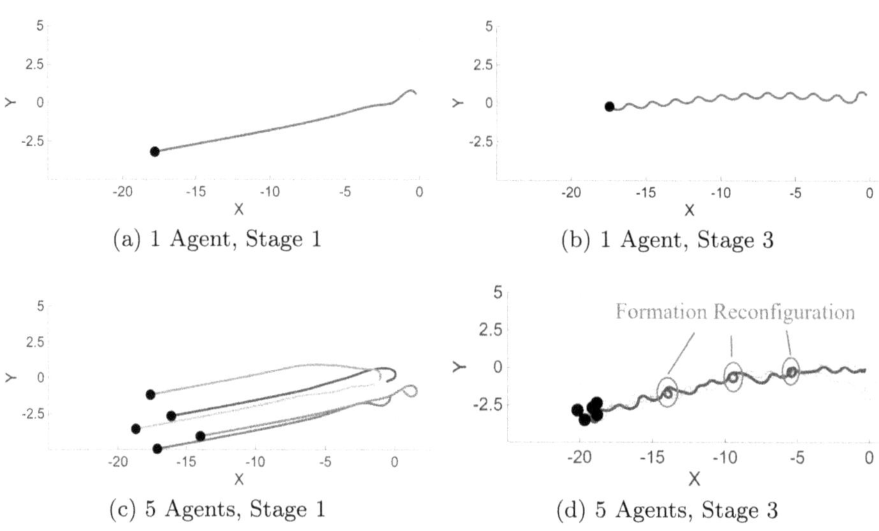

Fig. 6. Trajectories of the best controller from stage 1 (a, c) and stage 3 (b, d) in single- and five-agent setups. Also, (d) highlights the formation reconfiguration cycles in which agents take turns in the leading position.

So far, we have shown that the evolved controller achieves energy-efficient flocking with an emergent formation reconfiguration strategy and improved distance-battery trade-offs. However, these results alone do not reveal whether the controller actually exploits the internal battery state. To test whether battery awareness has any impact on the strategy that robots adopt, we compare the behaviour of an agent initialised normally with 100% battery to an agent initialised with 50% battery at the beginning of the simulation. The percentage wind speed of the grid cells where the agent travels, $U_{i,j}^{\%}$, is averaged over the simulation time. This parameter is chosen to quantify conservativeness; an agent that drives a lot in the front of the swarm will expose itself to much higher average $U_{i,j}^{\%}$ than an agent that tries to stay in the middle of the swarm shielded by others. Once again, we note that the robots do not have any onboard sensors for wind measurement. We ran 100 simulations with all agents initialized at full charge (100%) and recorded the average $U_{i,j}^{\%}$ along the trajectory of a representative agent. We then repeated the experiment, but this time with one agent initialized at half charge (50%) while all others remained at 100%. As shown in Fig. 5b and Table 4, the mean $U_{i,j}^{\%}$ for a normal agent was 38.7%, whereas an agent initialized with reduced battery travelled through regions with a lower mean $U_{i,j}^{\%}$ of 33.8%. A t-test confirmed the statistical significance of this difference ($p = 2.799e - 9$, $df = 198$). With this, we conclude that battery monitoring helps agents find adaptive strategies to increase the swarm's endurance.

The source code and the supplementary video are available in the Zenodo repository at https://doi.org/10.5281/zenodo.18602800.

5 Conclusion

We studied energy-efficient collective motion in a swarm of simple, memory-less ground robots. The swarm demonstrated emergent formation and dynamic formation reconfiguration, without these behaviours being explicitly encoded in the fitness function. Using a neural network controller with standard Hebbian plasticity, whose parameters were evolved via CMA-ES, the swarm learned to exploit local sensory readings and internal battery monitoring without explicit communication or wind sensing. The resulting controller outperformed a flocking baseline by 90% in terms of average achieved distance. A dedicated battery-awareness test showed that low-charge robots adapt by taking a conservative strategy through shielding themselves with other robots. Future works will investigate the minimal sensing and controller requirements that can manifest similar results. In addition, the impact of battery awareness on the learned strategies needs to be further investigated. For this matter, it is necessary to evolve a swarm that does not incorporate battery monitoring and see if similar behaviours can emerge.

Acknowledgments. The work of EF has been supported by the NYUAD Center for Artificial Intelligence and Robotics, funded by Tamkeen under the NYUAD Research Institute Award CG010, and by the NYUAD Center for Interdisciplinary Data Science & AI (CIDSAI), funded by Tamkeen under the NYUAD Research Institute Award CG016.

Disclosure of Interests. The authors have no competing interests to declare.

References

1. Andersson, M., Wallander, J.: Kin selection and reciprocity in flight formation? Behav. Ecol. **15**, 158–162 (2004). https://doi.org/10.1093/BEHECO/ARG109
2. Beaumont, F., Murer, S., Bogard, F., Polidori, G.: The aerodynamic mechanisms of the formation flight of migratory birds: a narrative review. Appl. Sci. **14**(13) (2024). https://doi.org/10.3390/app14135402
3. Beaver, L.E., Malikopoulos, A.A.: An overview on optimal flocking. Annu. Rev. Control. **51**, 88–99 (2021). https://doi.org/10.1016/j.arcontrol.2021.03.004
4. Blocken, B., et al.: Aerodynamic drag in cycling pelotons: new insights by CFD simulation and wind tunnel testing. J. Wind Eng. Ind. Aerodyn. **179**, 319–337 (2018). https://doi.org/10.1016/J.JWEIA.2018.06.011
5. Brambilla, M., Ferrante, E., Birattari, M., Dorigo, M.: Swarm robotics: a review from the swarm engineering perspective. Swarm Intell. **7**, 1–41 (2013). https://doi.org/10.1007/s11721-012-0075-2

6. Couzin, I., Krause, J., Franks, N., Levin, S.: Effective leadership and decision-making in animal groups on the move. Nature **433**, 513–516 (2005). https://doi.org/10.1038/nature03236

7. Debie, E., Kasmarik, K., Garratt, M.: Swarm robotics: a survey from a multi-tasking perspective. ACM Comput. Surv. **56** (2023). https://doi.org/10.1145/3611652

8. Dias, P.G.F., Silva, M.C., Rocha Filho, G., Vargas, P.A., Cota, L.P., Pessin, G.: Swarm robotics: a perspective on the latest reviewed concepts and applications. Sensors **21**, 1–30 (2021). https://doi.org/10.3390/s21062062

9. van Diggelen, F., Karagüzel, T.A., Rincon, A.G., Eiben, A.E., Floreano, D., Ferrante, E.: Emergent heterogeneous swarm control through Hebbian learning (2025). https://doi.org/10.48550/arXiv.2507.11566

10. Dimock, G.A., Selig, M.S.: The aerodynamic benefits of self-organization in bird flocks. In: 41st Aerospace Sciences Meeting and Exhibit. https://doi.org/10.2514/6.2003-608

11. Dorigo, M., Theraulaz, G., Trianni, V.: Swarm robotics: past, present, and future. Proc. IEEE **109**, 1152–1165 (2021). https://doi.org/10.1109/JPROC.2021.3072740

12. Elfwing, S., Uchibe, E., Doya, K., Christensen, H.I.: Biologically inspired embodied evolution of survival. In: 2005 IEEE Congress on Evolutionary Computation, vol. 3, pp. 2210–2216 (2005). https://doi.org/10.1109/CEC.2005.1554969

13. Ferrante, E., Turgut, A., Huepe, C., Stranieri, A., Pinciroli, C., Dorigo, M.: Self-organized flocking with a mobile robot swarm: a novel motion control method. Adapt. Behav. **20**, 460–477 (2012). https://doi.org/10.1177/1059712312462248

14. Friman, S.I., et al.: It pays to follow the leader: metabolic cost of flight is lower for trailing birds in small groups. Proc. Natl. Acad. Sci. **121**(26) (2024). https://doi.org/10.1073/pnas.2319971121

15. Haasdijk, E., Eiben, A.E., Winfield, A.F.T.: Individual, social, and evolutionary adaptation in collective systems. In: Handbook of Collective Robotics, pp. 437–496 (2013). https://doi.org/10.1201/B14908-16

16. Hansen, N., Ostermeier, A.: Completely derandomized self-adaptation in evolution strategies. Evol. Comput. **9**, 159–195 (2001). https://doi.org/10.1162/106365601750190398

17. Hassanalian, M., Mirzaeinia, A., Bawana, N., Heppner, F.: Energy management of echelon flying northern bald ibises with different wingspans and variable wingtip spacing. J. Bionic Eng. **19**, 44–61 (2022). https://doi.org/10.1007/S42235-021-00107-7

18. Leung, B., Haomachai, W., Pedersen, J.W., Risi, S., Manoonpong, P.: Bio-inspired plastic neural networks for zero-shot out-of-distribution generalization in complex animal-inspired robots (2025). https://doi.org/10.48550/arXiv.2503.12406

19. Liu, H., Liu, T., Cui, M., Shan, Y., Zhao, S., Huang, K.: An efficient position reconfiguration approach for maximizing lifetime of fixed-wing swarm drones. In: IEEE International Conference on Intelligent Robots and Systems, pp. 13922–13929 (2024). https://doi.org/10.1109/IROS58592.2024.10802362

20. Liu, H., Wei, M., Zhao, S., Cheng, H., Huang, K.: Energy efficient scheduling for position reconfiguration of swarm drones. IEEE Trans. Autom. Sci. Eng. **22**, 8400–8414 (2025). https://doi.org/10.1109/TASE.2024.3485681

21. Liu, W., Winfield, A., Sa, J., Chen, J., Dou, L.: Strategies for energy optimisation in a swarm of foraging robots. In: Şahin, E., Spears, W.M., Winfield, A.F.T. (eds.) SR 2006. LNCS, vol. 4433, pp. 14–26. Springer, Heidelberg (2007). https://doi.org/10.1007/978-3-540-71541-2_2

22. Mahdavi Nasab, S., et al.: Energy-efficient flocking (ants 2026, polimi) — matlab implementation (2026). https://doi.org/10.5281/zenodo.18602800
23. Mirzaeinia, A., Hassanalian, M., Lee, K., Mirzaeinia, M.: Energy conservation of v-shaped swarming fixed-wing drones through position reconfiguration. Aerosp. Sci. Technol. **94**, 105398 (2019). https://doi.org/10.1016/J.AST.2019.105398
24. Mirzaeinia, A., Heppner, F., Hassanalian, M.: An analytical study on leader and follower switching in v-shaped Canada goose flocks for energy management purposes. Swarm Intell. **14**, 117–141 (2020). https://doi.org/10.1007/S11721-020-00179-X
25. Olson, R.S., Hintze, A., Dyer, F.C., Knoester, D.B., Adami, C.: Predator confusion is sufficient to evolve swarming behavior. J. Roy. Soc. Interface **10**, 20130305 (2013). https://doi.org/10.1098/rsif.2013.0305
26. Ren, W., et al.: Efficient pipeline collaborative DNN inference in resource-constrained UAV swarm. In: IEEE Wireless Communications and Networking Conference, WCNC (2024). https://doi.org/10.1109/WCNC57260.2024.10570535
27. Roy, S., Mehmood, U., Grosu, R., Smolka, S.A., Stoller, S.D., Tiwari, A.: Learning distributed controllers for v-formation. In: Proceedings - 2020 IEEE International Conference on Autonomic Computing and Self-Organizing Systems, ACSOS 2020, pp. 119–128. Institute of Electrical and Electronics Engineers Inc. (2020). https://doi.org/10.1109/ACSOS49614.2020.00033
28. Trianni, V.: Evolutionary Swarm Robotics, vol. 108. Springer, Heidelberg (2008). https://doi.org/10.1007/978-3-540-77612-3
29. Vicsek, T., Zafeiris, A.: Collective motion. Phys. Rep. **517**(3), 71–140 (2012). https://doi.org/10.1016/j.physrep.2012.03.004
30. Voelkl, B., Fritz, J.: Relation between travel strategy and social organization of migrating birds with special consideration of formation flight in the northern bald ibis. Philos. Trans. Roy. Soc. B Biol. Sci. **372** (2017). https://doi.org/10.1098/RSTB.2016.0235
31. Weel, B., Haasdijk, E., Eiben, A.: The emergence of multi-cellular robot organisms through on-line on-board evolution. In: European Conference on the Applications of Evolutionary Computation, pp. 124–134. Springer (2012). https://doi.org/10.1007/978-3-642-29178-4_13
32. Wenguo, L., Winfield, A.F., Sa, J., Chen, J., Dou, L.: Towards energy optimization: emergent task allocation in a swarm of foraging robots. Adapt. Behav. **15**, 289–305 (2007). https://doi.org/10.1177/1059712307082088
33 Yang, J., Grosu, R., Smolka, S.A., Tiwari, A.: Love thy neighbor: V-formation as a problem of model predictive control. In: Desharnais, J., Jagadeesan, R. (eds.) 27th International Conference on Concurrency Theory (CONCUR 2016). Leibniz International Proceedings in Informatics (LIPIcs), vol. 59, pp. 4:1–4:5. Schloss Dagstuhl – Leibniz-Zentrum für Informatik, Dagstuhl, Germany (2016). https://doi.org/10.4230/LIPIcs.CONCUR.2016.4
34. Yasin, J.N., Mahboob, H., Haghbayan, M.H., Yasin, M.M., Plosila, J.: Energy-efficient navigation of an autonomous swarm with adaptive consciousness. Remote Sens. **13**(6) (2021). https://doi.org/10.3390/rs13061059
35. Zhang, Y., Lauder, G.V.: Energy conservation by collective movement in schooling fish. eLife **12** (2024). https://doi.org/10.7554/eLife.90352
36. Zhang, Y., Yi, N., Zhang, S., Ma, Y.: Energy consumption minimized task allocation with correlated data for symbiotic robotic swarm. In: 2023 IEEE 97th Vehicular Technology Conference (VTC2023-Spring), pp. 1–5 (2023). https://doi.org/10.1109/VTC2023-Spring57618.2023.10199239

Marine Surface Vehicle Formations in Confined Environments

Chanaka Thushitha Bandara$^{(\boxtimes)}$ and Herbert G. Tanner

Center for Autonomous and Robotic Systems (CARS), University of Delaware,
Newark, DE 19716, USA
`{chanaka,btanner}@udel.edu`

Abstract. This paper presents a navigation function-based formation control methodology for autonomous surface vehicles (ASVs) operating in confined aquatic environments with currents and obstacles. Three methodological advances facilitate field deployment: (i) a differentiable approximation of the minimum distance function eliminating control chattering while preserving collision avoidance, (ii) environmental workspace boundary avoidance through virtual agents extending collision avoidance to environmental constraints, and (iii) a receding horizon waypoint strategy accommodating nonholonomic constraints and minimum speed thresholds. Unlike existing approaches requiring fixed spatial coordinates, the proposed framework allows robots to drift with currents while maintaining desired geometric patterns. Validation through numerical simulations and field experiments with Jaiabot micro-ASVs demonstrates robust performance despite GPS uncertainty, communication latency, and environmental disturbances.

1 Introduction

Aquatic ecosystems, including lakes, rivers, and coastal areas, face mounting threats from climate change and human activity, creating an urgent need for efficient, large-scale environmental monitoring, spatial field estimation, and source seeking [5,6,11]. For such marine sensing applications, a sensor network approach offers significant advantages, yet successful implementation depends critically on effective network deployment and management strategies.

Consider the challenge of accurately estimating salinity levels in estuaries to monitor saltwater intrusion: environmental sensor-equipped ASVs (Fig. 1) provide a unique solution that enables timely, cost-efficient, and reconfigurable measurements at specific target locations. The effectiveness of such marine sensor network deployments hinges on precise sensor placement, whether defined relative to a fixed reference frame or through relative sensor configurations (see [1,13]). Measurement location critically influences subsequent sensor fusion and environmental quantity estimation.

This application context imposes particular requirements on formation control solutions. Indeed, strong environmental disturbances, powerful ambient currents, bilateral actuation limitations, communication constraints both in the field

© The Author(s), under exclusive license to Springer Nature Switzerland AG 2026
R. Groß et al. (Eds.): ANTS 2026, LNCS 16515, pp. 162–174, 2026.
https://doi.org/10.1007/978-3-032-26123-6_13

Fig. 1. A fleet of 13 Jaiabot micro-ASVs, equipped with water quality sensors, deployed in Lewes, DE.

and underwater, nontrivial vehicle kinematics, and varying workspace geometry along river banks with occasional obstacles (e.g., boats, floating piers, buoys) necessitate robust, feedback-based solutions that ensure collision avoidance without constraining sensors to fixed spatial configurations. A particular *navigation function*-based motion planning and control strategy [24] addresses most of these mission requirements, positioning it favorably compared to alternative approaches.

Within alternative approaches, early work coordinated autonomous underwater vehicles (AUVs) formations for ocean sampling using virtual body frameworks with field demonstrations in open coastal waters [9], and extensions to dynamic environments improved data collection via formation control, typically assuming reliable communication and relatively open spaces [12]. To address disturbances, sliding-mode strategies compensated for currents and modeling uncertainties [10], and synchronized path-following maintained formation geometry under strong flow, albeit with substantial communication requirements [19]. Despite additional demonstrations in survey-oriented multi-AUV deployments [21] and simulated SE(3) coordination using potential fields and virtual structures [33], validation in shallow, confined, obstacle-rich estuarine environments remains limited.

Traditional formation control strategies—including leader–follower schemes [4,7] combined with model predictive control (MPC) [26]—provide structured approaches for maintaining geometric formations. However, leader–follower methods can amplify disturbances and tracking errors throughout the formation [25], particularly when communication delays or environmental forces affect the leader's path, while MPC requires accurate models and reliable, low-latency feedback—conditions difficult to guarantee in dynamic, current-driven aquatic environments [20]. Recently, deep reinforcement learning has emerged as a data-driven alternative, showing promise in leader–follower formation control [14,28], collision avoidance, target tracking, and trajectory following [14–18,30]. However, these methods remain largely confined to simulation environments, exhibit sensitivity to model mismatch, and demand extensive computational training, making real-world deployment in dynamic aquatic settings challenging.

In this context, an artificial potential field (specifically, navigation function-based) formation controller [24] provides specific advantages: (i) allows the formation to flow along the river without fighting the current, (ii) leverages sensor position feedback to provide a robust control formulation, (iii) ensures collision avoidance between sensor platforms, and (iv) is frugal in terms of inter-vehicle communication needs. Yet this formulation lacks certain necessary features for this problem: (a) ensuring avoidance of collisions with environmental workspace boundaries, (b) accounting for vehicle nonholonomic constraints and turn radius limitations. Additionally, application-specific challenges absent from earlier implementations [24] must be addressed: (a) communication latency in field deployment, (b) positional uncertainty given typical GPS accuracy, and (c) disturbances from ambient environmental dynamics.

This paper thus offers several methodological innovations that extend and streamline the application of navigation function-based formation control for marine robots in field deployments. Specifically, the *contributions* of the reported work are in extending the navigation function-based formation control methodology to (i) allow for *differentiable* potential function approximations, (ii) include workspace boundary and internal *obstacle avoidance*, and (iii) introduce a receding horizon navigation layer to alleviate implementation problems related to *constrained vehicle kinematics*. These methodological improvements are tested in numerical simulations and validated experimentally in field trials with a fleet of micro-ASVs, Jaiabots (manufacturer's simulator results are omitted for brevity).

2   Problem Statement

The objective is to design a provably convergent decentralized feedback control law that enables a group of underactuated ASVs to fall into a formation specified by desired fixed relative positions. The ASVs must follow collision-free paths within a constrained workspace, while allowing their formation to shift under the potential influence of water current. Ignoring lateral drift (sway), we assume Dubins' car kinematics for an ASV:

$$\dot{x} = V \cos\theta \qquad\qquad \dot{y} = V \sin\theta \qquad\qquad \dot{\theta} = \omega \qquad (1)$$

where (x, y) denotes the vehicle's position, θ its heading, $0 < V < V_{\max}$ is its surge speed, and $|\omega| < \Omega$ is its bounded turning rate. We consider a group of $n > 1$ such vehicles and denote $\boldsymbol{p} \in \mathbb{R}^{2n}$ the stack vector of the (x, y) positions of all n ASVs. That is, if $\boldsymbol{p}_i \triangleq (x_i, y_i)^\mathsf{T}$ for $i = 1, \ldots, n$, then $\boldsymbol{p} = (x_1, y_1, \ldots, x_n, y_n)^\mathsf{T}$.

The desired formation is defined in terms of a set of desired relative position vectors $\boldsymbol{c}_{ij}$ with $i, j \in \{1, \ldots, n\}$, so that when $\boldsymbol{p}_i - \boldsymbol{p}_j = \boldsymbol{c}_{ij}$ for all $\boldsymbol{c}_{ij}$ specified, then the formation is assumed to have been achieved. The orientation θ_i of each ASV while in formation is immaterial. Thus if $\boldsymbol{q}_{ij} \triangleq \boldsymbol{p}_i - \boldsymbol{p}_j$ and we denote $\boldsymbol{q}$ the stack vector of those $\boldsymbol{q}_{ij}$ differences that have an associated $\boldsymbol{c}_{ij}$ formation control specification, then the formation control objective is achieved when $\|\boldsymbol{q} - \boldsymbol{c}\| = 0$, where c is the stack vector of relative position specifications, arranged in the order of their associated q_{ij} differences in q. Collision avoidance between ASVs is ensured if $\|q_{ij}(t)\| > 0$ for all $i, j \in \{1, \ldots, n\}$ and all time $t > 0$. For the sake of simplicity, let us assume that the bounded workspace in which the ASVs should operate is outlined by an ellipsoid $\mathcal{E}$. Then the problem requirement for workspace invariance (e.g., all ASVs being within the bounded workspace) is satisfied if $\inf_{s \in \mathcal{E}} \|p_i(t) - s\| > 0$ for all $i \in \{1, \ldots, n\}$ and $t > 0$.

In this context, the control objective is to construct control laws $V_i(p)$ and $\omega_i(p)$ for each ASV i, which *guarantee* that $\lim_{t \to \infty} \|q - c\| = 0$ while $\|q_{ij}\|$ and $\inf_{s \in \mathcal{E}} \|p_i - s\|$ is always bounded away from zero. Ideally, the solution can be implemented in a way that each ASV does not require position information from all other ASVs (the full p vector).

From an implementation standpoint, it would also be desirable to account for the fact that real ASVs cannot move arbitrarily slow, meaning that practically, $0 < v_{\min} < v < v_{\max}$.

3   Technical Approach

We build a multi-agent navigation function to bring the group of ASVs into formation for measurement collection while ensuring collision avoidance between ASVs and with environmental boundaries. Challenges we address include:

(a) The fact that the original methodology [24] does not provide for environmental boundary collision avoidance.
(b) That the resulting potential field control law does not account for limited turning rate constraints.
(c) That the nonsmooth control law can sometimes result in chattering.

Motivation for overcoming limitation (c) originates from consideration of the expected effect of chattering on rudder actuators and the non-negligible time constants in their control loops.

To realize objective (a), we introduce n additional *virtual* ASVs, which are uncontrollable and assumed moving along the workspace boundary, extending the group's position vector p to dimension $4n$. These virtual ASVs need not participate in the formation specification c unless constraining the formation relative to the boundary is desired. We associate each virtual ASV $i + n$ with real ASV i and position it at the point of minimum distance between ASV i and the boundary, naturally extending the collision avoidance behavior of the multi-agent potential field [24] to include workspace boundaries.

We define the scalar *goal function* for the formation:

$$\gamma(q) \triangleq \|q - c\|^2$$

which vanishes only when the ASVs are in their desired relative configuration, and the scalar *obstacle function*:

$$\beta(d(q)) \triangleq \log\left(\mu - a\exp\left(-(-r + d + d^2)^2\right)\right) \tag{2}$$

where a, r, and $\mu > 2$ are scalar coefficients, and $d = d(\boldsymbol{q})$ is the minimum distance between any pair of ASVs and between each ASV and its virtual pair:

$$d(\boldsymbol{q}) \triangleq \min \left\{ \min_{\substack{i \in \{1,\ldots,n\} \\ j \in \{1,\ldots,n\} \cup \{i+n\}}} \|\boldsymbol{q}_{ij}\| \right\} \tag{3}$$

Coefficient μ regulates the magnitude of function β, and together with parameter $\zeta > 0$, which determines the slope of β at distance d_0 where $\beta = 0$, is used to define r as [24]:

$$r = d_0^2 + d_0 - \frac{\zeta}{2(\mu - 1)(2d_0 + 1)}$$

Now given r, coefficient a is determined as

$$a = (\mu - 1) \exp\left((d_0^2 + d_0 - r)^2\right)$$

The multi-agent potential function is then constructed as

$$\hat{\varphi}(\boldsymbol{q}) = \frac{\gamma(\boldsymbol{q})}{\beta(\boldsymbol{q})^{1/\kappa}} \tag{4}$$

where $\kappa > 0$ is a scalar tuning parameter which, when chosen sufficiently large, ensures that (4) admits a unique minimum at the desired configuration, and has all other critical points in the free space [24] as saddles. With an appropriate choice of κ, the theoretical convergence and collision avoidance guarantees for (4) ensure that ASVs moving along the negated gradient of φ converge to the desired formation while following collision-free paths.

To avoid generalized gradients due to the nonsmooth nature of φ (since $d(\boldsymbol{q})$ is not everywhere differentiable) and achieve control objective (c), we *conservatively approximate* the minimum distance function (3) with the differentiable function

$$\mathfrak{d}(\boldsymbol{q}) \triangleq -\frac{1}{\rho} \log \left(\sum_{\substack{i \in \{1,\ldots,n\} \\ j \in \{1,\ldots,n\} \cup \{i+n\}}} \exp(-\rho \|\boldsymbol{q}_{ij}\|) \right) \tag{5}$$

which provides tighter under-approximations as $\rho > 0$ increases [27]. The conservative nature $\mathfrak{d}(\boldsymbol{q}) \leq d(\boldsymbol{q})$ preserves the collision avoidance properties of $\hat{\varphi}$ when in (2), d is replaced by $\mathfrak{d}$:

$$\varphi(\boldsymbol{q}) = \frac{\gamma(\boldsymbol{q})}{\beta(\mathfrak{d}(\boldsymbol{q}))^{1/\kappa}} \tag{6}$$

Of the three control objectives, ASV kinematic constraints are arguably the most challenging. Since the final vehicle orientation is of no particular significance, a look-ahead input-output feedback linearization approach [3] appears promising. However, with minimum turning radius constraints, this method will not always produce feasible solutions. Additionally, there are also *minimum speed* constraints since thruster input rates below a threshold produce no actuator motion. Such actuation constraints define bounded, finite-time reachable regions for the vehicle (Fig. 2).

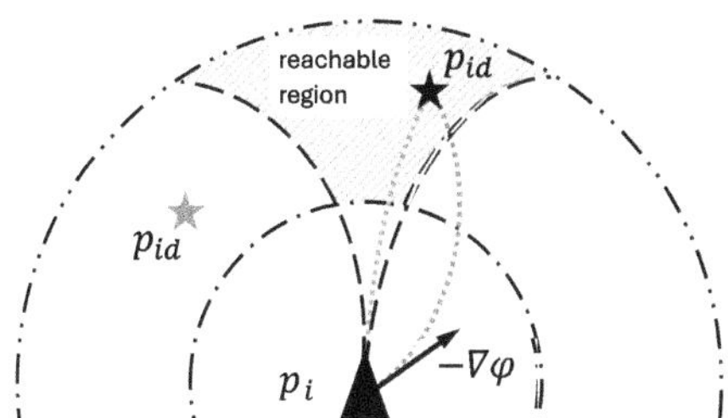

Fig. 2. A receding horizon strategy can mark waypoints (stars) along potential field flow lines. Some waypoints are reachable (black star) while others may not be (red star). The reachable region (shaded) accounts for minimum turning radius (black long-dash lines), minimum surge speed (black long-dash-dot line), and maximum surge speed (black long-dash-double-dot line). A feasible path (green dotted line) can lead to a reachable waypoint even when the integral line producing it (red dotted line) is kinematically infeasible. (Color figure online)

Figure 2 illustrates the effect of these speed constraints, highlighting the reachable (shaded) region for the ASV over a hypothesized time interval. The minimum turning radius restricts reachable points between two arcs (black long-dash lines), while the minimum surge speed introduces a "buffer zone" between the reachable region and the ASV. Maximum surge speed sets an upper distance limit. The red dotted line outside the shaded region represents a path the potential field could prescribe if the vehicle were unconstrained. A receding horizon approach can alleviate some of these challenges, because it can identify feasible motions to waypoints computed along kinematically infeasible potential field flow lines. Some waypoints may still be unreachable (red star in Fig. 2), but the feedback nature of the navigation function controller effectively compensates for those tracking errors since these waypoints are recomputed on the fly. Combining potential field-based formation control with receding horizon approaches has been explored in unmanned aerial vehicle (UAV) formations and validated *in simulation* [29,31].

Here, flow lines of the potential field are followed for a predetermined prediction horizon (integration time interval) to define a local waypoint for the ASV. The vehicle implements feasible control inputs to reach this waypoint, which updates before the next control cycle based on the ASV's new position. While the ASV will not follow the flow line exactly, this approach provides flexibility for local maneuvering and, with a relatively short prediction horizon and high control frequency, does not compromise safety. While infeasible waypoints can be generated since the field does not respect turning rate kinematic constraints and actuator deadzones, the majority of them appear within the GPS capture radius of the ASV, where the vehicle is assumed to have converged. In the case of infeasible waypoints outside the GPS capture radius, an appropriate choice of control horizon can still ensure the reduction of the navigation function within each such cycle, practically guaranteeing convergence [22].

The look-ahead receding horizon approach also alleviates the minimum surge speed constraint: small gradient vectors prescribing surge speeds below actuator dead zone thresholds would cause stalling, whereas a sufficiently long prediction horizon along even small gradients defines waypoints that keep the vehicle in motion. In cases of poor tuning or rapid formation dynamics, if a waypoint falls outside the reachable region, the ASV maneuvers to the closest feasible point on the boundary of its reachable region, with the waypoint updating at the next control cycle to correct the trajectory.

The local waypoint $\boldsymbol{p}_{id}[k]$ for ASV i at position $\boldsymbol{p}_i[k]$ is computed as

$$\boldsymbol{p}_{id}[k] = \boldsymbol{p}_i[k] - \int_0^T \nabla_{\boldsymbol{p}_i}\varphi\big(\boldsymbol{q}(\tau)\big)\mathrm{d}\tau \tag{7}$$

where T denotes the prediction horizon. What also motivates the approach of (7) is the Jaiabot communication architecture: each robot links only to the land-based hub, necessitating centralized fleet control with multiplexed communication. This introduces latencies of several seconds between pose measurement and command reception, during which the robot's state changes. The rationale behind (7) is to transfer some of the control authority back to the vehicle, and provide more robust steering that accounts for these implementation constraints.

Due to the receding horizon waypoint control law (7), φ may occasionally increase temporarily in the course of the prediction horizon as robots transition between intermediate waypoints, given that robots utilize their local low-level controllers rather than always moving along the negated gradient. While not observed in our Sect. 4.2 implementation, this remains possible. Still, it has been shown theoretically [22] that such intermittent increases do not pose stability issues provided these intermediate potential field-based waypoints are followed.

4   Validation

This section presents numerical (Subsect. 4.1) and experimental (Subsect. 4.2) results validating the proposed ASV formation control strategy. Numerical simulations model robots as single integrators to verify the geometric properties of the navigation function, while field trials with four Jaiabots at Lake Allure, PA evaluate performance under realistic kinematics, environmental boundaries, GPS uncertainty, communication latency, and disturbances. More details on hardware specifications and communication architecture are found elsewhere [2,8,23].

4.1   Numerical Simulations

Initial validation tests were performed in *Mathematica* by directly integrating the negated gradient of the navigation function (6), i.e., $-\nabla\varphi$, assuming unconstrained point-robot kinematics $\dot{p} = u$. These simulations isolate the geometric properties of the proposed navigation function and verify that it provides valid steering references prior to introducing vehicle kinematic constraints. Under these assumptions, the waypoint-based prediction strategy of (7) is not required.

Navigation-function parameters were set to $a = \exp(1) = 2.7183$, $\mu = 2$, $r = -1$, $\kappa = 1$, with minimum-distance approximation parameter $\rho = 10$. The desired formation consists of four agents arranged in a horizontal line with $10\,\text{m}$ spacing ($d_{12} = d_{23} = d_{34} = 10\,\text{m}$), with the final formation location determined by initial conditions. This line formation is motivated by estuarine salinity sensing, where vehicles are deployed across the river width to capture spatial salinity variations; sensing and sensor-fusion aspects are outside the scope of this paper.

Figure 3 summarizes representative simulation results. Figures 3(a) and 3(b) show the trajectories and inter-agent distances obtained using the proposed navigation-function-based controller. The results demonstrate convergence to the desired formation while maintaining collision-free motion.

For comparison, a baseline Jacobi-coordinate formation shape controller for marine surface vehicles [32] is also simulated. This method is chosen as being the "default" for marine vehicle formation control in support of a cooperative estimation task [32], which is ultimately the reason why the method reported was developed. The Jacobi-coordinate formation controller regulates formation geometry using relative inter-agent distances, but it lacks explicit inter-robot collision and boundary avoidance. As shown in Figs. 3(c) and 3(d), the baseline may converge faster due to shortest-path behavior, but it cannot prevent inter-agent distances from reaching zero.

4.2   Field Experiments

The field trials follow the setup of Sect. 4.1, with a line formation oriented $45°$ relative to the east–west axis, robots spaced $10\,\text{m}$ apart, and identical navigation function parameters. Experiments were conducted at Lake Allure, PA (Fig. 4(b)). A buoy served as a static obstacle, and the east lake boundary was modeled as an ellipse to represent shoreline constraints. Both obstacles and boundaries were implemented as virtual agents, with boundary interactions defined by the closest boundary point to each robot.

The initial configuration (Fig. 4(a)) was specified via waypoints with a $3\,\text{m}$ capture radius, introducing position uncertainty in the realized starting locations. Unlike point-robot simulations, real robots have orientation and kinematic constraints, preventing direct negated-gradient execution. We therefore employ the receding-horizon waypoint strategy of Sect. 3. Additionally, Jaiabot actuation limits impose $0 < v_{\min} < v < v_{\max}$, motivating the use of (7), which may still result in brief stops.

Figures 5(a)–5(d) show representative snapshots, illustrating the progression of trajectory evolution. Initial and final configurations (Figs. 5(a), 5(d)) confirm successful formation convergence. The robots maintained formation while drifting due to wind, demonstrating free-floating operation. Collision avoidance behavior is evident as robots separate during close encounters (Figs. 5(b)–5(c)).

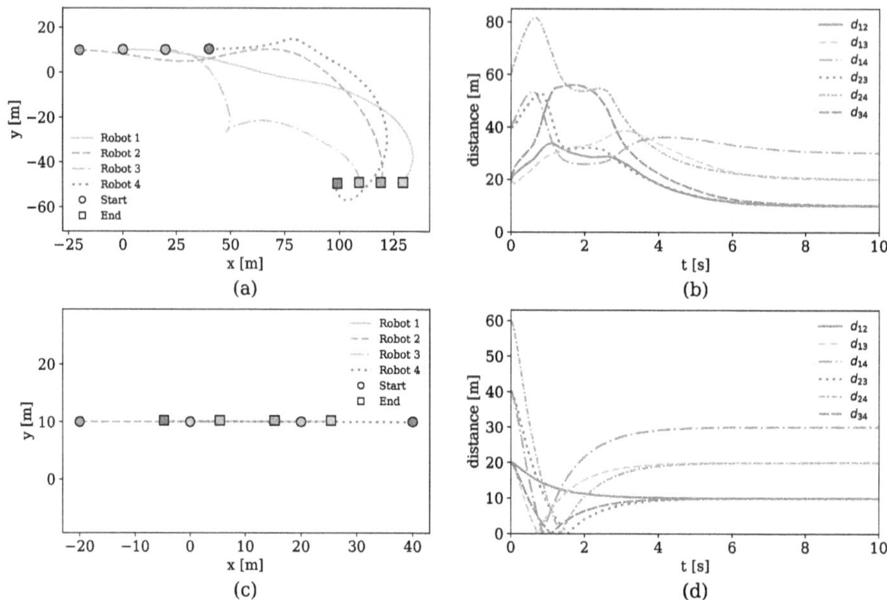

Fig. 3. Point-robot numerical simulation results: trajectories and inter-robot distances for the proposed controller (a–b) and the baseline Jacobi-coordinate formation shape controller [32] (c–d).

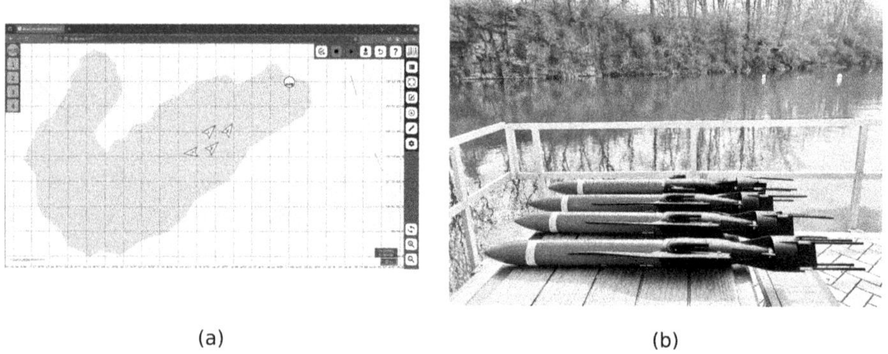

(a)   (b)

Fig. 4. (a) Initial configuration displayed on the Jaiabot web interface at Lake Allure, PA, and (b) Four Jaiabots prior to formation deployment at Lake Allure, PA.

Quantitative results in Fig. 6 confirm collision-free convergence, with positive minimum distances and decreasing $\varphi(\boldsymbol{q})$.

Several differences between simulation and field behavior arise from unmodeled hydrodynamics, GPS uncertainty, and actuator characteristics. These effects alter trajectories and final formation locations by design, as station-keeping against flow is undesirable for river deployments. Additionally, Jaiabots rest

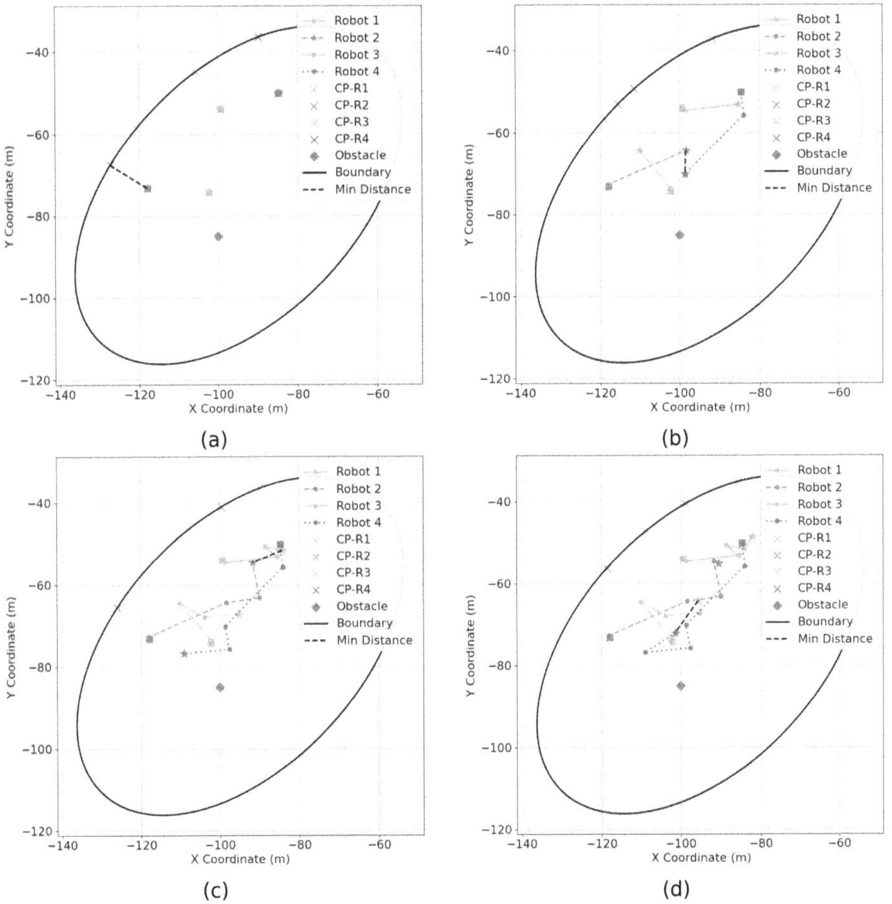

Fig. 5. Experimental validation in real-world lake environment at representative moments, showing robot paths, workspace boundaries, and virtual point-obstacle: (a) initial configuration, (b) Robots 2 and 4 in close proximity, (c) Robots 1 and 2 in close proximity, and (d) final configuration. Cross markers indicate closest boundary points for each robot.

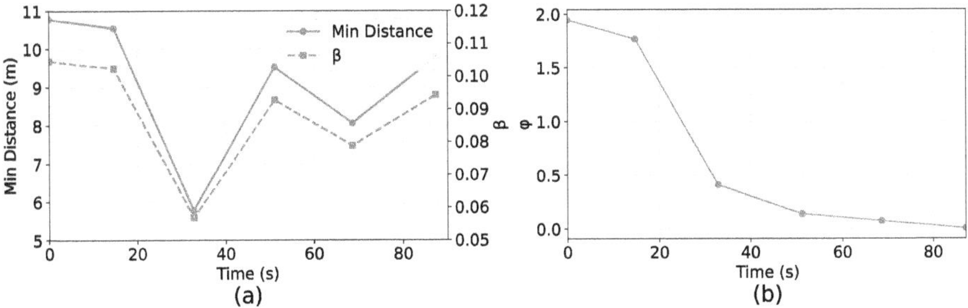

Fig. 6. (a) Minimum distance and obstacle function over time, and (b) multi-agent potential function over time during field tests.

nearly vertically when stopped, introducing intermittent orientation variation and discrepancies between true and estimated positions used for control.

5   Conclusions

This work demonstrates provable coordination of Jaiabot ASVs into specific geometric patterns without tying robots to pre-specified spatial locations—a useful capability for deployments in strong-current environments. The approach employs multi-robot artificial potential field methodology with formal guarantees of collision avoidance and formation convergence. While rooted in earlier work, this paper reports technical extensions overcoming switching control challenges and enabling incorporation of static environmental constraints and obstacles. The scheme is validated numerically and in field tests using a novel receding horizon waypoint methodology compatible with most ASV helm controllers, circumventing low-level actuator implementation challenges. Future work includes control architecture decentralization once hub-to-fleet broadcasting and vehicle-to-vehicle communication are established, and testing in open water estuaries where strong current effects can be fully assessed.

Acknowledgments. Funding for this project is provided through the USGS Next Generation Water Observing System (NGWOS) Research and Development program under award #G23AC00149-00. The authors would like to thank Matthew C. Gyves of the U.S. Geological Survey for his valuable support and coordination throughout the project. Any use of trade, firm, or product names is for descriptive purposes only and does not imply endorsement by the U.S. Government.

Disclosure of Interests. The authors have no competing interests to declare.

References

1. Akyildiz, I.F., Pompili, D., Melodia, T.: Underwater acoustic sensor networks: research challenges. Ad Hoc Netw. **3**(3), 257–279 (2005)
2. Baxevani, K., Bandara, C.T., Tanner, H.G.: Autonomous surface vehicle swarms with bifurcation-driven multi-behavioral dynamics. In: OCEANS 2025 - Great Lakes, pp. 1–7 (2025)
3. Baxevani, K., Otto, G.E., Trembanis, A.C., Tanner, H.G.: Optimal ASV path following for improved marine survey data quality. In: OCEANS 2023 Limerick, pp. 6861–6866 (2023)
4. Beard, R.W., McLain, T.W., Nelson, D.B., Kingston, D., Johanson, D.: Coordination variables, coordination functions, and cooperative timing missions. AIAA J. Guidance Control Dyn. **25**(1), 43–52 (2002)
5. Bresciani, M., Zacchini, L., Topini, A., Ridolfi, A., Costanzi, R.: Automatic target recognition and geolocalisation of natural gas seeps using an autonomous underwater vehicle. Control. Eng. Pract. **145**, 105864 (2024)
6. Budd, M., et al.: Probabilistic planning for AUV data harvesting from smart underwater sensor networks. In: 2022 IEEE/RSJ International Conference on Intelligent Robots and Systems (IROS), pp. 12051–12057 (2022)

7. Desai, J.P., Ostrowski, J.P., Kumar, V.: Modeling and control of formations of nonholonomic mobile robots. IEEE Trans. Robot. Autom. **17**(6), 905–908 (2001)
8. Faros, I., Tanner, H.G.: System identification and adaptive input estimation on the jaiabot micro autonomous underwater vehicle. arXiv preprint arXiv:2504.02005 (2025)
9. Fiorelli, E., Leonard, N.E., Bhatta, P., Paley, D.A., Bachmayer, R., Fratantoni, D.M.: Multi-AUV control and adaptive sampling in monterey bay. IEEE J. Oceanic Eng. **31**(4), 935–948 (2006)
10. Gao, Z., Guo, G.: Fixed-time sliding mode formation control of AUVs based on a disturbance observer. IEEE/CAA J. Automatica Sinica **7**(2), 539–545 (2020)
11. Joshi, B., Bandara, C., Poulakakis, I., Tanner, H.G., Rekleitis, I.: Hybrid visual inertial odometry for robust underwater estimation. In: OCEANS 2023 - MTS/IEEE U.S. Gulf Coast, pp. 1–7 (2023)
12. Leonard, N., Paley, D., Davis, R., Fratantoni, D., Lekien, F., Zhang, F.: Coordinated control of an underwater glider fleet in an adaptive ocean sampling field experiment in Monterey Bay. J. Field Robot. **27**, 718–740 (2010)
13. Leonard, N.E., Paley, D.A., Lekien, F., Sepulchre, R., Fratantoni, D.M., Davis, R.E.: Collective motion, sensor networks, and ocean sampling. Proc. IEEE **95**(1), 48–74 (2007)
14. Liang, Z., Qu, X., Zhang, Z., Chen, C.: Three-dimensional path-following control of an autonomous underwater vehicle based on deep reinforcement learning. Pol. Marit. Res. **29**(4), 36–44 (2022)
15. Martinsen, A.B., Lekkas, A.M.: Straight-path following for underactuated marine vessels using deep reinforcement learning. IFAC-PapersOnLine **51**(29), 329–334 (2018), 11th IFAC Conference on Control Applications in Marine Systems, Robotics, and Vehicles CAMS 2018
16. Martinsen, A.B., Lekkas, A.M., Gros, S.: Reinforcement learning-based NMPC for tracking control of ASVs: theory and experiments. Control. Eng. Pract. **120**, 105024 (2022)
17. Masmitja, I., et al.: Dynamic robotic tracking of underwater targets using reinforcement learning. Sci. Robot. **8**(80), eade7811 (2023)
18. Meyer, E., Heiberg, A., Rasheed, A., San, O.: Colreg-compliant collision avoidance for unmanned surface vehicle using deep reinforcement learning. IEEE Access **8**, 165344–165364 (2020)
19. Qu, X., Liang, X., Hou, Y., Li, Y., Zhang, R.: Finite-time sideslip observer-based synchronized path-following control of multiple unmanned underwater vehicles. Ocean Eng. **217**, 107941 (2020)
20. Shen, C., Shi, Y.: Distributed implementation of nonlinear model predictive control for AUV trajectory tracking. Automatica **115**, 108863 (2020)
21. Smith, R.N., Chao, Y., Li, P., Caron, D.A.: Persistent ocean monitoring with underwater gliders: Adapting sampling resolution. J. Field Robot. **28**(5), 714–741 (2011)
22. Tanner, H.G.: Relaxed stability conditions for switched systems with dwell time. Asian J. Control **16**(2), 313–320 (2014)
23. Tanner, H.G., Bandara, C.T., Gyves, M.C.: Partial system identification and sensor fusion with the jaiabot micro autonomous underwater vehicle. In: 2024 32nd Mediterranean Conference on Control and Automation (MED), pp. 167–172 (2024)
24. Tanner, H.G., Boddu, A.: Multiagent navigation functions revisited. IEEE Trans. Robot. **28**(6), 1346–1359 (2012)
25. Tanner, H.G., Pappas, G.J., Kumar, V.: Leader-to-formation stability. IEEE Trans. Robot. Autom. **20**(3), 433–455 (2004)

26. Tsourdos, A., White, B.A., Shanmugavel, M.: Cooperative Path Planning of Unmanned Aerial Vehicles. Wiley (2010)
27. Valbuena Reyes, L.A., Tanner, H.G.: Flocking, formation control, and path following for a group of mobile robots. IEEE Trans. Control Syst. Technol. **23**(4), 1268–1282 (2015)
28. Wang, S., Ma, F., Yan, X., Wu, P., Liu, Y.: Adaptive and extendable control of unmanned surface vehicle formations using distributed deep reinforcement learning. Appl. Ocean Res. **110**, 102590 (2021)
29. Wang, X., Yadav, V., Balakrishnan, S.N.: Cooperative UAV formation flying with obstacle/collision avoidance. IEEE Trans. Control Syst. Technol. **15**(4), 672–679 (2007)
30. Woo, J., Yu, C., Kim, N.: Deep reinforcement learning-based controller for path following of an unmanned surface vehicle. Ocean Eng. **183**, 155–166 (2019)
31. Yadav, I., Tanner, H.G.: Exact decentralized receding horizon planning for multiple aerial vehicles. In: Proceedings of the IEEE Conference on Decision and Control, pp. 5747–5752 (2021)
32. Zhang, F., Leonard, N.E.: Cooperative filters and control for cooperative exploration. IEEE Trans. Autom. Control **55**(3), 650–663 (2010)
33. Zhen, Q., Wan, L., Li, Y., Jiang, D.: Formation control of a multi-AUVs system based on virtual structure and artificial potential field on se(3). Ocean Eng. **253**, 111148 (2022)

Mitigating Latency and Partitioning Through Size Regulation in Blockchain-Enabled Robot Swarms

Raina Zakir$^{(\boxtimes)}$, Marco Dorigo , and Volker Strobel$^{(\boxtimes)}$

IRIDIA, Université Libre de Bruxelles, Brussels, Belgium
{raina.zakir,volker.strobel}@ulb.be, mdorigo@ulb.ac.be

Abstract. Blockchain technology has recently been integrated into robot swarms, providing the benefits of secure decentralized coordination and increased resilience against malicious agents. The security of blockchain technology relies on the consensus protocol, which ensures data consistency across the network. In robot swarms, however, changing network topologies and communication constraints can cause severe network partitioning. When such partitions occur, block production may be delayed or even halted, hindering the dissemination of information required for time-sensitive applications. In this work, we address the issue of delayed block production through adaptive swarm size control. We provide the first proof of concept for open swarms that self-regulate their swarm size during operation, based on acceptable block production delays. Our simulation results demonstrate that adaptive swarm size regulation effectively reduces latency, enabling the swarm to adapt its block production rate to acceptable task execution delays.

1 Introduction

Robot swarms are decentralized systems, typically composed of a large number of autonomous robots that coordinate to perform tasks [5,6]. Within such systems, self-organized collective behavior emerges from local interactions among the robots themselves and with their surrounding environment. The decentralized nature of robot swarms facilitates parallel task execution, which can provide fault tolerance against individual failures. However, studies have shown that robot redundancy and parallelization are not sufficient to achieve system robustness against misbehaving robots [29,30].

Recent research indicates that blockchain technology can improve the Byzantine fault tolerance of robot swarms by effectively identifying and neutralizing the actions of Byzantine robots (those whose behavior differs from their intended function). For instance, Strobel et al. [28] demonstrated the potential of blockchain-enabled robot swarms (using large swarms of up to 120 simulated robots) to maintain consensus in the presence of Byzantine agents through a collective sensing problem. Moroncelli et al. [15] showed that a blockchain-secured robot swarm can perform Simultaneous Localization and Mapping (SLAM) in

R. Groß et al. (Eds.): ANTS 2026, LNCS 16515, pp. 175–188, 2026.
https://doi.org/10.1007/978-3-032-26123-6_14

unknown environments while remaining resilient to Byzantine robots. Van Calck et al. [34] further presented a blockchain-based information market, in which robots trade data and penalize Byzantine behavior in a foraging scenario. Zhao et al. [41] proposed a generic framework that leverages the programmability of smart contracts to achieve consensus within a robot swarm in the presence of Byzantine robots, and illustrated its application in a foraging scenario. In these works, the blockchain is maintained collectively by the robots, with each robot functioning as a blockchain node in the decentralized network with its own version of the blockchain (see Sect. 2 for fundamentals of blockchain technology).

A blockchain consensus algorithm enables the swarm to reach an agreement on the validity of transactions and to add new blocks to the chain accordingly. Even though several consensus algorithms have been proposed over the years [17, 35, 36], most studies on blockchain-enabled robot swarms have adopted Proof-of-Authority (PoA) due to its lightweight design and computational efficiency [9, 19, 21, 28, 41]. Given the infancy of blockchain-enabled robot swarms, hardly any research has addressed issues of the underlying consensus protocol, in particular, the issue of delays in block production when using PoA. Recently, Simionato et al. [27] presented a study examining the security of blockchain-enabled robot swarms under network partitioning and proposed a framework for improving blockchain data consistency and enhancing the reliability of swarm coordination. This framework incorporates trigger rules (detection of delayed block production) and panic behaviors (temporarily increasing the robots' communication range) to reduce blockchain inconsistencies and unavailability in sparse networks. While temporarily increasing the communication range can be effective, it has limitations in real-world applications. For example, a panic behavior that switches the communication range from local (e.g., using Bluetooth) to more global (e.g., using Wi-Fi) may lead to high energy consumption and requires suitable robot hardware.

As an alternative, we propose introducing heterogeneity into the swarm by adding *relay robots*—lightweight and inexpensive blockchain nodes that enhance communication within the network. These relay nodes observe the environment and generate meaningful data, but do not produce blockchain blocks, as their purpose is to help facilitate data propagation and connectivity between otherwise sparse robots or network partitions. Relay robots can feature relatively larger, but still local communication ranges compared to block producers (called sealers in PoA, see Sect. 2), ensuring that transactions, messages, and blockchain updates continue to propagate steadily throughout the swarm even when direct links between sealers are unavailable. Depending on the application, relay robots can be integrated into the swarm in various ways, such as ground-based robots, aerial drones, or even stationary modules capable of maintaining robust communication links across the operational area.

In this work, we show that regulating swarm size through the addition or removal of ground-based relay robots enables the tuning of block production time according to application requirements. In general, swarm size regulation enables the adoption of different collective strategies based on the estimated group size, which may depend on factors such as speed, risk, or task complexity [10,13,14]. Although several studies have addressed group size regulation [2,8,18], in all these works, group size is typically assumed to be known a priori, disregarding problems that can occur during swarm operation, such as malfunctioning and malicious robots.

Swarm-size regulation also supports the scalability principle of swarm robotics by enabling the swarm to autonomously adjust its size based on system performance or task demands. In swarm robotics, scalability refers to the ability of decentralized controllers to operate effectively across different swarm sizes and adapt dynamically to changes caused by failures, malicious robots, or environmental factors. However, current blockchain-enabled swarm robotics implementations lack such adaptive scalability mechanisms.

To address this, we demonstrate adaptive swarm-size regulation and thus provide the first proof of concept of *open swarms* [30,34] where robots can join or leave the system (as opposed to traditional closed swarms, where the number of robots remains fixed). We implement and analyze the performance of our swarm using the ARGoS robot swarm simulator [24], demonstrating how relay robots can mitigate delays in block production of the robots' blockchains.

2 Blockchain Fundamentals

Blockchain technology enables peer-to-peer networks to reach consensus on shared data without requiring trust among participating nodes [1,16]. The blockchain is a decentralized ledger composed of sequentially linked blocks, beginning with a common genesis block. Each block records data generated by nodes called *transactions* and includes a cryptographic hash referencing its predecessor. By leveraging blockchain technology, tamper-proof algorithms can be executed in a distributed manner by the use of *smart contracts*. Robot nodes exchange information via blockchain transactions and can establish system-wide rules encoded within these smart contracts, enabling the distributed control and coordination of swarm behavior.

Using the Proof-of-Authority (PoA) consensus protocol [31], a designated set of N nodes, known as *sealers*, create new blocks at fixed intervals. After proposing a block, a sealer must wait for at least $\lfloor \frac{N}{2} \rfloor + 1$ subsequent blocks before producing another block. When multiple sealers generate blocks simultaneously (but potentially in different partitions), conflicting versions of the blockchain may arise due to differences in transactions or their ordering, resulting in what are known as *forks*. To resolve such conflicts, nodes agree on the chain with the highest difficulty: a difficulty of 2 is assigned to blocks produced by the preferred sealer (for each block, a preferred sealer is selected in a round-robin manner) and a difficulty of 1 to those produced by non-preferred sealers. Any attempt to modify an existing block in a blockchain invalidates all subsequent blocks (and, therefore, reduces the chain's overall difficulty), ensuring data integrity and tamper resistance.

Another characteristic of PoA is the minimum time required between consecutive blocks, known as the *block period*, which we set to a default of 15 s, following previous studies [21,27,28]. Setting the block time involves a trade-off: shorter block times enable real-time coordination but increase the risk of forks, causing temporary inconsistencies. Setting a minimum block period of 15 s ensures that the frequency of block production does not become excessively high, which would otherwise lead to greater communication, computation, and data storage costs, as well as to a higher rate of blockchain forks. The time elapsed between the creation of two successive blocks is referred to as the *block production time*, and the difference between the block production time and the block period defines the *block production delay*. In blockchain-enabled robot swarms, the block production time frequently exceeds the block period, as, due to the sparse connectivity and changing network topology of a robot swarm, a suitable block sealer is often temporarily unavailable.

One of the main challenges of integrating blockchain technology into a robot swarm is the constantly changing network topology of a swarm [7]. Blockchain technology was originally designed for networks of stationary nodes; however, in a swarm of robots, the nodes are mobile. Due to their limited communication range, robots can propose and validate new blocks only with nearby peers. Local communication, combined with potential malfunctions or breakdowns inherent to mobile systems, can result in disconnections among robots within the swarm. Such disconnections may disrupt blockchain operations by affecting block production, causing latency or even a complete halt in block generation—especially in PoA systems, where maintaining communication among sealers is essential for consensus. In fact, PoA relies on a small, fixed set of sealers that must exchange messages to propose, validate, and finalize blocks. Weak network links between sealers can prevent these messages from being transmitted efficiently, ultimately causing the chain to stall.

According to the CAP theorem, a distributed system experiencing a network partition (P) can only guarantee either consistency (C) or availability (A) [3]. When network connectivity is sparse, PoA is designed to prioritize consistency over availability, choosing to delay block production. While this delayed block production avoids excessive forks, it introduces latency that can impact task execution. Latency in block production is particularly critical in applications where robots rely on timely blockchain updates to coordinate actions or make decisions, rather than merely using the blockchain for data logging. Most previous approaches have relied on smart contracts to handle Byzantine faults in robot swarms [28,41]. However, these approaches fail to maintain availability under severe network partitioning—a situation that can also be exploited by an attacker to gain control of a relative majority of robots in the swarm.

An alternative approach to resolving network partitions and latency is to utilize distributed ledger technology frameworks that maintain transaction processing and consensus even during network partitions, such as DAG-based architectures [23,26] that allow concurrent transaction validation and asynchronous consensus without relying on sequential block production. For instance, the DAG-based distributed ledger framework IOTA includes a smart contract layer that operates on subnetworks, allowing contracts to execute independently while committing their results to the main chain, supporting both partition tolerance and parallel execution [12,25]. Similarly, SwarmDAG begins with multiple isolated blockchain views that emerge during network partitions and later merges them into a single DAG ledger once connectivity is restored, thereby preserving all locally collected data [22,33]. Avalanche, on the other hand, relies on a probabilistic consensus mechanism over a DAG of transactions, where nodes continuously sample and vote among peers until consensus emerges, achieving high throughput and rapid finality without central coordination [32]. Finally, Blockgraph is a DAG-based blockchain architecture specifically designed for mobile ad-hoc networks where consensus, block management, and group management are integrated, enabling nodes to maintain local progress even under intermittent connectivity and to synchronize seamlessly once communication resumes [4,37]. While DAG-based solutions improve partition tolerance, they face several issues, such as excessive data retention, which is unsuitable for resource-constrained robot swarms, and a lack of the inherent transaction ordering and immutability offered by linear blockchains. Overall, these distributed ledger technology frameworks prioritize partition tolerance over consistency and only offer limited support for smart contracts.

3   Experimental Methods

Scenario. In all experiments, we use a blockchain-enabled robot swarm in which the number of sealer robots is fixed during an experiment. The swarm's objective is to perform a task while maintaining a user-defined block production time of x seconds. As a test case, we adopt a collective sensing scenario widely used in previous studies [11,28–30,38,40]. The swarm aims to reach consensus on the percentage of white tiles in an environment covered with black and white tiles, where white tiles are grouped into two clusters and cover 25% of the arena. Each robot, equipped with a ground sensor, performs a random walk to estimate the proportion of white tiles. Sealer robots then broadcast their estimates as blockchain transactions within their 10 cm communication range. Relay robots, with an extended communication range of 50 cm, facilitate wider data exchange. A smart contract aggregates all estimate submissions and computes the collective estimate, as implemented in [28].

Setup. Our experiments are conducted in the ARGoS robot swarm simulator [24], using Pi-puck robots. The arena is a square environment of $3.61\,\mathrm{m}^2$, surrounded by walls (see Fig. 1A and supplementary video). Unless otherwise stated, each simulation experiment runs for 2,500 timesteps (1 timestep is equivalent to 1 s) and we perform 10 repetitions per setting. Each robot in the swarm functions as a blockchain node and only sealer robots are block producers in Toychain, a lightweight blockchain framework specifically designed for swarm robotics experiments [20]. Toychain implements the Proof-of-Authority consensus protocol, simulating Ethereum's Clique [31]. Its clock synchronization ensures

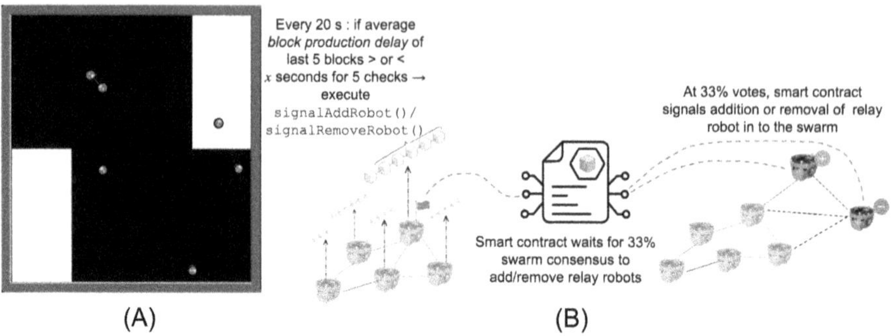

Fig. 1. Experimental setup. (A) Arena setup where Pi-puck robots estimate the proportion of white tiles via random walk. Each robot acts as a blockchain node using Toychain [20] to aggregate estimates. Communication ranges: 10 cm (sealers), 50 cm (relay robots). (B) Schematic of the size-regulation mechanism where robots adjust swarm size via smart contracts to maintain target block times and improve information flow in the collective sensing task in (A).

temporal consistency between the ARGoS simulation clock and blockchain operations. By using Toychain to simulate our blockchain, we obtain results in simulation faster than real-time while ensuring the results are transferable to real-world applications using the mature and established Ethereum framework because of the close modeling of Toychain's PoA after Ethereum's PoA [1]. All the code used for this study is open-source and available as supplementary material [39].

Initialization. The robots are randomly distributed in the arena at the start of each experimental run. The robots perform a random walk as in the previous blockchain-enabled swarm robotics studies [27–30]. To study the regulation of block production time in our system, we conduct three experiments.

In the first experiment, the required block production time x is set to be less than 60 s. We initialize a base swarm of six sealers forming a sparse network and observe how many relay robots are added over time to reduce the block production time under 60 s.

In the second experiment, we study a swarm of 30 robots (out of which 6 are sealers and 24 are relay robots). We examine how many robots need to be removed from the system to attain a block production time of more than 60 s and whether the swarm converges to a stable size.

In the third experiment, both addition and removal mechanisms are enabled to study how the swarm dynamically maintains the block production time between 50 s and 60 s. In all three experiments, there are six sealers in the swarm that cannot be removed.

As a baseline, we also conduct experiments with fixed swarm sizes of 6 and 24 robots (all of them being sealers) to demonstrate how increasing the swarm size improves block production times and, consequently, task execution times. At the beginning of each run, a new genesis block is created and distributed to all robots. This block contains the smart contract and the list of authorized sealers participating in the Proof-of-Authority consensus protocol.

Peering. In order to synchronize the blocks and transactions, the robot nodes use range-and-bearing sensors to identify peers within the communication range and use the Transmission Control Protocol (TCP) implemented in Toychain. Using TCP, robots share their node address with other robots within their communication range to establish peer-to-peer connections. Once robots are no longer within communication range, the corresponding connection is terminated.

Robot Controller. Every 20 s, each robot uses the most recent five blocks of its blockchain version and calculates the average time gap between the blocks to assess the block production time. In the first experiment, if the block production time exceeds 60 s after five consecutive readings, a robot sends a blockchain transaction invoking the `signalAddRobot()` function in the smart contract, signaling that an additional robot should be added to improve performance (see Fig. 1B). If 33% of the swarm flags for addition, a relay robot is introduced in the swarm. Conversely, in the second experiment, if blocks are being produced too quickly—i.e., the block production delay is less than 60 s— a robot invokes the `signalRemoveRobot()` function in the smart contract to remove a robot and avoid unnecessary resource usage. If 33% of the swarm flags for removal, the most recently added relay robot is removed from the swarm. In the third experiment, the robot swarm has to maintain the block production time between 50 and 60 s by adding or removing relay robots.

Performance Metrics. We evaluate the performance of our swarm size regulation behavior using the following metrics: (i) the *average block production time* is calculated by recording the rolling average of the last five blocks for each run, and then averaging these rolling averages across all runs of an experiment (ii) the *average number of robots* in the swarm over time (both sealers and relay robots) for all the runs of an experiment; (iii) the average *swarm estimate* computed as the mean of the average estimates from all runs at each time step, representing the collective sensing performance of the swarm; and (iv) the variance and standard deviation of swarm estimates across the runs in each experiment to assess how block production impacts the collective sensing of the environment.

4   Results

Before presenting the performance of our proposed swarm size modulation approach, which uses relay robots to mitigate block production delays, we first analyze how sparse connectivity affects swarm behavior. Figure 2A compares a swarm of 6 sealer robots (in green) and a swarm of 24 sealer robots (in blue) as they evolve over time toward the target mean value of the environment. The plots show both the average swarm estimate and its variability across experimental runs. A key observation is that the larger swarm converges and stabilizes

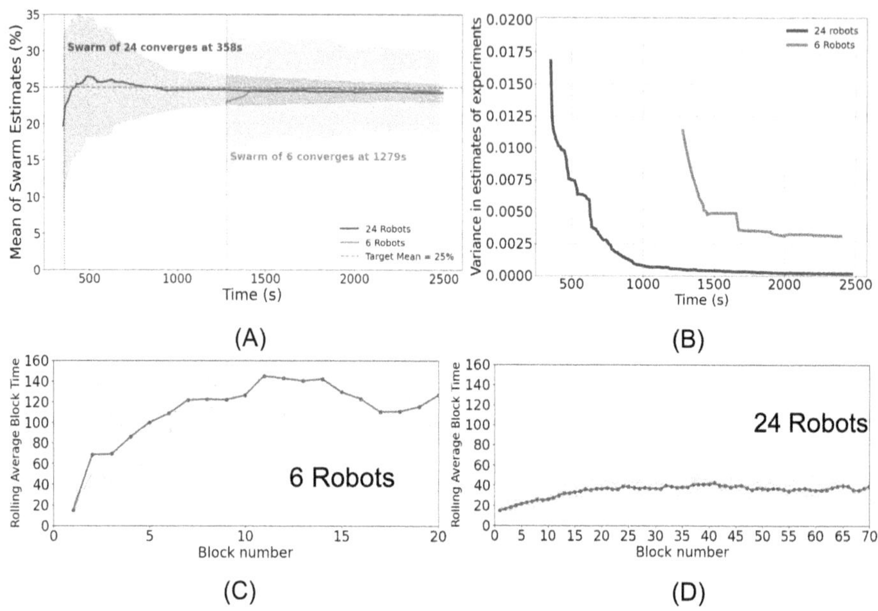

Fig. 2. Baseline experiments. (A) Average swarm estimates (indicating overall sensing performance) and standard deviation (showing variability across runs) over time for two experiments: a sparse swarm of 6 robots and a larger swarm of 24 robots. Vertical lines mark convergence times where the swarm's average remains within ±5% points of the 25% actual value. The average swarm estimate is computed from the experimental set at the time when all robots in each run have converged to a mean value. (B) The variance between the runs for 6 robots and a larger swarm of 24 robots. (C–D) Rolling average of block production times for the 6-robot swarm (C) and the 24-robot swarm (D). Each gray line represents one run, while the purple line shows the mean across all runs. (Color figure online)

around the target mean of 25% (within ±5% points) much earlier (at approximately 358 s) compared to the smaller swarm, which stabilizes at approximately 1,279 s. This delay can be attributed to the block production time (evident in Figs. 2C and 2D), which slows the propagation of estimates in the sparser swarm. Even after convergence, the smaller swarm exhibits notably higher variability, as shown by the variance plot in Fig. 2B.

To counter the high block production times observed in sparser swarms (Figs. 2C and 2D), we implement the robot controller presented in Sect. 2 (illustrated in Fig. 1B), which monitors block production time and dynamically adjusts swarm size through the addition of relay robots. Assuming an application requirement of maintaining block production time under 60 s, Fig. 3A shows how the production time gradually decreases and stabilizes under this threshold as relay robots are introduced in a swarm of six sealers over time. As shown in Fig. 3B, on average, 23 robots, including 17 relay robots, are required for the block production time to fall below 60 s. Notably, the stabilized block production

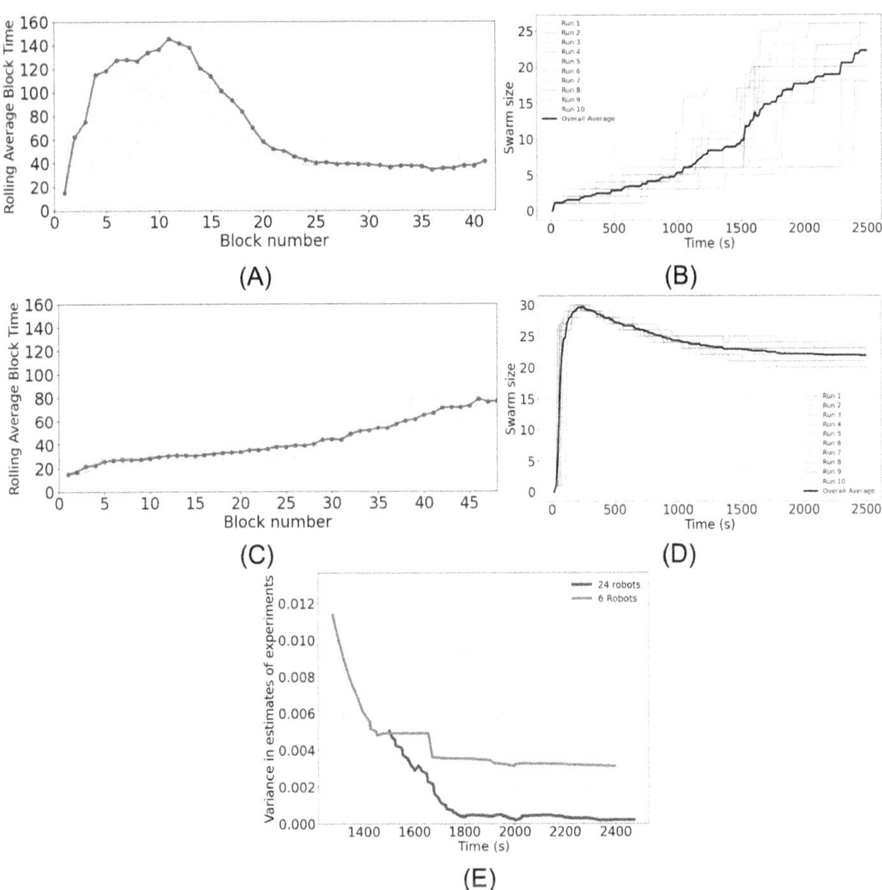

Fig. 3. Experiments 1 and 2. (A, C) Rolling average of block production times of last five blocks (y-axis) as the blocks are produced (x-axis) across multiple runs for two experimental conditions: swarms regulated to keep block time under 60 s (A) and above 60 s (C). In (A), each run begins with six sealer robots, while in (C) the initial swarm includes 30 robots (6 sealers and 24 relay robots). Gray lines represent individual runs, and the purple line shows the average of their rolling averages. (B, D) Evolution of swarm size (y-axis) over time (x-axis) for each run (orange) and the average swarm size (black) corresponding to the experiments in (A) and (C) obtained from the smart contract. (E) Comparison of variance in swarm estimate (y-axis) over time (x-axis) across individual runs between two cases: a fixed swarm of 6 sealers (experiments in Fig. 2C) and a dynamic swarm where robots can join to maintain block production under 60 s (as in A). (Color figure online)

time is not exactly 60 s but approximately 40 s (Fig. 3A). This occurs because robots compute a rolling average of the last five consecutive blocks every 20 s; when older blocks exhibit longer delays, the system tends to add more relay robots than strictly necessary. Additionally, sparser swarms tend to trigger the

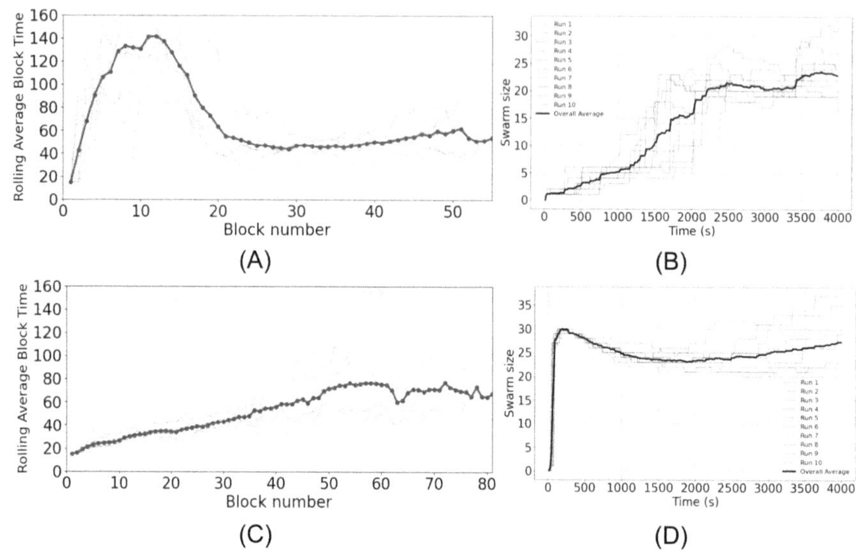

Fig. 4. Experiment 3. (A, C) Rolling average block production times of the last five blocks (y-axis) as the blocks are produced (x-axis) across multiple runs for two experimental setups where swarm size is regulated to maintain block times within 50–60 s. In (A), each run starts with six sealer robots, while in (C), the initial swarm includes 30 robots (6 sealers and 24 relay robots). Gray lines show individual runs, and the purple line indicates the average of the rolling averages across runs. (B, D) Evolution of swarm size (y-axis) over time (x-axis) for each run (orange) and the average swarm size (black) corresponding to the experiments in (A) and (C) obtained from the smart contract. The experimental runs to plot the figures (A-D) are run for 4,000 timesteps. (Color figure online)

addition of more robots than required, as the transactions that signal robot additions are delayed due to block production delays.

A complementary scenario is shown in Figs. 3C and 3D, where the goal is to increase the block production time beyond 60 s by removing relay robots. Also in this case, the final average delay exceeds the target (approximately 75 s) due to the same averaging effect from previous blocks. The average swarm size also converges to approximately 23 robots (7 relay robots are removed). Figure 3E compares the variance across experimental runs for a fixed swarm of six sealers (green; see Fig. 2B) and an open swarm that begins with six sealers but gradually adds relay robots (blue). The results clearly show that the swarm incorporating relay robots to mitigate block production delays exhibits lower variance—similar to the larger swarm of 24 robots shown in Fig. 2A.

For scenarios requiring precise control of block production delays, consistency must account for delays introduced by block generation. For example, Simionato et al. [27] used the length of blockchain forks as a measure of consistency. If delays exceed a threshold or exhibit high variance, they can cause undesirable slowdowns in task execution. To address this issue, we integrate dynamic swarm size monitoring, which enables the addition or removal of relay robots to maintain delays within a target range. In Figs. 4A and 4C, we set the required block production time between 50 s and 60 s. When the block production time exceeds 60 s, the robots trigger the addition of relay robots; if it falls under 50 s, relay robots are removed. We evaluate this approach in two scenarios: one with a swarm of six sealers and another with a swarm of 30 robots, comprising six sealers and 24 relay robots. In both cases, the block production time stabilizes at approximately 60 s. Figures 4B and 4D (in red) show the swarm size during individual runs, illustrating how it stabilizes while fluctuating in discrete steps to maintain block production within the target range.

5   Discussion and Conclusion

In applications where robots need to change their behavior based on blockchain data—such as voting, coordination, or task execution through smart contracts— timely availability of information across the swarm becomes critical. In this work, we have shown that the availability of such information cannot be guaranteed in sparse networks (resulting from low swarm density or large environments), thus leading to task execution delays.

To address this challenge in blockchain-enabled swarms, we introduced the concept of lightweight relay robots that do not seal blocks but instead enhance network connectivity among sealers while generating meaningful task-related data. Such a heterogeneous swarm, composed of both sealers and relay robots, established the connectivity required for reliable information propagation.

We demonstrated that the addition and removal of robots enables a swarm to balance the trade-off between information propagation speed and cost (in terms of number of robots) in a decentralized manner. Our results, therefore, highlight the ability of blockchain-enabled robot swarms to self-regulate their swarm size, enabling them to reach a target block production delay and data dissemination speed. Through this implementation of swarm-size regulation, we also provided a proof of concept for open swarms.

In future work, we aim to develop a comprehensive framework that accounts for different communication ranges for relay robots, supports integration across physically heterogeneous robots, and provides a mechanism to prevent Byzantine robots from joining the swarm when new members are added.

Acknowledgments. RZ, VS, and MD acknowledge support from the Belgian F.R.S.-FNRS, of which they are a FRIA doctoral researcher, a postdoctoral researcher, and a research director, respectively.

Disclosure of Interests. The authors have no competing interests to declare.

References

1. Buterin, V.: A next-generation smart contract and decentralized application platform. Ethereum Project White Paper (2014). https://ethereum.org/en/whitepaper/
2. Cambier, N., Frémont, V., Ferrante, E.: Group-size regulation in self-organised aggregation through the naming game. In: International Symposium on Swarm Behavior and Bio-Inspired Robotics (SWARM 2017) (2017)
3. Carrara, G.R., Burle, L.M., Medeiros, D.S.V., de Albuquerque, C.V.N., Mattos, D.M.F.: Consistency, availability, and partition tolerance in blockchain: a survey on the consensus mechanism over peer-to-peer networking. Ann. Telecommun. 163–174 (2020). https://doi.org/10.1007/s12243-020-00751-w
4. Cordova, D., Laube, A., Nguyen, T.M.T., Pujolle, G.: Blockgraph: a blockchain for mobile ad hoc networks. In: 4th Cyber Security in Networking Conference (CSNet 2020), pp. 1–8. IEEE (2020)
5. Dorigo, M., Birattari, M., Brambilla, M.: Swarm robotics. Scholarpedia **9**(1), 1463 (2014)
6. Dorigo, M., Theraulaz, G., Trianni, V.: Swarm robotics: past, present and future. Proc. IEEE **109**(7), 1152–1165 (2021)
7. Dorigo, M., Pacheco, A., Reina, A., Strobel, V.: Blockchain technology for mobile multi-robot systems. Nat. Rev. Electr. Eng. **1**(4), 264–274 (2024)
8. Firat, Z., Ferrante, E., Zakir, R., Prasetyo, J., Tuci, E.: Group-size regulation in self-organized aggregation in robot swarms. In: Dorigo, M., et al. (eds.) ANTS 2020. LNCS, vol. 12421, pp. 315–323. Springer, Cham (2020). https://doi.org/10.1007/978-3-030-60376-2_26
9. Gupta, H., Strobel, V., Pacheco, A., Ferrante, E., Natalizio, E., Dorigo, M.: Group-level behavioral switch in a robot swarm using blockchain. In: Swarm Intelligence – Proceedings of ANTS 2024 – 14th International Conference. LNCS, vol. 14987, pp. 98–111. Springer (2024)
10. Hamann, H., Reina, A.: Scalability in computing and robotics. IEEE Trans. Comput. **71**(6), 1453–1465 (2022)
11. Kaiser, T.K., Potten, T., Hamann, H.: Evolution of collective decision-making mechanisms for collective perception. In: IEEE Congress on Evolutionary Computation (CEC 2023), pp. 1–8. IEEE (2023)
12. Keramat, F., Peña Queralta, J., Westerlund, T.: Partition-tolerant and Byzantine-tolerant decision making for distributed robotic systems with IOTA and ROS2. IEEE Internet Things J. **10**(14), 12985–12998 (2023)
13. Kuckling, J., Luckey, R., Avrutin, V., Vardy, A., Reina, A., Hamann, H.: Do we run large-scale multi-robot systems on the edge? More evidence for two-phase performance in system size scaling. In: IEEE International Conference on Robotics and Automation (ICRA 2024), pp. 4562–4568. IEEE (2024)
14. Mondada, F., Bonani, M., Guignard, A., Magnenat, S., Studer, C., Floreano, D.: Superlinear physical performances in a SWARM-BOT. In: European Conference on Artificial Life, pp. 282–291. Springer (2005)
15. Moroncelli, A., Pacheco, A., Strobel, V., Lajoie, P.Y., Dorigo, M., Reina, A.: Byzantine fault detection in swarm-SLAM using blockchain and geometric constraints. In: Swarm Intelligence – Proceedings of ANTS 2024 – 14th International Conference. LNCS, vol. 14987, pp. 42–56. Springer (2024)
16. Nakamoto, S.: Bitcoin: a peer-to-peer electronic cash system (2008). https://bitcoin.org/bitcoin.pdf. Accessed 9 Nov 2023

17. Nguyen, G.T., Kim, K.: A survey about consensus algorithms used in blockchain. J. Inf. Process. Syst. **14**(1), 101–128 (2018)
18. O'Grady, R., Pinciroli, C., Christensen, A.L., Dorigo, M.: Supervised group size regulation in a heterogeneous robotic swarm. In: 9th Conference on Autonomous Robot systems and Competitions (ROBOTICA 2009), pp. 113–119 (2009)
19. Pacheco, A., Strobel, V., Reina, A., Dorigo, M.: Real-time coordination of a foraging robot swarm using blockchain smart contracts. In: Swarm Intelligence – Proceedings of ANTS 2022 – 13th International Conference. LNCS, vol. 13491, pp. 196–208. Springer (2022)
20. Pacheco, A., Denis, U., Zakir, R., Strobel, V., Reina, A., Dorigo, M.: Toychain: a simple blockchain for research in swarm robotics (2024). https://arxiv.org/abs/2407.06630
21. Pacheco, A., Strobel, V., Dorigo, M.: A blockchain-controlled physical robot swarm communicating via an ad-hoc network. In: Dorigo, M., et al. (eds.) ANTS 2020. LNCS, vol. 12421, pp. 3–15. Springer, Cham (2020). https://doi.org/10.1007/978-3-030-60376-2_1
22. Peña Queralta, J., Keramat, F., Salimi, S., Fu, L., Yu, X., Westerlund, T.: Blockchain and emerging distributed ledger technologies for decentralized multi-robot systems. Curr. Robot. Rep. **4**, 43–54 (2023)
23. Pervez, H., Muneeb, M., Irfan, M.U., Haq, I.U.: A comparative analysis of DAG-based blockchain architectures. In: 12th International Conference on Open Source Systems and Technologies (ICOSST 2018), pp. 27–34. IEEE (2018)
24. Pinciroli, C., et al.: ARGoS: a modular, parallel, multi-engine simulator for multi-robot systems. Swarm Intell. **6**(4), 271–295 (2012)
25. Salimpour, S., Keramat, F., Queralta, J.P.N., Westerlund, T.: Decentralized vision-based Byzantine agent detection in multi-robot systems with IOTA smart contracts. In: Foundations and Practice of Security: 15th International Symposium, FPS 2022, Revised Selected Papers, pp. 322–337. Springer (2023)
26. Santos De Campos, M.G., Chanel, C.P., Chauffaut, C., Lacan, J.: Towards a blockchain-based multi-UAV surveillance system. Front. Robot. AI **8**, 557692 (2021)
27. Simionato, G., Strobel, V., Cimino, M.G.C.A., Dorigo, M.: Analysis and mitigation of inconsistencies in blockchain-enabled robot swarms. In: IEEE/RSJ International Conference on Intelligent Robots and Systems (IROS 2025), pp. 166–172. IEEE Press (2025)
28. Strobel, V., Pacheco, A., Dorigo, M.: Robot swarms neutralize harmful Byzantine robots using a blockchain-based token economy. Sci. Robot. **8**(79), eabm4636 (2023)
29. Strobel, V., Castelló Ferrer, E., Dorigo, M.: Managing Byzantine robots via blockchain technology in a swarm robotics collective decision making scenario. In: Proceedings of the 17th International Conference on Autonomous Agents and MultiAgent Systems (AAMAS 2018), pp. 541–549 (2018)
30. Strobel, V., Castelló Ferrer, E., Dorigo, M.: Blockchain technology secures robot swarms: a comparison of consensus protocols and their resilience to Byzantine robots. Front. Robot. AI **7**, 54 (2020)
31. Szilágyi, P.: EIP-225: Clique proof-of-authority consensus protocol, Ethereum Improvement Proposals, No. 225 (2017). Available: https://eips.ethereum.org/EIPS/eip-225
32. Team Rocket, Yin, M., Sekniqi, K., Van Renesse, R., Sirer, E.: Scalable and probabilistic leaderless BFT consensus through metastability (2019). https://arxiv.org/abs/1906.08936

33. Tran, J.A., Ramachandran, G.S., Shah, P.M., Danilov, C.B., Santiago, R.A., Krishnamachari, B.: SwarmDAG: a partition tolerant distributed ledger protocol for swarm robotics. Ledger **4** (2019)
34. Van Calck, L., Pacheco, A., Strobel, V., Dorigo, M., Reina, A.: A blockchain-based information market to incentivise cooperation in swarms of self-interested robots. Sci. Rep. **13**, 20417 (2023)
35. Xiao, Y., Zhang, N., Lou, W., Hou, Y.T.: A survey of distributed consensus protocols for blockchain networks. IEEE Commun. Surv. Tutor. **22**(2), 1432–1465 (2020)
36. Xu, J., Wang, C., Jia, X.: A survey of blockchain consensus protocols. ACM Comput. Surv. **55**, 1–35 (2023)
37. Yang, C., Li, X., Yu, Y., Wang, Z.: Basing diversified services of complex IIoT applications on scalable block graph platform. IEEE Access **7**, 22966–22975 (2019)
38. Zakir, R., Dorigo, M., Reina, A.: Robot swarms break decision deadlocks in collective perception through cross-inhibition. In: Swarm Intelligence – Proceedings of ANTS 2022 – 13th International Conference. LNCS, vol. 13491, pp. 209–221. Springer (2022)
39. Zakir, R.: Supplementary material for paper 'Mitigating Latency and Partitioning through Size Regulation in Blockchain-Enabled Robot Swarms' (2025). Github Repository: https://github.com/rainazakir/size_regulation
40. Zakir, R., Dorigo, M., Reina, A.: Miscommunication between robots can improve group accuracy in best-of-n decision-making. In: IEEE/RSJ International Conference on Intelligent Robots and Systems (IROS 2024), pp. 9014–9021. IEEE Press (2024)
41. Zhao, H., et al.: A generic framework for Byzantine-tolerant consensus achievement in robot swarms. In: IEEE/RSJ International Conference on Intelligent Robots and Systems (IROS 2023), pp. 8839–8846. IEEE Press (2023)

Multi-Agent Reinforcement Learning of a Fault-Robust Controller in an Intralogistics Robot Swarm

Youssef Alboraei[1(✉)] [iD], Sabine Hauert[1] [iD], and Suet Lee[2] [iD]

[1] Bristol Robotics Laboratory, University of Bristol, Bristol, UK
youssef.alboraei@bristol.ac.uk
[2] University of Konstanz, Konstanz, Germany

Abstract. Robot faults are inevitable in swarm systems deployed in real-world applications, yet most fault mitigation approaches rely on explicit fault detection pipelines and hand-crafted recovery responses. We propose a novel Multi-Agent Reinforcement Learning (MARL) approach that learns a fault-robust controller by reactively mapping local state metrics directly to a set of predefined mitigation actions. We train a shared-parameter, recurrent MARL policy using Centralised Training with Decentralised Execution (CTDE) in a box transport task. In our approach, the same policy is used by both faulty and non-faulty robots, and in different fault conditions. Our learned policy demonstrates robustness to faults compared to a non-learning baseline, and scales to increasing numbers of faults not encountered during training. Results demonstrate that MARL provides a practical approach to robustness against faults in robot swarms, without relying on explicit fault detection.

1 Introduction

Multi-robot systems are increasingly deployed in domains where robustness and scalability are essential. These characteristics are usually attributed to robot swarms; they leverage decentralised control, local sensing, and simple interaction rules to yield emergent, system-level behaviours [8,44]. Yet, robustness to faults is not guaranteed by decentralisation and redundancy: mobility, actuation, sensing, or communication degradations in even a small fraction of robots can cascade to reduce throughput or stall tasks if not mitigated effectively [4,40,44].

Conventional fault-tolerance pipelines emphasise explicit detection and diagnosis followed by recovery. While effective in narrow settings, this approach can be brittle under partial observability, environmental variability, and scale [6]. Learning-based control offers an alternative where fault mitigation behaviours are selected dynamically based on local sensing [6,9,21]. Within this scope, MARL approaches are particularly effective for swarm systems because they handle partial observability, adapt to environmental uncertainties, and scale to large numbers of robots through autonomous learning mechanisms [5].

We present a novel application of MARL in learning a robust controller capable of handling different types and severities of faults. The controller learns

R. Groß et al. (Eds.): ANTS 2026, LNCS 16515, pp. 189–203, 2026.
https://doi.org/10.1007/978-3-032-26123-6_15

a direct mapping from local state metrics to a set of predefined mitigation actions, eliminating the need for fault detection or diagnosis steps. A single policy is trained to handle multiple fault types, and the same policy runs on all robots, faulty or non-faulty, enabling non-faulty robots to contribute to mitigation. We select Multi-Agent Proximal Policy Optimisation (MAPPO) for its demonstrated performance and sample efficiency in cooperative settings [42]. A centralised critic leverages shared information during training, while identical recurrent policies execute using only local observations. We evaluate on a box-transport task representative of intralogistics, where a swarm retrieves and delivers items to a goal region under mobility and manipulation faults.

2 Related Work

Approaches to fault tolerance in robot swarms can typically be separated into three sub-components: fault detection [9,11,22,36], diagnosis [28,30], and recovery [16,20,29]. In fault detection, emphasis is on exogenous pipelines by analysing externally observed data streams either through own local sensing or other swarm individuals [11]. Methods of fault detection have incorporated diverse paradigms including immune-inspired mechanisms that model biological immune responses [3,39], data-modeling approaches that learn patterns of nominal (or faulty) behaviours [17,18,22], and blockchain-assisted verification schemes that leverage distributed ledgers for tamper-proof fault records [34,35]. Fault diagnosis aims to characterise the faults once detection has occurred, allowing swarms to distinguish between different fault modes such as sensor failures, actuator faults, or software issues [11]. Recent research emphasises adaptive and online diagnostic systems that can dynamically identify faults in real-time using techniques inspired by biological immune systems, unsupervised learning, and model-based approaches [11,28,30].

In fault recovery, the objective is to restore the robot or swarm to optimal function after fault diagnosis. Common approaches include rule-based self-healing, trial-and-error selection from behavioural archives, local interventions, and simulated recovery actions such as power cycling, sensor/module replacement, or adaptive control strategies [16,29].

Alternative approaches have focused on designing swarm behaviours that inherently tolerate faults, embedding resilience directly into the collective control algorithms rather than relying on explicit detection and recovery mechanisms. Such approaches include: self-healing strategies for pattern formation [2,33]; adaptive control methods [13]; and evolutionary trial-and-error approaches generating archives of diverse behaviours [7].

In contrast, reactive fault mitigation strategies actively intervene when faults are detected. Examples include: immune-inspired methods for energy redistribution [38]; trust-aware mechanisms to isolate faulty robots [10,25]; and predictive maintenance to anticipate degradation [27].

In fault-related contexts, learning-based approaches have shown utility in adaptive fault detection, diagnosis, and recovery, where swarms can autonomously identify anomalies and recover functionality through self-organised strategies [12,14,29,32]. MARL frameworks leverage decentralised actor-critic architectures where agents learn policies based on local observations while critics access global state during training, enabling emergent coordination without explicit communication. Yet, the broader application of MARL within swarm robotics has mainly focused on coordination tasks such as formation control, flocking, and resource allocation rather than fault mitigation [5,31,41]. However, applying MARL to fault mitigation raises challenges: non-stationarity, credit assignment under sparse rewards, and the design of observation and action spaces that expose fault-relevant cues without relying on explicit fault identifiers [6]. CTDE, parameter sharing, and recurrent policies help address partial observability and improve sample efficiency [1,6,26]. On-policy actorcritic algorithms and their multi-agent variants show strong empirical performance in cooperative settings, with stability aids such as entropy regularisation and clipping constraints [42].

MAPPO extends the single-agent PPO algorithm to multi-agent settings through the CTDE paradigm [19,42]. In CTDE frameworks, agents learn decentralised policies based solely on local observations during execution, while critics access global state during training to guide coordinated learning, enabling stable convergence and mitigation of non-stationarity [1,43]. This paradigm has proven effective for swarm robotics applications, enabling scalability to large numbers of agents while maintaining stable learning dynamics and computational efficiency [37,42]. MAPPO has demonstrated success in various swarm coordination tasks, including planetary exploration [37], UAV cooperative trajectory planning [23], path planning for multi-mobile robots [24], and pursuit-avoidance in multi-robot systems [23], making it a promising candidate for fault mitigation where both local decision-making and global coordination are essential.

Despite these advances, the use of MARL to design swarm controllers, which are robust to multiple concurrent fault types, remains underexplored. Most existing work in fault-related learning approaches targets isolated components such as fault detection or recovery. Addressing this gap is especially relevant since MARL offers the potential for swarms to automatically discover mitigation strategies purely from local observations and emergent inter-agent coordination. Recent work explored evolving dynamic mitigation policies via neuroevolution, where both faulty and non-faulty robots successfully adapt their behaviour in response to faults without explicit detection or diagnosis phases [21]. This motivates our approach of learning a single MARL policy that directly maps local observations to fault mitigation across multiple possible mobility and manipulation faults.

3   Method

3.1   Task

We study collaborative single-transport in a $500 \times 500\,\mathrm{cm}$ warehouse with 10 homogeneous omnidirectional mobile robots and 10 boxes (see Fig. 1). Robots and boxes are spawned at random. The goal is to deliver boxes to a drop-off zone on one side of the warehouse in a decentralised manner. Robots execute a default random-walk controller: a random heading is sampled at each timestep to explore; a box is collected upon detection and released once the robot enters the drop-off zone. The scenario mirrors an experimental testbed of similar scale with a swarm of DOTS robots [15]. We use a custom C++ simulator with a Gym interface that allows exchange of observations, actions, and rewards data with the learning algorithm. The simulator advances with a fine internal timestep set to 0.02 s per iteration. The interface groups simulator iterations into one environment step via an iterations-per-step parameter. We set 100 iterations per step and a maximum episode length of 500 environment steps.

3.2 Fault Model

Faults are injected at the start of each episode and persist throughout. We study four types that affect mobility and manipulation, $\mathcal{F} = \{F_1, \ldots, F_4\}$, where:

- *F1* 0% maximum speed
- *F2* 10% maximum speed
- *F3* 50% maximum speed
- *F4* Cannot pick up boxes

These are a representative set of possible faults, most relevant to the task, which correspond to complete immobility, severe (10%) and moderate (50%) velocity caps, and failure to pick up boxes. A fault type is sampled and assigned to a subset of robots; non-faulty robots operate nominally. During training, both the fault type and the number of faulty robots are sampled at random per episode. We cap the number of faulty robots at 3 out of 10 to keep the learning problem manageable within limited compute. The same mitigation policy is applied to all robots regardless of fault status (no explicit fault identifier is provided).

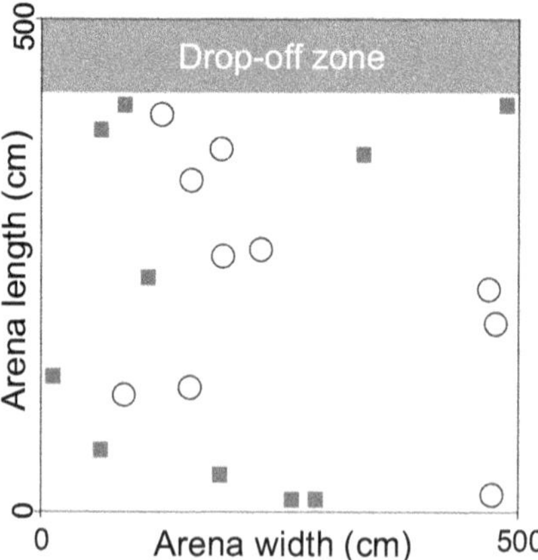

Fig. 1. Visualisation of the simulation environment showing robots as circles, boxes as blue squares, and the drop-off zone as a green strip of 75 cm length. (Color figure online)

3.3 Multi-agent Formulation

We model the system as a partially observable stochastic game (POSG) $G = \langle \mathcal{N}, \mathcal{S}, \{\mathcal{O}_i\}_{i \in \mathcal{N}}, \{\mathcal{A}_i\}_{i \in \mathcal{N}}, P, r, \gamma \rangle$ with homogeneous agents $\mathcal{N} = \{1, \ldots, n\}$, $n = 10$. At time t, agent i receives a local observation $o_i^t \in \mathcal{O}_i$ and selects a mitigation action $a_i^t \in \mathcal{A}_i$. The joint action influences the transition kernel $P(s^{t+1} \mid s^t, \mathbf{a}^t)$. A team-wide shared reward $r(s^t, \mathbf{a}^t)$ promotes throughput, with discount $\gamma \in (0, 1)$. We adopt MAPPO with CTDE and parameter sharing: a centralised critic consumes shared context during training, while at execution each robot runs the same recurrent actor policy using only its local observation history.

3.4 MARL Environment

Observation Spaces: Each agent uses a local observation vector of metrics capturing kinematic state and nearby entities [22]. The per-robot observation lies in $\mathbb{R}^{12}$ and includes:

<table>
<tr><td>

– *M1* Robot linear speed
– *M2* Nearest box distance
– *M3* Nearest robot distance
– *M4* Nearest wall distance
– *M5* Nearest box ID
– *M6* Nearest robot ID

</td><td>

– *M7* Nearest wall ID
– *M8* Robots count in range
– *M9* Boxes count in range
– *M10* Walls count in range
– *M11* Box ID carried by robot
– *M12* Has-box flag

</td></tr>
</table>

IDs are integer-coded, returning -1 when no entity is present; this enables lightweight entity reference without rich perceptual states, while distances and counts provide compact local context.

For centralised training, a shared observation concatenates all local observations with a compact global state enumerating the (x, y) positions of all robots and boxes; for n robots and m boxes, $O_{\text{shared}} \in \mathbb{R}^{12n+2n+2m}$, where $2n + 2m$ encodes global positions and $12n$ stacks the local vectors. This shared array feeds the centralised critic during training; execution remains decentralised.

Action Space: Mitigation is cast as a discrete action set of 13 options per robot, $\mathcal{A}_i = \{A_1, \ldots, A_{13}\}$, which modulate the default random-walk with motion biases, neighbour coordination, or task involvement:

<table>
<tr><td>

– *A1* No action (defer to baseline)
– *A2* Decrease speed 50%
– *A3* Stop moving
– *A4* Bias to nearest robot
– *A5* Bias to nearest box
– *A6* Bias to nearest wall

</td><td>

– *A7* Bias left
– *A8* Bias from nearest robot
– *A9* Bias from nearest box
– *A10* Bias from nearest wall
– *A11* Attract neighbour
– *A12* Repel neighbour
– *A13* Drop box

</td></tr>
</table>

This action set provides local, low-complexity primitives that learning can compose into system-level mitigation behaviours.

Reward Function: The per-step reward encourages efficient, cooperative box delivery while remaining simple enough to avoid over-engineering. It combines a shared box-delivery bonus R_{delivery} granted upon successful delivery of a box, an individual proximity shaping term $R_{\text{proximity}}$ that reduces reward sparsity and aids credit assignment by rewarding actions that move a box closer to the drop-off zone, and a small shared time penalty R_{time} to reward quicker completion; with weights w_{1-3} tuned during training:

$$R(s, a) = w_1\, R_{\text{delivery}} + w_2\, R_{\text{proximity}} - w_3\, R_{\text{time}}$$

3.5 MAPPO Implementation

Each agent's policy $\pi_\theta(a_i^t \mid h_i^t)$ is a multi-layer perceptron (MLP) followed by a gated recurrent unit (GRU) with a categorical head over mitigation actions. The centralised critic $V_\phi(O_{\text{shared}}^t)$ is an MLP mapping the shared observation to a scalar value. We use advantage normalisation (zero-mean, unit-variance scaling of $\hat{A}_t$ within each update to stabilise gradients and reduce sensitivity to reward scale) and gradient clipping (capping the global gradient norm to prevent occasional large updates; particularly important with recurrent policies under partial observability). Actors and critic have separate adaptive moment estimation (Adam) optimisers.

We train with an on-policy actor–critic objective using proximal policy optimisation (PPO)style clipping and generalised advantage estimation (GAE). For trajectories from parallel environments, the policy loss is

$$\mathcal{L}_\pi(\theta) = \mathbb{E}_t\Big[\min\Big(\rho_t(\theta)\, \hat{A}_t,\ \text{clip}(\rho_t(\theta), 1 - \epsilon, 1 + \epsilon)\, \hat{A}_t\Big)\Big] + \beta_{\text{ent}}\, \mathbb{E}_t\big[\mathcal{H}(\pi_\theta(\cdot \mid h^t))\big]$$

with importance ratio $\rho_t(\theta) = \pi_\theta(a^t \mid h^t)/\pi_{\theta_{\text{old}}}(a^t \mid h^t)$. The critic minimises $\mathcal{L}_V(\phi) = \mathbb{E}_t\big[(V_\phi(O_{\text{shared}}^t) - \hat{V}_t)^2\big]$, and the total loss is $\mathcal{L} = \mathcal{L}_\pi + c_V \mathcal{L}_V$. Here, ρ_t reweights samples collected under the behaviour policy; $\min(.)$ with the clipped ratio, $\text{clip}(.)$, defines a conservative surrogate that limits overly large policy updates, with ϵ setting the trust-region width. The entropy term $\beta_{\text{ent}}\mathbb{E}[\mathcal{H}(\pi_\theta(\cdot \mid h^t))]$ promotes exploration; the value loss $\mathcal{L}_V$ fits V_ϕ to boot-strapped targets $\hat{V}_t$ (from returns/GAE); and c_V controls the actorcritic trade-off.

Experience is gathered from E parallel simulator instances for T environment steps per update; an environment step aggregates multiple simulator iterations via the interface. One update (also called a learning iteration) therefore collects $E \times T$ transitions with the behaviour policy $\pi_{\theta_{\text{old}}}$. After each rollout we compute returns and GAE advantages on these $E \times T$ samples, then shuffle into minibatches and optimise for K epochs with Adam; during optimisation $\pi_{\theta_{\text{old}}}$ is held fixed in the PPO ratio, and is replaced by the new π_θ only after the update completes. Key hyperparameters are listed in Table 1.

Action selection is stochastic during training and greedy-with-noise at evaluation. Controlled seeding, observation normalisation, and gradient clipping are enabled throughout. A stochastic random-walk controller serves as the non-learning baseline under identical seeds.

Table 1. MAPPO key training hyperparameters.

Number of parallel simulator instances E	16
Algorithmic steps per rollout segment	500
Total environment steps for training	2×10^8
Optimisation epochs per update K	10
Minibatches per update	1
PPO ratio clipping ϵ	0.2
Policy learning rate (Adam)	7×10^{-4}
Critic learning rate (Adam)	1×10^{-3}
Entropy regularisation weight β_{ent}	0.015
GRU/MLP hidden width	128
Number of MLP layers (per head)	3
Orthogonal init gain	0.01
Frames stacked in observation	6
RNN backprop-through-time length	30

4 Results

4.1 MAPPO Performance

We conducted small-scale hyperparameter sweeps to ensure stable on-policy learning, following the guidelines outlined in [42]. We explored learning rate $\{3\times10^{-4},\ 7\times10^{-4},\ 10^{-3}\}$, entropy coefficient $\{0.005,\ 0.01,\ 0.015,\ 0.02\}$, clip range $\{0.1,\ 0.2,\ 0.3\}$, GRU hidden size $\{64,\ 128\}$, PPO epochs $\{5,\ 10\}$, and minibatches $\{1,\ 2\}$. The final configuration was selected by the median reward over the last 10 logged points, subject to no instability (e.g., diverging value loss or near-zero policy entropy). Training logs were recorded every five learning iterations; with 16 parallel instances and 500 steps per iteration, this yields one log point per 40,000 environment steps. Figure 2 shows the learning curve (average episode reward with a moving average): an initial rapid improvement is followed by a transient mid-training dip, after which performance recovers and trends upward, stabilising in a narrow band towards the end of training. This meets our convergence criterion (no upward trend over the final 10 logged points within the compute budget)[1].

We compare the learned policy against a stochastic random-walk baseline. For each fault type F_1F_4 and every admissible subset of faulty robots, we run 100 trials per condition. We use the same set of 100 random seeds across fault types and number of faults.

Performance is measured by the Normalised Cumulative Box Delivery Score (N-CBDS), the normalised area under the cumulative-deliveries curve:

---

[1] Hardware: Intel Core i7-12700 (8 P-cores, 4 E-cores, 20 threads), 32 GB DDR4-3200 RAM, NVIDIA GeForce RTX 3070 (8 GB); total wall-clock 13 h 20 m 52 s.

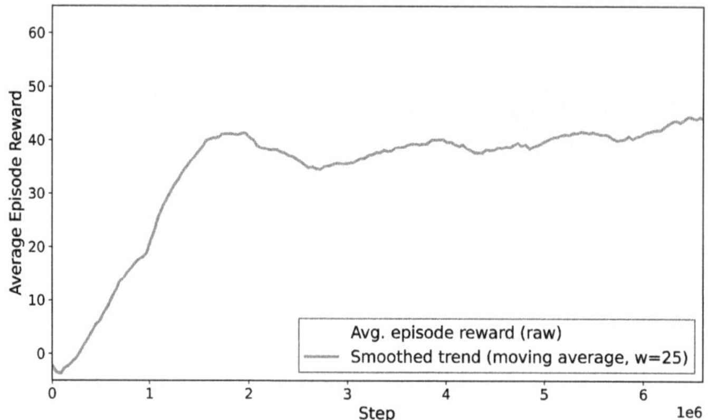

Fig. 2. MAPPO training curve showing average episode reward (dashed grey) with moving average (solid blue). Logged every five learning iterations (40,000 env steps). Fluctuations reflect controller stochasticity and random fault sampling. (Color figure online)

$$\text{N-CBDS} \;=\; \frac{1}{NT}\sum_{t=1}^{T} d(t)$$

where $d(t)$ counts the overall number of boxes delivered by the swarm up to step t, N is the number of boxes, and T is the fixed execution horizon; N-CBDS $\in [0,1]$, and higher values reward delivering earlier. Note that while the per-step reward function introduced in Sect. 3.4 provides a balance between immediate and long-term task progress to support learning, N-CBDS provides a direct performance indicator of the box delivery task for evaluation of the learned policies.

To test whether the policy improves over the baseline, we compare N-CBDS samples using a non-parametric rank test (MannWhitney U); we summarise direction and strength via a signed effect measure we term *mitigation power* as introduced in previous work [21,22]. Figure 3 presents per-condition distributions; Table 2 reports medians and deltas. Gains are strongest when agents are degraded but still operational (F_3, F_4), remain positive (but smaller) for mild slowdowns (F_2), and become fragile under widespread immobility (F_1).

Table 2. Per-fault median N–CBDS with absolute/relative deltas.

Fault condition	Baseline	Policy	Δ	% Δ
No fault	0.511	0.705	+0.194	+38.0%
F1: 0% speed	0.310	0.290	-0.020	-6.5%
F2: 10% speed	0.309	0.345	+0.036	+11.7%
F3: 50% speed	0.343	0.556	+0.213	+62.1%
F4: Cannot pick up	0.314	0.402	+0.088	+28.0%

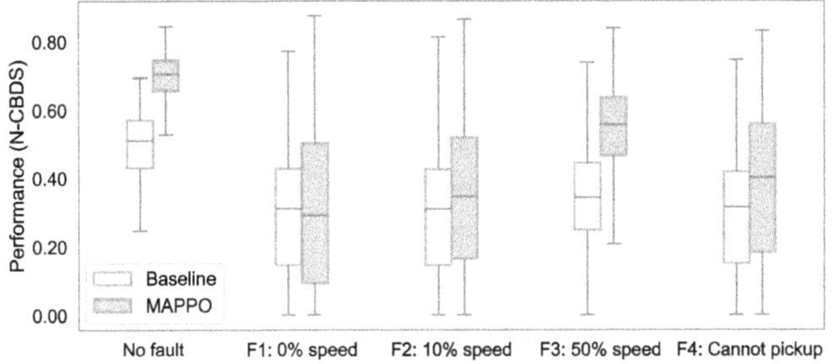

Fig. 3. Execution performance (N-CBDS); boxplots compare non-learning baseline (white) and learned MAPPO policy (green) across fault types. (Color figure online)

To understand how improvement scales with fault count, Fig. 4 shows mitigation power across fault types and numbers of faulty robots. For F_3 (50% speed) effects are strongly positive throughout ($\approx 0.70 - 0.92$), indicating robust coordination under moderate slowdowns. For F_4 (cannot pick up), benefits remain positive but taper as more robots lose manipulation ability (from ≈ 0.78 to ≈ 0.14, approaching neutral at the extreme). For F_2 (10% speed), the effect is positive at low counts, dips around the mid range, and can recover at the extreme, reflecting congestion sensitivity. The most challenging fault is F_1 (0% speed): advantages fade and turn negative once many agents are immobile.

4.2   Robustness Mechanism

We analyse action selection to uncover how robustness is realised. We sample actions selected by a faulty and a non-faulty robot for each trial and average across all trials, for each fault type. An action signature is produced for each

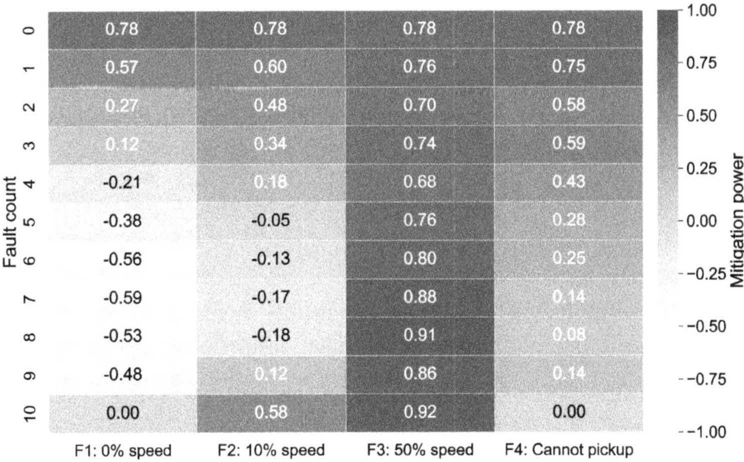

Fig. 4. Mitigation power (signed rank effect from Mann–Whitney U) vs. fault type and number of faulty robots.

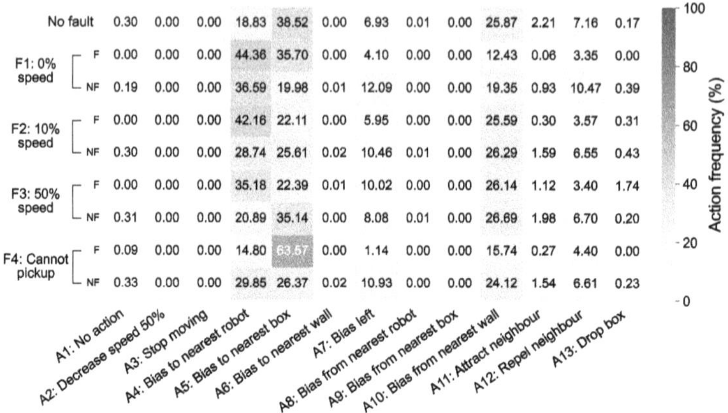

		A1	A2	A3	A4	A5	A6	A7	A8	A9	A10	A11	A12	A13
No fault		0.30	0.00	0.00	18.83	38.52	0.00	6.93	0.01	0.00	25.87	2.21	7.16	0.17
F1: 0% speed	F	0.00	0.00	0.00	44.36	35.70	0.00	4.10	0.00	0.00	12.43	0.06	3.35	0.00
	NF	0.19	0.00	0.00	36.59	19.98	0.01	12.09	0.00	0.00	19.35	0.93	10.47	0.39
F2: 10% speed	F	0.00	0.00	0.00	42.16	22.11	0.00	5.95	0.00	0.00	25.59	0.30	3.57	0.31
	NF	0.30	0.00	0.00	28.74	25.61	0.02	10.46	0.01	0.00	26.29	1.59	6.55	0.43
F3: 50% speed	F	0.00	0.00	0.00	35.18	22.39	0.01	10.02	0.00	0.00	26.14	1.12	3.40	1.74
	NF	0.31	0.00	0.00	20.89	35.14	0.00	8.08	0.01	0.00	26.69	1.98	6.70	0.20
F4: Cannot pickup	F	0.09	0.00	0.00	14.80	63.57	0.00	1.14	0.00	0.00	15.74	0.27	4.40	0.00
	NF	0.33	0.00	0.00	29.85	26.37	0.02	10.93	0.00	0.00	24.12	1.54	6.61	0.23

Fig. 5. Action selections frequencies (%) for the learned policy. Rows show faulty (F) and non-faulty (NF) agents per fault type; columns list actions A1A13. Proximity biases (A4/A5) dominate; wall avoidance (A10) is persistently active; heavy controls (A1A3) are rarely used.

fault type as well as for trials with no faults (Fig. 5). The policy mainly relies on local proximity steering (A4, A5) and wall avoidance (A10). Low-level overrides are rare (A1A3), and explicit neighbour forces (A11, A12) are near negligible.

Under manipulation failure F_4, faulty agents strongly select A5 (e.g., 63.6% vs 26.4%), coupled with the relatively high signature of A4 in non-faulty robots: faulty robots behave as mobile beacons attracting non-faulty robots to boxes. Under speed degradations F_1/F_2, faulty agents increase A4 (e.g., 44.4% for F_1 vs 36.6%), indicating a tendency to seek coordination; however, when many agents are immobile, congestion dominates; matching the mixed/negative mitigation power (Fig. 4).

We further quantify two complementary aspects that link behaviour to the observed outcomes: (i) whether non-faulty agents follow a stable, swarm-level coordination pattern across conditions; and (ii) whether faulty agents adjust their choices in a fault-conditioned manner. For each condition we compute a consistency signature (constructed from non-faulty agents only), i.e., a normalised frequency vector over the 13 actions, $p \in \Delta^{12} \subset \mathbb{R}^{13}$. Let $A = \{a_1, \dots, a_{13}\}$ be the action set and define the probability simplex, $\Delta^{12} := \{ \mathbf{p} \in \mathbb{R}^{13}_{\geq 0} \mid \mathbf{1}^{\top}\mathbf{p} = 1 \}$ A consistency signature is $\mathbf{p} = (p(a_1), \dots, p(a_{13}))^{\top} \in \Delta^{12}$, with $\sum_{a \in A} p(a) = 1$ and $p(a) \geq 0 \ \forall a \in A$.

To test if non-faulty behaviour is essentially unchanged across faults, we compare the non-faulty signature in a faulty condition c with the non-faulty signature in the no-fault condition using cosine similarity:

$$\cos\left(p_c^{\mathrm{NF}}, p_{\varnothing}^{\mathrm{NF}}\right) = \frac{\sum_a p_c^{\mathrm{NF}}(a)\, p_{\varnothing}^{\mathrm{NF}}(a)}{\left\|p_c^{\mathrm{NF}}\right\|_2 \left\|p_{\varnothing}^{\mathrm{NF}}\right\|_2}$$

Cosine focuses on the pattern of usage (scale-invariant on the simplex), which is appropriate for signatures. We observe near-identity with the no-fault pattern for all faults (F1 0.92, F2 0.97, F3 1.00, F4 0.97; 2 d.p.), indicating that non-faulty agents enact a stable proximity-based "flow rule" regardless of faults; consistent with improved performance for the "no fault" baseline in Table 2. In other words, non-faulty agents learn actions which optimise performance beyond baseline control.

To quantify how far faulty agents deviate from their non-faulty teammates within a fault type $f \in F$, we use the symmetric, bounded JensenShannon divergence (JSD, in bits):

$$\mathrm{JSD}\big(p_f^{\mathrm{F}} \,\|\, p_f^{\mathrm{NF}}\big) = \tfrac{1}{2}D_{\mathrm{KL}}\big(p_f^{\mathrm{F}} \,\|\, m_f\big) + \tfrac{1}{2}D_{\mathrm{KL}}\big(p_f^{\mathrm{NF}} \,\|\, m_f\big), \qquad m_f = \tfrac{1}{2}\big(p_f^{\mathrm{F}} + p_f^{\mathrm{NF}}\big)$$

with a small additive smoothing for rare actions. JSD is well-defined for discrete distributions with zeros and yields an interpretable distance in $[0, 1]$. Divergence is modest for speed degradations (F2 0.033, F3 0.041) and larger when capability is lost entirely (F1 0.058, F4 0.100). These values indicate small but systematic, fault-conditioned adjustments to behaviour on top of the global pattern.

Taken together, these statistics support a two-layer mechanism that explains the aggregate results (Table 2) and the mitigation-power map (Fig. 4): (i) a fault-agnostic, swarm-level coordination pattern enacted by non-faulty agents (high cosine similarity 0.92–1.00 to no-fault) that already improves throughput; and (ii) fault-conditioned adjustments by faulty agents whose direction matches task structure (A4 for mobility loss, A5 for pickup loss). Consequently, improvements are stronger where mobility or manipulation remain feasible (F3/F4), smaller but present under mild slowdowns (F2), and fragile when widespread immobility (F1) induces congestion that local proximity cues alone cannot resolve.

5   Conclusion

We introduced a novel MARL approach to learn a reactive and fault-robust controller in robot swarms that maps local observations to predefined mitigation actions, without an explicit fault detection step or scripted recovery. Concretely, a single shared recurrent MAPPO policy is trained under CTDE and executed identically on faulty and non-faulty robots, allowing the swarm to adapt online from purely local cues. We evaluated this in a warehouse box-transport task with 10 robots and 10 boxes, across mobility and manipulation faults. The learned policy consistently outperformed a non-learning baseline. Analysis of action usage reveals a two-layer mitigation mechanism: non-faulty robots enact a stable proximity/wall-avoidance "flow rule", boosting performance even in nominal conditions, while faulty robots make small but systematic, fault-conditioned adjustments. The policy scales beyond training (which capped faults per episode) to higher fault counts at test, and is built from low-level actions that are amenable to sim-to-real transfer on DOTS-scale testbeds. Overall, we successfully demonstrate that a single MARL policy can deliver robust performance in the presence of faults, by leveraging local signals and simple action primitives.

Disclosure of Interests. The authors have no competing interests to declare.

References

1. Amato, C.: An Introduction to Centralized Training for Decentralized Execution in Cooperative Multi-Agent Reinforcement Learning (2024). https://doi.org/10.48550/arXiv.2409.03052, http://arxiv.org/abs/2409.03052, arXiv:2409.03052
2. Arbuckle, D.J., Requicha, A.A.G.: Self-assembly and self-repair of arbitrary shapes by a swarm of reactive robots: algorithms and simulations. Auton. Robot. **28**(2), 197–211 (2010). https://doi.org/10.1007/s10514-009-9162-7
3. Bayar, N., Darmoul, S., Hajri-Gabouj, S., Pierreval, H.: Fault detection, diagnosis and recovery using artificial immune systems: a review. Eng. Appl. Artif. Intell. **46**, 43–57 (2015). https://doi.org/10.1016/j.engappai.2015.08.006, https://www.sciencedirect.com/science/article/pii/S0952197615001840
4. Bjerknes, J.D., Winfield, A.F.T.: On fault tolerance and scalability of swarm robotic systems. In: Martinoli, A., et al (eds.) Distributed Autonomous Robotic Systems, vol. 83, pp. 431–444. Springer, Heidelberg (2013). https://doi.org/10.1007/978-3-642-32723-0_31
5. Blais, M.A., Akhloufi, M.A.: Reinforcement learning for swarm robotics: an overview of applications, algorithms and simulators. Cogn. Robot. **3**, 226–256 (2023). https://doi.org/10.1016/j.cogr.2023.07.004, https://www.sciencedirect.com/science/article/pii/S2667241323000241
6. Bossens, D.M., Ramchurn, S., Tarapore, D.: Resilient robot teams: a review integrating decentralised control, change-detection, and learning. Curr. Robot. Rep. **3**(3), 85–95 (2022). https://doi.org/10.1007/s43154-022-00079-4, http://arxiv.org/abs/2204.10063, arXiv:2204.10063
7. Bossens, D.M., Tarapore, D.: QED: using quality-environment-diversity to evolve resilient robot swarms. IEEE Trans. Evol. Comput. **25**(2), 346–357 (2021). https://doi.org/10.1109/TEVC.2020.3036578, http://arxiv.org/abs/2003.02341, arXiv:2003.02341
8. Brambilla, M., Ferrante, E., Birattari, M., Dorigo, M.: Swarm robotics: a review from the swarm engineering perspective. Swarm Intell. **7**(1), 1–41 (2013). https://doi.org/10.1007/s11721-012-0075-2
9. Carminati, A., Azzalini, D., Vantini, S., Amigoni, F.: A distributed approach for fault detection in swarms of robots. In: Proceedings of the 23rd International Conference on Autonomous Agents and Multiagent Systems, AAMAS 2024, pp. 253–261. International Foundation for Autonomous Agents and Multiagent Systems, Richland, SC (2024). https://dl.acm.org/doi/10.5555/3635637.3662873
10. Cavorsi, M., Akgün, O.E., Yemini, M., Goldsmith, A., Gil, S.: Exploiting Trust for Resilient Hypothesis Testing with Malicious Robots (evolved version) (2023). https://doi.org/10.48550/arXiv.2303.04075, http://arxiv.org/abs/2303.04075, arXiv:2303.04075
11. Graham Miller, O., Gandhi, V.: A survey of modern exogenous fault detection and diagnosis methods for swarm robotics. J. King Saud Univ. Eng. Sci. **33**(1), 43–53 (2021). https://doi.org/10.1016/j.jksues.2019.12.005, https://www.sciencedirect.com/science/article/pii/S1018363919302995

12. Hart, E., Steyven, A.S.W., Paechter, B.: Evolution of a functionally diverse swarm via a novel decentralised quality-diversity algorithm. In: Proceedings of the Genetic and Evolutionary Computation Conference, pp. 101–108 (2018). https://doi.org/10.1145/3205455.3205481, http://arxiv.org/abs/1804.07655, arXiv:1804.07655

13. Hu, J., Turgut, A.E., Lennox, B., Arvin, F.: Robust formation coordination of robot swarms with nonlinear dynamics and unknown disturbances: design and experiments. IEEE Trans. Circuits Syst. II Express Briefs **69**(1), 114–118 (2022). https://doi.org/10.1109/TCSII.2021.3074705, https://ieeexplore.ieee.org/document/9409965

14. Hüttenrauch, M., Šošić, A., Neumann, G.: Deep reinforcement learning for swarm systems. J. Mach. Learn. Res. **20**(54), 1–31 (2019). http://jmlr.org/papers/v20/18-476.html

15. Jones, S., Milner, E., Sooriyabandara, M., Hauert, S.: DOTS: An Open Testbed for Industrial Swarm Robotic Solutions (2022). https://doi.org/10.48550/arXiv.2203.13809, http://arxiv.org/abs/2203.13809, arXiv:2203.13809

16. Khadidos, A., Crowder, R.M., Chappell, P.H.: Exogenous fault detection and recovery for swarm robotics. IFAC-PapersOnLine **48**(3), 2405–2410 (2015). https://doi.org/10.1016/j.ifacol.2015.06.448, https://www.sciencedirect.com/science/article/pii/S2405896315006874

17. Khaldi, B., Harrou, F., Cherif, F., Sun, Y.: Monitoring a robot swarm using a data-driven fault detection approach. Robot. Auton. Syst. **97**, 193–203 (2017). https://doi.org/10.1016/j.robot.2017.06.002, https://www.sciencedirect.com/science/article/pii/S0921889017300854

18. Khaldi, B., Harrou, F., Sun, Y., Cherif, F.: A measurement-based fault detection approach applied to monitor robots swarm. In: 2017 6th International Conference on Systems and Control (ICSC), pp. 21–26 (2017). https://doi.org/10.1109/ICoSC.2017.7958703, https://ieeexplore.ieee.org/document/7958703, iSSN: 2379-0067

19. Kraemer, L., Banerjee, B.: Multi-agent reinforcement learning as a rehearsal for decentralized planning. Neurocomputing **190**, 82–94 (2016). https://aquila.usm.edu/fac_pubs/15314

20. Lee, S., Hauert, S.: A data-driven method to identify fault mitigation strategies in robot swarms. In: International Conference on Swarm Intelligence. Springer, Cham (2024)

21. Lee, S., Hauert, S.: Evolving dynamic fault mitigation strategies in a robot swarm for collective transport. In: García-Sánchez, P., Hart, E., Thomson, S.L. (eds.) Applications of Evolutionary Computation, vol. 15612, pp. 305–322. Springer, Cham (2025). https://doi.org/10.1007/978-3-031-90062-4_19

22. Lee, S., Milner, E., Hauert, S.: A data-driven method for metric extraction to detect faults in robot swarms. IEEE Robot. Autom. Lett. **7**(4), 10746–10753 (2022). https://doi.org/10.1109/LRA.2022.3189789, https://ieeexplore.ieee.org/document/9826412

23. Li, J., Cao, S., Liu, X., Yu, R., Wang, X.: Trans-UTPA: PSO and MADDPG based multi-UAVs trajectory planning algorithm for emergency communication. Front. Neurorobot. **16**, 1076338 (2023). https://doi.org/10.3389/fnbot.2022.1076338, https://pmc.ncbi.nlm.nih.gov/articles/PMC9902498/

24. Li, S., Xiang, Y., Li, R., Zhao, Z., Zhang, H.: Imitation Learning based Alternative Multi-Agent Proximal Policy Optimization for Well-Formed Swarm-Oriented Pursuit Avoidance (2023). https://doi.org/10.48550/arXiv.2311.02912, http://arxiv.org/abs/2311.02912, arXiv:2311.02912

25. Liu, R., et al.: Trust-aware behavior reflection for robot swarm self-healing. In: Proceedings of the 18th International Conference on Autonomous Agents and MultiAgent Systems, AAMAS 2019, pp. 122–130. International Foundation for Autonomous Agents and Multiagent Systems, Richland, SC (2019)
26. Low, D., Zhou, Y.: Cooperative multi-agent reinforcement learning for robotic systems: a review. Multiagent Grid Syst. **21**(2), 96–123 (2025). https://doi.org/10.1177/15741702251370050
27. O'Keeffe, J.: Anticipating degradation: a predictive approach to fault tolerance in robot swarms. IEEE Robot. Autom. Lett. **10**(9), 8954–8961 (2025). https://doi.org/10.1109/LRA.2025.3592063, http://arxiv.org/abs/2504.01594, arXiv:2504.01594
28. O'Keeffe, J., Tarapore, D., Millard, A.G., Timmis, J.: Adaptive online fault diagnosis in autonomous robot swarms. Front. Robot. AI **5** (2018). https://doi.org/10.3389/frobt.2018.00131, https://www.frontiersin.org/journals/robotics-and-ai/articles/10.3389/frobt.2018.00131/full
29. Oladiran, O.O.: Fault Recovery in Swarm Robotics Systems using Learning Algorithms. PhD, University of York (2019). https://etheses.whiterose.ac.uk/id/eprint/27134/
30. O'Keeffe, J.: Detecting and diagnosing faults in autonomous robot swarms with an artificial antibody population model. Roy. Soc. Open Sci. **12**(10), 251252 (2025). https://doi.org/10.1098/rsos.251252, https://royalsocietypublishing.org/doi/10.1098/rsos.251252
31. Qiu, Y., Zhan, Y., Jin, Y., Wang, J., Zhang, X.: Sample-Efficient Multi-Agent Reinforcement Learning with Demonstrations for Flocking Control (2022). https://doi.org/10.48550/arXiv.2209.08351, http://arxiv.org/abs/2209.08351, arXiv:2209.08351
32. Rana, M.M., Ibrahim, U.M.: Exploring the role of reinforcement learning in area of swarm robotic. Eur. J. Electr. Eng. Comput. Sci. **8**(3), 15–24 (2024). https://doi.org/10.24018/ejece.2024.8.3.619, https://ejece.org/index.php/ejece/article/view/619
33. Rubenstein, M., Cornejo, A., Nagpal, R.: Robotics. Programmable self-assembly in a thousand-robot swarm. Science **345**(6198), 795–799 (2014). https://doi.org/10.1126/science.1254295
34. Strobel, V., Castelló Ferrer, E., Dorigo, M.: Managing byzantine robots via blockchain technology in a swarm robotics collective decision making scenario. In: Proceedings of the 17th International Conference on Autonomous Agents and MultiAgent Systems (2018). https://dspace.mit.edu/handle/1721.1/115883. Accepted 25 May 2018
35. Strobel, V., Pacheco, A., Dorigo, M.: Robot swarms neutralize harmful Byzantine robots using a blockchain-based token economy. Sci. Robot. **8**(79), eabm4636 (2023). https://doi.org/10.1126/scirobotics.abm4636, https://www.science.org/doi/10.1126/scirobotics.abm4636
36. Tarapore, D., Christensen, A.L., Timmis, J.: Generic, scalable and decentralized fault detection for robot swarms. PLoS ONE **12**(8), e0182058 (2017). https://doi.org/10.1371/journal.pone.0182058
37. Thai, Z.W., Balasubramani, P., Brand, C., Haines, A., DeLaurentis, D.A.: Study of swarm-based planetary exploration architectures using agent-based modeling. In: AIAA Scitech 2020 Forum. AIAA SciTech Forum, American Institute of Aeronautics and Astronautics (2020). https://doi.org/10.2514/6.2020-0075, https://arc.aiaa.org/doi/10.2514/6.2020-0075

38. Timmis, J., Ismail, A.R., Bjerknes, J.D., Winfield, A.F.T.: An immune-inspired swarm aggregation algorithm for self-healing swarm robotic systems. Biosystems **146**, 60–76 (2016). https://doi.org/10.1016/j.biosystems.2016.04.001, https://www.sciencedirect.com/science/article/pii/S030326471630034X
39. Timmis, J., Andrews, P., Hart, E.: On artificial immune systems and swarm intelligence. Swarm Intell. **4**(4), 247–273 (2010). https://doi.org/10.1007/s11721-010-0045-5
40. Winfield, A., Nembrini, J.: Safety in numbers: fault tolerance in robot swarms. Int. J. Model. Identif. Control **1**, 30–37 (2006). https://doi.org/10.1504/IJMIC.2006.008645
41. Xiao, J., Wang, Z., He, J., Yuan, G.: A graph neural network based deep reinforcement learning algorithm for multi-agent leader-follower flocking. Inf. Sci. **641**(C) (2023). https://doi.org/10.1016/j.ins.2023.119074
42. Yu, C., et al.: The Surprising Effectiveness of PPO in Cooperative, Multi-Agent Games (2022). https://doi.org/10.48550/arXiv.2103.01955, http://arxiv.org/abs/2103.01955, arXiv:2103.01955
43. Zhou, Y., et al.: Is Centralized Training with Decentralized Execution Framework Centralized Enough for MARL? (2025). https://doi.org/10.48550/arXiv.2305.17352, http://arxiv.org/abs/2305.17352, arXiv:2305.17352
44. Şahin, E.: Swarm robotics: from sources of inspiration to domains of application. In: Şahin, E., Spears, W.M. (eds.) Swarm Robotics. LNCS, pp. 10–20. Springer, Heidelberg (2005). https://doi.org/10.1007/978-3-540-30552-1_2

Multi-robot Visibility-Based Connected Exploration

Chetan Gadidesi$^{(\boxtimes)}$, Sean Klink, and Aaron T. Becker

Electrical and Computer Engineering, University of Houston, Houston, TX, USA
`{cgadides,scklink,atbecker}@cougarnet.uh.edu`

Abstract. We study the problem of deploying $|R|$ mobile robots to maximize visibility coverage in a polygonal workspace while maintaining a line-of-sight communication path to a home location. The environment contains opaque obstacles, and robots become *stationary* sensing nodes once placed. Each node exposes *visibility frontier windows*—open segments of the current visibility boundary—and available robots evaluate these windows to select the point that yields the largest *incremental* visible area. Robots bid their predicted gain, and a decentralized auction installs the highest bidder as the next stationary node, preserving a connected "min-link" backbone. The process repeats until all robots are placed or the environment is fully covered. We present the algorithm, its complexity, and communication requirements. Experiments on synthetic maps show rapid, monotone growth of visible area and effective distributed decision-making.

1 Introduction: Connected Visibility-Based Coverage

Autonomous exploration in unknown environments is a fundamental problem in robotics with critical applications ranging from search and rescue missions in hazardous environments to exploring maze-like cave systems. These tasks can be done in parallel, so multi-robot systems (swarms) are preferred for these tasks, offering significant advantages in speed, robustness, and efficiency. Our primary goal is maximum visibility coverage—a concept rooted in the classic Art Gallery Problem—while also staying connected in a network to avoid losing communication. We formulate this as an online, maximum-visibility, connected coverage problem, where a team of robots must iteratively plan placements within an unknown polygon to maximize the total area visible to the swarm. Coverage is defined as the net region visible to the robot swarm.

The main challenge in swarm-based coverage is to coordinate the swarm in a distributed manner toward an optimal placement of all robots. Further, the swarm must maintain a single component, line-of-sight communication network to share map data, so connected exploration is required. An exhaustive depth first search (DFS) could find a better placement sequence. However, DFS has exponential runtime that is computationally infeasible for online planning. Alternatively, a simple heuristic like moving to the largest frontier is fast but only locally optimal and can lead to poor coverage.

R. Groß et al. (Eds.): ANTS 2026, LNCS 16515, pp. 204–215, 2026.
https://doi.org/10.1007/978-3-032-26123-6_16

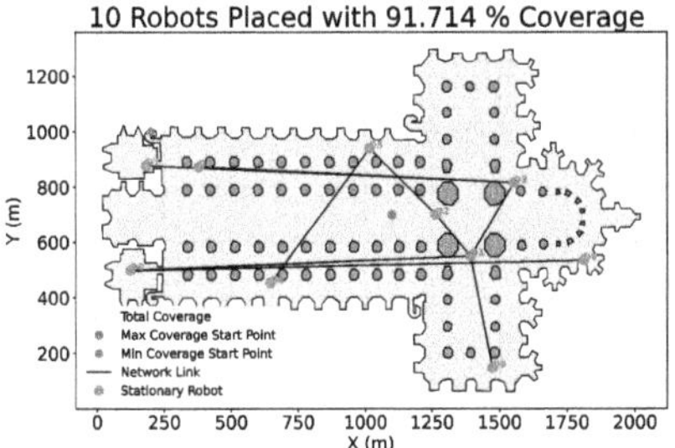

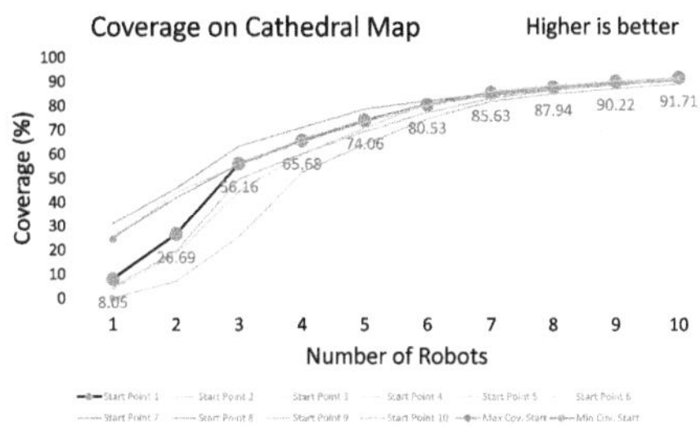

Fig. 1. Representative result: visibility-based connected exploration in *Cathedral* map with 10 robots. The percent coverage grows monotonically with the number of robots. The line-of-sight communication network is drawn with black lines.

This paper presents the Greedy-Auction Algorithm, a distributed online planner that overcomes the aforementioned challenges and computes a locally optimal step in each round, iteratively building a high-quality placement sequence to maximize coverage. Our algorithm models exploration as a round-based, distributed market. In each round, the swarm identifies available frontiers and holds an *auction* to efficiently assign available robots for evaluation. A distributed consensus is then used to greedily select the frontier that offers the maximum visibility gain. Finally, the closest available robot moves to the winning location. This process guarantees a connected, line-of-sight network, and the *sense-evaluate-consensus-act* cycle repeats until the fleet is fully deployed as illustrated in Fig. 1. See video overview[1]. The primary contributions of this work are:

- An online distributed exploration framework that combines fast triangulation-based visibility queries with an optimal greedy auction for efficient task allocation.
- Guaranteed line-of-sight connectivity between each robot, improving safety of the fleet.

2   Related Work

Visibility-Connectivity Problems. The Art Gallery Problem (AGP) seeks the minimum set of guards that collectively see an entire polygon with n_v vertices, beginning with Chvátal's classical $\lfloor n_v/3 \rfloor$ bound [5] and the extensive developments surveyed by O'Rourke [11]. The *Connected Art Gallery Problem* (CAGP) extends AGP by requiring that the visibility graph of guards be connected, a property relevant to robotics and surveillance systems that rely on line-of-sight communication. Ashok *et al.* [1] introduced a mobile, visibly connected formulation with centralized and distributed algorithms. These problems closely relate to our setting: we also seek coverage while ensuring a connected visibility backbone, but do so with greedy, online placement rather than global optimization.

---

[1] https://youtu.be/gxGc55g776I.

Algorithm [Ref.]	Conn.	Max Vis.	Online	Dist.	Exe.	Imp.
Frontier-based exploration [19]	✗	✗	✓	✗	✗	✓
Greedy submodular placement [13, 11]	✗	✗	✗	✗	✗	✓
Market-based multirobot coordination [7, 20]	✗	✗	✓	✓	✓	✓
Classical Art Gallery (guards) [6, 14]	✗	✓	✗	✗	✗	✗
Polygon Guarding with Orientation [18]	✗	✓	✗	✗	✓	✗
Watchman Route Problem (single) [5, 4]	✗	✓	✗	✗	✓	✗
Orthogonal Watchman Route w/ minimum-bends [10]	✗	✓	✗	✗	✓	✗
Multirobot Watchman Routes in Simple Polygon [12]	✗	✓	✗	✓	✓	✗
Visibly-Connected Guarding (CAGP mobile) [1]	✓	✓	✗	✓	✗	✗
Cooperative Guards in Polygons with Holes [2]	✓	✓	✗	✓	✗	✗
Our greedy algorithm (this work)	✓	✓	✓	✓	✓	✓

Fig. 2. Algorithmic Features Compared to This Work. Columns: (Conn.) maintains line-of-sight connectivity; (Max. Vis.) explicitly maximizes geometric visibility/coverage; (Online) incremental computation; (Dist.) distributed execution; (Exe.) considers execution time; (Imp.) considers if the algorithm was implemented or not.

Watchman Route Problem. The Watchman Route Problem (WRP) asks for a shortest path from which a moving observer can see the entire polygon. Introduced by Chin and Ntafos [4], variants include polynomial-time solutions for simple polygons [3], structural refinements [8], and fast approximations such as Tan's linear-time 2-approximation [14]. WRP provides a continuous analog to coverage problems and motivates multi-agent visibility strategies; our approach distributes this effort across multiple vantage points rather than optimizing a single route.

Frontier Exploration. Frontier-based exploration [15] expands free-space maps by selecting points on the boundary between explored and unknown space. Though highly influential, frontier methods typically operate on occupancy grids and rely on discrete adjacency. Our "windows" instead capture *exact* visibility boundaries in polygonal geometry, offering deterministic coverage guarantees absent from grid-based formulations.

Greedy Coverage and Submodularity. Greedy maximization is widely used for sensor placement and coverage due to strong approximation guarantees for monotone submodular objectives [9, 10]. Visibility gain is not strictly submodular but exhibits diminishing returns, making greedy selection effective in practice. Our approach follows this paradigm by maximizing incremental visible area at each step while preserving connectivity constraints.

Auction-Based Coordination. Market-based multirobot coordination [6, 16] assigns tasks through distributed bidding and offers scalable, low-overhead decision-making. Our distributed window-evaluation process resembles these frameworks but differs in coordination: while [12] achieves efficiency through emergent swarm behaviors and local reactive rules, our method employs explicit auction-based consensus and a shared incremental map. This transition from reactive to deliberative coordination enables the swarm to avoid redundant trajectories by focusing resources on the mathematically optimal frontier in each round.

Multiple papers were studied and compared to this work on the basis of five features as listed in Fig. 2.

3   Problem Formulation

Our goal is to maximize the net visible area, under the constraint that the robot must maintain a connected network. The connection is accomplished by assigning each new stationary node a parent that is the nearest visible stationary node, maintaining communication chains.

Let $P \subset \mathbb{R}^2$ be a 2D polygonal workspace with interior obstacles (holes). A viewpoint $x \in E$ sees the *visibility polygon* $\mathcal{V}(x) \subseteq P$. At iteration t, let

$$C_t = \bigcup_{i \in S_t} \mathcal{V}(x_i)$$

be the covered (visible) region from the set S_t of *stationary* robots placed so far. The boundary of C_t contains portions coincident with the environment boundary ∂P and portions that are interior to P. The *frontier windows* $\mathcal{W}_t = \{w\}$ are the maximal open segments on ∂C_t that are not within a small buffer of ∂P.

Given $|R|$ robots in total and one or more initially stationary at a home location, we iteratively:

1. extract $\mathcal{W}_t$ from C_t;
2. for each $w \in \mathcal{W}_t$ find $p^\star(w) \in w$ maximizing the *incremental gain* $g(w) =$ area$(\mathcal{V}(p^\star(w)) \setminus C_t)$;
3. conduct an auction among mobile robots evaluating candidate windows;
4. promote the highest bid to a new stationary robot; update $C_{t+1} = C_t \cup \mathcal{V}(p^\star)$.

The process stops when all robots are stationary or $\max_w g(w) \leq \varepsilon$.

4   Method

4.1   Visibility and Frontier Windows

We compute the visibility polygon $\mathcal{V}(x)$ for a robot at position x using Triangular Expansion [2]. The total coverage area, C_t, is the union of all visibility polygons from stationary robots. Frontiers are detected as segments of the boundary of C_t that do not overlap with the environment boundary, ∂P. In this paper, we use the term *visibility windows* to refer to these frontiers.

4.2   Frontier Task Generation

Each visibility window w represents a potential exploration task. For each window $w = [A, B]$, we discretize the parameter $\lambda \in (0, 1)$ (avoiding endpoints by a small margin), sample $p(\lambda) = A(1 - \lambda) + B\lambda$, and choose $p^\star(w)$ that maximizes the added visible area. In practice, our implementation uses the *visibility window*'s midpoint as a heuristic for $p^\star(w)$. Table 2 tests this heuristic.

4.3   Path Planning on Triangular Mesh

Robot motion is planned using an A* search algorithm on a graph $G(V, E)$ which is derived from the current total coverage area of C_t. Let $C_t \subset \mathbb{R}^2$ be the visibility polygon representing the current total coverage area. To contain query points that may lie on the boundary ∂C_t, we define a slightly inflated coverage polygon C_t' by growing C_t by a small constant. A constrained Delaunay triangulation $\mathcal{T} = \{\tau_1, \tau_2, ..., \tau_{n_t}\}$ is computed for C_t' and the graph G is constructed as a dual of $\mathcal{T}$ where n_t is the number of triangles in $\mathcal{T}$, the vertex set $V = \{v_i | v_i = \text{centroid}(\tau_i), \forall \tau_i \in \mathcal{T}\}$ is the set of all triangle centroids, an edge $e_{ij} = (v_i, v_j)$ exists in the edge set E if and only if their corresponding triangles $t_i, t_j \in \mathcal{T}$ are adjacent and the weight of an edge $w(e_{ij})$ is the Euclidean distance $\|v_i - v_j\|_2$. The start and end triangles, are identified by finding the nearest triangle centroid from the robot's position and the robot's target position using a k-d tree, which provides an $O(\log n_t)$ lookup.

4.4   Greedy Round with Auction

The core of our exploration strategy is a distributed, round-based greedy algorithm. The objective of each round is to deploy a robot from the fleet to a *visibility window* that offers the maximum visibility information gain. This is achieved through a round based auction that leverages a persistent cache to minimize redundancy.

4.5   Connectivity

The network topology is modeled as a connected graph (specifically, an exploration tree rooted at the home location). A new stationary robot is only deployed to a position $p^\star$ that lies on the *visibility window* of its parent stationary robot. This guarantees a line-of-sight link between every parent and child in the tree, ensuring that every robot is seen by at least one other robot.

5   Algorithm 1, Online Greedy Auction

Complexity. We precompute a triangulation of the environment in $O(n_v \log n_v)$ time (where n_v is the number of vertices of C_t) and reuse it for all visibility queries. In one greedy round, let M be the number of active windows and let each window be sampled at N points. A single visibility-polygon query costs $T_V = O(n_v)$ under our triangular-expansion method. Evaluating all samples costs

$$O(MNT_V) = O(MNn_v).$$

For a set of robots R, all remaining per-round operations—window extraction, consensus, assignment, and the A* step—run in $O(n_v)$, $O(|R|)$, $O(|R|^3)$, and $O(n_v \log n_v)$ time, respectively, and are dominated by the MN visibility evaluations for $|R| << n_v$. Thus the per-round complexity is $O(MNn_v)$, and the overall runtime scales linearly with the number of greedy rounds.

Algorithm 1. ONLINEGREEDYAUCTION(S_0, R, ε)

Input: initial stationary set S_0; robot set R; gain threshold ε
1: initialize triangulation $\mathcal{T}$ of the explored region from S_0
2: $C \leftarrow \bigcup_{i \in S_0} \mathcal{V}(x_i)$ $\triangleright$ current explored region
3: **for** $|R| - 1$ iterations **do**
4:      $\mathcal{W} \leftarrow$ EXTRACTFRONTIERWINDOWS$(C, \mathcal{T})$
5:      **if** $\mathcal{W} = \emptyset$ **then break**
6:      **end if**
7:      **while** $|\mathcal{W}| > 0$ **do**
8:          assign nearby windows in $\mathcal{W}$ to available robots using Hungarian Algorithm
9:          **for each** robot r assigned to window w **in parallel do**
10:             $(p^\star(w), g(w)) \leftarrow$ BESTPOINTONWINDOW$(w, C, \mathcal{T})$
11:             broadcast bid $\langle w, p^\star(w), g(w) \rangle$
12:             $\mathcal{W} \leftarrow \mathcal{W} \setminus w$
13:          **end for**
14:      **end while**
15:      $(\hat{w}, \hat{p}, \hat{g}) \leftarrow$ highest bid via max-consensus
16:      **if** $\hat{g} \leq \varepsilon$ **then break**
17:      **end if**
18:      promote winner as stationary node at $\hat{p}$ and connect to nearest parent
19:      update $\mathcal{T}$ and set $C \leftarrow C \cup \mathcal{V}(\hat{p})$
20: **end for**

---

6 Evaluation Protocol

We perform an evaluation across 100 map instances taken from the *dao* benchmark [13]. These are `.png` images that range in size from 26×27 to 656×1491. These environments—including mazes and indoor layouts—are converted to polygonal representations for visibility formulation. All results are averaged across the 100 maps.

6.1 Methods

We compare the performance of our primary Greedy-Auction Algorithm against two other methods:

- Only-Child Greedy-Auction: Differs in sensing methodology. Only *visibility windows* of the last-placed stationary robot are considered in the auction.
- Widest-Window Greedy-Auction: Differs in selection strategy. Rather than calculating the optimal gain $g^\star$, the algorithm selects the frontier with the largest geometric length.

6.2 Key Performance Metrics

The four primary metrics used to compare the performance of all algorithms are summarized below (Table 1):

Table 1. Key Performance Metrics (KPMs)

Metric	Definition	Purpose
Coverage (%) (E_{cov})	Total coverage percentage	Quantifies the coverage of the exploration strategy
Distance Cost (m) (C_{energy})	Sum of total distance traveled by all mobile robots	Provides a proxy for cumulative energy consumption
Computational Time Cost (s) (C_{comp})	Total wall-clock time spent on computation tasks	Measures algorithm's overhead and scalability
Travel Time Cost (s) (C_{exec})	Maximum individual travel time	Captures total execution time required for robot movement

6.3   Ablation Studies

We perform two ablation studies to isolate the contribution of individual design components:

- **Window Sampling Density (N):** Compares the coverage efficiency (E_{cov}) of the simple *midpoint heuristic* against increasing sampling densities ($N > 1$) to quantify the benefit of the *midpoint* heuristic.
- **Caching Known Frontiers:** Compares performance when the cache is enabled versus disabled. The goal is to quantify the reduction in *Energy Cost* (C_{energy}) realized by avoiding redundant re-evaluations. The Greedy-Auction algorithm employs a caching mechanism to minimize redundant computation by storing previously evaluated *visibility windows* and their gain $g(w)$. Since the explored map C_t expands over time, the potential gain from any cached window is monotonically non-increasing. Thus, the cached gain acts as an upper bound for the true gain. Consequently, cached frontiers are only queued for re-evaluation when their gain exceeds the maximum gain found among the newly detected frontiers.

7   Results

Our analysis comparing the performance of the Greedy-Auction (GA) against the Only-Child Greedy Auction (OCGA), and Widest Window (WW)—on multiple maps across four key metrics: coverage, distance cost, computational time cost and travel time cost is shown in Fig. 3.

Experiments were performed, varying the home location to understand dependence of coverage area on the number of samples along the frontier (N). Results in Table 2 show that the coverage area increases slightly ($<1\%$) with increase in samples, but the mean run-time increases linearly with the number of samples. We place each child sensor at the midpoint of a frontier to balance this tradeoff.

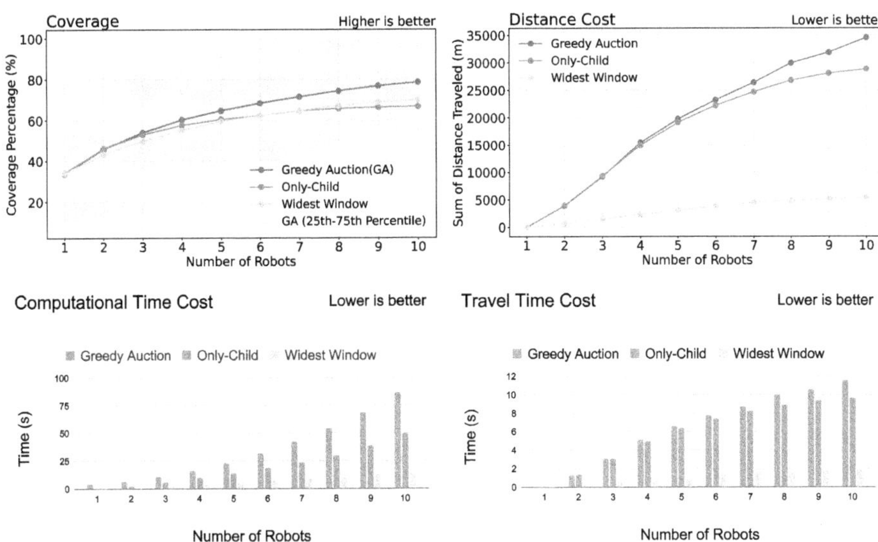

Fig. 3. Comparison of key performance metrics of Greedy-Auction against Only-Child GA and Widest Window over 100 maps. The Greedy Auction covers a higher percentage of the map compared to the other two at the expense of a higher overall cost.

Table 2. Frontier Sampling Strategies for *Cathedral* ($|R| = 10$ Robots, 15 Start Points).

Sampling Method	Mean Coverage (%)	Std. Dev. (±%)	Mean Time (s)
Midpoint	91.382	0.6391	26.78
3 Samples	91.459	0.5169	40.61
5 Samples	91.868	0.8648	67.68
9 Samples	92.027	0.6825	118.39

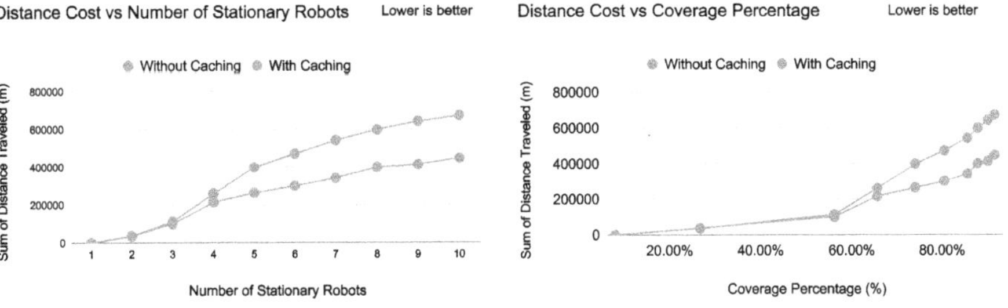

Fig. 4. Energy efficiency comparing the effect of caching known *visibility windows*.

Next we compare the performance of the *caching known frontiers* ablation in Fig. 4 and plot the sum of distance traveled by the robots with and without *caching. Caching* appears to reduce Distance Cost by 40.17%.

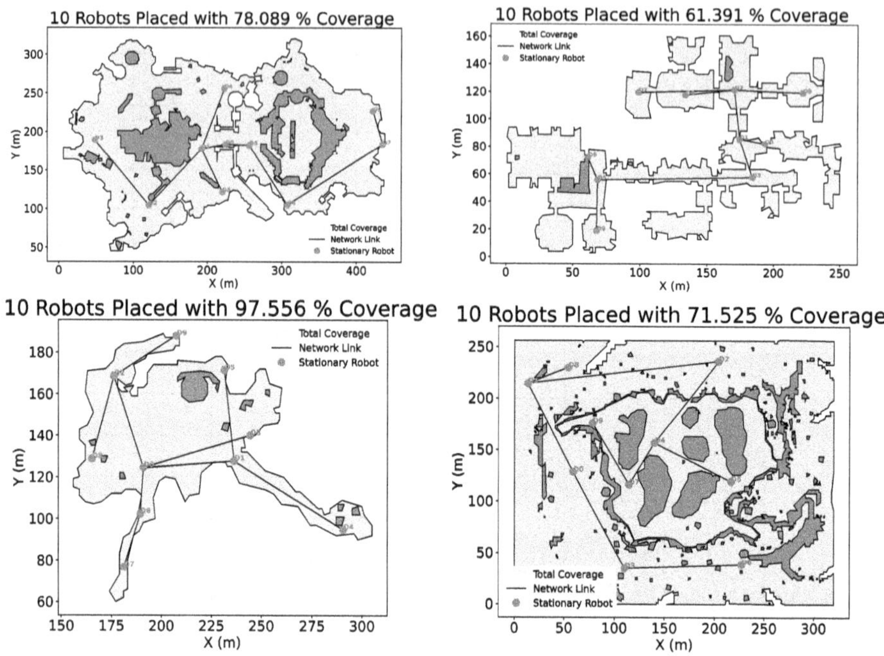

Fig. 5. Map results with 10 robots (4 of the 100 workspaces).

Figure 5 provides representative solutions from the simulation runs using the Greedy Auction algorithm showing how a swarm of robots can collaboratively cover complex unknown maps to maximize visibility coverage. As seen in Fig. 3, although the Greedy Auction is more expensive, computational time cost and travel time cost can be significantly reduced by using faster computers and robots respectively.

8   Discussion and Limitations

In this section we analyze the performance of the Greedy-Auction algorithm and discuss limitations and trade-offs considered.

8.1   Local Optimality and Computational Cost

The primary trade-off is sacrificing global optimality for faster computational performance. The Greedy-Auction algorithm is *greedy* because it selects the frontier that provides the maximum visibility gain for that single step. This myopic planning is fast, but it can be trapped in a local minimum. In contrast, the exhaustive DFS planner finds the globally optimal solution (restricted to using frontiers) but requires a combinatorial explosion of computation as shown

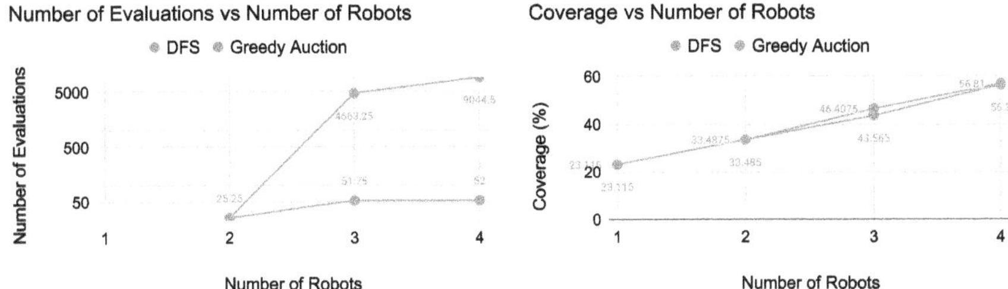

Fig. 6. Comparison between exhaustive DFS and proposed Greedy Auction algorithm (log scale) with 4 robots averaged over the 4 maps shown in Fig. 5, number of evaluations with each extra robot grows rapidly with diminishing increase in coverage.

in Fig. 6. It evaluates all possible sequences of placements to find the one that maximizes the total final coverage.

Let $|\mathcal{W}|$ be the number of frontiers and $|R|$ be the number of available robots. In the Greedy-Auction, the cost of each round is a polynomial dominated by $O(|R| \cdot |\mathcal{W}|)$ time while the exhaustive DFS explores a tree of depth $|R|$ with a branching factor of $|\mathcal{W}|$ and takes the form of an exponential with worst case time complexity of $O(|\mathcal{W}|^{|R|})$. This scaling becomes computationally infeasible.

8.2   The Frontier Placement Assumption

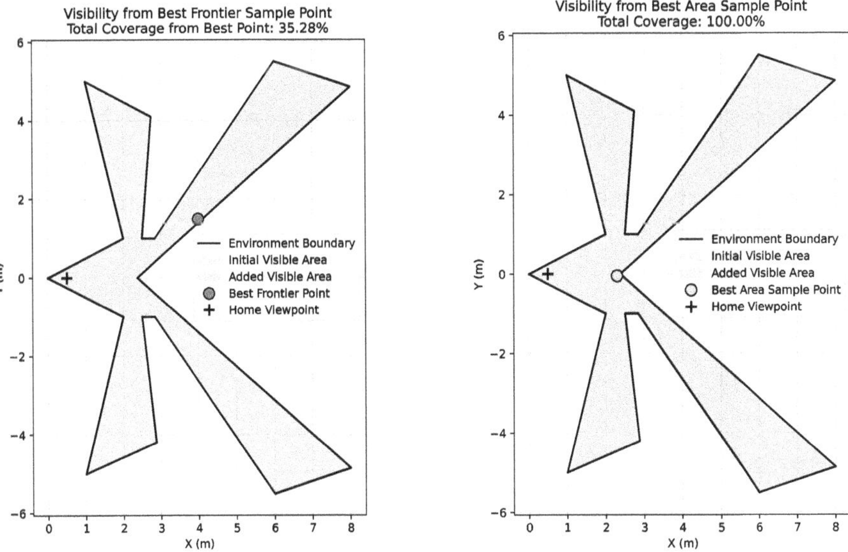

Fig. 7. The best point on window gives a total coverage of 35.28% but an interior point gives 100% visibility coverage.

In this paper, we assumed the best point to place a child robot while maintaining line of sight with its parent is on a frontier. This reduces the problem from searching a 2D region to searching a collection of 1D lines, but can be suboptimal as the optimal vantage point may not be on a frontier. Our BESTPOINTONWINDOW function finds the best point on the visibility window but does not search the interior. The answer can be far from optimal, as shown in Fig. 7.

9 Conclusion

In our trials, the proposed greedy visibility-based placement strategy achieves coverage comparable to an exhaustive DFS exploration, while requiring substantially less computation. By focusing computation on *visibility windows* and evaluating only a small set of promising viewpoints, the greedy approach scales efficiently even in large and cluttered environments, yet still produces coverage levels close to those of full search. Dividing the polygon into sectors for radial robot assignment reduced distance cost on the *Cathedral* map. However, the effectiveness of this strategy diminished on maps with limited free space.

Future work includes replacing the Hungarian assignment with a multi-vehicle routing planner [7] so that mobile robots can naturally divide the unexplored space into regions and visit them in a coordinated order. Incorporating such path-level optimization may further improve exploration efficiency and produce more realistic swarm behaviors in large-scale environments. Investigating moving stationary nodes to optimize coverage can also be studied.

GitHub Repository.   https://github.com/chetangadidesi/Multi-Robot-Visibility-Based-Connected-Exploration.

Acknowledgments. Research was sponsored in part by the DEVCOM Analysis Center, accomplished under Contract Number W911QX-23-D-0009 and the Army Research Laboratory, accomplished under Cooperative Agreement Number W911NF-23-2-0014. The views and conclusions contained in this document are those of the authors and should not be interpreted as representing the official policies, either expressed or implied, of the DEVCOM Analysis Center, the Army Research Laboratory, or the U.S. Government. The U.S. Government is authorized to reproduce and distribute reprints for Government purposes notwithstanding any copyright notation herein.

Disclosure of Interests. The authors have no competing interests to declare.

References

1. Ashok, B., Augustine, J., Mehekare, A., Ragupathi, S., Ramachandran, S., Sourav, S.: Guarding a polygon without losing touch. In: Richa, A.W., Scheideler, C. (eds.) SIROCCO 2020. LNCS, vol. 12156, pp. 91–108. Springer, Cham (2020). https://doi.org/10.1007/978-3-030-54921-3_6

2. Bungiu, F., Hemmert, M., Hershberger, J., Huang, K., Kröllert, A.: Efficient computation of visibility polygons. arXiv preprint cs.CG/1403.3905v1 (2014). https://doi.org/10.48550/arXiv.1403.3905
3. Carlsson, S., Jonsson, H., Nilsson, B.J.: Finding the shortest watchman route in a simple polygon. Discret. Comput. Geom. **22**, 377–402 (1999). https://doi.org/10.1007/PL00009475
4. Chin, W.P., Ntafos, S.: Optimum watchman routes. Inf. Process. Lett. **28**(1), 39–44 (1988). https://doi.org/10.1016/0020-0190(88)90141-X
5. Chvátal, V.: A combinatorial theorem in plane geometry. J. Comb. Theory Ser. B **18**(1), 39–41 (1975). https://doi.org/10.1016/0095-8956(75)90041-9
6. Dias, M.B., Zlot, R.M., Kalra, N., Stentz, A.: Market-based multirobot coordination: a survey and analysis. Proc. IEEE **94**(7), 1257–1270 (2006). https://doi.org/10.1109/JPROC.2006.876939
7. Didier, F., Perron, L., Mohajeri, S., Gay, S.A., Cuvelier, T., Furnon, V.: OR-tools' vehicle routing solver: a generic constraint-programming solver with heuristic search for routing problems. In: Congrès de la Société française de recherche opérationnelle et d'aide à la décision (ROADEF). Rennes, France (2023). https://roadef2023.sciencesconf.org/436822/document
8. Dror, M., Efrat, A., Lubiw, A., Mitchell, J.S.B.: Touring a sequence of polygons. SIAM J. Comput. **31**(1), 1–24 (2003). https://doi.org/10.1145/780542.780612
9. Krause, A., Singh, A., Guestrin, C.: Near-optimal sensor placements in Gaussian processes: theory, efficient algorithms and empirical studies. J. Mach. Learn. Res. **9**, 235–284 (2008). https://jmlr.org/papers/v9/krause08a.html
10. Nemhauser, G.L., Wolsey, L.A., Fisher, M.L.: An analysis of approximations for maximizing submodular set functions-I. Math. Program. **14**(1), 265–294 (1978). https://doi.org/10.1007/BF01588971
11. O'Rourke, J.: Art Gallery Theorems and Algorithms. International Series of Monographs on Computer Science. Oxford University Press (1987)
12. Stirling, T., Wischmann, S., Floreano, D.: Energy-efficient indoor search by swarms of simulated flying robots without global information. Swarm Intell. **4**(2), 117–143 (2010). https://doi.org/10.1007/s11721-010-0039-3
13. Sturtevant, N.: Benchmarks for grid-based pathfinding. Trans. Comput. Intell. AI Games **4**(2), 144–148 (2012). http://web.cs.du.edu/~sturtevant/papers/benchmarks.pdf
14. Tan, X.: A linear-time 2-approximation algorithm for the shortest watchman route in a simple polygon. Theoret. Comput. Sci. **384**(1), 1–13 (2007). https://doi.org/10.1016/j.tcs.2007.05.024
15. Yamauchi, B.: A frontier-based approach for autonomous exploration. In: Proceedings 1997 IEEE International Symposium on Computational Intelligence in Robotics and Automation, CIRA 1997. 'Towards New Computational Principles for Robotics and Automation', pp. 146–151 (1997). https://doi.org/10.1109/CIRA.1997.613851
16. Zlot, R., Stentz, A., Dias, M.B., Thayer, S.: Market-based multirobot coordination for complex tasks. In: Proceedings of the IEEE/RSJ International Conference on Intelligent Robots and Systems (IROS), pp. 3016–3023 (2002). https://doi.org/10.1177/0278364906061160

Plyo: AI-Assisted Lightning-Fast Communication for Robot Swarms

Martina Balbi[1,2(✉)], Lance Doherty[1], and Thomas Watteyne[1]

[1] Analog Devices, Boston, MA, USA
martina.balbi@analog.com
[2] Inria Paris, Paris, France

Abstract. Robot swarms rely on fast and reliable dissemination of control messages from a central orchestrator. Yet, achieving this over low-power wireless links is challenging. Mobility, interference, and link variability make some robots much harder to reach than others. We introduce *Plyo*, a relay-based flooding strategy in which only a small, carefully chosen subset of robots rebroadcasts orchestration messages. Selecting such relays is a difficult combinatorial problem, so we propose *PlyoNet*, a lightweight AI-based model that computes relay selections in a single forward pass. Across several swarm configurations, Plyo consistently matches a greedy relay selector in flooding performance while being orders of magnitude faster, achieving 2 ms inference on a MAX78000 microcontroller versus 440 ms for greedy on a microcontroller CPU. These results show that real-time, near-optimal relay-based TSCH flooding is feasible even on resource-constrained swarm orchestrators.

1 Introduction

Mobile robot swarms are increasingly used in applications such as environmental monitoring, precision agriculture, search-and-rescue, and coordinated industrial automation [8]. In many of these scenarios, a *central orchestrator* issues frequent downstream control messages to move robots to new waypoints, synchronize tasks, or trigger emergency stops. For safe and effective operation, these commands must reach *all* robots quickly and reliably despite mobility, interference, and rapidly changing connectivity.

Time-Synchronized Channel Hopping (TSCH) is a leading link-layer technology for low-power wireless systems, and an attractive foundation for swarm-scale deployments [4]. TSCH provides tight synchronization and predictable timing, and typically disseminates control traffic through *network-wide flooding*, where every robot rebroadcasts the orchestrator's packet. Although robust, this mechanism is inflexible: all nodes forward, the forwarding structure does not adapt to the instantaneous topology, and the weakest robot often dictates overall flood duration. As swarm size and mobility increase, flooding becomes slower and increasingly dominated by the most difficult-to-reach robot.

We introduce **Plyo**, a relay-based flooding mechanism for TSCH that replaces network-wide participation with a small, carefully chosen set of relay robots.

R. Groß et al. (Eds.): ANTS 2026, LNCS 16515, pp. 216–227, 2026.
https://doi.org/10.1007/978-3-032-26123-6_17

Rather than diffusing through every node, messages "jump" through a compact relay backbone targeted at maximizing the worst per-timeslot reception probability. Selecting such relays is a combinatorial problem that depends on instantaneous link qualities, which change rapidly under mobility.

To enable real-time relay selection, we propose *PlyoNet*, a lightweight neural scoring model that computes relay sets in a single forward pass. PlyoNet is trained via imitation learning to reproduce a greedy expert selector, achieving near-optimal flooding performance while running two orders of magnitude faster. This makes it suitable for deployment on microcontroller-class orchestrators, enabling relay sets to be recomputed at the timescale of TSCH slotframes.

2   Related Work

Flooding is a central mechanism in low-power wireless networks, and many TSCH systems rely on it to disseminate control traffic. Glossy [5] introduced concurrent transmission flooding and showed that tight slot-level synchronization can yield fast and reliable network-wide dissemination. Variants extend this approach to improve scalability, reduce latency or support distributed coordination [2,6]. In 6TiSCH networks, flooding is used for neighbor discovery, time synchronization, and schedule negotiation [9]. Orchestra [3] and related autonomous scheduling frameworks embed Glossy-style floods directly into TSCH schedules but retain the paradigm in which *every* node participates in every flood.

A key limitation is that flooding is treated as a fixed broadcast primitive, rather than tailored to the instantaneous topology. Every node forwards, the number of transmissions grows with swarm size, and the flood duration is dominated by the weakest robots. This is especially problematic in robot swarms, where mobility continually reshapes connectivity and leaves the downstream control channel vulnerable to the instantaneous worst-case robot. Existing TSCH-based systems, as explored in our previous work [1], do not explicitly optimize downstream flooding for mobile swarms, nor do they select a relay set that adapts to current link stabilities.

Beyond TSCH, reducing broadcast redundancy has been widely explored in classical wireless multi-hop networks. Approaches based on Connected-Dominating-Sets (CDS) [10] construct small relay backbones to reduce rebroadcast overhead in static ad hoc networks. While conceptually related, CDS techniques assume stable topologies, do not account for slotting and channel hopping, and are not designed to maximize per-timeslot reception probability.

To the best of our knowledge, no prior TSCH system constructs a minimal, connectivity-aware relay backbone for flooding, nor selects relays based on per-link stability matrices to optimize the worst-case downstream reception probability. Plyo is the first to formulate relay-based TSCH flooding as a max–min optimization problem and the first to provide a lightweight, embedded-friendly neural model capable of recomputing relay sets fast enough to track mobility in real time.

3   Problem Statement

Reliable and fast information flooding is a critical requirement in large robot swarms, where messages must propagate efficiently from a central orchestrator to the entire collective. In many practical settings, robots communicate over unreliable low-power wireless links whose packet delivery ratios (PDRs) depend on distance, multipath effects, and interference. We consider a TSCH flooding strategy in which a small set of *relay robots* rebroadcast orchestrator packets to the rest of the swarm. In this work, we focus specifically on two-hop flooding: a robot may receive the packet either directly from the orchestrator or from one relay within the same timeslot. Supporting longer relay chains would require additional transmission phases and a more complex flooding model, and is left for future work. The central question is *how to choose a set of K relays such that the TSCH flooding time is minimized?*

The flooding dynamics in our setting are dominated by the robot that is hardest to reach. Because flooding proceeds in repeated, identically structured timeslots, this worst robot is fully characterized by its per-timeslot probability of receiving the packet. Maximizing this probability directly minimizes the expected flooding time of the entire swarm.

3.1   Swarm Connectivity

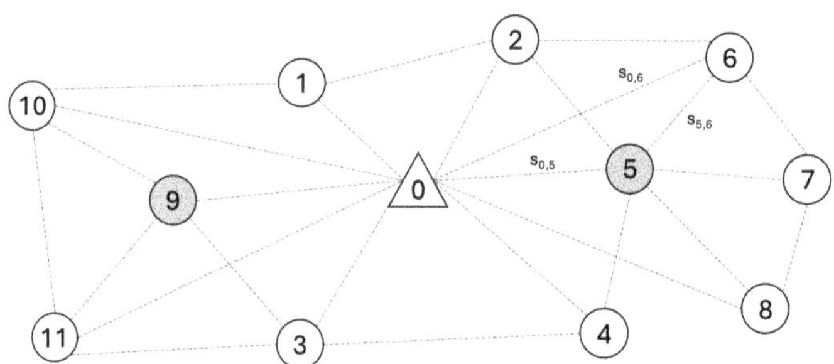

Fig. 1. Connectivity in a 10-robot, 1-orchestrator swarm.

We consider a network with node set $V = \{0, 1, \ldots, N\}$. This network of $N_{\text{nodes}} = N + 1$ **nodes** consists of $R = \{1, \ldots, N\}$ mobile **robots**, and one **orchestrator**. The orchestrator instructs the robots how to move to execute a mission. In Fig. 1, there are 10 robots (circles) and one orchestrator (triangle).

We define the **stability** as the fraction of link-layer frames sent by one device's radio that are correctly received by another. Let $s_{ij} \in [0, 1] \ \forall \ i, j \in V$ denote the stability from node i to node j. In Fig. 1, dotted lines indicate node pairs with non-zero stability, meaning that direct communication is physically possible. Stability reflects only the underlying radio link quality and is independent of higher-layer retries or relaying.

All pairwise stabilities are collected into the matrix

$$S = [s_{ij}]_{i,j=0}^{N} \in [0,1]^{N_{\text{nodes}} \times N_{\text{nodes}}}.$$

Although TSCH provides tight synchronization and channel hopping, packet success still depends on attenuation, interference, and environmental dynamics. The matrix S summarizes the underlying wireless behavior of the entire swarm at a given instant.

A **relay set** $R^* \subseteq R, |R^*| = K$, specifies the K robots that rebroadcast the orchestrator packet during each timeslot. Robots in R^* transmit once per timeslot in the relay phase, while all others serve solely as receivers.

3.2 Two-Phase TSCH Timeslot

With Plyo, flooding takes place in **every** TSCH timeslot by splitting each timeslot into two halves. In the first half, the orchestrator transmits the packet once. In the second half, the robots in the relay set R^* transmit.

Non-relay robots obtain two independent chances in each timeslot to receive the packet: one from the orchestrator in the first half, one from its preferred relay in the second half. Relay robots obtain a single chance per timeslot, coming from the orchestrator in the first half.

For a non-relay robot $i \notin R^*$, its preferred relay is the one with the strongest link towards it:

$$r_i^* = \arg \max_{r \in R^*} s_{ri}.$$

In one timeslot, robot i first attempts to receive from the orchestrator with success probability s_{0i}. If it fails, it may still receive from r_i^* in the second half with success probability $s_{r_i^* i}$, only if the relay received it from the orchestrator in the first half with probability $s_{0r_i^*}$. Assuming independence between these attempts, the per-timeslot success probability is

$$q_i(R^*) = 1 - (1 - s_{0i})(1 - s_{0r_i^*} s_{r_i^* i}), \qquad i \notin R^*.$$

Relay robots have a different structure. A relay $j \in R^*$ listens only in the first half, then transmits in the second, and thus has a single reception opportunity per timeslot, from the orchestrator:

$$q_j(R^*) = s_{0j}, \qquad j \in R^*.$$

The vector $q(R^*) = \{q_i(R^*)\}_{i \in R}$ can therefore be interpreted as the per-timeslot flooding reliability for all robots under relay set R^*.

During operation, the orchestrator always transmits on channel offset 0, while each relay uses a distinct offset during the second half, allowing up to 15 relays in practice given the 16 available TSCH channels. In parallel with flooding, every timeslot includes a scheduled uplink transmission from one robot to the orchestrator in a round-robin manner. When a robot is scheduled for uplink, it transmits instead of listening or relaying in that slot. The orchestrator maintains an up-to-date estimate of the stability matrix S from the delivery statistics of these continuous uplink packets, while robots periodically refine local estimates by overhearing uplink transmissions from nearby peers.

3.3 Flooding Time and Relay Selection Objective

Consider a robot i with per-timeslot success probability $q_i(R^*)$. The probability that robot i has *not* yet received the packet after t timeslots is $(1 - q_i(R^*))^t$. To guarantee reception with at least 99% probability, robot i requires

$$t_i(R^*) = \left\lceil \frac{\ln(0.01)}{\ln(1 - q_i(R^*))} \right\rceil.$$

Flooding completes only when every robot has received the packet, so the flooding time in timeslots $t_{\max}(R^*)$ is governed by the slowest robot. If Δ denotes the duration of a timeslot in milliseconds, the expected flooding time in milliseconds is $T_{0.99}(R^*) = t_{\max}(R^*)\,\Delta$. Since $t_i(R^*)$ is a strictly decreasing function of $q_i(R^*)$, minimizing $T_{0.99}(R^*)$ is therefore equivalent to maximizing the smallest per-timeslot success probability across all robots.

For a relay budget of K robots, the relay selection problem then reduces to choosing a subset $R^* \subseteq R, |R^*| = K$, that maximizes the worst per-timeslot success probability:

$$\max_{R^* \subseteq R,\, |R^*|=K} \; \min_{i \in R} q_i(R^*).$$

Because $q_i(R^*)$ differs between relay and non-relay robots, this objective trades off improving weak non-relays via good relay coverage and ensuring that each relay maintains a strong orchestrator link. The search space is combinatorial, and naive or greedy approaches become slow as N grows, motivating PlyoNet, an AI-assisted relay selection strategy presented in Sect. 4.2.

4 Plyo Architecture

The relay selection objective in Sect. 3.3 requires identifying, in real time, a subset of robots that maximizes the worst per-timeslot reception probability in the swarm. Exhaustive evaluation and even greedy search become prohibitively slow as the swarm grows. To address this, we introduce *Plyo*, a lightweight, AI-assisted scoring model that selects relays via a single forward pass.

Plyo is inspired by shared-parameter graph neural networks (GNNs), where each node is processed by the same encoder, but is specifically designed for embedded TSCH orchestrators. It therefore avoids message passing, neighborhood aggregation, and any operations that would be too computationally expensive for a microcontroller. Instead, Plyo constructs a relay-centric feature tensor from the stability matrix S, capturing for each potential relay how well it would contribute to flooding performance across the swarm. A small shared Convolutional Neural Network (CNN) then processes these relay feature maps and outputs a scalar score for every robot.

4.1   Relay-Centric Feature Tensor

Let node set V, orchestrator 0, robots R and stability matrix S be as presented in Sect. 3.1. For each relay candidate $r \in R$, Plyo builds a 3-channel feature map over all robot destinations $j \in R$:

- orchestrator-to-robot stability: $F_1(r, j) = s_{0j}$,
- relay-to-robot stability: $F_2(r, j) = s_{rj}$,
- two-hop path quality (orchestrator→relay→robot): $F_3(r, j) = s_{0r} s_{rj}$.

Each relay candidate has a feature matrix $F(r) \in \mathbb{R}^{3 \times N}$. Stacking these feature maps across all relay candidates yields:

$$X = \{F(r)\}_{r \in R} \in \mathbb{R}^{N \times 3 \times N}.$$

The first dimension indexes relay candidates r; the second the feature channels; the third the destination robots j. Conceptually, X encodes, for every relay, how it connects to all robots and how it can improve two-hop flooding paths.

4.2   PlyoNet: Convolutional Scoring Network

PlyoNet applies the same convolutional encoder to all relay feature maps. We view the scoring network as a function $f : \mathbb{R}^{N \times 3 \times N} \to \mathbb{R}^N$ that maps the feature tensor X to a score vector $\sigma = f(X) = \big(\sigma(1), \ldots, \sigma(N)\big)$, where $\sigma(r)$ is the score of relay candidate r.

The network consists of two 1D convolutions with ReLU activations:

$$H_1 = \mathrm{ReLU}\big(\mathrm{Conv1D}(X, 3 \to 96, \ \mathrm{kernel} = 5, \ \mathrm{pad} = 2)\big),$$
$$H_2 = \mathrm{ReLU}\big(\mathrm{Conv1D}(H_1, 96 \to 96, \ \mathrm{kernel} = 5, \ \mathrm{pad} = 2)\big),$$

yielding $H_2 \in \mathbb{R}^{N \times 96 \times N}$. PlyoNet then performs mean pooling across destination robots for each relay and applies a two-layer Multi-Layer Perceptron (MLP), producing one scalar score $\sigma(r)$ for every relay candidate.

4.3   Final Relay Selection

Once the score vector $\sigma \in \mathbb{R}^N$ is obtained, Plyo selects the relay set as

$$R^* = \mathrm{TopK}\{\sigma(r) : r \in R\}.$$

This top-K operation is deterministic and constitutes the final relay set used during flooding. Because the scoring pipeline is small, feed-forward, and free of message passing, Plyo can update relay selections at high frequency, enabling real-time adaptability to changing stability conditions while maintaining minimal computational overhead.

5   Training PlyoNet

PlyoNet is trained entirely through imitation learning, using labels produced by a high-quality greedy relay selector. This section describes how training data are generated, how expert labels are computed, and how models are trained for different swarm configurations.

5.1   Dataset Generation

Training data are obtained by sampling synthetic swarm configurations and computing expert relay sets using a greedy selector. Robot positions are drawn uniformly at random inside a square $200\ m \times 200\ m$ arena. For each scenario, link stabilities are computed directly from inter-robot distance using the Pister–Hack propagation model [7], yielding the full stability matrix $S \in [0, 1]^{N_{\mathrm{nodes}} \times N_{\mathrm{nodes}}}$.

We consider four combinations of robot count N and relay budget K:

$$(K, N) \in \{(6, 50), (6, 100), (15, 50), (15, 100)\}.$$

For each configuration, we generate 250,000 independent swarm instances with their stability matrix S. Each instance is labeled using a greedy relay selector to identify its near-optimal relay set R^* with $|R^*| = K$. Expert labels are stored as a binary membership vector

$$y_r = \begin{cases} 1, & r \in R^*, \\ 0, & r \notin R^*, \end{cases} \quad r \in R.$$

5.2   Greedy Selector for Expert Label Generation

The greedy relay selector used to label each dataset instance approximates the objective in Sect. 3.3. It constructs a relay set R^* by iteratively adding the robot that most improves the worst per-timeslot success probability (Algorithm 1).

5.3   Training and Inference

A separate PlyoNet model is trained for each (K, N) configuration. Datasets are split into 80% for training and 20% for validation. Training uses mini-batches, the Adam optimizer, gradient clipping, and early stopping based on validation loss.

Given the feature tensor X, PlyoNet outputs a real-valued score for each robot $\sigma = f(X) \in \mathbb{R}^N$, as explained in Sect. 4.2. These scores are trained to match the expert relay set by treating the problem as multi-label binary classification: each robot is either part of the expert relay set ($y_r = 1$) or not ($y_r = 0$). The training loss used is PyTorch's `BCEWithLogitsLoss()`, which compares the model's raw scores σ_r and the expert's binary labels y_r, and penalizes each robot independently if the model assigns too low a score to an expert relay or too high a score to a non-relay.

Algorithm 1. Greedy Relay Selection

Require: Stability matrix S, relay budget K
Ensure: Relay set R^*
1: $R^* \leftarrow \emptyset$
2: $(w, \mu) \leftarrow \text{Eval}(S, R^*)$ $\triangleright$ worst and mean PDR
3: **for** $k = 1$ to K **do**
4:      $\hat{c} \leftarrow$ nil; $\hat{\mu} \leftarrow -\infty$
5:      $c^* \leftarrow$ nil; $\mu^* \leftarrow -\infty$
6:      **for** each robot candidate $c \notin R^*$ **do**
7:          $(w', \mu') \leftarrow \text{Eval}(S, R^* \cup \{c\})$
8:          **if** $w' > w$ **then**
9:              $\hat{c} \leftarrow c$, $\hat{\mu} \leftarrow \mu'$
10:             $w \leftarrow w'$, $\mu \leftarrow \mu'$
11:          **else if** $w' = w$ **and** $\mu' > \hat{\mu}$ **then**
12:             $\hat{c} \leftarrow c$, $\hat{\mu} \leftarrow \mu'$
13:          **else if** $\mu' > \mu^*$ **then**
14:             $c^* \leftarrow c$, $\mu^* \leftarrow \mu'$
15:          **end if**
16:      **end for**
17:      **if** $\hat{c} =$ nil **then**
18:          $\hat{c} \leftarrow c^*$
19:          $(w, \mu) \leftarrow \text{Eval}(S, R^* \cup \{\hat{c}\})$
20:      **end if**
21:      $R^* \leftarrow R^* \cup \{\hat{c}\}$
22: **end for**
23: **return** R^*

At deployment time, the greedy selector is no longer required. Given a new stability matrix S, Plyo constructs the feature tensor X, performs a single forward pass to obtain the score vector σ, and selects the relay set as $R^* = \text{TopK}(\sigma)$. During training, we do not apply the TopK operation. The loss is computed directly on the per-robot scores σ_r and binary labels y_r, allowing gradients to flow through all network parameters.

6 Evaluation

We evaluate Plyo across all four swarm configurations considered in Sect. 5.1. For each configuration, we sample 1,000 stability matrices using the propagation and deployment model described in Sect. 5.1. For every instance, we compute the relay set using Plyo and compare the resulting flooding performance against three baselines: *before* (no relays), *random* (uniformly random selection of K relays), and *greedy* (the expert selector used to generate training labels). We report three metrics: (i) average per-robot per-timeslot PDR after relay selection, (ii) expected flooding time $T_{0.99}$ for the orchestrator's packet to reach all robots with 99% probability, and (iii) relay-selection runtime. All results are averaged across the 1,000 test networks.

6.1 Flooding Performance

Figure 2 reports the average per-robot PDR achieved after relay selection. By construction, the *before* condition performs the worst, with PDRs around 0.44 across all configurations, since each robot receives only a single transmission per

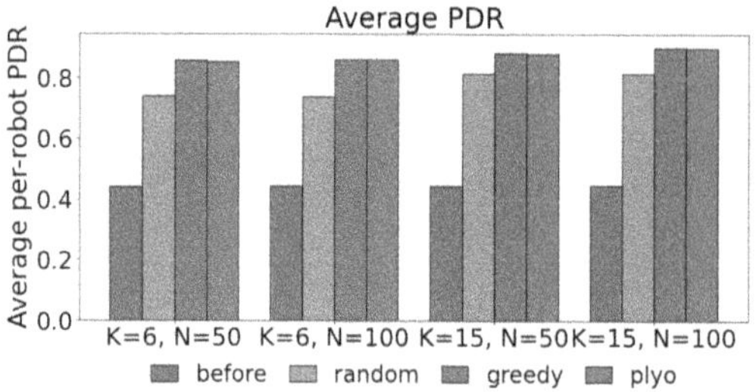

Fig. 2. Average per-robot PDR.

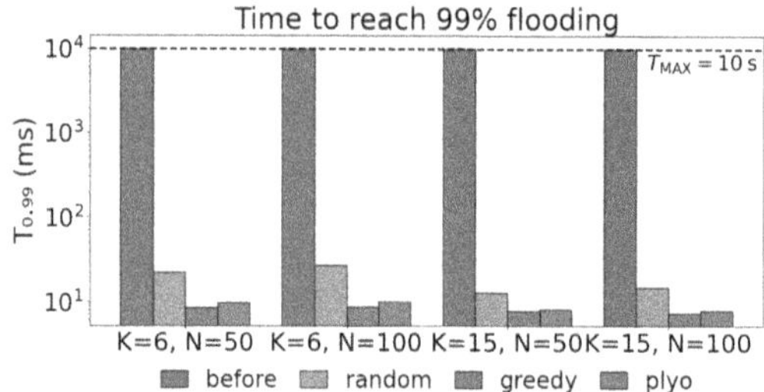

Fig. 3. Flooding time to 99% reliability.

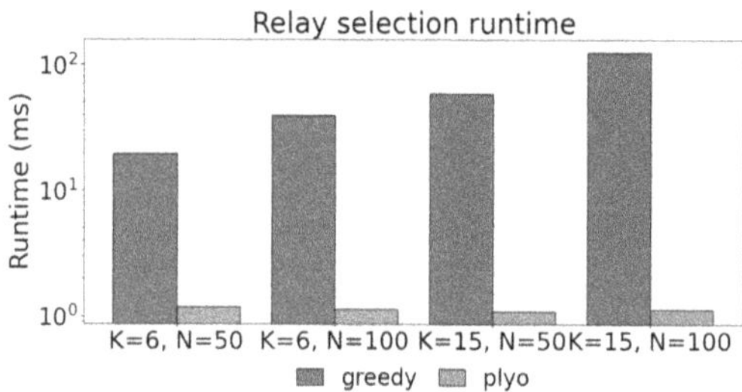

Fig. 4. Relay-selection runtime.

timeslot from the orchestrator. Random relay selection substantially improves performance, yielding PDRs between roughly 0.73 and 0.82 depending on (K, N), but it remains far from optimal and exhibits higher variability. The greedy selector achieves the highest PDRs overall, around 0.86–0.90 in our experiments. Plyo closely matches these values in every configuration, differing from the greedy selector by only 0.003–0.005 absolute PDR points. This confirms that the learned model accurately reproduces the greedy selector's selection behavior and consistently produces relay sets that achieve near-optimal per-timeslot reception probabilities across the swarm.

Using the analytical expression from Sect. 3.3, we compute the expected flooding time $T_{0.99}$ as follows. For each sampled stability matrix, we consider a protocol where the orchestrator repeatedly transmits the *same* control packet in consecutive TSCH timeslots, using the same relay set in every slot. For a given relay strategy, $T_{0.99}$ is the number of identical retransmissions required for the slowest robot to cross the 0.99 reception threshold, multiplied by the TSCH timeslot duration. Throughout this evaluation, we assume a TSCH timeslot of $\Delta = 1$ ms, so flooding time in milliseconds corresponds directly to the number of required retransmissions.

The results, summarized in Fig. 3, show a dramatic gap between the *before* condition and all relay-based strategies. Across all four (K, N) configurations, the flooding time without relays exceeds 10,000 ms, at which point we cap the plotted bars; the true flooding times are even larger. This occurs because in the *before* baseline some instances include robots with extremely weak or zero direct stability to the orchestrator, so their theoretical $T_{0.99}$ can be arbitrarily large or even infinite. Random relay selection improves performance substantially, reducing $T_{0.99}$ to the 13–26 ms range depending on the configuration. The greedy selector further reduces flooding time to about 7–9 ms. Plyo closely tracks the greedy selector across all cases, yielding flooding times in the range of 8–10 ms. The largest deviation from greedy is under 2 ms, confirming that Plyo consistently identifies relay sets that minimize the worst-case flooding time.

Comparing the two relay budgets also shows that increasing K from 6 to 15 yields consistently higher PDRs and shorter flooding times. For $N = 100$, the average per-robot PDR for greedy and Plyo increases from around 0.86 to about 0.90, and $T_{0.99}$ decreases by roughly 15%. This indicates that using a larger relay budget provides tangible gains in flooding reliability and latency, particularly in larger swarms.

6.2 Relay Selection Runtime

Figure 4 reports the runtime required to compute a relay set. All desktop measurements were obtained on a MacBook Air (M2) in Python: the greedy selector runs entirely on the CPU, while Plyo inference uses Apple's MPS hardware accelerator. Under this setup, greedy selection is the slowest approach and its cost increases rapidly with both swarm size and relay budget: from about 20 ms for $(K = 6, N = 50)$ to about 134 ms for $(K = 15, N = 100)$. In contrast, Plyo performs relay selection in approximately 1.06–1.12 ms across all configurations because inference requires only a single forward pass through a small CNN. In particular, it can be seen that increasing the relay budget from $K = 6$ to $K = 15$ more than doubles the greedy runtime, whereas Plyo's inference time remains essentially unchanged, making the larger relay budget practically viable only with the learned selector.

To evaluate embedded performance, we ported a $(K = 6, N = 45)$ model— the largest swarm configuration available on our development platform at the time—and executed Plyo using the MAX78000's on-chip CNN accelerator. End-to-end relay selection completes in approximately 2 ms, while the greedy selector—executed on the microcontroller's CPU—requires around 440 ms for the same configuration. Thus, on both desktop and embedded hardware, the comparison is structurally identical: a CPU-bound greedy algorithm versus an accelerator-backed Plyo inference pipeline. Plyo consistently provides a $20\times$–$120\times$ speedup, enabling real-time per-slotframe relay recomputation even on low-power orchestrators.

6.3 Model Size and Embedded Feasibility

Although a separate PlyoNet instance is trained for each (K, N) configuration, all models share the same architecture and thus contain the same number of trainable parameters. Thanks to the convolutional design, layer sizes depend on the number of feature channels rather than the swarm size, resulting in a fixed footprint of 53,985 parameters for every configuration.

This compact size greatly simplifies deployment on embedded platforms, since only a single memory footprint needs to be supported. On the MAX78000, the full model—including weights, intermediate buffers, and accelerator-friendly layout—fits comfortably within the available on-chip memory for the $(K = 6, N = 45)$ configuration used in our hardware tests. Combined with the millisecond-scale inference times reported above, this confirms that PlyoNet meets both computational and memory constraints for real-time relay selection on resource-limited robot-swarm orchestrators.

7 Conclusion

This paper presented Plyo, a relay-based flooding mechanism for TSCH that enables fast and reliable downstream communication in mobile robot swarms. By formulating relay selection as a max-min flooding problem and introducing PlyoNet—a lightweight neural model trained through imitation learning—we showed that high-quality relay sets can be computed in a single forward pass. Across four swarm configurations, Plyo matches the greedy expert in both average per-robot PDR and time to reach 99% reliability, typically differing by only a few thousandths and a few milliseconds, respectively. These results indicate that the structural patterns underlying effective relay sets can be captured by a compact neural model and reliably transferred from a greedy expert through imitation learning.

A key result is that Plyo achieves expert-level performance at a fraction of the computational cost. Greedy selection takes 20–134 ms depending on the configuration, while Plyo requires about 1 ms on a workstation and 2 ms on a MAX78000 microcontroller. This speed enables the orchestrator to recompute relay sets at the time scale of TSCH slotframes, providing real-time relay adaptation as connectivity evolves.

Plyo provides an efficient, adaptive downstream control channel suitable for applications requiring precise global coordination, such as mission-level updates in drone or ground-robot collectives, tightly synchronized operations in automated factories, and latency-critical safety mechanisms such as emergency-stop dissemination. Future work includes integrating Plyo into a full TSCH stack, validating the approach in a physical multi-robot testbed, and extending the current two-hop flooding design to multi-hop relay chains.

Acknowledgments. This document is issued within the frame and for the purpose of the OpenSwarm project. This project has received funding from the European Union's Horizon Europe Framework Programme under Grant Agreement No. 101093046. Views and opinions expressed are, however, those of the author(s) only, and the European Commission is not responsible for any use that may be made of the information it contains.

Disclosure of Interests. The authors have no competing interests to declare.

References

1. Balbi, M., Doherty, L., Watteyne, T.: A comprehensive survey on channel hopping and scheduling enhancements for TSCH networks. J. Netw. Comput. Appl. 104164 (2025)
2. Doddavenkatappa, M., Chan, M.C., Leong, B.: Splash: fast data dissemination with constructive interference in wireless sensor networks. In: 10th USENIX Symposium on Networked Systems Design and Implementation (NSDI 2013), pp. 269–282 (2013)
3. Duquennoy, S., Al Nahas, B., Landsiedel, O., Watteyne, T.: Orchestra: robust mesh networks through autonomously scheduled TSCH. In: Proceedings of the 13th ACM Conference on Embedded Networked Sensor Systems, pp. 337–350 (2015)
4. Fedrecheski, G., et al.: Mari allows connecting large scale robot swarms using TSCH over BLE and multiple independent gateways. In: International Conference on Embedded Wireless Systems and Networks-EWSN 2025 (2025)
5. Ferrari, F., Zimmerling, M., Thiele, L., Saukh, O.: Efficient network flooding and time synchronization with glossy. In: Proceedings of the 10th ACM/IEEE International Conference on Information Processing in Sensor Networks, pp. 73–84. IEEE (2011)
6. Landsiedel, O., Ferrari, F., Zimmerling, M.: Chaos: versatile and efficient all-to-all data sharing and in-network processing at scale. In: Proceedings of the 11th ACM Conference on Embedded Networked Sensor Systems, pp. 1–14 (2013)
7. Le, H.P., John, M., Pister, K.: Energy-aware routing in wireless sensor networks with adaptive energy-slope control. EE290Q-2 Spring, pp. 1–6 (2009)
8. Shahzad, M.M., et al.: A review of swarm robotics in a nutshell. Drones **7**(4), 269 (2023)
9. Vilajosana, X., Watteyne, T., Chang, T., Vučinić, M., Duquennoy, S., Thubert, P.: IETF 6tisch: a tutorial. IEEE Commun. Surv. Tutor. **22**(1), 595–615 (2019)
10. Wan, P.J., Alzoubi, K.M., Frieder, O.: Distributed construction of connected dominating set in wireless ad hoc networks. Mob. Netw. Appl. **9**(2), 141–149 (2004)

ROS-2-ARGoS Bridge: Scalable Simulations of Swarms of 1000 and More Robots

Sindiso Mkhatshwa[1,2]([✉])[iD], Tianfu Zhang[2][iD], Paolo Leopardi[1,2][iD], Heiko Hamann[1,2][iD], and Andreagiovanni Reina[1,2,3][iD]

[1] Centre for the Advanced Study of Collective Behaviour, Universität Konstanz, Konstanz, Germany
{sindiso.mkhatshwa,paolo.leopardi,heiko.hamann,
andreagiovanni.reina}@uni-konstanz.de
[2] Department of Computer and Information Science, Universität Konstanz, Konstanz, Germany
tianfu.zhang@uni-konstanz.de
[3] Department of Collective Behaviour, Max Planck Institute of Animal Behavior, Konstanz, Germany

Abstract. The Robot Operating System (ROS) is a widely adopted collection of software libraries and tools for designing and implementing robot control software. Its rapid growth has been driven by an active community that maintains an extensive ecosystem of reusable components, increasingly positioning ROS as a unifying framework bridging academic research and industrial applications. ROS 2 importantly enables decentralized, peer-to-peer communication, making it well suited for scalable and reliable multi-robot systems. Simulations play a critical role in the design and implementation of robotic systems prior to their real-world deployment. For large-scale robotic systems, simulation scalability, that is, the efficient simulation of many robots, is essential. However, existing ROS-based simulators are unable to scale to large numbers of robots, while highly scalable simulators lack integration with the ROS ecosystem. We introduce the ROS-2-ARGoS Bridge, a framework for simulating large-scale robotic systems running software based on ROS 2. We showcase its scalability through experiments with up to 1280 simulated robots that locally interact and coordinate their actions. As industries increasingly seek to scale up their robotic infrastructures, our open-source framework offers a timely and practical solution for simulating and designing large-scale multi-robot and swarm systems.

1 Introduction

Scalability is both a feature and a challenge in swarm robotics [10]. The decentralized coordination of robot swarms avoids bottlenecks and allows for maximally scalable system design. Reported swarm experiments involve up to $N = 10^3$ robots [9,30]. Scalability is still a challenge when swarm densities (i.e.,

© The Author(s), under exclusive license to Springer Nature Switzerland AG 2026
R. Groß et al. (Eds.): ANTS 2026, LNCS 16515, pp. 228–241, 2026.
https://doi.org/10.1007/978-3-032-26123-6_18

Fig. 1. A swarm of 320 simulated TurtleBot 3 robots flocking towards a light source.

number of robots per area) are critically high, shared resources (e.g., space or communication bandwidth) deplete and the system performance is decreased due to congestion or deadlocks [11,14].

Swarm robotics also has demanding requirements for the applied tooling. Commonly, swarm algorithms are iteratively developed, prototyped, and tested in robot simulators because for humans it is hard to anticipate the effects of many robot-robot interactions. This requires a 'meta-scalability,' that is, simulators of robot swarms also need to scale. Achieving system size scalability with state-of-the-art robot simulators is challenging [6]. Depending on simulation detail (e.g., robot model, physics engine), common limitations can be as low as swarm sizes of $N = 5$ or $N = 50$ robots [27]. Detailed simulations of many sensors and pair-wise robot interactions increase computational costs. In addition, common robot simulators do not always allow for easy parallelization on multi-core machines.

The demand for scalable tools is growing as industry increasingly adopts concepts from swarm robotics. Although swarm robotics research emerged over 20 years ago [3], large-scale robotic systems have only seen their real-world application in recent years. For example, they are employed in warehouse automation [12] and last-mile delivery [32]. Driven by economies of scale, we anticipate further efforts to scale up future robotic systems. However, the limitations of state-of-the-art robot simulators hinder development and add overhead by necessitating custom tool implementations for each use case.

Key tools besides simulators are software frameworks that provide a modular approach, hardware abstraction, and facilitate code sharing and reuse. For robotics, ROS 2 (Robot Operating System 2) is widely adopted [16] due to its distributed, message-based software architecture. Its modular design enables seamless substitution of simulated robots with real robot hardware without altering the underlying control logic, thus ensuring portability. Moreover, ROS 2 is also well-established in industry [18], bridging the gap between research and practical applications. Hence, there is a need for a scalable robot simulator that integrates ROS 2.

We address this technological gap by integrating ROS 2 with ARGoS 3 [26], one of the most scalable robot simulators [27]. Our ROS-2-ARGoS Bridge enables efficient large-scale simulations of robotics systems (see Fig. 1). Our software allows running the robot control software (i.e., robot algorithm) using ROS 2 libraries and executing physics-based simulations in ARGoS. ARGoS simulates sensor data acquisition and updates robots' physical states (e.g., robot position) as a consequence of robots' actuation and interactions with each other and the (potentially dynamic) environment. ROS2-based control software updates robots' internal states (e.g., algorithm variables) and computes the next actions (actuation activation) based on sensor data and internal state. Our ROS-2-ARGoS Bridge enables an efficient and scalable interaction between the two components. This integration supports broader adoption of scalable simulation tools within multi-robot research and may even provide industry with a coherent substitute to ad-hoc software solutions for modern large-scale multi-robot systems.

In Sect. 2, we give an overview of existing simulation platforms. In Sect. 3, we describe the bridge implementation, its components, and its main features. Section 4 details the available robotic platforms in ARGoS, and the integration of sensors and actuators with the ROS-2-ARGoS Bridge. In Sect. 5, we test the scalability of the proposed system with a series of experiments with up to 1280 simulated robots. We show that our ROS-2-ARGoS Bridge allows efficient simulation of large-scale robotics, making it a promising technology for future multi-robot and swarm robotics research, as described in the concluding Sect. 6.

2   Related Work

The field of multi-robot simulator development has witnessed significant advancements in recent years, driven by the need for scalable, efficient, and portable solutions to support complex robotic systems. As the scale of robotic applications grows, the ability to simulate thousands of robots while maintaining high performance (i.e., quick simulations) and ensuring realism (useful for seamless transition from simulation to real-world deployment) has become a critical challenge. In this section, we review the state of the art in multi-robot simulation, focusing on two key aspects: scalability and development/deployment challenges.

2.1   Scalability

In multi-robot simulation, the choice of the physics engine has a decisive impact on the simulation scale and performance. Currently, mainstream simulation software, such as Gazebo [13], Webots [19], and CoppeliaSim (previously known as V-REP) [29], relies on mature 3D physics engines [33] (e.g., ODE, Bullet), which are powerful but may face performance bottlenecks when dealing with thousands of robots. PyBullet is a simulator based on the Bullet physics engine and supports GPU acceleration, which can efficiently deal with large-scale physics computation but may still be limited by computational resources for the simulation of thousands of robots [7]. Stage is a lightweight simulator limited to 2.5 dimensions (thus supporting only a restricted number and types of sensors), although it offers high simulation speed [37]. In recent years, GPU-based physics engines have become a new trend in large-scale simulation. For example, AirSim and Genesis utilize GPU-accelerated physics engines that can efficiently handle complex 3D physical interactions and are suitable for large-scale multi-robot simulation [31,38]. However, these tools usually demand high-end computing hardware and require complex configuration and parameter optimization. ARGoS [25] is a simulator that can run quick large-scale simulations through a spatial partitioning parallel mechanism, dividing three-dimensional space into non-overlapping sub-regions assigned to independent physics engines. The system currently integrates four categories of physics engines (3D dynamic engines, 3D particle engines, 2D dynamic engines, and specialized engines), orchestrated by a unified entity state management interface. This architecture enables ARGoS to run rapid simulations of thousands of robots while fulfilling high-precision physical modeling requirements in specific scenarios [26].

Parallel computing is a key technology to support large-scale multi-robot simulation. Stage has high performance thanks to its lightweight 2.5D design, but it lacks support for parallel computing [37]. CoppeliaSim and MORSE's parallel computing capability mainly relies on the physics engine, leading to a marginal performance improvement [8,23]. Gazebo and Webots can benefit from both multi-thread and multi-device computation thanks to their integration with ROS 2 [17]. However, due to the constraints of their physics engine, parallel computing improvement remains limited and does not allow these simulators to scale to large numbers of robots. PyBullet supports multi-threading and GPU acceleration, which can efficiently handle large-scale physics computation, but it needs to rely on custom scripts for distributed simulation [7]. AirSim and Genesis excel in parallel computing, however, their configuration complexity and hardware requirements limit their wide adoption [31,38]. ARGoS has a significant advantage in multi-threaded and distributed computing as it can allocate simulation tasks to multiple CPU cores or computers, significantly improving simulation efficiency. ARGoS's event-driven mechanism further reduces unnecessary calculations, and its modular design and flexible configuration options make it easily adaptable to different speed and realism needs [27].

2.2 Simulated Robotic Platforms

ARGoS performs well in large-scale multi-robot simulation and, thanks to embedded cross-platform compilation, allows fast migration from simulation to real robots. However, such a high degree of consistency is mainly focused on a limited number of robotic platforms (e.g., Foot-bot, Kilobot, e-Puck, Thymio II, TurtleBot 3), resulting in the need to develop additional adaptation layers when migrating to other types of robots. Gazebo, Webots, and PyBullet, thanks to their ROS interface, leverage ROS's large community support and rich set of

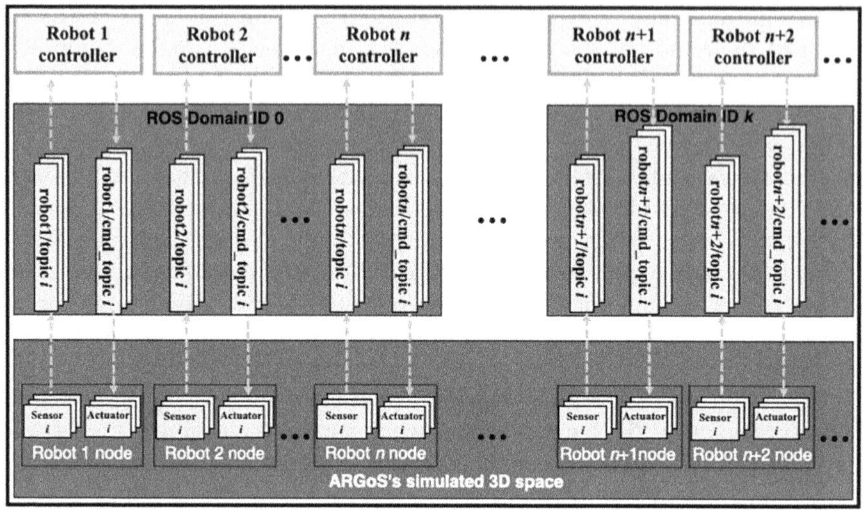

Fig. 2. An overview of the ROS-2-ARGoS Bridge framework. The ROS-2-ARGoS Bridge launches two ROS nodes for each simulated robot: one node is executed within ARGoS (blue rectangles on the bottom) and the other node is launched on the ROS side to execute the robot controller (green rectangles on the top). The two nodes of each robot exchange data through multiple ROS topics, one for each sensor and actuator that the robot is equipped with. (Color figure online)

hardware drivers available to access a wide range of commercially available sensors and actuators [2,21]. At the same time, ROS provides a complete tool chain (rviz, rqt, rosbag, etc.) that significantly simplifies debugging, testing, monitoring, and data playback. Its standardized communication mechanisms for topics, services and actions also offer efficient communication and coordination between (potentially heterogeneous) robots. We believe that our ROS-2-ARGoS Bridge framework can foster the adoption of ARGoS as a simulator for large-scale robotics and, in turn, spawn the integration in ARGoS of several new robotic platforms for multi-robot and swarm robotics applications.

3   Methods

The ROS-2-ARGoS Bridge handles efficient bidirectional data flow between the ARGoS simulator and the ROS 2-based controllers of each robot through a modular architecture. We first give an overview of the framework, then we describe the temporal workflow of the simulation, and finally, we give more details on the most critical system components.

3.1   System Architecture

The overall architecture of the system is illustrated in Fig. 2. The ARGoS simulator (blue component at the bottom) updates the 3D simulated space comprising robots (with their sensors and actuators) and environmental entities (e.g., walls, lights, objects) with potentially time-varying characteristics (e.g., changes in light intensities). The ROS-2-ARGoS Bridge launches two ROS nodes (i.e., two processes) per simulated robot: one runs within ARGoS, while the other executes the robot controller on the ROS side. The two nodes exchange data via the ROS's DDS (Data Distribution Service), more precisely, through dedicated ROS topics, one for each sensor and actuator that the robot is equipped with. Sensor topics are used to transfer sensor reading data from ARGoS to the robot controller, while actuator topics are used to transfer actuation control commands from the controller to ARGoS.

In the DDS, the primary mechanism for having different logical networks share a physical network is known as the ROS Domain ID. ROS 2 nodes within the same Domain ID can discover and communicate with each other, whereas ROS 2 nodes in different Domain IDs cannot. For each Domain ID, the DDS computes the UDP ports used for discovery and communication. Because each ROS 2 node uses two UDP ports, running several nodes in a single Domain ID may saturate the number of available ports on the computer. To avoid this limitation, robot nodes are distributed across multiple ROS Domain IDs. The assignment can be configured manually or automatically balanced by the framework across available Domain IDs. In our experiments, robots were automatically distributed with 50 robots per Domain ID, that is, (i.e., 100 nodes, each using two UDP ports). This strategy allows the system to scale up to large-scale simulations in the order of 10^3 robots, without requiring manual per-robot configuration.

Additionally, the ROS 2 DDS provides a distributed communication protocol, enabling the robot controllers to run on different computers or cluster nodes while interacting with the ARGoS simulator over the same ROS 2 network. Distributing the computation among different machines can potentially increase the simulation speed.

3.2 Temporal Workflow

The temporal workflow of a simulation is illustrated in Fig. 3, where we illustrate how various operations are executed by the three main system components (ARGoS, the Bridge, and ROS 2) and how data flows between them as time progresses (on the vertical axis, from top to bottom). The left column shows the typical sequence of phases of a simulation. The simulation is initialized (Init) by launching ARGoS and ROS 2, which loads the simulation environment and configures the ROS Domain, respectively. In the Setup phase, ARGoS starts the ROS-2-ARGoS Bridge, which is implemented as an ARGoS loop function. The bridge launches the robots' ROS nodes and configures the respective ROS topics.

The simulation then starts the Control Loop macro-phase, which repeats the two phases of Sensor Data Collection (SDC) and Control Command Execution and State Update (CCE&SU). During the SDC phase, ARGoS computes the simulated sensor readings, which are transmitted by the bridge to the ROS 2 controller via dedicated topics. The bridge also orchestrates time synchronization between ARGoS and ROS 2 by exposing the ARGoS simulation clock on a

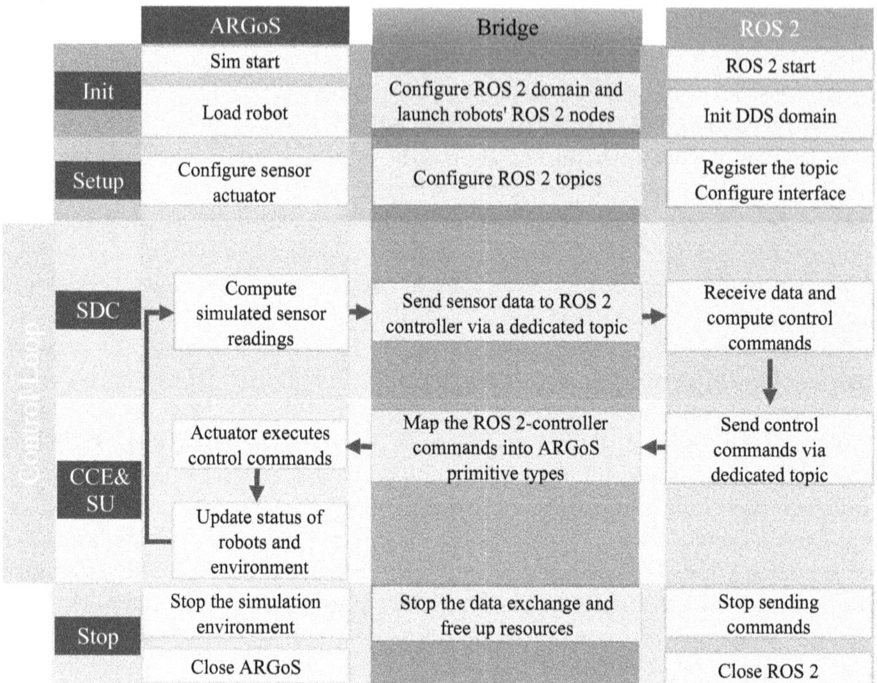

Fig. 3. Temporal workflow of a simulation where the ROS-2-ARGoS Bridge handles data exchange between the ARGoS simulator and the ROS 2 robot controller. Key phases include Init (initialization), Setup (configuration), SDC (sensor data collection, CCE&SU (control command execution and state update), and Stop (termination of the simulation).

dedicated/clock topic and by gating the advancement of each simulation tick on the completion of the corresponding ROS callbacks. ROS 2 controllers, therefore, perceive the same notion of time as ARGoS: the simulator pauses after providing sensor readings, waits for the controllers to process them and publish the resulting commands, and only then proceeds with the CCE&SU phase. Suppose a controller fails to respond before a configurable watchdog expires. In that case, the bridge records the violation, injects a safe fallback command (e.g., zero velocities, previous commands), and resumes the simulation to prevent the system from stalling. This mechanism guarantees deterministic replay, keeps ARGoS' clock authoritative even when ROS 2 nodes misbehave, and allows experiments to progress without manual intervention. In the CCE&SU phase, the bridge maps the received commands into ARGoS primitive types and forwards them to ARGoS for execution. Finally, ARGoS updates the state of the robots and the environment by executing the actuation commands (e.g., update robots' position) and any simulated temporal dynamics of the environment.

Eventually, when the termination condition is met (e.g., maximum simulation time is reached), ARGoS stops the simulation, the bridge halts data exchange, and ROS 2 shuts down (Stop phase).

3.3   Inter-robot Communication

In certain collective robotics application scenarios, especially in swarm robotics, it can be relevant to investigate the system dynamics when robots can only locally communicate. Such robots can only exchange messages with other robots (neighbors) located at a distance shorter than a given communication range. For example, robots may only be able to exchange messages by transmitting infrared signals to robots closer than 50 cm. Such local communication can improve the robotic system's scalability as saturation of the communication channel is prevented. However, because ROS 2 communication is handled through the DDS, robots (ROS nodes) in the same ROS Domain ID can always exchange data. Therefore, simulating distance-based inter-robot communication with traditional ROS-compatible simulators (e.g. Gazebo) can be complicated.

The ROS-2-ARGoS Bridge enables the seamless execution of ROS 2-based robot controllers with local inter-robot communication. During simulation, communication is handled analogously to sensors and actuators, exploiting distance-based neighbor selection. At each simulation step, ARGoS determines neighboring robots according to the communication device characteristics (e.g., Euclidean distance or line of sight), and copies the transmitted messages into the sensor data of those neighbors. The implementation of inter-robot communication mediated by ARGoS enables the simulation of both local and global communication, depending on application requirements and robot constraints.

4   Simulated Robotic Platforms

To run ROS-2-ARGoS simulations, the virtual model of the robot must be implemented in ARGoS. Each robot type is characterized by a specific set of sensors and actuators, which determine the external information accessible to the robot (e.g., environmental state) and how it changes its state (e.g., its positions) through physical interactions with the environment. The environment is simulated using a physics engine, and each robot's sensing and actuation must be modeled in the simulator. Like in any simulators, including realistic sensing and actuation noise requires dedicated tests to quantify such errors. Additionally, video visualization of the simulation requires a 3D model of the robot.

ARGoS already includes a bunch of models for popular robotics platforms, especially relevant for swarm robotics research. In addition to the Foot-bot [5], which is natively included in ARGoS, various plugins[1] allow simulating a variety of other popular robots, including Thymio II [28], Khepera IV [34], Turtle-Bot 3 [1], Kilobot [24], E-puck [20], and Crazyflie [35]. In our experiments,

---

[1] https://www.argos-sim.info/extensions.php.

we used the TurtleBot 3 [1], which is a robotic platform widely used in several research laboratories studying collective robotics, and is supported in both ARGoS and Gazebo, allowing us to compare the performances of the two simulators.

Robot models that are implemented in ARGoS can be interfaced with ROS 2 through a robot-specific ROS-2-ARGoS Bridge. As shown in Fig. 2, the only exchanged information regards sensors and actuators. Hence, our framework can be extended by mapping the data exchanged between ARGoS and ROS 2. More specifically, ARGoS's sensor data map to ROS 2's controller sensor input, and ARGoS's actuator input parameters map to ROS-2 actuation output. In each simulation, each robot can be configured by including the set of sensors and actuators needed for the given application scenario. In our open-source code,[2] we implemented ROS-2-ARGoS Bridge for a few relevant sensors and actuators: colored blob perspective camera sensor, infrared (IR) proximity sensor, ground-color sensor, light sensor, differential wheels, LED, range-and-bearing local communication, and LiDAR. We configured them for the Foot-bot and TurtleBot 3 robots. These same sensors and actuators, with different parameters and noise levels, can also model other robotic platforms, e.g., the Thymio II robot [28].

5 Simulation Experiments

We test the performance of our simulation approach in a classical swarm robotics task: flocking [36] (see a simulation screenshot in Fig. 1). This scenario has been widely studied in the literature and can be used as a building block for various applications, such as environmental monitoring, distributed sensing, and collective transport [4,39]. To implement flocking, where a group of robots flock in a hexagonal lattice towards a light source placed in the task environment, we use a generalization of the Lennard-Jones potential parameterized with the same values of [26] (code available in the same repository (see Footnote 2)).

We evaluate the scalability of our proposed framework using simulated TurtleBot 3 swarms of size $N \in \{3, 5, 10, 20, 40, 80, 160, 320, 640, 1280\}$ performing flocking. On Linux systems, the ROS-2-ARGoS Bridge framework can theoretically support up to 7200 robots due to ROS 2 constraints.[3] Specifically, ROS 2 provides 120 Domain IDs, each supporting up to 120 processes; since each robot requires two processes, this limits the total number of robots. Here, we run our tests with up to 1280 robots as a proof of concept. For all experiments, we performed 10 independent trials, each consisting of 600 simulation time steps. With a step size of 0.1 s, each trial corresponds to one simulated minute. We measured the time taken to run the simulation, as well as CPU and memory usage. As ARGoS supports multi-threaded execution, we ran our experiments both with and without multi-threading enabled. Because the simulation were run on a 12-core machine, ARGoS was configured to use 12 threads.

---

[2] https://github.com/CPS-Konstanz/argos3-ros2-bridge.
[3] https://docs.ros.org/en/jazzy/Concepts/Intermediate/About-Domain-ID.html.

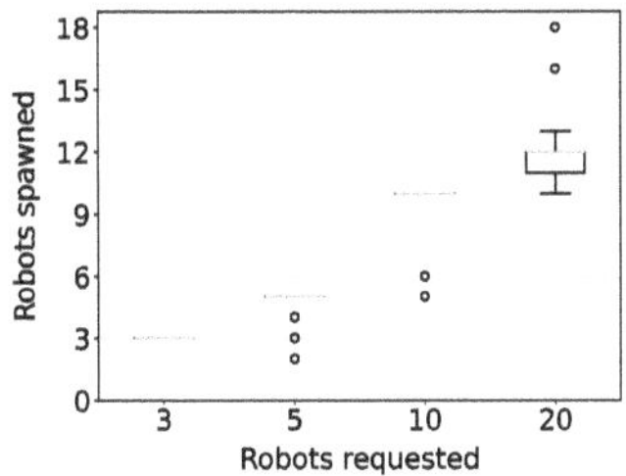

Fig. 4. Distribution of the number of robots successfully spawned in Gazebo across 100 simulation iterations for different swarm sizes. The orange line is the median, the box represents the interquartile range (IQR), the interval of the whiskers contains data points that are within 1.5 IQR, and circular markers indicate outliers. (Color figure online)

In our experiments, ROS 2 nodes were initialized with 100 ROS 2 nodes per ROS Domain ID, comprising 50 ARGoS nodes and 50 controller nodes. This setting was adopted to avoid conflicts with ephemeral ports at large population sizes. We used the default Eclipse Cyclone DDS settings for all experiments.

All simulations were conducted on a computer running Linux Ubuntu 22.04.5 LTS, equipped with an AMD® Ryzen 9 7900 processor featuring 12 cores, each supporting 2 threads for a total of 24 threads, as well as 32 GB of RAM.

We compare the performance of the proposed simulation framework with the most popular ROS 2-based simulator, Gazebo 11. We tested Gazebo's scalability by launching the simulator with an increasing number of TurtleBot 3 robots. We repeated each experiment 100 times and counted how many robots were successfully spawned after one minute. Figure 4 shows that Gazebo becomes unreliable beyond 3 robots and never succeeded in spawning 20 robots. Due to Gazebo's poor scalability performances, Gazebo experiments were restricted to the swarm sizes $N \in \{3, 5, 10\}$.

Figure 5 shows the average wall-clock time, CPU usage, and memory consumption for the flocking simulations with up to 1280 robots. The black dashed horizontal line denotes the real-time threshold (60 s), marking the point at which simulation time equals real-world time. Both Gazebo and our framework support simulation quicker than real-time (i.e., one simulated minute takes less than one real-world minute to be executed). However, for the same swarm sizes, Gazebo requires approximately eight times more execution time than our framework. ARGoS achieves faster-than-real-time performance for fewer than 30 robots (or 50 with multithreading). Overall, ARGoS's execution time scales approximately linearly with the swarm size N.

Gazebo uses more computation (linear increase) than our ARGoS framework, which shows sublinear scaling of CPU usage with increasing N. However, our framework uses more memory than Gazebo for the same swarm sizes. Interestingly, Gazebo's memory consumption decreased sharply for the largest swarm size (10 robots). On the other hand, our framework maintains a linear increase with N of the memory usage.

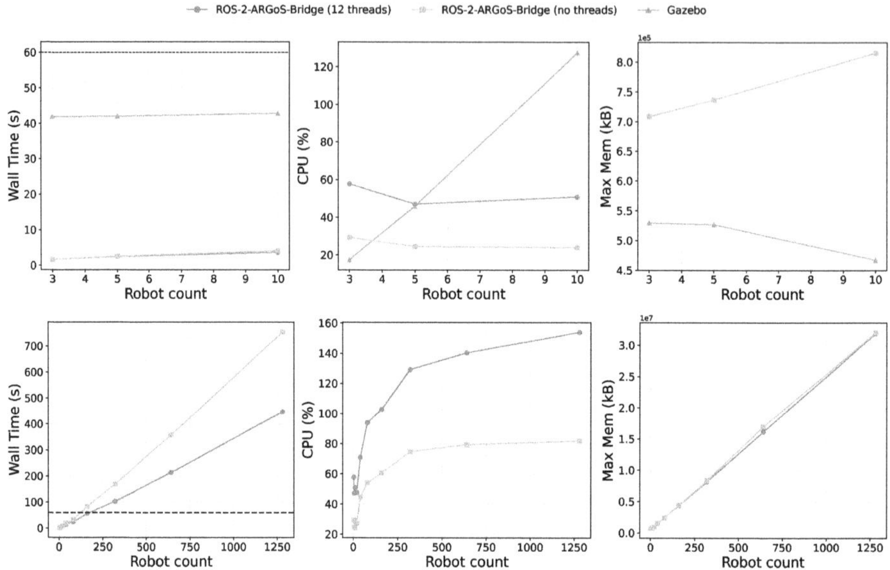

Fig. 5. Average wall clock time, CPU usage, and memory consumption for the ROS 2-based flocking simulations. (Top row) Performance comparison between Gazebo and the proposed simulation framework—ARGoS with ROS 2 Bridge with/without multi-threading. (Bottom row) Scalability performance of ARGoS in large-scale simulations.

6   Conclusion

This work presents the ROS-2-ARGoS Bridge, a scalable framework for large-scale multi-robot simulation. By bridging the high-performance, multi-threaded ARGoS simulator with the widely adopted ROS 2 ecosystem, our framework enables efficient and scalable simulation of large robot swarms.

Our results demonstrate that, in terms of scalability, our framework largely outperforms the state-of-the-art simulator for ROS-based robots, Gazebo. The proposed framework is computationally efficient and scales linearly with increasing swarm sizes, allowing physics-based simulations with over a thousand robots. We anticipate that the ROS-2-ARGoS Bridge will reduce development complexity, enhance code reusability, and streamline the transfer of swarm robotics algorithms from simulation to real-world applications. The proposed framework aims to accelerate the design, implementation, and testing of large-scale robotic systems beyond controlled lab environments, for example in automated warehouses and agricultural fields. Our approach supports the rapid expansion of real-world applications of swarm robotics.

Future work will investigate consolidating ROS components within a single process and leveraging intra-process communication to eliminate DDS-mediated UDP transport [22]. This approach is expected to reduce communication overhead and remove constraints such as limited UDP port availability, while preserving multi-threading capabilities and enabling distributed deployment via one ROS container per computer [15].

Acknowledgments. This work has been partially supported by the DFG under Germany's Excellence Strategy – EXC 2117-422037984. The authors thank Carlo Pinciroli for helpful discussions and Raina Zakir for testing the software and improving the GitHub installation documentation.

Disclosure of Interests. The authors have no competing interests to declare.

References

1. Amsters, R., Slaets, P.: Turtlebot 3 as a robotics education platform. In: Merdan, M., Lepuschitz, W., Koppensteiner, G., Balogh, R., Obdržálek, D. (eds.) RiE 2019. AISC, vol. 1023, pp. 170–181. Springer, Cham (2020). https://doi.org/10.1007/978-3-030-26945-6_16
2. Andreiev, A., Sotnik, S.: Comparative analysis of robotics platform: Webots, Coppeliasim and Gazebo. Technical report, Repository of Kharkiv National University of Radio Electronics (2024)
3. Beni, G.: From swarm intelligence to swarm robotics. In: Şahin, E., Spears, W.M. (eds.) SR 2004. LNCS, vol. 3342, pp. 1–9. Springer, Heidelberg (2005). https://doi.org/10.1007/978-3-540-30552-1_1
4. Berlinger, F., Gauci, M., Nagpal, R.: Implicit coordination for 3D underwater collective behaviors in a fish-inspired robot swarm. Sci. Robot. **6**(50), eabd8668 (2021)
5. Bonani, M., et al.: The marXbot, a miniature mobile robot opening new perspectives for the collective-robotic research. In: 2010 IEEE/RSJ International Conference on Intelligent Robots and Systems (IROS), pp. 4187–4193. IEEE (2010)
6. Choi, H., et al.: On the use of simulation in robotics: opportunities, challenges, and suggestions for moving forward. Proc. Natl. Acad. Sci. **118**(1), e1907856118 (2021)
7. Coumans, E., Bai, Y.: PyBullet, a Python module for physics simulation for games, robotics and machine learning (2016–2021). http://pybullet.org
8. Echeverria, G., Lassabe, N., Degroote, A., Lemaignan, S.: Modular open robots simulation engine: MORSE. In: IEEE International Conference on Robotics and Automation (ICRA), pp. 46–51. IEEE (2011)
9. Gauci, M., Ortiz, M.E., Rubenstein, M., Nagpal, R.: Error cascades in collective behavior: a case study of the gradient algorithm on 1000 physical agents. In: Proceedings of the 16th Conference on Autonomous Agents and MultiAgent Systems, pp. 1404–1412. IFAAMAS (2017)
10. Hamann, H.: Swarm Robotics: A Formal Approach. Springer, Cham (2018)
11. Hamann, H., Reina, A.: Scalability in computing and robotics. IEEE Trans. Comput. **71**(6), 1453–1465 (2021)
12. Ikumapayi, O.M., Laseinde, O.T., Elewa, R.R., Ogedengbe, T.S., Akinlabi, E.T.: Swarm robotics in a sustainable warehouse automation: opportunities, challenges and solutions. In: E3S Web of Conferences, vol. 552, p. 01080. EDP Sciences (2024)

13. Koenig, N., Howard, A.: Design and use paradigms for Gazebo, an open-source multi-robot simulator. In: 2004 IEEE/RSJ International Conference on Intelligent Robots and Systems (IROS) (IEEE Cat. No.04CH37566), vol. 3, pp. 2149–2154 (2004)
14. Kuckling, J., Luckey, R., Avrutin, V., Vardy, A., Reina, A., Hamann, H.: Do we run large-scale multi-robot systems on the edge? More evidence for two-phase performance in system size scaling. In: 2024 IEEE International Conference on Robotics and Automation (ICRA), pp. 4562–4568. IEEE (2024)
15. Macenski, S., Soragna, A., Carroll, M., Ge, Z.: Impact of ROS 2 node composition in robotic systems. IEEE Robot. Autom. Lett. **8**(7), 3996–4003 (2023)
16. Macenski, S., Foote, T., Gerkey, B., Lalancette, C., Woodall, W.: Robot operating system 2: design, architecture, and uses in the wild. Sci. Robot. **7**(66), eabm6074 (2022)
17. Mañas-Álvarez, F.J., Guinaldo, M., Dormido, R., Dormido-Canto, S.: Scalability of cyber-physical systems with real and virtual robots in ROS 2. Sensors **23**(13), 6073 (2023)
18. Maruyama, Y., Kato, S., Azumi, T.: Exploring the performance of ROS2. In: Proceedings of the 13th International Conference on Embedded Software (EMSOFT), pp. 1–10. IEEE (2016)
19. Michel, O.: Webots: symbiosis between virtual and real mobile robots. In: Heudin, J.-C. (ed.) VW 1998. LNCS (LNAI), vol. 1434, pp. 254–263. Springer, Heidelberg (1998). https://doi.org/10.1007/3-540-68686-X_24
20. Mondada, F., et al.: The e-puck, a robot designed for education in engineering. In: Proceedings of the 9th Conference on Autonomous Robot Systems and Competitions, vol. 1, pp. 59–65. IPCB: Instituto Politecnico de Castelo Branco, Portugal (2009)
21. Mower, C., et al.: ROS-PyBullet interface: a framework for reliable contact simulation and human-robot interaction. In: Proceedings of the 6th Conference on Robot Learning, PMLR, vol. 205, pp. 1411–1423. MLResearchPress (2023)
22. Naury, L., Gouguet, A., Lozenguez, G., Fabresse, L.: Communication isolation for multi-robot systems using ROS2. In: Proceedings of the 40th ACM/SIGAPP Symposium on Applied Computing, SAC 2025, pp. 850–858. ACM (2025)
23. Noori, F.M., Portugal, D., Rocha, R.P., Couceiro, M.S.: On 3D simulators for multi-robot systems in ROS: MORSE or Gazebo? In: 2017 IEEE International Symposium on Safety, Security and Rescue Robotics (SSRR), pp. 19–24. IEEE (2017)
24. Pinciroli, C., Talamali, M.S., Reina, A., Marshall, J.A.R., Trianni, V.: Simulating Kilobots within ARGoS: models and experimental validation. In: Dorigo, M., Birattari, M., Blum, C., Christensen, A.L., Reina, A., Trianni, V. (eds.) ANTS 2018. LNCS, vol. 11172, pp. 176–187. Springer, Cham (2018). https://doi.org/10.1007/978-3-030-00533-7_14
25. Pinciroli, C., et al.: ARGoS: a modular, multi-engine simulator for heterogeneous swarm robotics. In: Proceedings of the IEEE/RSJ International Conference on Intelligent Robots and Systems (IROS), pp. 5027–5034. IEEE (2011)
26. Pinciroli, C., et al.: ARGoS: a modular, parallel, multi-engine simulator for multi-robot systems. Swarm Intell. **6**, 271–295 (2012)
27. Pitonakova, L., Giuliani, M., Pipe, A., Winfield, A.: Feature and performance comparison of the V-REP, Gazebo and ARGoS robot simulators. In: Giuliani, M., Assaf, T., Giannaccini, M.E. (eds.) TAROS 2018. LNCS (LNAI), vol. 10965, pp. 357–368. Springer, Cham (2018). https://doi.org/10.1007/978-3-319-96728-8_30

28. Riedo, F., Chevalier, M., Magnenat, S., Mondada, F.: Thymio II, a robot that grows wiser with children. In: 2013 IEEE Workshop on Advanced Robotics and its Social Impacts, pp. 187–193. IEEE (2013)
29. Rohmer, E., Singh, S.P., Freese, M.: V-REP: a versatile and scalable robot simulation framework. In: IEEE/RSJ International Conference on Intelligent Robots and Systems (IROS), pp. 1321–1326. IEEE (2013)
30. Rubenstein, M., Cornejo, A., Nagpal, R.: Programmable self-assembly in a thousand-robot swarm. Science **345**(6198), 795–799 (2014)
31. Shah, S., Dey, D., Lovett, C., Kapoor, A.: AirSim: high-fidelity visual and physical simulation for autonomous vehicles. In: Hutter, M., Siegwart, R. (eds.) Field and Service Robotics. SPAR, vol. 5, pp. 621–635. Springer, Cham (2018). https://doi.org/10.1007/978-3-319-67361-5_40
32. Simoni, M.D., Kutanoglu, E., Claudel, C.G.: Optimization and analysis of a robot-assisted last mile delivery system. Transp. Res. Part E: Logist. Transp. Rev. **142**, 102049 (2020)
33. Smith, R.: Open dynamics engine (2006). https://ode.org/
34. Soares, J.M., Navarro, I., Martinoli, A.: The Khepera IV mobile robot: performance evaluation, sensory data and software toolbox. In: Reis, L., et al. (eds.) Robot 2015: Second Iberian Robotics Conference. AISC, vol. 417, pp. 767–781. Springer, Cham (2016). https://doi.org/10.1007/978-3-319-27146-0_59
35. Stolfi, D.H., Danoy, G.: An ARGoS plug-in for the Crazyflie drone. arXiv:2401.16948 (2024)
36. Turgut, A.E., Çelikkanat, H., Gökçe, F., Şahin, E.: Self-organized flocking in mobile robot swarms. Swarm Intell. **2**, 97–120 (2008)
37. Vaughan, R.: Massively multi-robot simulation in stage. Swarm Intell. **2**, 189–208 (2008)
38. Zhou, X., et al.: Genesis: a generative and universal physics engine for robotics and beyond (2024). https://github.com/Genesis-Embodied-AI/Genesis
39. Zhou, X., et al.: Swarm of micro flying robots in the wild. Sci. Robot. **7**(66), eabm5954 (2022)

Ten Years of the Collective Perception Benchmark in Swarm Robotics: Achievements and Challenges

Heiko Hamann[1,2(✉)] [iD] and Andreagiovanni Reina[1,2,3] [iD]

[1] Centre for the Advanced Study of Collective Behaviour, Universität Konstanz, Konstanz, Germany
[2] Department of Computer and Information Science, Universität Konstanz, Konstanz, Germany
`heiko.hamann@uni-konstanz.de`
[3] Department of Collective Behaviour, Max Planck Institute of Animal Behavior, Konstanz, Germany

Abstract. The collective perception scenario is an established swarm robotics task in which robots collectively infer a globally distributed environmental feature. The scenario is the most cited benchmark for collective decision-making in swarm robotics and has a 10-year history. Many variants of the original scenario have been proposed and studied. Many methods of collective decision-making have been tested against it. Given that the scenario was not initially intended as the defining benchmark, we summarize and analyze the literature and discuss the benefits and potential risks of a monoculture in benchmarking. We give a perspective on what could and should be improved in the future.

1 Introduction

Swarm robotics [19] generally lacks standardized benchmarks [23]. The collective perception (CP) scenario [57] is one of the few widely adopted testbeds and has been extensively used to evaluate methods that enable a swarm to reach consensus on the correct environmental state. In its original formulation, a swarm of robots operates on a grid where each tile (or grid cell) is either black or white (Fig. 1). The objective is to determine which color predominates across the entire environment. However, no individual robot has direct access to the global color distribution as each can collect evidence only from the tile beneath it. Although CP generalizes to a best-of-n problem (i.e., selecting the best discrete option from a finite set of size n), most studies focus on the binary case ($n = 2$).

Conceptually, the scenario relates to the classical cellular automata majority problem posed by Mitchell et al. [28], which asked whether a decentralized system can determine if black or white cells are initially in the majority. It is also related to the collective estimation problem studied by Morlino et al. [29], where the real-valued density of black tiles is estimated rather than reduced to a binary decision. The CP scenario represents a deliberately simplified perception

R. Groß et al. (Eds.): ANTS 2026, LNCS 16515, pp. 242–257, 2026.
https://doi.org/10.1007/978-3-032-26123-6_19

Fig. 1. Illustration of the CP scenario. Robots locally sample tile color on a black-and-white grid, form and communicate opinions, and reach a consensus on the majority color. The benchmark was intentionally designed to avoid spatial correlations, allowing for locally unbiased sampling and motion-induced mixing that approximate a well-mixed population, to compare best-of-n strategies.

task that differs from richer perception problems, such as multi-robot SLAM [27], where robots build maps and localize themselves, and complex semantic perception [26], which requires interpreting object features. Instead, CP isolates a core challenge of swarm cognition: how a distributed system can reliably aggregate noisy, local information to infer a macroscopic variable [29,43]; a process also observed in natural systems, such as insect colonies [17]. In applications, the macroscopic variable can be the presence or absence (or concentration) of a distributed resource (e.g., precious metals, pollutants), structural damage, or abnormal cell concentration (e.g., cancer cell detection). The CP scenario abstracts these problems into a model of distributed estimation and collective decision-making.

What the original authors of the CP scenario could not have anticipated ten years ago was its lasting influence. Its widespread adoption has improved comparability across collective decision-making methods, yet reliance on a single benchmark risks narrowing the design space. Although current approaches appear largely exploratory and show no clear signs of overfitting, the inflation of scenario variants and increasingly sophisticated algorithms complicates fair comparison. Over the past decade, CP has been extended from binary majority detection to density estimation, from uniform to spatially clustered environments, and from simple bio-inspired voting rules to Bayesian inference, evolutionary methods, reinforcement learning (RL), and blockchain-based robustness mechanisms. The complexity of communication models was expanded beyond 1-bit opinion exchange to include, for example, the statistical model parameters. While these novel methods advance the field, they also risk losing the benchmark's original simplicity. To move forward, we need a broader set of benchmarks that evaluate robustness, scalability, and security in a more systematic and comparable way.

We give an overview of the CP scenario, from its origin (Sect. 2) to various extensions in terms of the capabilities of the local perception units (i.e., the robots, Sect. 3), the environment to perceive (Sect. 4), and how to compare performance (Sect. 5). A meaningful benchmark requires not only a well-defined task and its variants (Sect. 4), but also explicit assumptions about the computational resources (robot capabilities, Sect. 3) to ensure a fair comparison. Moreover, the intended downstream use of information perceived by the swarm should inform the selection of models and evaluation metrics. We focus on three questions: which assumptions vary across studies, under which extensions prior conclusions no longer hold, and which metrics or generalizations remain underexplored.

2   Original Collective Perception Scenario

The original scenario by Valentini et al. [57] is formulated as a best-of-n problem with $n = 2$ options, that is, a binary collective decision-making problem. A swarm of robots operates in a bounded square arena whose floor is divided into a grid of black (b) and white (w) tiles, uniformly and randomly distributed in space (Fig. 1). The two colors correspond to the two decision options ($\mathcal{O} = \{b, w\}$), and their relative frequencies define the option quality (fill ratios ρ_b and $\rho_w = 1 - \rho_b$). The swarm's task is to collectively explore the environment and reach consensus (or a large majority) on the globally dominant option $o^* = \arg\max_{c \in \mathcal{O}} \rho_c$, that is, to determine whether $\rho_b > \rho_w$ or $\rho_b < \rho_w$. Robots cannot observe the global distribution ρ_b but can only take local measurements from ground sensors that detect the tile color beneath them. The CP scenario is meaningful only when individual estimations $\hat{\rho}_b^i$ are insufficiently reliable to determine the environmental state independently ($\mathbb{E}\big[(\hat{\rho}_b^i - \rho_b)^2\big] > 0$); otherwise, collaboration would neither improve the rate of correct perceptions of the true environmental state (i.e., perception accuracy) nor be required to reach an agreement. Because observations are strictly local and each robot samples only a small portion of the environment, individual estimates of the global distribution are often inaccurate. To enable a CP of the true environmental state, robots must exchange information. Each robot i maintains an opinion $o_i \in \{b, w\}$ about which color is more frequent and shares it locally through short-range communication. In the collective estimation variant, the swarm must agree on the real-valued density of black tiles, which defines the task as: $\min |\hat{\rho}_b^{\text{swarm}} - \rho_b|$ [29].

3   Robot Capabilities

Robot capabilities range from minimal machines that store, process, and exchange only a few bits of information to powerful robots capable of substantial computation. When comparing solutions, it is essential to consider the requirements each algorithm imposes on the robots. As robot platforms and algorithms vary widely, so do the capabilities assumed by different studies. In the following, we review existing work and outline research challenges and opportunities regarding how robot capabilities shape CP.

3.1   Computation, Communication Bandwidth, and Memory

The original scenario [57] compares three algorithms with minimal robot requirements. Robots can store a single opinion o_i and its estimated quality $\hat{\rho}^i$, communicate their preferred opinion o_i to nearby neighbors (not its quality), and process $M \geq 1$ messages. The simplest tested algorithm, the weighted voter model [58], restricts interaction to $M = 1$ message. Other tested algorithms are variants of the majority rule requiring $M \geq 3$ [59]. Under the majority rule, robots adopt the opinion held by the majority of their neighbors, whereas using the voter model, they copy the opinion of a randomly selected neighbor.

Many subsequent studies aimed to improve efficiency, particularly concerning the speed–accuracy tradeoff (see Sect. 5). The assumed robot capabilities of each study constrained the proposed algorithms and shaped their design methods.

Bio-Inspired Voting Algorithms. For very simple robots with minimal capabilities, effective solutions are bio-inspired. Zakir et al. [61,62] compare the weighted voter model with the cross-inhibition model, inspired by honeybee house-hunting. Cross-inhibition is identical to the weighted voter model, except that robots receiving neighbor votes for a different opinion transition to an uncommitted state. Cross-inhibition consistently outperforms the weighted voter model, producing more cohesive, stable, and faster decisions while retaining similar simplicity [61]. It also allows swarms to break symmetries and reach consensus in symmetric environments (i.e., options of equal quality), a setting in which the weighted voter model performs poorly.

Bayesian Algorithms. The 'Bayes Bot' approach of Ebert et al. [15] has a strong statistical foundation. Each robot acts as a Bayesian estimator, modeling the unknown fill ratio ρ_b with a Beta distribution ($\rho_b \sim Beta(\alpha, \beta)$), and continuously updating its posterior using both newly collected local binary observations and those received from neighbors. The algorithm adjusts its decision time to task difficulty, making decisions quickly when evidence is clear and slowly when it is ambiguous, while maintaining accuracy comparable to fixed-time methods.

Bayesian methods typically offer improved performance but require robots to compute and transmit more information. Shan and Mostaghim [47,48] make a particularly valuable contribution by conducting a careful and fair benchmarking of Bayesian approaches against other algorithms, explicitly accounting for the communication bandwidth required by each method, an aspect often overlooked. They introduce and evaluate several variants of Distributed Bayesian Belief Sharing (DBBS) [45,46], in which robots maintain Bayesian likelihoods over all hypotheses and exchange probabilistic beliefs rather than single-option votes. DBBS achieves high accuracy and fast consensus even with clustered features or reduced communication, at the cost of higher required bandwidth.

Other Bayesian-based approaches include Abdelli et al. [1], Chiu et al. (belief with PSO tuning) [11], and Bartashevich and Sanaz (evidence theory) [6,7].

Reinforcement Learning and Evolutionary Approaches. The only RL approach we are aware of is that of Hussein et al. [20], in which robots learn behaviors through a sequence of state–action–reward modules, producing a CP strategy that outperforms human-designed algorithms.

Evolutionary swarm robotics has been explored more extensively. Almansoori et al. [2,3] evolve small continuous-time recurrent neural networks that map locally sensed tile color and neighbor communication to the robot's opinion.

The evolved networks integrate perceptual and social information over time and outperform the weighted voter model.

Kaiser et al. [21] analyze how fitness functions shape evolved decision-making. By comparing task-independent (prediction-error minimization) and task-specific rewards, they find that the latter yield higher accuracy than the majority rule and the voter model, with decision times between the two.

Outlook. The original assumption of homogeneous robots and environments is limiting, and several studies have begun to relax it. A promising research direction is to leverage individual heterogeneity to improve group performance cost-effectively. If more sophisticated robots can achieve higher accuracy, speed, or cohesion than simpler ones, an important open question is whether similar performance can be reached by embedding only a small proportion of sophisticated robots within an otherwise simple swarm. Because simpler robots are typically cheaper to produce and operate, mixed swarms may offer practical and resource-efficient solutions. Early results suggest that heterogeneous swarms for CP are indeed a promising direction [64].

3.2   Communication Network

CP relies critically on information exchange among robots and, in general, the communication network topology can strongly influence collective decision-making dynamics [42]. In swarm robotics, communication is typically limited to interactions among neighbors. In the original study [57], robots move randomly, promoting spatial mixing of opinions and approximating a well-mixed state that minimizes spatial correlations between neighboring robots. Motion patterns and communication range jointly determine the communication topology.

Aust et al. [5] analyze the impact of communication range. A key counter-intuitive result is a less-is-more effect: with large communication ranges, the swarm loses the ability to integrate new evidence after option qualities change. High connectivity allows a majority favoring an outdated option to suppress minority discoveries before they spread. Reducing the communication range mitigates these lock-in effects.

Outlook. Future comparisons should incorporate network connectivity as a core factor. Such insights could inform decentralized control mechanisms that adapt communication range to improve performance (see metrics in Sect. 5).

3.3   Environmental Sensing

Robots sense only the color beneath them and estimate option qualities from local observations. In the original approach [57], all robots experience the same sensing noise; however, real-world deployments are unlikely to be so uniform [38]. Heterogeneity may be designed (e.g., by mixing robots of different sophistication or sensor types) or unintentionally through wear, manufacturing tolerances, calibration errors, or software and hardware faults.

Chin et al. [8–10] study a collective estimation variant of the problem in which robots have different, initially unknown, noise levels. By enabling robots to estimate both their own and other robots' noise levels, they can collectively weigh opinions inversely proportional to expected noise. Compared to approaches that ignore these differences, their method yields improved performance.

Outlook. A promising research track is that individuals may weigh option attributes differently, resulting in conflicting preferences within the swarm. Similarly, in nature, some ants prioritize darkness while others favor entrance size or number when evaluating nest sites [17]. Such settings can be modeled as multi-objective decision problems. Future work should extend the CP benchmark to examine how groups can resolve individual conflicts while still reaching consensus. This is relevant, for example, to robot teams in industrial applications when robots can be owned or configured by different stakeholders, potentially operating with differing objectives or incentives [60]. A benchmark could incorporate additional decision dimensions (e.g., ambient light or humidity, in addition to tile color) to study multi-objective CP.

4   Complex Environments

The original benchmark (Sect. 2) is simple and elegant, enabling clean comparisons between algorithms. Yet, advancing toward real-world applications requires consideration of more complex and realistic conditions.

4.1   Beyond Binary Decisions, $n > 2$ Options, and Continuous Options

Originally, the CP scenario focused on binary decisions ($n = 2$). This simplifies the analysis (e.g., the two option qualities can be expressed as a single ratio) and assumes that, when more options are present, the dynamics are dominated by competition between the two strongest alternatives. However, theoretical work indicates qualitative changes in the dynamics when $n > 2$ [13,41]. For $n > 2$, the environment can be characterized by fill ratios $\boldsymbol{\rho} = (\rho_1, \ldots, \rho_n)$, the CP task is then defined as a functional $f(\boldsymbol{\rho})$, and different objectives become possible. In particular, one may distinguish (a) best-of-n selection, identifying $o^* = \arg\max_j \rho_j$, (b) majority detection, determining whether $\exists j : \rho_j > 1/2$, or (c) full distribution estimation, reconstructing $\hat{\boldsymbol{\rho}} \approx \boldsymbol{\rho}$. Mostaghim and colleagues [7,48] compared several methods for best-of-n and full distribution estimation with up to $n = 10$ in simulations. While some methods scaled well, others exhibited substantial performance degradation as n increased, indicating the importance of studying $n > 2$.

Outlook. It remains an open question how to design a benchmark with $n \gg 2$ that remains elegant, analytically tractable, and focused on the most relevant conditions. A natural qualitative extension is going to continuous decision-making (i.e., collective estimation), where robots estimate real-valued quantities.

For example, the swarm needs to find consensus on the mean $\frac{1}{|\Omega|} \int_\Omega g(x)\,dx$ of a scalar field $g : \Omega \to \mathbb{R}$ within a bounded area $\Omega \subset \mathbb{R}^d$ [37]. This shift to collective estimation better matches realistic swarm-sensing tasks (e.g., mean pollutant concentration, temperature, or radiation level over an area) but also requires different methods, as categorical and continuous decisions pose fundamentally different challenges. One should also consider an early CP formulation [26] comparable to swarm SLAM [27], in which robots collaboratively scan and characterize objects to infer properties such as shape and function.

4.2 Spatial Heterogeneity

In the original scenario, black and white tiles are uniformly distributed, so any location provides a representative estimate of the fill ratio (Fig. 1).

Bartashevich and Mostaghim [6] introduce non-uniform tile color distributions and categorize them by clustering geometry (e.g., clusters, patches, strips). Whereas task difficulty in the original benchmark depends only on the fill ratio, they show that difficulty is also determined by how features are spatially arranged. The most challenging setting is the highly heterogeneous "half–half" environment (one side predominantly black, the other predominantly white).

Kelly et al. [24] study another form of spatial heterogeneity where communication quality varies across the environment. Some regions partially degrade messages, while others block communication entirely. Robots do not know where these communication-denied areas are or how large they are.

Outlook. Future work should extend the benchmark by incorporating a model of spatial correlation, enabling a systematic study of how tile distributions affect algorithmic performance while capturing patterns relevant to real-world environments. It would also be valuable to relate this scenario to best-of-n problems with spatially segregated options (e.g., site selection [35,56,58]). Analyses of spatial heterogeneity should further account for robot motion patterns and how these shape individual quality estimates and correlations among neighbors' observations.

4.3 Temporal Heterogeneity

In a static environment, a single robot could, in principle, solve CP optimally given enough time and memory to explore the entire space. In dynamic environments, however, swarms can detect changes and infer the state of the world far more quickly and accurately than any individual robot. Many decision-making algorithms nevertheless lock the swarm into a fixed consensus that cannot adapt to new evidence, as strong social reinforcement prevents revising earlier decisions. Studying time-varying environments is therefore essential for assessing robustness to reveal otherwise hidden limitations. Extensions to the benchmark introduce abrupt changes in option quality during runtime [5,15,33,34,64], enabling evaluation of swarm performance in dynamic environments where the best option suddenly switches.

Outlook. Only a few studies address dynamic environments, and the field still lacks a systematic treatment of time-varying conditions. Another important but largely unexplored aspect is the appearance and disappearance of options over time, as considered in other best-of-n scenarios [56]. Existing CP studies assume that robots know the option set $\mathcal{O}$ (e.g., black and white), but not the associated qualities. When the option set is unknown or changes over time, robots must first discover the available alternatives before estimating their qualities [25]. Research shows that adding independent option discovery causes several algorithms to fail, whereas cross-inhibition consistently reaches consensus quickly [61,62]. Incorporating discovery can be crucial for practical deployment, as real environments may feature dynamic and initially unknown options.

4.4 Byzantine Faults

A Byzantine fault occurs when a system component behaves arbitrarily or maliciously, sending inconsistent or deceptive information to others. Swarm robots must be robust to such faults. Therefore, several studies have investigated variants of the CP scenario that incorporate different adversarial conditions.

Malfunctioning and Malicious Robots. Robots that deviate from their specified behavior are typically referred to as Byzantine robots [14,54]. Such deviations may result from malicious attacks or from ordinary malfunctions due to wear, errors, or damage. Extensions of the CP benchmark, therefore, consider scenarios in which a fraction of the swarm is Byzantine.

Research has studied robustness against simple forms of Byzantine behavior, such as stubborn robots (also called zealots) [53–55,61]. Stubborn robots permanently hold a fixed opinion, ignore all social information, and continuously broadcast their chosen option. By never updating their state, they can inject a persistent bias into the swarm's information flow. Depending on their proportion and distribution, they can trap the swarm in a decision deadlock or push it toward the collective selection of an inferior option [61].

Two main strategies have emerged: (a) designing algorithms that are inherently robust to misbehaving agents and (b) developing mechanisms to detect and neutralize Byzantine robots. For (a), simple bio-inspired algorithms, such as cross-inhibition, have been shown to outperform the original solutions in the presence of zealots [61]. For (b), several works integrate methods for identifying faulty agents. A notable approach uses blockchain technology to maintain a shared reputation system and exclude low-reputation robots from the collective decision [39]. Early applications of blockchains in swarm robotics were demonstrated in CP [53] and collective estimation [54,55] scenarios with zealots, where smart contracts record votes, validate information, and automatically detect and blacklist inconsistent or malicious agents.

Miscommunication. Zakir et al. [63] study communication noise in cross-inhibition by including message corruption, where exchanged votes may be flipped. Counterintuitively, moderate noise can improve swarm accuracy by preventing premature convergence to suboptimal consensus, an effect confirmed through models, simulations, and 50-robot experiments. Excessive noise, however, prevents consensus, making miscommunication a tunable factor governing the speed-accuracy tradeoff.

Outlook. Ensuring robustness to adversarial or malfunctioning robots is essential for real-world deployment. While initial work addresses simple Byzantine behaviors, future research should tackle more sophisticated, potentially colluding attackers capable of steering consensus toward suboptimal outcomes.

5 Collective Perception Metrics

Comparison of alternative methods can be based on several alternative metrics.

5.1 Speed-Accuracy Tradeoffs and Beyond

Most studies focus on accuracy, the probability that the swarm reaches a consensus favoring the correct option. Accuracy is typically examined together with decision speed, the time required to reach consensus, revealing the speed-accuracy tradeoff: a swarm can only gain accuracy at the cost of time and vice versa. Less explored but equally important metrics include group cohesion [61,62], robustness to internal noise (e.g., sensing noise [9,10]) and external disturbances (e.g., zealots [61]), and adaptability to environmental changes [5,33,64].

Outlook. Relying solely on the speed-accuracy tradeoff may be too narrow, as it may conceal important strengths or weaknesses of algorithms. While accuracy offers a convenient binary assessment (correct/incorrect), complementary metrics, such as decision value (quality ρ of the chosen option) or decision regret (difference between the chosen option quality and the best quality), can provide better insights. Such metrics could reveal collective dynamics, such as value-sensitive responses [40,41], not yet examined in the CP benchmark.

5.2 Collective Perception as Part of Other Processes

The metrics discussed above evaluate CP in isolation, but in real applications, it would be embedded in a collective perception-action loop. Any perception would exist to initiate action [25].

Task Allocation. CP may function as one component of a more complex collective behavior. Ebert et al. [16] propose an algorithm enabling swarms to self-allocate dynamically across three independent perception tasks of differing difficulty. Instead, Fuady et al. [18] and Atasoy Bingöl et al. [4] study a task-allocation strategy to resize the robot group assigned to each perception task, increasing the number of robots for difficult tasks to boost accuracy and reducing it for easier tasks to save resources.

Localization and Hierarchical Tasks. In spatially heterogeneous environments, robots may require relative localization to interpret local observations correctly, coupling localization with perception. Soorati et al. [51] explicitly incorporate this requirement. Instead, Soma et al. [50] treat CP as an evidence-gathering layer in a best-of-2 decision problem, using it to estimate the qualities of two sites before making a site-selection decision based on those estimates.

Outlook. Although a few studies embed CP within richer collective behaviors, none extends the benchmark to allow the swarm to recognize when the perception task is complete. As Khaluf et al. [25] note, reaching a decision is not enough: a swarm must also detect that a decision has been reached so it can act on it. This decentralized awareness problem corresponds to quorum sensing, a mechanism observed in nature (e.g., social insects [36]) and explored in other swarm robotics contexts [12,30,32]. Quorum sensing requires defining what constitutes a collective decision: What threshold qualifies as a quorum? How long must it persist to avoid mistaking random fluctuations for genuine consensus? Incorporating quorum sensing into the benchmark highlights the importance of cohesion and stability. For example, voter-based models [57] typically yield only majorities due to stochastic fluctuations, whereas cross-inhibition [61] yields stable, cohesive majorities that could support reliable quorum detection. Future research should therefore couple perception with subsequent collective actions, rather than treating perception in isolation.

5.3 Hardware Testing

The CP benchmark has not yet been directly linked to a real-world application. Designed as a concise, non-spatial best-of-n problem, it favors analytical clarity over realism. A clear pathway to deployment has yet to be established. Future extensions will likely need either to move toward estimating more realistic features or to place stronger emphasis on hardware constraints. We next discuss work that takes the initial steps in this direction.

Despite the cost of physical experiments, many studies (including the original [57]) report results with real robots, for example, see [10,16,22,31,63]. Hardware experiments often reveal practical issues, such as unforeseen collective dynamics resulting from limited mixing or unreliable asynchronous communication.

One of the most sophisticated implementations is by Siemensma and Haghighat [49]. They realize the binary feature of the benchmark using vibrating and non-vibrating tiles on a metallic, actuated surface, with a swarm of up to ten miniature IMU-based vibration-sensing robots. Vibrating tiles are driven by stacked micro-motors, and because vibration propagates across the structure, robots must threshold and filter IMU readings to classify tile states. This setup represents a significant step toward real-world deployments and applications.

Outlook. Work on the CP benchmark has not yet translated into realistic application scenarios. The vibration-based system of Siemensma and Haghighat [49] represents a promising step toward structural health monitoring. Other potential applications lie in domains with severe sensing or communication constraints, such as underwater environments, as well as in agriculture or nanorobotics, where swarms may need to detect whether a distributed condition (e.g., pest presence or molecular concentration) exceeds a critical threshold before collectively triggering an autonomous intervention [44,52].

6 Discussion and Conclusion

Over the past decade, the CP scenario has served as a valuable reference task for studying collective decision-making in swarm robotics. Overall, the reviewed literature reflects a broad, exploratory effort along three main axes: modifying the capabilities of the robots (e.g., computation, memory, sensing, and communication bandwidth; Sect. 3), extending the perception task itself (e.g., spatially and temporally heterogeneous environments, adversarial settings, and multi-option or continuous problems; Sect. 4), and broadening the objectives and evaluation criteria beyond the classical speed-accuracy tradeoff (Sect. 5).

From this review, we draw three main conclusions. First, as expected, performance tends to improve with increased robot capabilities (e.g., richer internal state representations and more informative communication). Second, conclusions established under restrictive assumptions (homogeneous robots, static environments, and fully cooperative interactions) do not necessarily transfer well to more realistic conditions, such as spatial heterogeneity, dynamic environments, or adversarial agents. Third, there is no universally best approach: the relative ranking of algorithms depends strongly on the chosen objective and evaluation metrics (e.g., accuracy, decision time, robustness, cohesion, or adaptability), and methods optimized for one criterion can be suboptimal for another.

The shared CP scenario has helped compare methods and collectively advance the field by serving as a common reference task. However, we see two opposing risks: focusing too much on a single, highly abstract task may narrow the scope of studies, while the inflation of loosely defined variants without an overarching framework can limit meaningful comparisons. This creates a fundamental tension between balancing coherence and controlled diversity.

We argue for a more rigorous and structured benchmarking framework. Rather than treating CP as a single fixed scenario or as an unstructured collection of variants, it could be formalized as a benchmark family in which key assumptions are explicitly parameterized, including computational and memory resources, communication bandwidth and topology, spatial and temporal correlations, and the presence of adversarial agents. A systematic exploration of these dimensions would clarify which conclusions are robust and which are contingent on specific modeling choices. Initial steps toward unification already exist. For example, Zakir et al. [61] show that independent discovery, stubborn agents, and message corruption can be formulated as mathematically equivalent processes within a unified model. This formal equivalence helps consolidate seemingly distinct benchmark variants under a common analytical framework.

Future benchmarks should be guided by application-oriented realism to ensure that swarm robotics, as an engineering discipline, is oriented toward deployment. CP is too often studied in isolation, whereas applications require integrated perception–decision–action loops [25]. Our field would benefit from embedding CP within broader collective processes, linking it to the actions it informs and to other coordination mechanisms such as task allocation [16]. Initial work on hierarchical decision-making [50] and dynamic task allocation [18] offers promising starting points, but a systematic integration has not yet been initiated.

A community-driven benchmarking effort—with shared task definitions, parameter ranges, evaluation metrics, and reference implementations—could substantially improve reproducibility and comparability. Such an initiative would not replace CP, but situate it within a structured ecosystem of related benchmarks, balancing simplicity, generality, and realism. Swarm robotics must move beyond counting colors on a grid and toward enabling swarms to sense, interpret, and act within the complex, dynamic environments of real-world applications.

Acknowledgments. We acknowledge support from DFG Excellence Strategy – EXC 2117-422037984. We thank the anonymous reviewers for many helpful comments.

Disclosure of Interests. The authors have no competing interests to declare.

References

1. Abdelli, A., Yachir, A., Amamra, A., Khaldi, B.: Maximum likelihood estimate sharing for collective perception in static environments for swarm robotics. Robotica **41**(9), 2754–2773 (2023)
2. Almansoori, A., Alkilabi, M., Tuci, E.: A comparative study on decision making mechanisms in a simulated swarm of robots. In: IEEE Congress on Evolutionary Computation (CEC), pp. 1–8. IEEE (2022)
3. Almansoori, A., Alkilabi, M., Tuci, E.: On the evolution of adaptable and scalable mechanisms for collective decision-making in a swarm of robots. Swarm Intell. **18**(1), 79–99 (2024)
4. Atasoy Bingöl, S., Töpfer, T., Kosub, S., Hamann, H., Reina, A.: Optimal scalability-aware allocation of swarm robots: From linear to retrograde performance via marginal gains. IEEE Trans. Syst. Man Cybern. Syst. **56** (2026)
5. Aust, T., Talamali, M.S., Dorigo, M., Hamann, H., Reina, A.: The hidden benefits of limited communication and slow sensing in collective monitoring of dynamic environments. In: Dorigo, M., et al. (eds.) International Conference on Swarm Intelligence (ANTS). LNCS, vol. 13491, pp. 234–247. Springer, Cham (2022). https://doi.org/10.1007/978-3-031-20176-9_19
6. Bartashevich, P., Mostaghim, S.: Benchmarking Collective Perception: New Task Difficulty Metrics for Collective Decision-Making. In: Moura Oliveira, P., Novais, P., Reis, L.P. (eds.) EPIA 2019. LNCS (LNAI), vol. 11804, pp. 699–711. Springer, Cham (2019). https://doi.org/10.1007/978-3-030-30241-2_58
7. Bartashevich, P., Mostaghim, S.: Multi-featured collective perception with evidence theory: tackling spatial correlations. Swarm Intell. 83–110 (2021). https://doi.org/10.1007/s11721-021-00192-8
8. Chin, K.Y., Khaluf, Y., Pinciroli, C.: Minimalistic collective perception with imperfect sensors. In: IEEE/RSJ International Conference on Intelligent Robots and Systems (IROS), pp. 8862–8868. IEEE (2023)

9. Chin, K.Y., Pinciroli, C.: Adaptive self-calibration for minimalistic collective perception by imperfect robot swarms. arXiv:2410.21546 (2024)
10. Chin, K.Y., Pinciroli, C.: BayesCPF: Enabling collective perception in robot swarms with degrading sensors. arXiv:2504.04774 (2025)
11. Chiu, D., Nagpal, R., Haghighat, B.: Optimization and evaluation of a multi robot surface inspection task through particle swarm optimization. In: IEEE International Conference on Robotics and Automation (ICRA), pp. 8996–9002. IEEE (2024)
12. Cody, J.R., Adams, J.A.: An evaluation of quorum sensing mechanisms in collective value-sensitive site selection. In: International Symposium on Multi-Robot and Multi-Agent Systems (MRS), pp. 40–47. IEEE (2017)
13. Crosscombe, M., Lawry, J.: Collective preference learning in the best-of-n problem. Swarm Intell. **15**(1–2), 145–170 (2021)
14. Dorigo, M., Pacheco, A., Reina, A., Strobel, V.: Blockchain technology for mobile multi-robot systems. Nat. Rev. Electr. Eng. **1**(4), 264–274 (2024)
15. Ebert, J.T., Gauci, M., Mallmann-Trenn, F., Nagpal, R.: Bayes Bots: collective Bayesian decision-making in decentralized robot swarms. In: IEEE International Conference on Robotics and Automation (ICRA), pp. 7186–7192. IEEE (2020)
16. Ebert, J.T., Gauci, M., Nagpal, R.: Multi-feature collective decision making in robot swarms. In: Proceedings of the 17th International Conference on Autonomous Agents and MultiAgent Systems (AAMAS), pp. 1711–1719. IFAAMAS (2018)
17. Franks, N.R., Dornhaus, A., Metherell, B.G., Nelson, T.R., Lanfear, S.a.J., Symes, W.S.: Not everything that counts can be counted: ants use multiple metrics for a single nest trait. Proc. Royal Soc. B Biol. Sci. **273**(1583), 165–169 (2006)
18. Fuady, S., Tarapore, D., Soorati, M.D.: SubCDM: Collective decision-making with a swarm subset. In: IEEE International Conference on Intelligent Robots and Systems (IROS), pp. 2633–2638. IEEE (2025)
19. Hamann, H.: Swarm robotics: A formal approach. Springer, Cham (2018)
20. Hussein, A., Elsawah, S., Petraki, E., Abbass, H.A.: A machine education approach to swarm decision-making in best-of-n problems. Swarm Intell. **16**(1), 59–90 (2022)
21. Kaiser, T.K., Potten, T., Hamann, H.: Evolution of collective decision-making mechanisms for collective perception. In: IEEE Congress on Evolutionary Computation (CEC), pp. 1–8. IEEE (2023)
22. Karagüzel, T.A., Turgut, A.E., Eiben, A., Ferrante, E.: Collective gradient perception with a flying robot swarm. Swarm Intell. **17**(1), 117–146 (2023)
23. Kegeleirs, M., Birattari, M.: Towards applied swarm robotics: current limitations and enablers. Front. Robot. AI **12** (2025)
24. Kelly, T.G., Soorati, M.D., Zauner, K.P., Ramchurn, S.D., Tarapore, D.: Collective decision making in communication-constrained environments. In: IEEE/RSJ International Conference on Intelligent Robots and Systems (IROS), pp. 7266–7271. IEEE (2022)
25. Khaluf, Y., Simoens, P., Hamann, H.: The neglected pieces of designing collective decision-making processes. Front. Robot. AI **6** (2019)
26. Kornienko, S., Kornienko, O., Constantinescu, C., Pradier, M., Levi, P.: Cognitive micro-agents: individual and collective perception in microrobotic swarm. In: Proceedings of the IJCAI-05 Workshop on Agents in Real-Time and Dynamic Environments, pp. 33–42 (2005)
27. Lajoie, P.Y., Beltrame, G.: Swarm-SLAM: Sparse decentralized collaborative simultaneous localization and mapping framework for multi-robot systems. IEEE Robot. Autom. Lett. **9**(1), 475–482 (2023)

28. Mitchell, M., Crutchfield, J.P., Hraber, P.T.: Evolving cellular automata to perform computations: mechanisms and impediments. Phys. D **75**(1), 361–391 (1994)
29. Morlino, G., Trianni, V., Tuci, E.: Evolution of Collective Perception in a Group of Autonomous Robots. In: Madani, K., Dourado Correia, A., Rosa, A., Filipe, J. (eds.) Computational Intelligence. SCI, vol. 399, pp. 67–80. Springer, Heidelberg (2012). https://doi.org/10.1007/978-3-642-27534-0_5
30. Oddi, F., Reina, A., Trianni, V.: Minimalist protocols for quorum sensing in robot swarms. In: Hamann, H., et al. (eds.) International Conference on Swarm Intelligence (ANTS). LNCS, vol. 14987, pp. 141–154. Springer, Cham (2024). https://doi.org/10.1007/978-3-031-70932-6_11
31. Pacheco, A., Strobel, V., Dorigo, M.: A Blockchain-Controlled Physical Robot Swarm Communicating via an Ad-Hoc Network. In: Dorigo, M., et al. (eds.) ANTS 2020. LNCS, vol. 12421, pp. 3–15. Springer, Cham (2020). https://doi.org/10.1007/978-3-030-60376-2_1
32. Parker, C.A.C., Zhang, H.: Collective unary decision-making by decentralized multiple-robot systems applied to the task-sequencing problem. Swarm Intell. **4**(3), 199–220 (2010)
33. Pfister, K., Hamann, H.: Collective decision-making with Bayesian robots in dynamic environments. In: IEEE/RSJ International Conference on Intelligent Robots and Systems (IROS), pp. 7245–7250. IEEE (2022)
34. Pfister, K., Hamann, H.: Collective decision-making and change detection with Bayesian robots in dynamic environments. In: IEEE/RSJ International Conference on Intelligent Robots and Systems (IROS), pp. 8814–8819. IEEE (2023)
35. Prasetyo, J., De Masi, G., Ferrante, E.: Collective decision making in dynamic environments. Swarm Intell. 217–243 (2019). https://doi.org/10.1007/s11721-019-00169-8
36. Pratt, S.C.: Quorum sensing by encounter rates in the ant *Temnothorax albipennis*. Behav. Ecol. **16**(2), 488–496 (2005)
37. Raoufi, M., Hamann, H., Romanczuk, P.: Speed-vs-accuracy tradeoff in collective estimation: An adaptive exploration-exploitation case. In: International Symposium on Multi-Robot and Multi-Agent Systems (MRS), pp. 47–55. IEEE (2021)
38. Raoufi, M., Romanczuk, P., Hamann, H.: Individuality in swarm robots with the case study of Kilobots: Noise, bug, or feature? In: Proceedings of the Artificial Life Conference (ALIFE), p. 35. MIT Press (2023)
39. Reina, A.: Robot teams stay safe with blockchains. Nat. Mach. Intell. **2**, 240–241 (2020)
40. Reina, A., Bose, T., Trianni, V., Marshall, J.A.R.: Effects of Spatiality on Value-Sensitive Decisions Made by Robot Swarms. In: Groß, R., et al. (eds.) Distributed Autonomous Robotic Systems. SPAR, vol. 6, pp. 461–473. Springer, Cham (2018). https://doi.org/10.1007/978-3-319-73008-0_32
41. Reina, A., Marshall, J.A.R., Trianni, V., Bose, T.: Model of the best-of-N nest-site selection process in honeybees. Phys. Rev. E **95**(5), 052411 (2017)
42. Reina, A., Njougouo, T., Tuci, E., Carletti, T.: Speed-accuracy trade-offs in best-of-n collective decision making through heterogeneous mean-field modeling. Phys. Rev. E **109**(5), 054307 (2024)
43. Schmickl, T., Möslinger, C., Crailsheim, K.: Collective Perception in a Robot Swarm. In: Şahin, E., Spears, W.M., Winfield, A.F.T. (eds.) SR 2006. LNCS, vol. 4433, pp. 144–157. Springer, Heidelberg (2007). https://doi.org/10.1007/978-3-540-71541-2_10
44. Schranz, M., Umlauft, M., Sende, M., Elmenreich, W.: Swarm robotic behaviors and current applications. Front. Robot. AI **7** (2020)

45. Shan, Q., Mostaghim, S.: Collective Decision Making in Swarm Robotics with Distributed Bayesian Hypothesis Testing. In: Dorigo, M., et al. (eds.) ANTS 2020. LNCS, vol. 12421, pp. 55–67. Springer, Cham (2020). https://doi.org/10.1007/978-3-030-60376-2_5

46. Shan, Q., Mostaghim, S.: Discrete collective estimation in swarm robotics with distributed Bayesian belief sharing. Swarm Intell. **15**(4), 377–402 (2021). https://doi.org/10.1007/s11721-021-00201-w

47. Shan, Q., Mostaghim, S.: Benchmarking performances of collective decision-making strategies with respect to communication bandwidths in discrete collective estimation. In: Dorigo, M., et al. (eds.) International Conference on Swarm Intelligence (ANTS). LNCS, vol. 13491, pp. 54–65. Springer, Cham (2022). https://doi.org/10.1007/978-3-031-20176-9_5

48. Shan, Q., Mostaghim, S.: Many-option collective decision making: discrete collective estimation in large decision spaces. Swarm Intell. **18**(2), 215–241 (2024)

49. Siemensma, T., Haghighat, B.: Optimization of collective Bayesian decision-making in a swarm of miniaturized vibration-sensing robots. Swarm Intell. **20**, 1–32 (2026)

50. Soma, K., Vardharajan, V.S., Hamann, H., Beltrame, G.: Congestion and scalability in robot swarms: a study on collective decision making. In: International Symposium on Multi-Robot and Multi-Agent Systems (MRS), pp. 199–206. IEEE (2023)

51. Soorati, M.D., Krome, M., Mora-Mendoza, M., Ghofrani, J., Hamann, H.: Plasticity in collective decision-making for robots: Creating global reference frames, detecting dynamic environments, and preventing lock-ins. In: IEEE/RSJ International Conference on Intelligent Robots and Systems (IROS), pp. 4100–4105. IEEE (2019)

52. Stillman, N.R., Kovacevic, M., Balaz, I., Hauert, S.: In silico modelling of cancer nanomedicine, across scales and transport barriers. NPJ Comput. Mater. **6**(92) (2020)

53. Strobel, V., Castelló Ferrer, E., Dorigo, M.: Managing Byzantine robots via blockchain technology in a swarm robotics collective decision making scenario. In: Proceedings of the 17th International Conference on Autonomous Agents and Multiagent Systems (AAMAS), pp. 541–549. IFAAMAS (2018)

54. Strobel, V., Castelló Ferrer, E., Dorigo, M.: Blockchain technology secures robot swarms: A comparison of consensus protocols and their resilience to Byzantine robots. Front. Robot. AI **7** (2020)

55. Strobel, V., Pacheco, A., Dorigo, M.: Robot swarms neutralize harmful Byzantine robots using a blockchain-based token economy. Sci. Robot. **8**(79), eabm4636 (2023)

56. Talamali, M.S., Saha, A., Marshall, J.A.R., Reina, A.: When less is more: robot swarms adapt better to changes with constrained communication. Sci. Robot. **6**(56), eabf1416 (2021)

57. Valentini, G., Brambilla, D., Hamann, H., Dorigo, M.: Collective Perception of Environmental Features in a Robot Swarm. In: Dorigo, M., et al. (eds.) ANTS 2016. LNCS, vol. 9882, pp. 65–76. Springer, Cham (2016). https://doi.org/10.1007/978-3-319-44427-7_6

58. Valentini, G., Hamann, H., Dorigo, M.: Self-organized collective decision making: The weighted voter model. In: 13th International Conference on Autonomous Agents and Multi-Agent Systems (AAMAS), pp. 45–52. IFAAMAS (2014)

59. Valentini, G., Hamann, H., Dorigo, M.: Efficient decision-making in a self-organizing robot swarm: On the speed versus accuracy trade-off. In: 14th Interna-

tional Conference on Autonomous Agents and Multiagent Systems (AAMAS), pp. 1305–1314. IFAAMAS (2015)

60. Van Calck, L., Pacheco, A., Strobel, V., Dorigo, M., Reina, A.: A blockchain-based information market to incentivise cooperation in swarms of self-interested robots. Sci. Rep. **13**, 20417 (2023)

61. Zakir, R., Carletti, T., Dorigo, M., Reina, A.: Bio-inspired decision making in swarms under biases from stubborn robots, corrupted communication, and independent discovery. arXiv:2509.07561 (2025)

62. Zakir, R., Dorigo, M., Reina, A.: Robot swarms break decision deadlocks in collective perception through cross-inhibition. In: Dorigo, M., et al. (eds.) International Conference on Swarm Intelligence (ANTS). LNCS, vol. 13491, pp. 209–221. Springer, Cham (2022). https://doi.org/10.1007/978-3-031-20176-9_17

63. Zakir, R., Dorigo, M., Reina, A.: Miscommunication between robots can improve group accuracy in best-of-n decision-making. In: IEEE/RSJ International Conference on Intelligent Robots and Systems (IROS), pp. 9014–9021. IEEE (2024)

64. Zakir, R., Salahshour, M., Dorigo, M., Reina, A.: Heterogeneity can enhance the adaptivity of robot swarms to dynamic environments. In: Hamann, H., et al. (eds.) International Conference on Swarm Intelligence (ANTS). LNCS, vol. 14987, pp. 112–126. Springer, Cham (2024). https://doi.org/10.1007/978-3-031-70932-6_9

Tumblenauts: Towards a Bacteria-Inspired Robot Swarm for Intra-vehicular Space Inspection

Sneha Ramshanker[1]([✉]) [iD], Merihan Alhafnawi[1] [iD], Yushra Guffer[1] [iD], and Radhika Nagpal[1,2] [iD]

[1] Department of Mechanical and Aerospace Engineering, Princeton University, Princeton, NJ, USA
s.ramshanker@princeton.edu
[2] Department of Computer Science, Princeton University, Princeton, NJ, USA

Abstract. Tumblenauts are a swarm of minimalist, bacteria-inspired robots designed for collaborative inspection of pressurized microgravity habitats such as the International Space Station. Unlike current intra-vehicular robots that rely on complex, actuator-dense mechanisms for precise motion, the Tumblenauts use a stochastic run-and-tumble locomotion inspired by bacterial motility. This unique locomotion paradigm enables a simpler design, improves scalability, and greatly reduces actuation requirements, making the Tumblenauts among the smallest and least actuator-dense robots built for microgravity. In this paper, we present the design of the Tumblenaut, describe how it achieves run-and-tumble locomotion, and characterize its motion dynamics using Earth-based microgravity testbeds. Furthermore, using a data-driven simulation, we demonstrate how the Tumblenauts can perform a diverse set of inspection tasks by leveraging collective behavior. Specifically, we show that the swarm can collaboratively map environments, achieve directed navigation through a chemotaxis-inspired control mechanism, and make global inspection classification decisions by sharing information. As a new generation of space habitats is launched into orbit, we envision swarms of Tumblenauts run-and-tumbling within them, providing continuous monitoring and supporting the long-term sustainability of these stations.

1 Introduction

Space stations, once deployed, are designed to operate for decades [15]. The International Space Station (ISS) exemplifies this longevity, having supported scientific research for nearly 25 years. Today, a new generation of orbital habitats is emerging, including India's Bharatiya Antariksh Station [26], NASA's Lunar Gateway under the Artemis program [6], and Axiom Space's commercial modules [19]. Together, these platforms mark a new era of space infrastructure, with many designed to function autonomously and uncrewed for extended periods [12]. However, experience from the ISS has shown that long-duration missions

R. Groß et al. (Eds.): ANTS 2026, LNCS 16515, pp. 258–271, 2026.
https://doi.org/10.1007/978-3-032-26123-6_20

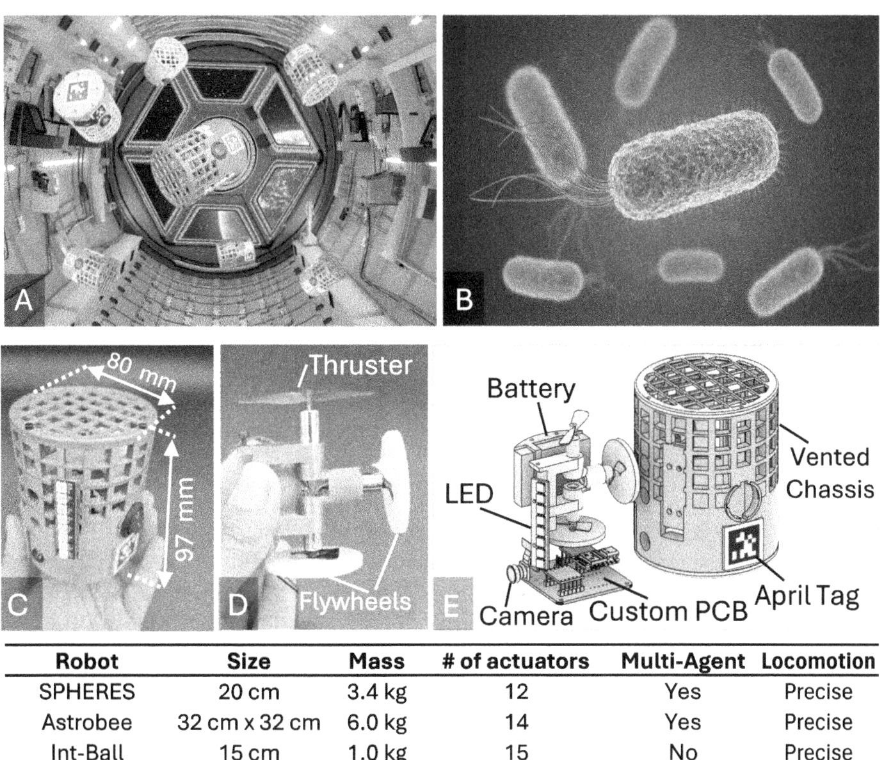

Robot	Size	Mass	# of actuators	Multi-Agent	Locomotion
SPHERES	20 cm	3.4 kg	12	Yes	Precise
Astrobee	32 cm x 32 cm	6.0 kg	14	Yes	Precise
Int-Ball	15 cm	1.0 kg	15	No	Precise
BFR	10 cm	0.2 kg	6	No	Precise
Tumblenauts	**8 cm x 10 cm**	**0.16 kg**	**3**	**Yes**	**Stochastic**

Fig. 1. *Tumblenauts* (A) Visualization of swarm operating inside a space station. (B) E. coli bacteria, the biological inspiration. (C) Robot dimensions. (D) Actuators: one thruster and two flywheels. (E) CAD model with labeled components. (Bottom Table) Comparison with other space robots: SPHERES [22], Astrobee [4], Int-Ball [23], BFR [17].

demand consistent inspection and maintenance to ensure safety and reliability, with recurring issues such as gas leaks often requiring complex human intervention [25]. This underscores a growing need for autonomous robotic systems [10] to monitor and maintain the structural health of space habitats.

In particular, free-flying robots designed for pressurized microgravity environments are emerging as powerful tools for intra-vehicular tasks within space stations. For example, NASA's Astrobee takes inventory and transports cargo [4], while JAXA's Int-Ball autonomously captures photo and video footage within the station [23]. Some of these robotic systems, such as NASA SPHERES [22] and NASA Astrobee [4], even demonstrate multi-robot coordination, working together to perform monitoring, inspection, and logistics tasks. Such cooperative systems are particularly effective for inspection, as they can operate in parallel, tolerate single-failures, and survey large areas with greater efficiency [20,28]. However, current single and multi-robot deployments are highly complex, incorporating numerous actuators and sophisticated control architectures in order to achieve extremely precise motions. This makes them energy-intensive, difficult to validate, and difficult to scale.

Meanwhile, in biological systems, we see a different paradigm. Bacterial swarms, for instance, move stochastically, drifting through spaces using run-and-tumble locomotion. They accomplish this form of random walk using a single flagellar actuator: during a "run", the bacterium's flagella rotate together to propel it forward, while during a "tumble", they reverse direction, causing the bacteria to randomly reorient [2]. Despite their remarkably simple actuation, stochastic motion combined with local interactions enables them to exhibit complex and intriguing emergent collective behaviors such as efficient exploration [29], gradient ascent [36], and quorum sensing [24]. Some engineered distributed systems also employ stochastic motion to operate efficiently in complex environments. For example, the ARGO float network in oceanography employs hundreds of minimally controlled drifting robots to provide long-term, high-frequency, global ocean observations—one of the most valuable sources of oceanographic data [5,30]. By leveraging stochasticity, each float has remarkable longevity, operating autonomously for three to five years on a single battery. Similarly, in microgravity, projects such as TESSERAE have investigated stochastic motion as a strategy for energy-efficient self-assembly of modular space habitats [11,31]. Here, free-flying tiles drift and interact stochastically until they connect, forming autonomous structures with minimal external control.

In this paper, we introduce the Tumblenaut, a minimalist, bacteria-inspired robot designed to autonomously inspect pressurized microgravity habitats, such as space stations, by leveraging collective behavior. Each robot moves stochastically, emulating the run-and-tumble locomotion of motile bacteria. By deliberately forgoing precise motion for stochastic behavior, we achieve a drastic reduction in mechanical complexity, making the Tumblenaut one of the smallest and least actuator-dense robots developed for microgravity. Moreover, the Tumblenauts are engineered for swarm deployment, emphasizing ease of manufacturing, scalability, and cooperative multi-robot functionality. This design philosophy is based on previous work in scalable swarm robotics [7,21,32], while extending to the unique constraints of microgravity.

The core contributions of this work are as follows. We present the design of the Tumblenauts (Sect. 2.1) and experimentally characterize their run-and-tumble locomotion using Earth-based microgravity testbeds (Sect. 2.2). Building on these results, we use a data-driven simulator to explore a family of collective behavior algorithms that demonstrate the autonomous inspection capabilities of the Tumblenauts (Sect. 3). We show that these stochastically moving robots can (a) collectively build environmental maps (b) perform directed navigation by climbing both real and artificial potentials using a chemotaxis-inspired motion controller (c) make rapid and accurate environmental classification decisions using collective information sharing. Together, these results highlight the flexibility and capability of the Tumblenauts as a minimalist robotic platform for intra-vehicular inspection. As a new generation of space habitats enters orbit, we envision swarms of Tumblenauts autonomously drifting through their interiors, providing scalable and resilient inspection for long-term space operations.

2 Design and Locomotion of the Tumblenauts

2.1 Robot Overview

A major design innovation of the Tumblenaut is its simple yet distinctive loco-motion mechanism. Unlike most free-flying space robots, which depend on 6–12 actuators for full-state control (see table in Fig. 1), the Tumblenaut achieves three-dimensional navigation with only three actuators by exploiting stochas-tic run-and-tumble motion. By deliberately trading precise position control for stochasticity, the Tumblenaut achieves a simpler, lighter, and more cost-effective design that scales well to large swarms.

Each Tumblenaut (Fig. 1) weighs 160 g, measures 80 mm in diameter and 97 mm in height, and can be manufactured for approximately USD 50 per unit. The robot achieves run-and-tumble locomotion using commercial quadrotor com-ponents. The run motion is generated by a motor–propeller thruster identical to that used in Crazyflie drones [27]. Similar propulsion systems are employed in other free-flying space robots such as Int-Ball [23], Astrobee [4], and BFR [17]. The three-dimensional tumbling motion is achieved using two 35 mm acrylic fly-wheels mounted orthogonally, each driven by a quadrotor motor. The flywheels generate torque using angular momentum conservation, the same principle used for attitude control in satellites [33] and for locomotion in some planetary robots such as TorqueCapsules [39] and Hedgehog [14]. This turning mechanism is sim-ple, eliminating the need for fluid interactions and relying solely on the rota-tion of internal masses. Critically, unlike previous free-flying robots that rely on sophisticated control architectures to maintain precise positioning and attitude, the Tumblenaut operates its actuators probabilistically, producing stochastic motion that reduces control complexity and enhances energy efficiency.

Each Tumblenaut is powered by a 3.7 V 1000 mAh Li-Po battery with USB and Qi wireless charging, and integrates a custom PCB featuring a XIAO ESP32S3-Sense microcontroller, dual DRV8833 motor drivers, OV2640 camera, MPU6050 IMU, SD card, and 8-LED Neopixel status strip. The robots commu-nicate via ESP-NOW and can use AprilTags for local neighbor identification and relative positioning. All components are enclosed within a 3D-printed chassis for safe operation near humans or sensitive equipment.

2.2 Characterizing Run and Tumble Motion

We characterize the run-and-tumble dynamics of the Tumblenaut using Earth-based testbeds that partially emulate microgravity conditions. In particular, we (a) quantify the thrust generated during runs and (b) the angular velocity during tumbles. These measurements are used to refine the robot's design and to predict

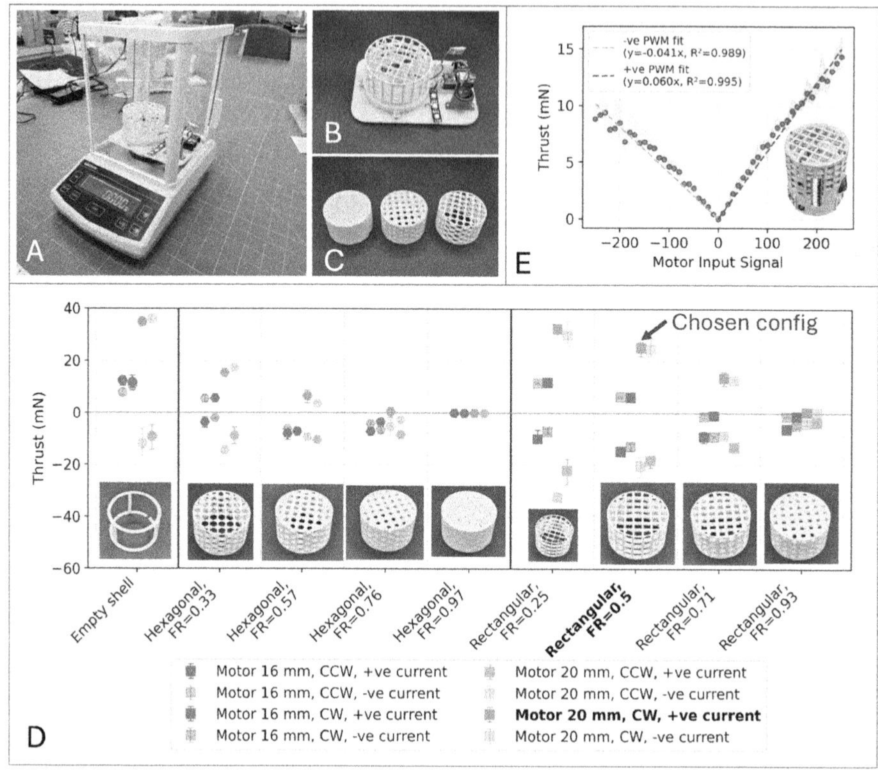

Fig. 2. *Thrust Characterization* (A) Precision scale for thrust measurement. (B) Rig for isolated thrust and venting tests. (C) Hexagonal vented chassis with varying fill ratios (FR). (D) Thrust test results comparing Bitcraze 16 mm and 20 mm motors, propeller directions (clockwise–CW, counterclockwise–CCW), and vent geometries. (E) Tumblenaut thrust vs. motor input signal (−255 to 255), where magnitude indicates power and sign indicates current polarity.

its dynamics in full microgravity using our data-driven simulator. Future work will involve verifying the robot's motion during a Zero-G flight.

Characterizing Run. To ensure safe operation near crew and sensitive equipment, all actuators in the Tumblenaut are enclosed within the chassis. This introduces complex fluid interactions, which we study by testing multiple venting and thruster configurations and using the results to refine the final Tumblenaut design. Thrust is then measured as a function of power, and secondary effects such as reaction torques are characterized. These results will inform run execution during upcoming Zero-G flights.

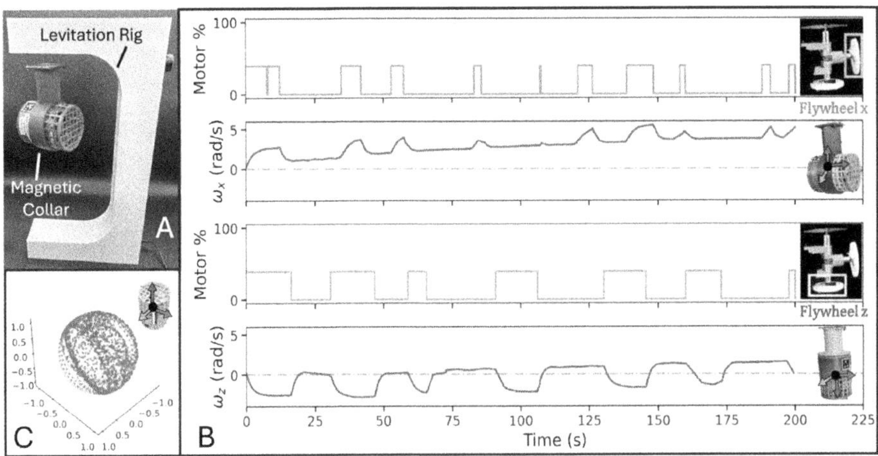

Fig. 3. *Tumbling Characterization* (A) Tumblenaut with magnetic collar suspended in the magnetic levitation system. (B) Flywheel motor input and corresponding measured angular velocities (ω_x, ω_z). (C) Thruster orientation over time reconstructed from the measured angular velocities in (B); red-x, green-y, blue-z axes. (Color figure online)

We measure thrust using a precision scale (Fig. 2A), following standard procedures for drones and other free-flying robots [23]. We systematically tested different thruster types (16 mm and 20 mm Bitcraze motors), propeller orientations (clockwise and counterclockwise), and vented shell geometries (rectangular vs. hexagonal, varying fill ratios), as shown in Figs. 2B–D. Rectangular vents with lower fill ratios produced greater thrust (Fig. 2D). The 20 mm motor outperformed the 16 mm version, with thrust direction determined by propeller orientation and current polarity. Based on these results, we selected a 20 mm motor with a clockwise propeller and a rectangular 0.5 fill-ratio venting pattern (8.5 mm vents) for the final Tumblenaut design, which offered a good balance between thrust efficiency and structural integrity.

We next analyze the relationship between thrust and power for the full Tumblenaut, which now includes internal components such as the flywheels and PCB (Fig. 2E). Motor power is controlled via a motor input signal ranging from –255 to 255, with the magnitude and sign setting the power level and current direction. The Tumblenaut produces up to 14 mN of thrust, which is comparable to other free-flying robots of similar scale, such as Int-Ball (1.5 mN; [23]) and BFR (12 mN; [17]). A clear linear relationship is observed between thrust and motor power for both current polarities. Unlike the isolated thruster tests, where reversing the current reversed the thrust direction, the full Tumblenaut generates positive thrust regardless of current polarity. This effect is also observed in other enclosed-fan robots such as BFR [17] and Int-Ball [23].

We also observed that the thruster generates a reaction torque, causing the robot to spin when activated. This effect was verified by suspending the robot in a magnetic levitation system (described in the next section) and recording its

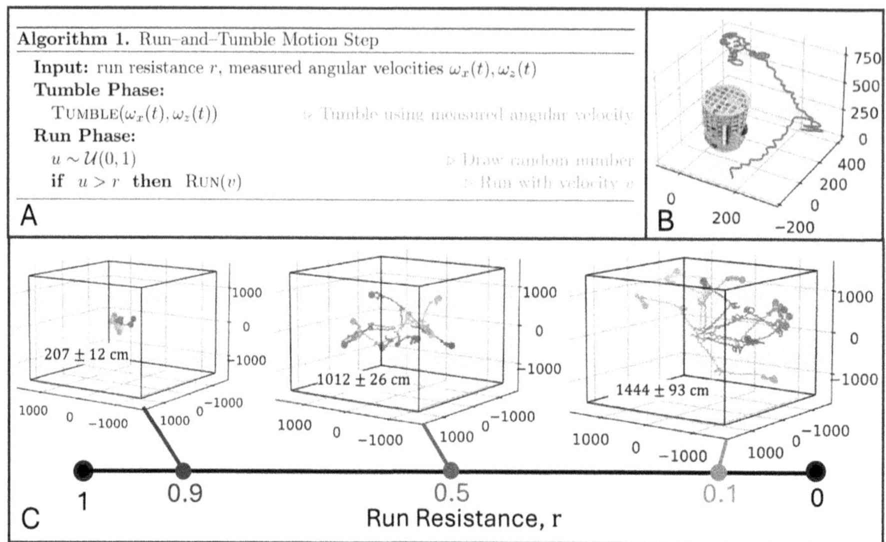

Fig. 4. *Run and Tumble Simulation* (A) Algorithm for a single run-and-tumble step. (B) Example Tumblenaut trajectory in the data-driven simulator. (C) 10 agent trajectories under varying run resistances; Text annotations in 3D figures show mean ± standard deviation of agent displacements from the origin over ten 100-s trials. All units are cm.

angular velocity using the onboard IMU. At 70% power, the robot can achieve a rotational speed of up to 8.73 rad/s. To counteract this angular velocity, we implemented a PID controller that reverses the propeller's rotation, maintaining thrust in the same direction while producing an opposing torque. Each run cycle begins with positive current to propel the robot forward, followed by PID-controlled counter-rotation to stop the robot from spinning (see supplementary video).

Characterizing Tumbling. In this section, we analyze the tumbling dynamics of the Tumblenaut, ensuring that its orientation uniformly spans the full range of directions in three-dimensional space. Uniform tumbling is critical for effective exploration, as any directional bias would reduce spatial coverage.

To characterize tumbling, the Tumblenaut is fitted with a magnetic collar and suspended in a magnetic levitation system (Fig. 3A and supplementary video). The magnetic field counteracts gravity, allowing the robot to rotate freely, replicating microgravity conditions along a single axis of rotation. Because the setup constrains motion to one axis at a time, we conduct two independent experiments measuring rotation about each flywheel axis (x and z). During each trial, the onboard IMU records angular velocity data, which is later combined in simulation to reconstruct the robot's full three-dimensional tumbling motion.

To achieve uniform tumbling, the two flywheel motors are toggled on (at 40% power) and off at random time intervals. Figure 3B presents a representative case of the two motor input signals and the resulting angular velocity outputs for each flywheel axis (x and z). Figure 3C plots the resulting orientation of the robot's z-axis, showing that it covers nearly the entire unit sphere. This confirms that the Tumblenaut tumbles relatively uniformly. A further advantage of this stochastic control approach is improved energy efficiency, since the motors are only intermittently active rather than running continuously.

Run and Tumble Locomotion in a Data-Driven Simulator. We now combine the experimental results from the previous sections to predict the run-and-tumble dynamics of the Tumblenaut in our data-driven simulator.

The Tumblenauts execute run-and-tumble motion by following the algorithm in Fig. 4A. The robot is assumed to run at $v = 82$ cm/s when the thruster is active and remain stationary otherwise. This value, estimated from thrust measurements, corresponds to the terminal velocity at roughly 20% motor power. We assume the robot is tumbling according to the angular velocity measurements presented in Fig. 3. We further add Gaussian noise with a standard deviation of 0.2 rad/s to simulate environmental perturbations and sensor variability. Figure 4B shows the trajectory of a single agent executing run-and-tumble motion. The current simulator is simplified, omitting key effects such as residual post-actuation velocity and assuming reflective boundary conditions. Future work will address these limitations using high-fidelity, physics-based simulators.

Tumblenauts can regulate their exploration dynamics by adjusting their run resistance r, which determines the probability that the thruster activates during motion. Figure 4C illustrates the exploration behavior of ten agents as run resistance is toggled. Robots with higher resistance remain close to their starting positions and explore less of the environment, whereas those with lower resistance travel farther and cover larger areas.

3   Leveraging Collective Behavior for Inspection

By leveraging collective behavior, the Tumblenauts serve as a powerful tool for intra-vehicular inspection. We highlight three ways stochastic swarm algorithms enable efficient inspection in microgravity. Using our data-driven simulator, we show that Tumblenauts can build measurement maps, navigate to regions of interest, and make inspection classification decisions (see y video).

3.1   Collective Data Mapping

We consider a collective mapping task in which the Tumblenaut swarm measures and reconstructs spatial maps of environmental quantities such as temperature, pressure, or gas concentration. This capability is essential for monitoring the structural and environmental health of space stations, enabling early anomaly detection and supporting long-term maintenance [9]. This application parallels ocean mapping with ARGO floats [5], where large arrays of drifting sensors generate global maps without explicit coordination.

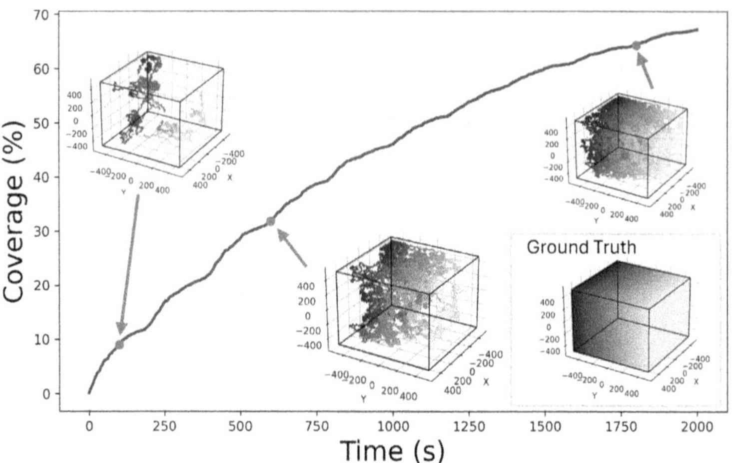

Fig. 5. *Collective Data Mapping.* Ten Tumblenauts map a 1000 m^3 environment (ISS-scale) under a linear potential. Insets show map progression over time; units in cm.

As an example, we task 10 randomly-positioned Tumblenauts with reconstructing the temperature field inside a confined, ISS-scale microgravity volume (1000m^3 [1]). Each robot independently performs run-and-tumble exploration with run resistance $r = 0.5$, logging temperature along its path. We assume the Tumblenauts have localization information and can upload data to a base station. The ground-truth temperature field is modeled as a simple linear gradient.

We evaluate mapping performance by measuring the swarm's spatial coverage over time (Fig. 5), defined as the percentage of unique 20 cm voxels visited by the agents. Even with simple random motion and without coordination, the swarm collectively reconstructs the temperature distribution, producing a high-resolution thermal map. Across ten 2000-s trials, the swarm reconstructed an average of $64.6 \pm 2.7\%$ of the ground truth map. Future work will extend this preliminary demonstration to physics-based space-station environments and conduct sensitivity and parameter-tuning studies for deployment optimization.

3.2   Directed Navigation Using Chemotaxis

Many long-duration inspection tasks require more control than purely stochastic motion. Inspired by bacterial chemotaxis [37,38], the Tumblenauts employ a Bacterial Chemotaxis Motion Controller (BCMC) to modulate their motion and climb local potential gradients to reach regions of interest. This enables purposeful navigation with stochastic motion.

The BCMC algorithm (Fig. 6A) adjusts the run-resistance r based on whether locally sensed conditions are improving. We show that BCMC enables Tumblenauts to localize defects such as leaks: in Fig. 6B, seven blue agents search for two gaussian leak sources using only local measurements of a normalized leak potential (e.g., air pressure). A leak is considered found when an agent enters within one standard deviation of the leak center ($\sigma_{leak} = 500$ cm). Even without a global map, inter-robot communication, or coordination, the agents find both leaks in all ten 400-s trials. In contrast, when the run resistance is fixed at $r = 0.1$, the swarm fails to find both leaks in any of the ten trials.

We can further generalize this to achieve a wide range of navigation goals by crafting artificial potentials. For example, an artificial Gaussian charging potential, $V = \exp\left(-\frac{\|p_{\text{agent}} - p_{\text{charge}}\|^2}{2\sigma_{charge}^2}\right)$, can attract agents toward a charging station, as seen by the red agents in Fig. 6B. Here, p_{agent} and p_{charge} denote the agent and charging-station positions, and σ_{charge} controls the size of the charging region. Similarly, a linear navigation gradient can guide Tumblenauts between different rooms (Fig. 6C). Moreover, these potentials can be dynamic. A robot might begin by following a leak-detection potential but, upon receiving a low-battery alert, switch to climbing a charging gradient instead (Fig. 6D).

Therefore, with BCMC, the Tumblenauts can achieve many of the directed navigation capabilities of controllable space robots like Astrobee [4] and Int-Ball [23], while preserving the simplicity and energy efficiency of stochastic agents.

3.3   Classifying Environments Using BayesBots Algorithm

Finally, we demonstrate that agents can leverage information sharing to make rapid and accurate decentralized inspection decisions, such as determining whether an environment requires maintenance. Specifically, we consider a scenario in which the robots must collectively decide whether the fraction of defective regions exceeds a critical threshold of 5%. A defective region may, for example, correspond to an area exhibiting abnormally high carbon concentration. A similar classification problem has previously been explored in two-dimensional settings [8,34], which we now extend to three dimensions.

In our setup, the environment is discretized into 1000 voxels (100 cm per side), each assigned a 10% probability of being defective (Fig. 6E). We employ a Bayesian decision-making framework in which the robots perform random walks through the environment (run resistance $r = 0.5$), recording binary measurements that indicate whether sampled voxels are defective. Each robot accumulates its own observations and information received from neighbors until it reaches sufficient confidence to classify the environment. The swarm's performance is evaluated based on the proportion of robots that correctly identify the environment as requiring maintenance and the time taken to reach this decision.

We find that information sharing greatly improves collective decision-making, allowing the swarm to perform better than isolated agents. In experiments spanning ten runs with ten randomly-positioned agents, the communicating swarm achieved a mean classification accuracy of 0.960 ± 0.097 and a decision time of 60.7 ± 27.9 s. Without communication, accuracy dropped to 0.920 ± 0.042 and the mean decision time increased to 534.3 ± 3.89 s. Further details on the Bayesian formulation, parameter sensitivity, and optimization are provided in [34,35].

BayesBots represents one of many cooperative algorithms for inspection that the Tumblenauts can employ. The Tumblenauts can support a broad spectrum of additional collective approaches, including those detailed in [3,13,16,18,28].

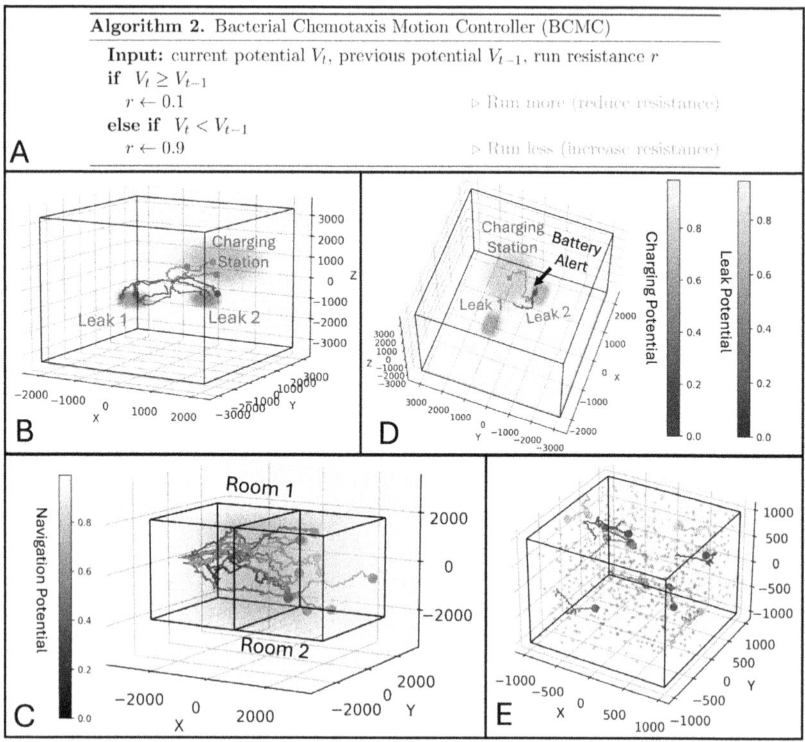

Fig. 6. *Directed Navigation and Environment Classification* (A) Single-step of BCMC algorithm showing how robots use potential measurements to adjust run resistance. (B) 7 blue agents climb a leak potential to locate leaks; 3 red agents follow a charging potential toward the charging station. (C) 10 agents navigate a linear potential to move across rooms. (D) An agent switches from climbing the leak potential to the charging potential upon getting a low-battery alert. (E) Ten agents using BayesBots to classify the environment as defective; red points denote defective voxels. All units in cm. (Color figure online)

4 Conclusion and Future Work

We present the Tumblenauts, a bacteria-inspired swarm of microgravity robots that leverages collective, stochastic motion for intravehicular inspection. Future work will validate Tumblenaut locomotion in Zero-G flights, characterize inspection strategies in physics-based space-station simulators, and conduct user studies on Tumblenaut–astronaut cohabitation. Finally, due to their low cost, we envision Tumblenauts as an accessible educational platform for space robotics.

Acknowledgments. Funded by NSF CMMI-2036359 and an Amazon Robotics Research Award. Following [40], we report manually compiled gender citation rates: 22.2% W (first author)/W (last author), 22.2% M/W, 25.0% W/M, 30.6% M/M.

Disclosure of Interests. The authors have no competing interests to declare.

References

1. International Space Station Facts and Figures - NASA, https://www.nasa.gov/international-space-station/space-station-facts-and-figures/, section: Humans in Space
2. Berg, H.C.: Random Walks in Biology. Princeton University Press (2025). google-Books-ID: LAtYEQAAQBAJ
3. Berman, S., Halasz, A., Hsieh, M., Kumar, V.: Optimized stochastic policies for task allocation in swarms of robots. IEEE Trans. Rob. **25**(4), 927–937 (2009). https://doi.org/10.1109/TRO.2009.2024997, http://ieeexplore.ieee.org/document/5161293/
4. Bualat, M., Barlow, J., Fong, T., Provencher, C., Smith, T.: Astrobee: developing a free-flying robot for the international space station. In: AIAA SPACE 2015 Conference and Exposition, p. 4643 (2015)
5. Chu, W.U., Mazloff, M.R., Verdy, A., Purkey, S.G., Cornuelle, B.D.: Optimizing observational arrays for biogeochemistry in the tropical Pacific by estimating correlation lengths. Limnol. Oceanogr. Methods **22**(11), 840–852 (2024). https://doi.org/10.1002/lom3.10641, https://onlinelibrary.wiley.com/doi/abs/10.1002/lom3.10641, _eprint: https://aslopubs.onlinelibrary.wiley.com/doi/pdf/10.1002/lom3.10641
6. Creech, S., Guidi, J., Elburn, D.: Artemis: An overview of NASA's activities to return humans to the moon. In: 2022 IEEE Aerospace Conference (AERO), pp. 1–7 (2022https://doi.org/10.1109/AERO53065.2022.9843277
7. Dorigo, M.: SWARM-BOT: an experiment in swarm robotics. In: Proceedings 2005 IEEE Swarm Intelligence Symposium, 2005. SIS 2005, pp. 192–200 (2005). https://doi.org/10.1109/SIS.2005.1501622, https://ieeexplore.ieee.org/document/1501622
8. Ebert, J.T., Gauci, M., Mallmann-Trenn, F., Nagpal, R.: Bayes bots: collective Bayesian decision-making in decentralized robot swarms. In: International Conference on Robotics and Automation (ICRA), pp. 7186–7192. IEEE (2020)
9. Ebert, J.T.: Distributed Decision-making Algorithms for Inspection by Autonomous Robot Collectives. Harvard University (2022)
10. Ekblaw, A., Coleman, C., Fish, S.: Into the ANTHROPOCOSMOS: A whole space catalog from the MIT Space Exploration Initiative. The MIT Press (2021)
11. Ekblaw, A., Paradiso, J.: Tesserae: Self-assembling shell structures for space exploration. Proc. IASS Ann. Symp. **2018**(1), 1–8 (2018). https://www.ingentaconnect.com/content/iass/piass/2018/00002018/00000001/art00007
12. Fuller, S., Lehnhardt, E., Zaid, C., Halloran, K.: Gateway program status and overview. J. Space Safety Eng. **9**(4), 625–628 (2022). https://doi.org/10.1016/j.jsse.2022.07.008, https://www.sciencedirect.com/science/article/pii/S2468896722000763
13. Hauert, S., Winkler, L., Zufferey, J.C., Floreano, D.: Ant-based swarming with positionless micro air vehicles for communication relay. Swarm Intell. **2**(2), 167–188 (2008). https://doi.org/10.1007/s11721-008-0013-5, https://doi.org/10.1007/s11721-008-0013-5
14. Hockman, B., Pavone, M.: Stochastic Motion Planning for Hopping Rovers on Small Solar System Bodies. In: Amato, N.M., Hager, G., Thomas, S., Torres-Torriti, M. (eds.) Robotics Research. SPAR, vol. 10, pp. 877–893. Springer, Cham (2020). https://doi.org/10.1007/978-3-030-28619-4_60

15. Jones, H., Hodgson, E., Kliss, M., Gentry, G.: How do lessons learned on the international space station (ISS) help plan life support for mars? In: 46th International Conference on Environmental Systems (2016)
16. Leonard, N., Fiorelli, E.: Virtual leaders, artificial potentials and coordinated control of groups. In: Proceedings of the 40th IEEE Conference on Decision and Control (Cat. No.01CH37228), vol. 3, pp. 2968–2973 (2001). https://doi.org/10.1109/CDC.2001.980728, https://ieeexplore.ieee.org/document/980728/
17. Liu, Y., Li, L., Li, H., Wang, X., Huang, Q., Ceccarelli, M.: A compact and low-actuator thrust system for microgravity flying robot in space stations. IEEE Trans. Industr. Electron. **72**(1), 629–638 (2025). https://doi.org/10.1109/TIE.2024.3401210, https://ieeexplore.ieee.org/document/10565905/
18. Lynch, N.A.: Distributed algorithms. Elsevier (1996)
19. Maender, C.: Beyond the ISS: The world's first commercial space station. In: In-Space Manufacturing and Resources: Earth and Planetary Exploration Applications, chap. 17. Wiley (2022). https://doi.org/10.1002/9783527830909.ch17, https://onlinelibrary.wiley.com/doi/abs/10.1002/9783527830909.ch17
20. Mataric, M.J.: Designing emergent behaviors: from local interactions to collective intelligence. In: Proceedings of the Second International Conference on From Animals to Animats 2 : Simulation of Adaptive Behavior: Simulation of Adaptive Behavior, pp. 432–441. MIT Press, Cambridge, MA, USA (Aug 1993)
21. McLurkin, J.: Speaking Swarmish: Human-Robot Interface Design for Large Swarms of Autonomous Mobile Robots. AAAI Spring Symposium: to Boldly Go Where No Human-Robot Team has Gone Before (2006)
22. Miller, D., et al.: SPHERES: a testbed for long duration satellite formation flying in micro-gravity conditions. In: Proceedings of the AAS/AIAA Space Flight Mechanics Meeting, vol. 105, pp. 167–179. Clearwater, Florida (2000)
23. Mitani, S., et al.: Int-Ball: crew-supportive autonomous mobile camera robot on ISS/JEM. In: 2019 IEEE Aerospace Conference, pp. 1–15 (2019). https://doi.org/10.1109/AERO.2019.8741689, https://ieeexplore.ieee.org/document/8741689/, iSSN: 1095-323X
24. Moreno-Gámez, S., Hochberg, M.E., van Doorn, G.S.: Quorum sensing as a mechanism to harness the wisdom of the crowds. Nat. Commun. **14**(1), 3415 (2023). https://doi.org/10.1038/s41467-023-37950-7, https://www.nature.com/articles/s41467-023-37950-7, publisher: Nature Publishing Group
25. NASA Office of Inspector General: Nasa's management of the international space station and efforts to commercialize low earth orbit (report no. ig-22-005). Inspection/Evaluation Report IG-22-005, National Aeronautics and Space Administration, Office of Inspector General, Washington, D.C., USA (2021). https://oig.nasa.gov/office-of-inspector-general-oig/ig-22-005/, issued November 30 2021
26. Phartiyal, B., Kumar, A., Shukla, S.: Martian/lunar analogue research station in india: Ladakh as a potential site. Current Sci. **128**(5) (2025), database: Academic Search Premier
27. Preiss, J.A., Honig, W., Sukhatme, G.S., Ayanian, N.: Crazyswarm: A large nano-quadcopter swarm. In: 2017 IEEE International Conference on Robotics and Automation (ICRA), pp. 3299–3304 (2017). https://doi.org/10.1109/ICRA.2017.7989376, https://ieeexplore.ieee.org/document/7989376/
28. Ramshanker, S., Ko, H., Nagpal, R.: Strategic sacrifice: self-organized robot swarm localization for inspection productivity. In: 17th International Symposium on Distributed Autonomous Robotic Systems (2024). https://doi.org/10.48550/arXiv.2411.09493, http://arxiv.org/abs/2411.09493, arXiv:2411.09493 [cs]

29. Rashid, S., Long, Z., Singh, S., Kohram, M., Vashistha, H., Navlakha, S., Salman, H., Oltvai, Z.N., Bar-Joseph, Z.: Adjustment in tumbling rates improves bacterial chemotaxis on obstacle-laden terrains. Proc. Natl. Acad. Sci. **116**(24), 11770–11775 (2019). https://doi.org/10.1073/pnas.1816315116, https://www.pnas.org/doi/full/10.1073/pnas.1816315116, publisher: Proceedings of the National Academy of Sciences
30. Riser, S., Freeland, H., Roemmich, D., et al.: Fifteen years of ocean observations with the global argo array. Nat. Clim. Change **6**, 145–153 (2016). https://doi.org/10.1038/nclimate2872
31. Rollock, A., Pommier, M., O'Hara, W., Ekblaw, A.: Development of a Flight-Scale TESSERAE Habitat Concept for Biotechnology Research Outpost Applications. In: 2024 International Conference on Environmental Systems (2024)
32. Rubenstein, M., Ahler, C., Nagpal, R.: Kilobot: A low cost scalable robot system for collective behaviors. In: 2012 IEEE International Conference on Robotics and Automation, pp. 3293–3298 (2012). https://doi.org/10.1109/ICRA.2012.6224638, https://ieeexplore.ieee.org/document/6224638/, iSSN: 1050-4729
33. Sidi, M.J.: Spacecraft Dynamics and Control: A Practical Engineering Approach. Cambridge Aerospace Series, Cambridge University Press, Cambridge (1997). https://doi.org/10.1017/CBO9780511815652, https://www.cambridge.org/core/books/spacecraft-dynamics-and-control/E9CAEE81CD09527C99497FA8C7C35B0A
34. Siemensma, T., Chiu, D., Ramshanker, S., Nagpal, R., Haghighat, B.: Collective Bayesian decision-making in a swarm of miniaturized robots for surface inspection. In: Hamann, H., et al. (eds.) Swarm Intelligence, pp. 57–70. Springer, Cham (2024). https://doi.org/10.1007/978-3-031-70932-6_5
35. Siemensma, T., Haghighat, B.: Optimization of Collective Bayesian Decision-Making in a Swarm of Miniaturized Vibration-Sensing Robots (2024). https://doi.org/10.48550/arXiv.2412.14646, arXiv:2412.14646 [cs]
36. Singh, S., Rashid, S., Navlakha, S., Bar-Joseph, Z.: Distributed Gradient Descent in Bacterial Food Search (2016)
37. Villa-Torrealba, A., Navia, S., Soto, R.: Kinetic modeling of the chemotactic process in run-and-tumble bacteria. Phys. Rev. E **107**(3), 034605 (2023). https://doi.org/10.1103/PhysRevE.107.034605, https://link.aps.org/doi/10.1103/PhysRevE.107.034605
38. Wang, C.C., Ng, K.L., Chen, Y.C., Sheu, P.C., Tsai, J.J.: Simulation of bacterial chemotaxis by the random run and tumble model. In: 2011 IEEE 11th International Conference on Bioinformatics and Bioengineering, pp. 228–233 (2011). https://doi.org/10.1109/BIBE.2011.41, https://ieeexplore.ieee.org/document/6089832/
39. Yang, W.Y., Zou, Y., Huang, J., Abujaber, R., Nakagaki, K.: TorqueCapsules: fully-encapsulated flywheel actuation modules for designing and prototyping movement-based and kinesthetic interaction. In: Proceedings of the 37th Annual ACM Symposium on User Interface Software and Technology, pp. 1–15. ACM, Pittsburgh PA USA (2024). https://doi.org/10.1145/3654777.3676364
40. Zurn, P., Bassett, D.S., Rust, N.C.: The citation diversity statement: a practice of transparency, a way of life. Trends Cogn. Sci. **24**(9), 669–672 (2020). https://doi.org/10.1016/j.tics.2020.06.009

Warmth and Competence in the Swarm: Designing Effective Human-Robot Teams

Genki Miyauchi[1]([envelope]) [ORCID], Roderich Groß[1,2] [ORCID], and Chaona Chen[3] [ORCID]

[1] School of Electrical and Electronic Engineering, University of Sheffield, Sheffield, UK
`g.miyauchi@sheffield.ac.uk`

[2] Department of Computer Science, Technical University of Darmstadt, Darmstadt, Germany
`roderich.gross@tu-darmstadt.de`

[3] School of Computer Science, University of Sheffield, Sheffield, UK
`chaona.chen@sheffield.ac.uk`

Abstract. As groups of robots increasingly collaborate with humans, understanding how humans perceive them is critical for designing effective human-robot teams. While prior research examined how humans interpret and evaluate the abilities and intentions of individual agents, social perception of robot teams remains relatively underexplored. Drawing on the competence–warmth framework, we conducted two studies manipulating swarm behaviors in completing a collective search task and measured the social perception of swarm behaviors when human participants are either observers (Study 1) and operators (Study 2). Across both studies, our results show that variations in swarm behaviors consistently influenced participants' perceptions of warmth and competence. Notably, longer broadcast durations increased perceived warmth; larger separation distances increased perceived competence. Interestingly, individual robot speed had no effect on either of the perceptions. Furthermore, our results show that these social perceptions predicted participants' team preferences more strongly than task performance. Participants preferred robot teams that were both warm and competent, not those that completed tasks most quickly. These findings demonstrate that human-robot interaction dynamically shapes social perception, underscoring the importance of integrating both technical and social considerations when designing robot swarms for effective human-robot collaboration.

1 Introduction

Swarm robotics is a rapidly growing field in which multiple robots work together as a team [11,12]. Unlike individual agents that maximize their own performance, robots in swarms prioritize collective goals, coordinating their actions to achieve outcomes that exceed the capability of any single robot [5,16,24,59]. As robots increasingly collaborate with humans, recent studies have explored human-swarm teaming, focusing primarily on improving objective performance metrics [19,27,41,47,48,56]. Less attention has been given to how humans perceive

R. Groß et al. (Eds.): ANTS 2026, LNCS 16515, pp. 272–286, 2026.
https://doi.org/10.1007/978-3-032-26123-6_21

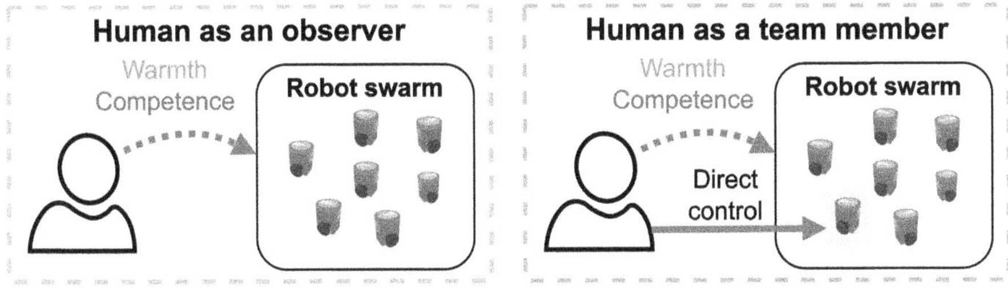

Fig. 1. Two studies were conducted where participants rated the perceived warmth and competence of swarms of robots. In the first (left), they only observe the swarm. In the second (right), they also control a member of the swarm.

and interact with swarms, despite the importance of such perceptions in shaping trust [43,48] and preferences for specific agents [9,17,34,35].

Humans naturally evaluate others along the dimensions of warmth and competence [13]. Competence reflects ability (e.g., intelligence, skill), while warmth reflects intent (e.g., friendliness, helpfulness). These dimensions also influence interactions with individual robots. For example, previous research suggest that agents perceived as both competent and warm are more trusted, whereas highly competent but low-warmth agents may be approached cautiously [17,30,34,46,54]. Prior work has largely focused on single-agent systems [35,54], but interactions with swarms may differ [9,22]. Understanding whether warmth and competence extend to human-swarm interaction is critical for effective swarm design.

In this paper, we make the following contributions[1]:

Social Perception Framework in Human-Swarm Interaction. We investigate warmth and competence as key dimensions of social perception in robot swarm behaviors, and examine how they shape both human perceptions of and interactions with robot swarms.

Influence of Human Involvement on Social Perception of Swarms. Across Studies 1 and 2 (see Fig. 1), we show that overall perceptions of robot swarms remain consistent across conditions, but human involvement as team members shifted their perception of the swarm behaviors. This highlights the dynamic nature of social perception in human-swarm interactions.

Team Preferences Beyond Objective Metrics. While both task performance and social perceptions influence team preference, we show that social perception has a stronger effect, highlighting the importance of designing robot swarms that prioritize socially preferred behaviors alongside task performance.

Initial Guidance for Designing Socially Preferred Swarm Behaviors. By manipulating robot parameters including speed, separation, and broadcast duration, we generated distinct swarm behaviors that were consistently perceived as highly warm and competent. These findings provide a foundation for the future design of socially preferred robot swarms.

---

[1] A selection of preliminary findings were reported in [39].

Swarm User Interface. We built SwarmUI, a user interface supporting human-swarm collaboration and controlled studies of social perception by manipulating swarm behaviors. SwarmUI will be released as an open-source tool to facilitate future research on human-swarm interaction.

This paper is organized as follows. Section 2 reviews related work on human social perception and human-swarm interaction. Section 3 introduces SwarmUI and the swarm behavior designs. Sections 4 and 5 present Studies 1 and 2, respectively. Finally, Sects. 6 and 7 conclude with discussion and implications.

2   Related Work

2.1   Fundamental Dimensions of Social Perception: Warmth and Competence

Research shows that warmth and competence are core dimensions of social perception shaping interactions at both individual and group levels [7,8,13]. These perceptions, sometimes expressed as stereotypes or biases [3,6,14,18] strongly influence engagement: people prefer interacting with those seen as both warm and competent, while competent but cold individuals may face cautious engagement or exclusion [13,15]. Notably, prior work shows that judgments of warmth and competence can depend on an individual's involvement in a group—for example, as an observer or as a team member. Individuals tend to perceive ingroup members as warmer than outgroup members, even when objective behavior is identical [6,14]. Research further indicates that judgments of competence and warmth are based on distinct factors. Competence is typically linked to an individual's or group's ability to perform tasks and tends to be relatively stable over time; a generally competent person or team may still be perceived as capable even after occasional failures. In contrast, warmth reflects moral and prosocial intentions, such as helping, cooperating, or prioritizing others' needs—which can be evaluated more independently of task performance [13,14].

2.2   Social Perception in Human-Swarm Interaction

A key characteristic of swarm robotics is its inherent robustness as a group, demonstrated in three ways: the swarms are typically relatively homogeneous, improving their tolerance to failures in individual members; control is decentralized, removing a single point of failure; and the swarm can self-organize to adapt dynamically to changing situations [61]. With the rapid advancement of swarm robotics, particularly in their ability to autonomously accomplish complex tasks, new challenges arise in designing systems that effectively support human-swarm collaboration. Recent research has primarily focused on enhancing the technical capabilities of swarm robots to enable collaborative tasks with single or multiple human partners [21,41]. Some studies in human-swarm interaction have focused on social perception through trust [1], psychophysiological effects [52], and users' calibration of reliance on swarm performance and its impact on task outcomes [33,60]. Other studies have focused on the expressive qualities of swarm motion, showing that coordinated movement patterns can convey "affective states" such as happiness or sadness [10,23,53,58]. However, it remains unclear how humans perceive the broader social characteristics of robot swarms, when behaviors are systematically varied, and whether these perceptions differ between observers and active team members.

To address these questions, we developed SwarmUI, a swarm user interface and paired this with physics-based simulations in which a swarm of robots collaboratively search for and approach locations of interest. Building on prior work in swarm behavior design [25,41], we created distinct robot team behaviors and investigated for the first time social perceptions across two studies (see Fig. 1): one in which participants acted as observers (Study 1) and one in which participants served as active team members (Study 2).

3   Methods

3.1   Swarm Behavior Design

We simulated a homogeneous swarm of 10 robots using the ARGoS simulator [50]. We used this swarm size to ensure observable collective behavior while keeping the swarm visually manageable for participants. Each robot is based on the e-puck [42], a mobile robot that has been widely used in swarm robotics due to its compact size, modular sensors, and reliable locomotion. The robot has a diameter of 7 cm and moves using a differential-wheel drive. It is equipped with eight proximity sensors positioned along its perimeter. We assume the robot can sense its global position but cannot communicate globally. Instead, it is equipped with a range-and-bearing board that enables local communication with neighboring robots (up to a range of 36 cm between the robot centers).

An overview of the experimental setup is shown in Fig. 2. The robots reside in a square arena of side length 150 cm, starting from uniformly random positions and orientations. Three seconds into the trial, a target region representing a location of interest appears at a random position. It is defined as a circular area of radius 25 cm. Each robot detects the position of the target region if its body resides therein. However, the robot is unaware of the locations of other robots. The objective for the swarm of robots is to all enter the target region as quickly as possible. To do so, each robot needs to explore the environment, discover the target either by itself or with the help from a team member, and move to it.

To enable all robots to efficiently arrive at the target location, we instructed the robots to perform the following three behaviors. The robots indicated their current behavior using distinct LED light patterns.

Explore. Each robot individually explores the arena using *ballistic motion* [25]. In this mode, a robot moves straight at a constant speed v and rotates on the spot for a random duration when it encounters an obstacle, such as walls (i.e., the arena boundary) or other robots. The direction of rotation is determined by which side the obstacle was detected; the robot will turn left if the obstacle was detected on the right side and vice versa. The walls are detected using proximity sensors with a range of 10 cm. Each robot maintains a desired separation

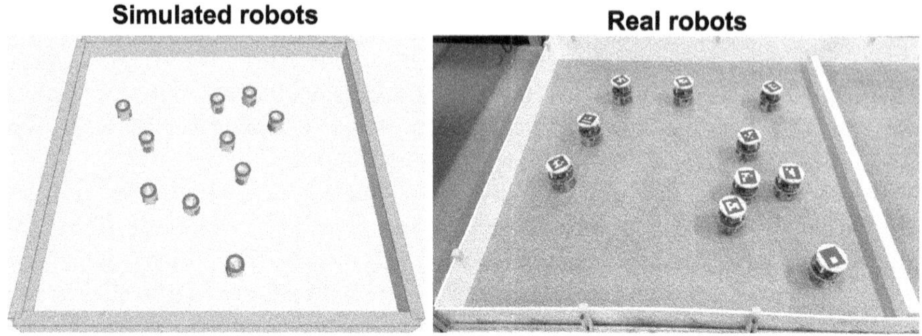

Fig. 2. Overview of the experimental setup. Left: We investigate swarms of simulated robots that explore a bounded environment to discover a hidden target region (not shown). Right: Real-world equivalent of the setup.

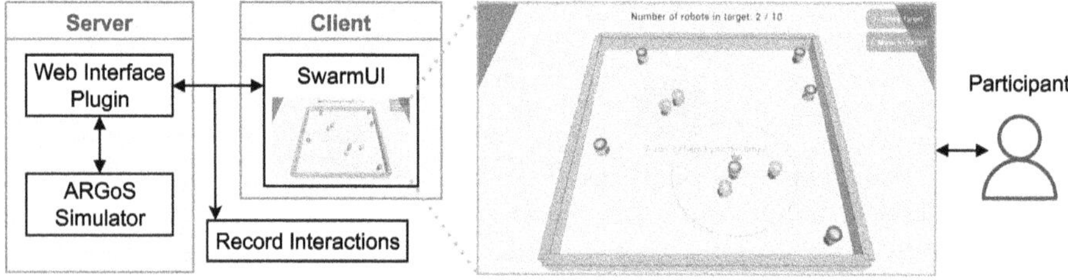

Fig. 3. Overview of the system architecture, including user interface SwarmUI as used in Study 2. The participant interacts with the swarm simulation via the user interface. They control one robot of the swarm.

distance d from other robots, measured using its range-and-bearing sensor. We used ballistic motion because it covers bounded areas more effectively than other random walk strategies while being simple to control [25].

Share Target. Once a robot discovers the target region, it starts sharing the target's location via local communication with neighboring robots for a predefined duration of T seconds. During this duration, the robot continues to move exactly as it would in the *Explore* mode. Any robot that is informed for the first time of the location of the target will also start sharing the location for T seconds. This approach helps to spread the information across the swarm.

Move to Target. After sharing the target's position for T seconds, the robot moves toward the target location. To do so, it realizes a flocking motion based on virtual potential forces, similarly to [40], where robots are attracted to a common target center while being repelled by each other. This allows the swarm of robots to cluster inside the target region regardless of the separation distance d, while avoiding collisions.

To elicit a range of group behaviors in the robot swarm, we systematically varied three core parameters of the aforementioned exploration strategy: *speed* $v \in$

$\{5.0, 7.5, 10.0, 12.5, 15.0\}$ cm/s, *separation distance:* $d \in \{4, 12, 20, 28, 36\}$ cm, and *local broadcast duration:* $T \in \{0, 4, 8, 12, 16\}$ s. The parameters were selected based on the physical capabilities of the e-puck robots and their expected impact on swarm behavior. The speed range reflects the feasible locomotion performance of the e-puck in real-world settings, ensuring that simulated behavior can be transferred to physical robots. Separation distance captures variations in the robots' ability to maintain spacing with each other, which directly influences group-level coordination. Local broadcast duration defines the temporal window during which a focal robot locally shares information with its peers, and varying it allows us to modulate how the information is spread across the swarm. Combining the five levels of each parameter yielded 125 robot team configurations. *Task performance* was measured as the time required for all robots in each team to reach the target region, with shorter times indicating better performance. Parameter checks confirmed that the selected parameters and their ranges produced a wide distribution of completion times (13–103 s, mean around 60 s) and that each parameter significantly affected task performance.

3.2 Swarm User Interface, SwarmUI

To allow users to interact with the swarm as team members (Study 2), we developed SwarmUI, a custom user interface for human-swarm interaction (see Fig. 3). Each participant controlled one robot via a web-based ARGoS plugin [49], while the remaining robots operated autonomously as described in Sect. 3.1. The source code is available from [38].

As shown in the screenshot of SwarmUI (See Fig. 3), the user-controlled robot was labeled "You" and surrounded by a red circle indicating its communication range. By default, the user-controlled robot remained in *Explore* mode, moving straight forward. Participants could steer the robot by holding the left or right keyboard keys, rotating it in place. This allowed users to control the robot's heading while maintaining the same speed as the remaining robots of the swarm. Participants can also switch between the three behaviors described in Sect. 3.1 using buttons at the top-right corner of SwarmUI. Pressing the button *"Share Target"* enabled the robot to broadcast the target location once it had discovered it, either directly, or through local communication by a peer. Pressing *"Move to Target"* directed the robot to navigate autonomously to and remain inside the target area for the remainder of the trial. Participants were instructed to press "Move to Target" only after they were satisfied that the target location had been shared with other robots and wanted their robot to move directly to the target.

3.3 Experimental Design

To examine the impact of human involvement on perceptions of robot swarms, we conducted two studies where participants acted as observers or active team members (see Fig. 1). Although a within-subjects design could allow direct comparisons within individuals, we ran separate studies to (1) recruit a larger, more diverse sample in Study 1 to identify features perceived as warm or competent, and (2) avoid carryover effects between roles [20, 26], ensuring clear separation and complementary insights across the studies.

4 Study 1: Perception of Robot Swarm Behaviors as an Observer

In Study 1, we aimed to examine whether the participants perceive different levels of warmth and competence when observing different robot swarm behaviors, and whether these social perceptions influence their preferences for selecting robots as potential teammates. Preliminary findings were reported in [39].

4.1 Participants

We recruited 90 online participants (hereafter referred to as observers) via Prolific (45 female, 45 male; $M_{\text{age}} = 29.6$ yrs, $SD_{\text{age}} = 4.5$ yrs). The sample size was chosen to ensure that each robot team was rated by at least 10 observers, providing sufficient data for stable estimation of stimulus-level effects in subsequent analysis. All observers reported normal or corrected-to-normal vision. Written informed consent was obtained from each observer prior to the study, and observers were compensated at a rate of £12/hour. The experimental protocol was approved by University of Sheffield Ethics Committee (Reference ID: 068772).

4.2 Procedure

Each observer first watched a short demonstration to familiarize themselves with the experimental setting and robot behaviors described in Sect. 3.1 (see Supplementary Video for an example clip). They were informed that the goal was for all robots to have reached the target region as quickly as possible. Observers then watched robot teams performing the task and rated each team on perceived warmth, competence, and team preference. We assessed perceptions of warmth ("How friendly, approachable, or cooperative is the group of robots?") and competence ("How capable, effective, and intelligent is the group of robots?") using 7-point Likert scales. The scale descriptions were adapted from [35], which evaluated the same dimensions in human–agent interaction. Each observer rated 15 randomly selected teams, with trials presented in random order. To reduce order effects, the rating sequence (i.e., warmth, competence, team preference) was counterbalanced across participants. After rating all teams, observers completed a brief post-task questionnaire and provided free-text responses describing robot behaviors they perceived as warm or competent.

4.3 Results

We first examined how swarm parameters (speed, separation, and broadcast) influenced perceptions of warmth and competence using a linear mixed-effects

Table 1. LME models of robot swarm parameters on warmth & competence. SE = standard error; t = t-statistic. Adapted from [39].

	predictor	estimate	SE	t	p-value
model for warmth ratings	speed	−0.002	0.020	−0.111	0.912
	separation	0.011	0.006	1.814	0.070
	broadcast	**0.043**	**0.012**	**3.565**	**0.0004**
model for competence ratings	speed	0.014	0.022	0.619	0.536
	separation	**0.018**	**0.007**	**2.564**	**0.010**
	broadcast	−0.013	0.014	−0.903	0.367

Significant predictors ($p < .05$) are highlighted in bold.

Table 2. LME model predicting team preference from social perceptions and task performance (standardized). SE = standard error; t = t-statistic. Adapted from [39].

predictor	estimate	SE	t	p-value
warmth	0.739	0.030	24.73	< 0.001
competence	0.924	0.031	29.70	< 0.001
task performance	0.121	0.024	5.02	< 0.001

Significant predictors ($p < .05$) are highlighted in bold.

model (LME) (see Table 1). Warmth was significantly predicted by broadcast duration ($p < 0.001$), with longer information sharing perceived as warmer. Competence was significantly influenced by separation distance ($p = 0.01$), with more dispersed robots perceived as more competent. No parameter interactions were significant (all $p > 0.10$), and robot speed had no significant effect on either dimension.

Previous research has shown that warmth and competence is a better predictor for participants' team preferences in human-agent collaboration than objective performance [17,35], suggesting that humans may prioritize perceived social traits over task outcomes in their team preferences. To test this, we modeled how team preference is predicted by warmth, competence, and task performance, using a similar LME analysis as above. Task performance was measured as the time to complete the task and thus reversed for interpretability (i.e., higher values = better performance). All predictors were standardized (z-scored) to allow comparison of effect sizes. As shown in Table 2, social perception ratings and objective task performance positively predicted team preference ($p < 0.001$ for all). Warmth ($\beta = 0.74$) and competence ($\beta = 0.92$) emerged as strong predictors, whereas task performance showed a significant but smaller effect ($\beta = 0.12$). This indicates that observers' preferences were driven more strongly by the social perceptions of the robot teams than by their objective performance.

Based on Study 1, we first divided all robot teams into four quadrants (1) high warmth–high competence, (2) low warmth–high competence, (3) high warmth–low competence, and (4) low warmth–low competence, using the median ratings of warmth and competence across all participants. Within each quadrant, we then ranked teams by the sum of their averaged warmth and competence scores and selected the top ten teams to ensure that Study 2 included robot teams with distinct behaviors.

5 Study 2: Perception of Robot Swarm Behaviors as an Operator

5.1 Participants

We recruited 16 participants (8 female, 8 male; $M_{\mathrm{age}} = 26.8$ yrs, $SD_{\mathrm{age}} = 9.9$ yrs). A priori power analysis for a repeated-measures ANOVA ($\alpha = 0.05$, power $= 0.8$) indicated that this sample size would be sufficient to detect medium-sized effects (i.e., $f = 0.25$). The inclusion criteria and ethical approval were identical to those described in Study 1.

5.2 Procedure

Each participant came to the lab and completed the task in person. The task instructions and the description of the social perception measures were kept consistent across all participants, following the same procedure as in Study 1. In each round, participants directly controlled one robot while the remaining robots were operated by the system using the same parameters as in Study 1. Participants used SwarmUI introduced in Sect. 3.2. They were instructed that the goal was for all robots to reach the target region as quickly as possible, with each round limited to 60 s. Following the procedure of a previous study on social perception in human–agent interactions [35], participants received a performance-based bonus of £0.50 for each successful round. In each round, participants rated the team on perceived warmth, competence, and joint effort. Here, we measured *joint effort* instead of team preference, because participants interacted with a new team in every round (i.e., irrelevant to their preference). The measurement of joint effort captured their sense of belonging to the team. Each participant completed 20 rounds, comprising five robot teams randomly sampled from each of the four groups identified in Study 1.

5.3 Results

Following the experiments for Study 2, we first examined whether participants' social perceptions of the teams were preserved overall. We included all trials in the analysis, except for one trial from a participant who did not successfully complete the task. Table 3 shows participants' ratings of warmth and competence for each group, averaged across robot teams and participants (1 = very low,

Table 3. Averaged ratings of warmth and competence in human—robot teamwork.

Group	Warmth (M±SD)	Competence (M±SD)
HighWarmth_HighCompetence	5.01 (1.50)	5.91 (1.08)
LowWarmth_HighCompetence	3.90 (1.82)	5.09 (1.57)
HighWarmth_LowCompetence	5.18 (1.37)	4.30 (1.52)
LowWarmth_LowCompetence	4.38 (1.66)	4.59 (1.43)
ANOVA F (df)	10.93 (3,316)	19.99 (3,316)
p-value	< .001	< .001

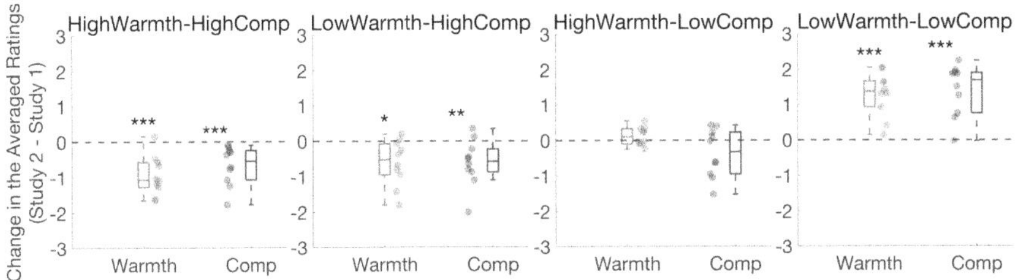

Fig. 4. Boxplots show the changes in warmth (red) and competence (blue) ratings between Study 1 and Study 2, with each dot representing an individual robot swarm team. Significance levels: $*p < 0.05$, $**p < 0.01$, $***p < 0.001$.

$7 =$ very high). A one-way ANOVA revealed significant differences in Study 2 ratings of both warmth and competence across the four groups (Warmth: $F(3, 316) = 10.93$, $p < 0.001$; Competence: $F(3, 316) = 19.99$, $p < 0.001$). Post-hoc Tukey HSD tests further confirmed significant differences in ratings for intended high vs. low warmth and competence teams, supporting the robustness of our results. These results suggest the robot swarm behaviors were robust across conditions, whether participants acted as observers or team members.

Although overall perceptions of the swarms were similar to Study 1, participants' perceptions shifted when they actively joined the teams. To assess this, we compared Study 2 ratings with Study 1 ratings for each group using two-sample t-tests. Figure 4 shows each group (labeled at the top of each subplot), with changes in warmth (red) and competence (blue) ratings. While general perceptions were largely preserved, interacting with the robots as team members shifted social perception. For instance, high-warmth, high-competence teams (leftmost subplot) were rated lower on both dimensions ($p < 0.001$), whereas low-warmth, low-competence teams (rightmost subplot) were rated higher ($p < 0.001$).

6 Discussion

Across two studies, we investigated how participants perceive warmth and competence in robot swarms under observation and direct control. Although direct control slightly modulated social perceptions of swarm behavior, the overall pattern of high versus low warmth and competence remained consistent across conditions. These findings demonstrate the robustness of our parameterized swarm behaviors across human–robot interaction contexts.

Social Perceptions of Robot Swarm Behaviors. Our results show that robot swarm behaviors elicit robust social perceptions, extending prior work on single agents [17,31,34,35,54]. While swarm-robotics research often prioritizes movement speed [10,22,57], our findings highlight two other parameters that significantly shape social perception. Within the parameter range tested in our study, larger separation distances were perceived as more competent, likely because the more distributed formations suggested improved exploration capability [2,29]. Longer broadcasting durations increased perceived warmth, as sustained broadcasting was often interpreted as robots "helping" each other [4,36] and signaled joint engagement [28,32,44]. These results offer practical guidance for designing more socially aware human–swarm interactions. Qualitative analysis of the post-task questionnaire responses revealed that participants consistently associated perceived warmth with prosocial, collective behaviors. In particular, warmth judgments were linked to robots' behaviors to share information and prioritize group success over individual efficiency. For example, participants highlighted behaviors associated with warmth: *"Robots went to share the target with others"*, *"I considered whether the robots which found the targets first would help other robots"*, and *"not going to the target straight away and moving around to share"*.

Social Perception Over Objective Performance in Team Preference. Our results show that social perceptions more strongly influenced team preferences than task performance. These results extend single-agent research to swarms, highlighting that optimizing task performance alone is insufficient for effective human-robot collaboration [17,35,51,54]. Designers should consider behaviors that convey warmth and collaboration, informed by more fine-grained, multidimensional assessments of social perception [4,45]. Future work can draw on human social behavior, natural systems, and variations in swarm size [52] to design swarms that are both effective and socially engaging [37,55].

7   Conclusion

In summary, our findings demonstrate that robot swarm behaviors elicit social perceptions of warmth and competence, which exert a stronger influence on human team preferences than task performance. Although active engagement in human–robot teams modulates these perceptions, robot parameters, including broadcasting duration and inter-robot distance, reliably shaped participants' perceptions during observation and collaboration. These findings underscore the importance of integrating technical and social considerations when designing robot swarms to ensure they are not only effective but also socially preferred.

Acknowledgments. This research was supported by the Horizon Europe OpenSwarm project (Grant No. 101093046) and Robotics Institute Germany (BMBF Grant No. 16ME1001). The views expressed do not necessarily reflect those of the funders.

Disclosure of Interests. The authors have no competing interests to declare.

References

1. Abu-Aisheh, R., et al.: Towards understanding the impact of swarm motion on human trust. In: 2025 34th IEEE International Conference on Robot and Human Interactive Communication (RO-MAN), pp. 2260–2265. IEEE (2025)
2. Bacula, A., Knight, H.: MoTiS parameters for expressive multi-robot systems: Relative motion, timing, and spacing. Int. J. Soc. Robot. **14**(9), 1965–1993 (2022)
3. Bargh, J.A.: The cognitive monster: The case against the controllability of automatic stereotype effects. Dual-Process Theories in Social Psychology (1999)
4. Carpinella, C.M., Wyman, A.B., Perez, M.A., Stroessner, S.J.: The robotic social attributes scale (RoSAS) development and validation. In: Proceedings of the 2017 ACM/IEEE International Conference on Human-Robot Interaction, pp. 254–262 (2017)
5. Cazenille, L., Toquebiau, M., Lobato-Dauzier, N., Loi, A., Macabre, L., Aubert-Kato, N., Genot, A.J., Bredeche, N.: Signalling and social learning in swarms of robots. Philos. Trans. A **383**(2289), 20240148 (2025)
6. Cuddy, A.J., Fiske, S.T., Glick, P.: The bias map: behaviors from intergroup affect and stereotypes. J. Pers. Soc. Psychol. **92**(4), 631 (2007)
7. Cuddy, A.J., Fiske, S.T., Glick, P.: Warmth and competence as universal dimensions of social perception: the stereotype content model and the bias map. Adv. Exp. Soc. Psychol. **40**, 61–149 (2008)
8. Czopp, A.M., Kay, A.C., Cheryan, S.: Positive stereotypes are pervasive and powerful. Perspect. Psychol. Sci. **10**(4), 451–463 (2015)
9. Dahiya, A., Aroyo, A.M., Dautenhahn, K., Smith, S.L.: A survey of multi-agent human-robot interaction systems. Robot. Auton. Syst. **161**, 104335 (2023)
10. Dietz, G., E, J.L., Washington, P., Kim, L.H., Follmer, S.: Human perception of swarm robot motion. In: Proceedings of the 2017 CHI Conference Extended Abstracts on Human Factors in Computing Systems, pp. 2520–2527 (2017)
11. Dorigo, M., Theraulaz, G., Trianni, V.: Reflections on the future of swarm robotics. Sci. Robot. **5**(49), eabe4385 (2020)
12. Dorigo, M., Theraulaz, G., Trianni, V.: Swarm robotics: past, present, and future [point of view]. Proc. IEEE **109**(7), 1152–1165 (2021)
13. Fiske, S.T., Cuddy, A.J., Glick, P.: Universal dimensions of social cognition: warmth and competence. Trends Cogn. Sci. **11**(2), 77–83 (2007)
14. Fiske, S.T., Cuddy, A.J., Glick, P., Xu, J.: A model of (often mixed) stereotype content: Competence and warmth respectively follow from perceived status and competition. In: Social Cognition, pp. 162–214. Routledge (2018)
15. Fiske, S.T., Xu, J., Cuddy, A.C., Glick, P.: (Dis) respecting versus (dis) liking: Status and interdependence predict ambivalent stereotypes of competence and warmth. J. Soc. Issues **55**(3), 473–489 (1999)
16. Hamann, H.: Swarm Robotics: A Formal Approach. Springer, Cham (2018). https://doi.org/10.1007/978-3-319-74528-2

17. Harris-Watson, A.M., Larson, L.E., Lauharatanahirun, N., DeChurch, L.A., Contractor, N.S.: Social perception in human-AI teams: Warmth and competence predict receptivity to ai teammates. Comput. Hum. Behav. **145**, 107765 (2023)
18. Hentschel, T., Heilman, M.E., Peus, C.V.: The multiple dimensions of gender stereotypes: A current look at men's and women's characterizations of others and themselves. Front. Psychol. **10**, 11 (2019)
19. Heuthe, V.L., Panizon, E., Gu, H., Bechinger, C.: Counterfactual rewards promote collective transport using individually controlled swarm microrobots. Sci. Robot. **9**(97), eado5888 (2024)
20. Ho, J., Min, J.: Causal inference in counterbalanced within-subjects designs. arXiv preprint arXiv:2505.03937 (2025)
21. Jang, I., Hu, J., Arvin, F., Carrasco, J., Lennox, B.: Omnipotent virtual giant for remote human-swarm interaction. In: 2021 30th IEEE International Conference on Robot & Human Interactive Communication (RO-MAN), pp. 488–494 (2021)
22. Kaduk, J., Cavdan, M., Drewing, K., Hamann, H.: From one to many: How active robot swarm sizes influence human cognitive processes. In: 2024 33rd IEEE International Conference on Robot and Human Interactive Communication (ROMAN), pp. 1207–1212. IEEE (2024)
23. Kaduk, J., Weilbeer, F., Hamann, H.: Emotional tandem robots: How different robot behaviors affect human perception while controlling a mobile robot. In: 2024 IEEE/RSJ International Conference on Intelligent Robots and Systems (IROS), pp. 2465–2470. IEEE (2024)
24. Karagüzel, T.A., Turgut, A.E., Eiben, A., Ferrante, E.: Collective gradient perception with a flying robot swarm. Swarm Intell. **17**(1), 117–146 (2023)
25. Kegeleirs, M., Garzón Ramos, D., Birattari, M.: Random Walk Exploration for Swarm Mapping. In: Althoefer, K., Konstantinova, J., Zhang, K. (eds.) TAROS 2019. LNCS (LNAI), vol. 11650, pp. 211–222. Springer, Cham (2019). https://doi.org/10.1007/978-3-030-25332-5_19
26. Keren, G.: Between-or within-subjects design: A methodological dilemma. In: A Handbook for data Analysis in the behaviorial Sciences, pp. 257–272. Psychology Press (2014)
27. Kolling, A., Walker, P., Chakraborty, N., Sycara, K., Lewis, M.: Human interaction with robot swarms: a survey. IEEE Trans. Human-Mach. Syst. **46**(1), 9–26 (2016)
28. Le Besnerais, A., Moore, J.W., Berberian, B., Grynszpan, O.: Sense of agency in joint action: a critical review of we-agency. Front. Psychol. **15**, 1331084 (2024)
29. Levillain, F., St-Onge, D., Zibetti, E., Beltrame, G.: More than the sum of its parts: Assessing the coherence and expressivity of a robotic swarm. In: 2018 27th IEEE International Symposium on Robot and Human Interactive Communication (RO-MAN), pp. 583–588. IEEE (2018)
30. Li, L., Li, Y., Song, B., Shi, Z., Wang, C.: How human-like behavior of service robot affects social distance: a mediation model and cross-cultural comparison. Behav. Sci. **12**(7), 205 (2022)
31. Liu, X.S., Yi, X.S., Wan, L.C.: Friendly or competent? The effects of perception of robot appearance and service context on usage intention. Ann. Tour. Res. **92**, 103324 (2022)
32. Loehr, J.D.: The sense of agency in joint action: an integrative review. Psychon. Bull. Rev. **29**(4), 1089–1117 (2022)
33. Lyons, J.B., Capiola, A., Adams, J.A., Mator, J.D., Cherry, E., Barrera, K.: Examining the human-centred challenges of human-swarm interaction. Philos. Trans. A **383**(2289), 20240140 (2025)

34. McKee, K.R., Bai, X., Fiske, S.T.: Humans perceive warmth and competence in artificial intelligence. Iscience **26**(8) (2023)
35. McKee, K.R., Bai, X., Fiske, S.T.: Warmth and competence in human-agent cooperation. Auton. Agent. Multi-Agent Syst. **38**(1), 23 (2024)
36. Mieczkowski, H., Liu, S.X., Hancock, J., Reeves, B.: Helping not hurting: Applying the stereotype content model and bias map to social robotics. In: 2019 14th ACM/IEEE International Conference on Human-Robot Interaction (HRI), pp. 222–229. IEEE (2019)
37. Mitri, S., Wischmann, S., Floreano, D., Keller, L.: Using robots to understand social behaviour. Biol. Rev. **88**(1), 31–39 (2013)
38. Miyauchi, G., Groß, R., Chen, C.: SwarmUI and robot controller source code (2025). https://github.com/genkimiyauchi/swarm-perception
39. Miyauchi, G., Groß, R., Chen, C.: Human perceptions of warmth and competence in swarm robot behavior. In: Companion Proceedings of the 21st ACM/IEEE International Conference on Human-Robot Interaction (HRI), Late Breaking Reports (2026)
40. Miyauchi, G., Lopes, Y.K., Groß, R.: Multi-operator control of connectivity-preserving robot swarms using supervisory control theory. In: 2022 International Conference on Robotics and Automation (ICRA), pp. 6889–6895. IEEE (2022)
41. Miyauchi, G., Lopes, Y.K., Groß, R.: Sharing the control of robot swarms among multiple human operators: A user study. In: 2023 IEEE/RSJ International Conference on Intelligent Robots and Systems (IROS), pp. 8847–8853. IEEE (2023)
42. Mondada, F., et al.: The e-puck, a robot designed for education in engineering. In: Proceedings of the 9th Conference on Autonomous robot Systems and Competitions, vol. 1, pp. 59–65. Castelo Branco: IPCB, Instituto Politécnico de Castelo Branco (2009)
43. Nam, C., Walker, P., Li, H., Lewis, M., Sycara, K.: Models of trust in human control of swarms with varied levels of autonomy. IEEE Trans. Human-Mach. Syst. **50**(3), 194–204 (2019)
44. Navare, U.P., Ciardo, F., Kompatsiari, K., De Tommaso, D., Wykowska, A.: When performing actions with robots, attribution of intentionality affects the sense of joint agency. Sci. Robot. **9**(91), eadj3665 (2024)
45. Nomura, T., Suzuki, T., Kanda, T., Kato, K.: Measurement of negative attitudes toward robots. Interaction Studies. Soc. Behav. Commun. Biol. Artif. Syst. **7**(3), 437–454 (2006)
46. Oliveira, R., Arriaga, P., Correia, F., Paiva, A.: The stereotype content model applied to human-robot interactions in groups. In: 2019 14th ACM/IEEE International Conference on Human-Robot Interaction (HRI), pp. 123–132. IEEE (2019)
47. Ordaz-Rivas, E., Torres-Treviño, L.: Improving performance in swarm robots using multi-objective optimization. Math. Comput. Simul. **223**, 433–457 (2024)
48. Orozco, J.A., Artemiadis, P.: Extracting human levels of trust in human-swarm interaction using EEG signals. IEEE Trans. Human-Mach. Syst. **54**(2), 182–191 (2024)
49. Patel, J., Sonar, P., Pinciroli, C.: On multi-human multi-robot remote interaction: a study of transparency, inter-human communication, and information loss in remote interaction. Swarm Intell. **16**(2), 107–142 (2022)
50. Pinciroli, C., et al.: ARGoS: a modular, parallel, multi-engine simulator for multi-robot systems. Swarm Intell. **6**(4), 271–295 (2012)
51. Pizzi, G., Vannucci, V., Mazzoli, V., Donvito, R.: I, chatbot! the impact of anthropomorphism and gaze direction on willingness to disclose personal information and behavioral intentions. Psychol. Mark. **40**(7), 1372–1387 (2023)

52. Podevijn, G., O'grady, R., Mathews, N., Gilles, A., Fantini-Hauwel, C., Dorigo, M.: Investigating the effect of increasing robot group sizes on the human psychophysiological state in the context of human–swarm interaction. Swarm Intell. **10**(3), 193–210 (2016)
53. Santos, M., Egerstedt, M.: From motions to emotions: Can the fundamental emotions be expressed in a robot swarm? Int. J. Soc. Robot. **13**(4), 751–764 (2021)
54. Scheunemann, M.M., Cuijpers, R.H., Salge, C.: Warmth and competence to predict human preference of robot behavior in physical human-robot interaction. In: 2020 29th IEEE International Conference on Robot and Human Interactive Communication (RO-MAN), pp. 1340–1347. IEEE (2020)
55. Sevillano, V., Fiske, S.T.: Warmth and competence in animals. J. Appl. Soc. Psychol. **46**(5), 276–293 (2016)
56. Shan, X., Jin, Y., Jurt, M., Li, P.: A distributed multi-robot task allocation method for time-constrained dynamic collective transport. Robot. Auton. Syst. **178**, 104722 (2024)
57. Song, W., Gao, Y., Quan, Q.: Speed and density planning for a speed-constrained robot swarm through a virtual tube. IEEE Robot. Autom. Lett. (2024)
58. St-Onge, D., Levillain, F., Zibetti, E., Beltrame, G.: Collective expression: how robotic swarms convey information with group motion. Paladyn, J. Behav. Robot. **10**(1), 418–435 (2019)
59. Sun, G., Zhou, R., Ma, Z., Li, Y., Groß, R., Chen, Z., Zhao, S.: Mean-shift exploration in shape assembly of robot swarms. Nat. Commun. **14**(1), 3476 (2023)
60. Wilson, J., Cet al.: Trustworthy swarms. In: Proceedings of the First International Symposium on Trustworthy Autonomous Systems, pp. 1–11. TAS '23, Association for Computing Machinery (2023)
61. Winfield, A.F., Swana, M., Ives, J., Hauert, S.: On the ethical governance of swarm robotic systems in the real world. Philos. Trans. A **383**(2289), 20240142 (2025)

Short Papers

Active Elastic Matter: 3D Collective Motion for Swarms

Ersin Keskin[1,2(✉)], Ali Emre Turgut[1,3(✉)], and Erol Şahin[1,4]

[1] Center for Robotics and Artificial Intelligence (ROMER), Middle East Technical University, Ankara, Turkey
ersin.keskin@metu.edu.tr
[2] Department of Robotics, Middle East Technical University, Ankara, Turkey
[3] Department of Mechanical Engineering, Middle East Technical University, Ankara, Turkey
[4] Department of Computer Engineering, Middle East Technical University, Ankara, Turkey

Abstract. Fluid-like volumetric collective motion in drone swarms with navigation, obstacle avoidance, and formation maintenance remains challenging. Existing potential-field-based approaches often lack stability guarantees and are largely restricted to two-dimensional formations. This paper proposes *Active Elastic Matter*, an extension of the *Active Elastic Sheet* method that (i) generalizes the elastic interaction model to volumetric 3D formations and (ii) incorporates estimated relative velocities and accelerations using an Extended Kalman Filter. These predictive interaction terms improve stability and robustness in dynamic environments. Simulation results demonstrate that Active Elastic Matter enables 3D formations to navigate narrow passages and dynamic obstacles while maintaining higher order and lower entropy compared to Active Elastic Sheet. Real-world experiments with Crazyflie drones further validate improved stability during narrow passage navigation.

1 Introduction

Flocking—the coherent and distributed movement of a swarm, such as a flock of starlings or a school of tuna, resembling a single super-organism—is a striking phenomenon in nature. Achieving such smooth collective motion in robotic swarms, where agents move in a common direction, avoid obstacles, and maintain a desired formation (a frequent requirement in swarm robotic systems), remains a challenging problem [3,7–9].

Most collective motion algorithms are developed using kinematic models and are primarily demonstrated in 2D environments [1,6]. Approaches such as [3] adjust an agent's motion based on the relative positions—and in some cases velocities—of neighboring agents. However, neglecting acceleration information often leads to degraded smoothness and robustness in dynamic environments. While collective motion in 3D has been explored [4], challenges related to noise reduction, motion prediction, and stability remain largely unaddressed.

R. Groß et al. (Eds.): ANTS 2026, LNCS 16515, pp. 289–296, 2026.
https://doi.org/10.1007/978-3-032-26123-6_22

In this paper, we extend the *Active Elastic Sheet* (AES) method [2,3], which models a swarm of robots as a 2D elastic sheet whose individuals are driven by forces generated through virtual springs and dampers based on relative inter-agent distances. The proposed method, termed *Active Elastic Matter* (AEM), extends AES in two key aspects: (i) it generalizes the framework to support volumetric 3D formations, and (ii) it incorporates estimated velocities and accelerations of neighboring agents—rather than relying solely on position information—using an Extended Kalman Filter (EKF).

2   Framework and Related Work

The AES model [3] represents agents as nodes of an elastic lattice connected by virtual springs, as illustrated in Fig. 1. Each agent interacts only with a local neighborhood, allowing the collective behavior to emerge in a fully decentralized manner.

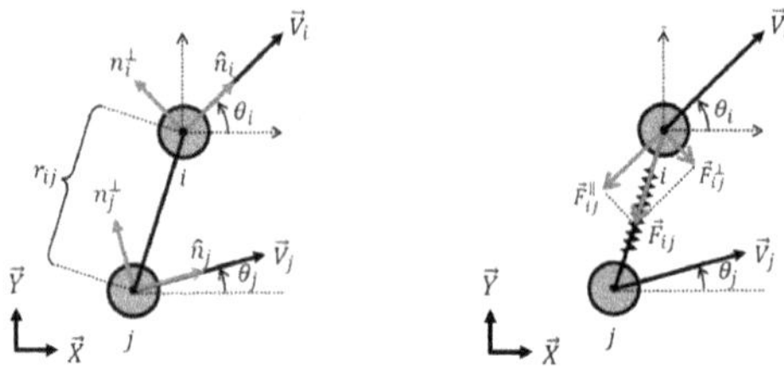

Fig. 1. Illustration of the AES model dynamics. v_i and v_j denote agent speeds, X and Y are the principal axes of the 2D plane, and θ_i is the heading angle of agent i. (Left) $\hat{n}$ and $\hat{n}^{\perp}$ are unit vectors parallel and perpendicular to the heading direction, and r_{ij} is the distance from agent i to agent j. (Right) $\boldsymbol{F}_{ij}$ is the force exerted on agent i by agent j, with $\boldsymbol{F}_{ij}^{\parallel}$ and $\boldsymbol{F}_{ij}^{\perp}$ denoting its parallel and perpendicular components.

The force acting on agent i due to its neighboring agents is defined as

$$\boldsymbol{F}_i = \sum_{j \in \mathcal{N}_i} -\kappa\big(r_{ij} - l_{ij}\big)\hat{r}_{ij},$$

where $\mathcal{N}_i$ denotes the neighbor set of agent i, $\boldsymbol{x}_i$ is the position of agent i, $\hat{r}_{ij} = (\boldsymbol{x}_j - \boldsymbol{x}_i)/\|\boldsymbol{x}_j - \boldsymbol{x}_i\|$ is the unit relative displacement vector, κ is the spring constant, and l_{ij} is the equilibrium spring length.

The resulting total force $\boldsymbol{F}_i = \sum_{j \in \mathcal{N}_i} \boldsymbol{F}_{ij}$ influences both the translational and rotational motion of the agent. Specifically, the agent dynamics are governed by

$$\dot{\boldsymbol{x}}_i = v_0 \hat{n}_i + \alpha\big(\boldsymbol{F}_i \cdot \hat{n}_i\big)\hat{n}_i,$$

$$\dot{\theta}_i = \beta\big(\boldsymbol{F}_i \cdot \hat{n}_i^{\perp}\big).$$

where θ_i denotes the heading angle of agent i, v_0 is the nominal forward speed, $\hat{n}_i$ and $\hat{n}_i^{\perp}$ are unit vectors parallel and perpendicular to the heading direction, and α and β are force-to-motion gain parameters.

By decomposing interaction forces into components parallel and perpendicular to the agent's heading, AES enables a group of agents to self-organize into a coherent and deformable 2D formation. Since AES relies solely on relative position information, it lacks predictive capability and is marginally stable in certain symmetric configurations [5].

3   Methodology

3.1   Active Elastic Matter Model

We extend the AES framework to 3D space and augment its interaction laws with relative velocity and acceleration terms. The resulting method, termed *Active Elastic Matter* (AEM), preserves the decentralized and physically interpretable structure of AES while enabling smoother and more stable collective motion.

The proposed model builds upon the velocity-augmented AES formulation of [2] by additionally incorporating acceleration-dependent interactions. Figure 2 illustrates the geometric interpretation of the three-dimensional extension.

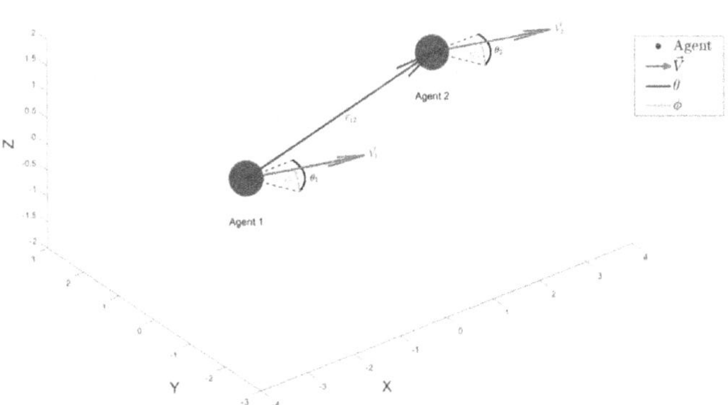

Fig. 2. Extension of AES into three-dimensional space through the introduction of the vertical Z axis. Relative angular displacements between two agents are represented by θ_{ij} in the $X\text{--}Y$ plane and ϕ_{ij} in the vertical plane.

For each agent i, the total interaction force is defined as

$$\boldsymbol{F}_i = \sum_{j \in \mathcal{N}_i} \left(-\kappa \left(\|\tilde{\boldsymbol{r}}_{ij}\| - l_{ij} \right) - b\|\tilde{\boldsymbol{v}}_{ij}\| - c\|\tilde{\boldsymbol{a}}_{ij}\| \right) \hat{r}_{ij}, \tag{1}$$

where $\tilde{\boldsymbol{r}}_{ij}$, $\tilde{\boldsymbol{v}}_{ij}$, and $\tilde{\boldsymbol{a}}_{ij} \in \mathbb{R}^3$ denote the estimated relative position, velocity, and acceleration between agents i and j, and b and c are velocity- and acceleration-dependent damping gains.

Translational motion follows the AES formulation, while orientation dynamics are extended to 3D with vertical heading dynamics are defined as

$$\dot{\phi}_i = \beta\left(\boldsymbol{F}_i \cdot \hat{n}_i^{\perp\perp}\right),$$

where $\hat{n}_i^{\perp\perp}$ is the orthogonal vector to forward and lateral heading.

3.2 Relative State Estimation

Agents measure only relative position information. To obtain the relative velocity and acceleration terms required by Eq. (1), each agent maintains a local EKF that estimates relative position, velocity, and acceleration from noisy range and bearing measurements to neighboring agents.

The estimator operates in a fully decentralized manner and mitigates noise amplification associated with numerical differentiation, enabling predictive interaction forces in dynamic environments.

3.3 Stability Analysis

We analyze local stability using a symmetric two-agent system, which captures the essential stability properties of both AES and AEM (Fig. 3).

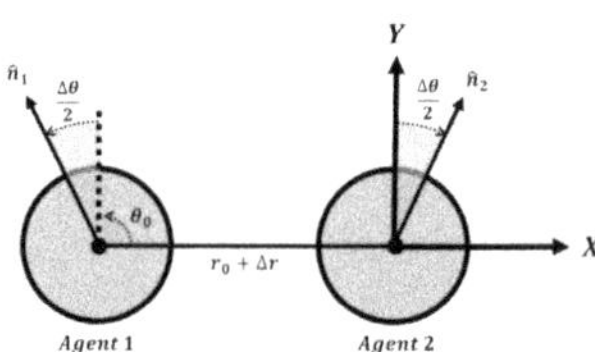

Fig. 3. Two-agent system exhibiting mirror symmetry.

Linearizing the relative dynamics around the equilibrium configuration for parallel motion ($\theta_0 = \pi/2$, $r_0 = l_0$) yields

$$\frac{d}{dt}\begin{pmatrix} \Delta r \\ \Delta\theta \end{pmatrix} = \begin{pmatrix} 0 & v_0 \\ -\dfrac{2\beta\kappa}{1+2\beta v_0 c} & -\dfrac{2\beta b v_0}{1+2\beta v_0 c} \end{pmatrix} \begin{pmatrix} \Delta r \\ \Delta\theta \end{pmatrix}.$$

The eigenvalues of the system matrix are

$$\lambda_{\pm} = \frac{-\dfrac{2\beta b v_0}{1+2\beta v_0 c} \pm \sqrt{\dfrac{4\beta^2 b^2 v_0^2}{(1+2\beta v_0 c)^2} - \dfrac{8\beta\kappa v_0}{1+2\beta v_0 c}}}{2}. \tag{2}$$

For the original AES formulation ($b = 0$, $c = 0$), the eigenvalues lie on the imaginary axis, indicating marginal stability [5]. In contrast, the velocity- and acceleration-dependent terms introduce damping that shifts the eigenvalues into the left half-plane, ensuring asymptotic stability for appropriate parameter choices.

4   Experiments

We evaluate the AEM framework in both simulation and real-world experiments to assess collective motion quality under spatial constraints and dynamic disturbances, and to validate the stabilizing effects.

Simulation experiments consider 3D formations navigating narrow passages and dynamic obstacles. Real-world experiments demonstrate the method using Crazyflie drones operating in a constrained indoor environment.

4.1   Performance Metrics

Collective motion quality is evaluated using *order* and *entropy*. The order metric

$$\psi = \left\| \frac{1}{N} \sum_{i=1}^{N} \hat{n}_i \right\|$$

quantifies directional alignment, where $\psi = 1$ indicates perfect coherence. The entropy-like metric is defined as a mean displacement measure,

$$S(t) = \frac{1}{N} \sum_{i=1}^{N} |x_i(t) - x_i'(0)|$$

which measures deviation from the initial formation, with lower values indicating stronger formation preservation.

4.2   Simulation Experiments

We simulate $N = 216$ agents initialized on a 3D octahedral lattice with $1\,\mathrm{m}$ inter-agent spacing. Parameters are set to $\alpha = 0.004$ m/(sN), $\beta = 0.12$ m/(sN), $v_0 = 0.002$ m/s, $k = 5$ N/m, $b = 250$ sN/m, and $c = 50$ s^{2}N/m, with b and c selected to satisfy the stability condition in Eq. (2).

Narrow Passage Navigation. The swarm encounters a donut-shaped narrow passage (Fig. 4). We compare the full AEM model against a position-only variant (AEM-, $b = 0$, $c = 0$). AEM- fails to traverse the passage and is reflected, accompanied by a rapid loss of order and increased entropy. In contrast, AEM adapts its shape, maintains cohesion, and successfully passes through the obstacle while preserving high order and low entropy.

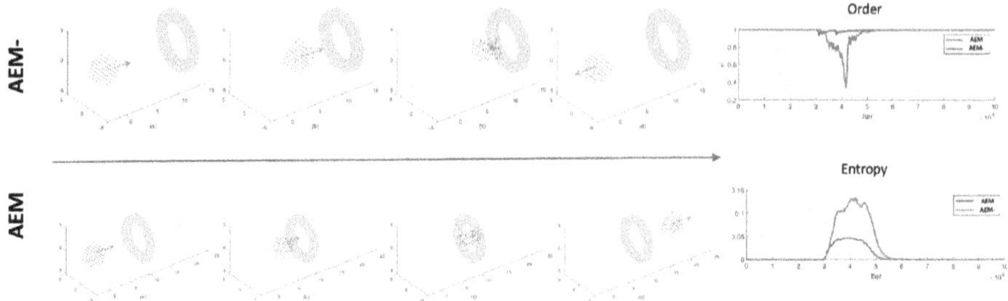

Fig. 4. AEM- fails to pass the narrow gap, while AEM successfully adapts its formation. Right: Order and entropy evolution.

Dynamic Intrusion. In the second scenario, a moving obstacle intrudes through the swarm (Fig. 5). The AEM- configuration exhibits a sharp loss of order followed by abrupt recovery, indicating insufficient damping. AEM responds smoothly to the disturbance and maintains sustained coherence, demonstrating improved robustness to dynamic perturbations.

Fig. 5. Dynamic intrusion scenario. AEM exhibits smoother adaptation and sustained order compared to AEM-.

4.3   Real-World Experiments

Real-world validation is conducted using five Crazyflie 2.1 drones tracked by a Vicon motion capture system with 12 cameras and controlled via the CrazySwarm framework. Interaction forces are computed from motion capture data and transmitted as position commands in real time.

A 2D formation is used to compare AEM against the AES[1] during narrow passage navigation (Fig. 6).

The AES-based swarm fails to traverse the passage due to limited damping and coordination. In contrast, AEM adapts its formation smoothly and successfully navigates the constrained region, confirming the practical benefits of

---

[1] For 2D formations with $b = 0$ and $c = 0$, AEM reduces to AES.

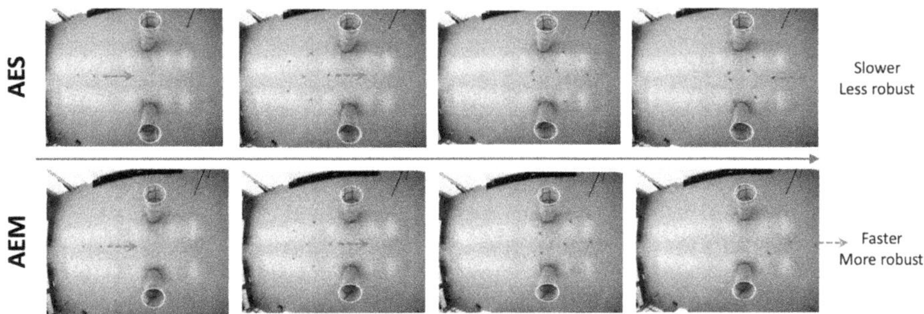

Fig. 6. Physical drone experiments. AES fails to sufficiently compress, while AEM successfully adapts and passes through the gap.

EKF-enhanced interaction dynamics. Due to arena size limitations and down-wash effects[2], three-dimensional real-world experiments could not be conducted.

5 Conclusion

This paper introduced *Active Elastic Matter*, a decentralized collective motion framework enabling drone swarms to move as coherent elastic formations in cluttered and dynamic environments. AEM extends the AES model in two key directions: it generalizes elastic interaction laws from planar lattices to volumetric three-dimensional formations, and it augments position-based interactions with relative velocity and acceleration estimates from decentralized EKF, introducing predictive damping that improves robustness and guarantees asymptotic stability.

Theoretical analysis showed that velocity- and acceleration-dependent interaction terms shift the system from marginal to asymptotically stable equilibria. Simulation results demonstrated that AEM allows dense 3D formations to adapt their shape, preserve coherence, and traverse narrow passages and dynamic disturbances, outperforming position-only models. Real-world experiments with Crazyflie nano-drones further validated these benefits, achieving smoother deformation and improved coordination during constrained navigation tasks. Overall, AEM provides a scalable and physically interpretable foundation for stable collective motion in three-dimensional robotic swarms.

Acknowledgement. We thank the Middle East Technical University, Scientific Research Projects Directorate (BAP) [grant number: ADEP-302-2024-11468]; and the European Union [RoboRoyale, grant number: 964492] for their support in the project.

Disclosure of Interests. The authors have no competing interests to declare.

---

[2] A drone being pushed towards the ground due to the downward air flow generated by another drone above it.

References

1. Aldana, M., Huepe, C.: Phase transitions in self-driven many-particle systems and related non-equilibrium models: a network approach. J. Stat. Phys. **112**(1–2), 135–153 (2003). https://doi.org/10.1023/A:1023675519930
2. Boz, İ.C.: Anticipation in Collective Motion of Robot Swarms. Master's thesis, Middle East Technical University (2021)
3. Ferrante, E., Turgut, A.E., Dorigo, M., Huepe, C.: Collective motion dynamics of active solids and active crystals. New J. Phys. **15**(9), 095011 (2013). https://doi.org/10.1088/1367-2630/15/9/095011
4. Karagüzel, T.A., van Diggelen, F., Garcia Rincon, A., Ferrante, E.: Self-organized flocking in three dimensions (2024). https://doi.org/10.1007/978-3-031-70932-6_12
5. Lin, G., Han, Z., Huepe, C.: Order-disorder transitions in a minimal model of active elasticity. New J. Phys. **23**(2), 023019 (2021). https://doi.org/10.1088/1367-2630/abe0da
6. Manju, M., Kant, C.: Ant colony optimization: a swarm intelligence based technique. Int. J. Comput. Appl. **73**(10), 30–33 (2013). https://doi.org/10.5120/12779-9387
7. Reynolds, C.W.: Flocks, herds and schools: a distributed behavioral model. ACM SIGGRAPH Comput. Graph. **21**(4), 25–34 (1987). https://doi.org/10.1145/37402.37406
8. Turgut, A.E., Boz, İC., Okay, İE., Ferrante, E., Huepe, C.: Interaction network effects on position- and velocity-based models of collective motion. J. R. Soc. Interface **17**(169), 20200165 (2020). https://doi.org/10.1098/rsif.2020.0165
9. Vicsek, T., Czirók, A., Ben-Jacob, E., Cohen, I., Shochet, O.: Novel type of phase transition in a system of self-driven particles. Phys. Rev. Lett. **75**, 1226–1229 (1995). https://doi.org/10.1103/PhysRevLett.75.1226

Adaptive Multi-robot Herding
via Dynamic Risk-Aware Angular
Repositioning

Leyre Remartinez[✉], Alejandro Perez-Yus, and Rosario Aragues

Instituto de Investigación en Ingeniería de Aragón, Universidad de Zaragoza,
Zaragoza, Spain
`leyre.remartinez.v@gmail.com, {alperez,raragues}@unizar.es`

Abstract. This article presents a control strategy for guiding a herd toward a goal region using a multi-robot system. In herding tasks, sheep act as noncooperative agents, combining aggregation tendencies with stochastic movements that complicate the guidance process. To overcome this challenge, we propose a cooperative control approach in which robots position themselves around the herd to exert pressure and steer it toward the target. The robots coordinate to encircle the herd, prioritizing areas with higher risk of escape, while the center of the robot formation is guided toward the goal. The effectiveness of the proposed strategy is validated through simulations, comparisons with state-of-the-art methods and real robotic experiments. Beyond demonstrating improved containment and more efficient guidance, the results highlight the method's ability to maintain order and cohesion within the group, adapt to dynamic herd configurations, respect inter-individual spacing, and achieve guidance in less time. These advantages position our strategy as a highly effective and scalable solution for advanced robotic herding tasks.

1 Introduction

Collective behavior emerges in many biological systems, where animals coordinate through local interactions. Sheep flocks represent an example of aggregation, in which individuals maintain cohesion and avoid dispersion, as described by Reynolds' flocking model [10]. Herding builds on this principle by using trained dogs to apply repulsive forces that guide livestock. With recent advances in robotics and multi-agent systems, there has been growing interest in reproducing this biologically inspired behavior using autonomous agents.

Prior work on noncooperative robotic herding has explored control strategies using single or multiple robotic herders. Vaughan [13] demonstrated duck herding with a single robot, while Lien *et al.* [6] proposed strategies based on robots occupying predefined positions. These ideas evolved into formation-based methods, including arc [3], V-shaped [4], and complete-circle herding [11], with further extensions for surrounding single evaders [2]. In contrast, the *Outmost Push* strategy [15] avoids fixed formations. Instead, robots concentrate their

R. Groß et al. (Eds.): ANTS 2026, LNCS 16515, pp. 297–305, 2026.
https://doi.org/10.1007/978-3-032-26123-6_23

efforts on sheep that are farthest from the goal region, as these individuals are considered more likely to escape. Other approaches explicitly separate the herding task into collection and driving phases [12], while decentralized strategies have been proposed for non-aggregating evaders [1]. A broader perspective on these and other strategies can be found in [7].

In this paper, we address the problem of guiding a swarm of agents toward a goal using mobile ground robots, referred to as *'sheep'* and *'dogs'*. It is particularly challenging due to nonlinear interaction and the high number of inter-agent forces. To simplify control design, we use a strategy in which robots surround the herd and apply pressure toward the goal. This coordinated behavior allows the system, composed of both sheep and dogs, to be modeled as a single non-holonomic agent with differential-drive dynamics.

Our approach is inspired by Pierson and Schwager's method [8], in which robots are distributed along an arc enclosing the herd. We extend it with a novel contribution in which robots dynamically adjust their positions, focusing on areas where sheep are closest to the formation's boundary, indicating dispersion risk. In addition, the system's velocity toward the goal is modulated based on the flock configuration. This responsiveness at both group and individual levels enables the dogs to prevent escapes more effectively than previous methods.

Our strategy is evaluated through simulations and compared with the Outmost Push method [15] and Pierson and Schwager's approach [8]. This comparison highlights the effectiveness of the proposed method, as it achieves higher containment, keeping the flock cohesive and within the desired region. In addition, the movement is more coordinated and ensures appropriate distance between agents to reduce collision risk. Finally, the approach is validated through real-robot experiments on the Robotarium platform [14], a remote experimental environment that enables testing on a team of ground mobile robots.

2　Problem Formulation

We consider a two-dimensional open space where $m \geq 1$ dogs guide $n \geq 1$ sheep toward a target region $\mathcal{O}_r \subset \mathbb{R}^2$, defined as a closed disk of radius r_{goal} centered at $\mathbf{p}_{\text{goal}}$. Let $\mathbf{y}_j \in \mathbb{R}^2$ and $\mathbf{x}_i \in \mathbb{R}^2$ denote the positions of dog j and sheep i, respectively. The task is completed when all sheep satisfy

$$\|\mathbf{x}_i - \mathbf{p}_{\text{goal}}\| \leq r_{\text{goal}}, \qquad \forall i \in \{1, \ldots, n\}.$$

Following [9], we use an aggregation method based on [5], which simulates group dynamics through local attraction and repulsion forces between agents. We extend it with two modifications to better capture sheep behavior. First, we propose that, for a sheep to consider another individual, in addition to being within its sensing radius, the other individual must also be a Voronoi neighbor, which means that their Voronoi cells must be adjacent. This additional constraint reflects the effect of natural occlusion, preventing responses to individuals positioned behind others. Second, a random component is added to the sheep's motion to reflect the unpredictability observed in animal behavior.

The goal is to design a control law for m dogs to drive n sheep from their initial positions to the goal region $\mathcal{O}_r$, assuming that dogs know the goal region, follow single-integrator dynamics and have a higher maximum speed than sheep.

3   Controller Design

The system, including dogs and sheep, is modeled as a single nonholonomic vehicle, allowing the use of differential-drive control techniques. This requires that the robots surround the flock during the entire process.

Motion Toward the Goal: We define the center of the circumference formed by the robots, $\mathbf{c} \in \mathbb{R}^2$, as a virtual reference. By controlling its motion from $\mathbf{p}_{\text{ini}}$ to $\mathbf{p}_{\text{goal}}$, the flock moves as a single vehicle. The relative pose between the virtual agent R and the goal G, ${}^G\mathbf{X}_R = ({}^Gx_R, {}^Gy_R, {}^G\theta_R)$, is used to define the unicycle control law:

$$v = \gamma \cdot k_\rho \cdot \rho, \qquad \omega = \gamma \cdot (k_\alpha \cdot \alpha + k_\beta \cdot \beta), \tag{1}$$

where k_ρ, k_α and k_β are control gains that must satisfy $k_\rho > 0$, $k_\beta < 0$ and $k_\alpha > k_\rho$, and ρ, α, and β are defined as follows:

$$\rho = \sqrt{({}^Gx_R)^2 + ({}^Gy_R)^2}, \quad -\beta = \operatorname{atan2}({}^Gy_R, {}^Gx_R) + \pi, \quad \alpha = -\beta - {}^G\theta_R. \tag{2}$$

A key contribution is the velocity modulation factor $\gamma \in (0, 1]$, which adapts the motion of the virtual agent R based on the risk escapes, determined by the minimum distance d_{min} between any sheep and the formation boundary:

$$\gamma = 1/(1 + e^{-k_\gamma(d_{\text{min}} - d_{\text{safe}})}), \tag{3}$$

where d_{safe} is a safety threshold and $k_\gamma > 0$ determines the response sharpness.

Over a time step T, the displacement of the virtual point $\mathbf{c}$ relative to R is:

$$\Delta x = (v/\omega)\sin(\omega T), \quad \Delta y = (v/\omega)\,(1 - \cos(\omega T)), \quad \Delta\theta = \omega T, \tag{4}$$

with the special case $\omega = 0$ corresponding to purely linear motion.

These local displacements are transformed into the global frame to update the global position of $\mathbf{c}$ at each iteration until it reaches $\mathbf{p}_{\text{goal}}$.

Dynamic Reposition of Robots to Cover High Risk Areas: The desired robot positions along the circumference of radius r are given by:

$$\hat{\mathbf{y}}_j = \mathbf{c} + r\left[\cos(\alpha_j), \sin(\alpha_j)\right]^\top \tag{5}$$

where α_j denotes the angle assigned to robot j on the circle.

Unlike traditional approaches [8], our strategy dynamically reallocates robots to high-risk regions. Algorithm 1 clusters sheep whose arc distance δ_{arc} is below a threshold. For example, in Fig. 1, sheep 2 and 6 are assigned to the same group. Algorithm 2 then computes the target angles α for each group. For a group with bounds θ_{ini} and θ_{fin}, the spanned arc length is $L = (\theta_{\text{fin}} - \theta_{\text{ini}})r$.

The set of target angles Θ_g is defined as follows:

Algorithm 1: Position Assignment to Risk Zones

Input: $\mathbf{x}$ (sheep positions), $\mathbf{c}$ (flock centroid), r (herding radius), n (number of sheep), m (number of dogs), $\delta_{\mathrm{arc}}^{\mathrm{th}}$ (arc-length threshold)

Output: Θ: list of target angles for the dogs

Compute distance of each sheep to $\mathbf{c}$: $d_i = \|\mathbf{x}^{(i)} - \mathbf{c}\|$

Compute distance to the circumference: $d_{\mathrm{circ}} = |d_i - r|$

Sort indices by d_{circ} (ascending): *sorted_indices*

groups $\leftarrow []$, *group_indices* $\leftarrow []$, $\Theta \leftarrow []$, $i \leftarrow 0$

while $|\Theta| < m$ **and** $i < n$ **do**

  Get index of current sheep: $j \leftarrow$ *sorted_indices*$[i]$

  Compute current angle: $\theta_j \leftarrow \mathrm{atan2}(y_j - y_c, x_j - x_c) \mod 2\pi$

  Compatible groups for sheep j: $G_{\mathrm{comp}} \leftarrow []$

  for $k \leftarrow 0$ **to** $|groups| - 1$ **do**

    $g \leftarrow groups[k]$

    foreach θ_g *in* g **do**

      Compute angular difference: $\delta\theta \leftarrow \min(|\theta_j - \theta_g|, 2\pi - |\theta_j - \theta_g|)$

      Compute arc length: $\delta_{\mathrm{arc}} \leftarrow \delta\theta \cdot r$

      if $\delta_{arc} < \delta_{arc}^{th}$ **then**

        $G_{\mathrm{comp}} \leftarrow G_{\mathrm{comp}} \cup \{k\}$; **break**

  if *isEmpty(G_{comp})* **then**

    groups $\leftarrow$ *groups* $\cup \{\theta_j\}$

    group_indices $\leftarrow$ *group_indices* $\cup \{j\}$

  else

    Merge *groups* in G_{comp} with $[\theta_j]$ and $[j]$

  if $i \geq m - 1$ **or** $i = n - 1$ **then**

    $\Theta \leftarrow$ `AssignAnglesToGroups`$(groups, r, \delta_{\mathrm{arc}}^{\mathrm{th}})$

  $i \leftarrow i + 1$

return Θ

- If $L < \delta_{\mathrm{arc}}^{\mathrm{th}}$, a single target angle is assigned $\Theta_g = \{\theta_{\mathrm{mid}}\}$, with $\theta_{\mathrm{mid}} = \theta_{\mathrm{ini}} + (\theta_{\mathrm{fin}} - \theta_{\mathrm{ini}})/2$.
- If $L \geq \delta_{\mathrm{arc}}^{\mathrm{th}}$, the target angles are uniformly distributed along the arc as $\Theta_g = \{\theta_{\mathrm{ini}} + i(\theta_{\mathrm{fin}} - \theta_{\mathrm{ini}})/s \mid i = 0, \ldots, s\}$, where $s = \lfloor L/\delta_{\mathrm{arc}}^{\mathrm{th}} \rfloor$ is the number of segments required.

Finally, the global set of target angles α aggregates the angles from all groups. Given these values, robot goal positions $\mathbf{y}_j$ are computed using Eq. (5). This process of detecting vulnerable areas and reassigning robots is repeated each iteration, allowing the formation to adapt to the flock's configuration.

Continuous Control of Robot Motion via Single Integrator: Each robot j follows a single-integrator model to reach its assigned target $\hat{\mathbf{y}}_j$. Let T be the high-level planner period, with discrete index $k \in \mathbb{N}$. Between planning steps, positions are updated at a finer time scale $\tau \in [kT, (k+1)T)$, keeping the target $\hat{\mathbf{y}}_j(kT)$ constant. Robot j evolves according to: $\mathbf{y}_j(\tau + 1) = (1 - K_p \cdot T) \cdot \mathbf{y}_j(\tau) + K_p \cdot T \cdot \hat{\mathbf{y}}_j(kT)$, where $\mathbf{y}_j(\tau) \in \mathbb{R}^2$ is the robot's position and $K_p \in (0, 1/T)$ a proportional gain.

Algorithm 2: `AssignAnglesToGroups` function

Input: *groups* (list of angle groups), r (radius), δ_{arc}^{th} (arc-length threshold)
Output: Θ: list of lists with assigned angles
$\Theta \leftarrow []$
foreach g *in groups* **do**
    if $|g| = 1$ **then**
        ⌊ Add g to Θ
    else
        Sort angles in group: $g \leftarrow \text{sort}(g)$
        Compute initial and final angles: θ_{ini} and θ_{fin}
        Compute angular span: $\delta\theta \leftarrow (\theta_{fin} - \theta_{ini}) \mod 2\pi$
        Compute arc length: $L \leftarrow \delta\theta \cdot r$
        if $L < \delta_{arc}^{th}$ **then**
            Compute mean angle: $\theta_{mid} \leftarrow (\theta_{ini} + \delta\theta/2) \mod 2\pi$
            ⌊ Add $[\theta_{mid}]$ to Θ
        else
            Compute number of segments: $s \leftarrow \lfloor L/\delta_{arc}^{th} \rfloor$
            Generate $s + 1$ equidistant angles between θ_{ini} and θ_{fin}
            ⌊ Add generated list of angles to Θ
return Θ

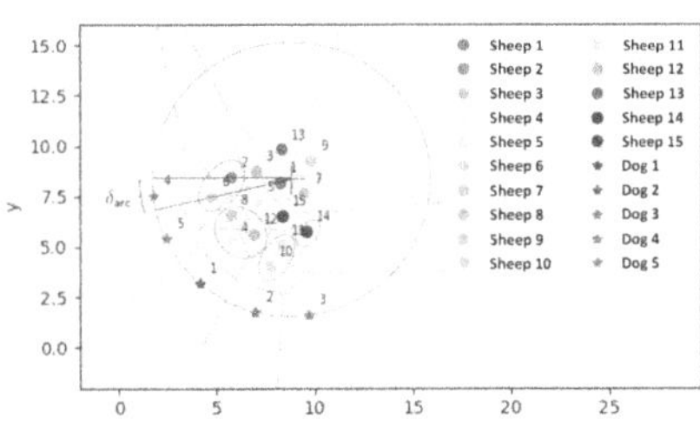

Fig. 1. Grouping of high-risk sheep based on angular proximity.

4 Experiments

The main experimental results are presented at https://youtu.be/vhrYr7Op-XM.

Regarding the simulations, to evaluate the proposed herding strategy we present two representative scenarios: the guidance of 1 and 30 sheep. Figure 2 illustrates the system behavior. In the first scenario, a single robot guides a sheep. In Fig. 2a, the robot anticipates its escape direction and positions itself to intercept while applying pressure toward the goal. In Fig. 2b, they reach the goal region and the robot prevents the sheep from leaving it. Figure 2c depicts the agents' trajectories. The second scenario considers 30 sheep and 5 robots.

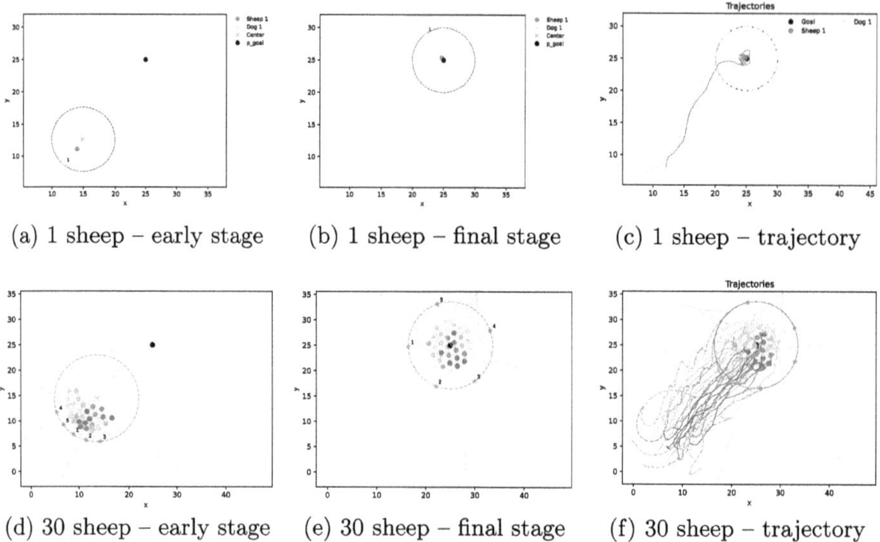

(a) 1 sheep – early stage   (b) 1 sheep – final stage   (c) 1 sheep – trajectory

(d) 30 sheep – early stage   (e) 30 sheep – final stage   (f) 30 sheep – trajectory

Fig. 2. Simulation results for single and 30 sheep herding scenarios. Sheep and dogs are represented by points (•) and asterisks (*), respectively.

Table 1. Comparison of strategies for guiding 1 and 30 sheep.

Metric	*Outmost Push*		Pierson and Schwager		Proposed Strategy	
	1 sheep	30 sheep	1 sheep	30 sheep	1 sheep	30 sheep
Number of robots	1	4	4	9	1	5
Time to reach goal (s)	28.35	33.95	25.70	30.05	25.80	31.75
Avg. sheep distance to goal (m)	17.21	25.07	18.11	21.06	17.02	20.91
Avg. dog distance to goal (m)	19.24	58.46	18.84	34.79	17.89	37.12
Min. dog–sheep distance (m)	0.93	1.18	2.54	1.32	3.12	1.96
Min. sheep–sheep distance (m)	–	0.52	–	0.95	–	1.04
Min. dog–dog distance (m)	–	1.09	–	2.88	–	2.39

In Fig. 2d, the robots surround the flock to prevent dispersion while guiding it toward the goal, which is reached in Fig. 2e. Figure 2f shows the agents' trajectories.

The proposed strategy is compared in the same scenarios with the *Outmost Push* method [15] and a modified version of Pierson and Schwager's approach [8] (see Table 1). While the latter preserves the original conceptual framework, we implement it using a new mathematical formulation adapted to our system. The modified Pierson and Schwager method does not react to sheep movements, requiring significantly more robots to achieve containment. Although robots travel shorter distances and maintain larger separations, these apparent advantages stem from the method's inability to react to escape attempts, resulting in

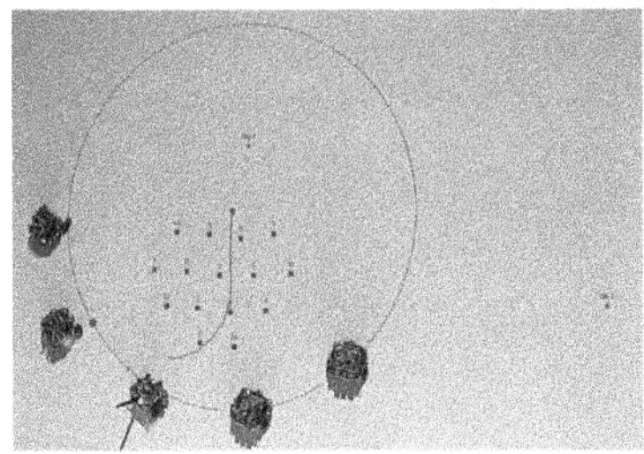 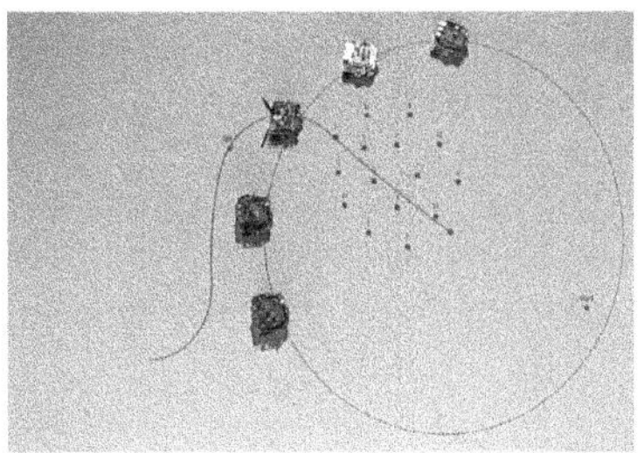

Fig. 3. Multi-goal herding experiment in Robotarium.

inferior overall performance. Compared with *Outmost Push*, our approach shows clear advantages in controlling the flock. During guidance, it ensures continuous containment and prevents dispersions, resulting in a more coordinated movement, even though more dogs are needed for larger flocks. At the goal, *Outmost Push* leaves robots inactive unless an escape occurs, while our strategy maintains active containment and avoids collisions. *Outmost Push* also has another important limitation that does not occur in the proposed strategy. When a sheep strays to the opposite side of the flock, the nearest robot attempts to reach it by crossing through the group, disrupting cohesion and causing dispersion. Overall, our method offers the best balance for effective herding. It performs particularly well when it is critical to keep all sheep within the goal region, without disrupting their behavior or causing collisions.

To evaluate the strategy under physical constraints, a set of experiments were conducted in the Robotarium, a remotely accessible multi-robot testbed at Georgia Tech that provides differential-drive robots for real-world validation experiments. We present an experiment in which 15 sheep, represented by ■, are guided through two sequential goals. The robots adapt their behavior as the flock transitions between regions, dynamically adjusting their positions to prevent escapes and ultimately maintain the sheep inside the final goal area. Two representative moments are shown in Fig. 3.

5   Conclusion

This paper presents a novel herding strategy that dynamically adapts robot positions around the flock, prioritizing regions with a higher risk of dispersion and adjusting velocities to reinforce containment near the boundary. Simulation and real-robot experiments show the effectiveness of the proposed method in containing the flock and guiding it toward the goal. Future work will focus on a more extensive comparison with recent methods, particularly in terms of scalability and efficiency, as well as on extending the approach to more complex environments involving obstacles and external agents.

Acknowledgement. This work was supported via project REMAIN S1/1.1/E0111 (Interreg Sudoe Programme, ERDF), via projects PID2021-124137OB-I00 and PID2024-159279OB-I00 funded by MICIU/AEI/10.13039/501100011033 and by ERDF/EU, and also, by the Gobierno de Aragón under Project DGA T45_23R.

Disclosure of Interests. The authors have no competing interests to declare.

References

1. Auletta, F., Fiore, D., Richardson, M.J., di Bernardo, M.: Herding stochastic autonomous agents via local control rules and online target selection strategies. Auton. Robot. **46**(3), 469–481 (2022). https://doi.org/10.48550/arXiv.2010.00386
2. Bacon, M., Olgac, N.: Swarm herding using a region holding sliding mode controller. J. Vib. Control **18**(7), 1056–1066 (2012). https://doi.org/10.1177/1077546311411346
3. Bennett, B., Trafankowski, M.: A comparative investigation of herding algorithms. In: Proceedings of Symposium on Understanding and Modelling Collective Phenomena (UMoCoP), pp. 33–38 (2012). https://doi.org/10.1007/978-3-319-39883-9_7
4. Fujioka, K.: Effective herding in shepherding problem in v-formation control. Trans. Inst. Syst. Control Inf. Eng. **31**(1), 21–27 (2018). https://doi.org/10.5687/iscie.31.21
5. Leccese, A., Gasparri, A., Priolo, A., Oriolo, G., Ulivi, G.: A swarm aggregation algorithm based on local interaction with actuator saturations and integrated obstacle avoidance. In: IEEE International Conference on Robotics and Automation, pp. 1865–1870 (2013). https://doi.org/10.1109/ICRA.2013.6630823
6. Lien, J.M., Bayazit, O., Sowell, R., Rodriguez, S., Amato, N.: Shepherding behaviors. In: IEEE International Conference on Robotics and Automation, vol. 4, pp. 4159–4164 (2004). https://doi.org/10.1109/ROBOT.2004.1308924
7. Long, N.K., Sammut, K., Sgarioto, D., Garratt, M., Abbass, H.A.: A comprehensive review of shepherding as a bio-inspired swarm-robotics guidance approach. IEEE Trans. Emerg. Top. Comput. Intell. **4**(4), 523–537 (2020). https://doi.org/10.1109/TETCI.2020.2992778
8. Pierson, A., Schwager, M.: Bio-inspired non-cooperative multi-robot herding. In: IEEE International Conference on Robotics and Automation (ICRA), pp. 1843–1849 (2015). https://doi.org/10.1109/ICRA.2015.7139438
9. Remartinez, L.: Simulación y control automático de rebaños mediante un sistema multi-agente. Escuela de Ingeniería y Arquitectura, Universidad de Zaragoza, Trabajo Fin de Grado (2025)
10. Reynolds, C.W.: Flocks, herds and schools: a distributed behavioral model. In: Proceedings of the 14th Annual Conference on Computer Graphics and Interactive Techniques, pp. 25–34 (1987). https://doi.org/10.1145/37402.37406
11. Song, H., et al.: Herding by caging: a formation-based motion planning framework for guiding mobile agents. Auton. Robot. **45**(5), 613–631 (2021). https://doi.org/10.1007/s10514-021-09975-8
12. Strömbom, D., et al.: Solving the shepherding problem: heuristics for herding autonomous, interacting agents. J. R. Soc. Interface **11**(100), 20140719 (2014). https://doi.org/10.1098/rsif.2014.0719

13. Vaughan, R., Sumpter, N., Henderson, J., Frost, A., Cameron, S.: Experiments in automatic flock control. Robot. Auton. Syst. **31**(1), 109–117 (2000). https://doi.org/10.1016/S0921-8890(99)00084-6
14. Wilson, S., et al.: The robotarium: globally impactful opportunities, challenges, and lessons learned in remote-access, distributed control of multirobot systems. IEEE Control Syst. Mag. **40**(1), 26–44 (2020). https://doi.org/10.1109/MCS.2019.2949973
15. Zhang, S., Lei, X., Duan, M., Peng, X., Pan, J.: A distributed outmost push approach for multirobot herding. IEEE Trans. Rob. **40**, 1706–1723 (2024). https://doi.org/10.1109/TRO.2024.3359528

Decentralized Multi-robot Coverage of Hemispherical Surfaces via Fortune-Based Partitioning

Mehdi Belal[1,2(✉)], Tiziano Manoni[1,3], Dario Albani[1], and Lorenzo Sabattini[2]

[1] Technology Innovation Institute (TII), Abu Dhabi, UAE
{mehdi.belal,tiziano.manoni,dario.albani}@tii.ae
[2] Department of Sciences and Methods for Engineering (DISMI), University of Modena and Reggio Emilia, Modena, Italy
{mehdi.belal,lorenzo.sabattini}@unimore.it
[3] Department of Computer Intelligence, Vrije Universiteit Amsterdam, Amsterdam, The Netherlands
t.manoni@vu.nl

Abstract. This paper presents a distributed framework providing high-level positioning guidance for multi-UAV systems operating on a hemispherical domain. Unlike conventional coverage approaches restricted to planar environments, the proposed method optimizes a coverage objective directly on the hemisphere, enabling three-dimensional viewpoint coordination around a dynamic target. Each UAV computes its motion using only locally available data, while the target position and a predefined probability density function remain independent of team size. The framework is validated through simulations and real-world experiments, demonstrating scalability and robustness.

1 Introduction

Multi-robot systems play an increasingly important role in real-world applications, where collaboration is required to cope with uncertainty and unpredictability [20]. Decentralization is a key enabler of scalability, fault tolerance, and uninterrupted operation, with demonstrated impact in precision agriculture [16], environmental monitoring [27], search and rescue [17], and industrial processes [7]. A fundamental task in these scenarios is area coverage, where robots must distribute over a region of interest. However, many practical deployments involve viewpoint coverage around a subject rather than planar tiling, as in aerial cinematography, cooperative observation, and infrastructure inspection. In such settings, coverage quality depends on angular diversity and rotational invariance. Modeling viewpoints as a hemisphere centered on the subject naturally captures these requirements and avoids distortions introduced by planar approximations. Most coverage approaches rely on Voronoi partitions and proximity graphs under assumptions of global knowledge and reliable communication [5,10,14,15,18,23]. Distributed schemes based on local perception

R. Groß et al. (Eds.): ANTS 2026, LNCS 16515, pp. 306–314, 2026.
https://doi.org/10.1007/978-3-032-26123-6_24

have been proposed to relax these assumptions [6,8], but extensions to curved domains remain limited. In this paper, we address decentralized viewpoint coverage directly on a hemispherical manifold. Given a static or moving subject and a predefined probability density function encoding deployment preferences, each UAV uses only local information to move along spherical geodesics toward its assigned region. The approach is scalable with team size and robust to agent additions and removals. In details, the main contributions can be summarized as follows: (i) We propose a methodology to partition hemispherical domains and perform coverage control, building upon Voronoi-based methods for two-dimensional environments. (ii) The proposed methodology is scalable with respect to the number of drones and area size, and robust to formation variations. (iii) We validate the proposed methodology in simulations and real-world experiments with a fleet of quadrotor UAVs.

1.1 Related Work

Coverage and formation control in non-planar spaces have been explored in the context of aerial cinematography and cooperative observation. Prior work has addressed camera motion planning and formation control for multi-UAV systems [13,22], as well as greedy and Voronoi-based coordination strategies [4,25]. However, these approaches often neglect scalability and computational complexity, which are critical for large teams. While decentralized coverage control with limited sensing and communication has been extensively studied in planar environments [21], relatively few works address coverage directly on curved manifolds. In contrast to planar formulations and greedy methods, we operate directly on a hemispherical manifold, optimizing a solid-angle objective with a decentralized update rule and explicitly discussing the complexity of spherical Voronoi maintenance.

2 Control

The coverage control mechanisms based on Lloyd's algorithm follow an iterative procedure designed to minimize a cost function [2,3,21], by assigning vehicles to their corresponding spatial partitions. In our work, we extend Fortune's algorithm [12] to a three-dimensional context defined over a spherical—or hemispherical—surface. Fortune's algorithm provides an efficient method for generating Voronoi diagrams. While the core structure of the algorithm remains analogous to the original two-dimensional formulation, it incorporates a modified distance metric and accounts for the curvature and topology of the spherical domain. Details on the computational complexity will be discussed subsequently. In contrast to prior formulations, our contribution here is the integration of a sweep-plane spherical Voronoi update with a centroid computation tailored to solid-angle densities.

2.1 Notation

Let $\mathcal{P} = \{p_1, \ldots, p_n\} \subset \mathbb{R}^3$ denote the set of agent positions. We consider coverage on the unit sphere $S^2 = \{p \in \mathbb{R}^3 : \|p\| = 1\}$ (or the hemisphere obtained by restricting to $z > 0$). The geodesic distance between two points $p, q \in S^2$ is defined as $d(p, q) = \arccos(p \cdot q)$. Given $\mathcal{P}$, the spherical Voronoi diagram is denoted by $\mathcal{V}(\mathcal{P}) = \{\mathcal{V}_i\}_{i=1}^n$, where each Voronoi cell is defined as

$$\mathcal{V}_i = \{\hat{r} \in S^2 : d(\hat{r}, p_i) < d(\hat{r}, p_j), \ \forall j \neq i\}. \tag{1}$$

Two agents are Voronoi neighbors if their cells share a boundary. The corresponding proximity graph is given by the Delaunay graph $\mathcal{G}_D(\mathcal{P})$. Throughout the paper, $\phi : S^2 \to \mathbb{R}_{\geq 0}$ denotes a probability density function defined on the surface, and integrals over $\mathcal{V}_i$ are taken with respect to the spherical surface measure.

2.2 Proposed Control Methodology

Following [2,3,8,21], coverage control minimizes an objective that spreads agents according to a surface density function $\phi(\mathbf{q})$:

$$\mathcal{H}(\mathcal{P}) = -\sum_{i=1}^n \int_{\bar{\mathcal{V}}_i} \|\mathbf{q} - \mathbf{p}_i\|^2 \, \phi(\mathbf{q}) \, d\mathbf{S}, \tag{2}$$

Higher values of $\mathcal{H}(\mathcal{P})$ correspond to configurations that better match the desired density. Inspired by planar Voronoi coverage and spherical sweep methods [26], we evaluate the objective on spherical Voronoi cells and use the resulting centroids as motion targets on S^2. Each robot is thus linked to its corresponding partition. To solve this optimization, one can calculate the gradient of $\mathcal{H}$, yielding: $\frac{\partial \mathcal{H}_V}{\partial \mathbf{p}_i}(\mathcal{P}) = 2 \, M_{\mathcal{V}_i} \left(C_{\mathcal{V}_i} - \mathbf{p}_i\right)$, where $M_{\mathcal{V}_i}$ and c_i represent, respectively, the mass and centroid in the Voronoi region $V_i \subset \mathcal{Q}$ for robot i located at $\mathbf{p}_i$, with ϕ being the density function within V_i. The mass and centroid values are computed as: $M_{\mathcal{V}_i} = \int_{\mathcal{V}_i} \phi(\mathbf{q}) \, dS$, $c_i = \frac{\int_{\mathcal{V}_i} q \, \phi(q) \, dS}{\int_{\mathcal{V}_i} \phi(q) \, dS}$. For further insights, see [9]. We consider a multi-robot setup of n agents navigating in a three-dimensional environment. The motion of each robot is described by a single-integrator model, with its position $\mathbf{p}_i \in \mathbb{R}^3$ evolving as:

$$\dot{\mathbf{p}}_i = \mathbf{u}_i, \tag{3}$$

where $\mathbf{u}_i \in \mathbb{R}^3$ is the control input, for $i = 1, \ldots, n$. The collection of all robot positions is $\mathcal{P} = \{\mathbf{p}_1, \ldots, \mathbf{p}_n\}$.

For single-integrator dynamics, Lloyd's method drives each agent toward the centroid of its Voronoi cell. Configurations satisfying $\mathbf{p}_i = c_i$ are centroidal Voronoi tessellations (CVTs) [10], which locally maximize $\mathcal{H}(\mathcal{P})$. The exact Voronoi partitioning $\mathcal{V}(\mathcal{P})$ of the region $\mathcal{Q}$ is assumed to be continuously updated in an iterative process—under the assumption that the region $\mathcal{Q}$ is known or that each robot is able to measure it. The network of the group of robots is defined by the Delaunay proximity graph $\mathcal{G}_D(\mathcal{P})$. To compute the i-th component of the $\mathcal{H}_\mathcal{V}(\mathcal{P})$ function, it is necessary for robot i to know its own position and the positions of its neighbors over the graph $\mathcal{G}_D(\mathcal{P})$. Usually the positions of all the robots are assumed to be known or measurable.

2.3   Algorithm and Complexity

Algorithm 1. Lloyd's Algorithm on the Sphere

Require: $\mathcal{P} = \{p_1, \ldots, p_n\} \subset S^2$, density $\phi : S^2 \to \mathbb{R}_+$
1: **for** $k = 1, 2, \ldots$ **do**
2:     **Voronoi Diagram** $\mathcal{V}(\mathcal{P}) \leftarrow$ spherical sweep [26]
        Sort $\mathcal{P}$ by latitude, process site/circle events
        Maintain beach curve, update cells $\mathcal{V}_i \subset S^2$
3:     **for** $i = 1$ to n **do**
4:         $c_i \leftarrow \dfrac{\int_{\mathcal{V}_i} q\,\phi(q)\,dS}{\int_{\mathcal{V}_i} \phi(q)\,dS}$ // *weighted centroid*
5:         $p_i \leftarrow \dfrac{c_i}{\|c_i\|}$ // *normalize to S^2*
6:     **end for**
7: **end for**
8: **return** $\mathcal{P}$

The proposed Algorithm 1 is carried out using Fortune's algorithm, a sweep-plane procedure for constructing the Voronoi diagram of a finite set of points, which runs in $O(n \log n)$ time, where n is the number of sites [12,26]. The overall computational cost can be analyzed by considering two primary components: (i) the construction of the Voronoi diagram on the sphere via a plane sweep, and (ii) the computation of the centroid of each Voronoi region. The plane sweep algorithm proposed by Zheng et al. [26] has a time complexity of $\mathcal{O}(n \log n)$ and space complexity of $\mathcal{O}(n)$, where n is the number of generators. Following the Voronoi construction, the algorithm computes the centroid c_i of each region $\mathcal{V}_i$ according to the weighted formula: $c_i = \dfrac{\int_{\mathcal{V}_i} q\,\phi(q)\,dS}{\int_{\mathcal{V}_i} \phi(q)\,dS},$ followed by: $c_i \leftarrow \frac{c_i}{\|c_i\|}$. Assuming numerical integration over each Voronoi cell is performed using m evaluation points, the centroid update for all n regions has a total complexity of $\mathcal{O}(nm)$. The standard practice in centroidal Voronoi literature assumes m to be fixed or bounded by a small constant—i.e. approximate integrals [11], resulting in a centroid computation phase of linear complexity with respect to n. Therefore, the total cost per iteration is $\mathcal{O}(n \log n + nm)$, which simplifies to $\mathcal{O}(n \log n)$ when $m = \mathcal{O}(1)$. Figure 1 shows practical methodologies for c_i computation.

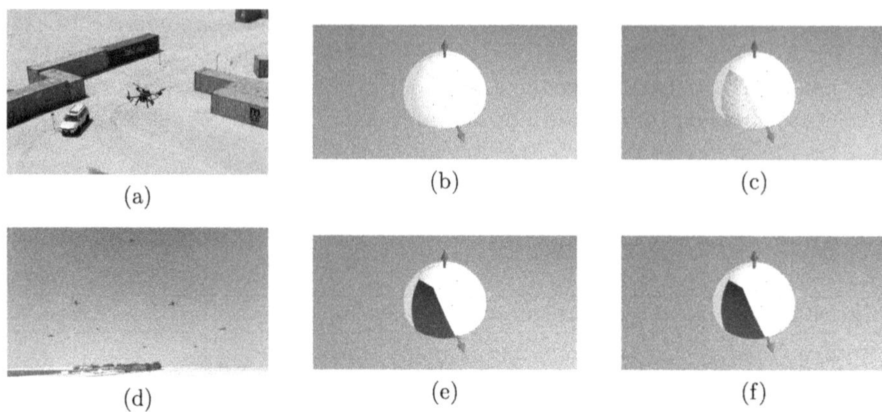

Fig. 1. Practical centroid computation: (a), (d) drones during the experiment, (b) geometric centroid with reprojection onto the sphere; (c),(e),(f) density-weighted geodesic Gaussian centroid, approximating $\int_{V_i} w(x)\, x\, dA$ via spherical micro-triangles and exact area computation [24].

2.4   Control Refinement

Each robot's control input can be determined via Lloyd's method [9]: $\mathbf{u}_i = k(c_i - \mathbf{p}_i)$, where $k \in \mathbb{R}_{>0}$ is a proportional gain. Since the pure Lloyd step can exhibit overshoot/oscillations in practice, inspired by field implementations [1,19], we introduce a nonlinear gain k_s that moderates corrections near the goal and preserves fast convergence far from it. Specifically, k_s is formulated by combining two overlapping sigmoid functions whose shape yields a gentler pull near the goal position while still ensuring rapid, smooth convergence from farther away: $k_s = \dfrac{1}{1+e^{\left(\frac{e_i}{s}+s\right)}} + \dfrac{1}{1+e^{-\left(\frac{e_i}{s}-s\right)}}$. Here, e_i is the positional error for the i-th agent, and $s \in \mathbb{R}$ governs how sharply the sigmoids change.

3   Experiments

To validate the proposed methodology, the algorithm was evaluated through both simulation and real-world experiments with UAVs. The control strategy was implemented in C++ using the Robot Operating System (ROS) for both simulated and physical deployments. In simulation, a Software-In-The-Loop environment was used, with each UAV executing coverage control, low-level flight control, inter-agent communication, and PX4 integration in a dedicated thread. Field experiments were conducted at a remote test site in the Al Dhafra region of the Abu Dhabi Emirate (UAE), using custom quadrotor UAVs developed at the Technology Innovation Institute (TII). Each platform features a 60 cm carbon-fiber airframe, a Pixhawk 6X flight controller, and an NVIDIA Jetson Orin NX onboard computer. Inter-UAV communication is achieved via a 2.4 GHz radio link. An overview of the experimental setup is shown in Figs. 2a, 2d. To maintain

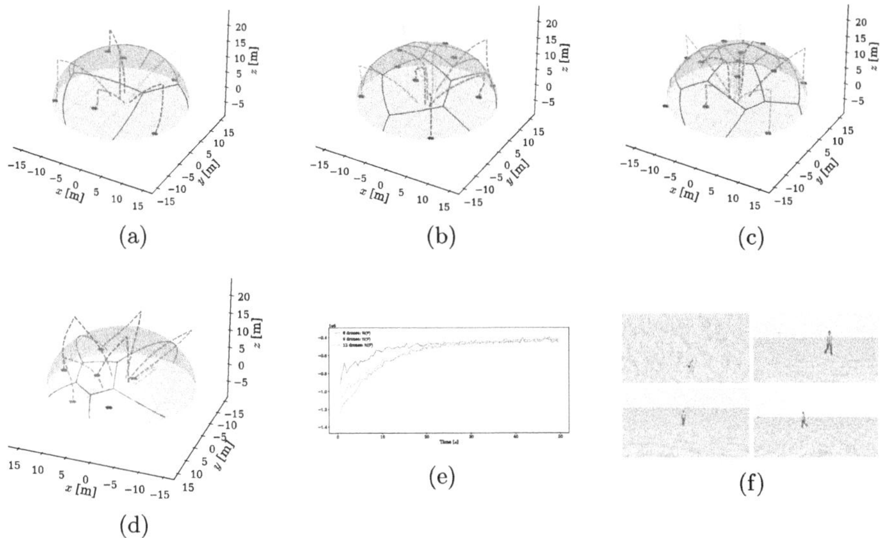

Fig. 2. Sub-figures (a)(c) show simulated hemispherical coverage with 6, 9, and 12 drones. In (d), trajectories with $\phi(q) \neq 1$. In (e), $\mathcal{H}(\mathcal{P})$ statistics over 10 runs. In (f), simulated camera views from 4 drones.

camera alignment with the target, yaw orientation is actively regulated by augmenting the control state with the yaw angle ψ and applying a PID controller to its first-order dynamics, allowing joint regulation of translational velocity $\dot{\mathbf{p}}$ and yaw rate $\dot{\psi}$. While simulations impose no dynamic constraints, real-world experiments limit the ground speed to $8\,\mathrm{m/s}$. A planar coverage phase is executed during take-off and landing to ensure safe transitions, while collision avoidance during hemispherical operation is inherently ensured by the Voronoi-based spatial partitioning.

4   Evaluation

Computing the value of the optimization function defined in (2), we evaluate the geometric notion of *configuration optimality* [3,8]. This metric quantifies the proximity of the current robot configuration to the centroidal Voronoi configuration, where the weighting is defined by the probability density function $\phi(q)$ for each point $q \in Q$. Figure 2e reports the average values of the function $\mathcal{H}(\mathcal{P})$ across multiple experimental trials. The results indicate that the agent configuration tends to optimize the configuration optimality metric once the drones have dispersed and reached a steady state. One direct way to assess how close a configuration of n sites $\mathcal{P}$ is to a CVT is to compare each site $\mathbf{p}_i$ with the centroid $\mathbf{c}_i$ of its Voronoi cell V_i, i.e., to evaluate the discrepancy targeted by (2). In an ideal CVT, every site coincides with its cell centroid, $\mathbf{p}_i = \mathbf{c}_i$ for all i. We define the per-site displacement $E_i = \|\mathbf{p}_i - \mathbf{c}_i\|$, and aggregate it into a

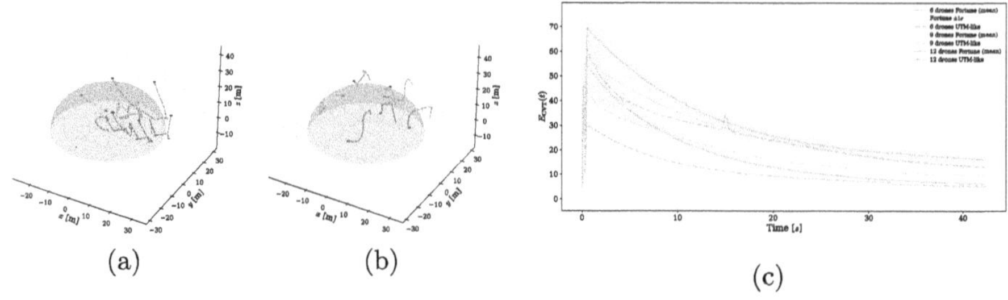

Fig. 3. Sub-figures (a)(b) show a field experiment with 8 drones, from takeoff to hemispherical coverage and adaptation. Sub-figure (c) reports $E_{\mathrm{CVT}}(\mathcal{P})$ for 6, 9, and 12 drones on a 15 m hemisphere.

configuration-level score $E_{\mathrm{CVT}}(\mathcal{P}) = \sum_{i=1}^{n} E_i$, which vanishes if and only if the configuration is centroidal.

As a baseline with comparable computational complexity, we evaluate a planar proxy-based coverage method. Points on the hemispherical surface are mapped to a local planar domain using an equirectangular-like projection centered at a reference location, enabling standard planar Voronoi coverage computation in $O(n \log n)$ via Fortune's algorithm. The resulting centroids are then mapped back to the hemispherical surface. This projection is neither conformal nor equal-area, and geometric distortions increase with distance from the reference point; however, when the reference is chosen near the operational region, the mapping provides a reasonable local approximation. Figure 3c reports the error for configurations with 6, 9, and 12 drones, comparing the two coverage methodologies. After mapping the centroids back to the hemispherical surface, the planar proxy yields exact alignment in the ideal case. By contrast, the sweep-plane approach produces a polyhedral approximation of the surface, resulting in higher error due to off-surface effects. Nevertheless, both methods exhibit asymptotic convergence toward zero error. The sweep-plane formulation additionally offers finer control and avoids projection-induced distortions.

5   Conclusions

This paper presented a decentralized coverage control strategy on hemispherical surfaces that preserves the $O(n \log n)$ complexity of planar approaches while enabling flexible viewpoint guidance via Gaussian density functions. The method is scalable, robust to dynamic changes, and suitable for realistic multi-UAV deployments. Future work includes handling multiple POIs, time-varying density functions $\phi(q, t)$, and extending Fortune-based constructions to more general curved surfaces.

Disclosure of Interests. The authors have no competing interests to declare.

References

1. Albani, D., Manoni, T., Saska, M., Ferrante, E.: Distributed three dimensional flocking of autonomous drones. In: 2022 International Conference on Robotics and Automation (ICRA), pp. 6904–6911. IEEE (2022)
2. Belal, M., Albani, D., Sabattini, L.: Understanding the role of time-varying targets in adaptive distributed area coverage control. In: International Symposium on Experimental Robotics, pp. 239–249. Springer, Cham (2023)
3. Bertoncelli, F., Belal, M., Albani, D., Pratissoli, F., Sabattini, L.: On limited-range coverage control for large-scale teams of aerial drones: Deployment and study. In: International Symposium on Distributed Autonomous Robotic Systems, pp. 333–346. Springer, Cham (2022)
4. Bucker, A., Bonatti, R., Scherer, S.: Do you see what i see? coordinating multiple aerial cameras for robot cinematography. In: 2021 IEEE International Conference on Robotics and Automation (ICRA), pp. 7972–7979. IEEE (2021)
5. Bullo, F., Cortés, J., Martinez, S.: Distributed Control of Robotic Networks: A Mathematical Approach to Motion Coordination Algorithms. Princeton University Press, Princeton (2009)
6. Cao, M., Hadjicostis, C.: Distributed algorithms for voronoi diagrams and application in ad-hoc networks. UIUC Coordinated Science Laboratory, Technical report UILU-ENG-03-2222, DC-210 (2003)
7. Cortés, J., Egerstedt, M.: Coordinated control of multi-robot systems: a survey. SICE J. Control, Meas. Syst. Integr. **10**(6), 495–503 (2017)
8. Cortes, J., Martinez, S., Bullo, F.: Spatially-distributed coverage optimization and control with limited-range interactions. ESAIM: Control, Optim. Calculus Var. **11**(4), 691–719 (2005)
9. Cortes, J., Martinez, S., Karatas, T., Bullo, F.: Coverage control for mobile sensing networks. IEEE Trans. Robot. Autom. **20**(2), 243–255 (2004)
10. Du, Q., Emelianenko, M., Ju, L.: Convergence of the Lloyd algorithm for computing centroidal voronoi tessellations. SIAM J. Numer. Anal. **44**(1), 102–119 (2006)
11. Du, Q., Faber, V., Gunzburger, M.: Centroidal voronoi tessellations: applications and algorithms. SIAM Rev. **41**(4), 637–676 (1999)
12. Fortune, S.: A sweepline algorithm for voronoi diagrams. In: Proceedings of the Second Annual Symposium on Computational Geometry, pp. 313–322 (1986)
13. Galvane, Q., et al.: Directing cinematographic drones. ACM Trans. Graph. (TOG) **37**(3), 1–18 (2018)
14. Guruprasad, K., Dasgupta, P.: Distributed voronoi partitioning for multi-robot systems with limited range sensors. In: 2012 IEEE/RSJ International Conference on Intelligent Robots and Systems, pp. 3546–3552. IEEE (2012)
15. He, C., Feng, Z., Ren, Z.: Distributed algorithm for voronoi partition of wireless sensor networks with a limited sensing range. Sensors **18**(2), 446 (2018)
16. Kim, J., Kim, S., Ju, C., Son, H.I.: Unmanned aerial vehicles in agriculture: a review of perspective of platform, control, and applications. IEEE Access **7**, 105100–105115 (2019)
17. Kumar, V., Michael, N.: Opportunities and challenges with autonomous micro aerial vehicles. Int. J. Robot. Res. **31**(11), 1279–1291 (2012)
18. Laventall, K., Cortés, J.: Coverage control by multi-robot networks with limited-range anisotropic sensory. Int. J. Control **82**(6), 1113–1121 (2009)
19. Manoni, T., Albani, D., Horyna, J., Petracek, P., Saska, M., Ferrante, E.: Adaptive arbitration of aerial swarm interactions through a gaussian kernel for coherent group motion. Front. Robot. AI **9**, 1006786 (2022)

20. Parker, L.E.: Multi-robot team design for real-world applications. In: Distributed Autonomous Robotic Systems, vol. 2, pp. 91–102. Springer, Cham (1996)
21. Pratissoli, F., Capelli, B., Sabattini, L.: On coverage control for limited range multi-robot systems. In: IEEE/RSJ International Conference on Intelligent Robots and Systems (IROS) (2022)
22. Tallamraju, R., et al.: Active perception based formation control for multiple aerial vehicles. IEEE Robot. Autom. Lett. **4**(4), 4491–4498 (2019)
23. Teruel, E., Aragues, R., López-Nicolás, G.: A practical method to cover evenly a dynamic region with a swarm. IEEE Robot. Autom. Let. **6**(2), 1359–1366 (2021)
24. Toda, A.A.: Radii of the inscribed and escribed spheres of a simplex. Int. J. Geom **3**, 5–13 (2014)
25. Xu, X., Shi, G., Tokekar, P., Diaz-Mercado, Y.: Interactive multi-robot aerial cinematography through hemispherical manifold coverage. In: 2022 IEEE/RSJ International Conference on Intelligent Robots and Systems (IROS), pp. 11528–11534. IEEE (2022)
26. Zheng, X., Ennis, R., Richards, G.P., Palffy-Muhoray, P.: A plane sweep algorithm for the voronoi tessellation of the sphere. Electron. Liq. Crystal Commun. (e-LC) (2011)
27. Zhou, B., Xu, H., Shen, S.: Racer: rapid collaborative exploration with a decentralized multi-UAV system. IEEE Trans. Rob. **39**(3), 1816–1835 (2023)

Distributed Analytic Center Selection for Resilient Control of Multi-robot Systems with Imperfect Communication Channels

Gennaro Notomista$^{(\boxtimes)}$ [ID]

Department of Electrical and Computer Engineering, University of Waterloo, Waterloo, ON, Canada
gennaro.notomista@uwaterloo.ca

Abstract. This paper presents a constrained-control synthesis algorithm amenable for distributed multi-robot decision making. The proposed approach is based on a newly introduced controller selection method named analytic center selection which results in a dynamically defined controller that is able to ensures the satisfaction of state constraints. The controller synthesis lends itself to be distributed among a network of agents using state-of-the-art distributed optimization techniques. Resilience of the controller to imperfect communication channels among the robots is demonstrated in simulation.

1   Introduction

The ability of multi-robot systems to continue to cooperatively execute desired tasks even in presence of imperfect communication channels is fundamental in a variety of applications, including remote sensing and precision agriculture [20], search and rescue [15], mining [14], and space exploration [11]. In these scenarios, survivability—intended as the property of remaining functional, even though at the expense of the quality of task execution—is an essential feature. In dynamical system theory, survivability is typically intended as the satisfaction of a number of constraints on the state of the system [7]. Several of approaches have been proposed to achieve survivability, in order to characterize whether systems naturally satisfy state constraints or, if not, to control them to do so.

Viability is commonly employed as a tool to analyze and satisfy state constraints [2]. A trajectory of the state, $x : \mathbb{R} \to \mathbb{R}^n : t \mapsto x(t)$ is viable when

$$\forall t \quad x(t) \in K(t), \tag{1}$$

where $K(t)$ is the viability subset at time t. While viability theory provides tools to analyze constraint satisfaction, it typically results in computationally expensive algorithms. For this reason, viability theory is generally not amenable for online implementation, which is paramount in the application scenarios mentioned above. Similar considerations hold for optimal control approaches, where

R. Groß et al. (Eds.): ANTS 2026, LNCS 16515, pp. 315–323, 2026.
https://doi.org/10.1007/978-3-032-26123-6_25

trajectories that satisfy the constraint (1) are optimized based on a cost functional to be minimized.

Optimization-based techniques have emerged as a popular technique to synthesize control inputs signals in order to satisfy state constraints. Recent developments in the set-invariance theory based on control barrier functions allows for computationally efficient synthesis of control inputs $u : \mathbb{R} \to \mathbb{R}^m : t \mapsto u(t)$ that result in the satisfaction of constraints on the state [1]. State trajectory infinite-dimensional optimization is then turned into control input finite-dimensional optimization problem $\min_{u'}\{c(u') : u' \in C(x(t))\}$, where $c : \mathbb{R}^m \to \mathbb{R}$ is a cost function, and the constraint set $C(x(t))$ is such that a control input function $u(t)$ selected in $C(x(t))$ results in a state trajectory $x(t)$ evolving in the viable subset (1). The computational advantage, however, comes at the cost of a myopic controller synthesis strategy—whereby the control input at time t, $u(t)$, is selected based on the state at time t, $x(t)$, in the set $C(x(t))$—as well as feasibility problems. As a matter of fact, the optimization-based nature of the controller has led to several studies on the feasibility of its evaluation and several approaches have been devised in order to ensure it (e.g. [5,17]).

In this paper we propose a new constrained-control synthesis algorithm which is suitable for distributed multi-robot system operations. The approach combines the benefits of viability theory (long-term state constraint satisfaction) and optimization-based techniques (computational efficiency). Moreover, the formulation as an unconstrained optimization problem lends itself to design a distributed optimization algorithm that can be solved collaboratively by robots in a team to collectively satisfy state constraints. Central to the proposed algorithm is a new selection method for set-valued maps, which we named *analytic center selection*, constructed based on the notion of analytic center from convex analysis [3]. Applying this selection strategy to controller synthesis leads to the analytic center controller selection. After defining it, we cast the process of synthesizing it as a dynamic feedback optimization scheme which takes the form of an unconstrained optimization problem [6,10]. We then provide a distributed algorithm that allows multi-robot systems to calculate the optimal controller required to satisfy desired behavior constraints. We then show how the proposed algorithm naturally endows the multi-robot system with resilience with respect to lossy and asynchronous communication channels.

2   Mathematical Modeling

Let us start by considering the input affine system dynamics

$$\dot{x}(t) = f(x(t)) + g(x(t))u(t), \tag{2}$$

where $x(t) \in \mathbb{R}^n$ is the state, $u(t) \in \mathbb{R}^m$ is the input, $f : \mathbb{R}^n \to \mathbb{R}^n$ and $g : \mathbb{R}^n \to \mathbb{R}^{n \times m}$ are Lipschitz continuous vector fields. The motivation for focusing on such dynamical systems stems from the observation that, in many applications of teams of mobile robots, the robotic platforms are modeled via input affine dynamics.

We assume that the evolution of the system (2) is subject to the state constraints (1) and further that we can represent the set $K(t)$ in (1) as the intersection of zero superlevel sets of control barrier functions [1]. Such constraints are intended to represent desired behaviors for the robots to execute. To this end, let $B_i : \mathbb{R}^n \to \mathbb{R}$, $i = 1, \ldots, M$ be control barrier functions. The set of control inputs that guarantee the forward invariance of $\bigcap_{i=1}^{M} \{x' : B_i(x') \geq 0\}$ is given by:

$$C(x(t)) = \{u' : A(x(t))u' \leq b(x(t))\}, \tag{3}$$

where $A(x(t))$ and $b(x(t))$ are the stack of $-L_g B_i(x(t))$ and $\gamma_i(B_i(x(t))) + L_f B_i(x(t))$, respectively. The functions $\gamma_1, \ldots, \gamma_M$ are of class $\mathcal{K}$, and $L_f B_i$ and $L_g B_i$ denote the Lie derivatives of B_i in the direction of the vector fields f and g, respectively. Notice that, owing to the comparison lemma, the structure of the system dynamics is inherited by the input constraint sets: input affine dynamics (2) lead to input affine constraints (3).

It is then natural to select a control input satisfying the constraints (3) using an optimization-based formulation. For instance, in many applications, the min-norm controller, solution of the following convex quadratic program, is considered:

$$\underset{u'}{\text{minimize}} \ \|u'\|^2 \text{ subject to } A(x(t))u' \leq b(x(t)). \tag{4}$$

The feasibility of such optimization problem has been the focus of several existing works and many different approaches have been proposed in order to ensure recursive feasibility of optimization problems similar to (4) (see [5,17], just to name a few). Nevertheless, another aspect to consider when dealing with such optimization-based controllers is their regularity. It is well known, for instance, that $u^\star(x(t))$, solution of (4), might not be a Lipschitz continuous function [13]. This drawback limits their practical application, where non-regularity of control input or state trajectories may result in the loss of survivability. Such results can be seen as instances of regularity conditions for selections from parametrized set-valued maps.

Continuing with this analogy, finding a controller for the system (2) that satisfies the constraints defined by the set $C(x(t))$ in (3) leads to the selection of a trajectory for the following differential inclusion: $\dot{x}(t) \in F_{cl}(x(t))$, where $F_{cl}(x(t)) = f(x(t)) + g(x(t))C(x(t))$ is a set-valued map associating to each $x(t) \in \mathbb{R}^n$ the subset $F_{cl}(x(t)) \subset \mathbb{R}^n$. The differential inclusion defined above is parametrized by the feedback map $x(t) \mapsto C(x(t))$. The controller synthesis process can be then realized by first selecting a trajectory for the differential inclusion, and then finding a controller $u(t) \in C(x(t))$ to execute it. Among the several selections from set-valued maps, the one defined below is related to the min-norm controller solution of (4).

Definition 1 (Minimal selection [2]). *Let F be a set-valued map from a metric space $\mathcal{X}$ to a Hilbert space $\mathcal{Y}$. The mapping $x \mapsto \text{argmin}_{y \in F(x)} \|y\| =: m(F(x))$ is the <u>minimal selection</u> from F.*

With the formalism introduced above, the analysis of the regularity of optimization/based controllers can be moved from the study of optimization problems to that of selections of differential inclusions. In the next section, the analytic center controller selection is introduced and its regularity is studied. Afterwards, in Sect. 4, an algorithm for the distributed computation of the analytic center controller is proposed.

3 Analytic Center Controller Selection

In this section, we define a new selection from set-valued maps which is amenable for distributed multi-robot control. The controller will be obtained from an unconstrained optimization program which can be distributed among a network of communication agents using state-of-the-art distributed optimization techniques. To this end, let us start by recalling the definition of Lipschitz continuous set-valued maps.

Definition 2 (Lipschitz continuous set-valued map [2]). *Let F be a set-valued map from a metric space $\mathcal{X}$ to a metric space $\mathcal{Y}$. F is a Lipschitz continuous set-valued map if there exists a constant $L \geq 0$ such that $\forall x, x' \in \mathcal{X}, F(x) \subset F(x') + Ld(x, x')B$, where $d(x, x')$ is the distance between x and x' in $\mathcal{X}$, and B is the unit ball in $\mathcal{Y}$.*

The set-valued map $x(t) \mapsto C(x(t))$, with $C(x(t))$ defined in (3) is Lipschitz continuous. Therefore, the control synthesis turns into a trajectory selection problem. It is interesting to note that, while there are types of selections that are guaranteed to be Lipschitz continuous if the set-valued maps are Lipschitz continuous, commonly used ones—such as the minimal selection—are not Lipschitz continuous. An example of Lipschitz continuous selection is the barycentric selection [2]. One could therefore think of leveraging this selection to compute state or input trajectories for systems to be employed in multi-robot autonomy applications. However, while there exist fast and accurate algorithms to compute the barycenter of a convex polyhedron (e.g., [9,12])—as, for instance, the one defined by $C(x(t))$ in (3)—, in this paper we introduce a new selection process which is both computationally efficient, and, at the same time, distributable among a network of agents communicating among each other. In order to do so, the following definition recalls the notion of analytic center of a set of linear inequalities, used in convex analysis.

Definition 3 (Analytic center [3]). *The analytic center of a set of linear inequalities $a_i^T v \leq b_i, \quad i = 1, \ldots, M$, where $a_i \in \mathbb{R}^m, b_i \in \mathbb{R}$ for all i, is defined as the optimal point of the following unconstrained convex optimization problem: $\min_v \{ -\sum_{i=1}^{M} \log(b_i - a_i^T v) \}$.*

Based on the analytic center of a set of linear inequality, the analytic center selection from set-valued maps is defined as follows.

Definition 4 (Analytic center selection). *Let $A(x(t)) \in \mathbb{R}^{M \times m}$ and $b(x(t)) \in \mathbb{R}^M$, and let the i-th row of $A(x(t))$ and the i-th element of $b(x(t))$*

be denoted by $a_i(x(t))$ and $b_i(x(t))$, respectively. The <u>analytic center selection</u> from the set-valued map $C(x(t))$ defined in (3) is the map

$$x(t) \mapsto \operatorname*{argmin}_{v} \; -\sum_{i=1}^{M} \log(b_i(x(t)) - a_i(x(t))^T v). \tag{5}$$

Given its definition as the minimizer of the logarithmic barrier cost function, provided that the constraints are differentiable functions of the state, the analytic center selection is differentiable with respect to the parameters of the constraints encoding the behaviors of the robots, namely the state of the latter. This translates to the desirable property of a smooth dependence with respect to undesirable changes in the robots' state. In the following, the process of selecting a control input using the analytic center selection provided in Definition 4 will be referred to as the Analytic Center Controller (ACC) selection. Moreover, for the analytic center selection to be well defined, we will assume the set $C(x(t))$ in (3) has non-empty interior along the system state trajectories $x(t)$.

4   Distributed Analytic Center Controller Selection

In this section, we propose a distributed algorithm to evaluate the ACC map in (5). Let us introduce the following optimization problem, which is solved in (5) to compute the controller:

$$\min_{v} -\sum_{i=1}^{M} \log(b_i(x(t)) - a_i(x(t))^T v). \tag{6}$$

This is an unconstrained optimization program whose cost at time t depends, in general, on the state of all the robots, $x(t)$.

In this paper, we consider state constraints that define the set $C(x(t))$ in (3) such that $a_i(x(t))$ and $b_i(x(t))$, for all i, only couple $x_j(t)$, the state of robot j, with $\{x_k(t)\}_{k \in \mathcal{N}_j}$, i.e. the states of robots that are able to communicate with robot j, $\mathcal{N}_j$ being the set of robots which share a communication channel with robot j. This assumption holds for all decentralized multi-robot tasks, which include, among others, consensus-like algorithms (like rendez-vous, alignment, leader follower, and formation control) and coverage control [4]. With this assumption, the optimization problem (6) is a partition-based optimization problem, where the cost function has the same sparsity structure as the communication graph among the robots [18].

When deploying multi-robot systems in the real world, the communication channel among them is likely to be lossy and asynchronous. In these settings, it is still desirable to be able to compute the ACC which minimizes the cost in (6), even at the expense of a decrease in the convergence speed of the solution algorithm. This is precisely what is provided by the *resilient gradient descent* algorithm proposed in [19], which is implemented as follows:

$$u_j \leftarrow u_j - \epsilon \sum_{k \in \mathcal{N}_j \cup \{j\}} \hat{\rho}_k^{(j)}, \tag{7}$$

where $\epsilon > 0$, and $\hat{\rho}_k^{(j)}$ is the last available value of the gradient of the cost function in (6) with respect to the state of robot k. This quantity is computed by robot k itself based on the last available information received from its neighbors and is asynchronously communicated to robot j. Note that, when $j = k$, the gradient $\hat{\rho}_j^{(j)}$ can be computed on board of robot j with the last available information received asynchronously from its neighbors.

The cost function in (6) is also twice differentiable. Hence, the solution algorithm has local exponential convergence, although with a rate of convergence which is typically lower than a distributed gradient descent under perfect communication [19]. The properties of resilience that this algorithm exhibits with respect to imperfect communication channels is demonstrated in the following section where consensus-like algorithms are implemented on a simulated robotic swarm with imperfect sensing and communication channel.

5   Simulations

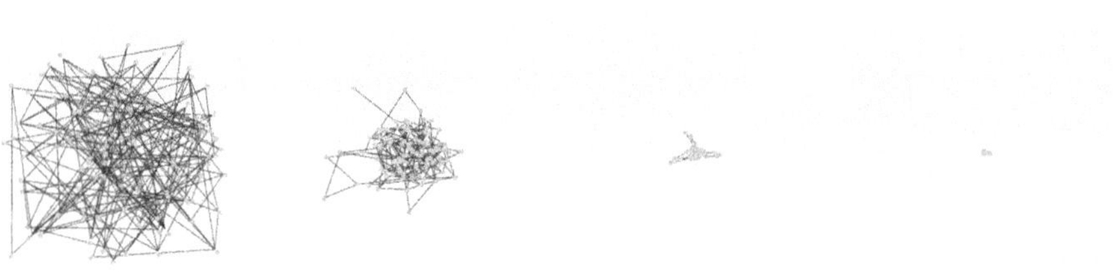

Fig. 1. Sequence of snapshots recorded during the course of the simulation of a rendez-vous task.

Fig. 2. This figure shows a sequence of snapshots similar to the one in Fig. 1 where the robots are controlled to align towards a common direction.

As a prototype for distributed multi-robot operations, in this section we consider the behaviors that characterize Reynolds' boids [16], in particular cohesion and alignment. Recently, optimization-based techniques developed using control barrier functions have allowed for the execution of such behaviors using a constraint-based approach [8]. In the simulations we show, the behaviors of the boids are encoded as constraints whose analytic center is computed in order to control the robots to achieve cohesion and alignment.

In order to achieve the cohesion behavior, we define the following control barrier functions $B_{c,i}(x(t)) = -\sum_{j \in \mathcal{N}_i} \|x_i(t) - x_j(t)\|^2$, $\quad \forall i$, where $x_i(t) \in \mathbb{R}^2$ is the velocity-controlled position of robot i at time t, i.e. $\dot{x}_i(t) = u_i(t)$. The alignment behavior is defined by the following control barrier functions $B_{a,i}(x(t)) = -\sum_{j \in \mathcal{N}_i} \|\theta_i(t) - \theta_j(t)\|^2$, $\quad \forall i$, where $\theta_i(t) \in [0, 2\pi]$ is the velocity-controlled orientation of robot i at time t. In this case, the kinematics of the robots are modeled as a Dubin's car, i.e. $\dot{x}_i(t) = \begin{bmatrix} \dot{p}_{x,i}(t) & \dot{p}_{y,i}(t) & \dot{\theta}_i(t) \end{bmatrix}^T = \begin{bmatrix} \bar{v} \cos\theta_i(t) & \bar{v} \sin\theta_i(t) & u_i(t) \end{bmatrix}^T$, where $p_{x,i}(t)$ and $p_{y,i}(t)$ denote the components of the position of robot i at time t and $\bar{v}$ is a constant longitudinal velocity at which the robots move.

The snapshots recorded during the course of two simulations are reported in Figs. 1 and 2. In both simulations, an imperfect communication channel among the robots is considered. This is meant to represent packet losses, delays, and asynchronous data exchanges. In the simulations, this is effectively realized by randomly drawing, at each iteration, a communication graph from a collection of connected graphs.

In Fig. 1, the robots (yellow dots), starting from random initial positions in the environment, are able to meet at a common location. This is achieved executing the ACC selection of the constraint set constructed from the control barrier functions $B_{c,i}$. The snapshots are recorded at fixed time intervals to illustrate the rate of convergence of the resilient gradient descent algorithm (7), which is capable of coping with imperfect communication. The communication channels are shown in the snapshots as blue lines connecting the robots that share a communication channel.

In a similar fashion, Fig. 2 demonstrates the execution of the alignment behavior obtained by implementing the ACC selection from the set of constraints built using the control barrier functions $B_{a,i}$. In this case, the robots are depicted as yellow triangles to also show their heading. The sequence of snapshots shows that alignment is successfully achieved and the robots are able to swarm towards a common direction.

6   Conclusions

In this paper, we presented a novel control synthesis algorithm suitable for enforcing state constraints in distributed multi-robot systems. The approach combines the benefits of techniques based on viability theory, in terms of long-term constraint satisfaction, with those of distributed optimization, in terms of computational complexity. The resilience of the proposed distributed algorithm with respect to imperfect communication among robots is achieved via a modified gradient-based optimization algorithm. Simulations demonstrate the implementation of the proposed control synthesis framework in order to achieve typical coordinated swarm behaviors.

Acknowledgement. This work has been partially supported by the NSERC Discovery Grant RGPIN-2023-03703.

Disclosure of Interests. The author has no competing interests to declare.

References

1. Ames, A.D., Coogan, S., Egerstedt, M., Notomista, G., Sreenath, K., Tabuada, P.: Control barrier functions: theory and applications. In: 2019 18th European Control Conference (ECC), pp. 3420–3431. IEEE (2019)
2. Aubin, J.P., Cellina, A.: Differential Inclusions: Set-Valued Maps and Viability Theory. Springer, Heidelberg (1984)
3. Boyd, S.P., Vandenberghe, L.: Convex Optimization. Cambridge University Press, Cambridge (2004)
4. Cortés, J., Egerstedt, M.: Coordinated control of multi-robot systems: a survey. SICE J. Control, Meas. Syst. Integr. **10**(6), 495–503 (2017)
5. Cortez, W.S., Dimarogonas, D.V.: Correct-by-design control barrier functions for Euler-Lagrange systems with input constraints. In: 2020 American Control Conference (ACC), pp. 950–955. IEEE (2020)
6. Francois, G., Bonvin, D.: Measurement-based real-time optimization of chemical processes. In: Advances in Chemical Engineering, vol. 43, pp. 1–50. Elsevier (2013)
7. Hellmann, F., Schultz, P., Grabow, C., Heitzig, J., Kurths, J.: Survivability of deterministic dynamical systems. Sci. Rep. **6**(1), 29654 (2016)
8. Hengstebeck, C., Jamieson, P., Van Scoy, B.: Extending boids for safety-critical search and rescue. Franklin Open **8**, 100160 (2024)
9. Kallay, M.: Computing the moment of inertia of a solid defined by a triangle mesh. J. Graph. Tools **11**(2), 51–57 (2006)
10. Kelly, F.P., Maulloo, A.K., Tan, D.K.H.: Rate control for communication networks: shadow prices, proportional fairness and stability. J. Oper. Res. Soc. **49**(3), 237–252 (1998)
11. Leitner, J.: Multi-robot cooperation in space: a survey. In: 2009 Advanced Technologies for Enhanced Quality of Life, pp. 144–151 (2009)
12. Mirtich, B.: Fast and accurate computation of polyhedral mass properties. J. Graph. Tools **1**(2), 31–50 (1996)
13. Morris, B.J., Powell, M.J., Ames, A.D.: Continuity and smoothness properties of nonlinear optimization-based feedback controllers. In: 2015 54th IEEE Conference on Decision and Control (CDC), pp. 151–158. IEEE (2015)
14. Puche, V.V., Verma, K., Fumagalli, M.: Underground multi-robot systems at work: a revolution in mining. arXiv preprint arXiv:2509.16267 (2025)
15. Queralta, J.P., et al.: Collaborative multi-robot search and rescue: planning, coordination, perception, and active vision. IEEE Access **8**, 191617–191643 (2020)
16. Reynolds, C.W.: Flocks, herds and schools: a distributed behavioral model. In: Proceedings of the 14th Annual Conference on Computer Graphics and Interactive Techniques, pp. 25–34 (1987)
17. Squires, E., Pierpaoli, P., Egerstedt, M.: Constructive barrier certificates with applications to fixed-wing aircraft collision avoidance. In: 2018 IEEE Conference on Control Technology and Applications (CCTA), pp. 1656–1661. IEEE (2018)
18. Testa, A., Carnevale, G., Notarstefano, G.: A tutorial on distributed optimization for cooperative robotics: from setups and algorithms to toolboxes and research directions. In: Proceedings of the IEEE (2025)

19. Todescato, M., Bof, N., Cavraro, G., Carli, R., Schenato, L.: Partition-based multi-agent optimization in the presence of lossy and asynchronous communication. Automatica **111**, 108648 (2020)
20. Zarco-Tejada, P.J., Berni, J.A., Suárez, L., Fereres, E.: A new era in remote sensing of crops with unmanned robots. SPIE Newsroom **10**(2.1200812), 1438 (2008)

Escaping the Trap: Benchmarking Swarm Gradient-Following in Geometrically Constrained Environments

Kian Andrew Busico[1], Lilly Schwarzenbach[2], Fares Abu-Dakka[1], and Eliseo Ferrante[1,2]

[1] Department of Computer Science, New York University Abu Dhabi, Abu Dhabi, United Arab Emirates
[2] Department of Computer Science, Vrije Universiteit Amsterdam, Amsterdam, The Netherlands
`ef2698@nyu.edu`

Abstract. Following an environmentally constrained path in a timely fashion can be crucial for swarms in scenarios such as disaster response or emergency evacuation. In such situations, swarms must rapidly follow potentially challenging paths while not losing cohesion. We benchmark a robust, decentralized gradient-following behavior against varying path sinuosity, and swarm size. The swarm races to reach a minimum distance in a fixed time budget. We measure the success rate and the mean completion time. Our findings show that the algorithm allows the swarm to successfully reach the target line in the allotted time as long as the swarm size is relatively small. Furthermore, we find that the algorithm handles low and medium degrees of sinuosity well but struggles with high sinuosity, where the turns become too sharp. This work is the first to study swarm racing in constrained environments, revealing that "more is not always better": larger swarms hinder rapid path traversal. This paves the way for future research on scale-invariant racing collective behaviors.

1 Introduction

In recent years, swarm robotics has emerged as a robust approach to handle complex collective navigation tasks, drawing inspiration from biological systems where agents interact solely based on local sensing and communication [4,15]. Recent work has demonstrated collective convergence toward targets and gradient-following behaviors in swarm robotics, often under static or gently varying environmental conditions [8,9].

However, real-world applications face more challenging conditions. For example, scenarios such as disaster response [1,6,11] require rapid collective movement through constrained and complex environments, e.g., to assess the situation, bring supplies to victims, or lead them out of danger [6]. Gradient-following is particularly applicable in these contexts, as swarms must often navigate by tracking environmental scalar fields such as heat intensity, chemical concentrations, or dynamic safety potentials rather than relying on global positioning or

R. Groß et al. (Eds.): ANTS 2026, LNCS 16515, pp. 324–331, 2026.
https://doi.org/10.1007/978-3-032-26123-6_26

preexisting maps [9]. This poses significant challenges, particularly in terms of maintaining speed, agility, and success when the path is geometrically difficult, for instance, when it features constricted passages or sharp high-curvature turns.

This research is based directly on recent work [8,9] that introduced a decentralized gradient-following algorithm: individual robots in a swarm were equipped with a scalar sensor, able to perceive the local scalar intensity of a gradient (e.g. the light intensity in real drone experiments), and the group as a whole was able to follow the gradient to the location that had the highest concentration, using only local range and bearing sensors and no global information [9]. In [8], the approach was adapted to work fully onboard of the drones and was able to achieve dynamic source tracking.

Karagüzel *et al.* [8] established the foundations for collective gradient perception without global positioning, while Vásárhelyi *et al.* [16] successfully addressed flocking in constrained environments outdoor. More recently, work has been published on high-speed flocking in an open environment without the need to follow a specific path [2,7]. Swarming in constrained environments has also been explored, but without an explicit speed requirement [5,13,17]. Despite high speed flocking and constrained environments having been studied in isolation, the joint ability of a swarm to perform high speed evacuation along a geometrically constrained path perceivable only using a scalar sensor remains an open question.

This paper addresses this gap by conducting a systematic empirical study to benchmark the algorithm [8] in this new race-like context. The central research question is: How does the algorithm performance perform when key parameters of the swarm and its environment are varied? In this study, we specifically investigate the effect of two key factors: (i) path sinuosity and (ii) swarm size.

2   Methodology

Our methodology for self-organized flocking utilizes the decentralized gradient-following algorithm from Karagüzel *et al.* [8] as a base. We then design a novel systematic benchmarking framework to evaluate the performance of this algorithm in a new, time-critical race task, which is presented in Sect. 3.

The two main building blocks of the algorithm, adopted from [8], are collective motion and the localization of the emergent source. The algorithm is fully decentralized, and the collective motion of the swarm emerges from local interactions and individual scalar-based sensing of an environmental gradient such as a lava-like field.

The core logic is based on adaptive social spacing. Each agent computes the desired distance from its neighbors based on its locally sensed light intensity. The agent's *social spacing* parameter is calculated as:

$$\sigma_i = \sigma_L + \left(\frac{L_s - L_{min}}{L_{max} - L_{min}} \right)^{0.1} \cdot \sigma_r \tag{1}$$

where σ_L is the base spacing, σ_r is the variable spacing range or the modulation range, and 0.1 is a fine-tuned parameter found in Karagüzel et al. [8]. This σ_i is then used to calculate the desired distance:

$$d_{des_i} = \sigma_i \sqrt{2} \tag{2}$$

This mechanism means agents in the brighter area prefer to be closer together, while agents reading lower light intensities in darker areas desire more space, moving farther from the swarm, thus emergently pushing the swarm to the dark areas as the rest of the swarm follows to maintain flocking. In the original setup, the task was simply to drive the agents towards the lightest (or darkest) region of the environment, in the presence of dynamic and/or bimodal gradients [8]. As explained in Sect. 3, the novelty of the present paper is to consider a gradient whereby the lightest region of the environment is curvilinear and surrounded by a gradient; thus, the main research question is whether a swarm originally conceived for emergent gradient sensing can also slide along the lightest region at high speed.

Once the desired distance is calculated under the effect of gradient modulation, it is used to calculate the proximal control force $\boldsymbol{p}_i$, which is based on a modified Lennard-Jones potential:

$$\boldsymbol{p}_i = \sum_{m \in N} -\epsilon \left[2 \frac{\sigma_i^4}{(d_i^m)^5} - \frac{\sigma_i^2}{(d_i^m)^3} \right] e^{j\phi_i^m} \tag{3}$$

where d_i^m is the distance to neighbor m (among those within the sensing range D_p), ϵ is the potential's strength, and $e^{j\phi_i^m}$ is the 2D unit vector to the neighbor, expressed in complex notation.

Another important component used in self-organized collective motion is alignment control, which when present is used to have the swarm align in a common direction. The alignment control vector $\boldsymbol{h}_i$ is found by summing the headings of neighbors within the alignment control communication range D_a with the heading of the focal agent i, and normalizing the result.

$$\boldsymbol{h}_i = \frac{\angle e^{j\theta_0} + \sum_{m \in N} \angle e^{j\theta_m}}{||\angle e^{j\theta_0} + \sum_{m \in N} \angle e^{j\theta_m}||} \tag{4}$$

The heading of agent m located in the communication range D_a of i is $\angle e^{j\theta_i^m}$. The heading of the focal agent i is $\angle e^{j\theta_0}$. Headings are calculated with respect to a common frame of reference for all agents and shared in that way, e.g. we assume that agents are equipped with a digital compass or equivalent device [14] or are able to detect a shared directional signal (such as a light source) [3].

The proximal force control $\boldsymbol{p}_i$ and the alignment control vector $\boldsymbol{h}_i$ are combined using the standard linear combination of vectors:

$$\boldsymbol{f}_i = \alpha \boldsymbol{p}_i + \beta \boldsymbol{h}_i. \tag{5}$$

This final vector $\boldsymbol{f}_i$ is then translated into two scalar components, one parallel (f_x) and one perpendicular (f_y) to the direction of motion (considering the agent's local reference frame), and those two components are used to calculate the linear (U_i) and angular (ω_i) velocity commands for the agent:

$$U_i = K_1 f_x + u_{add}, \tag{6}$$

$$\omega_i = K_2 f_y. \tag{7}$$

Following the reference work [8], we use the baseline parameters (see Table 1).

Table 1. Simulation and Control Parameters

Parameter	Value	Parameter	Value
Control Gains		*Interaction Potentials*	
Linear Velocity Weight (K_1)	0.08	Proximal Weight (α)	2.0
Angular Velocity Weight (K_2)	0.2	Alignment Weight (β)	1.0
Forward Bias (u_{add})	0.05 m/s	Lennard-Jones Weight (ϵ)	12.0
Spacing Parameters		*System Frequency*	
Base Spacing (σ_L)	0.3	Control Frequency	48 Hz
Variable Spacing (σ_r)	0.5	Simulation Frequency	240 Hz
Sigma Range (σ)	$[0.3, 0.8]$		

3 Experimental Setup

We test this algorithm's performance in a simulated environment using the PyBullet physics engine, with agents modeled as Crazyflie 2.1 nano-drones. All motion is constrained to 2 dimensions, representing flight at a fixed altitude.

The Race Task: The environment consists of a $20\,\text{m} \times 4\,\text{m}$ arena. A pre-defined curvilinear path (a sine curve) is represented by an "inverted" light gradient, with the lowest intensity $(L = 0)$ on the path's centerline, increasing to the maximum $(L = 255)$ off the path. The swarm's task is to navigate from a starting area (near $X = 1\,\text{m}$) to a finish line as quickly as possible. To ensure a fair comparison, the task definition adapts the parameters of the simulation in two ways:

1. **Adaptive Finish Line:** The finish line's X coordinate FL_x is adaptive, based on the formula $FL_x = L - R_S - \epsilon_R$, where L is the arena length, R_S is the swarm radius, and $\epsilon_R = 0.2$ is a tolerance. The swarm radius is determined by d_des multiplied by the number of rings in the swarm formation (e.g. 1 ring for a swarm up to 7 robots and 2 rings for a swarm up to 37 robots. We consider a run successful if the swarm center of mass (COM) trespasses the finish line at coordinate FL_x. This accounts for the swarm's physical size (through its radius) and measures the time for the entire swarm body to approach the end of the map.

2. **Scaled Max Duration:** To isolate the variable of completion time from success rate, the maximum allowed duration of a run is scaled with swarm size to account for increased coordination overhead. We use a baseline of 300 s for $n = 7$ and scale it up proportionally for larger swarms.

We utilize two primary metrics: 1) Success Rate, the percentage of runs that the swarm COM successfully reaches its calculated finish line within its allotted scaled duration, and 2) Mean Completion Time (s) for those successful runs.

Experimental Variables: We benchmark the algorithm's performance by varying two key parameters, running 50 trials for each combination (baseline map can be seen in Fig. 1):

- **Path Cycles (Flexibility) :** Using the baseline swarm ($n = 7$) and width ($\approx$ 2 m), we vary the path's cycles by testing cycles $= [1, 2, 4]$. These correspond to physical wavelengths of $\lambda = 20\,\mathrm{m}$ (low), $\lambda = 10\,\mathrm{m}$ (medium), and $\lambda = 5\,\mathrm{m}$ (high).
- **Swarm Size (Scalability):** We test swarm sizes of $n = [7, 10, 19, 37]$ because these sizes have the potential to form concentric rings akin to a honeycomb structure. The baseline map (wavelength $\lambda = 20\,\mathrm{m}$ from cycles $= 1$, effective width $\approx 2\,\mathrm{m}$) is used.

4   Results and Discussion

We present our findings in four parts, corresponding to the baseline and our two experimental variables: path complexity and swarm size.

4.1   Baseline Performance

The baseline performance for our study uses the simplest version of our race task: a small swarm ($n = 7$), and low sinuosity ($\lambda = 20\mathrm{m}$). Under these baseline conditions, the swarm achieved a 100% success rate over 50 runs, with a mean completion time of 174.33 s (std. dev. 17.14 s). This result confirms the algorithm's effectiveness for this simple task and provides a robust benchmark for the following experiments. Figure 1 shows us the trajectory of the swarm centroid for this baseline condition and how the swarm retained the collective motion from the start to the end of the gradient map.

4.2   The Effect of Path Complexity (Wavelength and Sinuosity)

To investigate the algorithm's sensitivity to the path's sinuosity, we again use the $n = 7$ swarm on the baseline-width path. The high-sinuosity $\lambda = 5\mathrm{m}$ path was designed as a stress test, and Table 3 reveals it successfully induced a performance collapse to a 6% success rate. This failure demonstrates a systematic control-system imbalance: the path's sharp turns command a high angular velocity (ω_i)

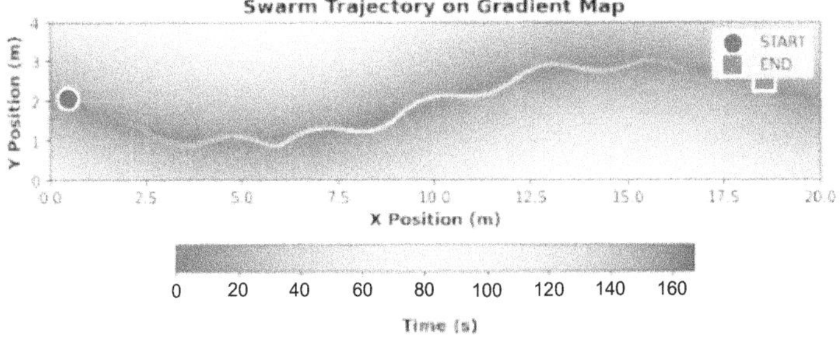

Fig. 1. Swarm centroid trajectory for baseline conditions.

that conflicts with the algorithm's low forward bias. This conflict, which we call a turning stall, might have caused the swarm to pivot in place, lose its heading, and deviate from the path. This test critically confirms that the algorithm's default control parameters, tuned for the source-tracking task in [8], are not suited for this high-curvature race task (Table 2).

Table 2. Effect of Path Sinuosity on Performance

Cycles	Wavelength (λ)	Success Rate (50 runs)	Mean Completion Time (s)
1	20m (Low)	100%	174.33 s
2	10m (Medium)	100%	190.80 s
4	5m (High)	6%	262.08 s

4.3 The Effect of Scalability (Swarm Size)

Finally, we analyzed the algorithm's performance as a function of swarm size, using the baseline map (low sinuosity, medium width). The results show a clear trade-off between swarm size and performance. As shown in Table 4, performance degrades as swarm size increases. We observe two distinct effects. First, there is a strong positive correlation between swarm size and mean completion time: the $n = 37$ swarm is $\approx 30\%$ slower than the $n = 7$ swarm. We attribute this to an effect we call social drag. In denser swarms, agents must spend more time resolving local proximal forces, which impedes the collective's overall forward motion. Second, the success rate drops to 74% for the $n = 37$ swarm. Our analysis suggests this is due to social deformation: in larger, denser swarms, the ideal honeycomb-like structure often breaks, causing the swarm to deform into an elliptical shape. This is a result of the fact that the huge swarm sizes are significantly larger than the gradient on the map, and in the case of 37 drones, some of them go backward or forward to where the gradient is. An example of such a case can be seen in Fig. 2 where the swarm changes shape to obtain minimum average gradient and stays in the path.

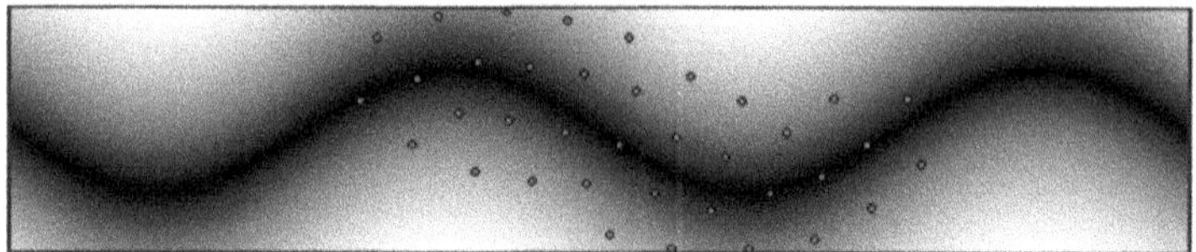

Fig. 2. Adaptation of swarm position when number of drones is 37.

Table 3. Effect of Swarm Size on Mission Success Rate

Number of Drones	Success Rate (%)	Mean Completion Time (s)
7	100	174.33
10	100	180.17
19	100	205.10
37	74	226.24

5　Conclusion

Our overall results indicate that the algorithm, while effective under baseline conditions, shows significant performance degradation when scaled to larger swarms or presented with geometrically challenging paths. This suggests that the algorithm's baseline parameters, tuned for source-tracking, represent a critical factor in its performance. In particular, swarm size is a crucial factor for a swarm's success in race tasks. If the swarm is too big, it becomes slow and loses its ability to adapt to quick-changing paths such as paths with sharp turns.

Future work should further investigate the algorithm for this new class of high-speed evacuation tasks focusing on small swarms on different path geometries and its application in three-dimensional spaces. In addition, the benefits of breaking up the swarm into smaller groups and coordinating between them for narrow or complex paths might also warrant further investigation. Finally, an interesting direction to investigate is how to achieve scale invariant [10] swarm racing algorithms: a swarm should be able to achieve scalable racing performance independently of the swarm size while being able to cope with arbitrary environmental complexities. To achieve this, it is likely that we need to resort to reinforcement learning and other state of the art methods such as those that are deployed in the field of competitive autonomous drone racing [12].

Acknowledgments. This work is supported in part by the NYUAD Center for Artificial Intelligence and Robotics (CAIR), funded by Tamkeen under the NYUAD Research Institute Award CG010, and by the NYUAD Center for Interdisciplinary Data Science & AI (CIDSAI), funded by Tamkeen under the NYUAD Research Institute Award CG016.

Disclosure of Interests. The authors have no competing interests to declare.

References

1. Abraham, L., et al.: Swarm robotics in disaster management. In: 2019 International conference on innovative sustainable computational technologies (CISCT), pp. 1–5. IEEE (2019)
2. Boldrer, M., Kratky, V., Walter, V., Saska, M.: Swarming in the wild: a distributed communication-less Lloyd-based algorithm dealing with uncertainties. arXiv preprint arXiv:2504.18840 (2025)
3. Ferrante, E., et al.: A self-adaptive communication strategy for flocking in stationary and non-stationary environments. Nat. Comput. $\mathbf{13}$(2), 225–245 (2014)
4. Ferrante, E., et al.: Self-organized flocking with a mobile robot swarm: a novel motion control method. Adapt. Behav. $\mathbf{20}$(6), 460–477 (2012)
5. Gaydamaka, A., et al.: Dynamic topology organization and maintenance algorithms for autonomous UAV swarms. IEEE Trans. Mob. Comput. $\mathbf{23}$(5), 4423–4439 (2023)
6. Hafid, A., Hocine, R., Guezouli, L.: Analyzing swarm robotics approaches in natural disaster scenarios: a comparative study. In: 2024 1st International Conference on Innovative and Intelligent Information Technologies (IC3IT), pp. 1–6. IEEE (2024)
7. Horyna, J., et al.: Fast swarming of UAVS in GNSS-denied feature-poor environments without explicit communication. IEEE Rob. Autom. Lett. $\mathbf{9}$(6), 5284–5291 (2024)
8. Karagüzel, T.A., Retamal, V., Cambier, N., Ferrante, E.: From shadows to light: a swarm robotics approach with onboard control for seeking dynamic sources in constrained environments. IEEE Rob. Autom. Lett. $\mathbf{9}$(1), 127–134 (2024). https:// doi.org/10.1109/LRA.2023.3331897
9. Karagüzel, T.A., Turgut, A.E., Eiben, A.E., Ferrante, E.: Collective gradient perception with a flying robot swarm. Swarm Intell. $\mathbf{17}$(1), 117–146 (2023). https:// doi.org/10.1007/s11721-022-00220-1
10. Khaluf, Y., Ferrante, E., Simoens, P., Huepe, C.: Scale invariance in natural and artificial collective systems: a review. J. R. Soc. Interface $\mathbf{14}$(136), 20170662 (2017)
11. Kumar, T.R., et al.: Swarm robotics for search and rescue operations in disaster zones using particle swarm optimization (PSO) algorithms. In: 2025 International Conference on Networks and Cryptology (NETCRYPT), pp. 870–875. IEEE (2025)
12. Loquercio, A., et al.: Learning high-speed flight in the wild. Sci. Rob. $\mathbf{6}$(59), eabg5810 (2021)
13. Nathan, R.J.A.A., Strand, S., Mehrwald, D., Shutin, D., Bimber, O.: An autonomous drone swarm for detecting and tracking anomalies among dense vegetation. arXiv preprint arXiv:2407.10754 (2024)
14. Turgut, A.E., Çelikkanat, H., Gökçe, F., Şahin, E.: Self-organized flocking in mobile robot swarms. Swarm Intell. $\mathbf{2}$(2–4), 97–120 (2008)
15. Vicsek, T., Zafeiris, A.: Collective motion. In: Proceedings of the Physics Reports Symposium. PR '12, Elsevier, Amsterdam, Netherlands (2012).https://doi.org/10.1016/j.physrep.2012.03.004
16. Vásárhelyi, G., et al.: Optimized flocking of autonomous drones in confined environments. Sci. Rob. $\mathbf{3}$(20), eaat3536 (2018). https://doi.org/10.1126/scirobotics.aat3536
17. Zhang, X., et al.: Bio-inspired fission-fusion control and planning of unmanned aerial vehicles swarm systems via reinforcement learning. Appl. Sci. $\mathbf{14}$(3), 1192 (2024)

FDA Flocking: Future Direction-Aware Flocking via Velocity Prediction

Hossein B. Jond[(✉)][iD] and Martin Saska[iD]

Department of Cybernetics, Czech Technical University in Prague, Prague, Czechia
`{hossein.barghi.jond,martin.saska}@cvut.cz`

Abstract. Understanding self-organization in natural collectives such as bird flocks inspires swarm robotics, yet most flocking models remain reactive, overlooking anticipatory cues that enhance coordination. Motivated by avian postural and wingbeat signals, as well as multirotor attitude tilts that precede directional changes, this work introduces a principled, bio-inspired anticipatory augmentation of reactive flocking termed *Future Direction-Aware* (FDA) flocking. In the proposed framework, agents blend reactive alignment with a predictive term based on short-term estimates of neighbors' future velocities, regulated by a tunable blending parameter that interpolates between reactive and anticipatory behaviors. This predictive structure enhances velocity consensus and cohesion-separation balance while mitigating the adverse effects of sensing and communication delays and measurement noise that destabilize reactive baselines. Simulation results demonstrate that FDA achieves faster and higher alignment, enhanced translational displacement of the flock, and improved robustness to delays and noise compared to a purely reactive model. Future work will investigate adaptive blending strategies, weighted prediction schemes, and experimental validation on multirotor drone swarms.

1 Introduction

The self-organization of large groups of agents into coherent spatiotemporal patterns—such as bird flocks and fish schools—emerges from local perception-based interactions that produce collective motion without centralized control. Reynolds' Boids model [18] captured this through three reactive rules: cohesion (proximity maintenance), separation (collision avoidance), and alignment (velocity matching). Subsequent influential models, including Vicsek [22], Cucker-Smale [8], Couzin's zonal scheme [7], and various multi-agent robotic swarms [9,11,17,23], largely retain these reactive principles.

However, purely reactive approaches, which respond only to instantaneous neighbor states, struggle to replicate the smooth, anticipatory coordination observed in biological flocks. Empirical studies show that birds use subtle postural adjustments, wing orientations, and wingbeat signals to predict neighbors' impending maneuvers, enabling coherent propagation of turns and minimizing

R. Groß et al. (Eds.): ANTS 2026, LNCS 16515, pp. 332–340, 2026.
https://doi.org/10.1007/978-3-032-26123-6_27

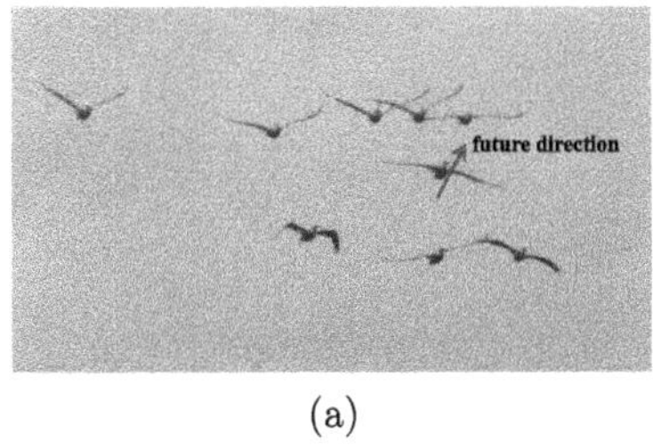

(a)

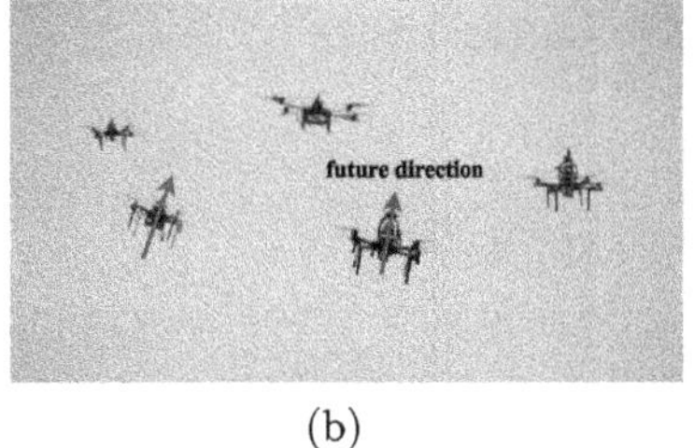

(b)

Fig. 1. Anticipatory cues in natural and engineered collectives: (a) In bird flocks, individuals signal impending maneuvers via body posture and wing alignment, which precede direction changes. Neighbors interpret these cues to predict their future direction, ensuring smooth coordination; (b) In multirotor drones, attitude tilting (pitch and roll) acts as an analog, as drones must tilt before accelerating in a new direction, providing an implicit cue of future velocity.

damping of directional information [1,3–6]. Reactive models (e.g., Vicsek) dissipate such predictive cues, leading to less robust collective turns and reduced performance under realistic conditions. This biological insight motivates augmenting reactive rules with anticipation, as explored in recent visual servoing and robotic swarm research using optic flow or learned features [14,15,19].

We provide a principled, bio-inspired anticipatory augmentation of reactive flocking—termed Future Direction-Aware (FDA) flocking—and characterize its performance under sensing and communication imperfections. Drawing from natural flocks, where postural and wingbeat cues forecast future velocities [10], and from multirotor drones, where attitude tilting (pitch/roll) signals intended acceleration [21], FDA agents blend reactive alignment with a predictive term based on short-term neighbor velocity estimates. A tunable blending parameter balances immediate feedback against forward-looking adjustments, yielding improved velocity consensus, cohesion-separation balance, and collision avoidance, while mitigating the adverse effects of perception/communication delays and sensor noise that destabilize purely reactive models [2,16,20,21,24]. Figure 1 illustrates these anticipatory cues in birds and drones, highlighting their role in enabling predictive coordination.

Simulations demonstrate that the FDA achieves faster and higher alignment, steadier centroid trajectories, and substantially less performance degradation under perturbations compared to the reactive baseline. While the current model uses uniform averaging of predictions (potentially missing nuanced weighting of stronger cues as in biology), future extensions will include adaptive blending, weighted prediction schemes, and real-world robotic validation.

The remainder of this paper is organized as follows. Section 2 reviews the baseline reactive flocking model. Section 3 presents the FDA framework, velocity prediction, and extensions for delay and noise. Section 4 reports simulation results on performance and robustness. Section 5 concludes with key insights and future directions.

2 Reactive Flocking

Consider $n \geq 2$ agents indexed by $\mathcal{N} = \{1, \ldots, n\}$ in $\mathbb{R}^m$. Each agent $i \in \mathcal{N}$ has position $\mathbf{p}_i$, velocity $\mathbf{v}_i$, and acceleration/control $\mathbf{u}_i$ in $\mathbb{R}^m$. Its neighborhood is $\mathcal{N}_i = \{j \neq i \mid \|\mathbf{p}_j - \mathbf{p}_i\| \leq r_i\}$, with interaction radius $r_i > 0$.

The flocking model is based on [12] and is given by

$$
\begin{cases}
\dot{\mathbf{p}}_i & = \mathbf{v}_i, \quad \dot{\mathbf{v}}_i = \mathbf{u}_i, \\
\mathbf{u}_i & = \sum_{j \in \mathcal{N}_i} \psi(\|\mathbf{p}_j - \mathbf{p}_i\|)(\mathbf{p}_j - \mathbf{p}_i) + \phi_i \sum_{j \in \mathcal{N}_i} (\mathbf{v}_j - \mathbf{v}_i),
\end{cases}
\tag{1}
$$

where $\psi(\|\mathbf{p}_j - \mathbf{p}_i\|) = 1 - \frac{\delta_i |\mathcal{N}_i|}{\|\mathbf{p}_j - \mathbf{p}_i\|}$, $\|\mathbf{p}_j - \mathbf{p}_i\| > 0$, $\phi_i = \frac{1}{|\mathcal{N}_i|}$, $\mathcal{N}_i \neq \emptyset$, are the interaction weights, $\delta_i \geq 0$ is the spatial offset, and $|\mathcal{N}_i|$ is the neighborhood size. Velocity and control inputs are obtained via smooth saturation as

$$
\mathbf{x}_i = x_i^{\max} \tanh \left(\frac{\|\mathbf{x}_i^{\mathrm{cmd}}\|}{x_i^{\max}} \right) \frac{\mathbf{x}_i^{\mathrm{cmd}}}{\|\mathbf{x}_i^{\mathrm{cmd}}\|},
\tag{2}
$$

where $\mathbf{x}_i^{\mathrm{cmd}} \in \{\mathbf{v}_i^{\mathrm{cmd}}, \mathbf{u}_i^{\mathrm{cmd}}\}$ is the commanded (unsaturated) input, $\mathbf{x}_i \in \{\mathbf{v}_i, \mathbf{u}_i\}$ is the applied (saturated) input and $x_i^{\max} \in \{v_i^{\max}, u_i^{\max}\}$ is the corresponding maximum magnitude (with the convention $\mathbf{0}/\|\mathbf{0}\| = \mathbf{0}$).

The model balances cohesion-separation via interaction weight ψ and alignment via ϕ. For cohesion-separation, $\psi < 0$ (repulsive) when $\|\mathbf{p}_j - \mathbf{p}_i\| < \delta_i |\mathcal{N}_i|$ ensures short-range repulsion; $\psi > 0$ (attractive) when $\|\mathbf{p}_j - \mathbf{p}_i\| > \delta_i |\mathcal{N}_i|$ promotes long-range attraction; and $\psi = 0$ at $\|\mathbf{p}_j - \mathbf{p}_i\| = \delta_i |\mathcal{N}_i|$ marks equilibrium spacing. Smaller δ_i yields denser formations, larger δ_i looser ones, with built-in collision avoidance. The alignment weight $\phi > 0$ drives velocity consensus.

The purely reactive flocking model in (1) uses instantaneous neighbor states, whereas anticipating neighbor motions improves coordination in both natural and engineered systems. We therefore propose the FDA framework, in which agents integrate short-horizon velocity predictions of neighbors—obtained via communication or estimation—directly into the interaction rules, thereby enhancing collective dynamics. The approach is detailed in the next section.

3 FDA Flocking with Velocity Prediction

Agent i has access to the current states of neighbors $j \in \mathcal{N}_i$: $\mathbf{p}_j$, $\mathbf{v}_j$, and $\mathbf{u}_j$ (via estimation or communication). It predicts the velocity as

$$
\mathbf{v}_j^{\mathrm{pred}} = \mathbf{v}_j + t_i^{\mathrm{ph}} \mathbf{u}_j,
\tag{3}
$$

where $t_i^{\mathrm{ph}} > 0$ is the prediction horizon. The result is saturated by (2).

The FDA flocking model, incorporating velocity predictions into agent interactions, is given by

$$
\mathbf{u}_i = \sum_{j \in \mathcal{N}_i} \psi(\|\mathbf{p}_j - \mathbf{p}_i\|)(\mathbf{p}_j - \mathbf{p}_i)
$$

$$
+ (1 - \theta_i)\phi_i \sum_{j \in \mathcal{N}_i} (\mathbf{v}_j - \mathbf{v}_i) + \theta_i \phi_i \sum_{j \in \mathcal{N}_i} (\mathbf{v}_j^{\mathrm{pred}} - \mathbf{v}_i),
\tag{4}
$$

where $\theta_i \in [0,1]$ blends current ($\theta_i = 0$, reactive) and predicted ($\theta_i = 1$, fully anticipatory) alignment terms.

The predictive velocity term $\mathbf{v}_j^{\mathrm{pred}}$ in (4) serves as a mathematical analogue to anticipatory signals, encoding intended motion directions akin to birds' postural cues or drones' rotor tilts. By blending reactive and predictive alignment via θ_i, the model mimics natural collectives and supports engineered swarms, where such cues facilitate smoother trajectory corrections and emergent coordination without relying solely on current states.

In quadrotor swarms, the quantities used to form $\mathbf{v}_j^{\mathrm{pred}}$ correspond to directly sensed or communicated signals (e.g., acceleration reconstructed from onboard tilt (pitch/roll) measurements that determine thrust direction together with thrust magnitude inferred from propeller speeds), rather than relying on explicit state observers or filter-based estimation.

3.1   Alignment Convergence Under Prediction

To gain insight into how velocity prediction affects alignment, consider the idealized case of steady-state flocking under the following assumptions: (i) fixed, connected interaction graph, (ii) no control saturation, (iii) uniform prediction horizon t^{ph} and uniform blending parameter θ across agents, (iv) cohesion-separation forces at equilibrium (negligible contribution to velocity dynamics), and (v) absence of delay and noise. Under near-alignment conditions, where cohesion-separation terms vanish at equilibrium and saturation effects are inactive, the FDA control law (4) admits the approximation

$$\dot{\mathbf{v}}_i \approx \phi \sum_{j \in \mathcal{N}_i} \left[(1-\theta)(\mathbf{v}_j - \mathbf{v}_i) + \theta(\mathbf{v}_j + t^{\mathrm{ph}}\dot{\mathbf{v}}_j - \mathbf{v}_i) \right] = \phi \sum_{j \in \mathcal{N}_i}(\mathbf{v}_j - \mathbf{v}_i) + \theta\phi t^{\mathrm{ph}} \sum_{j \in \mathcal{N}_i}\dot{\mathbf{v}}_j,$$

where $\dot{\mathbf{v}}_j \approx \mathbf{u}_j$. In vector form, with $\mathbf{v} = [\mathbf{v}_1^\top, \ldots, \mathbf{v}_n^\top]^\top$, the Laplacian $\mathbf{L}$, and adjacency matrix $\mathbf{A}$, the collective velocity dynamics, after rearrangements, become

$$\dot{\mathbf{v}} \approx -\phi\big(\mathbf{I} + \theta\phi t^{\mathrm{ph}}(\mathbf{A} \otimes \mathbf{I}_m)\big)^{-1}(\mathbf{L} \otimes \mathbf{I}_m)\mathbf{v}.$$

For a connected graph, $\mathbf{L}$ has one zero eigenvalue (consensus subspace) and positive eigenvalues elsewhere. The matrix $\mathbf{I} + \theta\phi t^{\mathrm{ph}}\mathbf{A}\otimes\mathbf{I}_m$ is invertible for typical (small) values of $\theta\phi t^{\mathrm{ph}}$. The resulting system matrix is negative semi-definite on the disagreement subspace, so velocity differences $\mathbf{v}_i - \mathbf{v}_j$ decay exponentially to zero—i.e., asymptotic velocity consensus (alignment) is preserved.

The predictive term effectively preconditions the consensus dynamics, accelerating convergence for moderate t^{ph} and θ. However, excessively large prediction horizons with large blending weights can push eigenvalues toward instability, imposing a practical trade-off between anticipatory benefit and robustness. This analysis provides theoretical support for the observed faster and more robust alignment in FDA flocking (in Sect. 5) while highlighting the limits of naive long-horizon prediction.

3.2 Incorporation of Delay and Noise

In realistic settings, agents experience communication/measurement delays and sensor noise. For agent i, the delayed states of neighbor j are $\mathbf{p}_j^{\tau_i}$, $\mathbf{v}_j^{\tau_i}$, and $\mathbf{u}_j^{\tau_i}$ (shifted by agent-specific delay $\tau_i \geq 0$). Delayed states are used directly; FDA predicts via open-loop extrapolation of delayed velocity using delayed acceleration. The perceived states are further corrupted by zero-mean Gaussian noise, $\tilde{\mathbf{p}}_j^{\tau_i} = \mathbf{p}_j^{\tau_i} + \mathbf{n}_{p,ij}, \tilde{\mathbf{v}}_j^{\tau_i} = \mathbf{v}_j^{\tau_i} + \mathbf{n}_{v,ij}, \tilde{\mathbf{u}}_j^{\tau_i} = \mathbf{u}_j^{\tau_i} + \mathbf{n}_{u,ij}$, with $\mathbf{n}_{p,ij} \sim \mathcal{N}(\mathbf{0}, \sigma_p^2\mathbf{I})$, $\mathbf{n}_{v,ij} \sim \mathcal{N}(\mathbf{0}, \sigma_v^2\mathbf{I})$, $\mathbf{n}_{u,ij} \sim \mathcal{N}(\mathbf{0}, \sigma_u^2\mathbf{I})$, and σ_p, σ_v, and σ_u represent the respective noise intensities. The resulting FDA control law under delay and noise becomes

$$
\begin{aligned}
\mathbf{u}_i = &\sum_{j \in \mathcal{N}_i} \psi\big(\|\tilde{\mathbf{p}}_j^{\tau_i} - \mathbf{p}_i\|\big)\big(\tilde{\mathbf{p}}_j^{\tau_i} - \mathbf{p}_i\big) \\
&+ (1 - \theta_i)\phi_i \sum_{j \in \mathcal{N}_i} \big(\tilde{\mathbf{v}}_j^{\tau_i} - \mathbf{v}_i\big) + \theta_i\phi_i \sum_{j \in \mathcal{N}_i} \big(\tilde{\mathbf{v}}_j^{\mathrm{pred}} - \mathbf{v}_i\big),
\end{aligned}
\tag{5}
$$

where $\tilde{\mathbf{v}}_j^{\mathrm{pred}} = \tilde{\mathbf{v}}_j^{\tau_i} + t_i^{\mathrm{ph}}\tilde{\mathbf{u}}_j^{\tau_i}$ (and saturated as before).

By extrapolating from delayed and noisy data, the predictive term reduces the adverse impact of communication lag—by approximating neighbors" near-future states—and attenuates high-frequency stochastic perturbations through short-horizon forward projection. This bio-inspired mechanism, motivated by anticipatory cues observed in natural flocks, enhances robustness to timing errors and measurement uncertainty without relying on explicit delay estimators or noise filtering.

4 Simulation Results

To validate the FDA flocking framework—motivated by predictive postural cues observed in birds and drones—simulations compare it against the reactive model. Simulations use $n = 10$ agents in 3D space over $T = 25\,\mathrm{s}$ with time step $dt = 0.02\,\mathrm{s}$. Each agent employs a prediction horizon $t_i^{\mathrm{ph}} = 1\,\mathrm{s}$ and experiences a communication delay $\tau_i = 0.4\,\mathrm{s}$. The prediction horizon is chosen in line with common practice in short-horizon predictive control for fast dynamical systems; smaller horizons reduce the FDA model toward the reactive baseline, while larger horizons amplify prediction errors and may destabilize collective motion. The delay duration reflects typical sensing and communication latencies reported for multirotor drone swarms. Agent dynamics are bounded by $v_i^{\mathrm{max}} = 4\,\mathrm{m/s}$ and $u_i^{\mathrm{max}} = 8\,\mathrm{m/s}^2$, representative of common multirotor platforms; these bounds primarily affect transient timing rather than qualitative flocking behavior. Initial positions are sampled uniformly from $[0, 10)^m$, and initial velocities are drawn i.i.d. from $\mathcal{N}(\mathbf{0}, 1)$. The interaction radius $r_i = 7.5\,\mathrm{m}$ and spatial offset $\delta_i = 1$ are selected to yield an average neighborhood size of approximately 4–7 agents, consistent with biological and robotic swarm studies. The blending parameter $\theta_i = 0.8$ is chosen to emphasize the predictive component; smaller values smoothly recover reactive flocking behavior.

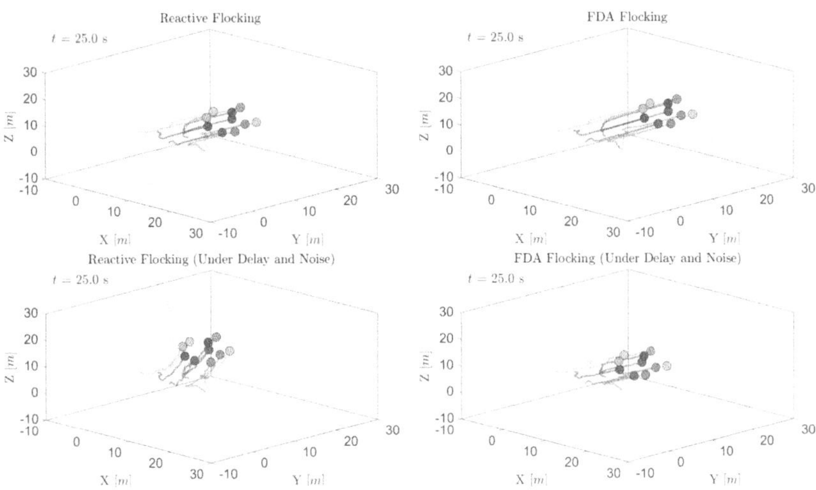

Fig. 2. 3D agent trajectories over $t \in [0, 25]$ s: reactive (left) and FDA (right); nominal conditions (top) and with delay and noise (bottom).

Flocking performance is compared between the reactive and the FDA variant using the following metrics: (i) *directional alignment* ($\gamma \in [-1, 1]$): average pairwise cosine similarity of velocities between each agent and its neighbors (averaged across the flock), where values near 1 indicate strong velocity coherence [13]; (ii) *inter-agent distances*: minimum, mean, and maximum pairwise distances between agents; and (iii) *flock centroid path length* (S): total distance traveled by the flock centroid over the simulation. Both reactive and FDA flocking achieve strong alignment and cohesion under nominal conditions (top row, Fig. 2), from the same random initialization. Animations are shown in the supplementary video (top row). The corresponding time histories in Fig. 3 (top row) compare (a) alignment γ, (b) inter-agent distances, and (c) centroid trajectories with S. Subfigures (a)–(c) highlight the FDA's efficiency. In (a), FDA reaches peak γ earlier with consistently higher values, aiding cohesion via prediction. As shown in (b), both models yield comparable distance profiles. Centroids in (c) align, with FDA's S being 40% larger. Multiple runs confirm these trends.

A second scenario incorporates delays and time-varying zero-mean Gaussian noise in position, velocity, and acceleration data to assess FDA robustness (Fig. 2, bottom row; supplementary video, bottom row). Noise standard deviations vary asynchronously to mimic environmental fluctuations, $\sigma_p = 0.5 + 0.10 \sin(5t)$ m, $\sigma_v = 0.2 + 0.05 \sin(5t + \pi/4)$ m/s, $\sigma_u = 0.1 + 0.02 \sin(5t + \pi/2)$ m/s^2. The time histories in Fig. 3 (bottom row) show that FDA exhibits only minor performance degradation under these adverse perturbations. Although delays and noise slow alignment, the predictive structure of the FDA enables the collective motion to maintain near-nominal alignment and centroid stability. In contrast, the reactive model does not consistently achieve full alignment and exhibits lower efficiency, with centroid trajectories deviating substantially from

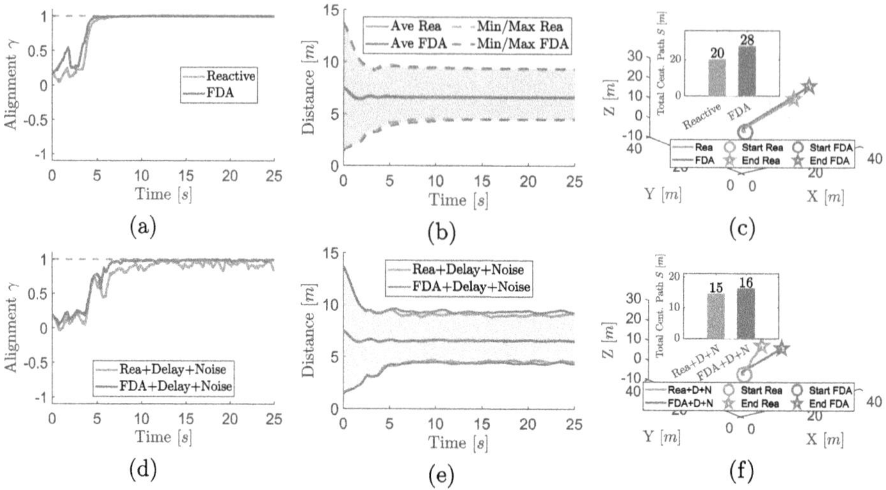

Fig. 3. Metrics for reactive and FDA flocking: nominal (top) vs. delay + noise (bottom). (a,d) alignment γ; (b,e) inter-agent distances; (c,f) centroid paths with length S.

nominal behavior. For both models, inter-agent distance profiles remain largely comparable to nominal conditions. These results demonstrate the robustness of the FDA under sensing and communication constraints.

5 Conclusion

We introduced Future Direction-Aware (FDA) flocking, a bio-inspired anticipatory extension of reactive flocking that enables proactive coordination. FDA blends reactive alignment with a predictive term via a tunable blending parameter, balancing immediate feedback with forward-looking adjustments. Simulations confirm FDA's advantages over the reactive baseline, including faster and higher alignment and substantially less performance degradation under adverse perturbations (delay and Gaussian noise). FDA enhances the robustness of collective motion under realistic sensing and communication constraints, supporting its potential for scalable deployment in aerial robotic swarms. Limitations of the current model include uniform averaging of velocity predictions, which may overlook biologically observed differential weighting of stronger directional cues. Future work will explore weighted prediction schemes and empirical validation.

Acknowledgments. This work was funded by the Czech Science Foundation (GAČR) under research project no. 23-07517S and the European Union under the project Robotics and Advanced Industrial Production (reg. no. CZ.02.01.01/00/22_008/0004590).

Disclosure of Interests. The authors have no competing interests to declare.

References

1. Ballerini, M., et al.: Empirical investigation of starling flocks: a benchmark study in collective animal behaviour. Anim. Behav. **76**(1), 201–215 (2008)
2. Casas, V., Mitschele-Thiel, A.: On the impact of communication delays on UAVs flocking behavior. In: 2018 IEEE Wireless Communications and Networking Conference Workshops (WCNCW), pp. 67–72. IEEE (2018)
3. Castro, D., Ruffier, F., Eloy, C.: Modeling collective behaviors from optic flow and retinal cues. Phys. Rev. Res. **6**(2), 023016 (2024)
4. Cavagna, A., et al.: Scale-free correlations in starling flocks. Proc. Natl. Acad. Sci. **107**(26), 11865–11870 (2010)
5. Cavagna, A., et al.: Flocking and turning: a new model for self-organized collective motion. J. Stat. Phys. **158**(3), 601–627 (2015)
6. Cavagna, A., Giardina, I., Grigera, T.S.: The physics of flocking: correlation as a compass from experiments to theory. Phys. Rep. **728**, 1–62 (2018)
7. Couzin, I.D., Krause, J., James, R., Ruxton, G.D., Franks, N.R.: Collective memory and spatial sorting in animal groups. J. Theor. Biol. **218**(1), 1–11 (2002)
8. Cucker, F., Smale, S.: Emergent behavior in flocks. IEEE Trans. Autom. Control **52**(5), 852–862 (2007)
9. Han, W., Wang, J., Wang, Y., Xu, B.: Multi-UAV flocking control with a hierarchical collective behavior pattern inspired by sheep. IEEE Trans. Aerosp. Electron. Syst. **60**(2), 2267–2276 (2024)
10. Hoetzlein, R.C.: Flock2: a model for orientation-based social flocking. J. Theor. Biol. **593**, 111880 (2024)
11. Jond, H.B.: Bearing-distance flocking with zone-based interactions in constrained dynamic environments. J. Comput. Sci. **87**, 102574 (2025)
12. Jond, H.B.: A minimal model for emergent collective behaviors in autonomous robotic multi-agent systems. IEEE Trans. Cognitive Dev. Syst. (2025)
13. Jond, H.B.: Position-based flocking for robust alignment. In: Proceedings of the 9th International Symposium on Swarm Behavior and Bio-Inspired Robotics (SWARM 2025). Göttingen, Germany (Sep 2025), pp. 23–25 (2025)
14. Mezey, D., et al.: Purely vision-based collective movement of robots. NPJ Rob. **3**(1), 11 (2025)
15. Moshtagh, N., Michael, N., Jadbabaie, A., Daniilidis, K.: Vision-based, distributed control laws for motion coordination of nonholonomic robots. IEEE Trans. Rob. **25**(4), 851–860 (2009)
16. Munz, U., Papachristodoulou, A., Allgower, F.: Delay-dependent rendezvous and flocking of large scale multi-agent systems with communication delays. In: 2008 47th IEEE Conference on Decision and Control, pp. 2038–2043. IEEE (2008)
17. Olfati-Saber, R.: Flocking for multi-agent dynamic systems: algorithms and theory. IEEE Trans. Autom. Control **51**(3), 401–420 (2006)
18. Reynolds, C.W.: Flocks, herds and schools: a distributed behavioral model. In: Proceedings of the 14th Annual Conference on Computer Graphics and Interactive Techniques. pp. 25–34 (1987)
19. Schilling, F., Schiano, F., Floreano, D.: Vision-based drone flocking in outdoor environments. IEEE Rob. Autom. Lett. **6**(2), 2954–2961 (2021)
20. Shi, X., Avila-Martinez, E.J., Li, Y., Shi, L.: Flocking dynamics for cooperation multi-agent networks subject to intermittent communication. Expert Syst. Appl. **292**, 128620 (2025)

21. Vásárhelyi, G., et al.:Optimized flocking of autonomous drones in confined environments. Sci. Rob. **3**(20), eaat3536 (2018)
22. Vicsek, T., Czirók, A., Ben-Jacob, E., Cohen, I., Shochet, O.: Novel type of phase transition in a system of self-driven particles. Phys. Rev. Lett. **75**(6), 1226 (1995)
23. Virágh, C., et al.: Flocking algorithm for autonomous flying robots. Bioinspiration biomimetics **9**(2), 025012 (2014)
24. Wang, X., Wang, L., Wu, J.: Impacts of time delay on flocking dynamics of a two-agent flock model. Commun. Nonlinear Sci. Numer. Simul. **70**, 80–88 (2019)

FORMICA: Decision-Focused Learning for Communication-Free Multi-robot Task Allocation

Antonio Lopez, Jack Muirhead, and Carlo Pinciroli[✉]

Department of Robotics Engineering, Worcester Polytechnic Institute, Worcester, MA 01609, USA
{alopez3,jmuirhead,cpinciroli}@wpi.edu

Abstract. Most multi-robot task allocation methods rely on communication to resolve conflicts and reach consistent assignments. In environments with limited bandwidth, degraded infrastructure, or adversarial interference, existing approaches degrade sharply. We introduce a learning-based framework that achieves high-quality task allocation without any robot-to-robot communication. The key idea is that robots coordinate implicitly by predicting teammates' bids. While analytical predictions assume idealized conditions (uniform distributions, known bid functions), our learned approach adapts to task clustering and spatial heterogeneity. We train bid predictors end-to-end to minimize *Task Allocation Regret* rather than prediction error. To scale to large swarms, we develop a mean-field approximation, reducing complexity from $O(NT)$ to $O(T)$. We call our approach *FORMICA: Field-Oriented Regret-Minimizing Implicit Coordination Algorithm*. Experiments show FORMICA substantially outperforms a natural analytical baseline. Training requires only 21 s on a laptop, enabling rapid adaptation to new environments.

1 Introduction

Task allocation methods have achieved remarkable success in multi-robot systems, yet they share a common vulnerability: a strong dependency on communication. In distributed settings, methods such as the Consensus-Based Bundle Algorithm (CBBA) [5] and its variants [3,13] require that robots eventually exchange winning bids and timestamps to resolve conflicts. When robots operate underwater where bandwidth is severely limited [2], in disaster zones with damaged infrastructure, or under adversarial jamming, this dependency becomes a critical limitation. Reduced-communication approaches exist [8,18], yet to the best of our knowledge, no existing method achieves decentralized task allocation *completely without communication* while retaining the performance benefits of optimization-based allocation.

DISTRIBUTION STATEMENT A. Approved for public release; distribution is unlimited. OPSEC10388.

The central insight of this paper is that robots can coordinate implicitly if they can predict each other's behavior. This idea echoes classical notions of implicit coordination in biological swarms and recent work on machine theory of mind [1,19]. At swarm scale, however, manually engineering such predictive models becomes infeasible. Instead, robots must *learn* to predict each other: A capability we call a *swarm theory of mind*.

We present a market-based approach in which each robot computes bids for tasks and uses a learned model to estimate the competing bids of other robots. We call our method FORMICA: *Field-Oriented Regret-Minimizing Implicit Coordination Algorithm*. Inspired by the *Smart Predict-then-Optimize (SPO)* framework [10,17], FORMICA trains bid predictors to minimize *Task Allocation Regret* (TAR), the loss of performance due to coordination failures. To scale to large swarms, we employ a mean-field approximation: instead of predicting individual robot bids—which would require $O(NT)$ estimates per robot—each robot predicts the *distribution* of bids across the swarm, reducing complexity to $O(T)$.

Experiments show that our method substantially outperforms a natural analytical baseline in which robots select locally highest-valued tasks. In scenarios with 16 robots and 64 tasks, our approach improves system reward by approximately 17% and approaches the optimal solution obtained via MILP. When deployed on much larger scenarios (256 robots, 4096 tasks), the same model improves performance by about 7% over the analytical approach, demonstrating scalability and strong generalization.

2   Related Work

Multi-robot Task Allocation. Market-based methods such as CBBA [5] achieve strong performance in decentralized settings but require communication to resolve conflicts [3,13]. Recent learning-based approaches combine graph neural networks with reinforcement learning [14] or attention mechanisms [7,12], but all assume periodic communication or global broadcasts. For communication-free allocation, Dai *et al.* [6] use game-theoretic equilibria, but cannot learn from data or optimize for allocation quality.

Smart Predict-then-Optimize. Elmachtoub and Grigas [10] introduced SPO to train predictors that minimize *decision regret* rather than prediction error. Extensions include generalization bounds [9], interpretable models [11], and applications to routing, scheduling, and inventory management [17]. *Critically, all existing SPO work addresses single-agent, centralized problems.*

Communication-Free Coordination. Several approaches achieve multi-robot coordination without explicit messaging. Swarm intelligence methods use stigmergy [20] or reactive rules [2,22]. Wang and Schwager [21] enable manipulation through force sensing. For multi-agent prediction, work spans opponent modeling [1,4] to machine theory of mind [19]. However, learning to predict bid values specifically for communication-free task allocation—and training these predictors end-to-end to minimize allocation regret—remains unexplored.

3   Methodology

In this Section we present our approach. For a discussion that includes the full derivation of the presented equations refer to [16].

3.1   Problem Formulation

We consider N robots allocating $T > N$ tasks, where robot i computes bid $b_{i,j}$ for task j. The binary variable $x_{i,j}$ is 1 if robot performs task j and 0 otherwise. Since robots cannot communicate, robot k estimates competitors' bids $\hat{b}^k_{-k,j}(\theta^k)$ and locally solves:

$$x^{k,\star} = \underset{x^k}{\mathrm{argmax}} \quad \sum_{j=1}^{T} x^k_j \cdot \max\left(0, b_{k,j} - \hat{b}^k_{-k,j}\right) \qquad \text{(LOCOBJ)}$$

$$\text{subject to} \quad \sum_{j=1}^{T} b_{k,j} x^k_j \leq C_k,$$

The central question is how to tune θ^k. A natural choice minimizes prediction error (e.g., MSE). However, estimation errors are not equally consequential: underestimating a competitor's bid on a high-value task causes conflicts; overestimating bids on low-value tasks causes unnecessary abstention; errors on tasks where robot k is uncompetitive have negligible effect. We instead minimize *Task Allocation Regret (TAR)*: the loss in collective reward due to unallocated tasks. This connects our approach to the *Smart Predict-then-Optimize (SPO)* framework [10,17], extending it for the first time to a distributed, multi-agent setting.

3.2   The 2-Robot Case

To make the optimization differentiable, we relax binary assignments using a soft allocation function (SAF). Via Lagrangian relaxation of (LOCOBJ), a robot k takes task j when $b_{k,j} - \lambda^k b_{k,j} > \hat{b}_{-k,j}$, where $\lambda^k b_{k,j}$ is the opportunity cost and $\hat{b}_{-k,j}$ is the bid of the other robot. We embed this condition in a differentiable softmax:

$$\tilde{x}^k_j(\theta_k) = \frac{\exp\left\{\beta \cdot \left(b_{k,j} - \hat{b}^k_{-k,j} - \lambda^k b_{k,j}\right)\right\}}{\sum_{j'=1}^{T} \exp\left\{\beta \cdot \left(b_{k,j'} - \hat{b}^k_{-k,j'} - \lambda^k b^k_{k,j'}\right)\right\}} \cdot C_k. \qquad \text{(SAF)}$$

β controls sharpness and $\tilde{x}^k_j/C_k$ is the probability robot k takes task j. We apply a capacity-true normalization so that $\sum_j b_{k,j} \tilde{x}^k_j = C_k$, consistent with the knapsack constraint. For two robots, TAR is:

$$\mathcal{L}_{\mathrm{TAR}}\left(\theta_1,\theta_2\right) = \sum_{j=1}^{T} b_j \cdot \left(1 - \frac{\tilde{x}_j^1}{C_1}\right) \cdot \left(1 - \frac{\tilde{x}_j^2}{C_2}\right). \tag{TAR-2}$$

We minimize this via a primal-dual algorithm: the primal update tunes θ^k (with λ^k fixed), and the dual update tunes λ^k (with θ^k fixed). The primal gradient reduces to:

$$\frac{\partial \mathcal{L}_{\mathrm{TAR}}}{\partial \theta_k} = \sum_{j=1}^{T} \frac{\partial \mathcal{L}}{\partial \tilde{x}_j^k} \cdot \frac{\partial \tilde{x}_j^k}{\partial \hat{b}_{-k,j}^k} \cdot \frac{\partial \hat{b}_{-k,j}^k}{\partial \theta_k} = \beta \cdot \sum_{j=1}^{T} b_j \cdot \underbrace{\left(1 - \frac{\tilde{x}_j^{-k}}{C_{-k}}\right)}_{\hat{q}_j^k} \cdot \frac{\tilde{x}_j^k}{C_k} \cdot \left(1 - \tilde{x}_j^k\right).$$

where $\hat{q}_j^k$ is robot's k estimate that no competitor takes task j. The gradient is largest when: (a) the task is high-value; (b) it risks being uncovered; and (c) the allocation is uncertain ($\tilde{x}_j^k \approx 0.5$). Notably, these are the cases where accurate prediction matters most. The dual update is $\lambda^k \leftarrow \lambda^k + \alpha \left(\sum_j b_{k,j}\tilde{x}_j^k - C_k\right)$.

3.3   The N-Robot Case

Individual bid estimation scales as $O(NT)$ and becomes intractable for large swarms. As $N \to \infty$, individual identities become irrelevant, so robot k needs only estimate the *bid density function* $\rho_j(b)$, i.e., the fraction of robots with bid b for task j. We define $\hat{h} \triangleq \sup\{b : \rho_j(b) > 0\}$ (the estimated maximum competing bid) and rewrite (SAF) as:

$$\tilde{x}_j^k(\theta_k) = \frac{\exp\left\{\beta \cdot \left(b_{k,j} - \hat{h}_j^k - \lambda^k b_{k,j}\right)\right\}}{\sum_{j'=1}^{T} \exp\left\{\beta \cdot \left(b_{k,j'} - \hat{h}_{j'}^k - \lambda^k b_{k,j'}^k\right)\right\}} \cdot C_k. \tag{SAF-MF}$$

The probability that robot k has the highest bid on task j is given by $\hat{q}_j^k = \exp\left\{-N \int_{b_{k,j}}^{\infty} \rho_j(b)db\right\}$, using the Poisson approximation for large N. The mean-field TAR becomes:

$$\mathcal{L}_{\mathrm{TAR}}(\theta_k) = \sum_{j=1}^{T} b_j \cdot \left(1 - \frac{\tilde{x}_j^k}{C_k}\right) \cdot \hat{q}_j^k, \tag{TAR-MF}$$

and its gradient is

$$\frac{\partial \mathcal{L}_{\mathrm{TAR}}}{\partial \theta_k} = \beta \underbrace{\sum_{j=1}^{T} b_j \cdot \hat{q}_j^k \cdot \left(1 - \frac{\tilde{x}_j^k}{C_k}\right) \cdot \frac{\tilde{x}_j^k}{C_k} \cdot \frac{\partial \hat{h}_j^k}{\partial \theta_k}}_{\text{Term A}} + \underbrace{\sum_{j=1}^{T} b_j \cdot \left(1 - \frac{\tilde{x}_j^k}{C_k}\right) \cdot \frac{\hat{q}_j^k}{\theta_k}}_{\text{Term B}}.$$

Table 1. Performance comparisons.

(a) Performance at training scale (16 robots, 64 tasks)

Method	Objective	Coverage (%)	Ratio to AMF	Ratio to MILP
MILP	7.22 ± 0.25	89.6 ± 4.1	1.70 ± 0.12	1.00
FORMICA (ours)	5.01 ± 0.48	54.3 ± 5.6	1.17 ± 0.11	0.69 ± 0.07
AMF	4.27 ± 0.28	73.6 ± 5.7	1.00	0.59 ± 0.04

(b) Large-scale generalization (256 robots, 4096 tasks)

Method	Objective	Coverage (%)	Ratio to AMF
FORMICA (ours)	90.14 ± 7.86	42.3 ± 3.9	1.07 ± 0.01
AMF	84.32 ± 7.09	39.2 ± 3.5	1.00

Note: MILP is computationally infeasible at this scale.

The gradient now has two terms: Term A (same structure as the 2-robot case) encourages accurate max-bid prediction; Term B encourages coverage on tasks robot k does not take, and is large when a high-value task risks being unallocated. This approximation reduces complexity to $O(T)$—only and must be computed per task—and allows training a single shared network that scales across swarm sizes.

Analytical Baseline. In a task allocation scenario with uniform robot distribution, $\rho_j(b)$ has a closed-form solution derived from the geometry of equal-bid contours:

$$\rho_j(b) = \frac{2\pi R_j}{|\Omega| \cdot b^2} \cdot \left(\frac{R_j}{b} - \epsilon \right). \tag{AMF}$$

where R_j is the reward for completing task j, Ω is the environment area, and ϵ is the fixed cost to perform the task. This *Analytical Mean Field (AMF)* baseline represents the best performance achievable under idealized (uniform, stationary) assumptions, and isolates the value of learned corrections.

3.4   Training Algorithm

Training consists of two phases. **Phase 1 (supervised):** A Set Transformer [15] takes the tasks encoded as $[x_j/W, y_j/W, R_j/\bar{R}, 1/\ell, \log N]$ and outputs per-task densities $\hat{\rho}(b')$ over B log-spaced bins, trained to minimize cross-entropy against empirical histograms. Bids are normalized using characteristic length $\ell = \sqrt{|\Omega|/N}$, $W \times H$ is the environment size, and $\bar{R}$ is the average reward. **Phase 2 (decision-focused):** Starting from Phase 1 weights, we refine via TAR. For each sampled scenario and robot k: (a) compute $\hat{h}_j$ as a soft quantile of ρ_j; (b) compute $\hat{q}_j^k$ by integrating $\hat{\rho}_j$ above $b_{k,j}$; (c) perform soft allocation

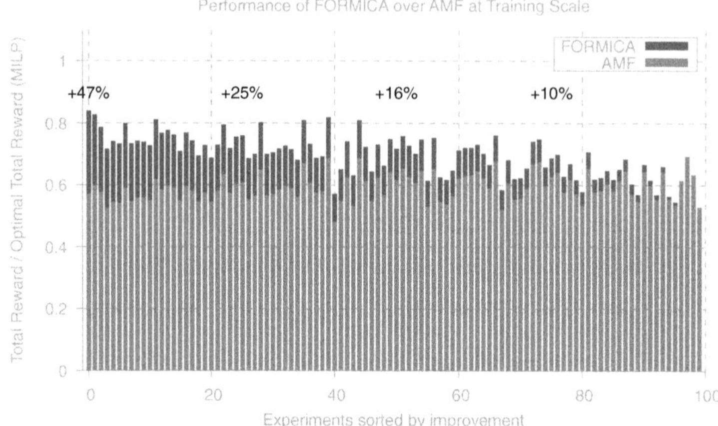

Fig. 1. Performance comparison: FORMICA vs AMF as a ratio over MILP. The percentages shown in black indicate the performance improvement of FORMICA over AMF.

and compute $\mathcal{L}_{\mathrm{TAR}}$. The primal update backpropagates through $\hat{\rho}_j$ and $\hat{h}_j$ only; the dual update adjusts $\lambda \leftarrow \lambda + \eta \left(\sum_j b_{k,j} \tilde{x}_j^k - C_k \right)$.

4   Experimental Evaluation

We consider in a scenario inspired by garbage collection. Each task j at position $\mathbf{p}_j$ has reward $R_j \sim \mathcal{U}[6, 24]$. For robot i at position $\mathbf{p}_i$, the bid is $b_{i,j} = R_j/(\|\mathbf{p}_i - \mathbf{p}_j\| + \varepsilon)$ where $\varepsilon = 0.5$. Each robot has capacity $C_k = 0.5$ on the sum of accepted bids. The global objective is to maximize $\sum_j \max_i (b_{i,j} x_{i,j})$ subject to capacity constraints and at-most-one-robot-per-task.

Training Configuration. We train on $N = 16$ robots and $T = 64$ tasks in a 300×200 workspace with clustered task distribution (6 Gaussian clusters, $\sigma = 0.15 \cdot \min(W, H)$). The hyperparameters were as follows:

- bin config: $B = 64$, $b' \in [0.02, 64]$;
- Phase 1: $p_1 = 400$ steps, $\alpha = 3 \times 10^{-3}$;
- Phase 2: $p_2 = 1200$ steps, $\beta = 3.5$, $q_h = 0.70$, $\Delta b' = 1.6$, $\gamma = 0.08$, $\eta = 10^{-3}$

The entire training took approximately $21\,\mathrm{s}$ on a laptop equipped with an 11th Gen Intel(R) Core(TM) i7-1185G7 @ 3.00GHz (3.00 GHz).

Baselines. *(1) Analytical Mean Field (AMF):* Each robot uses the closed-form bid density (AMF). This represents the best performance achievable using perfect analytical predictions under idealized assumptions. Comparing against (AMF) isolates the value of learned corrections to handle non-uniform distributions, task clustering, and other deviations from mean-field assumptions. *(2)*

MILP: For small-scale scenarios only, we solve a Mixed-Integer Linear Program using CBC to provide a near-optimal upper bound.

Metrics. We evaluate: (1) Global objective $\sum_j \max_i(b_{i,j} x_{i,j})$; (2) Task coverage (fraction with ≥ 1 robot); (3) Performance ratio ($\text{obj}_\text{method}/\text{obj}_\text{baseline}$).

Training Scale Results. We evaluate on fresh scenarios from the training distribution: 16 robots, 64 tasks, 300×200 workspace. Figure 1 and Table 1(a) compare performance across $N = 100$ test scenarios. FORMICA achieves an average objective of 5.01 ± 0.48, compared to 4.27 ± 0.28 for the AMF baseline (approximately 17% improvement; paired t-test, $p \ll 10^{-6}$) and 7.22 ± 0.25 for the MILP upper bound. This corresponds to $69.4 \pm 6.9\%$ of the MILP objective for FORMICA versus $59.2 \pm 4.3\%$ for AMF. FORMICA achieves 54% coverage versus AMF's 74%, yet delivers 17% higher objective. This reveals decision-focused learning's key advantage: optimizing directly for reward rather than prediction accuracy leads to *strategic task abandonment*. The method learns to sacrifice low-value coverage to secure high-value tasks: a clear instance of *decision-focused learning*. FORMICA outperforms AMF in $96/100 = 96\%$ of test scenarios. In clustered configurations, FORMICA successfully predicts high competition and reallocates robots to underserved regions, while the AMF baseline fails to capture the actual bid distribution, leading to conflicts and missed coverage.

Large-Scale Generalization. We deploy the same network on $N = 256$ robots and $T = 4096$ tasks in a 3000×2000 workspace ($10\times$ larger in each dimension). This represents $16\times$ more robots, $64\times$ more tasks, and $100\times$ larger workspace area. FORMICA outperforms AMF in every scenario we tested ($1000/1000$) with an average improvement of approximately $\sim 6.9\%$ in the objective (90.14 ± 7.86 vs. 84.32 ± 7.09; paired t-test, $p \ll 10^{-10}$; Table 1(b)). While the relative gain is smaller than at training scale—expected as the mean-field approximation becomes more accurate as N increases—the consistency demonstrates successful transfer of learned corrections across scales. It also increases coverage from $39.2 \pm 3.5\%$ to $42.3 \pm 3.9\%$.

5   Conclusions

We have presented FORMICA, a learning-based framework for multi-robot task allocation that achieves high-quality coordination without robot-to-robot communication, avoiding reliance on stable, bandwidth-rich links unavailable in underwater, disaster, or adversarial environments.

We contribute (i) the first application of decision-focused learning to multi-agent coordination, training predictors end-to-end to minimize Task Allocation Regret and focus on consensus-critical errors; (ii) a mean-field approximation reducing complexity from $O(NT)$ to $O(T)$, enabling a model trained on 16 robots to generalize to 256 with gains; and (iii) empirical evidence that implicit coordination can rival communication, improving performance by 17% over an analytical baseline at training scale and 7% on swarms $16\times$ larger, a *swarm theory of mind* where each robot models teammates' decisions internally.

Future work includes heterogeneity, dynamic arrivals, alternative utilities, obstacle/boundary effects, full SPO gradients through coverage probabilities, and emergent specialization. Beyond task allocation, this combination may apply to formation control, collaborative manipulation, or distributed sensing.

Acknowledgments. This work was supported by the Automotive Research Center (ARC), a US Army Center of Excellence for modeling and simulation of ground vehicles, under Cooperative Agreement W56HZV-24-2-0001 with the US Army DEVCOM Ground Vehicle Systems Center (GVSC).

Disclosure of Interests. The authors have no competing interests to declare.

References

1. Albrecht, S.V., Stone, P.: Autonomous agents modelling other agents: a comprehensive survey on the predicted utility of opponent models. Artif. Intell. **258**, 66–109 (2018)
2. Berlinger, F., Gauci, M., Nagpal, R.: Implicit coordination for 3D underwater collective behaviors in a fish-inspired robot swarm. Sci. Rob. **6**(50), eabd8668 (2021)
3. Buckman, N., Choi, H.L., How, J.P.: Partial replanning for decentralized dynamic task allocation. AIAA Scitech 2019 Forum p. 0915 (2019)
4. Carmel, D., Markovitch, S.: Learning models of intelligent agents. In: AAAI/IAAI, vol. 1, pp. 62–67 (1996)
5. Choi, H.L., Brunet, L., How, J.P.: Consensus-based decentralized auctions for robust task allocation. IEEE Trans. Rob. **25**(4), 912–926 (2009)
6. Dai, W., Lu, H., Xiao, J., Zheng, Z.: Task allocation without communication based on incomplete information game theory for multi-robot systems. J. Intell. Rob. Syst. **94**(3), 841–856 (2019)
7. Dai, X., et al.: Heterogeneous multi-robot task allocation with temporal and capacity constraints. IEEE Rob. Autom. Lett. **10**(2), 1–8 (2025)
8. Dias, M.B., Zlot, R., Kalra, N., Stentz, A.: Market-based multirobot coordination: a survey and analysis. Proc. IEEE **94**(7), 1257–1270 (2006)
9. El Balghiti, O., Elmachtoub, A.N., Grigas, P., Tewari, A.: Generalization bounds in the predict-then-optimize framework. Adv. Neural Inf. Process. Syst. **32** (2019)
10. Elmachtoub, A.N., Grigas, P.: Smart predict, then optimize. Manage. Sci. **68**(1), 9–26 (2022)
11. Elmachtoub, A.N., Liang, J.C.N., McNellis, R.: Decision trees for decision-making under the predict-then-optimize framework. In: International Conference on Machine Learning, pp. 2858–2867. PMLR (2020)
12. Goarin, M., Loianno, G.: Graph neural network for decentralized multi-robot goal assignment. IEEE Rob. Autom. Lett. **9**(5), 4051–4058 (2024)
13. Johnson, L., Ponda, S., Choi, H.L., How, J.: Asynchronous decentralized task allocation for dynamic environments. In: Infotech@ Aerospace 2011, p. 1441. American Institute of Aeronautics and Astronautics (2011)
14. Lai, M., et al.: RoboBallet: planning for multirobot reaching with graph neural networks and reinforcement learning. Sci. Robot. **10**(106), eads1204 (2025)
15. Lee, J., et al.: Set transformer: a framework for attention-based permutation-invariant neural networks. In: International Conference on Machine Learning, pp. 3744–3753. PMLR (2019)

16. Lopez, A., Muirhead, J., Pinciroli, C.: FORMICA: decision-focused learning for communication-free multi-robot task allocation (2026). https://arxiv.org/abs/2602.18622
17. Mandi, J., et al.: Decision-focused learning: foundations, state of the art, benchmark and future opportunities. J. Artif. Intell. Res. **80**, 1623–1701 (2024)
18. Quinton, F., Lesire, C., Grand, C.: Market approaches to the multi-robot task allocation problem: a survey. J. Intell. Robot. Syst. **107**(2), 29 (2023)
19. Rabinowitz, N.C., et al.: Machine theory of mind. In: International Conference on Machine Learning, pp. 4218–4227. PMLR (2018)
20. Theraulaz, G., Bonabeau, E.: A brief history of stigmergy. Artif. Life **5**(2), 97–116 (1999)
21. Wang, Z., Schwager, M.: Multi-robot manipulation without communication. In: Distributed Autonomous Robotic Systems: The 12th international symposium, pp. 135–149. Springer (2016)
22. Werfel, J., Petersen, K., Nagpal, R.: Designing collective behavior in a termite-inspired robot construction team. Science **343**(6172), 754–758 (2014)

From Pheromones to Policies: Reinforcement Learning for Engineered Biological Swarms

Aymeric Vellinger$^{(\boxtimes)}$, Nemanja Antonic , and Elio Tuci

Department of Computer Science, University of Namur, Namur, Belgium
aymeric.vellinger@unamur.be
https://www.unamur.be/

Abstract. Swarm intelligence emerges from simple local interactions. We show a formal equivalence between pheromone-mediated aggregation in *C. elegans* and reinforcement learning: stigmergic signals implement distributed rewards and cross-learning updates. Using a foraging model grounded in empirical data, we reproduce *C. elegans* patch-selection in static environments. In dynamic settings, persistent pheromones create positive feedback that hinders adaptation by locking swarms to outdated sites. Computational bandit experiments reveal that implementing heterogeneity through a minority of exploratory, pheromone-insensitive agents restores plasticity and enables rapid task switching. Thus, behavioural heterogeneity balances exploration-exploitation and implements swarm-level extinction of obsolete strategies. Our results reinterpret stigmergy as externalised memory for collective credit assignment and link synthetic biology with RL-driven swarm control, pointing to programmable living systems capable of resilient decision-making.

1 Introduction

Collective animal behaviour illustrates how large groups accomplish sensing, decision making and actuation that far exceed the cognitive or energetic capacity of the individuals that compose them. These examples have inspired swarm intelligence, a biologically inspired, self-organised and decentralised problem-solving paradigm in which simple agents encode local interaction rules, enabling the collective to exhibit coherent and adaptive behaviour without any agent possessing global knowledge or acting as a central controller.

In artificial intelligence a parallel idea appears at the level of a single agent. Reinforcement learning (RL), as conceptualised by Sutton and Barto [14], synthesises psychological principles of Thorndike's law of effect (trial-and-error learning), optimal control theory from engineering, and operant conditioning paradigms. Thus, what swarms exhibit at the population level and what a single RL agent exhibits at the individual level are two scales of the same cognitive learning dynamic: decentralised, incremental hypothesis testing driven by

R. Groß et al. (Eds.): ANTS 2026, LNCS 16515, pp. 350–357, 2026.
https://doi.org/10.1007/978-3-032-26123-6_29

environment. A direct consequence of treating learning as continual model revision is adaptability (i.e., the capacity to maintain competent behaviour under changing conditions). In animal conditioning, extinction denotes the decay of a conditioned response when reinforcement ceases. Balancing knowledge consolidation and extinction [11], therefore amounts to regulating exploration-exploitation [17]. Achieving that balance is central to designing swarm systems that remain resilient, sample-efficient, and cognitively coherent over long horizons. For instance, theoretical models have shown that heterogeneity enhances optimal decision-making [3].

Even if swarm robotics shows promising engineering solutions, it falls short in facing natural environments [7]. This gap motivates the exploration of biological animal robots [4], where living organisms themselves constitute the agents. In this context, *Caenorhabditis elegans* (*C. elegans*) with its fully mapped neural connectome consisting of 302 neurons [16] emerges as a favorable candidate. This neural simplicity, combined with emerging techniques in neuro-synthetic biology [12], opens opportunities for creating bioengineered *C. elegans* as swarm agents. By genetically manipulating synaptic connectivity [13] and constructing in vivo gene circuits [9], it may become feasible to systematically alter collective behaviours, thus transforming *C. elegans* populations into a programmable biological swarm of robots.

C. elegans occurs in diverse natural and laboratory strains that span a behavioural continuum. The canonical laboratory reference strain $N2$ has been demonstrated to be almost entirely *solitary*, whereas strains carrying the low-activity allele of the neuropeptide-receptor gene $npr - 1$ adopt a more *social* collective behaviour, i.e., clustering in clumps at the food interface [5]. Nonetheless, even these *social* worms exhibit little beyond simple aggregation, far from the elaborate tasks of eusocial or subsocial insects [2]. It is conceivable, however, that pheromone-based communication could be harnessed to engineer much more elaborate collective behaviour [1], allowing us to treat *C. elegans* populations as programmable biological robots whose coordination is mediated by tunable chemical signals.

Our study forges a formal bridge between engineered stigmergy (i.e., coordination via environmentally deposited pheromones) and RL, and examines how environmental volatility and population heterogeneity shape swarm adaptability in pheromone-guided foraging. We show the equivalence between pheromone-driven swarming dynamics and the Cross Learning update rule (validated against published in-vivo data), quantify the consensus-adaptability trade-off under environmental shifts, and demonstrate that a minority of exploration-oriented individuals sustains plasticity by enabling swarm-level extinction.

2 Model

We develop our model based on the empirical framework described in [10], with the aim of integrating pheromone-based communication into a swarm of *C. elegans*.

The intrinsic attractiveness of a food patch i with bacterial density D_i is given by the sigmoidal function

$$A_i = \sqrt{H} \, \frac{1 + 4 \left(\frac{D_i}{D_{\text{attract}}} \right)^k}{H + 4 \left(\frac{D_i}{D_{\text{attract}}} \right)^k}, \tag{1}$$

where bacterial attractiveness A_i is time-invariant and H controls the dynamic range, k the steepness of the response, and D_{attract} the characteristic density.

To model stigmergic reinforcement, we define the pheromone-induced modulation of patch attractiveness as

$$B_i(t) = 1 + \tau_i(t), \tag{2}$$

where $\tau_i(t)$ denotes the amount of pheromone present at site i at time t. Thus, pheromones linearly amplify the intrinsic attractiveness of a patch.

Although pheromone sensing can be nonlinear and context-dependent [6], we adopt this linear formulation for analytical tractability.

The probability of worms aggregating at the ith food patch, in an environment with M patches, is then given by

$$P_i(t) = \frac{B_i(t)\, A_i}{\sum_{j=1}^{M} B_j(t)\, A_j}. \tag{3}$$

We now characterise the temporal evolution of pheromone concentration. The quantity of pheromone at patch i evolves according to

$$\tau_i(t+1) = \rho\, \tau_i(t) + \Delta_{k,i}(t), \tag{4}$$

where the deposition term depends on individual decisions:

$$\Delta_{k,i}(t) = \begin{cases} Q, & \text{if agent } k \text{ selects patch } i, \\ 0, & \text{otherwise.} \end{cases} \tag{5}$$

Here, $0 \le \rho \le 1$ denotes the pheromone persistence rate, and $Q \ge 0$ is the amount of pheromone deposited upon selecting a patch. Together, these dynamics capture how local decisions reinforce patch attractiveness over time, driving collective aggregation through positive stigmergy.

3   Learning

In a multi-armed bandit with M actions, an agent maintains a policy $\pi(t) = (\pi_1(t), \ldots, \pi_M(t))$, where $\pi_i(t)$ denotes the probability of selecting action i at time t. After selecting action k and receiving reward r_k, the policy is updated as

$$\pi_i(t+1) = \pi_i(t) + \alpha\, r_k \begin{cases} 1 - \pi_i(t), & \text{if } i = k, \\ -\pi_i(t), & \text{otherwise,} \end{cases} \tag{6}$$

where α is the learning rate.

We now establish how pheromone-mediated aggregation induces a reinforcement-learning update of patch-selection probabilities when agents (worms) act sequentially.

At time t, the probability of selecting patch i is given by Eq. 3. When a worm selects patch k at time t, it deposits pheromone Q at that site, yielding $\tau_k(t+1) = \rho\,\tau_k(t) + Q$, while pheromones at all other sites decay as $\tau_i(t+1) = \rho\,\tau_i(t)$.

Substituting these dynamics into the expression of $P_i(t+1)$ and regrouping the chosen and unchosen cases (derivations in the Supplement [15]) yields the update rule:

$$P_i(t+1) = P_i(t) + QR_k(t) \begin{cases} 1 - P_i(t), & \text{if } i = k, \\ -P_i(t), & \text{otherwise,} \end{cases} \tag{7}$$

with

$$R_k(t) = \frac{A_k}{\rho \sum_{j=1}^{M} \tau_j(t) A_j + Q A_k}. \tag{8}$$

Equation 7 is mathematically equivalent to the Cross Learning update (Eq. 6), where the reward signal is implicitly implemented through environmental stigmergy. In this interpretation, pheromone deposition acts as a distributed reinforcement mechanism, and the population distribution across patches corresponds to the agent's policy.

This mechanism explains how local decisions can give rise to collective learning: actions that lead to higher bacterial payoff leave stronger pheromone traces, which bias subsequent choices and drive convergence toward optimal sites. However, purely positive feedback also induces a risk of lock-in under changing conditions, as persistent pheromones slow the extinction of outdated collective preferences. High pheromone persistence therefore hinders adaptation unless mechanisms promoting exploration are introduced.

Although worms act sequentially in our formulation, the equivalence holds at the population level due to the ergodicity of cross-learning dynamics, ensuring statistical equivalence with parallel updates. In simulations, pheromone accumulation is implemented via a finite replay buffer that approximates the total pheromone mass $\sum_j \tau_j(t)$.

4   Results

We present three types of experiments using the reinforcement learning model. The first experiment aims to validate our model, while the other two focus on the swarm's response in dynamic environments.

4.1   Model Validation in Static Environment

We evaluate the model in a stateless multi-armed bandit and in a two-state bandit where rewards have Gaussian noise $\sigma = 0.1$ and are permuted at epoch $T = \Delta$. We initialise the policy with $\pi_1 = 0.9$ and $\pi_i = \frac{0.1}{M-1}$ for $i \geq 2$.

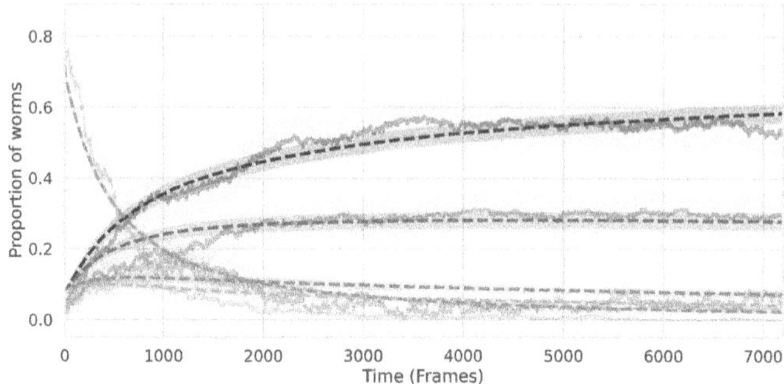

Fig. 1. Proportion of worms at each food patch over time. Solid lines: experimental mean over 58 videos (299 worms total); shaded: 95% bootstrap CI; dashed: model. Patch optical densities are $D \in \{0.2, 0.1, 0.05, 0.025\}$, respectively blue, purple, pink and orange; an additional curve represents the proportion of worms outside patches in grey.

To validate our model, we compare its predictions with empirical data gathered from controlled experiments in [10]. In these experiments, four food patches were arranged in a square at 1.2 cm from the center of a plate. Each patch contained *E. coli OP*50 at distinct densities: 0.2, 0.1, 0.05, and 0.025 (measured as Optical Density). In each trial, worms were placed in the center of the plate, and their distribution across patches was recorded over 7200 seconds. We compared the results of the experiment with the prediction of our model in the multi-armed stateless bandit setting.

Figure 1 displays the average time evolution of the proportion of worms present in each patch as well as those outside the patches, approximating an Ideal Free Distribution (IDF) [8].

We found the best-fit parameters using Differential Evolution (DE). The parameters found for the Attractiveness sigmoid function are: $H = 51.5, k = 0.29, D_{attract} = 0.003$. The pheromone secretion parameter (i.e., the learning rate) of the model was also adjusted to best fit the data, therefore Q was set to 0.02. With these parameters, our model achieved an MSE of 2.595E−2.

4.2   Adaptation to Dynamic Environments

To investigate the swarm's adaptability under changing conditions, we consider a dynamic environment in which patch attractiveness changes abruptly at time $t = \Delta$.

Before the switch ($t < \Delta$), the environment is in its first state: arm a_1 has attractiveness $r_1 = 0$, arm a_2 has attractiveness $r_2 = A(D = 1) = 2.22$, and arm a_3 has attractiveness $r_3 = 0$.

At time $t = \Delta$, the environment transitions to a second state. In this new state, arm a_1 remains non-rewarding ($r_1 = 0$), arm a_2 becomes non-rewarding ($r_2 = 0$), and arm a_3 becomes the only attractive option, with $r_3 = A(D = 1) = 2.22$.

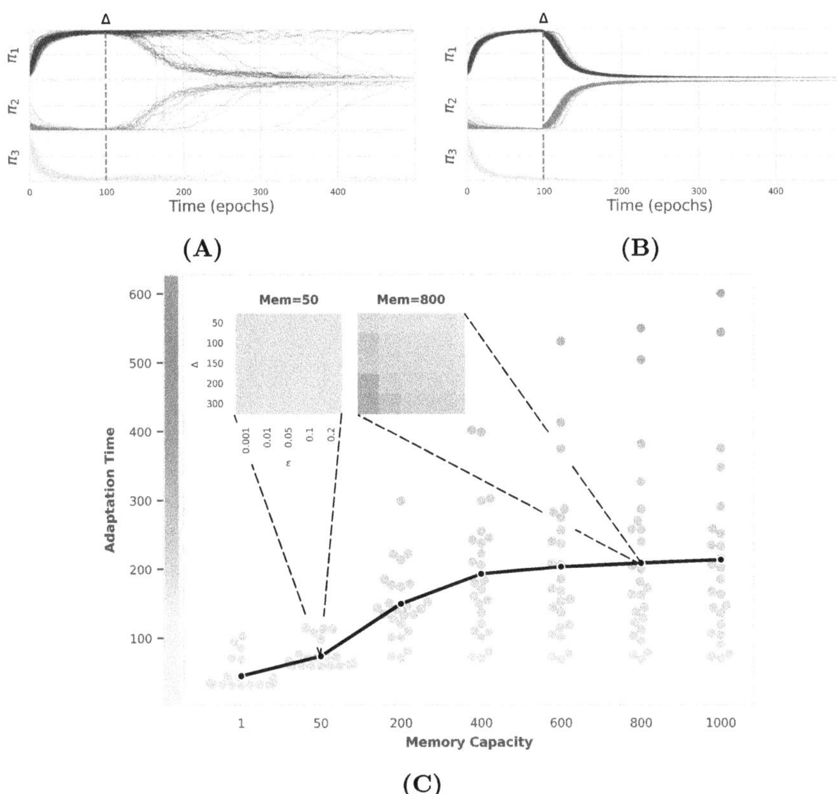

Fig. 2. Adaptation dynamics in a dynamic three-arm two-state bandit task. (A) Policy evolution in a homogeneous population. (B) Policy evolution in a heterogeneous population with a fraction $\epsilon = 0.1$ of exploratory individuals that ignore pheromones. In (A-B), both populations operate in a two-state multi-armed bandit with three arms, start fully distributed on a_1, aggregate at a_2, and experience an environmental switch at epoch $\Delta = 100$ (red vertical line), after which a_3 becomes the only rewarding option. (C) Mean Time to Adapt (MTA) in the same task. The swarm plot shows MTA as a function of pheromone memory (black line: mean over 5 runs, 1000 epochs). Heatmaps report MTA across exploratory fraction $\epsilon \in \{0.001, 0.01, 0.05, 0.1, 0.2\}$ (x-axis) and switch time $\Delta \in \{50, 100, 150, 200, 300\}$ (y-axis).

Using this setup with $\Delta = 100$, *Memory size*= 350 (i.e., Buffer size), maximum number of epochs $T = 500$, and number of runs $N = 100$, we first examined a homogeneous population. In Fig. 2A-B, we show the evolution of the policy across arms. In the homogeneous case (Fig. 2A), 13% of the runs successfully aggregated at the new spot after the state change. This limited success arises from the swarm's strong positive stigmergic reinforcement: the continuous deposition of pheromones sustains a positive feedback loop that can trap the swarm at the first spot, even after its attractiveness has dropped to zero. We therefore introduce a fraction ϵ of exploratory individuals that ignore pheromones and rely solely on bacterial attractiveness.

In the heterogeneous population, we assume that $1 - \epsilon$ of the *C. elegans* can both sense and secrete pheromones, while ϵ are blind to pheromones but still secrete them. Hence, the exploratory group relies solely on bacterial density for navigation. Figure 2B shows that introducing $\epsilon = 0.1$ exploratory individuals leads to a 100% success rate in reaching and aggregating at the final spot. These findings highlight the importance of exploratory agents in avoiding local attractor traps created by purely attractive pheromone-driven learning.

We quantify the swarm's response to an environmental switch using the Mean Time to Adapt (MTA):

$$\text{MTA} = \frac{1}{N} \sum_{i=1}^{N} \min\{k \geq 0 \; : \; \pi_3(\Delta + k) \geq 0.9\}, \tag{9}$$

If the threshold is not reached before the terminal time T, the adaptation time is set to $T - \Delta$.

Figure 2C summarises adaptation as a function of pheromone memory, switch time Δ, and exploratory fraction ϵ. Larger memory increases lock-in and requires larger ϵ to recover fast switching, whereas short memory yields consistently low MTA across Δ and ϵ.

5   Conclusion

We presented a framework linking pheromone-mediated coordination and RL. By deriving an update rule equivalent to cross-learning, we showed that positive stigmergy acts as an implicit reward, turning collective aggregation into distributed learning where the environment stores reinforcement history.

This shared feedback structure explains efficient convergence in static environments and lock-in in dynamic ones unless exploration and extinction mechanisms are present. We showed that a small fraction of exploratory, pheromone-insensitive individuals restores flexibility, enabling the swarm to revise outdated strategies.

Overall, our results bridge biological learning, swarm dynamics, and RL, and provide design principles for programmable biohybrid collectives capable of adaptive behaviour in volatile environments.

Acknowledgments. The BABots project has received funding from the Horizon Europe, PathFinder European Innovation Council Work Programme under grant agreement No 101098722. Views and opinions expressed are however those of the authors only and do not necessarily reflect those of the European Union or European Innovation Council and SMEs Executive Agency (EISMEA).

Disclosure of Interests. The authors have no competing interests to declare.

References

1. Antonic, N., Vellinger, A., Tuci, E.: Chemotactic swarming of C. elegans as a collective decision-making process. In: Italian Workshop on Artificial Life and Evolutionary Computation, pp. 56–69. Springer (2024)
2. Antonic, N., Vellinger, A., Tuci, E.: On collective behavior in C. elegans. Front. Neurorobotics **19**, 1689332 (2025). https://doi.org/10.3389/fnbot.2025.1689332
3. Antonic, N., Zakir, R., Dorigo, M., Reina, A.: Collective robustness of heterogeneous decision-makers against stubborn individuals. In: AAMAS, pp. 68–77 (2024)
4. BABots: BABots: The design and control of small swarming biological animal robots (2024). https://babots.eu/. Accessed 02 Oct 2026
5. de Bono, M., Bargmann, C.I.: Natural variation in a neuropeptide Y receptor homolog modifies social behavior and food response in C. elegans. Cell **94**(5), 679–689 (1998). https://doi.org/10.1016/S0092-8674(00)81609-8
6. Dal Bello, M., Pérez-Escudero, A., Schroeder, F.C., Gore, J.: Inversion of pheromone preference optimizes foraging in C. elegans. eLife **10**, e58144 (2021). https://doi.org/10.7554/eLife.58144
7. Dorigo, M., Theraulaz, G., Trianni, V.: Swarm robotics: past, present, and future. Proc. IEEE **109**(7), 1152–1165 (2021). https://doi.org/10.1109/JPROC.2021.3072740
8. Houston, A.I., McNamara, J.M.: Switching between resources and the ideal free distribution. Anim. Behav. **35**(1), 301–302 (1987)
9. Kukhtar, D., Fussenegger, M.: Synthetic biology in multicellular organisms: opportunities in nematodes. Biotechnol. Bioeng. **120**(8), 2056–2071 (2023). https://doi.org/10.1002/bit.28497
10. Madirolas, G., et al.: Caenorhabditis elegans foraging patterns follow a simple rule of thumb. Commun. Biol. **6**(1), 841 (2023). https://doi.org/10.1038/s42003-023-05220-3
11. Quirk, G.J., Mueller, D.: Neural mechanisms of extinction learning and retrieval. Neuropsychopharmacology **33**(1), 56–72 (2008). https://doi.org/10.1038/sj.npp.1301555
12. Rabinowitch, I.: Synthetic biology in the brain: a vision of organic robots. In: Artificial Life Conference Proceedings, pp. 654–655. MIT Press (2019). https://doi.org/10.1162/isal_a_00236
13. Rabinowitch, I., Colón-Ramos, D.A., Krieg, M.: Understanding neural circuit function through synaptic engineering. Nat. Rev. Neurosci. **25**(2), 131–139 (2024). https://doi.org/10.1038/s41583-023-00777-8
14. Sutton, R.S., Barto, A.G.: Reinforcement Learning: An Introduction. MIT Press, Cambridge, MA (1998)
15. Vellinger, A.: Supplementary material for pheromones to policies: RL for biological swarms. Zenodo (2025). https://doi.org/10.5281/zenodo.17639367
16. White, J.G., Southgate, E., Thomson, J.N., Brenner, S.: The structure of the nervous system of the nematode Caenorhabditis elegans. Philos. Trans. R. Soc. Lond. B Biol. Sci. **314**(1165), 1–340 (1986). https://doi.org/10.1098/rstb.1986.0056
17. Yogeswaran, M., Ponnambalam, S.G.: Reinforcement learning: exploration-exploitation dilemma in multi-agent foraging task. Opsearch **49**(3), 223–236 (2012). https://doi.org/10.1007/s12597-012-0077-2

GMM-PACO: Gaussian Mixture Models and Pareto-Based Ant Colony Optimization for Multi-objective Feature Selection

Anna Krysta, Inès Alaya[✉], and Tristan Cazenave[✉]

LAMSADE, Université Paris Dauphine - PSL, Paris, France
anna.krysta@dauphine.eu, ines.alaya@parisnanterre.fr,
tristan.cazenave@lamsade.dauphine.fr

Abstract. In this paper, we propose GMM-PACO, a novel Ant Colony Optimization (ACO) for multi-objective feature selection. This algorithm explicitly models each feature using Gaussian Mixture Models (GMMs) to capture distributional characteristics. Our heuristic function integrates mutual information with the Wasserstein distance between feature distributions to evaluate feature relevance and redundancy. GMM-PACO simultaneously optimizes classification accuracy, feature subset size, and redundancy using Pareto dominance. Extensive evaluations on multiple UCI datasets with k-nearest neighbors (KNN) classifier demonstrate improvements over existing methods in both subset compactness and classification accuracy.

1 Introduction

Feature selection (FS) aims to identify the most relevant features in order to improve model performance and reduce complexity. This study focuses on multi-objective FS, aiming to find feature subsets that balance three conflicting goals: maximizing classification accuracy, minimizing redundancy, and minimizing the number of selected features.

Ant Colony Optimization (ACO) [8] is used in this work for multi-objective FS. Existing ACO-based FS methods often rely on simplistic statistical assumptions and lack robust feature modeling or clear convergence criteria, which can lead to suboptimal subsets or unstable performance across datasets. To address these limitations, we propose a novel multi-objective FS framework that integrates Gaussian Mixture Models (GMMs) [3] and Pareto optimization into the ACO search process. Our contributions include:

- A novel multi-objective ACO-based FS framework using Gaussian Mixture Models (GMMs) to model feature distributions.
- An entropy-based stopping criterion that guides the selection process.

R. Groß et al. (Eds.): ANTS 2026, LNCS 16515, pp. 358–366, 2026.
https://doi.org/10.1007/978-3-032-26123-6_30

- A heuristic function combining mutual information (MI) and Wasserstein distance (WD) [23] to evaluate feature relevance and redundancy.
- A pheromone update rule based on accuracy and normalized by subset size.

The remainder of the paper is structured as follows. Section 2 reviews related work on ACO and FS methods. Section 3 introduces our proposed method, along with definitions and pseudocode. Section 4 presents the experiments and comparative results. Finally, Sect. 5 concludes with findings and future directions. The code is available at: https://github.com/annkry/GMM-PACO.

2 Related Work

Feature selection (FS) is a key dimensionality reduction technique that selects a subset of original features. Multi-objective FS typically balances competing goals such as minimizing subset size, prediction error, computational cost, or redundancy. Pareto-based approaches are widely used to identify a set of non-dominated solutions, forming the Pareto front, which represents optimal trade-offs among the objectives. These approaches have been successfully applied to classical combinatorial problems such as the multi-objective knapsack problem [2] and the traveling salesman problem with Time Windows [19]. For multi-objective FS problem, PMFS [15] combines relevance and redundancy with crowding distance to maintain diversity. PEFS [16] aggregates filter rankings and applies Pareto selection, while 2OMF [12] uses a two-step approach that combines mutual information with classifier stability.

Nature-inspired algorithms are widely applied in FS for their ability to search large search spaces. A multi-objective Artificial Bee Colony (MOABC) algorithm [14] explores both binary and continuous variants. ACO-based approaches such as ACOFS [17] select features probabilistically, with heuristic updates based on information gain, subset size, and accuracy. FSvACO [10] uses cosine similarity for transitions, while MLACO [21] extends ACO to multi-label FS using feature-class similarity and Pearson correlation. UFSACO [22] applies inverse cosine similarity and another work [18] proposes a multi-objective ACO using non-dominated solutions for pheromone updates and crowding for diversity preservation. Many ACO-based FS methods rely on simple heuristic functions, which can limit their ability to handle complex data structures and dependencies among features. Gaussian Mixture Models (GMMs) [3] offer a way to better capture such complexity by modeling feature distributions as mixtures of Gaussian distributions. Prior work has applied GMMs in FS outside of metaheuristics. For example, [1] surveys FS techniques for GMMs and Hidden Markov Models, while [11] introduces a GMM-based FS method using a relevance index. Most of these methods are single-objective and lack global search capabilities.

3 Proposed Method

In this section, we introduce our proposed method for solving the FS problem using the ACO algorithm and describe the pseudocode.

Algorithm 1. GMM-PACO pseudocode

Input: dataset
Output: Pareto front
 1: Preprocessing features
 2: Compute pairwise Wasserstein distances between feature GMMs
 3: **Initialize** pheromone levels τ_j
 4: **while** max iterations not reached **do**
 5:    **for** each ant k **do**
 6:       Start at a random feature
 7:       **while** stopping probability far from uniform **do**
 8:          Ant k selects a feature with transition probability P_j^k
 9:       **end while**
10:    **end for**
11:    Evaluate objectives: classification accuracy, subset size, redundancy
12:    Update Pareto set and pheromone levels
13: **end while**
14: **return** final Pareto set

3.1 Overview of GMM-PACO Framework

Algorithm 1 outlines our proposed ACO method. In preprocessing, feature values are discretized using equal-width binning and MI is computed. For each feature, GMM parameters are estimated via the Expectationâ€“Maximization (EM) algorithm [7] until likelihood convergence and pairwise Wasserstein-1 distances between GMMs are approximated using the Sinkhorn algorithm [6]. Feature pheromones are initialized using normalized maximum cosine similarity to class labels. During optimization, each ant incrementally constructs a feature subset until transition probabilities become nearly uniform, guided by a heuristic combining mutual information and Wasserstein-based redundancy. The Pareto set is updated each iteration: the Chebyshev score [25] selects the best solution in the first iteration and Pareto dominance is applied thereafter. Pheromone levels are finally updated using our accuracy-based rule normalized by subset size.

3.2 Gaussian Mixture Models for Features Modeling

We define GMM associated with each feature f_j within a dataset as

$$p_j(x) = \sum_{m=1}^{M} \pi_{jm}\, \mathcal{N}(x \mid \mu_{jm}, \sigma_{jm}^2),$$

where π_{jm} are the mixture weights, $\sum_m \pi_{jm} = 1$, M is the number of mixtures, and

$$\mathcal{N}(x \mid \mu, \sigma^2) = \frac{1}{\sqrt{2\pi\sigma^2}} \exp\left(-\frac{(x-\mu)^2}{2\sigma^2}\right)$$

is the Gaussian probability density function. Real-world datasets often contain features that have complex and multimodal patterns, making simplistic single-distribution assumptions inadequate [20]. The GMM allows capturing these intricate structures by representing the distribution of each feature through a weighted sum of several Gaussian components.

3.3 Heuristic Function

The heuristic function we define aims at guiding ants towards promising feature selections by balancing two critical aspects: relevance and diversity. Formally, we express it as follows

$$\eta_j(t) = \lambda \cdot \frac{\mathrm{MI}(f_j, Y)}{\max_k \mathrm{MI}(f_k, Y)} + (1 - \lambda) \cdot \frac{\mathrm{WWD}(f_j, S(t))}{\max_j \mathrm{WWD}(f_j, S(t))},$$

where λ balances the importance of mutual information, that is, feature relevancy, with feature redundancy, that is, the Wasserstein distance between feature GMM distributions. The heuristic combines two components. The first component assesses the relevance of a feature f_j to the target class label random variables Y by measuring the mutual information (MI) and is defined as $\mathrm{MI}(X, Y) = \sum_x \sum_y p(x, y) \log \left(\frac{p(x,y)}{p(x)p(y)} \right)$, where $p(x, y)$ is the joint probability of observing $X = x$ and $Y = y$, and $p(x)$ and $p(y)$ are the marginal probabilities of X and Y, respectively. High MI values indicate strong relationships between the feature and the class labels. To ensure numerical stability and fair comparison, MI is normalized by the highest MI observed across all features.

The second component encourages feature diversity within the currently built solution $S(t)$, ensuring that newly selected features are distinct from those already chosen. This diversity is measured using a weighted Wasserstein distance (WWD), defined as $\mathrm{WWD}(f_j, S(t)) = \sum_{k=1}^{|S(t)|} \tilde{w}_k \cdot \mathrm{WD}(p_{t_k}, p_j),$

where $\mathrm{WD}(p_{t_k}, p_j)$ is the entropic-regularized Wasserstein-1 distance between the GMM of previously selected feature f_{t_k} and the candidate feature f_j. The weighting scheme $\tilde{w}_k$ exponentially decays, giving more importance to recently selected features

$$\tilde{w}_k = \frac{\exp\left(-\gamma_w(|S(t)| - k)\right)}{\sum_{s=1}^{|S(t)|} \exp\left(-\gamma_w(|S(t)| - s)\right)}$$

with $\gamma_w > 0$ controlling the decay rate. A higher γ_w gives greater weight to recent selections, dynamically adapting feature diversity.

3.4 Pheromone Update

Another component of the ACO algorithm is the pheromone levels. Initially, we compute for each feature a similarity score

$$s_j = \max_c \frac{\mathbf{x}_j^\top \mathbf{y}^{(c)}}{\|\mathbf{x}_j\|_2 \|\mathbf{y}^{(c)}\|_2} = \max_c \frac{\sum_{i=1}^n x_{ij}\, \delta_{y_i,c}}{\sqrt{\sum_{i=1}^n x_{ij}^2}\, \sqrt{n_c}},$$

where x_{ij} is the value of feature j in sample i, $\delta_{y_i,c} = 1$ if $y_i = c$, and n_c is the number of samples in class c. These scores are then linearly normalized to initialize the pheromones. In each iteration of the ACO algorithm, we update the pheromone levels and apart from the typical ρ-declined part, we define it to be an accuracy deposit normalized by a number of selected features. Formally, the pheromone update rule is defined as

$$\tau_j \leftarrow (1 - \rho) \cdot \tau_j + \mathbf{1}_{\{\text{feature } j \in \text{sol}_k\}} \frac{\text{acc}_k}{|\text{sol}_k|},$$

where $\mathbf{1}_{\{A\}} = 1$ if A is true, and $\mathbf{1}_{\{A\}} = 0$ otherwise, ρ is the evaporation rate $(0 < \rho < 1)$, sol_k is the set of selected features of k-th ant that had the highest accuracy in a given iteration, $|\text{sol}_k|$ is the number of selected features and acc_k is the accuracy of a classifier using only the selected features for k-th ant.

3.5 Feature Selection Stopping Criteria

In every iteration, an ant chooses a subset of features until the selection probabilities are close to becoming uniform. The motivation is that when all the features have the same probability of being selected, they would not introduce any new information to the currently chosen feature subset, since no feature is significantly different from the remaining features. To monitor this, we measure the entropy of the transition probabilities and define a probabilistic stopping condition based on the level of uniformity. First, we define the normalized entropy for the k-th ant as

$$U_t^k = \frac{- \sum\limits_{j \in R_t} P_j^k(t) \log P_j^k(t)}{\log |R_t|},$$

where R_t is the set of remaining candidate features at a given time t, and $P_j^k(t) = \frac{[\tau_j(t)]^\alpha \cdot [\eta_j(t)]^\beta}{\sum_{l \in N^k(t)} [\tau_l(t)]^\alpha \cdot [\eta_l(t)]^\beta}$ is the probability of the k-th ant selecting feature j, where $N^k(t)$ is the set of features not yet selected at time t and the parameters (α, β) control the influence for pheromone and heuristic information. Now, the probabilistic stopping probability is as follows

$$P_{\text{stop}}^k(t) = \frac{1}{1 + \exp\left(-\gamma(U_t^k - \theta)\right)},$$

where $\theta \in [0, 1]$ denotes the entropy threshold controlling when the stopping probability becomes significant and $\gamma > 0$ is a scaling parameter that controls the steepness of the stopping probability function. An ant would stop adding new features when a random variable r sampled from a uniform distribution $\mathcal{U}(0, 1)$ is smaller than the stopping probability $P_{\text{stop}}^k(t)$.

3.6 Pareto Optimization

In multi-objective feature selection, we consider three objectives: minimizing $1 - \text{accuracy}$ after classification with a given feature subset, minimizing the number of selected features, and minimizing redundancy. Redundancy is computed for a subset $S = \{f_{t_1}, f_{t_2}, \ldots, f_{t_m}\}, m = |S|$, as the negative average pairwise WD between feature GMMs:

$$\text{subset\_redundancy}(S) = -\frac{1}{\binom{m}{2}} \sum\limits_{1 \leq a < b \leq m} \text{WD}(p_{t_a}, p_{t_b}).$$

Table 1. Comparison of the average best f-score values of the KNN model on different datasets before and after feature selection using our proposed approach.

Dataset	Before feature selection		After feature selection		
	# of features	f-score	# of features	f-score	
WDBC	30	0.907	5.6	**0.949**	(+)
Dermatology	34	0.694	7.8	**0.923**	(+)
Ionosphere	34	0.747	4.8	**0.933**	(+)
Arrhythmia	279	0.122	6.2	**0.302**	(+)
Wine	13	0.742	4.4	**1.000**	(+)
Hepatitis	19	0.395	7	**0.859**	(+)
Spambase	57	0.411	7	**0.459**	(+)
Madelon	500	0.664	11.6	**0.899**	(+)

Our goal is to find a Pareto set of feature subsets. In the first iteration, when the Pareto set is empty, the Chebyshev score [25] is computed as $\max_i \frac{f_{a,i}-z_i^*}{z_i^{\text{nad}}-z_i^*+\varepsilon}$, where $f_{a,i}$ is the value of objective i for solution a, z_i^* and z_i^{nad} are the ideal and nadir values, and ε ensures numerical stability. The solution with the smallest Chebyshev score is added to the Pareto set. In subsequent iterations, ant solutions are evaluated individually using Pareto domination: a solution is added if it is non-dominated with respect to the current set and any dominated solutions are removed. Consequently, multiple non-dominated solutions may be added in one iteration, while dominated ones are pruned.

4   Experiments

This section presents numerical results and comparisons with existing methods.

4.1   Experimental Setup

We use high-dimensional datasets from the Physics and Chemistry, and Health and Medicine domains of the UCI Machine Learning Repository [9]. Experiments ran for 1000 ACO iterations with 25 ants and parameters $\alpha = 1.0$, $\beta = 4.0$ and $\rho = 0.01$ chosen via a small grid search, while remaining parameters were set through preliminary experiments. Feature subsets were evaluated using a k-nearest neighbors (KNN) classifier [5] with $k = 5$ to compute classification accuracy.

F-Score Evaluation. We evaluate the average best f-scores of GMM-PACO with KNN before and after feature selection, using a 2/3 training and 1/3 testing split with 5 runs per dataset, as the low variance across runs indicates stable performance. Table 1 reports the average best achieved f-scores, with the highest

Table 2. Comparison of GMM-PACO using the KNN model. Each cell reports accuracy followed by the average number of selected features, separated by a semicolon, except for the first column. The second column shows KNN accuracy using all features.

Dataset	5-NN acc	ABC-ER	ABC-Fit2$_{2C}$	LFS	GSBS	GMM-PACO
Ionosphere	83.02	92.12; 12	91.74; 12	90.48; 6	89.52; 29	**94.15; 3**
Madelon	64.67	72.91; 252	72.20; 248	71.03; **7**	74.88; 250	**87.17**; 11
Musk 1	76.22	**83.11**; 83	82.32; 81	80.71; 12	82.86; 124	79.09; **11**
Musk 2	96.11	81.52; 82	81.54; 81	82.87; **8**	80.24; 122	**94.44**; 9
Opt Digits	98.70	98.10; 41	98.22; 37	97.86; 32	**98.75**; 38	93.03; **15**
Hill-Valley	54.52	54.13; 48	54.92; 45	55.49; 9	54.40; 95	**56.45; 6**

values in bold. GMM-PACO consistently selects significantly smaller feature subsets. Wilcoxon signed-rank tests [24] were applied at two levels: (1) per dataset, comparing best f-scores across runs before and after feature selection (with $+$ indicating significance at $p < 0.05$) and (2) across datasets using average best f-scores. GMM-PACO improved f-scores, with a statistically significant cross-dataset result ($p = 0.008 < 0.05$).

Comparison with Other Methods (Cross-Validation). In Table 2, we compare GMM-PACO with ABC-ER and ABC-Fit2$_{2C}$ [14], LFS [13], and GSBS [4]. They were chosen to represent diverse single-objective feature selection methods, covering both metaheuristic and greedy strategies. The experiments consisted of 30 runs following a 70/30 train-test split, where feature subsets were selected based on the average 10-fold cross-validation accuracy on the training set and test accuracy was reported afterward. GMM-PACO achieves comparable or higher accuracy, while selecting significantly fewer features. These results can be attributed to GMM-PACO's ability to better capture feature redundancy via distributional similarity, which allows the selection of compact yet highly discriminative feature subsets.

5   Conclusion

We proposed GMM-PACO, a feature selection method combining a probabilistic stopping rule, a mutual informationâĂŞ and Wasserstein-based heuristic and a pheromone update favoring high-performing subsets. It was evaluated on multiple UCI datasets using a KNN classifier with hold-out and cross-validation, achieving competitive or superior accuracy with fewer features and statistically significant improvements by Wilcoxon tests. Future work includes exploring other classifiers, refining the heuristic and analyzing dataset conditions where the method performs best or is outperformed.

Disclosure of Interests. The authors have no competing interests to declare.

References

1. Adams, S., Beling, P.: A survey of feature selection methods for gaussian mixture models and hidden Markov models. Artif. Intell. Rev. **52**, 1739–1779 (2019). https://doi.org/10.1007/s10462-017-9581-3
2. Alaya, I., Solnon, C., Ghedira, K.: Ant colony optimization for multi-objective optimization problems. In: 19th IEEE International Conference on Tools with Artificial Intelligence(ICTAI 2007), vol. 1, pp. 450–457 (2007). https://doi.org/10.1109/ICTAI.2007.108
3. Bishop, C.M.: Pattern Recognition and Machine Learning (Information Science and Statistics). Springer-Verlag, Heidelberg (2006)
4. Caruana, R., Freitag, D.: Greedy attribute selection. In: Proceedings of the Eleventh International Conference on International Conference on Machine Learning, ICML'94, pp. 28–36. Morgan Kaufmann Publishers Inc., San Francisco (1994)
5. Cover, T., Hart, P.: Nearest neighbor pattern classification. IEEE Trans. Inf. Theory **13**(1), 21–27 (1967). https://doi.org/10.1109/TIT.1967.1053964
6. Cuturi, M.: Sinkhorn distances: lightspeed computation of optimal transport. In: Burges, C., Bottou, L., Welling, M., Ghahramani, Z., Weinberger, K. (eds.) Advances in Neural Information Processing Systems, vol. 26. Curran Associates, Inc. (2013). https://proceedings.neurips.cc/paper_files/paper/2013/file/af21d0c97db2e27e13572cbf59eb343d-Paper.pdf
7. Dempster, A.P., Laird, N.M., Rubin, D.B.: Maximum likelihood from incomplete data via the EM algorithm. J. R. Stat. Soc. Ser. B **39**, 1–38 (1977). http://web.mit.edu/6.435/www/Dempster77.pdf
8. Dorigo, M., Stützle, T.: Ant Colony Optimization. Bradford Company, Michigan (2004)
9. Dua, D., Graff, C.: UCI machine learning repository (2017). http://archive.ics.uci.edu/ml
10. Eroglu, D.Y., Akcan, U.: An adapted ant colony optimization for feature selection. Appl. Artif. Intell. **38**(1), 2335098 (2024). https://doi.org/10.1080/08839514.2024.2335098
11. Fu, Y., Liu, X., Sarkar, S., Wu, T.: Gaussian mixture model with feature selection: an embedded approach. Comput. Ind. Eng. **152**, 107000 (2021). https://doi.org/10.1016/j.cie.2020.107000. https://www.sciencedirect.com/science/article/pii/S0360835220306707
12. Grandchamp, E., Abadi, M., Alata, O.: A pareto front approach for feature selection. In: Proceedings of the 5th International Conference on Pattern Recognition Applications and Methods, ICPRAM 2016, pp. 334–342. SCITEPRESS - Science and Technology Publications, Lda (2016). https://doi.org/10.5220/0005752603340342
13. Gütlein, M., Frank, E., Hall, M., Karwath, A.: Large-scale attribute selection using wrappers. In: 2009 IEEE Symposium on Computational Intelligence and Data Mining, pp. 332 – 339 (2009). https://doi.org/10.1109/CIDM.2009.4938668
14. Hancer, E., Xue, B., Zhang, M., Karaboga, D., Akay, B.: Pareto front feature selection based on artificial bee colony optimization. Inf. Sci. **422**(C), 462–479 (2018). https://doi.org/10.1016/j.ins.2017.09.028
15. Hashemi, A., Bagher Dowlatshahi, M., Nezamabadi-pour, H.: An efficient pareto-based feature selection algorithm for multi-label classification. Inf. Sci. **581**, 428–447 (2021). https://doi.org/10.1016/j.ins.2021.09.052. https://www.sciencedirect.com/science/article/pii/S002002552100983X

16. Hashemi, A., Bagher Dowlatshahi, M., Nezamabadi-pour, H.: A pareto-based ensemble of feature selection algorithms. Expert Syst. Appl. **180**, 115130 (2021). https://doi.org/10.1016/j.eswa.2021.115130. https://www.sciencedirect.com/science/article/pii/S0957417421005716
17. Kabir, M.M., Shahjahan, M., Murase, K.: A new hybrid ant colony optimization algorithm for feature selection. Expert Syst. Appl. **39**(3), 3747–3763 (2012). https://doi.org/10.1016/j.eswa.2011.09.073. https://www.sciencedirect.com/science/article/pii/S0957417411013960
18. Ke, L., Feng, Z., Xu, Z., Shang, K., Wang, Y.: A multiobjective ACO algorithm for rough feature selection. In: 2010 Second Pacific-Asia Conference on Circuits, Communications and System, vol. 1, pp. 207–210 (2010). https://doi.org/10.1109/PACCS.2010.5627071
19. Lallouet, N., Cazenave, T., Enderli, C.: Pareto-NRPA: a novel Monte-Carlo search algorithm for multi-objective optimization (2025). https://doi.org/10.48550/arXiv.2507.19109
20. Murphy, K.P.: Machine Learning: A Probabilistic Perspective. The MIT Press, Cambridge (2012)
21. Paniri, M., Dowlatshahi, M.B., Nezamabadi-pour, H.: MLACO: A multi-label feature selection algorithm based on ant colony optimization. Knowl.-Based Syst. **192**, 105285 (2020). https://doi.org/10.1016/j.knosys.2019.105285. https://www.sciencedirect.com/science/article/pii/S0950705119305805
22. Tabakhi, S., Moradi, P., Akhlaghian, F.: An unsupervised feature selection algorithm based on ant colony optimization. Eng. Appl. Artif. Intell. **32**, 112–123 (2014). https://doi.org/10.1016/j.engappai.2014.03.007. https://www.sciencedirect.com/science/article/pii/S0952197614000621
23. Villani, C.: Topics in Optimal Transportation. Graduate studies in mathematics, American Mathematical Society (2003). https://books.google.pl/books?id=idyFAwAAQBAJ
24. Wilcoxon, F.: Individual comparisons by ranking methods. Biometr. Bull. **1**(6), 80–83 (1945). http://www.jstor.org/stable/3001968
25. Zhang, Q., Li, H.: MOEA/D: a multiobjective evolutionary algorithm based on decomposition. IEEE Trans. Evol. Comput. **11**(6), 712–731 (2007). https://doi.org/10.1109/TEVC.2007.892759

Heterogeneous Visco-Elastic Cyber-Physical Swarm Exploration Algorithm in an Unknown Environment

Fatemeh Rekabi Bana[1(✉)], Mazen Bahaidarah[2], and Farshad Arvin[1]

[1] Department of Computer Science, Durham University, Durham, UK
`fatemeh.rekabi-bana@durham.ac.uk`
[2] Department of Electrical and Electronics Engineering, King Abdulaziz University,
Jeddah, Saudi Arabia

Abstract. This paper presents a heterogeneous viscoelastic cyber-physical swarm exploration algorithm for navigating robot groups in unknown, obstacle-filled environments. The framework integrates physical agents aware of a target coordinate with a surrounding layer of cyber agents that process environmental measurements and prevent collisions through viscoelastic interactions. Built on a structured, stable, and robust formulation, the method guarantees asymptotic stability of the collective motion and robustness to bounded perturbations. A hybrid control strategy enables agents to switch between normal operation and stagnation-recovery modes, helping the swarm avoid deadlock, maintain cohesion, and pass through narrow spaces without prior map knowledge. Monte Carlo simulations show that the algorithm consistently achieves alignment, stable cohesion, and collision-free exploration under sensing noise, varied swarm compositions, and different target coordinates in an unknown maze. The results demonstrate that the cyber-physical viscoelastic architecture provides adaptability and resilience, offering a scalable and analytically validated approach to autonomous exploration.

1 Introduction

Swarm intelligence offers a scalable and robust paradigm for coordinating large groups of simple agents, inspired by collective behaviours in nature such as bird flocks, fish schools, and insect colonies [17,22]. Although bio-inspired algorithms show adaptability for exploration, monitoring, and distributed decision-making, practical deployment is challenged by limited onboard resources, uncertain interactions, and the difficulty of providing formal guarantees for stability and robustness [14,26]. Prior works modelled biological interactions and flocking behaviours [6,20,29], yet their nonlinear dynamics hinder analytical validation. Other heuristic, fuzzy, or reinforcement-learning-based approaches [2,21] often lack tractable stability guarantees. Conversely, multi-agent system (MAS) control provides rigorous tools such as Lyapunov theory and graph-theoretic analysis [9,18,24,25], although these methods become computationally demanding

R. Groß et al. (Eds.): ANTS 2026, LNCS 16515, pp. 367–375, 2026.
https://doi.org/10.1007/978-3-032-26123-6_31

for large-scale swarms. Viscoelastic interaction models offer a bridge between these paradigms by enabling structured coordination through simple local rules [13,19], but previous active-elastic-sheet (AES) methods exhibit marginal stability and performance variability in heterogeneous settings [3,4,31]. Addressing these limitations is essential for reliable cyber-physical swarms in unknown environments. Swarm robotics includes bio-inspired foraging, flocking, and pheromone-based coordination [10,11], which offer decentralisation and scalability but limited stability guarantees [7]. MAS approaches provide structured control and communication [28,30], although their complexity restricts application to large swarms of simple robots [1]. Statistical and continuum-based models, including Fokker–Planck formulations [16], support macroscopic predictions but do not ensure agent-level stability. Viscoelastic swarm models have recently gained interest for enabling simple physics-inspired local coordination [12,19]. While analytical stability under heterogeneity has been investigated [23], their behaviour in complex environments remains largely unexplored. Robustness analyses commonly rely on Monte Carlo simulations [15] and complementary sensitivity studies [27], providing key insights for reliable real-world deployment. In this paper, we propose a heterogeneous viscoelastic cyber-physical swarm exploration algorithm that ensures stable collective motion, building on [5,23]. The method assigns only a subset of agents to track target points, while others coordinate through local viscoelastic couplings. Although [23] provides explicit parameter conditions for asymptotic stability and ISS under bounded perturbations and small delays, its evaluation was restricted to simple, obstacle-free settings. The main contributions of this paper are: (i) extending that algorithm to coordinate a heterogeneous swarm of physical and cyber agents in a maze environment, and (ii) enabling physical robots to share environmental measurements through distributed computational cyber nodes. Extensive Monte Carlo simulations demonstrate robustness to sensing noise and environmental uncertainties, supporting exploration and navigation in unknown workspaces.

2   Cyber-Physical Swarm Search

The cyber-physical swarm search framework extends the viscoelastic coordination model for exploring maze-like environments without prior maps. The swarm consists of physical agents, aware of target coordinates, and cyber agents forming a distributed sensory layer for obstacle avoidance. Cyber agents process environmental data from physical agents' sensors to estimate proximity to walls and exert viscoelastic virtual forces that prevent collisions and guide motion. This coupling improves efficiency, adaptability, and robustness over map-based or potential-field methods [8]. The viscoelastic formulation ensures smooth attraction-repulsion transitions. Under stagnation, physical agents apply a corrective goal-directed term, while cyber agents switch to an exploration mode with a small stochastic velocity to escape deadlock. As a result, the swarm maintains cohesion and achieves effective target search.

3   Collective Motion Control in Cyber-Physical Swarm Search

This section presents the collective motion behaviour for target search and navigation in unknown environments. Each agent follows a second-order model with acceleration commands from agent-agent and agent-environment interactions.

3.1   Agent Dynamics and Interaction Model

For a swarm of N_{ag} agents, agent i evolves as

$$\ddot{\mathbf{r}}_i = \mathbf{F}_i, \quad \mathbf{F}_i = \sum_{j \in \mathcal{N}_i} \mathbf{f}_{ij} + \mathbf{f}_{oi}, \quad \mathbf{f}_{ij} = -k_{ij}(\mathbf{r}_{ij} - \mathbf{l}_{ij}) - c_{ij}(\dot{\mathbf{r}}_{ij} - \dot{\mathbf{l}}_{ij}), \tag{1}$$

where $\mathbf{r}_i \in \mathbb{R}^2$ is the position, $\mathcal{N}_i$ the neighbourhood, $\mathbf{f}_{ij}$ the viscoelastic interaction, and $\mathbf{f}_{oi}$ the environment/target interaction. Also, $\mathbf{r}_{ij} = \mathbf{r}_j - \mathbf{r}_i$ and desired offset $\mathbf{l}_{ij}$; $k_{ij}, c_{ij} \in \mathbb{R}^{2\times 2}$ are stiffness and damping.

3.2   Environmental Interaction Force for Cyber and Physical Agents

Cyber agents interact with the environment via a viscoelastic virtual force $\mathbf{f}_{oi} \in \mathbb{R}^2$ decomposed along local wall normal/tangent directions for obstacles $l \in \mathcal{V}_i$:

$$\mathbf{f}_{oi} = \sum_{l \in \mathcal{V}_i} \left(-k_n d_n^l \mathbf{n}_i^l - c_n(\dot{\mathbf{r}}_i \cdot \mathbf{n}_i^l)\mathbf{n}_i^l - k_t(\dot{\mathbf{r}}_i \cdot \mathbf{t}_i^l)\mathbf{t}_i^l \right), \tag{2}$$

where d_n^l is the shortest distance to the wall, $\mathbf{n}_i^l$ the unit normal, $\mathbf{t}_i^l$ the unit tangent, and k_n, c_n, k_t regulate collision avoidance and wall-following. For physical agents, the attraction toward target points is $\mathbf{f}_{tgt,i} = -\gamma_i^k(\mathbf{r}_i - \mathbf{l}_i) - \gamma_i^c(\dot{\mathbf{r}}_i - \dot{\mathbf{l}}_i) + \ddot{\mathbf{l}}_i$ with gains γ_i^k, γ_i^c.

3.3   Switching Between Normal and Stagnation Modes

Under normal conditions, both physical and cyber agents follow the viscoelastic law. Stagnation is detected by

$$\mathrm{Stg}(k) = \begin{cases} 1, & \text{if } (C_1 \vee C_2 \vee C_3) \wedge C_4, \\ 0, & \text{otherwise,} \end{cases} \quad \begin{cases} C_1 : \|v_c(k)\| < \varepsilon_p, \\ C_2 : \|p(k)\| < \varepsilon_p, \\ C_3 : c_{\mathrm{mov}}(k) \le 0.1, \\ C_4 : S_c(k) \ge T_s, . \end{cases} \tag{3}$$

with $v_c(k) = \|\mathbf{c}(k) - \mathbf{c}(k-1)\|$, $p(k) = d_{tgt}^c(k-1) - d_{tgt}^c(k)$, $d_{tgt}^c(k) = \|\mathbf{c}(k) - \mathbf{p}_t\|$, and $c_{\mathrm{mov}}(k) = \|\mathbf{c}(k) - \mathbf{m}(k)\|$, $\mathbf{m}(k) = \frac{1}{20}\sum_{j=k-20}^{k} \mathbf{c}(j)$. When stagnation is detected, control switches:

1) Stagnation in Physical Agents:

$$\mathbf{f}_{\mathrm{tgt},i}^* = \kappa_i \left\| \frac{\mathbf{f}_{\mathrm{tgt},i}}{\|\mathbf{f}_{\mathrm{tgt},i}\|} \cdot \frac{\mathbf{t}_i^{cls}}{\|\mathbf{t}_i^{cls}\|} \right\| \mathbf{f}_{\mathrm{tgt},i}, \tag{4}$$

where $\mathbf{t}_i^{cls}$ is the unit tangent of the closest boundary and $\kappa_i \in \mathbb{R}$.

2) Stagnation in Cyber Agents: with resultant viscoelastic force $\mathbf{F}_{\text{total},i} \in \mathbb{R}^2$, exploration gain $\beta = 0.05$, and random direction $\mathbf{d}_{explr,i} = \begin{bmatrix} \cos(\alpha_i) \\ \sin(\alpha_i) \end{bmatrix}$ with $\alpha_i = \Delta_\alpha(2\xi_i - 1)$ where $\xi_i \sim \mathcal{U}(0,1)$ and $\Delta_\alpha = 30°$. These ensure escape from deadlock while preserving cohesion.

3.4   Collective Motion Dynamics

Let $\mathbf{R} = col\{\mathbf{r}_i\} \in \mathbb{R}^{2N_{ag}}$, $\dot{\mathbf{R}} = col\{\dot{\mathbf{r}}_i\}$, and $\mathbf{U}^* = col\{\mathbf{F}_i^*\}$. With desired geometry $\mathbf{L} = col\{\mathbf{l}_i\}$, then $\mathbf{E} = \mathbf{R} - \mathbf{L}$ and $\dot{\mathbf{E}} = \dot{\mathbf{R}} - \dot{\mathbf{L}}$. The collective input is

$$\mathbf{U}^* = \left[-(\mathbf{K}_{\mathcal{G}} + \mathbf{\Gamma}) \; -\mathbf{C}_{\mathcal{G}} \right] \begin{bmatrix} \mathbf{E} \\ \dot{\mathbf{E}} \end{bmatrix} + \ddot{\mathbf{L}} + \mathbf{F}_o^*, \text{ where } \mathbf{F}_o^* = col\{\mathbf{f}_{oi}^*\} \text{ is the environmental}$$

term after switching. With $\mathcal{G}$ a static, undirected, connected graph and Laplacian $\mathcal{L}_{\mathcal{G}}$, we have $\mathbf{K}_{\mathcal{G}} = \mathbf{k}_s \otimes \mathcal{L}_{\mathcal{G}}$, $\mathbf{C}_{\mathcal{G}} = \mathbf{c}_s^{\mathcal{G}} + diag\{\gamma_i^c\}$, $\mathbf{\Gamma} = diag\{\gamma_i^k\}$, with $\mathbf{k}_s \in \mathbb{R}^{2 \times 2}$ and $\mathbf{c}_s^{\mathcal{G}} \in \mathbb{R}^{2N_{ag} \times 2N_{ag}}$. The collective dynamics are

$$\begin{bmatrix} \dot{\mathbf{R}} \\ \ddot{\mathbf{R}} \end{bmatrix} = \mathbf{A} \begin{bmatrix} \mathbf{R} \\ \dot{\mathbf{R}} \end{bmatrix} + \mathbf{B}\left(-(\mathbf{K}_{\mathcal{G}} + \mathbf{\Gamma})\mathbf{E} - \mathbf{C}_{\mathcal{G}}\dot{\mathbf{E}} + \ddot{\mathbf{L}} + \mathbf{F}_o^* \right), \tag{5}$$

$$\mathbf{A} = \begin{bmatrix} [\mathbf{0}]_{2N_{ag} \times 2N_{ag}} & \mathbb{I}_{2N_{ag}} \\ [\mathbf{0}]_{2N_{ag} \times 2N_{ag}} & [\mathbf{0}]_{2N_{ag} \times 2N_{ag}} \end{bmatrix}, \quad \mathbf{B} = \begin{bmatrix} [\mathbf{0}]_{2N_{ag} \times 2N_{ag}} \\ \mathbb{I}_{2N_{ag}} \end{bmatrix}. \tag{6}$$

Here, $\mathbf{F}_o^*$ aggregates normal/tangential wall forces and stochastic exploration (for cyber agents) and the perturbed target force (for physical agents), acting as bounded perturbations that preserve collective stability within the Lyapunov framework of the viscoelastic model.

3.5   Cyber-Physical Swarm Coordination

Define the weighted state error $\mathbf{S} = \begin{bmatrix} \Lambda & [\mathbf{0}]_{2N_{ag} \times 2N_{ag}} \\ [\mathbf{0}]_{2N_{ag} \times 2N_{ag}} & \mathcal{Q} \end{bmatrix} \begin{bmatrix} \mathbf{E} \\ \dot{\mathbf{E}} \end{bmatrix}$, with $\Lambda, \mathcal{Q} \in \mathbb{R}^{2N_{ag} \times 2N_{ag}} > 0$. Using (5), results $\dot{\mathbf{S}} = \underbrace{\begin{bmatrix} [\mathbf{0}]_{2N_{ag} \times 2N_{ag}} & \Lambda \\ -\mathcal{Q}(\mathbf{K}_{\mathcal{G}} + \mathbf{\Gamma}) & -\mathcal{Q}\mathbf{C}_{\mathcal{G}} \end{bmatrix}}_{\mathcal{A}_s} \begin{bmatrix} \mathbf{E} \\ \dot{\mathbf{E}} \end{bmatrix} +$

$\Delta_{\mathcal{E}}$, where $\Delta_{\mathcal{E}} = \mathbf{BF}_o^*$. A Lyapunov candidate ensuring asymptotic stability for the unperturbed system is $V = \frac{1}{2}\mathbf{S}^T\mathbf{PS}$, $\mathbf{P} = \begin{bmatrix} (\mathbf{K}_{\mathcal{G}} + \mathbf{\Gamma})^{-1} & \Lambda^{-1} \\ \Lambda^{-1} & \mathcal{Q}^{-1} \end{bmatrix}$, [23] with $\mathbf{P}$ symmetric positive definite under the same sufficient conditions as [23]. Its derivative is $\dot{V} = \mathbf{S}^T\mathbf{P}\dot{\mathbf{S}} = \mathbf{S}^T\mathbf{P}\mathcal{A}_s\mathbf{S} + \mathbf{S}^T \begin{bmatrix} \Lambda & \mathbf{0} \\ \mathbf{0} & \mathcal{Q} \end{bmatrix} \mathbf{P}\Delta_{\mathcal{E}}$. For $\Delta_{\mathcal{E}} = \mathbf{0}$, the first term

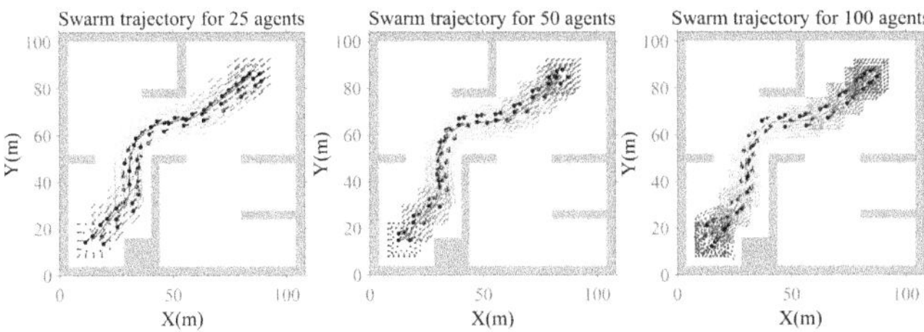

Fig. 1. Swarm trajectories for varying swarm sizes. Solid lines show the mean path with variability bounds; black markers are physical robots and coloured quivers are cyber agents. (Color figure online)

is negative definite, yielding asymptotic convergence to $\mathbf{S} = \mathbf{0}$ [23]. For $\Delta_{\mathcal{E}} \neq \mathbf{0}$, treat $\mathbf{F}_o^*$ as a bounded perturbation $\|\Delta_{\mathcal{E}}\| \leq \delta_{\max}$ so that, following [23], if

$$\|\mathbf{S}\| > \mathcal{X}(\|\Delta_{\mathcal{E}}\|) = \frac{1}{(1-\varepsilon)\sigma_{\max}(\mathcal{A}_s)}\|\Delta_{\mathcal{E}}\|, \quad 0 < \varepsilon < 1, \tag{7}$$

then $\dot{V} < 0$ for all $\mathbf{S} \neq 0$, and the system is Input-to-State Stable (ISS) with respect to $\Delta_{\mathcal{E}}$. Hence, environmental and exploration-induced perturbations do not compromise the stability of the cyber-physical swarm, which remains robust, collision-free, and cohesive in unstructured environments.

4   Results and Discussion

This section presents the simulation results used to evaluate the proposed coordination algorithm. Two scenarios were tested. In the first, the swarm size varies while the number of physical agents remains fixed, illustrating the role of cyber agents in navigation and collision avoidance. In the second, the swarm size is fixed and the number of physical agents varies to assess performance as the ratio of physical to cyber agents changes. The simulations were performed using swarm sizes of $N_{ag} \in \{25, 50, 100\}$ with a fixed number of four physical agents, and alternatively with $N_{Pag} \in \{2, 10, 20\}$ while keeping $N_{ag} = 100$. The interaction parameters were set to a neighbourhood radius of $4\,\mathrm{m}$, a spring constant of $k = 0.05$, an attraction coefficient of $\gamma = 0.075$, a sensing radius of $2\,\mathrm{m}$ with measurement noise of $\pm 5\%$, and an arena of size $100\,\mathrm{m} \times 100\,\mathrm{m}$.

Each physical agent uses a $120°$ range sensor with measurement noise. For each scenario, 100 Monte Carlo simulations were conducted. The first set of trajectories, shown in Fig. 1, demonstrates successful navigation for all swarm sizes. As seen in Fig. 1, larger numbers of cyber agents provide stronger protection and more conservative motion near obstacles. Alignment and cohesion [3] are shown in Fig. 2. In all cases, alignment stabilises after roughly 200 time steps, and cohesion remains bounded, although transient differences appear for 100 agents. The second scenario varies the number of physical agents while the total swarm size is fixed. Figure 3 shows that increasing physical agents reduces the cyber-agent protection layer, allowing robots to move closer to obstacles,

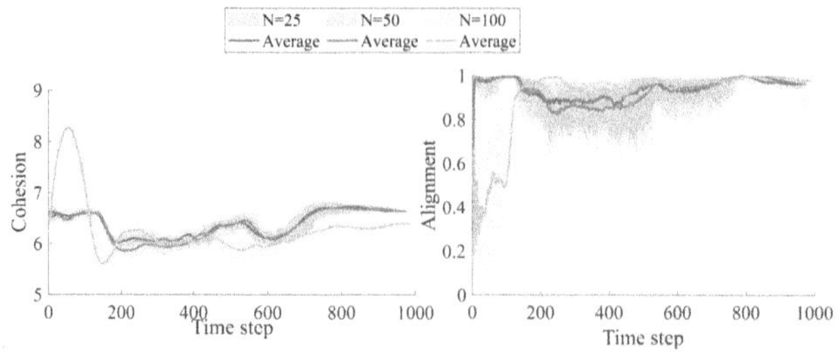

Fig. 2. Alignment and cohesion indices for the first scenario.

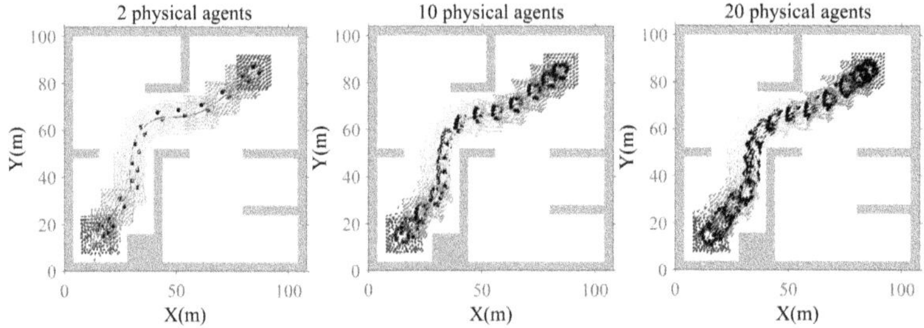

Fig. 3. Swarm trajectories for varying numbers of physical agents.

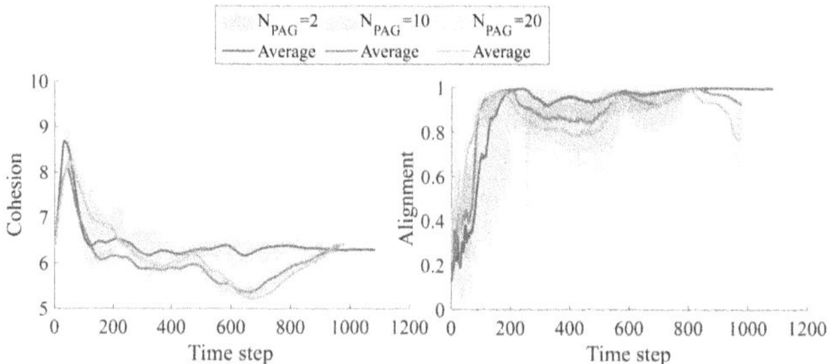

Fig. 4. Alignment and cohesion in the second scenario.

particularly at corners. Nevertheless, Fig. 4 confirms that alignment and cohesion remain effectively unchanged, indicating reliable collective behaviour when the physical-agent ratio is below 0.2. To evaluate performance in different maze regions, both scenarios were repeated for the target [68 25]. As shown in Fig. 5, swarm size strongly affects clearance in tight U-turn sections; smaller swarms show reduced safety margins. The trajectories for different numbers of physical agents (Fig. 6) demonstrate that the proposed framework continues to guide the swarm through narrow corridors without collisions.   Overall, the results show that the cyber-physical viscoelastic framework ensures stable maze navigation, maintains alignment and cohesion, and adapts reliably to changes in swarm size, physical-agent ratio, and target location.

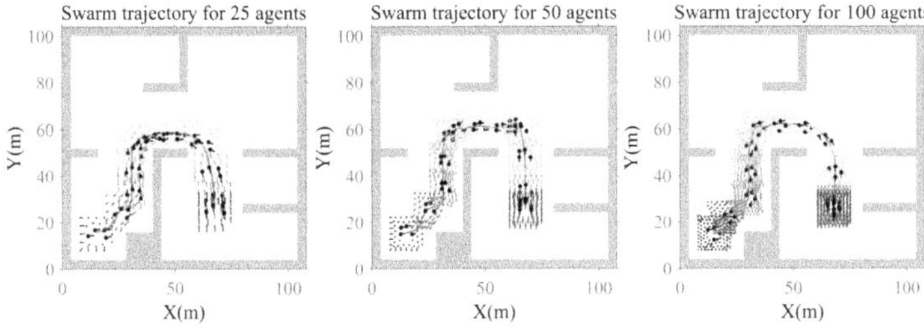

Fig. 5. Swarm trajectories for varying swarm sizes (second target).

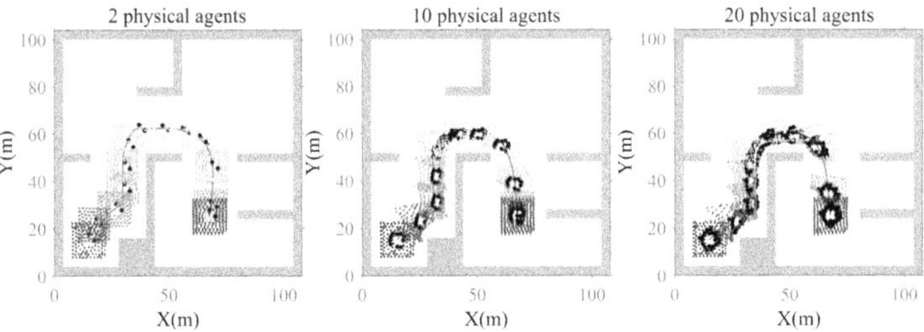

Fig. 6. Swarm trajectories for varying physical-agent numbers (second target).

5 Conclusion

This paper presented a viscoelastic swarm coordination framework that enables heterogeneous physical-cyber teams to navigate unknown environments. Cyber agents process local measurements to provide environmental perception, while physical agents follow viscoelastic interactions for collective motion. Two simulation scenarios evaluated the effects of swarm size and the number of physical agents. The Monte Carlo results showed that the algorithm reliably navigates an unknown maze under sensing uncertainties, with the number of cyber agents strongly influencing safety near sharp corners. In contrast, the number of physical agents has a limited impact provided their fraction remains around 20%. Although the framework demonstrates effective coordination in complex, unmapped environments, future work will focus on systematic optimisation of stagnation detection and recovery using machine learning and parameter tuning.

Disclosure of Interests. The authors have no competing interests to declare.

References

1. Alqudsi, Y., Makaraci, M.: Exploring advancements and emerging trends in robotic swarm coordination and control of swarm flying robots: a review. Proc. Inst. Mech. Eng. Part C: J. Mech. Eng. Sci. (2025)
2. Azzam, R., Boiko, I., Zweiri, Y.: Swarm cooperative navigation using centralized training and decentralized execution. Drones (3) (2023)

3. Bahaidarah, M., Bana, F.R., Turgut, A.E., Marjanovic, O., Arvin, F.: Optimization of a self-organized collective motion in a robotic swarm. In: Swarm Intelligence (2022)
4. Bahaidarah, M., Marjanovic, O., Rekabi-Bana, F., Arvin, F.: An optimised robot swarm flocking with genetic algorithm. In: IEEE International Conference on Mechatronics and Automation (ICMA) (2023)
5. Bahaidarah, M., Rekabi-Bana, F., Marjanovic, O., Arvin, F.: Swarm flocking using optimisation for a self-organised collective motion. Swarm Evol. Comput. (2024)
6. Berlinger, F., Gauci, M., Nagpal, R.: Implicit coordination for 3d underwater collective behaviors in a fish-inspired robot swarm. Sci. Rob. **6**(50) (2021)
7. Bijli, M.K., Verma, P., Singh, A.P.: A systematic review on the potency of swarm intelligent nanorobots in the medical field. Swarm Evol. Comput. (2024)
8. Brambilla, M., Ferrante, E., Birattari, M., Dorigo, M.: Swarm robotics: a review from the swarm engineering perspective. Swarm Intell. (2013)
9. Cui, Y., Chen, Y., Yang, D., Shu, Z., Huang, T., Gong, X.: Resilient formation tracking of spacecraft swarm against actuation attacks: a distributed Lyapunov-based model predictive approach. IEEE Trans. Syst. Man Cybern. Syst. (2023)
10. Dratnal, M., Danys, L., Martinek, R.: Bio-inspired optimization methods for visible light communication: a comprehensive review. Artif. Intell. Rev. (2025)
11. Duan, H., Huo, M., Fan, Y.: From animal collective behaviors to swarm robotic cooperation. Natl. Sci. Rev. (2023)
12. Eguchi, M., Nishimura, M., Yoshida, S., Hiraki, T.: Robot swarm control based on smoothed particle hydrodynamics for obstacle-unaware navigation. In: 2024 IEEE/RSJ International Conference on Intelligent Robots and Systems (IROS) (2024)
13. Ferrante, E., Turgut, A.E., Dorigo, M., Huepe, C.: Collective motion dynamics of active solids and active crystals. New J. Phys. (2013)
14. Hamann, H.: Swarm Robotics: A Formal Approach. Springer Cham (2018)
15. Janila, J., Lenin Fred, A.: Multi-robot assisted communication service in disaster areas using fractional chameleon swarm algorithm. In: Communications in Statistics-Simulation and Computation (2025)
16. Lin, R., Kim, S., Egerstedt, M.: Heterogeneous collaborative pursuit via coverage control driven by Fokker-Planck equations. IEEE Trans. Rob. (2025)
17. Long, N.K., Sammut, K., Sgarioto, D., Garratt, M., Abbass, H.A.: A comprehensive review of shepherding as a bio-inspired swarm-robotics guidance approach. IEEE Trans. Emerg. Topics Comput. Intell. (2020)
18. Maldonado, D., Cruz, E., Torres, J.A., Cruz, P.J., Benitez, S.D.P.G.: Multi-agent systems: a survey about its components, framework and workflow. IEEE Access (2024)
19. McGuire, L., Schuler, T., Otte, M., Sofge, D.: Viscoelastic fluid-inspired swarm behavior to reduce susceptibility to local minima: the chain siphon algorithm. IEEE Rob. Autom. Lett. (2021)
20. Na, S., et al.: Bio-inspired artificial pheromone system for swarm robotics applications. Adapt. Behav. (2021)
21. Nhu, T., Hung, P.D., Ho, V.A., Ngo, T.D.: Fuzzy-based distributed behavioral control with wall-following strategy for swarm navigation in arbitrary-shaped environments. IEEE Access (2021)
22. Parpinelli, R.S., Plichoski, G.F., Silva, R.S.D., Narloch, P.H.: A review of techniques for online control of parameters in swarm intelligence and evolutionary computation algorithms. Int. J. Bio-Insp. Comput. (2019)

23. Rekabi-Bana, F., Bahaidarah, M., Marjanovic, O., Arvin, F.: Lyapunov stability-driven control algorithm for heterogeneous multi-robot coordination. IEEE Trans. Autom. Sci. Eng. (2025)
24. Rekabi-Bana, F., Shirazi, F.A., Sadigh, M.J.: Distributed nonlinear h_∞ control algorithm for multi-agent quadrotor formation flying. ISA Trans. (2020)
25. Rekabi-Bana, F., Shirazi, F.A., Sadigh, M.J., Saadat, M.: Distributed output feedback nonlinear h_∞ formation control algorithm for heterogeneous aerial robotic teams. Rob. Auton. Syst. (2021)
26. Shi, P., Yan, B.: A survey on intelligent control for multiagent systems. IEEE Trans. Syst. Man Cybern. Syst. (2020)
27. Smith, R.C.: Uncertainty quantification: theory, implementation, and applications (2024)
28. Ulrich, J., et al.: Autonomous tracking of honey bee behaviors over long-term periods with cooperating robots. Sci. Rob. (2024)
29. Wang, X., Lu, J.: Collective behaviors through social interactions in bird flocks. IEEE Circ. Syst. Maga. (2019)
30. Xu, L., Almahri, S., Mak, S., Brintrup, A.: Multi-agent systems and foundation models enable autonomous supply chains: opportunities and challenges. IFAC-PapersOnLine (2024)
31. Zheng, Y., Huepe, C., Han, Z.: Experimental capabilities and limitations of a position-based control algorithm for swarm robotics. Adapt. Behav. (2022)

How Swarms Differ: Challenges in Collective Behaviour Comparison

André Fialho Jesus[1,2]([✉]) [iD] and Jonas Kuckling[1,2,3] [iD]

[1] Department of Computer and Information Science, University of Konstanz, Konstanz, Germany
{andre.jesus,jonas.kuckling}@uni-konstanz.de
[2] Centre for the Advanced Study of Collective Behaviour, University of Konstanz, Konstanz, Germany
[3] Zukunftskolleg, University of Konstanz, Konstanz, Germany

Abstract. Collective behaviours often need to be expressed through numerical features, e.g., for classification or imitation learning. This problem is often addressed by proposing an ad-hoc feature set for a particular swarm behaviour context, usually without further consideration of the solution's resilience outside of the conceived context. Yet, the development of automatic methods to design swarm behaviours is dependent on the ability to measure quantitatively the similarity of swarm behaviours. Hence, we investigate the impact of feature sets for collective behaviours. We select swarm feature sets and similarity measures from prior swarm robotics works, which mainly considered a narrow behavioural context and assess their robustness. We demonstrate that the interplay of feature set and similarity measure makes some combinations more suitable to distinguish groups of similar behaviours. We also propose a self-organised map-based approach to identify regions of the feature space where behaviours cannot be easily distinguished.

1 Introduction

A central problem of automatic design methods for swarm robotics applications is how to measure the similarity between different collective behaviours. In particular, the similarity between collective behaviours has been explored in the context of novelty search [6], classification [16] and imitation learning [1,5]. Yang et al. [16] propose a set of swarm features and use several machine learning methods to recognise collective behaviours, including flocking and random walk. Gomes and Christensen [6] provide two measures of swarm behaviour similarity. Alharthi et al. [1] provide a set of swarm features to an evolutionary algorithm tasked to correctly reconstruct the behaviour tree that simulated the original collective behaviour. The same authors extend the previous approach

---

Supplementary Information The online version contains supplementary material available at https://doi.org/10.1007/978-3-032-26123-6_32.

Table 1. Feature sets considered in this work.

ALHARTHI2022 [1]: maximum swarm shift • center of mass • swarm mode index • longest path • maximum radius • average local density • average nearest neighbour distance • beta index. GOMES2013 [6]: boid x • boid y • boid vx • boid vy. YANG2023 [16]: collision count • flock density • grouping • straggler count • order • subgroup count. GHARBI2023 [5]: neighbour shortest distances.

---

by proposing a new set of environmental imprint features [2]. Gharbi et al. [5] proposed a swarm feature set for inverse reinforcement learning that was reused in a similar context in a follow-up paper by Szpirer et al. [14].

While humans can recognise different collective behaviours with relative ease [16], automatic methods need to rely on numerical features describing the collective behaviour (e.g., [1,5,16]). Usually, the feature sets are developed in an ad-hoc fashion, targeting a particular behavioural context. As a result, it is unclear if these feature sets hold beyond the context in which they are proposed. This limits their usability in fully automatic design [3]. Consequently, we explore different ad-hoc feature sets and their implications in comparing collective behaviours. In particular, we focus on computing similarity (or distance) measures and classification. Similarity measures provide us with an immediate numerical value that can be used in fully automatic methods. Classification addresses a slightly different aspect of behavioural similarity. By focusing on the differences between behaviour classes, it highlights the feature set's discriminative power.

2 Methodology

Collective Behaviours. We consider six collective behaviours that are typically associated with spatial organisation and coordinated motion [13]. The behaviours are executed on a swarm of massless points in an otherwise empty environment. We control the initial placement of the agents and subsequently the execution of the (deterministic) behaviours through a random seed. The agents' speeds are kept constant to facilitate the comparison of behaviours. We consider two variants of the flocking coordinated motion: the *Reynolds* boids model [11] and the *Vicsek* model [15]. For spatial organisation behaviours, we consider *aggregation* (inspired by Kaiser et al. [7]), *dispersion* (inspired by Kaiser et al. [7]), and two variants of random walk: *ballistic motion* and *Brownian motion* (following Kegeleirs et al. [8]). See the supplementary video for the example trajectories of the collective behaviours. In terms of similarity, we expect that the flocking behaviours are identified as highly similar to each other. *Aggregation* should have a moderate similarity degree to either flocking behaviour, and the two random walks and *dispersion* should, for the most part, be dissimilar to them.

Feature Sets. We utilise the previously defined collective behaviours to compute and extract four feature sets from the literature (see Table 1). We hypothesise that different feature sets yield measurable trade-offs in the similarity assessment and classification. For the full details of the features, please consult the original sources. "Alharthi2022" [1, 2] offers a comprehensive set of eight swarm-level features and has been previously used to assess the similarity of collective behaviours. "Gomes2013" [6] offers a set of agent-level features, based on their sensor and actuator information, which has been used to derive generic measures of collective behaviour. "Yang2023" [16] comprises six swarm-level features, which have been used to classify collective behaviours of boid-like particles. Note that in "Yang2023", we opted to discard the diffusion feature as we were unable to find a definitive source on how to compute it. Lastly, we consider "Gharbi2023" [5, 14], a set of environment-based agent-level features. We acknowledge that the construction of this feature set degenerates to only inter-robot distances in our environment. We opted, however, to include this feature set as a lower baseline to put the performance of other feature sets into context.

Similarity Assessment. We consider the impact of the swarm features on four similarity measurements: cosine similarity, Euclidean distance, combined state count [6], and sampled average state [6]. *Cosine similarity* is a standard measure to quantify similarity using vector representations. Due to the construction of our features, the cosine similarity scores are between $[0, 1]$, where 1 refers to perfectly equal features. Likewise, the *Euclidean distance* is another standard measure of similarity. As a distance measure, two identical feature vectors will have a distance of 0. The *combined state count* method (see [6]) discretises the swarm feature set (describing the state space) and counts the number of times any swarm member is in a given state. When the behaviours are identical, it leads to a score of 0 and 1 when they do not have anything in common. The *sampled average state* method (see [6]) summarises each feature by averaging its value over all robots and splitting it over several time windows. Since it is a distance measure, the closer to 0, the more similar the behaviours are.

Explainable Classification. The similarity and distance measures do not provide insights towards which features are important to distinguish behaviours or why certain behaviours score high similarity while being visually distinct. Therefore, we consider a explainable classification algorithm to gain further insights into these questions. In particular, we employ a self-organising map (SOM) for classification. Self-organising maps [9, 10] are a type of prototype-based classifiers trained through the competitive learning paradigm [12]. The map topology allows us to define an inter-node distance between units. During the training phase, the *best matching unit* for each training sample is selected. The weights associated with the best-matching unit and its neighbours are adjusted towards the training sample. After training, the nodes' classification labels are extracted according to the "majority voting" strategy [4]. In case of a tie for the node label choice, one of the tied labels is selected randomly, and when a node has no samples assigned to it, the most commonly assigned class label amongst the SOM nodes is used as the default class.

3   Experimental Setup

All behaviours are executed in a 500px × 500px environment that can either be bounded (agents cannot pass beyond the boundaries) or unbounded (agents that pass beyond a boundary appear on the other side). For more behaviour simulation details, consult the supplementary video. We collect data for each behaviour in three settings: 40b with 40 agents in a bounded environment, 30b with 30 agents in the same bounded environment and 40u with 40 agents in an unbounded environment. In each setting, each behaviour is simulated 50 times, from different initial positions (as defined by the random seed). We minimise initialisation artefacts that can lead to noisy classification samples by removing the first 250 steps of each simulation. We compute the four feature sets for every swarm state. As we consider varying swarm sizes, leading to feature set vectors of different sizes (using "Gomes2013" and "Gharbi2023"), we perform a random subsampling schema and only consider 30 agents' features for the experimental configurations 40b and 40u. The dataset and the experimental setup are available at https://kondata.uni-konstanz.de/radar/en/dataset/18h2w28a9d6sm1eq and https://github.com/alfjesus3/swarm_behaviour_sim.

The experimental setup for the similarity assessment and classification follows. The threshold of the swarm mode index feature in the "Alharthi2022" is set to 0.5. The discretisation in the *combined state count* measure is set to low/medium/high with a threshold of 1×10^{-2} as suggested in the original paper [6]. The *sampled average state* measure uses a sampling window of 10 to allow for a averaging of 1 simulation second. Across all similarity measures, the behaviour pairs are compared using the same initial conditions, which leads to comparisons of the same behaviour achieving a perfect measure score. Therefore, the same-behaviour pairs are omitted from the results.

The hyperparameters for the SOM have been chosen by a grid search. The map topology is rectangular, with 46 by 46 nodes. The neighbourhood prototype spreading is Gaussian, and the prototype activation function is Euclidean. The train-test split for the classification task is $80\% - 20\%$. The training took 180000 SOM update steps with a learning rate of 0.1. Additionally, each classification sample is a time-series of 5 sequential simulation steps ($0.5\,\text{s}$) and the corresponding numerical class label from 1–6. For more reliable classification results, the SOM scores are averaged over 3 independently created and trained models.

4   Results

Similarity. Figure 1 shows the similarity scores between behaviour pairs. The *cosine similarity* values (Fig. 1) display the lowest score variability even for behaviours that should, for the most part, be dissimilar, such as flocking and *dispersion*. In line with the scores spread issue, the absolute similarity values are meaningless by themselves. The "Alharthi2022" similarity values display some confusion since the *aggregation* (based on neighbours attraction) and *dispersion* (based on neighbours repulsion) pair has a score of 0.86, which is higher than the *Reynolds* and *Vicsek* pair score of 0.83 ± 0.02 (both flocking behaviours). I.e.,

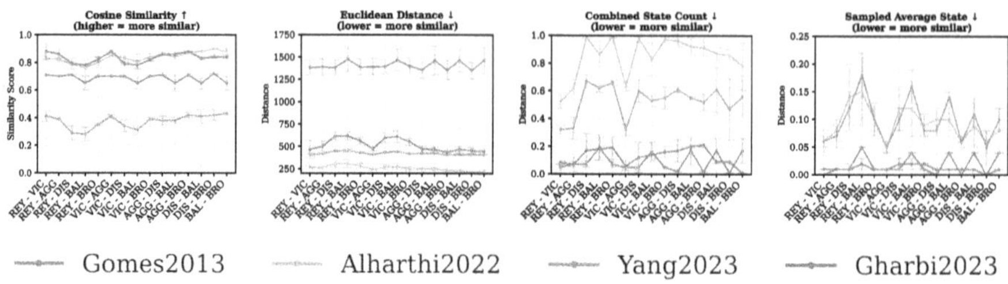

Gomes2013   Alharthi2022   Yang2023   Gharbi2023

Fig. 1. Similarity assessment for all behaviour pairs. Lines represent the mean scores and the standard deviation over 50 independent simulations.

Table 2. Classification scores, averaged over three independent runs.

		Feature Sets			
Model	Metric	Alharthi2022 [1]	Gomes2013 [6]	Yang2023 [16]	Gharbi2023 [5]
SOM	Train accuracy	0.489 ± 0.003	$\mathbf{0.595 \pm 0.005}$	0.500 ± 0.003	0.444 ± 0.009
	Test accuracy	0.442 ± 0.005	$\mathbf{0.494 \pm 0.016}$	0.455 ± 0.013	0.345 ± 0.005

two visually very distinct behaviours (that are often treated as opposites) score higher similarity than two variants of what is arguably the same behaviour. See the behaviour trajectories in the supplementary video for further visual aid.

The *combined state count* measure provides the highest score variability, as visually depicted in Fig. 1. Like in the other similarity measures results, the values in absolute terms are meaningless. The "Alharthi2022" feature set is the only set that clearly separates the flocking behaviours (*Reynolds* and *Vicsek*) and the *aggregation* behaviour. Additionally, this feature set displays dissimilarity pairs near 1 when there is not much behavioural resemblance, like in flocking–*dispersion* or flocking–*Brownian motion*. Again, some feature sets suffer from ambiguities, e.g., in the "Gomes2013" feature set, the *aggregation–dispersion* pair has a score of 0.02 while the flocking behaviours pair (0.08 ± 0.01).

The *Euclidean distance* measure between the behaviour pairs is outlined in Fig. 1. In general, it deviates from the distances obtained through the *sampled average state* measure since the two feature sets with the lowest average distances, namely "Alharthi2022" and "Yang2023", are the feature sets with the highest average distance in the latter measure. The "Gomes2013" feature set displays the highest distance average and standard deviation (error bars).

The *sampled average state* measure provides a distance between the behaviour features (see Fig. 1). This measure averages over the features of all the agents of the swarm, and subsequently, it averages over all the simulation steps per time window. Therefore, there is a noticeable difference in the similarity scores between the swarm-level feature sets ("Alharthi2022" and "Yang2023") and the agent-level feature sets ("Gomes2013" and "Gharbi2023") since the latter are represented by a single agent instead of the N agents.

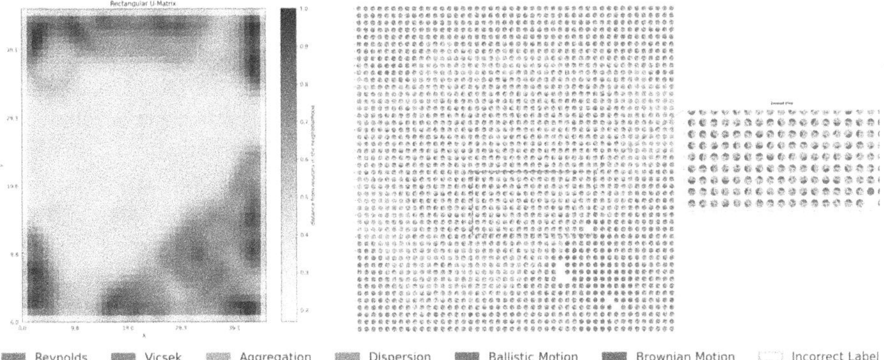

Fig. 2. Analysis of the first seed "Gomes2013" based SOM. Left: the inter-node Euclidean distances. Right: the training classification.

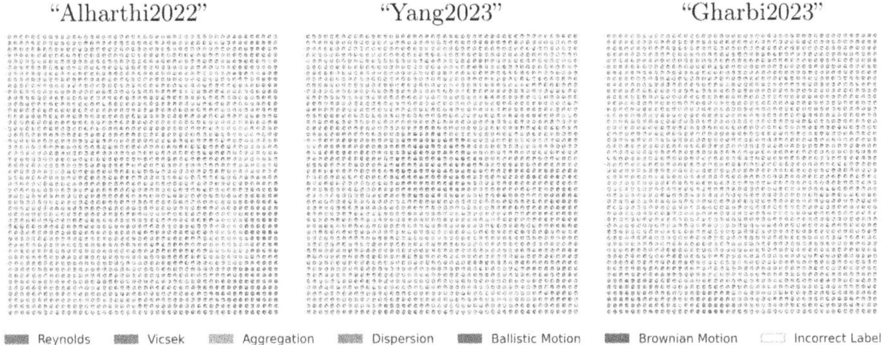

Fig. 3. Analysis of the first seed SOMs on the training samples. The node colour indicates the true label, and the grey contour indicates incorrect labels. The corresponding inter-node distance maps are available in the video. (Color figure online)

Explainable Classification. Table 2 shows the average scores of the classifiers. The "Gomes2013" (see Fig. 2) feature set achieves the highest accuracy scores as it contains the exact positions and velocities of all agents (i.e., there is no compression of the swarm representation). However, the accuracy is still relatively low ($\approx 50\,\%$ test accuracy). The *ballistic motion* and flocking behaviours are primarily represented in the corners (Fig. 2, right), while the centre area displays confusion in disentangling the representation of *aggregation*, *dispersion*, and *Brownian motion*. The confusion in the classification of the flocking behaviours is expected, given the discriminatory power of the selected feature sets. Looking at the inter-node distances (Fig. 2, left), we see that the corner regions show higher inter-node distances, while in the centre region the distances are much smaller. This is an indicator that the misclassification is not a result of a lack of training data. The prototypes' closeness implies that any confusion stems from the fact that samples were similar (under the Euclidean distance).

The "Alharthi2022" SOM in Fig. 3 displays a clearer node label separation for the *dispersion* behaviour. The inter-node distances are more evenly distributed when compared to "Gomes2013". The "Yang2023" feature set (see Fig. 3) based classifier can separate more clearly the nodes with the *ballistic motion* label. The inter-node distances are comparable, except on the centre cluster that contains the majority of the *Brownian motion* nodes. These nodes often misclassify the *dispersion* behaviour. The "Gharbi2023" feature set performs the worst in terms of classification accuracy. This is somewhat expected, as it only considers agents' shortest distances. This accuracy gap can be, in part, explained by the lack of clear clusters of nodes in the SOM (see Fig. 3). Additionally, the low similarity scores variability across all the measures might relate to SOM misclassification. The poor performance implies that we may need to augment this feature set to help disambiguate the map's topological arrangement.

5   Discussion and Conclusion

In this work, we have investigated the effect of four feature sets from the literature on similarity assessments and classification of collective behaviours. Our results show that often-used measures, like Euclidean distance or cosine similarity, perform poorly when used to assess the similarity of collective behaviours. Distance measures particularly designed for swarm robotics (e.g., [6]) appear to be better suited to compare similarities of collective behaviour. Additionally, our results show that the most suitable feature set depends heavily on the selected similarity measure and that similarity or distance scores are influenced at least as strongly by the measure as by the compared behaviours. This highlights the need for future research on the interaction of feature sets and similarity measures.

Our classification experiments further highlight the difficulties of finding appropriate feature sets. The test accuracies of all trained self-organised maps are below 50 %. Closer inspection of the SOM prototypes revealed that similar behaviours (e.g., *Reynolds* and *Vicsek* flocking) were often confused, contributing to the lower accuracy. However, even visually distinct behaviours, such as *dispersion* and *aggregation*, were often matched to the same prototypical units. This further highlights the fact that selecting features that best represent the collective behaviour is a challenging task. In particular, there is a lack of consistency between the different similarity measures and classification predictors on what features are most useful to discriminate the behaviours. Our work on self-organised maps provides first insights into this problem, but in the future, we must develop more robust tools to find and choose appropriate features.

Acknowledgments. AFJ and JK acknowledge support from the Carl-Zeiss-Foundation, the DFG through Germany's Excellence Strategy-EXC 2117-422037984 and the Centre for the Advanced Study of Collective Behaviour (CASCB). JK acknowledges support from the Zukunftskolleg.

Disclosure of Interests. The authors have no competing interests to declare.

References

1. Alharthi, K., Abdallah, Z.S., Hauert, S.: Automatic extraction of understandable controllers from video observations of swarm behaviors. In: Dorigo, M., et al. (eds.) Swarm Intelligence: 13th International Conference, ANTS 2022, vol. 13491, pp. 41–53. Springer, Cham (2022). https://doi.org/10.1007/978-3-031-20176-9_4
2. Alharthi, K., Abdallah, Z.S., Hauert, S.: Ghost swarms: learning swarm rules from environmental changes alone. In: Xue, B., Manzoni, L., Bakurov, I. (eds.) Genetic Programming: 28th European Conference, EuroGP 2025, Held as Part of EvoStar 2025, Trieste, Italy, 23–25 April 2025, Proceedings. Lecture Notes in Computer Science, vol. 15609. Springer, Cham (2025). https://doi.org/10.1007/978-3-031-89991-1_1
3. Birattari, M., Ligot, A., Hasselmann, K.: Disentangling automatic and semi-automatic approaches to the optimization-based design of control software for robot swarms. Nat. Mach. Intell. **2**(9), 494–499 (2020). https://doi.org/10.1038/s42256-020-0215-0
4. Coelho, D.N., Barreto, G.A., Medeiros, C.M.S.: Detection of short circuit faults in 3-phase converter-fed induction motors using kernel SOMs. In: 2017 12th International Workshop on Self-Organizing Maps and Learning Vector Quantization, Clustering and Data Visualization (WSOM), pp. 1–7. IEEE, Piscataway (2017). https://doi.org/10.1109/WSOM.2017.8020016
5. Gharbi, I., Kuckling, J., Garzón Ramos, D., Birattari, M.: Show me what you want: inverse reinforcement learning to automatically design robot swarms by demonstration. In: 2023 IEEE International Conference on Robotics and Automation (ICRA), pp. 5063–5070. IEEE, Piscataway (2023). https://doi.org/10.1109/ICRA48891.2023.10160947
6. Gomes, J., Christensen, A.L.: Generic behaviour similarity measures for evolutionary swarm robotics. In: Blum, C. (ed.) GECCO'13: Proceedings of the 15th Annual Conference on Genetic and Evolutionary Computation, pp. 199–206. ACM, New York (2013). https://doi.org/10.1145/2463372.2463398
7. Kaiser, T.K., Begemann, M.J., Plattenteich, T., Schilling, L., Schildbach, G., Hamann, H.: ROS2SWARM – a ROS 2 package for swarm robot behaviors. In: 2022 IEEE International Conference on Robotics and Automation (ICRA), pp. 6875–6881. IEEE (2022). https://doi.org/10.1109/ICRA46639.2022.9812417
8. Kegeleirs, M., Garzón Ramos, D., Birattari, M.: Random walk exploration for swarm mapping. In: Althoefer, K., Konstantinova, J., Zhang, K. (eds.) Towards Autonomous Robotic Systems: 20th Annual Conference, TAROS 2019. Lecture Notes in Computer Science, vol. 11650, pp. 211–222. Springer, Cham (2019). https://doi.org/10.1007/978-3-030-25332-5_19
9. Kohonen, T.: Self-organized formation of topologically correct feature maps. Biol. Cybern. **43**(1), 59–69 (1982). https://doi.org/10.1007/BF00337288
10. Kohonen, T.: The self-organizing map. Neurocomputing **21**, 1–6 (1990)
11. Reynolds, C.W.: Flocks, herds and schools: a distributed behavioral model. In: SIGGRAPH'87: Proceedings of the 14th Annual Conference on Computer Graphics and Interactive Techniques, vol. 21, pp. 25–34. ACM, New York (1987). https://doi.org/10.1145/37401.37406
12. Rumelhart, D.E., Zipser, D.: Feature discovery by competitive learning. Cogn. Sci. **9**(1), 75–112 (1985). https://doi.org/10.1207/s15516709cog0901_5
13. Schranz, M., Umlauft, M., Sende, M., Elmenreich, W.: Swarm robotic behaviors and current applications. Front. Robot. AI **7**, 36 (2020). https://doi.org/10.3389/frobt.2020.00036

14. Szpirer, J., Garzón Ramos, D., Birattari, M.: Automatic design of robot swarms that perform composite missions: an approach based on inverse reinforcement learning. In: 2024 IEEE/RSJ International Conference on Intelligent Robots and Systems (IROS), pp. 5791–5798. IEEE, Piscataway (2024). https://doi.org/10.1109/IROS58592.2024.10801506
15. Vicsek, T., Czirók, A., Ben-Jacob, E., Cohen, I., Shochet, O.: Novel type of phase transition in a system of self-driven particles. Phys. Rev. Lett. **75**(6), 1226–1229 (1995). https://doi.org/10.1103/PhysRevLett.75.1226
16. Yang, S., Samarasinghe, D., Arukgoda, A., Abpeikar, S., Lakshika, E., Barlow, M.: Automatic recognition of collective emergent behaviors using behavioral metrics. IEEE Access **11**, 89077–89092 (2023). https://doi.org/10.1109/ACCESS.2023.3304682

Knowledge Distillation-Driven Federated Learning as a Service for Resource-Constrained Edge Intelligence

Filippo Vannella[1(✉)], Tianyue Chu[1(✉)], David Solans Noguero[1], and Sotirios Spantideas[2]

[1] Telefonica Research, 08029 Barcelona, Spain
`{filippo.vannella,tianyue.chu,david.solansnoguero}@telefonica.com`
[2] National and Kapodistrian University of Athens, Psachna, 34400 Evia, Greece
`sospanti@uoa.gr`

Abstract. Federated Learning as a Service (FLaaS) enables large-scale, privacy-preserving training across heterogeneous edge devices but incurs significant deployment and communication overhead when distributing high-capacity models. This paper introduces the integration of *server-side knowledge distillation* into FLaaS, producing compact student models that are deployed for federated training and inference. Distillation is implemented as a configurable service within the FLaaS orchestration layer and operates offline prior to federated training, preserving existing client-side logic. Experiments on CIFAR-10 show that FLaaS+KD reduces model transmission size by 88.8% and deployment energy by nearly 90%, at the cost of an approximate 21% reduction in accuracy. These results demonstrate that centralized KD enables scalable, energy-efficient, and privacy-preserving deployment in resource-constrained federated and edge environments.

Keywords: Federated Learning as a Service · Knowledge Distillation

1 Introduction

Federated Learning (FL) enables decentralized clients to collaboratively train Machine Learning (ML) models while keeping raw data local, making it key for privacy-preserving learning on edge and mobile devices [7,15]. However, as model complexity and the number of participating clients grow, FL systems face severe communication and deployment bottlenecks, particularly when distributing large global models to resource-constrained devices [2,14,20].

Federated Learning as a Service (FLaaS). [9] provides a service-oriented framework that orchestrates large-scale federated training across heterogeneous mobile devices. By abstracting communication, aggregation, and client

---

F. Vannella, T. Chu—Equal Contribution.

© The Author(s), under exclusive license to Springer Nature Switzerland AG 2026
R. Groß et al. (Eds.): ANTS 2026, LNCS 16515, pp. 385–393, 2026.
https://doi.org/10.1007/978-3-032-26123-6_33

coordination behind a unified control layer, FLaaS enables scalable and privacy-compliant deployment of FL across multiple applications and devices [8].

Knowledge Distillation (KD). [3,5,16] compresses high-capacity models (*teachers*) into lightweight ones (*students*) by transferring their semantic behavior rather than their parameters. This produces compact models that retain competitive accuracy while reducing the model size, making KD well suited for deployment and communication-efficient learning in federated settings [3,13].

Motivation. However, as model sizes increase, FLaaS must also address deployment-time communication and inference costs, which are often overlooked in training-centric FL systems. Distributing large global models to edge devices incurs significant bandwidth and energy overheads, particularly in swarm and multi-agent environments. Despite this, existing FLaaS frameworks lack integrated mechanisms for lightweight model deployment.

Contributions. We integrate server-side KD into FLaaS through an *offline distillation phase*, producing lightweight student models for federated training and inference. The proposed design operates entirely at the system level, preserving standard FL workflows and client-side logic while enabling automated model compression and deployment. Experiments on CIFAR-10 show that FLaaS+KD reduces model size by 88.8% and transmission energy by nearly 90%, substantially improving deployability across heterogeneous edge environments. FLaaS-KD is released as open-source to facilitate reproducibility and further research[1].

2   Related Work

Federated Learning Foundations. FL enables multiple decentralized clients to collaboratively train a shared global model while keeping raw data localized and private [7]. Classical FL algorithms, such as FedAvg [15], rely on the iterative exchange of model parameters between clients and the server, aggregating updates to produce a refined global model. Although this paradigm preserves privacy at the data level, it suffers from high communication costs, especially when applied to deep architectures [18].

Knowledge Distillation and Model Compression. KD [5], transfers the knowledge of a large teacher model to a smaller student network by aligning their output distributions. KD has since become a key technique for deploying compact yet accurate models on devices with limited resources [3], providing significant gains in inference efficiency, latency, and energy consumption. These properties make KD well suited to edge intelligence where training large models requires high communications and inference costs.

Federated Knowledge Distillation. The intersection of FL and KD has produced a class of algorithms referred to as Federated Knowledge Distillation (FKD) [12]. Early works, such as FedMD [11], trained models by exchanging logits instead of full model parameters, reducing communication costs. Other

---

[1] https://github.com/TianyueChu/FLaaS-Server.

works, including ensemble-based schemes [6] and training frameworks such as FedGKT [4], decoupled client and server to support heterogeneous devices. However, these methods typically perform KD *during* the federated training process. Instead, our *system* layer integration targets the pretraining phase.

3   System Design

3.1   FLaaS Architecture

Legacy FlaaS. The FLaaS architecture [8] comprises four modules: (*i*) the *admin interface* for configuration and experiment management (model, rounds, etc.); (*ii*) the *global server*, orchestrating rounds and aggregating client updates; (*iii*) the *notification and coordination service* that synchronizes clients; and (*iv*) the set of *mobile clients* that train locally via the FLaaS Software Development Kit (SDK). This modular design enables cross-application participation, multi-tenancy, and heterogeneous devices while keeping client-side logic unchanged.

Extending FLaaS with KD. We extend FLaaS with a server-side KD module integrated into the orchestration layer. During project registration, users specify teacher and student architectures together with KD hyperparameters via the admin interface. The global server invokes the KD sub-module which loads the pretrained teacher, executes the distillation stage on a server-held buffer, and outputs a distilled student head, which is the initial global model used in the standard FLaaS round workflow. This integration preserves the federated logic while extending the server-side model preparation pipeline (Fig. 1).

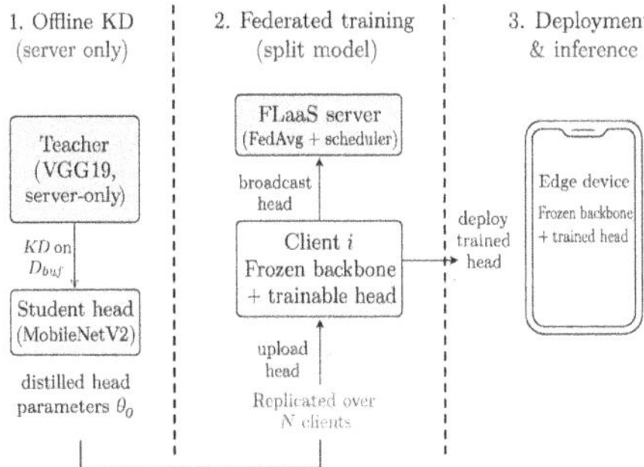

Fig. 1. FLaaS+KD workflow. 1. Offline KD from a server-side teacher to a student head. 2. federated training of the student head on N clients with a frozen backbone. 3. deployment of the trained head to edge devices for inference.

3.2   Knowledge Distillation in FLaaS

Split Model. In the following, we adopt a generic split model $f(\cdot) = h(g(\cdot; \psi); \theta)$ where the *feature extractor* $g(\cdot; \psi)$ is shared and *frozen* on devices, while only the *classifier head* $h(\cdot; \theta)$ is trained; ψ and θ denote the parameters for the feature extractor and the classifier head, respectively.

Student and Teacher Models. We denote by $f_T(x) = h_T(g(\cdot; \psi); \theta_T)$ the (pre-trained) *teacher* and by $f_S(x) = h_S(g(\cdot; \psi); \theta_S)$ the (untrained) *student model*. The pretrained global *teacher* $f_T(\cdot) = h_T(g(\cdot; \psi); \theta_T)$ serves as the high-capacity source from which a smaller, resource-efficient *student* head is distilled.

Data. The KD step is entirely centralized and does not involve federated client data. Let $\mathcal{D} = \{(x_s, y_s)\}_{s \in [S]}$ denote a generic dataset, where x_s denotes a feature vector, y_s denotes a label from a finite set, and S is the dataset size. Before the FL phase, the server reserves a centralized *held-out buffer* $\mathcal{D}_{\mathrm{buf}} \subset \mathcal{D}$.

KD Training. The student is trained to match the teacher's softened output distribution using the standard KD objective [5]. Let $z_T(x)$ and $z_S(x)$ denote the teacher and student *logits*, i.e., the pre-softmax outputs of their classifier heads. We define the corresponding softened class-probability vectors $p_T^{(\tau)}(x) = \mathrm{softmax}(z_T(x)/\tau), p_S^{(\tau)}(x) = \mathrm{softmax}(z_S(x)/\tau)$, where $\tau > 0$ is a temperature parameter. The KD loss combines two components: (i) a standard cross-entropy term ($\mathcal{L}_{\mathrm{CE}}$) that aligns the student with the ground-truth label, and (ii) a Kullback-Leibler divergence term (KL) that aligns the student's softened predictions with those of the teacher. Following [5], the objective minimized over the student parameters θ_S is

$$\mathcal{L}_{\mathrm{KD}} = \mathbb{E}_{(x,y) \sim \mathcal{D}_{\mathrm{buf}}} \left[(1 - \beta)\, \mathcal{L}_{\mathrm{CE}}(y,\, p_S^{(1)}(x)) \; + \; \beta\, \tau^2\, \mathrm{KL}(p_T^{(\tau)}(x) \,\|\, p_S^{(\tau)}(x)) \right],$$

where $\beta \in [0, 1]$ balances the relative weight of hard and soft supervision. The teacher weights θ_T remain frozen at this stage; only the student head is updated.

Deployment. After distillation, the student replaces the teacher as the deployable global model and is distributed to clients for both federated training and inference, reducing deployment-time communication and latency.

3.3   Federated Learning in FLaaS

FLaaS[1] [8] orchestrates the federated training phase between the server and a set of N clients, indexed by $i \in \{1, \ldots, N\} \triangleq [N]$. The training follows the standard federated learning phases [15], as described next.

Model. We reuse the split model $f(\cdot) = h(g(\cdot; \psi); \theta)$ introduced in Sect. 3.2, with a shared, frozen feature extractor $g(\cdot; \psi)$ on devices and a trainable classifier head $h(\cdot; \theta)$. At the beginning of federated training, we set the global head to the distilled student parameters, i.e., $\theta \leftarrow \theta_S$. For notational simplicity, we omit the student subscript in the remainder of the FL phase and write θ instead; this corresponds to the student head obtained from the KD stage.

---

[1] Although FlaaS supports cross-app training, in the following, we describe the method for a single-app training scenario for simplicity. The methods can be easily generalized to the cross-app training scenario (see [8]).

Data. Starting from the dataset $\mathcal{D} = \{(x_s, y_s)\}_{s \in [S]}$ and the KD buffer $\mathcal{D}_{\text{buf}}$ defined in Sect. 3.2, we partition the remaining samples $\mathcal{D} \setminus \mathcal{D}_{\text{buf}}$ across clients. Each client i holds a private subset $\mathcal{D}_i \subset \mathcal{D} \setminus \mathcal{D}_{\text{buf}}$ that never leaves the device.

Federated Learning. At each communication round $t \geq 1$, the server selects a fraction C out of N clients as the set $\mathcal{N}_t \subseteq [N]$, where $\mathcal{N}_t$ denotes the set of participating clients at round t. The server broadcasts the current head parameters θ_t to these clients. Each client i initializes $\theta_{t,i}^{(0)} \leftarrow \theta_t$ (superscripts $^{(\cdot)}$ denote local epoch) and performs E local epochs over mini-batches $\mathcal{B} \subseteq \mathcal{D}_i$ to minimize over mini-batches $\mathcal{B} \subseteq \mathcal{D}_i$ to minimize $F_i(\theta) = \frac{1}{|\mathcal{D}_i|} \sum_{(x,y) \in \mathcal{D}_i} \ell\big(h(g(x; \psi); \theta), y\big)$, where ℓ is the local cross-entropy loss and the feature extractor $g(\cdot; \psi)$ is *frozen* on device. More precisely, each client performs gradient descent steps indexed by $e = 0, \ldots, E - 1$ (with weight decay λ_t, step size η) on $\mathcal{B}$ as $\theta_{t,i}^{(e+1)} = \theta_{t,i}^{(e)} - \eta\Big(\frac{1}{|\mathcal{B}|} \sum_{(x,y) \in \mathcal{B}} \nabla_\theta \ell\big(h(g(x; \psi); \theta_{t,i}^{(e)}), y\big) + \lambda_t \theta_{t,i}^{(e)}\Big)$. After E epochs, every client returns $\theta_{t,i} \leftarrow \theta_{t,i}^{(E)}$ and the server aggregates as $\theta_{t+1} = \sum_{i \in \mathcal{N}_t} \frac{|\mathcal{D}_i|}{\sum_{j \in \mathcal{N}_t} |\mathcal{D}_j|} \theta_{t,i}$.

4 Experimental Setup

Evaluation Objective. We evaluate server-side KD within FLaaS. The main evaluation objectives are: (i) to verify that KD produces a compact student model suitable for on-device training and inference; and (ii) to demonstrate that FLaaS-KD reduces communication and energy costs.

Task and Datasets. We use CIFAR-10 [10] with a non-IID Dirichlet split $(\alpha = 0.5)$ across $N = 10$ clients. Each client holds 150 training samples; the server reserves 5,000/1,000 samples for KD train/evalution.

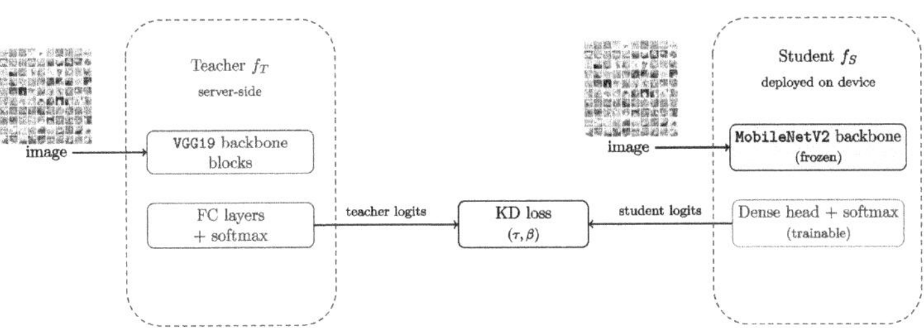

Fig. 2. Student and teacher architectures. The MobileNet base (`bottleneck.tflite`) remains frozen on device, while the lightweight head (`train_head.tflite`) is trained locally and uploaded each round.

Model Architectures. We instantiate the split model from Sect. 3 as presented in using the Fig. 2:

- **Teacher** $f_T(\cdot; \theta_T)$: a `VGG_19` model [19] pretrained on CIFAR-10 (loaded via `torch.hub` [1]), used only during the server-side KD training stage to distill the student model described next.
- **Student** $f_S(\cdot; \theta_S)$: a `MobileNetV2` backbone [17] initialized from ImageNet-pretrained weights, followed by a *single* dense (linear) head and softmax. The backbone is frozen; KD trains the head centrally on the server, and the resulting student is broadcast at the start of federated training.

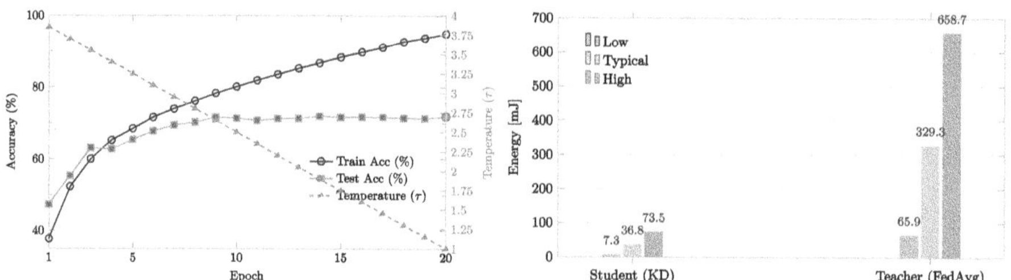

(a) Student train/test accuracy (left axis) and temperature schedule τ (right axis).

(b) Transmission energy [mJ] for different network scenarios.

Fig. 3. Experimental results for (a) KD training and (b) transmission energy.

On-Device Training in FLaaS. Each client executes a split model using the `transfer_api` built on TensorFlow Lite. The frozen MobileNetV2 backbone is packaged as `bottleneck.tflite`, while the trainable dense head is provided as `train_head.tflite` together with `optimizer.tflite` and `inference.tflite`. During FL rounds, clients update the head weights only, consistent with the split-model design described in Sect. 3. The implementation therefore transmits only the head parameters each round.

Federated Configuration and KD Parameters. We emulate $N = 10$ Android clients with $E = 20$ local epochs (SGD: $m = 0.9$, $B = 20$, $\eta = 3 \times 10^{-3}$) and FedAvg aggregation [15]. KD uses linear τ annealing ($3.8 \rightarrow 1.0$) and $\beta = 0.3$.

5   Results and Discussion

We evaluate the integration of centralized KD within FLaaS along three axes: (*i*) offline KD training performance, (*ii*) model compression and deployment efficiency, and (*iii*) system-level resource usage.

5.1   KD Training

Figure 3(a) shows the training and test accuracy of the distilled student across KD epochs. The final student reaches a test accuracy of $\approx 71.9\%$, compared to 93.39% for the VGG19 teacher. This corresponds to a trade-off of approximately 21.5 percentage points in accuracy for an almost $9\times$ reduction in model size and the associated communication and energy savings.

5.2   Energy Consumption Analysis

As shown in Fig. 3(b), downloading the distilled student model consumes under 12% of the energy required for the teacher across all evaluated network regimes (*low*, *typical*, and *high* throughput). In the typical throughput setting, energy consumption drops from ~ 329.3 mJ to ~ 36.8 mJ, quantifying the deployment-time savings enabled by KD.

5.3   Model Compression and Transmission Efficiency

Table 1 reports server-side profiling metrics for the teacher and KD student including number of parameters, Wall Time, Central Processing Unit (CPU) time, Average CPU utilization, Peak Resident Set Size (RSS) and energy consumed. These values refer to the full models distributed to devices. The teacher contains 20,565,834 parameters (78.5 MB), while the KD student contains 2,236,682 parameters (8.76 MB), yielding an 88.8% reduction in model size. This reduces deployment-time download duration by 65%, CPU time by 95%, average CPU load by 82%, and peak RSS by 32%. As FLaaS exchanges only model heads, KD primarily reduces the cost of deploying and updating global models.

Table 1. Server-side profiling for teacher and KD student models.

Model	Parameters	Wall Time [s]	CPU Time [s]	Avg CPU [%]	Peak RSS [MB]	Energy [mJ]
Student	2,236,682($8.76MB$)	1.522	0.210	18.6	345.31	36.75
Teacher	20,565,834($78.53MB$)	4.354	4.443	102.5	508.22	329.38

5.4   Latency and Scalability

With total round time expressed as $T_{\mathrm{round}} = T_{\mathrm{train}} + T_{\mathrm{upload}} + T_{\mathrm{download}}$, download can dominate when distributing large models. Replacing the teacher with the KD student reduces T_{download} roughly by $|\theta_S|/|\theta_T|$, consistent with Table 1.

6　Conclusion and Future Work

This paper introduced the integration of *server-side knowledge distillation* into the FLaaS framework, enabling lightweight model deployment in federated learning without modifying client-side logic. By performing KD centrally, prior to federated training, FLaaS+KD produces compact student models suitable for efficient on-device training and inference. Experiments on CIFAR-10 demonstrate that the distilled student achieves competitive accuracy ($\approx 72\%$) while reducing model size by nearly 88% and transmission energy by almost 90%. These results highlight the suitability of KD for scalable deployment in edge and swarm-based federated systems. Future work includes adaptive teacher-student coordination, dynamic distillation schedules, and multi-teacher extensions.

Acknowledgments. This research was funded by the European Union under TaRDIS (GA 101093006) and XTRUST-6G (GA 101192749). Views and opinions expressed are those of the author(s) only and do not necessarily reflect those of the European Union, the European Commission, or the Smart Networks and Services Joint Undertaking.

Disclosure of Interests. The authors have no competing interests to declare.

References

1. Chen, Y.f.: pytorch-cifar-models: Pretrained cifar-10/100 models for pytorch. https://github.com/chenyaofo/pytorch-cifar-models, torchHub model used: `cifar10_vgg19_bn`. Accessed 18 Nov 2025
2. Dritsas, E., Trigka, M.: Federated learning for IoT: a survey of techniques, challenges, and applications. J. Sens. Actuator Netw. **14**(1), 9 (2025)
3. Gou, J., Yu, B., Maybank, S., Tao, D.: Knowledge distillation: a survey. Int. J. Comput. Vision **129**(6), 1789–1819 (2021)
4. He, C., Annavaram, M., Avestimehr, S.: Group knowledge transfer: federated learning of large CNNs at the edge. In: Proceedings of NeurIPS (2020)
5. Hinton, G., Vinyals, O., Dean, J.: Distilling the knowledge in a neural network. In: NeurIPS Deep Learning Workshop (2015)
6. Itahara, S., Nishio, T., Yonetani, R., Koda, Y.: Distillation-based semi-supervised federated learning for on-device personalization. IEEE Trans. Neural Netw. Learn. Syst. (2023)
7. Kairouz, P., et al.: Advances and open problems in federated learning. Found. Trends Mach. Learn. **14**(1–2), 1–210 (2021)
8. Katevas, K., Perino, D., Kourtellis, N.: FLaaS – practical federated learning as a service for mobile applications. In: Proceedings of HotMobile '22, pp. 130–137 (2022)
9. Kourtellis, N., Katevas, K., Perino, D.: FLaaS: federated learning as a service. In: Proceedings of the 1st Workshop on Distributed Machine Learning, pp. 7–13 (2020)
10. Krizhevsky, A.: Learning multiple layers of features from tiny images. Tech. rep., University of Toronto (2009). https://www.cs.toronto.edu/~kriz/learning-features-2009-TR.pdf

11. Li, D., Wang, J., Liang, Y., Jin, B., Zhang, J.: FedMD: heterogeneous federated learning via model distillation. In: NeurIPS Workshop on Federated Learning for Data Privacy and Confidentiality (2019)
12. Li, Q., Wen, Z., He, B., et al.: Federated learning with knowledge distillation. IEEE Internet Things J. **8**(5), 3459–3471 (2021)
13. Liu, H.I., et al.: Lightweight deep learning for resource-constrained environments: a survey. ACM Comput. Surv. **56**(10), 1–42 (2024)
14. Liu, Y., Zhang, X., Huo, L., Wu, J., Guizani, M.: Swarm learning and knowledge distillation empowered self-driving detection against threat behavior for intelligent IoT. IEEE Trans. Mob. Comput. **23**(6), 7117–7134 (2023)
15. McMahan, B., Moore, E., Ramage, D., Hampson, S., y Arcas, B.A.: Communication-efficient learning of deep networks from decentralized data. In: Proceedings of AISTATS (2017)
16. Romero, A., Ballas, N., Kahou, S.E., Chassang, A., Gatta, C., Bengio, Y.: FitNets: hints for thin deep nets. In: Proceedings of ICLR (2015)
17. Sandler, M., Howard, A., Zhu, M., Zhmoginov, A., Chen, L.C.: MobileNetV2: inverted residuals and linear bottlenecks. In: Proceedings of CVPR (2018)
18. Sattler, F., Wiedemann, S., Müller, K.R., Samek, W.: Robust and communication-efficient federated learning from Non-IID data. IEEE Trans. Neural Netw. Learn. Syst. (2019)
19. Simonyan, K., Zisserman, A.: Very deep convolutional networks for large-scale image recognition. In: International Conference on Learning Representations (2015)
20. Wen, J., Zhang, Z., Lan, Y., Cui, Z., Cai, J., Zhang, W.: A survey on federated learning: challenges and applications. Int. J. Mach. Learn. Cybern. **14**(2), 513–535 (2023)

Modeling Information Propagation in Robot Swarms Through Epidemiological Models

Giuseppe A. Patarino[1]([envelope]) [iD], Volker Strobel[1] [iD], Himank Gupta[1,2] [iD], and Marco Dorigo[1] [iD]

[1] IRIDIA, Université Libre de Bruxelles, Brussels, Belgium
{giuseppe.patarino,volker.strobel,himank.gupta}@ulb.be, mdorigo@ulb.ac.be
[2] Technology Innovation Institute, Abu Dhabi, UAE

Abstract. Information propagation in robot swarms is critical for coordinated behavior, since collective actions depend on the exchange of messages among robots. However, a predictive model linking the swarm parameters to the dynamics of information propagation has yet to be established. We introduce an epidemiology-inspired approach based on the Susceptible–Infected model to predict information propagation in mobile robot swarms executing random walks. The propagation rate is empirically related to robot density, communication range, and motion speed, yielding a predictive model that accurately reproduces the temporal evolution of the informed fraction across diverse swarm configurations.

1 Introduction

A robot swarm consists of multiple autonomous robots that cooperate without centralized control, relying instead on local sensing and short-range communication with nearby robots. This decentralized architecture provides fault tolerance and scalability, making robot swarms well suited for tasks such as distributed sensing and search and rescue operations [2,5,6]. The swarm performance often depends on how efficiently information generated by individual robots propagates through local interactions. A detection made by a single robot becomes actionable only after it reaches a sufficiently large subset of the swarm via short-range wireless links enabled by robot mobility. For tasks requiring synchronized behaviors, a triggering message must propagate rapidly enough through the swarm to ensure coordination [8,10,15]. Predicting how fast such information propagates as a function of swarm parameters remains an open problem. Analytical modeling is complicated by stochastic robot motion and intermittent communication, which give rise to dynamic, time-varying interaction networks. To address this, we adopt the Susceptible–Infected (SI) model [11,12], an epidemiological framework that captures the probabilistic nature of pairwise transmission while retaining analytical tractability. This model provides a compact representation of swarm-level information propagation. In our SI model, robots are classified as either susceptible (uninformed) or infected (informed), and infected robots transmit information to neighboring robots, thereby enabling propagation to other susceptible robots in the swarm. The model is governed by the contact rate β, defined as the probability per unit time that a robot encounters and informs another robot, and by the initial informed fraction i_0, which represents the fraction of robots expected to have at least one informed neighbor at the beginning of the propagation process. In this work, we express β and i_0 as functions of key swarm parameters: the robot density ρ, the communication range r, and the mean robot speed v. The proposed model thus links these parameters to the temporal evolution of the fraction of informed robots, showing how they affect encounter rates and, consequently, information propagation over time. We validate the model through simulations in which robots perform random walks, a widely used mobility pattern in swarm robotics.

2   Related Work

A recent review of communication in multi-robot systems identifies the limited rate of information propagation as a key scalability bottleneck and emphasizes the challenges posed by local communication in robot swarms [7]. Because connectivity within the swarm changes over time as a consequence of the robots' movements and their local-only interactions, predicting how information will propagate is challenging. Analytical models are therefore needed to describe the dynamics of information propagation under time-varying connectivity. In epidemiology, foundational works formalize compartmental models such as the Susceptible–Infected framework, where the contact rate β governs the speed of information propagation [11,12]. In swarm robotics, however, few studies explicitly adopt an SI formulation and relate the contact rate β to measurable physical parameters. Notably, Arai et al. [1] derive a contact-rate expression under random-walk mobility, whereas Correll and Martinoli [3] develop a probabilistic encounter model that relates spatial configuration and motion dynamics to interaction frequency. To characterize proximity-based connectivity in spatially distributed swarms, we adopt the framework of random geometric graphs (RGGs), in which nodes are uniformly distributed in space and edges are formed between nodes separated by a distance of at most r. In this framework, connectivity is governed by the expected number of nodes λ within distance r, defined as $\lambda = \rho\pi r^2$, which serves as a measure of local network connectivity. As λ increases beyond critical connectivity thresholds, the network transitions from a fragmented regime to a connected one [9,13]. Our approach integrates analytical derivation with extensive ARGoS simulations [14] to establish and empirically validate a predictive mapping between physical swarm parameters and information propagation dynamics. We evaluate the theoretical contact-rate expression across diverse swarm configurations and quantify how accurately the resulting SI dynamics reproduce the observed propagation curves.

3   Predictive Model

We derive a predictive model to describe the macroscopic dynamics of information propagation in a swarm of mobile robots performing a random walk with obstacle avoidance in a confined square arena. The formulation is based on the assumptions that communication is local, lossless, and limited to a range r, and that information propagates only through pairwise contacts between robots that come within communication range. Under these assumptions, the propagation process is primarily determined by the robot density ρ, communication range r, and average speed v. We assume a well-mixed population, such that each robot has, on average, an equal chance of encountering any other robot over time. Following random geometric graph theory [13], local connectivity can be characterized by $\lambda = \rho \pi r^2$, which denotes the average number of neighboring robots within communication range. Thresholds in λ mark the transition from fragmented to connected regimes [4,9]. The expected number of informed neighbors of a randomly chosen robot at time t is $\lambda_I(t) = \rho \pi r^2 i(t)$, where $i(t)$ is the fraction of informed robots at time t. Here, λ quantifies the average number of neighbors per robot, while $\lambda_I(t)$ represents the subset of those neighbors that are informed at time t. Assuming that robot positions are uniformly and independently distributed, the number of informed neighbors within range can be modeled as a Poisson random variable with mean $\lambda_I(t)$. Therefore, the probability that at least one informed robot is within range at time t (contact probability) is $P(t) = 1 - e^{-\rho \pi r^2 i(t)}$. The rate of information propagation scales with the encounter frequency, which increases with robot speed v. Accordingly, using the contact probability and the uninformed fraction $(1 - i)$, the dynamics of the informed fraction are

$$\frac{di}{dt} = v\,(1 - i(t))\,P(t) = v\,(1 - i(t))\left(1 - e^{-\rho \pi r^2 i(t)}\right). \tag{1}$$

Equation (1) links the spatial configuration and mobility of the swarm to the temporal dynamics of information propagation. To obtain a tractable analytical form valid in the early propagation phase, when the expected number of informed neighbors is small, we linearize the exponential term using its first-order Taylor expansion, $1 - e^{-\rho \pi r^2 i(t)} \approx \rho \pi r^2 i(t)$ which holds when the expected number of informed neighbors is small $(\rho \pi r^2 i(t) \ll 1)$. This approximation captures the initial growth, where encounters are rare and independent. Substituting the linearized expression into Eq. (1) yields

$$\frac{di}{dt} = v\,\rho\,\pi r^2\,(1 - i(t))i(t), \tag{2}$$

and expressing the contact rate as $\beta = v\,\rho\,\pi r^2$, Eq. (2) can be rewritten to obtain the canonical SI model [12]

$$\frac{di}{dt} = \beta\,(1 - i(t))i(t), \tag{3}$$

whose closed-form solution is the logistic function

$$i(t) = \frac{1}{1 + \left(\frac{1-i_0}{i_0}\right) e^{-\beta t}}. \tag{4}$$

The theoretical contact rate β describes the early propagation regime, where encounters are sparse and the exponential term in Eq. (1) can be linearized. Beyond this regime, the linear approximation no longer holds, as the growing density of informed neighbors increases the probability of multiple simultaneous contacts. To account for these deviations while preserving physical interpretability, we generalize both the contact rate and the effective initial informed fraction as power-law functions of the swarm parameters:

$$\beta = c_0\, v^{c_1} \rho^{c_2} r^{c_3}, \qquad i_0 = c_4\, \rho^{c_5} r^{c_6}. \tag{5}$$

This formulation preserves the physical dependence on speed, robot density, and communication range, while allowing each parameter to contribute differently to encounter frequency and early-stage information spreading. Although a single robot is initially informed, the effective initial fraction i_0 captures early connectivity effects induced by density and communication range.

4 Experimental Validation

This section presents the experimental validation of the proposed model, the simulation setup, the explored parameter space, and the evaluation of predictive accuracy. The comparison between model predictions and simulation results assesses the model's ability to reproduce the observed propagation dynamics across different robot densities, communication ranges, and speeds.

4.1 Experimental Setup

All experiments are performed using the ARGoS simulator [14] with swarms of e-puck robots executing a random walk with obstacle avoidance in a square, enclosed arena. Each robot moves at a constant speed and updates its heading every 5 s by drawing a direction uniformly at random from $[0, 2\pi)$. Robot trajectories are adjusted in the vicinity of obstacles and neighboring robots to ensure collision avoidance. The robot density ρ is defined as the number of robots divided by the arena area. We set the number of robots N in the swarm to $N = 100$, and the arena size is scaled to achieve the desired density value. At the beginning of each simulation, a single robot is randomly designated as informed, while all others are initialized as susceptible. Information exchange occurs only between neighboring robots within the communication range r and is modeled as deterministic when within range under ideal, noise-free conditions. Bandwidth limitations, packet collisions, and message loss are not explicitly modeled. The parameter space was explored by varying the robot density

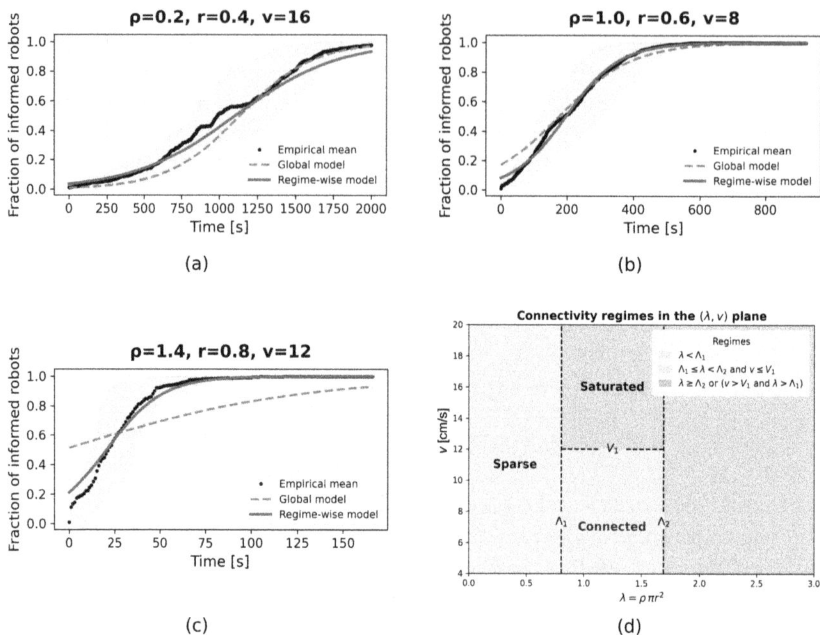

Fig. 1. Propagation curves for (**a**) sparse, (**b**) connected, and (**c**) saturated regimes. (**d**) Partition of the configuration space in the (λ, v) plane.

$\rho \in [0.2, 1.4]$ robots/m^2, the communication range $r \in [0.2, 1.4]$ m, and the robot speed $v \in [4, 20]$ cm/s, using uniform sampling steps of 0.2 for ρ and r, and 4 for v, resulting in 245 distinct parameter combinations. For each configuration (ρ, r, v), ten independent simulation runs with different random seeds were performed. For each parameter combination, the fraction $i(t)$ of informed robots was measured over time and sampled every $\Delta t = 1$ s over a total duration of $T = 2,000$ s. The resulting propagation curves were averaged across 10 different runs. Model fitting and evaluation were performed using 5-fold cross-validation over the resulting configurations, ensuring that each fold contained a representative sample of the parameter space. Each averaged propagation curve is fitted to the analytical SI solution given by Eq. (4) using nonlinear least-squares regression to estimate the parameters i_0 and β.

4.2 Results

Global Model. We evaluate how the SI formulation (see Eq. (4)) reproduces the propagation dynamics. The model is fitted by estimating the coefficients appearing in Eq. (5) using nonlinear least-squares regression. The propagation curves generated with the fitted coefficients show good agreement with the cross-validated test data ($R^2_{\mathrm{mean}} = 0.944$, $\mathrm{RMSE}_{\mathrm{mean}} = 0.082$), indicating that the model captures the main trends across the parameter space. Deviations became more pronounced at the boundaries of the parameter space. When the robot

Table 1. Mean model performance on training and test sets.

Model	Training Set		Test Set	
	RMSE ± Std	R^2	**RMSE ± Std**	R^2
Global	0.077 ± 0.003	0.952	0.082 ± 0.011	0.944
Regime-wise	0.048 ± 0.001	0.981	0.055 ± 0.005	0.975
Sparse	0.051 ± 0.001	0.980	0.060 ± 0.001	0.972
Connected	0.032 ± 0.001	0.990	0.038 ± 0.006	0.985
Saturated	0.050 ± 0.002	0.964	0.055 ± 0.008	0.954

swarm is sparsely connected, the model underestimates the contact rate, and the fitted curves start rising too late (Fig. 1a). In contrast, in high-connectivity, the model overestimates the initial contact rate by increasing i_0 rather than capturing the shape of the curve through a larger β (Fig. 1c).

Regime-Wise Model. The observed deviations motivate a partitioning of the configuration space into three regions, within each of which the model exhibits similar performance. These regions correspond to three qualitatively different deviation patterns: a sparse regime, a connected regime, and a saturated regime, which reflect distinct levels of network connectivity. The propagation regimes are defined by the expected number of neighbors $\lambda = \rho \pi r^2$ and the robot speed v, which respectively determine the number of possible interactions and the rate at which they are explored over time. Two thresholds Λ_1 and Λ_2 are introduced on λ to distinguish between sparse, connected, and saturated interaction conditions, while a single threshold V_1 on v accounts for the fact that, for a given level of connectivity, faster robot motion effectively increases how connected the interaction network becomes. Based on these thresholds, the configuration space is partitioned into three regimes: the *sparse* ($\lambda < \Lambda_1$), the *connected* ($\Lambda_1 \leq \lambda < \Lambda_2$ and $v \leq V_1$), and the *saturated* ($\lambda \geq \Lambda_2$ or ($v > V_1$ and $\lambda > \Lambda_1$)) regimes. Through a grid search, the threshold values are determined to minimize the RMSE variance within each candidate partition, ensuring that configurations grouped within the same regime exhibit similar fitting errors. The determined threshold values are: $\Lambda_1 \approx 1.5$, $\Lambda_2 \approx 4.5$, $V_1 \approx 12$ cm/s. After the thresholds were determined, the model was refitted independently within each regime. The regime-wise fitting led to a substantial improvement in model accuracy on the training set, reducing the mean RMSE from 0.082 for the global model to an average of 0.055 across the regime-wise model, as summarized in Table 1. Figure 1 summarizes the regime-wise analysis. Panels (a–c) present propagation curves for each regime, comparing empirical data (black curve), the global (red curve), and the regime-wise model (blue curve). Panel (d) shows the partition of the (λ, v) space obtained from the threshold search, which defines three connectivity regimes based on the expected neighborhood size and speed. The regime-wise formulation accurately reproduces the temporal evolution of information propa-

Table 2. Fitted coefficients for the global and regime-wise models.

Model	c_0	c_1	c_2	c_3	c_4	c_5	c_6
Global	0.0034	0.679	0.844	0.207	0.337	1.305	2.642
Sparse	0.0037	0.660	0.974	0.510	0.111	0.325	0.733
Connected	0.0073	0.853	1.705	2.648	0.214	1.846	2.987
Saturated	0.0050	0.953	2.003	2.73	0.314	1.550	3.298

gation, as confirmed by the cross-validated performance. The global formulation achieved a mean RMSE $= 0.082 \pm 0.011$, while the regime-wise model further reduced the error to a mean RMSE $= 0.055 \pm 0.005$, confirming that the regime-wise formulation provides better predictive performance across all connectivity regimes. The three identified regimes delineate distinct domains of swarm connectivity and information propagation. In the *sparse* regime, propagation is slow due to fragmented local clusters and correspondingly small contact rates β. In the *connected* regime, the swarm parameters lie in the range where the well-mixed assumption holds best. In the *saturated* regime, increasing λ or v no longer affects the dynamics, as the propagation saturates almost instantaneously. The regime-wise model highlights how different connectivity levels govern the macroscopic behavior of information propagation in robot swarms. The fitted coefficients of the predictive expressions in Eq. 5 are reported in Table 2.

5   Conclusion

This study introduced and validated a predictive model of information propagation in robot swarms, inspired by epidemiological dynamics that capture the temporal evolution of the informed fraction of robots through the initial informed fraction i_0 and the contact rate β. By linking these variables to propagation dynamics, the formulation provides a predictive tool capable of forecasting information propagation across a broad range of swarm configurations. The regime-based structure improves predictive accuracy and reveals how swarm mobility determines information-transfer efficiency. Beyond its predictive capacity, the proposed formulation also serves a diagnostic purpose: It enables the identification of distinct operational regimes from physical parameters. This diagnostic capability allows the model to guide the design and tuning of robot swarms to achieve desired propagation performance under specific constraints. Future work will extend this formulation to scenarios involving structured motion, heterogeneous communication conditions, and environmental perturbations.

Acknowledgments. The Service Public de Wallonie Recherche supported this work under grant no. 2010235 (ARIAC, DigitalWallonia4.AI). V. Strobel and M. Dorigo acknowledge support from the Belgian F.R.S.–FNRS.

Disclosure of Interests. The authors have no competing interests to declare.

References

1. Arai, T., Yoshida, E., Ota, J.: Information diffusion by local communication of multiple mobile robots. In: Proceedings of the IEEE Systems Man and Cybernetics Conference, vol. 4, pp. 535–540. IEEE Press (1993)
2. Brambilla, M., Ferrante, E., Birattari, M., Dorigo, M.: Swarm robotics: a review from the swarm engineering perspective. Swarm Intell. **7**(1), 1–41 (2013)
3. Correll, N., Martinoli, A.: Modeling and designing self-organized aggregation in a swarm of miniature robots. Int. J. Robot. Res. **30**(5), 615–626 (2011)
4. Dall, J., Christensen, M.: Random geometric graphs. Phys. Rev. E **66**(1), 016121 (2002)
5. Dorigo, M., Birattari, M., Brambilla, M.: Swarm robotics. Scholarpedia **9**(1), 1463 (2014)
6. Dorigo, M., Theraulaz, G., Trianni, V.: Swarm robotics: past, present and future. Proc. IEEE **109**(7), 1152–1165 (2021)
7. Gielis, J., Shankar, A., Prorok, A.: A critical review of communications in multi-robot systems. Curr. Robot. Rep. **3**(4), 213–225 (2022)
8. Gupta, H., Strobel, V., Pacheco, A., Ferrante, E., Natalizio, E., Dorigo, M.: Group-level behavioral switch in a robot swarm using blockchain. In: Swarm Intelligence – Proceedings of ANTS 2024 – Fourteenth International Conference. Lecture Notes in Computer Science, vol. 14987, pp. 98–111. Springer (2024)
9. Haenggi, M., Andrews, J.G., Baccelli, F., Dousse, O., Franceschetti, M.: Stochastic geometry and random graphs for the analysis and design of wireless networks. IEEE J. Sel. Areas Commun. **27**(7), 1029–1046 (2009)
10. Hayat, S., Yanmaz, E., Bettstetter, C., Brown, T.X.: Multi-objective drone path planning for search and rescue with quality-of-service requirements. Auton. Robot. **44**(7), 1183–1198 (2020)
11. Hethcote, H.W.: The mathematics of infectious diseases. SIAM Rev. **42**(4), 599–653 (2000)
12. Keeling, M.J., Eames, K.T.D.: Networks and epidemic models. J. R. Soc. Interface **2**(4), 295–307 (2005)
13. Penrose, M.D.: Random Geometric Graphs, Oxford Studies in Probability, vol. 5. Oxford University Press, Oxford (2003)
14. Pinciroli, C., et al.: ARGoS: a modular, parallel, multi-engine simulator for multi-robot systems. Swarm Intell. **6**(4), 271–295 (2012)
15. Trianni, V., Nolfi, S., Dorigo, M.: Hole avoidance: experiments in coordinated motion on rough terrain. In: Intelligent Autonomous Systems 8 – IAS 8, pp. 29–36. IOS Press, Amsterdam, The Netherlands (2004)

On the Cost of Evolving Task Specialization in Multi-Robot Systems

Paolo Leopardi[1,2](✉) [ID], Heiko Hamann[1,2] [ID], Jonas Kuckling[1,2] [ID],
and Tanja Katharina Kaiser[3] [ID]

[1] Centre for the Advanced Study of Collective Behaviour, University of Konstanz,
Konstanz, Germany
[2] Department of Computer and Information Science, University of Konstanz,
Konstanz, Germany
{paolo.leopardi,heiko.hamann,jonas.kuckling}@uni-konstanz.de
[3] Department of Computer Science and Artificial Intelligence, University of
Technology Nuremberg, Nuremberg, Germany
tanja.kaiser@utn.de

Abstract. Task specialization can lead to simpler robot behaviors and higher efficiency in multi-robot systems. Previous works have shown the emergence of task specialization during evolutionary optimization, focusing on feasibility rather than costs. In this study, we take first steps toward a cost-benefit analysis of task specialization in robot swarms using a foraging scenario. We evolve artificial neural networks as generalist behaviors for the entire task and as task-specialist behaviors for subtasks within a limited evaluation budget. We show that generalist behaviors can be successfully optimized while the evolved task-specialist controllers fail to cooperate efficiently, resulting in worse performance than the generalists. Consequently, task specialization does not necessarily improve efficiency when optimization budget is limited.

1 Introduction

Swarm robotics [8,11] often relies on simple behaviors (e.g., reactive). Task specialization can scale task complexity by dividing labor while keeping individual behaviors simple, as seen in biological systems such as ant colonies [13,29]. However, task specialization is only effective when tasks can be partitioned while reducing the requirements for the specialized behaviors. These behaviors can be hand-coded, learned, or optimized using evolutionary optimization [3,18,30], and task specialization may even emerge naturally [7,10,20].

In this work, we study the cost of enabling task specialization and whether task-specialized behaviors can evolve under the same evaluation budget. While most prior work focuses on feasibility, we take first steps toward a cost-benefit analysis of task specialization in realistic swarm robotics use cases. We argue that task decomposition can destroy synergies in robot-environment interactions, introduce brittle interfaces, and make generalist policies easier to optimize than specialists in some settings. This mirrors Nolfi's distinction between monolithic

R. Groß et al. (Eds.): ANTS 2026, LNCS 16515, pp. 402–410, 2026.
https://doi.org/10.1007/978-3-032-26123-6_35

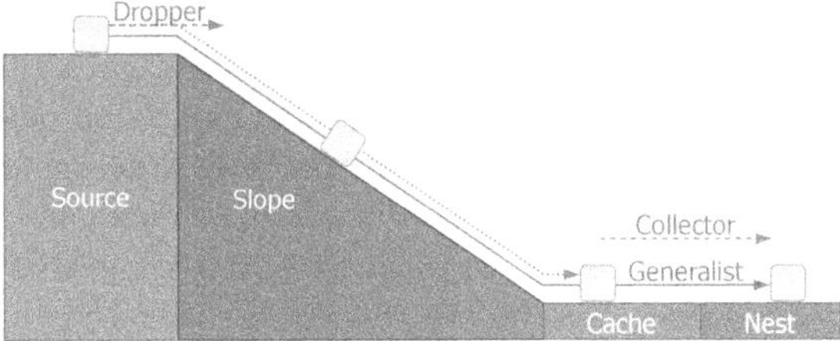

Fig. 1. Overview of the foraging task: Robots have to transport objects (squares) from the source across a slope to the nest. The task can either be executed by each robot individually (generalist) or shared between robots (dropper and collector).

and decomposed, modular controllers [23,24]. Moreover, for n subtasks, evolving n specialized controllers splits the evaluation budget E to E/n per controller, rather than using the full budget for one controller.

Using the foraging task of leafcutter ants as defined by Ferrante et al. [10], we compare evolved generalist controllers to task-specialist controllers without pre-defined primitives and under a limited evaluation budget. Our results quantify the opportunity cost [25]: under the same scarce evaluation budget, generalists achieve comparable or better performance at lower complexity. This is particularly relevant for real robots, where sim-to-real transfer often limits evaluation budgets due to computational constraints.

2 Related Work

Task partitioning and allocation is widely studied in swarm robotics. Challenges include coalition formation, resource management, and task interdependencies. Coalition formation concerns allocating groups of homogeneous [14] or heterogeneous [28] robots to tasks, often requiring many tasks to be handled by few robots without causing deadlocks. Resource management matters when allocation incurs a cost, such as energy [15], requiring task allocation strategies to balance potential gains against failure risk. In interdependent tasks, some (sub-)tasks depend on others [4], so robots allocated to downstream tasks contribute only after upstream tasks are sufficiently addressed. Foraging scenarios, where robots must find and transport resources, include all these challenges.

Inspired by the foraging behavior of insects, threshold models [17] have the robots observe and accumulate stimuli over time. Once the accumulated stimuli reach a threshold, the robots switch their behavior, e.g., they switch from waiting to foraging [6,15,17] or switch between subtasks [4,19,26,27]. Pini et al. [27] investigated the emergence of task specialization in a threshold-based model. Robots could either perform a generalist strategy, foraging items from the source into the nest, or learn to partition the task by using a cache. Depending on the properties of the environment (i.e., the cost of performing the generalist strategy), the swarm learned to either remain generalists or partition the task.

Other works study how task specialization emerges through artificial evolution and reinforcement learning. Researchers investigate the environmental conditions that benefit specialized behaviors over generalist ones [10,21] or how task allocation in homogeneous systems differs from heterogeneous ones [7,31]. Ferrante et al. [10] evolve the control software of a homogeneous robot swarm using predefined low-level behavioral primitives and show that task specialization is evolutionary stable, that is, swarms with successful task specialization do not revert to generalist behavior. Overall, however, specialized heterogeneity outperforms homogeneous systems [21,31], with heterogeneity either being predefined [7] or emerging during the design process [21]. Hiraga et al. [12] evolve controllers for manually defined subtasks and an arbitrator controller for subtask selection. This hierarchical structure outperforms controllers based on a single artificial neural network (ANN) by favoring collaborations among robots. Furthermore, it overcomes the bootstrapping and deception problem shown by the single ANN-based controller.

3 Task, Experimental Setup, and Methods

3.1 Task Description

We study a foraging task inspired by leafcutter ants harvesting leaves from trees [10]. Our environment has four areas (Fig. 1): source, slope, cache, and nest. M objects O_m, $m \in M$ are initially randomly distributed in the source. A swarm of N robots has to retrieve objects from the source and transport them to the nest. When dropped on the slope, objects slide down into the cache. Robots can exploit the slope to deliver objects faster to the cache. The performance of the swarm is measured by the number of objects C^T_{Nest} brought to the nest within an evaluation time T. Following Balch [1], we formalize C^T_{Nest} by

$$C^T_{\text{Nest}} = \sum_{m=1}^{M} H(O_m, t_0 + T, \text{Nest}), \tag{1}$$

$$H(O_m, t, \mathcal{A}) = \begin{cases} 1, & \text{if object } O_m \text{ is in area } \mathcal{A} \text{ at time } t \\ 0, & \text{otherwise} \end{cases} \tag{2}$$

with start time t_0 and $H(O_m, t, \mathcal{A})$ indicating if object O_m is in area $\mathcal{A}$ at time t.

The foraging task can be performed by two strategies: (i) each robot executes the full task alone, that is, it collects an object from the source and brings it back to the nest (*generalist*), or (ii) robots split the task into two interdependent subtasks. *Droppers* specialize in moving objects to the cache by exploiting the slope, and *collectors* specialize in transporting them from the cache to the nest.

3.2   Experimental Setup

We run our experiments in the open-source simulator Gazebo [16].

Arena.   We use an $4\,\mathrm{m} \times 7.5\,\mathrm{m}$ arena with a $1.5\,\mathrm{m}$-long nest, $1\,\mathrm{m}$-long cache and source areas, and a $4\,\mathrm{m}$-long slope. Three light sources indicate the nest. Cylinders (height: $0.06\,\mathrm{m}$, radius: $0.1\,\mathrm{m}$, weight: $1\,\mathrm{kg}$) are used as objects. Seven objects are randomly placed in the source at the beginning of each experiment.

Robot.   We use the differential-drive TurtleBot 4 and extend it with an emulated grasping mechanism, where objects automatically attach and release in specific areas depending on the behavior. Generalists and droppers attach objects in the source and release them in the nest and on the slope, respectively, while the collector attaches objects in the cache and releases them in the nest. Each robot can grasp only one object at a time, however, multiple objects can be pushed at once. We use the robot's seven infrared (IR) sensors normalized to $[0, 1]$, and its $360°$ 2D LiDAR capped to $1\,\mathrm{m}$. To reduce the number of sensor values, we divide the LiDAR readings into eight sectors and take the minimum reading of each sector. To detect the area a robot is currently in, we emulate four ground sensors. Each outputs a discrete value based on the current area: 0.2 for the nest, 0.4 for the cache, 0.6 for the slope, and 0.8 for the source. In addition, we place three light sensors on the top of the robot to detect the current light gradient relative to it. The possible light directions—front, right, left, and back—are mapped to the values 0.2, 0.4, 0.6, and 0.8, respectively. We add Gaussian noise to the IR sensors and the LiDAR. For the ground sensors, the correct area encoding is returned only with an 85% probability. The likelihood of returning the encoding of another area decreases the farther the area is from the true area.

Control Architecture.   Each robot is controlled by a fully-connected feedforward ANN, whose weights are optimized through evolution. It has one hidden layer of eight neurons, outputs a linear velocity v and an angular velocity ω, and has 21 inputs $s_1, \ldots, s_{21}$: $s_1, \ldots s_7$ are the normalized IR readings, $s_8, \ldots, s_{15}$ are the preprocessed LiDAR values, $s_{16}, \ldots, s_{19}$ are the ground sensor readings, s_{20} is the preprocessed light sensor value, and s_{21} is a binary value indicating whether the robot is currently grasping an object.

3.3   Evolution

We optimize ANN weights using a simple evolutionary algorithm [9], where genomes directly encode for weights. Initial weights are uniformly sampled from $[-0.5, 0.5]$. We use a population size of 100, tournament selection with a tournament size of 2, elitism of 1, one repetition, no crossover, and run evolution for 100 generations. Each gene is mutated with a 2% probability using Gaussian mutation with zero mean and standard deviation of 0.2. Initial robot poses and object placement are randomized across generations. As the foraging task does not require close robot collaboration, we argue that the three robot behaviors (see Sect. 3.1) can be evolved individually. Thus, we use only a single robot during optimization. We vary the simulated evaluation time T_{eval} and the configuration of the environment (i.e., initial robot pose and initial object placement) based on the behavior being evolved. For the generalist, we set $T_{\text{eval}} = 4\,\text{min}$, the robot is initialized in either the nest or the cache, and objects are positioned in the source. For the dropper and collector, we set $T_{\text{eval}} = 1\,\text{min}$. The dropper starts in the source with objects, while the collector starts in either the nest or the cache, with objects placed in the cache. We use longer evaluations for the generalist because they need to traverse the full arena to deliver items to the nest.

For the generalist and the collector behaviors, fitness is defined as the number of objects C_{Nest}^{T} in the nest at the end of the run at time T_{eval} (see Eq. 1). We define fitness F_G for the generalist and fitness F_C for the collector behaviors as

$$F_G = F_C = C_{\text{Nest}}^{T} = \sum_{m=1}^{M} H(O_m, t_0 + T_{\text{eval}}, \text{Nest}) \,. \tag{3}$$

For droppers, we use the number of objects on the cache, as defined by

$$F_D = \sum_{m=1}^{M} H(O_m, t_0 + T_{\text{eval}}, \text{Cache}) \,. \tag{4}$$

These aggregate fitness functions measure task success without rewarding specific behaviors [22]. We ran evolutions on two PCs, one with an AMD Ryzen 9 7900 CPU and a NVIDIA GeForce RTX 4070/4080, and another one with an Intel i5 and an NVIDIA GeForce RTX 4070 Ti Super. Each run took about 10 days for a generalist and 2 days for each specialist. We limited experiments to three independent runs each for the generalist, dropper, and collector.

3.4 Post-evaluation

We post-evaluate both foraging strategies (see Sect. 3.1) using the best genomes from the last generation of each evolutionary run. Controllers are tested with $N = 2$ robots in two settings: (i) homogeneous pairs of generalists sharing the same evolved weights, and (ii) mixed pairs composed of one dropper and one collector. We combine the droppers and collectors in the order of their evolution (i.e., the first evolved dropper with the first evolved collector, etc.). In addition, we evaluate the best of the three evolved droppers and collectors together. We test each configuration in ten random trials with 7 objects and an evaluation time of 5 min. In each trial, one robot begins in a random pose in the nest (generalist or collector) while the other starts in the source (generalist or dropper).

4 Results

4.1 Evolution

All three behaviors (see Sect. 3.1) are successfully evolved. Generalists require 30 generations before consistently achieving non-zero fitness, reaching a mean

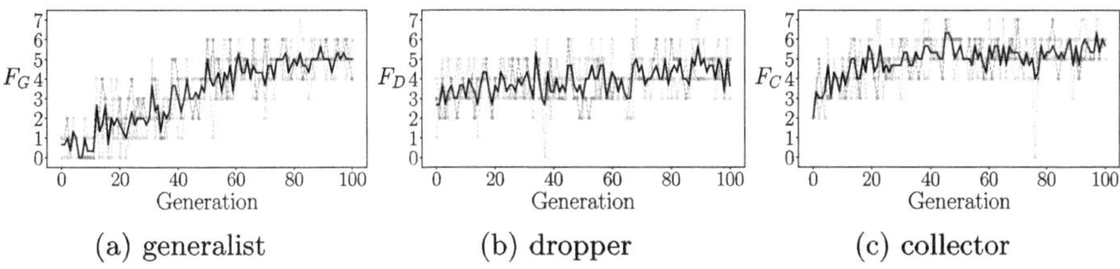

(a) generalist   (b) dropper   (c) collector

Fig. 2. Best fitness (Eqs. 3, 4) for the generalists, droppers, and collectors over 100 generations. Dashed lines: different independent evolutionary runs; black line: mean.

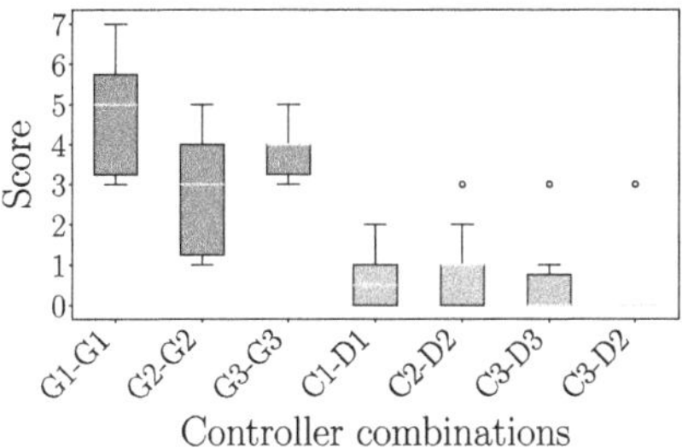

Fig. 3. Performance of groups of 2 robots. Letters indicate the subtask performed (generalist G, dropper D, collector C), numbers indicate the evolutionary run. Each letter-number pair is associated with a robot.

fitness of 5 for the best evolved individuals of the last generation. Within 30 generations, droppers and collectors steadily reach mean scores of 4 and 4.7, respectively. However, their fitness curve is flatter than for the generalist (see Fig. 2). These differences likely stem from the initial conditions and behavior complexity. Generalists are initialized in the nest and must first learn to navigate to the source. Since our aggregate fitness function F_G does not reward intermediate progress toward the source, evolution takes several generations before object collection reliably emerges. By contrast, droppers and collectors are initialized close to the objects, so even circular movements can yield non-zero fitness early on. This may, however, allow less robust behaviors to persist.

4.2   Post-evaluation

Next, we post-evaluate the three evolved behaviors in a multi-robot scenario (see Sect. 3.4). Letters indicate the behavior with generalists G, droppers D, collectors C, and numbers the evolutionary run of the respective best individual. The overall best evolved dropper emerged in evolution 2. The collectors C2 and C3 have equal performance. For the evaluation of the overall best evolved individuals, we consider the combinations of D2 and C2 and of D2 and C3.

Generalists outperform task-partitioned groups (see Fig. 3). The combination of the best evolved individuals, C3-D2, achieved the worst score, while C2-D2 performed the best among task-specialist groups. The differences can be explained by the behaviors of C2 and C3. C2 covers the cache area more homogeneously, while C3 shows circular movements at one side of the cache. Consequently, C2 may collect objects that spread over the entire cache, making it more reliable than C3. The performance gap between generalist and task-specialist groups mainly stems from the interdependence between the specialist subtasks. Both dropper and collector must perform reliably, while poor performance in either directly limits maximum achievable system performance. For example, even if the dropper delivers all objects quickly to the cache, success still depends on the collector bringing them to the nest. In contrast, generalists can complete the full task independently and contribute directly to system performance. Moreover, generalists must find and grasp each object once, whereas specialists require both, dropper and collector, to do so. Limiting these actions can improve performance if the dropper-collector cooperation is inefficient.

Another factor is the difference between the evolutionary setup, which employs one robot, and the multi-robot scenario, where two robots share the same arena. For generalists, this can reduce performance as robots may interfere with each other. Droppers and collectors operate at opposite ends of the same arena. If a robot leaves its area, it encounters sensor inputs not seen during optimization, which leads to unexpected behaviors and eventually reduces system performance.

5   Discussion and Conclusion

Task specialization can improve efficiency in multi-robot systems. However, our results show that its optimization cost does not always outweigh the benefits of the task decomposition. Under a fixed evaluation budget, generalist behaviors can outperform task-specialized controllers due to robot-environment and robot-robot interactions. Alternative evolutionary settings or more advanced controllers [12] may improve behavior quality, but better overall performance is not guaranteed. In our scenario, object finding and grasping seems to be challenging and is required twice as often in the task-specialized case, which can reduce system performance. This supports Nolfi's claim [23] that monolithic approaches may outperform decomposition and integration approaches when the overall behavior emerges from complex interactions.

In future work, we will study whether larger evaluation budgets enable more effective task-specialized behaviors. We aim to conduct a comprehensive cost-benefit analysis comparing generalist and task-specialized behaviors. To accelerate evolution, we will switch to a more scalable simulator [5], and address the potentially larger sim-to-real gap via a multi-level modeling approach [2], progressing from low to high-fidelity simulators and finally to real robots.

Acknowledgments. PL, HH, and JK acknowledge support from DFG through Germany's Excellence Strategy-EXC 2117-422037984 and Centre for the Advanced Study of Collective Behaviour (CASCB), University of Konstanz, Konstanz, Germany. JK acknowledges support from the Zukunftskolleg and the Carl-Zeiss-Foundation.

Disclosure of Interests. The authors have no competing interests to declare.

References

1. Balch, T.: Taxonomies of Multirobot Task and Reward. Robot Teams: From Diversity to Polymorphism, pp. 23–35 (2002)
2. Baumann, C., Birch, H., Martinoli, A.: Leveraging multi-level modelling to automatically design behavioral arbitrators in robotic controllers. In: IEEE/RSJ International Conference on Intelligent Robots and Systems (IROS), pp. 9318–9325 (2022)
3. Bongard, J.C.: Evolutionary robotics. Commun. ACM **56**(8), 74–83 (2013)
4. Brutschy, A., Pini, G., Pinciroli, C., Birattari, M., Dorigo, M.: Self-organized task allocation to sequentially interdependent tasks in swarm robotics. Auton. Agent. Multi-Agent Syst. **28**(1), 101–125 (2014)
5. Calderón-Arce, C., Brenes-Torres, J.C., Solis-Ortega, R.: Swarm robotics: simulators, platforms and applications review. Computation **10**(6), 80 (2022)
6. Castello, E., Yamamoto, T., Nakamura, Y., Ishiguro, H.: Foraging optimization in swarm robotic systems based on an adaptive response threshold model. Adv. Robot. **28**(20), 1343–1356 (2014)
7. van Diggelen, F., De Carlo, M., Cambier, N., Ferrante, E., Eiben, G.: Emergence of specialised collective behaviors in evolving heterogeneous swarms. In: International Conference on Parallel Problem Solving from Nature (PPSN), pp. 53–69. Springer, Cham (2024)
8. Dorigo, M., Theraulaz, G., Trianni, V.: Swarm robotics: past, present, and future [point of view]. Proc. IEEE **109**(7), 1152–1165 (2021)
9. Eiben, A.E., Smith, J.E.: Introduction to Evolutionary Computing. Springer, Heidelberg (2015)
10. Ferrante, E., Turgut, A.E., Duéñez-Guzmán, E., Dorigo, M., Wenseleers, T.: Evolution of self-organized task specialization in robot swarms. PLoS Comput. Biol. **11**(8), 1–21 (2015)
11. Hamann, H.: Swarm Robotics: A Formal Approach. Springer, Heidelberg (2018)
12. Hiraga, M., Wei, Y., Yasuda, T., Ohkura, K.: Evolving autonomous specialization in congested path formation task of robotic swarms. Artif. Life Robot. **23**(4), 547–554 (2018). https://doi.org/10.1007/s10015-018-0483-5
13. Hölldobler, B., Wilson, E.O.: The Superorganism: The Beauty, Elegance, and Strangeness of Insect Societies. W. W. Norton and Company, New York (2008)
14. Ijspeert, A.J., Martinoli, A., Billard, A., Gambardella, L.M.: Collaboration through the exploitation of local interactions in autonomous collective robotics: the stick pulling experiment. Auton. Robot. **11**(2), 149–171 (2001)
15. Kernbach, S., Nepomnyashchikh, V.A., Kancheva, T., Kernbach, O.: Specialization and generalization of robot behaviour in swarm energy foraging. Math. Comput. Model. Dyn. Syst. **18**(1), 131–152 (2012)
16. Koenig, N., Howard, A.: Design and use paradigms for gazebo, an open-source multi-robot simulator. In: IEEE/RSJ International Conference on Intelligent Robots and Systems (IROS), vol. 3, pp. 2149–2154. IEEE (2004)
17. Krieger, M.J., Billeter, J.B.: The call of duty: self-organised task allocation in a population of up to twelve mobile robots. Robot. Auton. Syst. **30**(1–2), 65–84 (2000)
18. Kuckling, J.: Recent trends in robot learning and evolution for swarm robotics. Front. Robot. AI **10**, 1134841 (2023)
19. Lee, W., Vaughan, N., Kim, D.: Task allocation into a foraging task with a series of subtasks in swarm robotic system. IEEE Access **8**, 107549–107561 (2020)

20. Li, L., Martinoli, A., Abu-Mostafa, Y.S.: Emergent specialization in swarm systems. In: International Conference on Intelligent Data Engineering and Automated Learning, pp. 261–266. Springer, Cham (2002)
21. Montanier, J.M., Carrignon, S., Bredeche, N.: Behavioral specialization in embodied evolutionary robotics: why so difficult? Front. Robot. AI **3**, 38 (2016)
22. Nelson, A.L., Barlow, G.J., Doitsidis, L.: Fitness functions in evolutionary robotics: a survey and analysis. Robot. Auton. Syst. **57**(4), 345–370 (2009)
23. Nolfi, S.: Adaptation as a more powerful tool than decomposition and integration: experimental evidences from evolutionary robotics. In: IEEE International Conference on Fuzzy Systems Proceedings, vol. 1, pp. 141–146 (1998)
24. Nolfi, S., Floreano, D.: Evolutionary Robotics: The Biology, Intelligence, and Technology of Self-Organizing Machines. MIT Press, Cambridge (2000)
25. Paglieri, F., Parisi, D., Patacchiola, M., Petrosino, G.: Investigating intertemporal choice through experimental evolutionary robotics. Behav. Process. **115** (2015)
26. Pang, B., Song, Y., Zhang, C., Wang, H., Yang, R.: Autonomous task allocation in a swarm of foraging robots: an approach based on response threshold sigmoid model. Int. J. Control Autom. Syst. **17**(4), 1031–1040 (2019)
27. Pini, G., Brutschy, A., Frison, M., Roli, A., Dorigo, M., Birattari, M.: Task partitioning in swarms of robots: an adaptive method for strategy selection. Swarm Intell. **5**(3), 283–304 (2011)
28. Prorok, A., Hsieh, M.A., Kumar, V.: The impact of diversity on optimal control policies for heterogeneous robot swarms. IEEE Trans. Rob. **33**(2), 346–358 (2017)
29. Taborsky, M.: The evolution of division of labour: preconditions and evolutionary feedback. Philos. Trans. B **380**(1922), 20230262 (2025)
30. Trianni, V.: Evolutionary Swarm Robotics - Evolving Self-Organising Behaviours in Groups of Autonomous Robots, Studies in Computational Intelligence, vol. 108. Springer, Berlin (2008)
31. Tuci, E.: Evolutionary swarm robotics: genetic diversity, task-allocation and task-switching. In: International Conference on Swarm Intelligence, pp. 98–109. Springer, Cham (2014)

Online Self-calibration of Robotic Swarm Motility Phases via Social Learning with Fast Transmission

Leo Cazenille[1]([✉])(iD), Salman Houdaibi[2](iD), and Nicolas Bredeche[1,3]([✉])(iD)

[1] Sorbonne Université, CNRS, ISIR, 75005 Paris, France
leo.cazenille@gmail.com
[2] Université Libre de Bruxelles, 1050 Brussels, Belgium
[3] Sorbonne Université, CNRS, IBPS, LJP, 75005 Paris, France
nicolas.bredeche@sorbonne-universite.fr

Abstract. Collective motion in swarm robotics is often designed from homogeneous, physics-inspired rules, yet real swarms must operate in confined arenas where boundaries reshape local interactions and where robots exhibit heterogeneous sensor and motor biases. We introduce an online, fully decentralized self-calibration framework that tunes microscopic control parameters so that the swarm reaches a desired macroscopic motility phase. Building on social learning, we add a fast-transmission mechanism that rapidly disseminates clearly better controllers through local interactions, complementing slower mutation–selection updates. Using a motility model combining alignment, density-dependent crowding, and collective U-turn propagation, we show in simulation that swarms self-calibrate from random initial behavior to reliably achieve several target phases (flocking, disordered gas, clustering, and gas–solid coexistence) in a disk arena. Fast transmission substantially accelerates convergence and improves robustness to heterogeneity, enabling rapid phase control without any central coordination.

1 Introduction

Swarm robotics [5,23] studies how large groups of simple robots, each following local rules and using short-range communication, can self-organize into robust and scalable collectives. Much of the theory of collective motion, in both active matter [17,31,32] and swarm robotics, is grounded in homogeneous equation-based models such as the Vicsek and Toner–Tu families [35,36], where identical point agents evolve in periodic geometries. These models are invaluable for understanding phase transitions. However, when a fixed set of controller parameters is transferred to physical or realistic robot swarms, the resulting dynamics depend strongly on arena geometry (walls, bottlenecks, corners) [2,26,34] and hardware biases, so each new arena or bias regime often requires expert retuning. Figure 1 illustrates this point: the same hand-crafted controller, tuned for flocking, produces markedly different motility patterns with differing hardware bias regimes.

R. Groß et al. (Eds.): ANTS 2026, LNCS 16515, pp. 411–419, 2026.
https://doi.org/10.1007/978-3-032-26123-6_36

Low-level calibration (e.g. PID) does not solve this problem [21]: sensor and motor characteristics drift during experiments, heading control degrades under noisy orientation estimates, and small systematic biases alter behavior. Controllers that appear robust in simulation can yield very different macroscopic statistics [15] when deployed under realistic heterogeneity and geometry constraints. This motivates a shift from hand-crafted parameter sets to *online self-calibration* of microscopic control parameters based on macroscopic behavior [12,19,27].

There exists a class of evolutionary optimization algorithms, called social learning (SL) [1,6–8,37], that enable embodied, online, distributed optimization in robot swarms. While successful for tasks such as phototaxis or foraging, they are not suited to optimizing motility patterns that require locally homogeneous behavior (e.g., flocking) while preserving genotypic diversity to compensate for hardware biases. We postulate that Horizontal Information Transfer (HIT), the flagship SL algorithm [18], converges too slowly with rewards that depend on neighbors' behavior (diluted credit assignment). To address this, we introduce a *fast transmission* (FT) mechanism operating on a shorter time scale: when a high-performing genotype is far superior, it is quickly copied by neighbors. Inspired by cultural transmission [4,24], epidemiological spreading [20,29], and horizontal gene transfer [14,33], FT allows successful "behavioral strains" to propagate quickly while evolutionary dynamics maintain exploration and heterogeneity.

To validate this approach, we introduce the ACU motility model (Alignment with Crowding and U-turns), which combines (i) Vicsek-style alignment with angular noise [36], (ii) density-dependent speed modulation inspired by motility-induced phase separation (MIPS) [9,16], and (iii) propagating collective U-turns reminiscent of those observed in fish schools [13,22,25,28]. This low-dimensional model generates flocking, disordered gas, compact clusters, and MIPS-like coexistence of dense and dilute phases, and remains implementable on resource-constrained robots. We deploy ACU with HIT+FT in simulation targeting the Pogobots [30], open-hardware circular robots executed in the Pogosim simulator [11] which reproduce collisions through a 2D physics engine. We show that the swarm *self-calibrates* its motility parameters online to reach target macroscopic dynamics across heterogeneous robots. Implementation details and code used are available at [10].

2   Motility Model: Alignment with Crowding and U-Turns

We consider N planar self-propelled agents with states (x_i, y_i, θ_i), commanded linear speed $v_i \in [0, 1]$, heading θ_i and set of current neighbors $\mathcal{N}_i(t)$.

Kinematics: $\mathrm{d}x_i = v_i \cos\theta_i\, \mathrm{d}t, \qquad \mathrm{d}y_i = v_i \sin\theta_i\, \mathrm{d}t.$

Vicsek Alignment Target. Let $\theta_i^\star(t)$ be the commanded heading with $\theta_i^\star(t) = \theta_i^{\mathrm{vic}}(t)$ but overridden during U-turns (see below): $\theta_i^{\mathrm{vic}}(t) = \arg\left(e^{j\theta_i(t)} + \sum_{k \in \mathcal{N}_i(t)} e^{j\theta_k(t)}\right).$

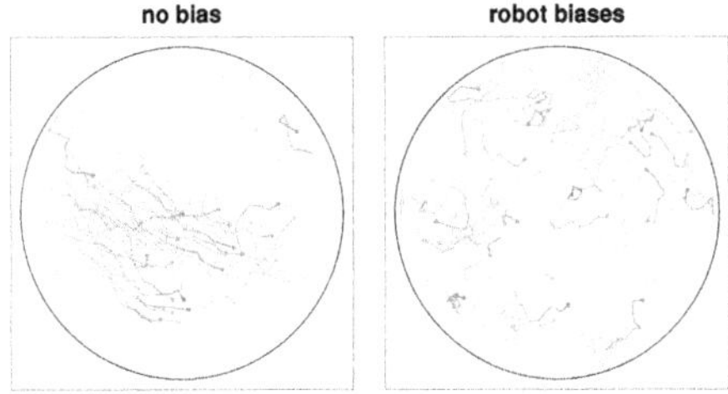

Fig. 1. Representative traces of 60 robots driven by the ACU motility model robots over 30 s in disk arenas, respectively without and with biases across motors and heading sensors (thus influencing PID control). Color intensity represent different time steps (brightest: present time). We use the following parameters, corresponding to a flocking dynamics: $v_0 = 1.0$, $\beta = 0.82$, $\sigma = 0.20$, $\phi_{\mathrm{norm}} = 0.70$, $d_{\mathrm{crowd}} = 0.0$. The arenas have a surface of 2.0×10^6 mm^2 within walls, robots have a radius of 26.5 mm and can communicate 133 mm from center to center.

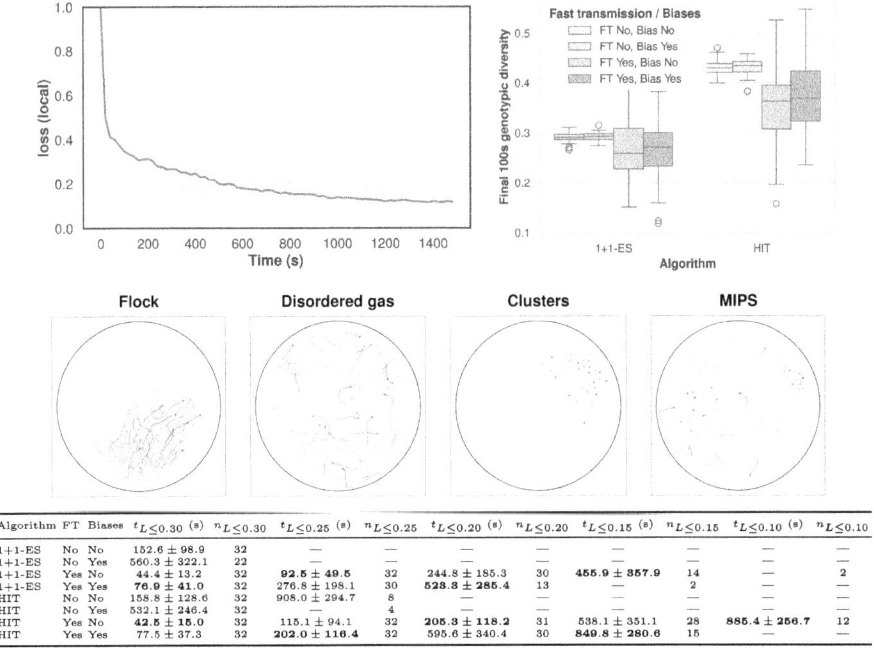

Algorithm	FT	Biases	$t_{L \leq 0.30}$ (s)	$n_{L \leq 0.30}$	$t_{L \leq 0.25}$ (s)	$n_{L \leq 0.25}$	$t_{L \leq 0.20}$ (s)	$n_{L \leq 0.20}$	$t_{L \leq 0.15}$ (s)	$n_{L \leq 0.15}$	$t_{L \leq 0.10}$ (s)	$n_{L \leq 0.10}$
1+1-ES	No	No	152.6 ± 98.9	32	—	—	—	—	—	—	—	—
1+1-ES	No	Yes	560.3 ± 322.1	22	—	—	—	—	—	—	—	—
1+1-ES	Yes	No	44.4 ± 13.2	32	$\mathbf{92.5 \pm 49.5}$	32	244.8 ± 185.3	30	$\mathbf{455.9 \pm 357.9}$	14	—	2
1+1-ES	Yes	Yes	$\mathbf{76.9 \pm 41.0}$	32	276.8 ± 198.1	30	$\mathbf{523.3 \pm 285.4}$	13	—	2	—	—
HIT	No	No	158.8 ± 128.6	32	908.0 ± 294.7	8	—	—	—	—	—	—
HIT	No	Yes	532.1 ± 246.4	32	—	4	—	—	—	—	—	—
HIT	Yes	No	$\mathbf{42.5 \pm 15.0}$	32	115.1 ± 94.1	32	$\mathbf{205.3 \pm 118.2}$	31	538.1 ± 351.1	28	$\mathbf{885.4 \pm 256.7}$	12
HIT	Yes	Yes	77.5 ± 37.3	32	$\mathbf{202.0 \pm 116.4}$	32	595.6 ± 340.4	30	$\mathbf{849.8 \pm 280.6}$	15	—	—

Fig. 2. HIT-FT results. **Top Left**: representative example of loss score evolution for the HIT+FT case (here for the Clusters goal) over 32 runs. **Top Right**: Genotypic (v_0, β, σ, ϕ_{norm}, d_{crowd}) diversity of all optimizer cases, over the last 100 s of all goals and runs. **Middle**: representative examples of 60-robot traces (with no robot biases) targeting all four considered goals. Color intensity represent different time steps (brightest for present time). **Bottom** Comparison of simulation results across 32 runs per case: time (in simulation seconds) to reach loss targets 0.30 to 0.10 (mean $\pm$ std), and number of runs n reaching each target (across runs, bias regime and goals, min. time in bold). Only combinations with ≥ 5 runs reaching a target are considered ("—" if less).

Heading SDE. With alignment gain $\beta > 0$ and angular diffusion $\sigma \geq 0$, $d\theta_i = 10\beta \sin\big(\theta_i^\star(t) - \theta_i(t)\big)\, dt + 10\sigma\, dW_i(t)$, where W_i is a standard Wiener process. We multiply β and σ by 10 to have all parameters in the $[0,1]$ domain, easing the optimization process of the next Sec.

Crowding-Based Speed Command. Given a base speed $v_0 \in [0,1]$, let $d_i(t) = |\mathcal{N}_i(t)|$ be the neighbor count, $N_{\text{tgt}} > 0$ a target neighbor count, $w_n \geq 1$ a width, and $d_{\text{crowd}} \in [0,1]$ the slowdown depth: $v_i(t) = v_0\Big[(1 - d_{\text{crowd}}) + d_{\text{crowd}} \min\Big(1, \frac{|d_i(t) - N_{\text{tgt}}|}{w_n}\Big)\Big] \in [0,1]$. For $|d_i(t) - N_{\text{tgt}}| < w_n$, the crowding term reduces the speed around the target density (e.g., to create clusters), whereas for $|d_i(t) - N_{\text{tgt}}| \geq w_n$ the agent simply moves at the base speed v_0 (no crowding).

Cluster U-Turn. We attach IR LED strips to walls so that they periodically emit a message "I am a wall" to the robots. A U-turn triggers at the rising edge of a wall-avoidance event at time t_i^0, with heading $\theta_i(t_i^0)$, selecting a target $\theta_i^{\text{ut}} := \big(\theta_i(t_i^0)+\phi\big) \bmod 2\pi$, $\phi := 2\pi\,\phi_{\text{norm}} \in [0, 2\pi)$. and activating $\theta_i^\star(t) = \theta_i^{\text{ut}}$ for a fixed duration $\tau_{\text{ut}} > 0$: $t \in [t_i^0, t_i^0+\tau_{\text{ut}}] \Rightarrow \theta_i^\star(t) = \theta_i^{\text{ut}}$, $t > t_i^0+\tau_{\text{ut}} \Rightarrow \theta_i^\star(t) = \theta_i^{\text{vic}}(t)$. During activation, robot i broadcasts $(\theta^{\text{ut}}, t^0)$; any neighbor receiving a newer message adopts the same $(\theta^{\text{ut}}, [t^0, t^0 + \tau_{\text{ut}}])$, yielding a sequential "domino-like" propagation of collective U-turns.

The parameter ϕ_{norm} controls the angular offset of the collective reorientation relative to the agent's current heading, expressed as a fraction of a full turn. A value $\phi_{\text{norm}} = 0.5$ corresponds to $\phi = \pi$ and thus induces a full reversal of the agent's direction. Smaller values produce partial reorientations: for instance, $\phi_{\text{norm}} \approx 0.2$ yields a turn of about 72°, which empirically promotes wall-following trajectories rather than direct reversal.

Equation-based models typically assume homogeneous agents. Here, each robot has its own hardware biases, so behavior varies across individuals. Figure 1 shows representative time-evolution of robot motion with different bias regimes, using a parameter set targeting flocking with wall avoidance. This suggests that **hand-crafted parameter sets are not robust in practice**, motivating the self-calibration mechanism described in the next section.

3   Self-calibrating Swarm with Fast Transmission (FT)

This section describes the self-adaptive controller that *optimizes* the parameters of a ACU model online. We run an online optimizer on every robot (either 1+1-ES or HIT, described below), that will **slowly** improve their local ACU parameters. Alongside the optimizer, we implement a novel "Fast transmission" (FT) mechanism (contribution of this article) that clones clearly-better neighbors with a small acceptance probability gate. FT causes fast, *wave-like* propagation of winning genotypes in just a few communication hops, while remaining robust to noise . This gives an optimization process that operate at **two different time-scales**, with both fast percolation and slow incremental random noise. This lets the swarm quickly exit local optima and coordinate toward targets that require both genotypic/phenotypic convergence and structured inhomogeneities (e.g., robot hardware bias, dual persistence for MIPS-like regimes), which standard decentralized optimizers fail to achieve at realistic timescales.

Local Phenotypical Statistics Computed on Each Robot: Robots periodically compute local statistics, that serve as heuristics of the desired global statistics corresponding to the target behavioral goal. Each robot i maintains local, normalized phenotypical statistics in $[0,1]$: $s_i^{\mathrm{loc}} = (P_i, W_i, \Pi_i, N_i)$.

Rayleigh-corrected Local Polarization. Let $\theta_i(t)$ be robot i's heading and $\theta_j(t)$ the heading of neighbor $j \in \mathcal{N}_i(t)$ at time t, with $d_i(t) = |\mathcal{N}_i(t)|$. Robot i first computes the average heading vector over itself and its current neighbors,

$$\hat{\mathbf{m}}_i(t) = \frac{1}{1 + d_i(t)}\Big((\cos\theta_i(t), \sin\theta_i(t)) + \sum_{j \in \mathcal{N}_i(t)} (\cos\theta_j(t), \sin\theta_j(t))\Big),$$

and its modulus $R_i(t) = \|\hat{\mathbf{m}}_i(t)\| \in [0,1]$. To compensate the finite-sample bias of $R_i(t)$ for small $d_i(t)$, we use a Rayleigh correction with

$R_{0,i}(t) = \frac{\sqrt{\pi}}{2\sqrt{1 + d_i(t)}}, P_i(t) = \frac{R_i(t) - R_{0,i}(t)}{1 - R_{0,i}(t)}$

Thus $P_i(t) \approx 0$ when headings are locally isotropic, and $P_i(t) \approx 1$ when robot i and its neighbors are strongly aligned (e.g., flocking).

Wall/U-turn Ratio. Let W_i denote the ratio of time robot i spend over an optimization evaluation window of duration $T_{\mathtt{eval}}$ in either (i) in local wall-avoidance mode, or (ii) in the U-turn mode triggered by a wall hit.

Neighbor-persistence Score. Robot i maintains, for each neighbor $j \in \mathcal{N}_i(t)$, the time $a_{ij}(t)$ elapsed since j first entered its neighborhood and has remained continuously visible. This age is normalized by a time constant $\tau_{\mathtt{pers}}$ and clipped at 1. The neighbor-persistence score is the average normalized age. With $d_i(t) > 0$, $\Pi_i(t) = \frac{1}{d_i(t)} \sum_{j \in \mathcal{N}_i(t)} \min\Big(\frac{a_{ij}(t)}{\tau_{\mathtt{pers}}}, 1\Big)$. Hence $\Pi_i(t) \approx 1$ when robot i keeps the same neighbors for at least $\tau_{\mathtt{pers}}$ (solid-like), and $\Pi_i(t) \approx 0$ when neighbors frequently change (gas-like regime).

Neighbor Count. Finally, $N_i(t)$ is the neighbor count $d_i(t)$ normalized to $[0,1]$.

Per-robot Online Optimization: Given target goals $G = (\hat{P}, \hat{W}, \hat{\Pi}, \hat{N})$ with nonnegative weights $\Omega = (\omega_P, \omega_W, \omega_\Pi, \omega_N)$, we define per-objective "goodness" scores for robot i as $s_x(t) = 1 - 2|x_i(t) - \hat{x}|, x \in \{P, W, \Pi, N\}$, using the fact that all variables are normalized to $[0,1]$. The weighted utility of robot i is $U_i(s_i^{\mathrm{loc}}(t)) = \frac{\omega_P s_{P,i}(t) + \omega_W s_{W,i}(t) + \omega_\Pi s_{\Pi,i}(t) + \omega_N s_{N,i}(t)}{|\omega_P| + |\omega_W| + |\omega_\Pi| + |\omega_N|}$ and the corresponding bounded local loss is $L_i(s_i^{\mathrm{loc}}(t)) = \frac{1 - U_i(s_i^{\mathrm{loc}}(t))}{2} \in [0,1]$. Robots minimize the **local** loss $L_i^{\mathrm{loc}}(t) := L_i(s_i^{\mathrm{loc}}(t))$. Each step, robot i accumulates $L_i^{\mathrm{loc}}(t)$ over an evaluation window of $T_{\mathtt{eval}}$ s, preceded by maturation guard $T_{\mathtt{quiet}}$. The objective function is the time-averaged loss over this window.

Each robot i runs an optimizer over the **genotype**: $g = (\beta, \sigma, v_0, \phi_{\text{norm}}, d_{\text{crowd}}) \in [0,1]^5$, from the ACU model. After each T_{eval}-window end, robot i tells the achieved loss L_i to its optimizer, obtains a new g and broadcast $\langle g, \text{epoch}, L_i \rangle$ in its periodic messages. Neighbors record these remote candidates for their own optimizers. The two considered optimizers are described as follows.

Horizontal Information Transfer **(HIT)** [18] is an embodied-evolution / social-learning algorithm [7,37] in which robots optimize their policy online **by exchanging and mutating subsets** of their controller parameters rather than full genomes. Each agent evaluates its current genome using a task-specific reward accumulated over a sliding window of length eval_T. Communication is disabled during this maturation period so that only fully evaluated policies participate in selection. When two mature agents meet, the one with the lower sliding-window score adopts $z \approx \alpha^{\text{HIT}} n$ randomly chosen parameter values from the better neighbor's genome, where $\alpha^{\text{HIT}} \in [\alpha^{\text{HIT}}_{\text{min}}, \alpha^{\text{HIT}}_{\text{max}}]$ is the transfer rate controlling the fraction of copied parameters. After transfer, all parameters are perturbed by additive Gaussian noise with standard deviation σ^{HIT}. The transfer rate itself evolves by copying the neighbor's α^{HIT}, mutating it with variance $(\alpha^{\text{HIT}}_{\sigma})^2$. The slow nature of HIT genome exchange **stabilizes reward evaluation and credit assignment**.

The **1+1-ES** [3] baseline is a classical (1+1) Evolution Strategy that maintains a single parent solution and, at each iteration, generates a single offspring by adding Gaussian noise with step-size σ to all parameters. Contrarily to HIT, with 1+1-ES, **robots do not exchange genomes and optimization is purely local.** The global mutation step-size is initialized to σ_0, then adapted online based on the observed success of offspring. If the offspring achieves a better objective value than its parent, it replaces the parent. Step-size updates follow a standard multiplicative rule controlled by the learning rate c_σ, allowing the algorithm to automatically adapt its exploration scale to the local fitness landscape.

Fast Transmission (FT): Thresholded Probabilistic Cloning: On top of the slow parameter search performed by the optimizer, we add a *fast transmission* rule that can immediately copy a clearly better neighbor's genotype. Let L_i be robot i's current loss and L_j^{adv} the loss advertised by a neighbor j. We define the relative improvement $I = \frac{L_i - L_j^{\text{adv}}}{\max(L_i, \varepsilon)}$, with $\varepsilon = 10^{-5}$. A neighbor is considered *strictly better* if $I > \tau$, where $\tau \in [0,1]$ is an improvement threshold. If i has already reached its target loss L_{target}, it will not accept any clone.

Given a base acceptance probability $p_0 \in [0,1]$, the FT rule is: $p_{\text{accept}} = p_0$ if $I > \tau$ and $L_i > L_{\text{target}}$, and $p_{\text{accept}} = 0$ otherwise. On acceptance, robot i immediately clones neighbor j's genotype $g_j = (\beta, \sigma, v, \phi_{\text{norm}}, d_{\text{crowd}})$ and reseeds its optimizer at that point. This creates fast-moving "information fronts" that spread high-performing genotypes across the swarm in $O(\text{diameter})$ hops, while the gate τ and the stochastic factor p_0 dampen fragile cascades.

4   Results

We validate the FT mechanism in a disk arena (Fig. 1) using two optimizers: 1+1-ES (no genome exchange) and HIT (social learning). Both minimize a multiobjective loss targeting four collective goals: flocking (alignment), disordered gas (no alignment or clustering), clusters, and MIPS (coexistence of dense and dilute phases) – see [10] for parameter values. All experiments test both presence and absence of hardware biases.

Figure 2-Bottom reports the mean time (across runs, bias regimes, and goals) to reach target loss values and the proportion of successful runs. Without FT, convergence to $L \leq 0.30$ is significantly slower (≈ 150âĂŞ850s) than with FT (≈ 40âĂŞ75s), and lower losses are not reached within 1500 s. FT consistently achieves $L \leq 0.25$, and HIT-FT reaches $L \leq 0.15$. Since $L = 0$ may be unattainable in this setup, we define success at $L_{\texttt{target}} = 0.15$. Figure 2-Top-Left shows a representative HIT-FT trajectory, where loss plateaus around $L \approx 0.20$ at 1000 s before further gradual improvement.

Genotypic diversity is quantified as the variance of robot genotypes g. Figure 2-Top-Right shows that diversity depends on both optimizer (higher with HIT than 1+1-ES) and FT (larger variance). Without FT, robots tend to converge toward a single sub-optimum with 1+1-ES, whereas HIT maintains diversity through incremental genome exchange. In non-FT cases, diversity remains similar across biases and goals; with FT, diversity adapts to task demands, acting as an adaptive diversity regulation mechanism.

Figure 2-Middle presents representative trajectories obtained with HIT-FT, demonstrating successful adaptation across all configurations.

5   Discussions and Conclusion

Here we presented two contributions: (1) the ACU motility algorithm combining Alignment, Crowding and U-Turns, enabling a wide range of collective phases in robot swarms; and (2) a fast self-adaptive mechanism that accelerates local or social learning of target collective dynamics.

Fast Transmission resembles an epidemic spread of elite individuals, complementing slow mutationâĂŞselection dynamics. As soon as a highly performing genotype appears, FT rapidly propagates it across the interaction network, recentering local optimizers on that basin of attraction and drastically reducing time spent evaluating poor genomes. It also enables fast escape from local optima, since copying is immediate and does not require long evaluation windows. This induces strong early selection pressure, as successful lineages multiply exponentially via FT. Once a low-loss regime is reached, selection weakens, noise and motor-bias adaptation dominate, and HIT continues injecting mutations. The result is ongoing neutral drift along the plateau, maintaining a rich polymorphism of genotypes achieving similar collective performance.

Our approach constitutes a first step toward complex self-adaptive swarms with decentralized online learning. Future work will validate HIT-FT on real

Pogobot robots, leveraging the shared C API between Pogosim and hardware to ease transfer. We also plan to use percolation-style analyses to characterize the joint effects of fast transmission and slower HIT diffusion on swarm learning, and to study the impact of hyperparameters (e.g., genome size, transmission rate, FT parameters). Formal convergence guarantees and adaptation bounds remain open theoretical questions. Extensions to more complex goals and controllers (equation-based or neural) are possible, as well as studying adaptation across changing tasks or environments.

Acknowledgments. This work was supported by the SSR project funded by the Agence Nationale pour la Recherche under Grant No ANR-24-CE33-7791. We thank J. Fersula, A. Loi, K. Amini, L. Polachini and J. Botoko Ekila for meaningful comments.

Disclosure of Interests. The authors have no competing interests to declare.

References

1. Ben Zion, M.Y., Fersula, J., Bredeche, N., Dauchot, O.: Morphological computation and decentralized learning in a swarm of sterically interacting robots. Sci. Robot. **8**(75), eabo6140 (2023)
2. Beppu, K., Maeda, Y.: Exploring order in active turbulence: geometric rule and pairing order transition in confined bacterial vortices. Biophys. Physicobiol. **19**, e190020 (2022)
3. Beyer, H., Arnold, D.: Theory of evolution strategies—a tutorial. Theoretical Aspects of Evolutionary Computing, pp. 109–133 (2001)
4. Boyd, R., Richerson, P., Henrich, J.: The cultural niche: why social learning is essential for human adaptation. PNAS **108**, 10918–10925 (2011)
5. Brambilla, M., Ferrante, E., Birattari, M., Dorigo, M.: Swarm robotics: a review from the swarm engineering perspective. Swarm Intell. **7**(1), 1–41 (2013)
6. Bredeche, N., Fontbonne, N.: Social learning in swarm robotics. Philos. Trans. R. Soc. B **377**(1843), 20200309 (2022)
7. Bredeche, N., Haasdijk, E., Prieto, A.: Embodied evolution in collective robotics: a review. Front. Robot. AI. **5**, 12 (2018)
8. Bredeche, N., Montanier, J., Liu, W., Winfield, A.: Environment-driven distributed evolutionary adaptation in a population of autonomous robotic agents. Math. Comput. Model. Dyn. Syst. **18**(1), 101–129 (2012)
9. Cates, M., Tailleur, J.: Motility-induced phase separation. Annu. Rev. Condens. Matter Phys. **6**(1), 219–244 (2015)
10. Cazenille, L., Houdaibi, S., Bredeche, N.: Self-adaptive phase control in robotic swarms using social learning with fast transmission. https://github.com/leo-cazenille/ACU-selfadapt (2025), Accessed 20 Nov 2025
11. Cazenille, L., Macabre, L., Bredeche, N.: Pogosim-a simulator for pogobot robots. arXiv:2509.10968 (2025)
12. Chin, K., Pinciroli, C.: Adaptive self-calibration for minimalistic collective perception by imperfect robot swarms. arXiv preprint arXiv:2410.21546 (2024)
13. Crosato, E., et al.: Informative and misinformative interactions in a school of fish. Swarm Intell. **12**(4), 283–305 (2018). https://doi.org/10.1007/s11721-018-0157-x

14. Croucher, N., Mostowy, R., Wymant, C., Turner, P., Bentley, S., Fraser, C.: Horizontal dna transfer mechanisms of bacteria as weapons of intragenomic conflict. PLoS Bio. **14**(3), e1002394 (2016)
15. Duarte, M., Costa, V., Gomes, J., Rodrigues, T., Silva, F., Oliveira, S., Christensen, A.: Evolution of collective behaviors for a real swarm of aquatic surface robots. PLoS ONE **11**(3), e0151834 (2016)
16. Fily, Y., Marchetti, M.: Athermal phase separation of self-propelled particles with no alignment. PRL **108**(23), 235702 (2012)
17. Fodor, E., Marchetti, M.: The statistical physics of active matter: from self-catalytic colloids to living cells. Phys. A: Stat. Mech. Appl. **504**, 106–120 (2018)
18. Fontbonne, N., Dauchot, O., Bredeche, N.: Distributed on-line learning in swarm robotics with limited communication bandwidth. In: CEC, pp. 1–8. IEEE (2020)
19. Francesca, G., Birattari, M.: Automatic design of robot swarms: achievements and challenges. Front. Robot. AI **3**, 29 (2016)
20. Fraser, C., Riley, S., Anderson, R., Ferguson, N.: Factors that make an infectious disease outbreak controllable. Proc. Natl. Acad. Sci. **101**(16), 6146–6151 (2004)
21. Garcia-Saura, C.: Self-calibration of a differential wheeled robot using only a gyroscope and a distance sensor. arXiv preprint arXiv:1509.02154 (2015)
22. Gautrais, J., et al.: Deciphering interactions in moving animal groups (2012)
23. Hamann, H.: Swarm robotics: a formal approach, vol. 221. Springer (2018)
24. Henrich, J.: Cultural transmission and the diffusion of innovations: adoption dynamics indicate that biased cultural transmission is the predominate force in behavioral change. Am. Anthropol. **103**(4), 992–1013 (2001)
25. Herbert-Read, J., Buhl, C., Hu, F., Ward, A., Sumpter, D.: Initiation and spread of escape waves within animal groups. RSOS **2**(4), 140355 (2015)
26. Knippenberg, T.: Active matter under static and dynamic confinement (2025)
27. Kuckling, J.: Recent trends in robot learning and evolution for swarm robotics. Front. Robot. AI **10**, 1134841 (2023)
28. Lecheval, V., Jiang, L Tichit, P., Sire, C., Hemelrijk, C., Theraulaz, G.: Social conformity and propagation of information in collective u-turns of fish schools. Proc. R. Soc. B: Biol. Sci. **285**(1877), 20180251 (2018)
29. Lloyd-Smith, J., Schreiber, S., Kopp, PEand Getz, W.: Superspreading and the effect of individual variation on disease emergence. Nature **438**(7066), 355–359 (2005)
30. Loi, A., et al.: Pogobot: an open-source, low-cost robot for swarm robotics and programmable active matter (2025)
31. Marchetti, M., et al.: Hydrodynamics of soft active matter. RMP **85**(3), 1143–1189 (2013)
32. Ramaswamy, S.: The mechanics and statistics of active matter. Annu. Rev. Condens. Matter Phys. **1**(1), 323–345 (2010)
33. Soucy, S., Huang, J., Gogarten, J.: Horizontal gene transfer: building the web of life. Nat. Rev. Gen. **16**(8), 472–482 (2015)
34. Telezki, V., Klumpp, S.: Simulations of structure formation by confined dipolar active particles. Soft Matter **16**(46), 10537–10547 (2020)
35. Toner, J., Tu, Y.: Long-range order in a two-dimensional dynamical XY model: how birds fly together. PRL **75**(23), 4326 (1995)
36. Vicsek, T., Czirók, A., Ben-Jacob, E., Cohen, I., Shochet, O.: Novel type of phase transition in a system of self-driven particles. PRL **75**(6), 1226 (1995)
37. Watson, R., Ficici, S., Pollack, J.: Embodied evolution: distributing an evolutionary algorithm in a population of robots. RAS **39**(1), 1–18 (2002)

Re-Solving the Shepherding Problem: Lead When Possible, Herd When Necessary

Daniel Strömbom[(✉)][iD], Julianna Hoitt, and Cameron Cloud

Department of Biology, Lafayette College, Easton, PA, USA
`stroembp@lafayette.edu`

Abstract. Designing systems for autonomous transport of groups of living agents has received a lot of attention in recent years due to a wealth of important potential applications. Biomimetic approaches are often sought, and a range of herding algorithms, inspired by how dogs herd sheep, as well as leadership algorithms mimicking leader-follower systems, have been introduced. However, they suffer from a common problem: shepherding algorithms require that agents evade the shepherd, and leading algorithms require that agents follow. This can cause problems in real-world applications where the behavioral responses of the agents to a transporter are likely to be heterogeneous over both long and short timescales. Here, we introduce an algorithm that adaptively switches between leading and herding depending on the response it receives from the agents to mitigate this problem. We show via simulation that this mixed algorithm can transport groups with any follower and evader composition, and we compare its performance with lead-only and herd-only algorithms. We also show that the mixed algorithm can deal with groups where individual agents randomly switch their strategy over time, as long as sufficient time is provided to complete the task relative to the switching rate. Given that our algorithm overcomes issues associated with herd-only and lead-only algorithms and might also, as a side effect, mitigate the issue of habituation to robotic transporters, it takes us one step closer to realizing many of the proposed applications for these types of algorithms.

1 Introduction

Guiding or leading a group of individuals to a specific location is a task regularly performed by animals across taxa [39,42], ranging from primates leading troops to foraging sites [34] and sheepdogs herding flocks [7,26], to ants guiding or carrying conspecifics during nest relocation [10,20]. Understanding these phenomena is of interest not only in biology but also for engineering, as autonomous systems capable of transporting groups of inanimate objects or living agents have a wide range of potential applications [25], including wildlife conservation, environmental remediation, livestock management, crowd control, evacuation, and multi-robot coordination [6,9,11,13,15,21–23,27,35,40,44].

R. Groß et al. (Eds.): ANTS 2026, LNCS 16515, pp. 420–428, 2026.
https://doi.org/10.1007/978-3-032-26123-6_37

Biomimetic approaches to collective transport are therefore common, with most recent work focusing on shepherding inspired by sheepdog behavior [29]. Numerous shepherding algorithms have been studied in simulation [1,3,27,28,30, 32,36,38], and several have been implemented on robotic platforms transporting inanimate or living agents [12,37,41]. Transport via leadership has also been explored [8], and robotic leaders have been shown to elicit following behavior in a variety of animal systems [14,33]. While effective in specific settings, both approaches share a fundamental limitation: herding requires agents to evade the transporter, whereas leading requires agents to follow it.

In natural groups, however, individuals often exhibit heterogeneous and context-dependent behavioral responses [24], which may change over time due to habituation [12] and can undermine the effectiveness of purely herd-based or leader-based strategies. Beyond these two modes, nature also exhibits mixed transport strategies that can be described as "lead when possible and force, carry, or herd when necessary," as observed in some ant species during nest relocation [10]. This biomimetic alternative has not yet been considered in the context of autonomous collective transport of living agents, despite its potential relevance for many proposed applications [25].

At the same time, a growing body of work has begun to address heterogeneity explicitly, considering differences in responsiveness, social affiliations, or behavioral rule sets [4,5,17–19]. These studies provide valuable insights into specific forms of heterogeneity but often rely on increasingly specialized control rules layered onto existing shepherding architectures. A complementary biomimetic perspective is that robust transport in nature frequently emerges from simple interaction mechanisms rather than progressively elaborate ones, a principle that has been explicitly exploited in earlier herding models [38]. Extending shepherding algorithms developed for different transport contexts [1,27,28,36] to incorporate alternative transport modes may therefore yield both more robust solutions and deeper theoretical insight into the autonomous transport of unwilling or variably responsive agents.

2   Model and Results

Here we introduce an algorithm for a transporter that adaptively switches between herding and leading depending on the response it receives from the agents. More specifically, we extend the shepherding model in [38] by adding a new mode of operation 'lead' that the transporter will autonomously and adaptively switch to from 'herding' if it detects that agents are following it. Another modification made here is that the (sheep-like) agents now adopt one of two strategies: 'follow' or 'evade' the transporter, and we introduce a parameter p that represents the proportion of followers in the group of agents. We note that when $p = 0$ (no followers) our new transporter algorithm is identical to the shepherding algorithm in [38], when $p = 1$ (all followers) the transporter will only lead, and for any p in $(0,1)$ the transporter will employ the 'mixed' strategy where it leads if at least one agent is following and herds if no agent is following.

We also introduce a parameter π that represents the probability that an agent will switch strategy on each timestep.

To study how the performance of the mixed, herd-only, and lead-only algorithms depends on the proportion of followers in a group, we ran simulations for values of p from 0 to 1 and measured the time to completion and the proportion of agents delivered to the target. The mixed algorithm successfully delivers all agents for all proportions $p \in [0, 1]$ within the allotted time (Fig. 1AB). In contrast, the herd-only algorithm succeeds only when all agents are evaders ($p = 0$), since the presence of any followers prevents the transporter from maintaining an effective driving position. Conversely, the lead-only algorithm succeeds only when all agents are followers ($p = 1$); if evaders are present, the transporter can guide the followers to the target but cannot induce the remaining agents to approach. The mixed algorithm avoids both failure modes by leading whenever at least one agent follows and reverting to herding otherwise, thereby guiding followers to the target before herding the remaining evaders.

To examine robustness to time-varying behavior, we next considered agents that stochastically switch between evading and following. For moderate switching rates (up to $\pi \approx 0.01$ per timestep), the mixed algorithm reliably delivers all agents within the fixed time horizon (Fig. 1C). As the switching rate increases further, the fixed time limit becomes insufficient and the success rate decreases. Removing the time constraint shows that the algorithm nevertheless succeeds even for high switching rates, including cases where agents switch strategy on average every other timestep (Fig. 1D).

See the Methods section for a more detailed description of the model and simulation protocols.

3   Discussion

Biomimetic solutions for autonomous transport of groups of inanimate and living agents are highly desirable because of the wealth of potential applications [25]. Most proposed algorithmic solutions to these problems involve herding [29], inspired by how sheepdogs herd sheep, and to a lesser degree leading, which is a ubiquitous phenomenon in social animal groups [39, 42]. However, both of these approaches suffer from a common issue that may render them ineffective for real-world applications: they are typically unable to deal with behavior-wise heterogeneous groups, in particular groups containing a mix of evaders and followers, or groups with individuals that may change behavioral strategies over time. Here we have extended a well-known shepherding algorithm to autonomously lead when possible and herd when necessary to mitigate this problem.

We establish that the mixed algorithm always succeeds regardless of the proportion of followers in a group if given sufficient time to complete the task (see Fig. 1). Unlike herding and leading that only succeed in the extremes when either all are followers or all are evaders. For any given group composition, the mixed algorithm will attempt to move the agents towards the target in one of two ways and will proceed with whichever works at a given time, and because of this its success does not rely on agents being strictly evading or strictly following.

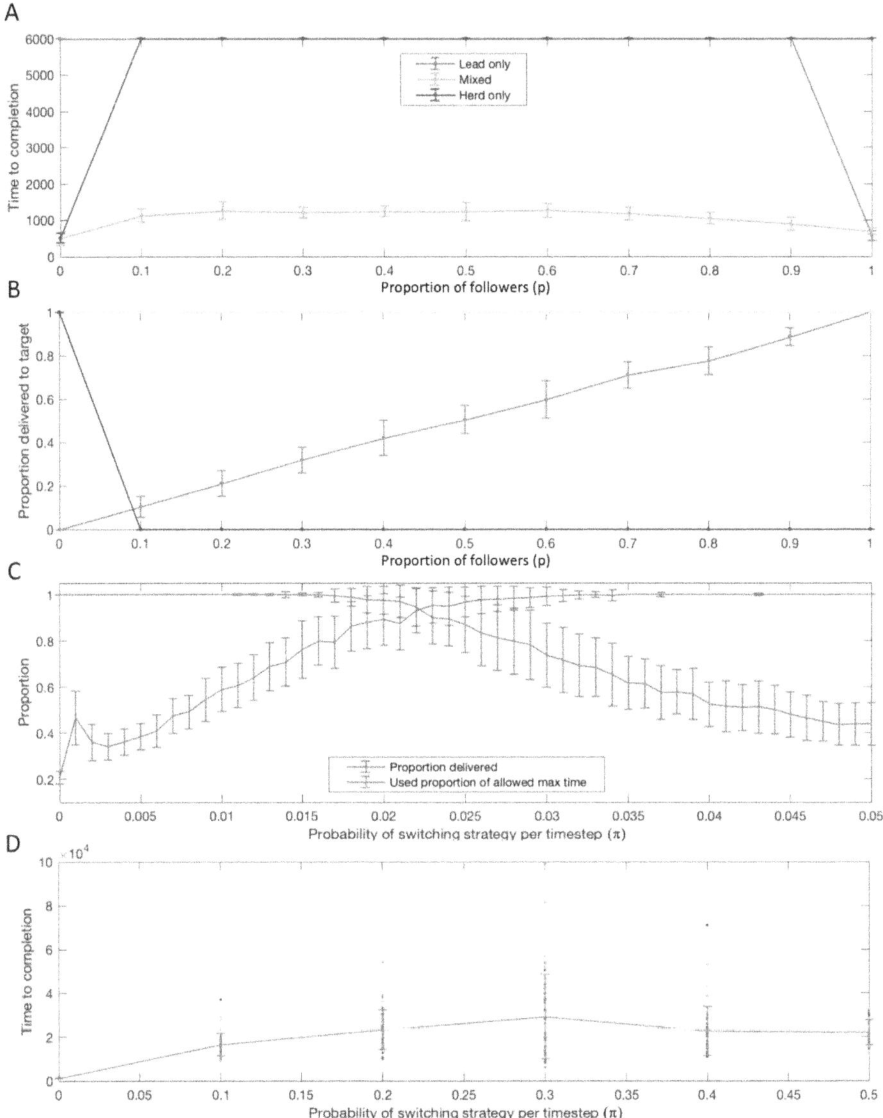

Fig. 1. Performance of the algorithms. (A)-(B) Comparison of the original herd-only algorithm, a lead-only algorithm, and the mixed 'lead when possible, herd when necessary' algorithm with respect to time to completion (A), and proportion of agents delivered to target (B), as a function of proportion of followers (p). (C) Performance of the mixed algorithm when agents switch strategy with probability π per timestep. We see that for π up to 0.01 the algorithm delivers all agents to the target within the allotted time, but as the rate of strategy switches increases the mixed algorithm's capacity to deliver the agents to the target within the allotted time decreases. (D) Time to completion for the mixed algorithm for π from 0 to 0.5. The red curve indicates mean completion time, the bars represent the standard deviation, and the dots represent the actual completion times from each simulation. We note that the mean completion time for all π is around or below 20000 timesteps and that overall only a few individual simulations that take far longer than that to complete.

One practical issue with herding by robots is habituation, in particular, the agents may initially evade the robot but over time habituate and stop evading it [12], in which case a herd-only algorithm will stop working (see Fig. 1). The mixed strategy may mitigate, or even exploit, habituation effects in transported animals. First, because it will switch between trying to lead and herd, if it receives ambiguous responses from the agents, which may make the transporter appear less predictable and therefore delay habituation. Secondly, if leading is attempted it may turn out that the agents can be led, in which case the more costly mode of transportation, herding, might be unnecessary. For animals, herding is also based on a fear response which may lead to stress [43] and an increased risk of injury during transport. If the animals could instead be led, or persuaded to be led, this may improve animal welfare. In fact, it has been shown that some animals can be trained or persuaded to follow a robot [14,33], and perhaps the task of making animals follow an appropriate transporter is easier than coercing them to move via herding in some situations. We also note that there is anecdotal evidence that a sheepdog can lead a flock of sheep [2] rather than herd them, and if the same dog could transport sheep using a combination of both these modes that would represent a direct real-world example of the mixed strategy. Finally, we note that the 'lead' mode in the algorithm does not depend on the real-world motivation of the agents for following the transporter. It can work equally well when animals are following the transporter because they perceive it as a leader or as a threat that they are trying to chase away. For example, the chasing and mobbing behavior seabirds have been observed to exhibit towards drones [16] may potentially be exploited to 'lead' them away. As with much prior work on autonomous collective transport, our results are obtained in simulation, which enables systematic exploration of heterogeneous and time-varying agent responses. We note, however, that closely related shepherding mechanisms have previously been implemented on simple robotic platforms and shown to robustly transport and reorganize objects under dynamic conditions when given sufficient time to complete the task [37].

Given the shortcomings of herd-only and lead-only approaches, it is clear that new types of collective transport algorithms are required to achieve success with many of the proposed real-world applications for these systems, and to advance theoretical approaches beyond the current state of the art described, for example, in [25,31]. In particular, algorithms that not only are robust to standard intrinsic or extrinsic noise, but also to substantial strategy differences in the individuals to be transported over both short and longer timescales given habituation [12] and behavioral heterogeneity [24] issues. Recent work has begun to address specific forms of heterogeneity, for example, differences in social affiliations [4,5], responsiveness to the transporter [18,19], or behavioral rule sets [17], often by adding tailored control elements to existing shepherding architectures. These contributions are important, but often target particular scenarios and can increase control complexity. A complementary biomimetic perspective is that robust herding and guidance in nature often arises from simple interaction principles rather than from growing layers of specialized rules. Following this view, our mixed lead-herd approach introduces only a minimal switching mechanism informed by natural transport strategies, but nevertheless accommodates a fundamental axis of heterogeneity: whether individuals are attracted to or repelled from the transporter, potentially in a time-dependent manner. From a computational perspective, our adaptive switching mechanism introduces negligible overhead relative to standard shepherding algorithms, as it requires only monitoring the sign of the relative motion of the closest agent and does not scale with group size beyond computations already present in the baseline model. We see this as an initial step toward more general, biomimetic "third-wave" transport algorithms that remain effective across a wide range of heterogeneous behavioral responses, and that may complement and extend existing specialized approaches.

4   Methods

4.1   Model

Here we describe how we extend the shepherding model of [38] to implement a mixed "lead when possible, herd when necessary" transport strategy.

In the original model, N sheep-like agents are herded by a single shepherd toward a target in an unbounded two-dimensional space. The position of the shepherd at time t is denoted by $\bar{S}_t$, and the position of agent i by $\bar{A}_{i,t}$. Agents farther than a distance r_s from the shepherd perform small random movements, while agents within r_s are repelled from the shepherd and attracted toward the center of mass of their n nearest neighbors. Short-range agent-agent repulsion is also included. Under these interactions, the heading of agent i at time $t+1$ is given by

$$\bar{H}_{i,t+1} = h\hat{H}_{i,t} + c\hat{C}_{i,t} + \rho_a\hat{R}^a_{i,t} + \rho_s\hat{R}^s_{i,t}, \tag{1}$$

where $\hat{H}_{i,t}$ is the normalized heading at time t, $\hat{C}_{i,t}$ is the direction toward the local center of mass, and $\hat{R}^a_{i,t}$ and $\hat{R}^s_{i,t}$ denote agent-agent and shepherd repulsion directions, respectively (see [38] for details).

Our first modification is to generalize the shepherd into a transporter, relative to which agents may adopt one of two behavioral strategies. Evading agents follow the dynamics in Eq. 1, while following agents instead experience attraction toward the transporter, yielding

$$\bar{H}_{i,t+1} = h\hat{H}_{i,t} + c\hat{C}_{i,t} + \rho_a\hat{R}^a_{i,t} + \rho_s\hat{F}^s_{i,t}, \tag{2}$$

where $\hat{F}^s_{i,t} = -\hat{R}^s_{i,t}$. The two agent types therefore differ only in the sign of the transporter interaction.

Herding motion follows the standard collection-driving strategy of [38]: when the group is sufficiently cohesive, the transporter moves to a driving position behind the group relative to the target; otherwise, it collects the most distant agent by moving to a collection position. Our second modification is that the transporter dynamically switches from herding to leading when it detects that the closest agent is approaching rather than evading. In this case, the transporter adopts a heading directly toward the target and leads the following agent(s) until no agents continue to approach, at which point it resumes herding behavior. As in the original shepherding framework, the transporter is assumed to have access to the positions of all agents relative to itself and the target, with the additional ability to infer whether the closest agent is approaching or receding based on changes in relative distance over time; no explicit knowledge of agent strategies (follower or evader) or overall group composition is assumed.

4.2 Simulation Protocols

The target location is always located at the origin $(0,0)$ and the N agents are initially assigned random positions in the upper right region of an $L \times L$ square and the transporter is released from near the target location in the lower left of this square. The heading update weights in Eqs. 1 and 2 are $h = 0.5$, $\rho_a = 2$, $\rho_s = 1$, $c = 1.5$ (Cf Table 1 in [38]) and we use $L = 100$ and $N = 46$ to match the simulation setup used to compare the original model to the empirical study [26]. Using this common setup we ran three types of simulations (A), (B) and (C) here. (A) Simulations where the evader and follower status of each agent remains constant through the entire simulation to compare the herd-only, lead-only, and mixed algorithms. For each algorithm we ran 100 trials of up to 6000 timesteps for each proportion of followers p from 0 to 1 in increments of 0.1 and measured the number of timesteps it took for the algorithm to complete the task (if it did, else 6000 was recorded) and the proportion of agents that was delivered to the target within the time limit. At the start of each simulation, each agent was randomly assigned to be a follower with probability p (and thus an evader with probability $1 - p$). The agents that were assigned to be evaders updated their headings using Eq. 1, and those assigned to be followers updated their headings using Eq. 2, throughout the entire simulation. The 6000-timestep limit was chosen based on pilot simulations to ensure completion well before this time. Simulations of this type were used to create Figs. 1AB. (B)-(C) Simulations where the evader and follower status of each agent (may) change throughout the simulation for the mixed algorithm only. At the start of each simulation, each agent is randomly assigned to be a follower with probability 0.5 so that on average half of the agents start off as followers and half evaders. Then, at each subsequent timestep each agent will switch strategy with probability π, where switching strategy corresponds to changing the update rule between Eqs. 1 and 2. (B) Here we ran 100 simulations for each strategy switch rate π from 0 to 0.05 in increments of 0.001 and measured task completion time and delivery success within 6000 timesteps. (C) Here we ran 100 simulations for each strategy switch rate π from 0 to 0.5 in increments of 0.1, measuring completion time without a time limit (Figs. 1CD).

Code Availability. https://github.com/danielstrombom/Lead-Herd.

Disclosure of Interests. The authors have no competing interests to declare.

References

1. Auletta, F., Fiore, D., Richardson, M.J., di Bernardo, M.: Herding stochastic autonomous agents via local control rules and online target selection strategies. Auton. Robot. **46**(3), 469–481 (2022)
2. Bell, J.: Worlds worst sheepdog. https://www.youtube.com/watch?v=p-9-3DtUzug, Accessed 23 Oct 2025
3. Bennett, B., Trafankowski, M.: A comparative investigation of herding algorithms. In: Proc. Symp. on Understanding and Modelling Collective Phenomena (UMoCoP), pp. 33–38 (2012)
4. Bennett, C.: Heterogeneity in multi-agent systems. Ph.D. thesis, University of Bristol (2024)
5. Bennett, C., Bullock, S., Lawry, J.: Demonstrating the differential impact of flock heterogeneity on multi-agent herding. In: Annual Conference Towards Autonomous Robotic Systems, pp. 147–157. Springer (2021)
6. Brenner, M., Wijermans, N., Nussle, T., de Boer, B.: Simulating and controlling civilian crowds in robocup rescue. In: Proc of RoboCup 2005: Robot Soccer World Cup IX (2005)
7. Coppinger, L., Coppinger, R.: Dogs for herding and guarding livestock. In: Livestock handling and transport, pp. 245–260. CABI Wallingford UK (2014)
8. Couzin, I.D., Krause, J., Franks, N.R., Levin, S.A.: Effective leadership and decision-making in animal groups on the move. Nature **433**(7025), 513–516 (2005)
9. Desholm, M., Kahlert, J.: Avian collision risk at an offshore wind farm. Biol. Let. **1**(3), 296–298 (2005)
10. Dornhaus, A., Franks, N.R., Hawkins, R., Shere, H.: Ants move to improve: colonies of leptothorax albipennis emigrate whenever they find a superior nest site. Anim. Behav. **67**(5), 959–963 (2004)
11. Endangered Wildlife Trust: EWT airport safety project. Tech. rep., (1999). www.ewt.org.za/programmes/WTP/air.html
12. Evered, M., Burling, P., Trotter, M., et al.: An investigation of predator response in robotic herding of sheep. Int. Proc. Chemic. Biologic. Environ. Eng. **63**, 49–54 (2014)
13. Fàbregas, M.C., Fosgate, G.T., Ganswindt, A., Bertschinger, H., Meyer, L.C.: Unforeseen consequences of conservation management practices: case study on herding rhino as an anti-poaching measure. Anim. Conserv. **24**(3), 412–423 (2021)
14. Faria, J.J., et al.: A novel method for investigating the collective behaviour of fish: introducing 'robofish'. Behav. Ecol. Sociobiol. **64**, 1211–1218 (2010)
15. Fingas, M.F.: The basics of oil spill cleanup. Lewis Publishers, 2nd edn. (2001)
16. Frixione, M.G., Salvadeo, C.: Drones, gulls and urbanity: Interaction between new technologies and human subsidized species in coastal areas. Drones **5**(2), 30 (2021)
17. Fujioka, A., Ogura, M., Wakamiya, N.: Shepherding algorithm for heterogeneous flock with model-based discrimination. Adv. Robot. **37**(1–2), 99–114 (2023)
18. Hepworth, A.J., Hussein, A.S., Reid, D.J., Abbass, H.A.: Contextually aware intelligent control agents for heterogeneous swarms. Swarm Intell. **18**(4), 275–310 (2024)
19. Himo, R., Ogura, M., Wakamiya, N.: Iterative shepherding control for agents with heterogeneous responsivity. Math. Biosci. Eng. **19**(4), 3509–3525 (2022)
20. Hölldobler, B., Wilson, E.O.: The ants. Harvard University Press (1990)
21. Hughes, R.L.: A continuum theory for the flow of pedestrians. Transp. Res. Part B Methodol. **36**(6) (2002)

22. Hughes, R.L.: The flow of human crowds. Ann. Rev. Fluid Mech. **35**(1) (2005)
23. Isobe, M., Helbing, D., Nagatani, T.: Experiment, theory, and simulation of the evacuation of a room without visibility. Phys. Rev. E **69** (2004)
24. Jolles, J.W., King, A.J., Killen, S.S.: The role of individual heterogeneity in collective animal behaviour. Trends Ecol. Evolution **35**(3), 278–291 (2020)
25. King, A.J., et al.: Biologically inspired herding of animal groups by robots. Methods Ecol. Evol. **14**(2), 478–486 (2023)
26. King, A.J., et al.: Selfish-herd behaviour of sheep under threat. Curr. Biol. **22**(14), R561–R562 (2012)
27. Li, X., Huang, H., Savkin, A.V., Zhang, J.: Robotic herding of farm animals using a network of barking aerial drones. Drones **6**(2), 29 (2022)
28. Lien, J., Bayazit, O.B., Sowell, R.T., Rodriguez, S., Amato, A.M.: Shepherding behaviors. IEEE Proc Robot. Autom., 4159–4164 (2004)
29. Long, N.K., Sammut, K., Sgarioto, D., Garratt, M., Abbass, H.A.: A comprehensive review of shepherding as a bio-inspired swarm-robotics guidance approach. IEEE Trans. Emerging Top. Comput. Intell. **4**(4), 523–537 (2020)
30. Miki, T., Nakamura, T.: An effective simple shepherding algorithm suitable for implementation to a multi-mobile robot system. IEEE Proc Innov. Comput. Inf. Control **3**, 161–165 (2006)
31. Papadopoulou, M., et al.: Active interactions between animals and technology: Biohybrid approaches for animal behaviour research. Animal Behav, 123160 (2025)
32. Paranjape, A.A., Chung, S.J., Kim, K., Shim, D.H.: Robotic herding of a flock of birds using an unmanned aerial vehicle. IEEE Trans. Rob. **34**(4), 901–915 (2018)
33. Romano, D., Donati, E., Benelli, G., Stefanini, C.: A review on animal-robot interaction: from bio-hybrid organisms to mixed societies. Biol. Cybern. **113**(3), 201–225 (2019)
34. Schaller, G.E.: The mountain gorilla: ecology and behavior (1963)
35. Schultz, A., Adams, W.: Continuous localization using evidence grids. In: IEEE Proc International Conference on Robotics and Automation (ICRA), vol. 4, pp. 2833–2839 (1998)
36. Song, H., et al.: Herding by caging: a formation-based motion planning framework for guiding mobile agents. Auton. Robot. **45**(5), 613–631 (2021). https://doi.org/10.1007/s10514-021-09975-8
37. Strömbom, D., King, A.J.: Robot collection and transport of objects: a biomimetic process. Front. Robot. AI, 48 (2018)
38. Strömbom, D., et al.: Solving the shepherding problem: heuristics for herding autonomous, interacting agents. J. R. Soc. Interface **11**(100), 20140719 (2014)
39. Sumpter, D.J.: Collective animal behavior. Princeton University Press (2010)
40. Turgut, A.E., H. Celikkanat, F. Gökce, E.S.: Self-organized flocking in mobile robot swarms. Swarm Intell. **2**, 97–120 (2008)
41. Vaughan, R., Sumpter, N., Frost, A., Cameron, S.: Robot sheepdog project achieves automatic flock control. In: Proc. Fifth International Conference on the Simulation of Adaptive Behaviour (1998)
42. Ward, A., Webster, M.: Sociality: the behaviour of group-living animals, vol. 407. Springer (2016)
43. Yaxley, K.J., Joiner, K.F., Abbass, H.: Drone approach parameters leading to lower stress sheep flocking and movement: sky shepherding. Sci. Rep. **11**(1), 7803 (2021)
44. Zahugi, E.M., M.M. Shanta, T.V.P.: Oil spill cleaning up using swarm of robots. Adv. Comput. Inf. Technol. **178**, 215–224 (2013)

Scalable Foraging: A Paired Body and Controller Design for Foraging Robots

Andrew Vardy$^{(\boxtimes)}$ and Marius Seidl

Memorial University of Newfoundland, St. John's, Canada
`av@mun.ca`

Abstract. We propose a paired physical and controller design for a swarm of simple robots attempting to collect objects and convey them to a goal region. We show that a robot body featuring a curved tail, combined with a simple state machine controller, enables scalable foraging even in a highly congested environment. Through numerical experiments, we compare our approach to a benchmark controller that uses omnidirectional movement and predictive collision avoidance. Our results demonstrate that the proposed approach cannot converge as quickly as the benchmark at low robot densities, but comes to surpass it at high densities. These findings highlight the value of integrating physical design with controller design to achieve scalability in robot swarms.

Keywords: Swarm robotics · Foraging · Scalability

1 Introduction

A scalable robot swarm would have the ability to tackle problems of varying size just by adjusting the number of robots deployed [3]. However, it is well-known that congestion between robots is a significant barrier to progress.

In this paper we propose the paired design of the physical bodies and the controller for a swarm of simple robots attempting to collect objects and convey them to a goal region. This is the foraging problem, which has been studied extensively in robotics [8,11], but also in biology [16] and multi-agent systems [18]. In particular, we are interested in scalable foraging—gathering objects even when the density of robots is high, since it is commonly observed that adding more robots leads to diminishing returns even at moderate robot densities [2,9]. Most of the work in this domain seeks computational solutions: reducing time spent in avoiding other robots by state estimation & planning [15], communication [1,5,15], and explicit collaboration [1,5]. However, we take a different approach in line with the concepts of mechanical intelligence [17] and induced phase changes [10] by a paired body/controller design which maintains the robots' ability to collect objects, even while mired in traffic. Our approach contrasts previous work where selecting one ideal robot-density was part of the co-designing process [13], or the behaviours were not tailored to crowded environments [6]

© The Author(s), under exclusive license to Springer Nature Switzerland AG 2026
R. Groß et al. (Eds.): ANTS 2026, LNCS 16515, pp. 429–437, 2026.
https://doi.org/10.1007/978-3-032-26123-6_38

Figure 1 depicts our robot's design, which is based on a differential-drive platform. The robot's body exists within a circular outer shell called the halo. Robots may butt up against each other, but will still be able to rotate on the spot. The halo prevents robots from interpenetrating, but pucks can fit underneath it. Within the halo are sensors to detect the presence of pucks. A curved tail on the back of the robot can interact with pucks through three behaviours. In the *Sweep* behaviour, the robot rotates clockwise, moving the puck along an arc towards the goal. At the end of a *Sweep*, the puck may now be positioned to be pushed directly to the goal via the *Plow* behaviour. However, if movement in that direction is blocked, some incremental progress can still be made by rotating counter-clockwise via the *Lash* behaviour. When the density of robots is low, *Sweep* and *Plow* suffice to convey pucks to the goal. However, in the presence of congestion, the *Lash* behaviour allows progress to be made by pushing pucks through the liminal space between the robots and beneath their halos.

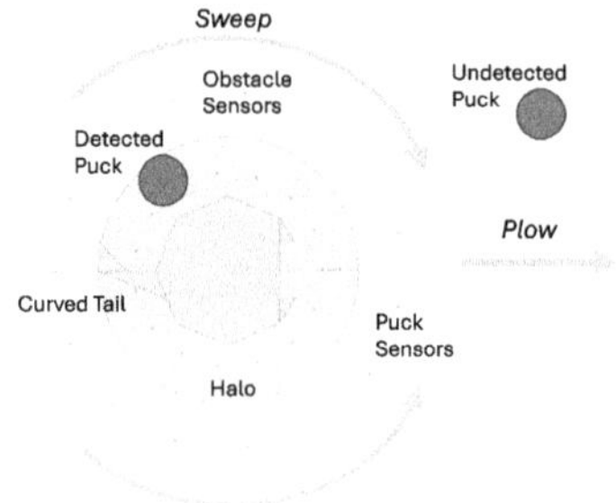

Fig. 1. Our curved-tail robot design, as represented in simulation.

Beyond the specific behaviours implemented by our controller, our results support what we term the *principle of locality*: robots in a swarm should, as far as possible, perform useful work where they are. Local sensing and communication are already central assumptions in swarm robotics [3,11] but this principle highlights the idea of doing work locally. Related ideas appear in work on embodied intelligence and morphological computation, where physical structure and local dynamics are exploited to simplify control and coordination [7,12]. In the context of robots manipulating objects, we can further refine the principle of locality: when long-range motion is impeded by congestion, robots can remain productive by manipulating and reconfiguring nearby objects.

2   Methodology

2.1   Proposed Controller

The proposed controller is a finite state machine, that implements the behaviours *Sweep*, *Plow* and *Lash* referred to earlier, as well as simple obstacle avoidance. The controller's five states are summarized below:

TURN_TO_ANGLE Turn towards a target angle.
READY Move straight. Evaluate conditions to initiate interaction with pucks.
SWEEP Turn clockwise to catch a puck within halo and bring it closer to goal.
PLOW Move to goal, while veering left or right to minimize the angle to goal.
LASH Turn counter-clockwise to push a puck within halo directly towards goal.

There is a distinction between states and the behaviours they are meant to implement. For example, to perform the *Plow* behaviour, the robot might begin in the READY state, then notice that a sensed puck is already aligned with the goal. It then transitions to TURN_TO_ANGLE to turn toward that puck. Once the turn is complete, it switches to PLOW to push that puck to the goal.

Figure 2 depicts the state machine. Transitions are based on the set of predicates described in Table 1. Several of these predicates require knowledge of the angle and distance to the goal. We assume this information is provided to the robots directly or can be inferred from sensory data (e.g. visual homing [19]).

The **attackable** predicate plays a central role. We use *attack* as the broader term for both *Plow* and *Lash*. The attackable predicate means that a puck is aligned with the goal. The robot chooses to initiate a *Plow* or a *Lash* depending on whether an obstacle is blocking the direction towards the goal.

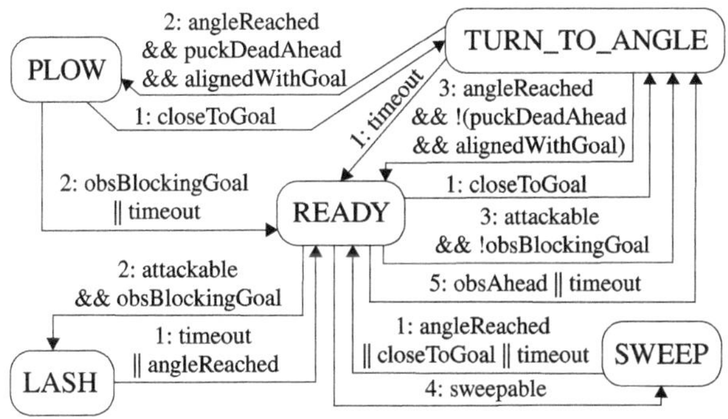

Fig. 2. State machine of proposed controller.

Figure 3 provides examples of the *Sweep*, *Plow* and *Lash* behaviours Given the robots' curved tails, we refer to this as the *Curtail* approach.

Table 1. Predicates derived from sensory data.

Name	Description
alignedWithGoal	Robot is aligned with (i.e. pointing at) the goal.
angleReached	Robot has arrived at the target angle ($\pm$ a threshold).
attackable	Amongst all active puck sensors, find the one most aligned with the goal. If this active puck sensor's angular difference with the goal < a threshold, then attackable is true.
closeToGoal	The centre of the robot has crossed into the goal region.
obsAhead	Obstacle sensors at the front of the robot have been triggered.
obsBlockingGoal	Obstacle sensors close to angle of the goal have been triggered.
puckDeadAhead	A puck is detected immediately in front of the robot.
timeout	The maximum dwell time within the state has elapsed.
sweepable	We have determined that a detected puck would be closer to the goal after a *Sweep* movement.

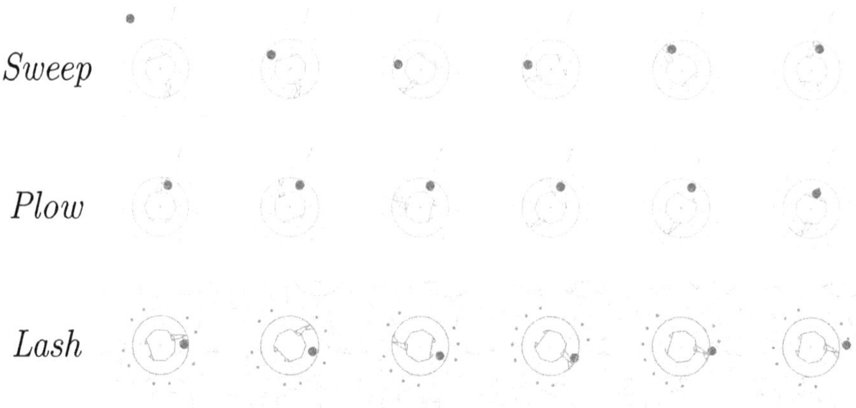

Fig. 3. The three behaviours that act upon pucks.

2.2   Benchmark Controller

The benchmark controller is meant to represent a more traditional approach to foraging, where congestion is avoided by communication and accounting proactively for the movements of other robots. For consistency, the benchmark controller is also a state machine. States TURN_TO_ANGLE and READY operate in the same manner as the Curtail controller. Their purpose for the benchmark controller is to search for pucks. Once a puck is found, the HOME state is entered (described below). After a puck has been delivered to the goal region, the ESCAPE state selects a random velocity to move away from the goal.

Within the HOME state, the method of Reciprocal Velocity Obstacles (RVO) is used to drive the robot towards the goal region while avoiding other robots [14].

This controller serves only as a benchmark and is given certain advantages:

- In the HOME and ESCAPE states, the robots are controlled by RVO and are not subject to kinematic constraints.
- Whenever the benchmark controller senses a puck, we remove the puck closest to the front of the robot, emulating an abstract version of puck grasping.
- Whenever entering the goal region while carrying a puck, the puck is teleported to the centre of the goal region. Pucks in the goal region are protected by a virtual circular obstacle, preventing any 'accidental' robot incursions.

The *Benchmark* approach is implemented on robots with a circular inner body and halo of the same radii as for the proposed robot design.

3   Numerical Experiments

Numerical experiments were conducted using our custom C++ simulation based on box2d, a two-dimensional physics engine intended for games but used in many

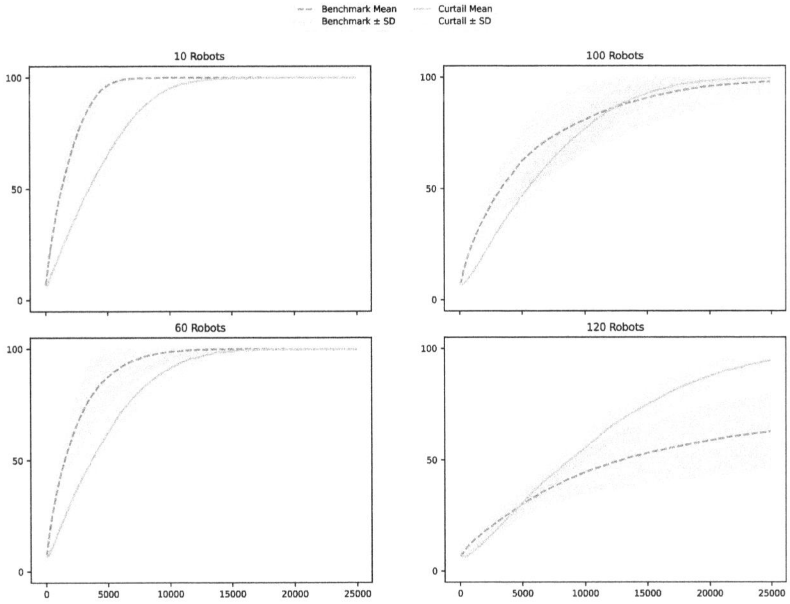

Fig. 4. Number of pucks collected as a function of time for varying numbers of robots. The shaded regions depict ± one standard deviation from the mean.

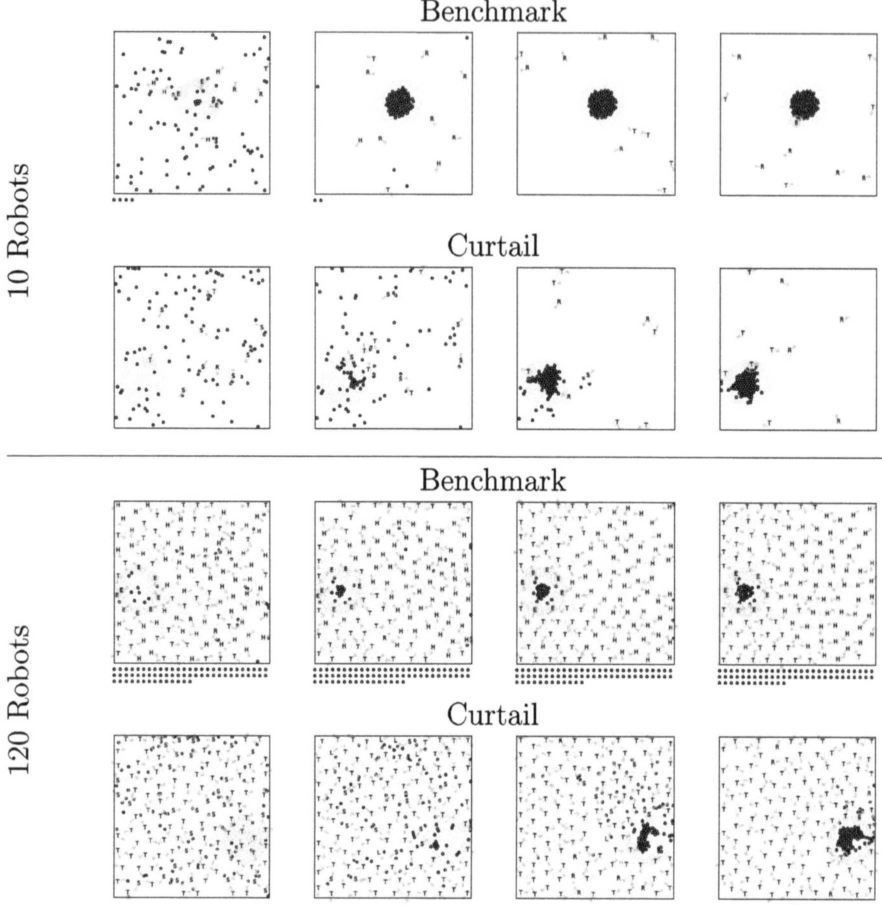

Fig. 5. Snapshots of the lowest-performing trials for 10 and 120 robots. Temporarily removed pucks (Benchmark only) are shown at the bottom of each frame.

robotic applications [4]. Using one robot inner diameter as our basic unit, the test arena is 20×20 and contains 100 pucks of diameter 0.3. The goal region is a circle with diameter 6. The robots, pucks, and the goal region are all assigned random positions at the beginning of each trial. Each trial is run for 25,000 time steps and every experiment consists of 100 trials.

Figure 4 show the performance of both the Benchmark and Curtail methods while varying the number of robots. When the number of robots is 10 or 60 the Benchmark clearly offers quicker convergence, while both methods converge on the target of 100 pucks collected. However, at 100 robots the gap in performance shrinks and the Curtail method converges on a slightly higher value, with less variation. As we progress to 120 robots, the Curtail method maintains a similar rate of convergence, while the Benchmark converges slower and to a lower value.

Note that if the number of robots is increased much beyond 120 they become unable to move and no method can make progress.

Figure 5 show snapshots of the simulation's progress for 10 and 120 robots. The trials shown are the lowest-performing trials in terms of the final number of pucks collected. The overall results are similar for 10 robots (top two rows), but we can also see that the Benchmark method more rapidly accumulates pucks. At this low robot-density, the Curtail method moves most pucks to the goal via the *Plow* behaviour. With 120 robots (bottom two rows) the Benchmark method has stalled. Only 34 of the 100 pucks have been delivered to the goal region. The remaining 66 pucks have been picked up by robots who are now in the HOME state (indicated by 'H' in the figure). All 66 of these robots are trying to reach the goal region, but are blocked by each other and by 6 robots in the ESCAPE state, which are attempting to leave the goal region. On the other hand, the Curtail method has still managed to deliver 85 pucks to the goal.

4   Conclusions

This paper introduced a paired physical and controller design for scalable foraging in robot swarms, focusing on performance in highly congested environments. By combining a simple differential-drive robot with a curved tail and a finite state machine controller implementing the *Sweep*, *Plow*, and *Lash* behaviours, we demonstrated that effective object collection can be maintained even as robot density increases. Numerical experiments showed that while a benchmark controller using omnidirectional movement and predictive collision avoidance (via the Reciprocal Velocity Obstacles method) performs well at low densities, its performance degrades under congestion. In contrast, our approach sustains higher performance by enabling robots to continue manipulating objects despite close packing and limited mobility.

These findings highlight the importance of co-designing physical morphology and control strategies to address scalability challenges in swarm robotics. Rather than relying solely on complex planning or communication, simple embodied strategies can yield robust collective performance. Our approach also exemplifies the principle of locality, which may prove to be a useful design principle for any task where the work of a robot swarm can be partitioned by location, without the need for explicit coordination.

Future work will explore the application of the proposed approach to related tasks such as object sorting and planar construction. It will also be necessary to demonstrate an implementation on physical robots. Finally, it would also be interesting to assess the controller for susceptibility to sensor noise and other sim-to-real challenges.

Acknowledgments. This work was funded by the Natural Sciences and Engineering Research Council of Canada (NSERC) Discovery Grant program (application RGPIN-2024-04451).

Disclosure of Interests. The authors have no competing interests to declare.

References

1. Argote-Gerald, J., Miyauchi, G., Trodden, P., Groß, R.: On the Benefits of Robot Platooning for Navigating Crowded Environments, vol. 34, pp. 259–272. Springer, Cham (2026)
2. Beckers, R., Holland, O., Deneubourg, J.L.: From local actions to global tasks: stigmergy and collective robotics. In: Artificial Life IV, pp. 181–189. MIT Press, Cambridge, MA (1994)
3. Brambilla, M., Ferrante, E., Birattari, M., Dorigo, M.: Swarm robotics: a review from the swarm engineering perspective. Swarm Intell. $7(1)$, 1–41 (2013)
4. Chuck, C., et al.: Robot air hockey: a manipulation testbed for robot learning with reinforcement learning. arXiv preprint arXiv:2405.03113 (2024)
5. Drogoul, A., Ferber, J.: From tom thumb to the dockers: some experiments with foraging robots. In: From Animals to Animats 2: Proceedings of the Second International Conference on Simulation of Adaptive Behavior, pp. 451–459 (1993)
6. Ferrante, E., Turgut, A.E., Duéñez Guzmán, E., Dorigo, M., Wenseleers, T.: Evolution of self-organized task specialization in robot swarms. PLoS Comput. Biol. $11(8)$, e1004273 (2015)
7. Hauser, H., Ijspeert, A.J., Füchslin, R.M., Pfeifer, R., Maass, W.: Towards a theoretical foundation for morphological computation with compliant bodies. Biol. Cybern. $105(5)$, 355–370 (2011)
8. Kaminka, G.A., Douchan, Y.: Heterogeneous foraging swarms can be better. Front. Robot. AI 11, 1426282 (2025)
9. Kuckling, J., Luckey, R., Avrutin, V., Vardy, A., Reina, A., Hamann, H.: Do we run large-scale multi-robot systems on the edge? more evidence for two-phase performance in system size scaling. In: IEEE International Conference on Robotics and Automation (ICRA). (Accepted) (2024). https://doi.org/10.48550/arXiv.2310.11843
10. Li, S., et al.: Programming active cohesive granular matter with mechanically induced phase changes. Sci. Adv. 7, eabe8494 (2021)
11. Lu, Q., Fricke, G.M., Ericksen, J.C., Moses, M.E.: Swarm foraging review: closing the gap between proof and practice. Curr. Robot. Reports, 1–11 (2020)
12. Pfeifer, R., Bongard, J.C.: How the Body Shapes the Way We Think: A New View of Intelligence. MIT Press, Cambridge, MA (2006)
13. Salman, M., Ligot, A., Birattari, M.: Concurrent design of control software and configuration of hardware for robot swarms under economic constraints. PeerJ Comput. Sci. 5, e221 (2019)
14. Snape, J., Guy, S.J., Van Den Berg, J., Manocha, D.: Smooth coordination and navigation for multiple differential-drive robots. In: Experimental Robotics: The 12th International Symposium on Experimental Robotics, pp. 601–613. Springer (2014)
15. Steels, L.: Cooperation between distributed agents through self-organisation. In: International Conference on Intelligent Robots and Systems (IROS) (1990)
16. Stephens, D.W., Brown, J.S., Ydenberg, R.C.: Foraging: behavior and ecology. University of Chicago Press (2007)
17. Wang, T., et al.: Mechanical intelligence simplifies control in terrestrial limbless locomotion. Sci. Robot. 8, eadi2243 (2023)

18. Zedadra, O., Jouandeau, N., Seridi, H., Fortino, G.: Multi-agent foraging: state-of-the-art and research challenges. Complex Adaptive Syst. Model. **5**(1), 1–24 (2017)
19. Zeil, J., Boeddeker, N., Stürzl, W.: Visual Homing in Insects and Robots, pp. 87–100. Springer Berlin Heidelberg, Berlin, Heidelberg (2010). https://doi.org/10.1007/978-3-540-89393-6_7

Split Over n Resource Sharing Problem: Are Fewer Capable Agents Better Than Many Simpler Ones?

Karthik Soma[1,2]([✉]) [iD], Mohamed S. Talamali[2] [iD], Genki Miyauchi[2] [iD],
Giovanni Beltrame[1] [iD], Heiko Hamann[3] [iD], and Roderich Groß[2,4] [iD]

[1] MIST Lab, Polytechnique Montréal, Montreal, Canada
`karthik.soma@polymtl.ca`
[2] School of Electrical and Electronic Engineering, The University of Sheffield,
Sheffield, UK
[3] Department of Computer and Information Science, University of Konstanz,
Konstanz, Germany
[4] Department of Computer Science, Technical University of Darmstadt, Darmstadt,
Germany

Abstract. In multi-agent systems, should limited resources be concentrated into a few capable agents or distributed among many simpler ones? This work formulates the split over n resource sharing problem where a group of n agents equally shares a common resource (e.g., monetary budget, computational resources, physical size). We present a case study in multi-agent coverage where the area of the disk-shaped footprint of agents scales as $1/n$. A formal analysis reveals that the initial coverage rate grows with n. However, if the speed of agents decreases proportionally with their radii, groups of all sizes perform equally well, whereas if it decreases proportionally with their footprints, a single agent performs best. We also present computer simulations in which resource splitting increases the failure rates of individual agents. The models and findings help identify optimal distributiveness levels and inform the design of multi-agent systems under resource constraints.

1   Introduction

Artificial systems must operate with limited resources. These resources could be concentrated into a single agent. Alternatively, they could be divided among multiple agents. For example, consider a system designer with a limited monetary budget to purchase robots for a given mission. If opting for a single-agent system, they could afford a high-spec robot featuring advanced actuation, sensing, and computational resources. However, if opting for a system comprising many agents, they could only afford robots of substantially lower cost (per unit) featuring lower quality actuation, sensing, and computational resources.

This paper formulates the aforementioned dilemma as the *split over n resource sharing problem* (see Fig. 1), where n agents are assumed to each possess an equal share of a limited resource. The problem addresses a fundamental

R. Groß et al. (Eds.): ANTS 2026, LNCS 16515, pp. 438–446, 2026.
https://doi.org/10.1007/978-3-032-26123-6_39

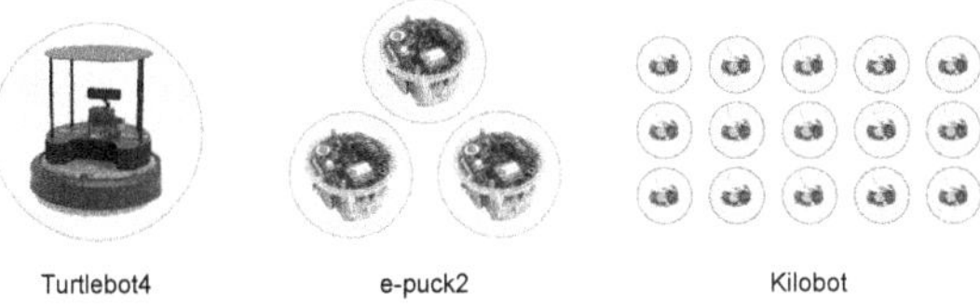

Fig. 1. Split over n resource sharing problem. A finite resource is equally shared among n robots; What is the optimal n? Different values of n might correspond to different robot platforms, for example, Turtlebot4 [1], e-puck2 [9], and Kilobot [14].

question in swarm intelligence: given a fixed resource, what is the optimal level of distributiveness?

The split over n resource sharing problem differs from the vast literature in the field of swarm intelligence that focuses on the optimal group size under the assumption of an effectively unlimited supply of identical robots. For example, will 5, 50, or 500 robots of a particular design yield the best performance? Such studies [10,11] provide models and answers for questions about optimal group size or swarm density (robots/area). These models show an initial increase of system performance with increasing number of robots and robot density that can even be superlinear, that is, doubling the number of robots results in more than doubled system performance [10]. There is an optimal number of robots (and density) at which system performance is maximized. Increasing the number of robots beyond this critical value leads to performance degradation due to congestion or interference [16].

This paper investigates the split over n resource sharing problem in the context of a spatial coverage task [3,6,13], where agents must visit all locations of the environment collectively. Spatial coverage tasks are fundamental to many real-world applications, such as vacuuming floors and mapping. As coverage depends on both footprint and mobility, it serves as a benchmark for this study.

The contributions of this work are threefold. First, we formulate the split over n resource sharing problem, the solution to which may inform optimal level of distributiveness in multi-robot system design assuming a constant resource budget. Second, we present a multi-agent coverage case study incorporating practical miniaturization constraints, such as reduced mobility and higher failure rates. Third, we formally model the system and reveal conditions under which the optimal level of distributiveness is minimal, maximal, or irrelevant.

2 Formulation of the Split Over n Resource Sharing Problem

We assume a periodic environment of size $p \times p$ arbitrary units. It is populated by n identical, disk-shaped agents. Let $A > 0$ denote the shared resource, representing the combined footprint of all agents. Hence, the resource (i.e., footprint) per agent is A/n. Each agent has a continuous position in 2-D space and an

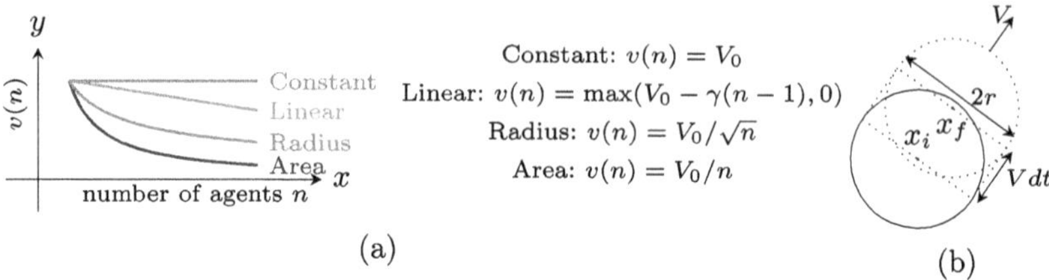

Fig. 2. (a) The four velocity profiles as functions of n. (b) Area covered by a disk-shaped agent of radius r moving forward with velocity V.

orientation. It propels by alternating between (i) moving forward with velocity v for δ time steps, and (ii) rotating instantaneously by angle θ (in rad). δ is drawn from a power-law distribution and turning angles θ from a wrapped Cauchy distribution to realize a random walk [7], given by:

$$P_\alpha(\delta) \propto \delta^{-(\alpha+1)},\ 0 < \alpha \leq 2\,. \qquad f_w(\theta; \mu, \rho) = \frac{1}{2\pi}\frac{1-\rho^2}{1+\rho^2 - 2\rho\cos(\theta-\mu)}$$

We consider Brownian random motion [7] ($\rho = 0$, $\mu = 0$, $\alpha = 2$) and investigate four velocity profiles that capture practical conditions where footprint miniaturization imposes limits on the maximum achievable velocity of smaller sized agents (see Fig. 2a):

1. *constant*: an agent's velocity is constant, V_0, that is, irrespective of the group size (n);
2. *linear*: an agent's velocity is V_0 if $n = 1$, however, as n increases, it decreases proportionally until reaching zero;
3. *radius*: an agent's velocity is proportional to $\frac{1}{\sqrt{n}}$. Hence, it is proportional to the radius of its footprint, which is $\sqrt{\frac{A}{n\pi}}$;
4. *area*: an agent's velocity is proportional to $\frac{1}{n}$. Hence, it is proportional to the area of its footprint, which is $\pi\sqrt{\frac{A}{n\pi}}\sqrt{\frac{A}{n\pi}} = \pi\frac{A}{n\pi} = \frac{A}{n}$.

To determine the area covered, we discretize the environment into $m \times m$ square cells. At any given time, an agent senses all cells whose centers lie within its footprint.

The coverage percentage up to time t is given as:

$$c(t) = \frac{\sum_{i=1}^{m}\sum_{j=1}^{m}P_{i,j}(t)}{m^2} \cdot 100 \qquad P_{i,j}(t) = \begin{cases} 1 & \text{if cell } (i,j) \text{ covered} \\ 0 & \text{otherwise} \end{cases}$$

Let t_f denote the first time at which the coverage reaches 100%, where $t_f = \inf\{t \in \mathbb{R}^+ \,|\, c(t) = 100\}$ and inf denotes the infimum, or the greatest lower bound. The objective is to find the optimal level of distributiveness (n): $\underset{n}{\mathrm{argmin}}\ t_f$.

Table 1. Initial coverage rates for various velocity profiles (from Fig. 2a).

Constant	Linear
$\frac{d\mathcal{P}_0}{dt} \propto 2\sqrt{\frac{An}{\pi}} \cdot V_0 \propto \sqrt{n}$	$\frac{d\mathcal{P}_0}{dt} \propto 2\sqrt{\frac{An}{\pi}} \cdot \left(V_0 - \gamma(n-1)\right) \propto a\sqrt{n} - bn^{3/2}$
Radius	Area
$\frac{d\mathcal{P}_0}{dt} \propto 2\sqrt{\frac{An}{\pi}} \cdot \frac{V_0}{\sqrt{n}} \propto \mathcal{P}_c$	$\frac{d\mathcal{P}_0}{dt} \propto 2\sqrt{\frac{An}{\pi}} \cdot \frac{V_0}{n} \propto \frac{1}{\sqrt{n}}$

3   Formal Analysis

We derive the initial coverage rates for the four velocity profiles, ignoring overlaps with other agents. Let $\mathcal{P}_0^f$ and $\mathcal{P}_0^i$ denote the area that an agent had covered after and prior to a given placement, respectively, and r denotes its radius. An agent covers new area at a rate proportional to its diameter and velocity (see Fig. 2b). Therefore, as $r = \sqrt{\frac{A}{n\pi}}$, the initial collective coverage rate $\frac{d\mathcal{P}_0}{dt}$ of all agents is:

$$d\mathcal{P}_0 \propto n \times (\mathcal{P}_0^f - \mathcal{P}_0^i)$$
$$d\mathcal{P}_0 \propto n \times (V dt 2r + \pi r^2 - \pi r^2)$$
$$\frac{d\mathcal{P}_0}{dt} \propto n \times 2r \times v(n) \propto 2 \times \sqrt{\frac{An}{\pi}} \times v(n)$$

Table 1 presents the initial coverage rates for all velocity profiles.

4   Simulation Results

This section uses computer simulations to evaluate how different levels of distributiveness affect coverage performance for disk-shaped agents (see Sect. 2) under no gradual motion, varying velocity profiles, failure rates, and collisions. Each configuration was tested across 30 different initial conditions. The cumulative coverage percentage $c(t)$ achieved by the agents was recorded using tools from the OpenCV library [2]. We use a no-split agent velocity: $V_0 = 0.005$ units/step, a linear velocity-profile slope: $\gamma = 4 \times 10^{-6}$, and an environment of size: $p \times p = 1 \times 1$ sq. units discretized into $m \times m = 1000 \times 1000$ cells. The total footprint is fixed at $A = \pi \times 0.1^2$ sq. units.

4.1   Effect of No Gradual Motion

We investigate the scenario in which agents can instantly appear in any random position in the environment without undergoing gradual movement. This experiment isolates the effect of resource splitting from other influences, such as velocity profiles and physical collisions altering the course. These experiments

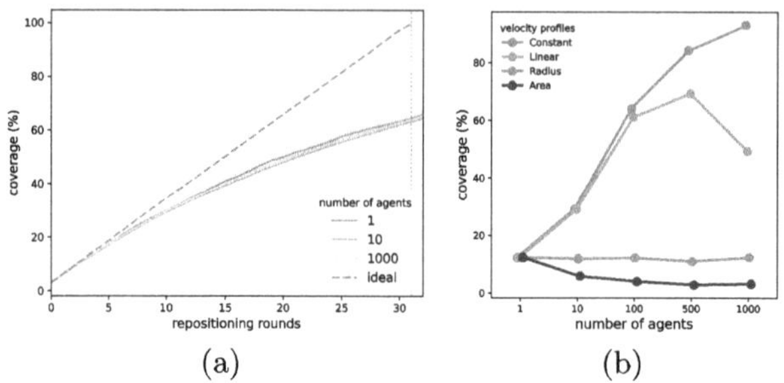

Fig. 3. (a) Coverage trends when agents instantly relocate to random positions (b) Coverage at 100th simulation step with various velocity profiles.

use the parameters described above, except the total number of cells is increased to $10^4 \times 10^4$. Moreover, coverage is reported once per *repositioning round*, that is, each time the entire group has been repositioned. As seen in Fig. 3a, the coverage trends are identical across all group sizes. Coverage initially even match ideal rates, corresponding to perfect avoidance of revisiting explored regions (i.e., coverage rate of A per round). However, after a few rounds, the coverage achieved for every group size begins to deviate from the ideal rates, as overlaps with already visited regions increase and the probability of visiting unvisited cells decreases proportionally to the overall coverage.

4.2   Effect of Velocity Profiles

We investigate the effects of velocity profiles (see Fig. 2a). We first examine the initial performance, reporting coverage percentages at the 100th simulation step. As shown in Fig. 3b, the coverage trends match those of the formal analysis in Table 1. In particular:

Constant: Coverage increases monotonically with the number of splits. For the group sizes considered, 1000 agents achieve the highest coverage, indicating that the optimal group size tends toward ∞ agents, consistent with Table 1. In practice, this suggests distributing resources among as many agents as possible.

Linear: Of the group sizes tested, $n = 500$ agents achieve the highest coverage, implying that the optimal group size lies between the two extremes (1 and ∞). To understand this behavior, consider the relationship between coverage rate and $\sqrt{n}$ from Table 1, which takes the form $y = ax - bx^3$, where y is the coverage rate, $x = \sqrt{n}$, $a, b > 0$ and $n \geq 1$. This cubic equation attains its local maximum at $x = \sqrt{\frac{a}{3b}}$, or equivalently, at $n = \frac{a}{3b}$. For the parameters in our setup, this corresponds to $n = 417$ (and $n = 500$ is the closest from the set of tested agent numbers).

Radius: Coverage remains nearly constant across all group sizes. This indicates that an increase in benefit from distributiveness compensates the reduced mobility of an individual agent at larger group sizes.

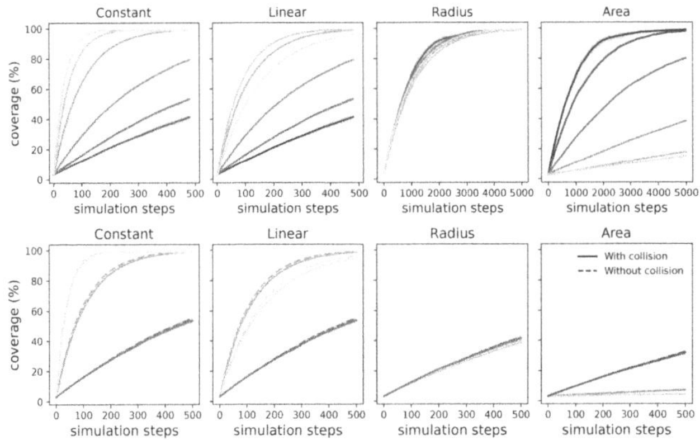

Fig. 4. Coverage trends across velocity profiles. The top row shows collision-free results for 1, 2, 10, 100, 500, and 1000 agents; the bottom row shows results with collisions for 2, 100, and 1000 agents. In each profile, colour intensity encodes group sizes, with darker shades indicating fewer agents.

Area: Coverage decreases as the group size (n) increases, showing that it is optimal to keep all resources within a single agent.

These trends persist beyond the initial steps, as seen in the top row of Fig. 4. In the constant profile, coverage increases from the darkest to the lightest shade of red (group sizes $1 \rightarrow 1000$). For the linear profile, the performance order is as follows: the second-lightest green (500 agents) achieve the highest coverage, followed by 100, 1000, 10, 2, and 1 agents that perform in decreasing order thereafter. In the radius profile, all shades remain nearly identical, reflecting the uniform coverage across group sizes. In the area profile, coverage decreases from the darkest to the lightest purple ($1 \rightarrow 1000$).

4.3   Effect of Collisions

While the previous sections discarded the effect of collisions, this section quantifies their impact. In multi-robot systems, when robots are about to collide, they typically slow down and rotate away from each other until the situation is resolved, after which they resume their task at the original velocity [8]. These robot-robot interferences commonly accumulate to long-term [15] and global effects [11,15]. We approximate this behavior by decreasing an agent's velocity proportionally to the overlap between its footprint and that of any colliding neighboring agents, while ignoring heading corrections. To prevent deadlocks, a residual velocity is maintained even in the case of full overlap.

We evaluate the effect of collisions on all velocity profiles. As shown in the bottom row of Fig. 4, there is no significant decrease in coverage for experiments where the total footprint split over n agents is $A = \pi \times 0.1^2$ sq. units, and the coverage trends closely resemble those observed in the top row of Fig. 4.

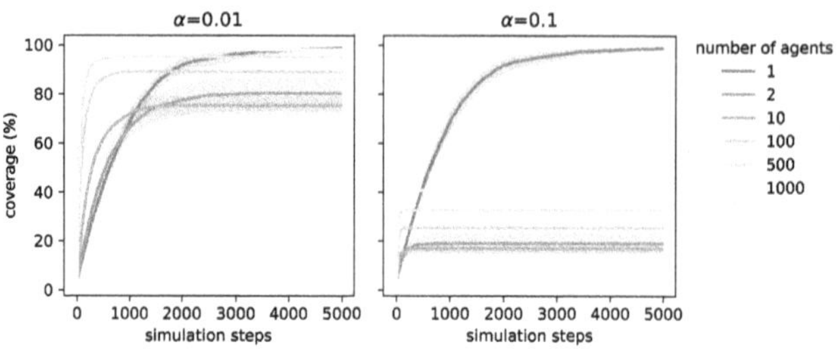

Fig. 5. Coverage trends for different failure rates (left: $\alpha = 0.01$ and failure rate $k < 0.007$; right: $\alpha = 0.1$ and failure rate $k \leq 0.05$). α controls the rate at which failure rate approaches its maximum failure rate $\beta = 0.1$, where $k(n) = \beta(1 - \frac{1}{n^\alpha})$.

For larger footprints, deviations may increase due to the higher impact of an individual overlap with other agents.

Notably, unlike classical scalability studies [10,16], where a fixed footprint per agent leads to congestion-induced performance degradation as group size grows, agent density remains constant here. Nevertheless, except for the constant velocity profile, increasing n still reduces agent velocities, emulating congestion like effects.

4.4   Effect of Failures

Typically, in swarm robotics, increasing the number of robots introduces miniaturization-related risks [12,17] that may cause agents to fail over the course of the experiment [4,5]. In this section, we model such effects through a failure rate $k(n)$ that depends only on n. At each simulation step, we sample a uniform random number $r \sim \mathcal{U}(0,1)$ for every agent, and if $r < k(n)$, the agent ceases motion and does not contribute to coverage thereafter. We define $k(n) = \beta(1 - \frac{1}{n^\alpha})$, which is a non-linear, monotonically increasing function with a horizontal asymptote. For any $\alpha > 0$ and $\beta \geq 0$, the failure rate for $n = 1$ is 0. Hence, a sole robot would always be assumed fault-free. $\beta > 0$, determines the maximum failure rate for $n \to \infty$. α controls how rapidly the failure rate approaches β as n increases (except for $n = 1$).

The experiment compares the performance of a single agent with zero failure probability to that of multi-agent groups with failure rate $k(n)$. We use $\beta = 0.1$ and $\alpha \in \{0.01, 0.1\}$ in this study. All agents have constant velocity $V_0 = 0.005$ units/step.

As shown in Fig. 5, for small $\alpha = 0.01$, large group sizes (e.g., 1000 agents) remain robust to failures and consistently outperform a single agent, whereas small groups eventually fall behind due to a larger proportion of agents failing. For the large $\alpha = 0.1$ and for the same n, the failure rate approaches β more rapidly, causing agents to fail earlier in the simulation. Under this condition, a single agent overtakes every group size n even before covering a significant proportion of the environment.

5   Conclusions

In this work, we formulated the split over n resource sharing problem. It explores a fundamental question in swarm robotics: What level of distributiveness is optimal? We presented a case study built around a simple coverage task. We formally derived the initial coverage rates for a range of velocity profiles. Through a series of computer simulations, we showed that technological constraints due to miniaturization, such as reduced mobility and increased failure rates, shift the optimal level of distributiveness. Depending on the type of robots available, our findings could inform system designers in determining whether a single highly capable robot, several moderately capable robots, or a large group of smaller, less capable robots would be most effective for a coverage task. Future work will investigate the performance of heterogeneous robot swarms, combining highly capable and less capable robots. We will also study how these findings translate to physics-based simulations, assessing whether the observed trends hold.

Acknowledgments. This research was supported in part by the Mitacs Globalink Research Award, BMBF (Robotics Institute Germany; grant no. 16ME1001) and EU Horizon Europe Framework Programme ("OpenSwarm"; grant no. 101093046).

Disclosure of Interests. The authors have no competing interests to declare.

References

1. Amsters, R., Slaets, P.: Turtlebot 3 as a Robotics Education Platform, pp. 170–181 (2020). https://doi.org/10.1007/978-3-030-26945-6_16
2. Bradski, G.: The opencv library. In: Dr. Dobb's Journal of Software Tools (2000)
3. Breitenmoser, A., Martinoli, A.: On combining multi-robot coverage and reciprocal collision avoidance. Springer Tracts in Advanced Robotics, vol. 112, p. 49–64. Springer Japan, Tokyo (2016). https://doi.org/10.1007/978-4-431-55879-8_4, https://infoscience.epfl.ch/handle/20.500.14299/127959
4. Caprari, G., Estier, T., Siegwart, R.: Fascination of down scaling-Alice the sugar cube robot. In: Proceedings of The IEEE International Conference on Robotics and Automation (ICRA), Workshop on Mobile Micro-Robots (2000)
5. Chin, K.Y., Khaluf, Y., Pinciroli, C.: Minimalistic collective perception with imperfect sensors. In: 2023 IEEE/RSJ International Conference on Intelligent Robots and Systems (IROS), pp. 8862–8868. IEEE (2023)
6. Choset, H.: Coverage for robotics - a survey of recent results. Ann. Math. Artif. Intell. **31**(1), 113–126 (2001)
7. Dimidov, C., Oriolo, G., Trianni, V.: Random walks in swarm robotics: an experiment with kilobots, pp. 185–196 (2016). https://doi.org/10.1007/978-3-319-44427-7_16
8. Goldberg, D., Matarić, M.J.: Interference as a tool for designing and evaluating multi-robot controllers. In: Proceedings of the Fourteenth National Conference on Artificial Intelligence and Ninth Conference on Innovative Applications of Artificial Intelligence, pp. 637–642 (1997)

9. Gonçalves, P., et al.: The e-puck, a robot designed for education in engineering. In: Proceedings of the 9th Conference on Autonomous Robot Systems and Competitions, vol. 1 (2009)
10. Hamann, H.: Superlinear scalability in parallel computing and multi-robot systems: shared resources, collaboration, and network topology. In: Berekovic, M., Buchty, R., Hamann, H., Koch, D., Pionteck, T. (eds.) Architecture of Computing Systems - ARCS 2018, pp. 31–42. Springer International Publishing, Cham (2018)
11. Hamann, H., Reina, A.: Scalability in computing and robotics. IEEE Trans. Comput. **71**(6), 1453–1465 (2022). https://doi.org/10.1109/TC.2021.3089044
12. Pfeiffer, C.: Fundamental efficiency limits for small metallic antennas. IEEE Trans. Antennas Propag. **65**(4), 1642–1650 (2017)
13. Ramesh, M., Imeson, F., Fidan, B., Smith, S.L.: Anytime replanning of robot coverage paths for partially unknown environments. IEEE Trans. Rob. **40**, 4190–4206 (2024). https://doi.org/10.1109/TRO.2024.3454417
14. Rubenstein, M., Ahler, C., Nagpal, R.: Kilobot: a low cost scalable robot system for collective behaviors. In: 2012 IEEE International Conference on Robotics and Automation, pp. 3293–3298 (2012). https://doi.org/10.1109/ICRA.2012.6224638
15. Schroeder, A., Trease, B., Arsie, A.: Balancing robot swarm cost and interference effects by varying robot quantity and size. Swarm Intell. **13**(1), 1–19 (2019)
16. Soma, K., Vardharajan, V.S., Hamann, H., Beltrame, G.: Congestion and scalability in robot swarms: a study on collective decision making. In: 2023 International Symposium on Multi-Robot and Multi-Agent Systems (MRS), pp. 199–206 (2023). https://doi.org/10.1109/MRS60187.2023.10416793
17. Yang, C., Van Der Drift, E., French, P.: Review of scaling effects on physical properties and practicalities of cantilever sensors. J. Micromech. Microeng. **32**(10), 103002 (2022)

Swarming from Vision Data Only: A Comparative Study of Imitation and Reinforcement Learning

Yu Zhou[1]([⊠])[iD], Jo Plested[2], Kathryn Kasmarik[2], and Matt Garratt[1][iD]

[1] School of Engineering and Technology, University of New South Wales, Canberra, Australia
{yu.zhou8,m.garratt}@unsw.edu.au
[2] School of Systems and Computing, University of New South Wales, Canberra, Australia
{j.plested,kathryn.kasmarik}@unsw.edu.au

Abstract. This paper presents two novel approaches to learning swarming collective motion from vision data using both Reinforcement Learning and Imitation Learning. Both methods are trained with an identical dataset, network architecture and visual observation input to compare their ability to generate collective behaviours. A simulated environment is developed in Gazebo with a group of three ground vehicles performing flocking motion to validate the experiments. Comparative results reveal the characteristics of each method, including group, order and violation metrics. This study provides insights into the trade-offs between stability and adaptability in learning-based swarm control, offering guidance for future vision-based swarming systems.

1   Introduction

Collective behaviours in swarm robotics, such as flocking [25], formation control [8], and aggregation [6], are inspired by biological systems and support tasks including navigation [27], area coverage [9], and search and rescue [7]. In robotic systems [11,12], such coordination typically requires relative localisation or access to a global reference frame. As a result, many approaches rely on external coordination systems such as motion capture [22], GNSS [2], UWB [28], multi-sensor fusion [13], or inter-agent communication. While effective, these methods depend on infrastructure or communication bandwidth that may be unavailable in real-world or resource-constrained environments. In contrast, natural swarms rely solely on local perception, such as vision or sound [1]. Rule-based models, including Reynolds' Boids [16], can generate stable formations with accurate measurements but degrade when only visually information is available [21].

Learning-based approaches reduce reliance on hand-crafted rules, with reinforcement learning (RL) and imitation learning (IL) being the widely explored paradigms. RL enables agents to autonomously discover control policies through

R. Groß et al. (Eds.): ANTS 2026, LNCS 16515, pp. 447–455, 2026.
https://doi.org/10.1007/978-3-032-26123-6_40

interaction, offering strong adaptability but often requiring careful reward design and substantial computational resources [10]. IL learns policies from expert demonstrations, enabling faster convergence and smoother control, but typically generalises poorly beyond the training distribution [18]. Evolutionary methods have also been explored in swarm robotics [23], though they often require extensive offline optimisation. Recent studies demonstrate decentralised flocking and formation using RL [3,4,14,20,26], but many assume access to privileged state information or are restricted to discrete actions. Vision-based approaches either require additional depth sensing [27] or are limited in behavioural diversity [18], while purely vision-based collective motion using raw images has only recently been explored [15]. Despite this progress, two gaps remain: few studies systematically compare RL and IL under identical sensory inputs and architectures, and the performance of these methods under noisy, vision-derived observations remains unclear. We compare RL and IL for vision-only swarm control in a unified framework, where a single learning agent uses omnidirectional vision while other robots follow Boids rules. The contributions are: (i) a vision-based IL method without explicit relative position measurements; (ii) an RL formulation with a unified architecture and reward design; and (iii) a controlled comparison highlighting trade-offs in stability and adaptability.

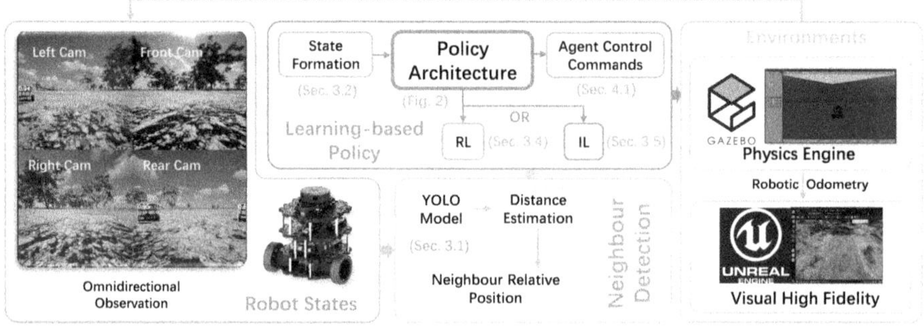

Fig. 1. Overview of the proposed pipeline for using either RL or IL for vision-based swarm control. Both modules process multi-camera visual inputs to produce velocity commands for an agent in a swarm.

2   Method

The design of our IL and RL algorithms for vision-only swarming is shown in Fig. 1. The neighbour detection part processes RGB images to infer the relative position of other swarm members. This data is combined with the linear and angular velocities of the agent and input to the RL or IL module. For RL, we employ the Proximal Policy Optimisation (PPO) [19] algorithm with an actor-critic network structure to train the policy and output the control velocity for the agent in the next time step. For IL, the DAgger algorithm [17] is used to aggregate the dataset when the agent deviates from the expert trajectories.

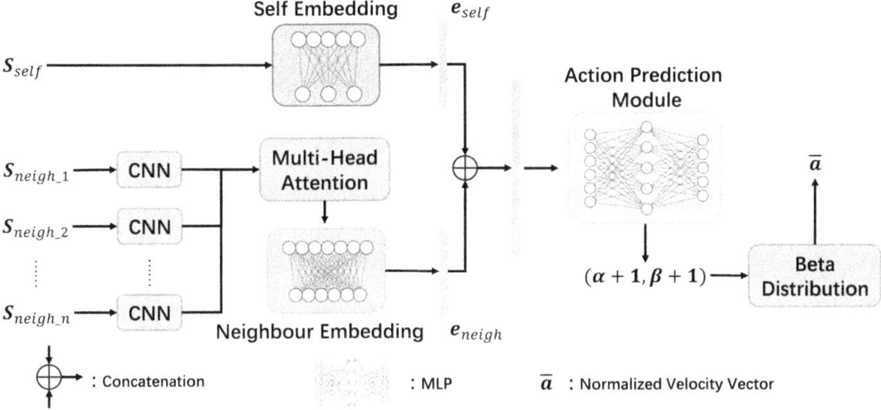

Fig. 2. Model architecture of the proposed RL and IL frameworks.

2.1 Swarm Member Perception System

This work uses camera data as the sole sensing modality. Experiments are conducted in Gazebo and Unreal Engine 5 using TurtleBot3 Burger robots. The learning agent is equipped with four cameras providing omnidirectional coverage, capturing images at resolution I and frequency f_c. The images are stitched and processed by a YOLOv8-based detector [24], trained on a task-specific dataset to detect surrounding robots. Each detected bounding box with height h_{bbox} and centre coordinates (c_x, c_y) is converted to relative spatial information. The object depth is estimated as $Z = (h_{\mathrm{real}} \cdot f_y)/h_{\mathrm{bbox}}$, and the corresponding 3D position in the local camera frame is computed as $\begin{bmatrix} x_c \ y_c \ z_c \end{bmatrix}^T = Z \begin{bmatrix} c'_x/f_x \ -c'_y/f_y \ 1 \end{bmatrix}^T$. The 2D position in the agent frame is obtained via $\begin{bmatrix} x_a \ z_a \end{bmatrix}^T = R_y(\theta_{\mathrm{cam}}) \begin{bmatrix} x_c \ z_c \end{bmatrix}^T$. The relative distance is computed as $r = \sqrt{x_a^2 + z_a^2}$, and each detected robot is represented as $\begin{bmatrix} \cos\theta \ \sin\theta \ r \end{bmatrix}$. Neighbour identities are maintained implicitly by associating detections across consecutive frames based on minimal spatial displacement in image coordinates. The parameters are detailed in Table 2.

2.2 Model Design

The design of the state input S for both IL and RL is defined as follows. The agent state is given by $S_{\mathrm{self}} = [v_{\mathrm{linear}}, \omega_{\mathrm{angular}}]^T$. For neighbour i, the state is represented as a temporal sequence $S_{\mathrm{neigh}(i)} = [S_{\mathrm{neigh}(i)}^{t-(N_t-1)}, S_{\mathrm{neigh}(i)}^{t-(N_t-2)}, \ldots, S_{\mathrm{neigh}(i)}^{t}]^T$, with each time step encoded as $S_{\mathrm{neigh}(i)}^{t} = [\cos(\theta_i), \sin(\theta_i), r_i]^T$. When a neighbour is temporarily not detected, its most recent observation is retained in the history buffer for up to N_t frames and reused until the detection reappears. The model architecture (Fig. 2) consists of a temporal convolution module, a multi-head attention module, and MLP-based embeddings, as summarised in Table. 1. Temporal dependencies in each neighbour's observation history are

Table 1. Network architecture of the proposed model. MHA: Multi-head Attention. AAP1D: 1D Adaptive Average Pooling. LN: Layer Norm

Module	Layer/Stage	Structure	Dimensions/Details
Temporal-Conv	Conv-1	Conv-ReLU	$80 \times N_t \to 64 \times N_t$
	Conv-2	Conv-ReLU	$64 \times N_t \to 64 \times N_t$
	Conv-3	Conv-ReLU	$64 \times N_t \to 32 \times N_t$
	Pooling	AAP1D	$32 \times N_t \to 32 \times 1$
Attention	Self-Attn	MHA	$(B, N-1, 32)$
	Pooling	Mean pooling	$(B, N-1, 32) \to (B, 32)$
MLPs	Neighbour Embed	Linear-ReLU-LN	$32 \to 64 \to 64$
	Self Embed	Linear-ReLU-LN	$2 \to 64 \to 64$
Action Head	Action Head	Linear-ReLU-LN-Linear	$128 \to 128 \to 128$
		ReLU-Linear-Softplus	$128 \to 256 \to 4$

encoded using dilated 1D convolutions and adaptive average pooling. A 4-head self-attention module aggregates neighbour features, which are fused with the agent's self-embedding and passed to the action head to parameterise a beta distribution [5]. Normalised actions are mapped to bounded velocity commands $[V, \, \omega]^T = [v_{\lim}V_{\mathrm{norm}}, \, 2\omega_{\lim}\omega_{\mathrm{norm}} - \omega_{\lim}]^T$. This formulation enforces bounded actions and allows explicit control over velocity limits. Compared to Gaussian policies, beta-distribution policies avoid boundary bias and converge faster in bounded continuous control tasks [5].

2.3   Reinforcement Learning

The RL framework adopts PPO with an actorcritic architecture, where the actor and critic share the same network structure (Fig. 2). The PPO clip ratio is set to $PPO_{\mathbf{clip}}$, and both networks are trained using the ADAM optimiser with learning rate l_r. The reward at each time step is defined as $r = r_{\mathrm{vel}} + r_{\mathrm{srv}}$, combining a velocity-matching term and a safety penalty. The velocity match reward is given by

$$r_{\mathrm{vel}} = \frac{V_{\mathrm{agent}} \cdot V_{\mathrm{reyn}}}{|V_{\mathrm{agent}}| \, |V_{\mathrm{reyn}}|} \cdot \min\left(e^{-\frac{(V_{\mathrm{agent}} - V_{\mathrm{reyn}})^2}{2\sigma^2}}, 1\right), \tag{1}$$

which encourages alignment in both direction and magnitude between the agent velocity $V_{\mathrm{agent}} = (v_{\mathrm{agent}(x)}, v_{\mathrm{agent}(y)})$ and the reference Boids velocity V_{reyn} (see Sect. 3.1). The parameter σ controls sensitivity to speed mismatch. A safety range penalty is applied as $r_{\mathrm{srv}} = -100 \cdot \mathbf{1}\{\mathrm{dist}_c > R_{\mathrm{coh}} \text{ or } \mathrm{dist}_c < R_{\mathrm{col}}\}$, penalising the agent when its distance from the swarm centre dist_c exceeds the cohesion range or falls within the collision range.

Table 2. Training and experiment parameters

Param.	Value	Desc.	Param.	Value	Desc.
N	3	Robot Number	N_s^{max}	6000	Max Steps
E_{RL}	2400	RL Episodes	E_{IL}	10	IL Episodes
N_t	10	History Buffer	K	22	DAgger Iters
k_a	1	Align Gain	k_c	2	Cohesion Gain
k_s	2	Separate Gain	PPO_{clip}	0.1	PPO Clip
R_{col}	$0.26\,\mathrm{m}$	Collision	R_{coh}	$5.0\,\mathrm{m}$	Cohesion
l_r	2×10^{-4}	Learning Rate	B	128	Batch Size
v_{lim}	$0.22\,\mathrm{m/s}$	Linear Vel.	ω_{lim}	$2.84\,\mathrm{rad/s}$	Angular Vel.
σ	0.05	Sensitivity Gain	λ	0.001	Entropy
h_{real}	$0.192\,\mathrm{m}$	Robot Height	f_c	$1/30\,\mathrm{s}$	Camera Hz
I	$480\times480\times3$	Image Scale	f_x or f_y	240	Focal x or Focal y

2.4 Imitation Learning

The IL method shares the same network architecture, input representation, and beta distribution policy as the RL actor. It follows the DAgger framework [17], in which the learned policy π_θ interacts with the environment for K iterations while the expert π_E provides reference actions computed from Boids velocity (see Sect. 3.1). Early stopping is applied to mitigate over-fitting. The actor network is parametrized as a beta distribution to generate bounded continuous actions as defined in Sect. 2.2. Compared to standard DAgger, the loss function $\mathcal{L}_{\mathrm{DAgger}}(\theta)$ is augmented with an entropy regularisation term $\lambda H(\pi_\theta)$, encouraging exploration during early training. Prior to the DAgger iterations, E_{IL} episodes are collected and used to initialise the policy.

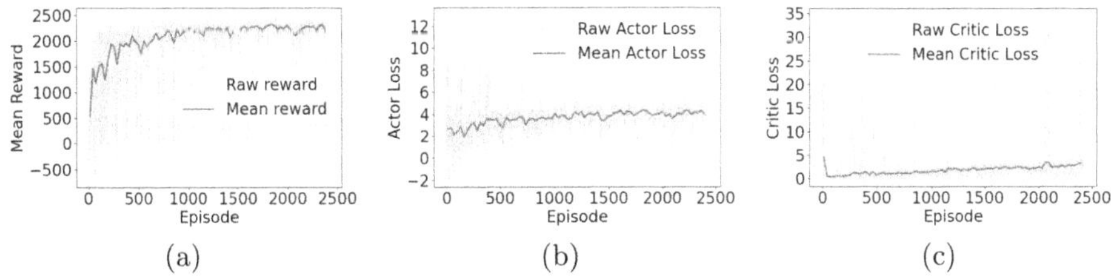

Fig. 3. Learning curves of the proposed RL model during training. (Left Image) mean episode reward, (b) actor loss and (c) critic loss.

3   Experiments

3.1   Training Setup

Agents are trained in an $18\,\text{m} \times 18\,\text{m}$ obstacle-free environment. At the start of each episode, robots are randomly initialised within a central $4\,\text{m} \times 4\,\text{m}$ region with random headings. One agent is controlled by the learned policy, while the remaining agents follow Reynolds' Boids model [16]. For non-learning agents, flocking behaviour is generated by cohesion, separation, and alignment forces. For a swarm of N robots (excluding the learning agent), robot R_i has position p_i^t and velocity v_i^t at time t. The Boids velocity update is given by $v_i^{t+1} = v_i^t + k_c v_{i(\text{coh})}^t + k_s v_{i(\text{sep})}^t + k_a v_{i(\text{alig})}^t + v_{i(\text{wall})}^t$, where k_c, k_s, and k_a are gain parameters and $v_{i(\text{wall})}^t$ provides wall repulsion. The resulting flocking velocity is converted to linear and angular commands as $V = \|v_i\|$ and $\omega = k_\omega\big(\text{atan2}(v_{i(y)}, v_{i(x)}) - \theta\big)$, where $v_i = (v_{i(x)}, v_{i(y)})$ is the world-frame velocity and θ is the robot heading. Training parameters are listed in Table 2. Policies are trained in Gazebo at $10\times$ simulation speed on an NVIDIA RTX 4000 Ada Generation GPU for approximately $10\,\text{h}$. Each run lasts up to 6000 steps with a control interval of $1/30\,\text{s}$. The linear speed of non-learning agents is fixed at $0.15\,\text{m/s}$. RL training curves are shown in Fig. 3.

Table 3. Performance comparison (mean $\pm$ 95% Confidence Interval).

Scenario	Method	G (m)	O	V (%)
Walled	RL	0.62 ± 0.02	114.47 ± 25.16	0.00 ± 0.00
	IL	0.62 ± 0.01	172.70 ± 29.14	0.01 ± 0.00
	Boids	0.62 ± 0.01	36.15 ± 4.55	0.00 ± 0.00
Circle	RL	0.43 ± 0.19	198.18 ± 72.25	0.00 ± 0.00
	IL	0.43 ± 0.17	220.15 ± 94.16	0.01 ± 0.00
	Boids	0.44 ± 0.17	137.03 ± 56.55	0.00 ± 0.00
Sine	RL	0.28 ± 0.09	71.81 ± 27.78	0.00 ± 0.00
	IL	0.27 ± 0.09	98.14 ± 28.09	0.01 ± 0.02
	Boids	0.31 ± 0.00	39.89 ± 11.05	0.00 ± 0.00
Random	RL	0.31 ± 0.00	117.87 ± 19.07	0.00 ± 0.00
	IL	0.29 ± 0.09	121.84 ± 45.47	0.01 ± 0.01
	Boids	0.30 ± 0.02	58.18 ± 11.48	0.00 ± 0.00

3.2   Environments and Performance Metrics

Four scenarios are evaluated: **Walled**, **Circle**, **Sine**, and **Random** (Fig. 4). Each scenario is tested over ten trials with randomised initial conditions for all robots (including the Learning agent and Non-learning agents: Robot 1 and Robot 2). Performance is evaluated using three metrics: *Group* cohesion G (Eq. 2), *Order* O (Eq. 3), and *Violation* rate V (Eq. 4).

$$G = \sum_{t=T_0}^{T_0+N_s} \frac{\frac{1}{N}\sum_{i=1}^{N} \|p_i - p_{\text{mean}}\|}{N_s}, \quad p_{\text{mean}} = \frac{1}{N}\sum_{i=1}^{N} p_i \tag{2}$$

$$O = \sum_{t=T_0}^{T_0+N_s} \frac{\frac{1}{N}\sum_{i=1}^{N} \|v_i - v_{\text{mean}}\|}{N_s}, \quad v_i = [v_x, v_y] \tag{3}$$

$$V = \sum_{t=T_0}^{T_0+N_s} \frac{\frac{1}{N}\sum_{i=1}^{N} \mathbf{1}\{\text{dist}_i < R_{\text{col}}\}}{N_s} \tag{4}$$

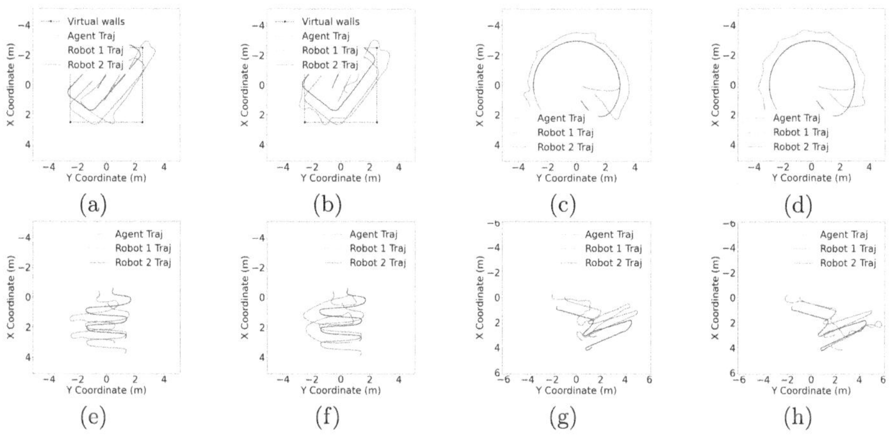

Fig. 4. Robot trajectories under four scenarios: (a) Walled RL (b) Walled IL, (c) Circle RL (d) Circle IL, (e) Sine RL (f) Sine IL (g) Random RL (h) Random IL.

4 Conclusion

This paper compared reinforcement learning (RL) and imitation learning (IL) for achieving swarm collective motion using only onboard omnidirectional vision, without access to global state information. Experiments across four motion scenarios demonstrate that both learning approaches can produce stable, collision-free flocking behaviour, confirming the feasibility of decentralised vision-only swarm coordination. Quantitative results (Table 3) show that RL and IL achieve comparable group cohesion (G) across all scenarios, with violation rates (V) remaining near zero, indicating safe and stable behaviour. However, IL consistently exhibits higher order (O), particularly in dynamic scenarios such as Random motion, reflecting reduced alignment with instantaneous swarm velocity changes. In contrast, RL adapts more effectively to changing swarm dynamics through exploration and the proposed reward formulation, and demonstrates more consistent performance, as evidenced by narrower confidence intervals in the Circle and Sine scenarios. Compared to the Boids baseline, both learning-based methods show increased disorder, highlighting the challenge of inferring relative motion from vision-derived observations. Overall, IL offers fast convergence and stable control when high-quality demonstrations are available, making it suitable for resource-constrained systems. RL, while more computationally demanding, provides stronger adaptability and robustness to previously unseen motion patterns, suggesting better long-term scalability. Although the Boids model achieves higher coordination efficiency (O), it relies on noise-free state information that is typically unavailable in vision-limited or infrastructure-free settings.

Disclosure of Interests. The authors have no competing interests to declare.

References

1. Basiri, M., Schill, F., Lima, P., Floreano, D.: On-board relative bearing estimation for teams of drones using sound. IEEE Robot. Autom. Lett. **1**(2), 820–827 (2016)
2. Causa, F., Fasano, G., Grassi, M.: GNSS-aware path planning for UAV swarm in complex environments. In: 2019 IEEE 5th International Workshop on Metrology for AeroSpace (MetroAeroSpace), pp. 661–666 (2019)
3. Chen, Y.F., Everett, M., Liu, M., How, J.P.: Socially aware motion planning with deep reinforcement learning. In: 2017 IEEE/RSJ International Conference on Intelligent Robots and Systems (IROS), pp. 1343–1350 (2017)
4. Chen, Y.F., Liu, M., Everett, M., How, J.P.: Decentralized non-communicating multiagent collision avoidance with deep reinforcement learning. In: 2017 IEEE International Conference on Robotics and Automation (ICRA), pp. 285–292 (2017)
5. Chou, P.W., Maturana, D., Scherer, S.: Improving stochastic policy gradients in continuous control with deep reinforcement learning using the beta distribution. In: International Conference on Machine Learning, pp. 834–843. PMLR (2017)
6. Correll, N., Martinoli, A.: Modeling and designing self-organized aggregation in a swarm of miniature robots. Int. J. Robot. Res. **30**(5), 615–626 (2011)
7. Din, A., Jabeen, M., Zia, K., Khalid, A., Saini, D.K.: Behavior-based swarm robotic search and rescue using fuzzy controller. Comput. Electr. Eng. **70**, 53–65 (2018)
8. Fang, Z., Chen, T., Shen, T., Jiang, D., Zhang, Z., Li, G.: Multi-agent generative adversarial interactive self-imitation learning for AUV formation control and obstacle avoidance. IEEE Robot. Autom. Lett. (2025)
9. Ghanem, R., Ali, I.M., Abpeikar, S., Kasmarik, K., Garratt, M.: Optimizing and predicting swarming collective motion performance for coverage problems solving: A simulation-optimization approach. Eng. Appl. Artif. Intell. **139**, 109522 (2025)
10. Hussein, A., Petraki, E., Abbass, H.A.: Swarm imitation learning from observations. IEEE Trans. Emerg. Top. Comput. Intell. (2025)
11. Li, X., Wang, J., Xu, Q., Wang, H., Yang, K., Mao, D.: Extended state observer based iteration learning fault-tolerant control scheme for AUV. In: Global Oceans 2020: Singapore–US Gulf Coast, pp. 1–8. IEEE (2020)

12. Li, X.G., Wang, H.D., Li, M., Karkoub, M.: A linear extended state observer-based fuzzy fault tolerant controller for autonomous underwater vehicle. In: 2019 IEEE Symposium Series on Computational Intelligence (SSCI), pp. 3265–3271 (2019)
13. Li, Z., Jiang, C., Gu, X., Xu, Y., Cui, J., et al.: Collaborative positioning for swarms: a brief survey of vision, LiDAR and wireless sensors based methods. Defence Technol. **33**, 475–493 (2024)
14. Matta, M., et al.: Q-RTS: a real-time swarm intelligence based on multi-agent Q-learning. Electron. Lett. **55**(10), 589–591 (2019)
15. Mezey, D., et al.: Purely vision-based collective movement of robots. NPJ Robot. **3**(1), 11 (2025)
16. Reynolds, C.W.: Flocks, herds and schools: a distributed behavioral model. In: Proceedings of the 14th Annual Conference on Computer Graphics and Interactive Techniques, pp. 25–34 (1987)
17. Ross, S., Gordon, G., Bagnell, D.: A reduction of imitation learning and structured prediction to no-regret online learning. In: Proceedings of the Fourteenth International Conference on Artificial Intelligence and Statistics, pp. 627–635. JMLR Workshop and Conference Proceedings (2011)
18. Schilling, F., Lecoeur, J., Schiano, F., Floreano, D.: Learning vision-based flight in drone swarms by imitation. IEEE Robot. Autom. Lett. **4**(4), 4523–4530 (2019)
19. Schulman, J., Wolski, F., Dhariwal, P., Radford, A., Klimov, O.: Proximal policy optimization algorithms. arXiv preprint arXiv:1707.06347 (2017)
20. Singla, A., Padakandla, S., Bhatnagar, S.: Memory-based deep reinforcement learning for obstacle avoidance in UAV with limited environment knowledge. IEEE Trans. Intell. Transp. Syst. **22**(1), 107–118 (2019)
21. Soria, E., Schiano, F., Floreano, D.: The influence of limited visual sensing on the Reynolds flocking algorithm. In: 2019 Third IEEE International Conference on Robotic Computing (IRC), pp. 138–145 (2019)
22. Tran, V.P., Garratt, M.A., Kasmarik, K., Anavatti, S.G.: Dynamic frontier-led swarming: multi-robot repeated coverage in dynamic environments. IEEE/CAA J. Autom. Sinica **10**(3), 646–661 (2023)
23. Trianni, V., Nolfi, S., Dorigo, M.: Evolution, self-organization and swarm robotics. In: Blum, C., Merkle, D. (eds.) Swarm Intelligence. Natural Computing Series, pp. 163–191. Springer, Heidelberg (2008). https://doi.org/10.1007/978-3-540-74089-6_5
24. Varghese, R., Sambath, M.: YOLOv8: a novel object detection algorithm with enhanced performance and robustness. In: 2024 International Conference on Advances in Data Engineering and Intelligent Computing Systems (ADICS), pp. 1–6. IEEE (2024)
25. Vásárhelyi, G., Virágh, C., Somorjai, G., Nepusz, T., Eiben, A.E., Vicsek, T.: Optimized flocking of autonomous drones in confined environments. Sci. Robot. **3**(20), eaat3536 (2018)
26. Xie, L., Wang, S., Markham, A., Trigoni, N.: Towards monocular vision based obstacle avoidance through deep reinforcement learning. arXiv preprint arXiv:1706.09829 (2017)
27. Xu, Z., Han, X., Shen, H., Jin, H., Shimada, K.: NavRL: learning safe flight in dynamic environments. IEEE Robot. Autom. Lett. (2025)
28. Zhou, X., et al.: Swarm of micro flying robots in the wild. Sci. Robot. **7**(66), eabm5954 (2022)

User-Centred Design of Multi-UAV Swarm Interfaces for Firefighting UAVs

Alexander McConville[1(✉)] [iD], Georgios Tzoumas[1] [iD], Lucio R. Salinas[1,3] [iD], Marcela Munera[2] [iD], and Sabine Hauert[1] [iD]

[1] University of Bristol, Bristol, UK
`a.mcconville@unsw.edu.au`
[2] University of the West of England, Bristol, UK
[3] Instituto de Automática (INAUT), National University of San Juan (UNSJ) - CONICET, San Juan, Argentina

Abstract. In this work, we develop a user interface to manage a swarm of large fixed-wing Uncrewed Aerial Vehicles (UAVs) for firefighting applications through a user-centered design process. We conduct Wizard of Oz studies with nine firefighters and drone operators to collect end-user data on their ideal system for use in a wildfire scenario. This data is then translated into features and design drivers implemented in a prototype interface for swarm firefighting. The interface is evaluated through a usability study in which six participants provide feedback and score the interface, resulting in an overall usability rating of 'Good' with a System Usability Scale (SUS) score of 76.25. We find that end users in this application are more concerned with producing the desired effect than with controlling individual UAVs. This finding provides a useful insight for the design of future multi-UAV systems, suggesting a reduced emphasis on micro-managing the fleet.

1 Introduction

Increasing wildfire frequency driven by changing climate conditions [19] is intensifying impacts on communities [26] and placing growing demands on fire services. Uncrewed Aerial Vehicles (UAVs) are being adopted to support wildfire response through aerial monitoring and large-area coverage [13,18]. In UAV wildfire response, past research has focused on optimising search, monitoring, and coordinating multi-UAV systems [23]. Despite their effectiveness, most systems remain limited to passive observation [20]. Single UAV deployments have demonstrated their operational value [17], while ongoing work explores active fire engagement to reduce risk to crewed aircraft [24].

The effectiveness of multi-UAV and swarm systems depends strongly on interface design. Human-swarm interaction research emphasises balancing global control with local intervention [3], with studies highlighting the role of situational awareness and intuitive interaction [20,23]. Misaligned or complex systems, however, can hinder adoption in safety-critical environments [22]. User-centred design has proven effective in improving usability and acceptance in domains

R. Groß et al. (Eds.): ANTS 2026, LNCS 16515, pp. 456–464, 2026.
https://doi.org/10.1007/978-3-032-26123-6_41

such as healthcare and vehicle safety [6,12]. This work therefore adopts a User-Centred Design (UCD) approach, emphasizing continuous user involvement to align system functionality with operational needs, guided by ISO 9241-210:2019 [1,7,9].

This work contributes empirically grounded design guidance for human-swarm interfaces in wildfire response, derived from domain experts and validated via usability testing. The results demonstrate that firefighters prefer expressing intent in terms of desired operational effects, relying on autonomous swarm behaviours rather than continuous individual UAV control, with implications for future multi-robot system interface design.

2 Concept Multi-UAV Swarm System Description

The interface was designed for wildfire monitoring and engagement using swarms of large fixed-wing UAVs, based on the Windracers ULTRA platform [25]. ULTRA has a 10 m wingspan, a 100 kg payload, and an operational range of approximately 1000 km. Equipped with fire-sensing payloads and water or retardant delivery, multiple aircraft operate as a coordinated swarm under firefighter supervision. Engagement behaviours, interaction methods, and system autonomy were defined iteratively through a user-centred design (UCD) process.

System requirements were determined using a Wizard of Oz (WOz) study, in which experimenters manually controlled system behaviours to enable rapid exploration of interaction concepts without requiring full implementation. This approach is well established in usability research for refining functionality prior to development [2,8,14,16]. Following interface development, a usability study was conducted. Usability was defined in terms of effectiveness, efficiency, and user satisfaction [10,11], as no comparative interfaces were evaluated, the study focused primarily on user satisfaction.

3 Wizard of Oz Study

This study aimed to elicit user information, interaction, and system behaviour requirements for multi-UAV operations. A custom multi-UAV simulation was developed in which users interacted with a simplified system representation and verbally described desired information access, objectives, and preferred methods for directing the swarm.

The simulation followed an operational workflow, defining a search area, launching UAVs, monitoring for fires, managing multiple concurrent incidents, responding to airspace incursions, and recovering all UAVs. A moderator guided task progression, while a "wizard" behind the scenes translated user commands into system responses.

Qualitative data were coded by interface component, mission phase, and feature requirements were identified through frequency analysis. These requirements informed the design of system functionalities, interaction methods, and behaviours, guided by established uncrewed search-and-rescue interface design principles [21].

Participants included five UAV operators and four firefighters from the Lancashire Fire and Rescue Service drone unit. All participants had prior experience with multirotor UAV systems.

3.1   Wizard of Oz Study Results

Across the WOz studies, participants consistently preferred limited direct control of individual UAVs, relying instead on autonomous behaviours. Manual control was considered necessary only during faults, indicating strong operator willingness to delegate fine-grained control to the swarm.

Participant feedback was categorised by mission segment and category: information, interaction methods, and autonomous agent behaviours, producing three feature lists per segment. Grouping and counting comment frequencies generated a prioritised set of user needs shown in Table 1, which guided feature selection and refinement for upcoming flight trials.

Table 1. Summarised primary feature list from the WOz study broken down by type of feature (n representing the frequency of the response, with multiple mentions by the same participant being counted individually).

Visual Information	Interaction Method	Vehicle Behaviours
Weather display - wind speed/direction (n = 8)	A method to define drop lines and direct drops with Go/No Go option (n = 12)	Automatic trajectory generation based on desired task (n = 14)
Audio and visual notification cues (n = 13)	Click for individual vehicle information (n = 6)	Survey grid was the most preferred search pattern (n = 9)
Colour-based status indication (n = 23)	Click for individual vehicle control (n = 26)	Automatic return to base on failure (n = 5)
Vehicle data available but hidden (n = 28)	Global control of the swarm (n = 10)	Loiter on fire when detected (n = 4)
Access to vehicle data feeds (n = 9)		Redistribute swarm when vehicles are removed (n = 4)

For visual displays, operators required flexible information control, including switching map types, showing search regions, and visualising aircraft positions. Interaction preferences reflected multi-level control, reinforcing [3] findings in earlier work where participants wanted to command the swarm at a high level, for example, issuing a single "land" command with autonomous sequencing, while retaining the ability to intervene with individual UAVs during faults. Access to individual sensor feeds, such as UAV camera views, was also requested for monitoring critical events. Desired autonomous behaviours focused on safe and effective operation, including collision avoidance, area containment, adaptive search coverage, and automatic task scheduling. Overall, responses emphasised controlling the effect rather than micromanaging individuals, highlighting the importance of intuitive high-level interaction and reliable autonomous behaviour.

3.2   Interface Design and Development

The graphical user interface was implemented in Python using the Kivy framework. The interface supports operator awareness of swarm state and rapid transitions between swarm-level and individual UAV control. The interactive map shown in Fig. 1 shows each UAV with an icon indicating position and heading, with colour coding for system states, white for normal, red for fire detection, yellow for sense-and-avoid or geo-fence responses, and blue to highlight a selected vehicle. A persistent agent status panel Section A in Fig. 1 provides an overview of all UAVs, including UAV numbers and swarm activity, at all times.

Operators can select UAVs directly on the map, opening a platform panel with detailed status, mode controls, sensor data, and waypoint commands, reflecting the need to shift control granularity based on task demands [3]. Audio cues supplement visual alerts for fire events, triggering a ping sound and a red highlight on the detecting agent's node in the status panel to capture attention when operators are focused elsewhere [4].

Two fire engagement methods were implemented based on firefighter feedback. The direct drop represented in Fig. 2(a) lets operators specify a drop point and approach vector, with the system assigning the most suitable UAV to execute the water or retardant drop autonomously. The drop line allows operators to define a control line by selecting two points on the map, with the swarm autonomously planning flight paths to slow fire progress by providing a fire break using water or retardant, as shown in Fig. 2(b). Multi-agent coordinated drops are supported but were not included in usability testing.

Controls are arranged in three regions to simplify interaction: Section A for individual vehicle panels, Section B for swarm-level controls containing mode controls, and search and fire-drop behaviours. Section C contained controls for visual display settings such as map style, sensor ranges, and overlays. This layout reduces nested menus, minimises misclicks, and accelerates training, supporting efficient swarm management and situational awareness.

4   Usability Study

The system interface was evaluated in a moderated usability study. Participants first completed a ten-minute scripted training session introducing the interface, available information, and actions, without mentioning specifics that would be necessary in the tasks of the study.

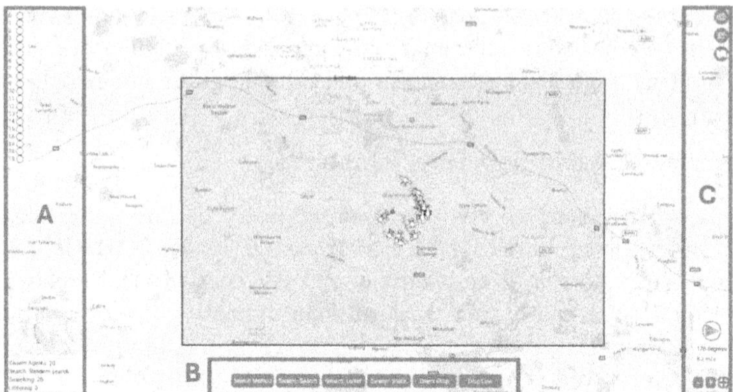

Fig. 1. The interface developed based on the desired features from the WOz study, where A) shows the status panel and swarm information, B) shows the swarm interaction controls for managing the swarm as a whole, and C) shows the visual display controls.

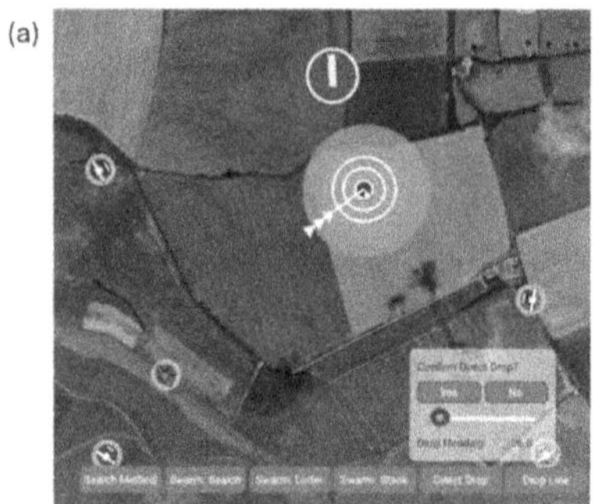
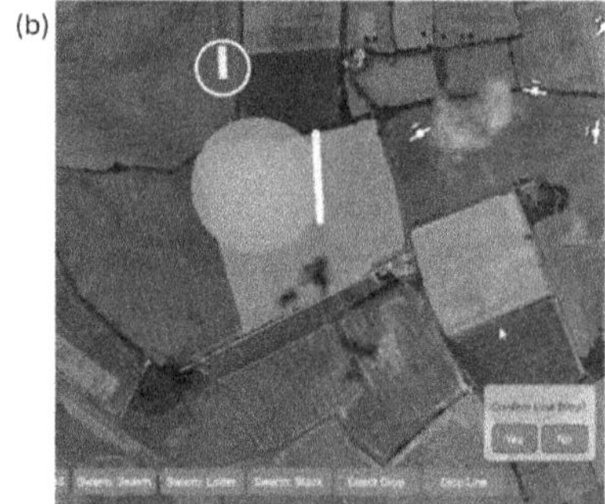

Fig. 2. The designed interaction methods for wildfire engagement and mitigation strategies based on the user inputs from the WOz study. The Drop point (a) requiring a location and approach bearing and Drop line (b) requiring a start and point defined by the operator, both approaches require positive confirmation to confirm the action.

Participants then completed a series of moderator-guided tasks. Each task was timed from prompt to completion, and participants were encouraged to think aloud, describing where they expected to find information and the anticipated outcome of their actions. Screen activity and audio were recorded.

Following task completion, participants provided qualitative feedback on intuitive and problematic interface elements, completed the System Usability Scale (SUS) questionnaire [5], and answered demographic questions.

Tasks required participants to: change the map visual style; modify swarm search behaviour; remove search visualisations; activate the fire sensor range indicator; locate and zoom in on a detected fire; define a direct and control line drop; select a specific UAV; determine its heading and altitude; command an individual UAV to land; and set all UAVs to Loiter mode.

These tasks exercised the core interface components, including map and visual controls, swarm-level management of 20 UAVs, individual vehicle control, and fire-related actions.

To support operation at this scale, several assumptions were made: UAVs autonomously manage flight stability and collision avoidance, maintain fixed altitudes throughout the operation, and operate at sufficiently separated altitude bands to prevent interaction.

Six male participants took part in the usability study, with some overlap with the WOz study. Participant backgrounds ranged from PhD students to a commercial flight instructor, all with prior experience in robotics and UAVs, however, no firefighters were available for the usability study.

4.1   Usability Study Results

The usability study gathered both qualitative user feedback and quantitative task-timing data. Error types and participant comments were counted to identify unclear or weak areas of the interface. As shown in Fig. 3(a) five main themes emerged: feedback, control/latency, display clarity, misclicks, and training failures. Most issues stemmed from insufficient feedback from the system and uncertainty in whether the command had been received, followed by control delays and system latency. Display clarity also affected performance, due to different preferences in map style and the visibility of overlays being impacted, while the low number of misclicks suggests this design goal was largely met. One participant noted the need for more training before the study.

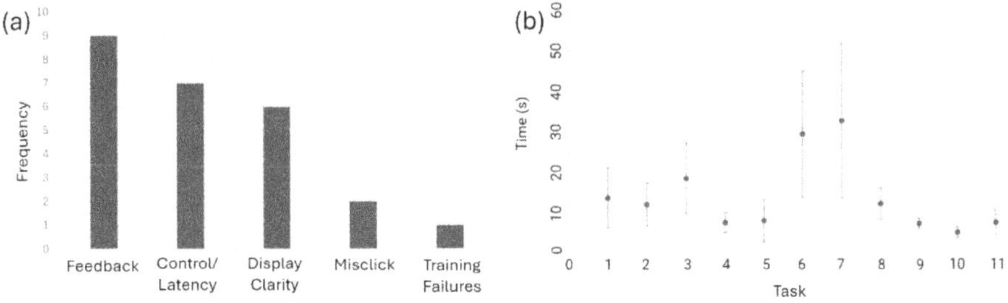

Fig. 3. Summary results from the Usability Study, where (a) shows the frequency of errors and themes of comments and (b) mean and standard deviation of task timing in seconds.

Task timing results in Fig. 3(b) show that Tasks 6 and 7, direct drops and drop-line generation, took the longest time, they were also the tasks that produced the most errors. While these tasks are the most complex and action-intensive, the elevated error rate indicates a need for improvements in how they are implemented.

SUS scores ranged from 65 to 87.5, with a mean of 76.25 out of 100, and a standard deviation of 8.26, putting the result in the"Good" range [15]. Convergence in new errors, total errors, and participant comments suggests the sample size was sufficient to identify primary usability issues with the current iteration. Overall, participants found the system intuitive with minimal training.

The agent status panel was well received, with users valuing its clean layout and dual interaction modes. However, several visual elements, particularly the wind direction indicator and element opacity, require refinement to maintain clarity across different map styles.

The interface supports situational awareness through effective colour coding and accessible swarm information, enabling users to filter large volumes of data and quickly assess system state. However, latency and overly sensitive zoom controls led to misclicks and user frustration.

Finally, access to richer sensor data and more detailed system feedback would improve decision-making. While the interface is generally clean and functional, future iterations should incorporate stronger feedback, additional confirmations for actions that would affect overall swarm behaviour, and predictive visualisations of vehicle state and position to increase user confidence and overall effectiveness.

5 Conclusion

This work applied user-centered design to develop a swarm UAV wildfire interface. WOz study data identified firefighter requirements and informed feature implementation, resulting in a highly usable interface that achieved a "Good" SUS rating in a single iteration. The design also aligned swarm behaviours with operator expectations rather than developer assumptions. From the WOz study, it was clear that users are more focused on producing the desired result than low-level control, this makes it vital to design interfaces that allow users to effectively express their intent to the system.

For the next iteration, key improvements include reducing system latency, providing more feedback to minimise errors and frustration, and adding confirmations to verify actions across the system. These refinements target interface performance and clarity, rather than the broader interaction, control, and information-display principles established through user input.

Acknowledgments. GT and SH are funded by Horizon Europe Project 101070918 supported by UKRI grant number 10038942.

Disclosure of Interests. The authors have no competing interests to declare.

References

1. Ergonomics of human-system interaction-human-centred design for interactive systems. Tech. rep. (2019). www.iso.org
2. Alce, G., Wallergård, M., Hermodsson, K.: WozARd: A wizard of Oz method for wearable augmented reality interaction-a pilot study. Adv. Hum Comput Interact. **2015** (2015). https://doi.org/10.1155/2015/271231
3. Bjurling, O., Granlund, R., Alfredson, J., Arvola, M., Ziemke, T.: Drone swarms in forest firefighting: a local development case study of multi-level human-swarm interaction. In: ACM International Conference Proceeding Series. Association for Computing Machinery (2020). https://doi.org/10.1145/3419249.3421239
4. Brimner, S.S., et al.: Assessing flight information priority by flight phase for us army future vertical lift platforms. In: Proceedings of the Human Factors and Ergonomics Society, vol. 67, pp. 27–31. SAGE Publications Inc. (2023). https://doi.org/10.1177/21695067231192421
5. Brooke, J.: SUS-a quick and dirty usability scale. Tech. rep. (1996). https://www.researchgate.net/publication/319394819
6. Cacciabue, P.C., Martinetto, M.: A user-centred approach for designing driving support systems: the case of collision avoidance. Cogn. Technol. Work **8**(3), 201–214 (2006). https://doi.org/10.1007/s10111-006-0039-7
7. Chammas, A., Quaresma, M., Mont'Alvão, C.: A closer look on the user centred design. In: Procedia Manufacturing, vol. 3, pp. 5397–5404. Elsevier B.V. (2015). https://doi.org/10.1016/j.promfg.2015.07.656
8. Dahlbick, N., J6nsson, A., Ahrenberg, L.: Wizard of Oz stadies l W-language interfaces need for wizard of oz studies. Tech. rep. (1993)
9. Den Buurman, R.: User-centred design of smart products. In: Ergonomics, vol. 40, pp. 1159–1169. Taylor & Francis Ltd (1997). https://doi.org/10.1080/001401397187676
10. Hornbæk, K.: Current practice in measuring usability: challenges to usability studies and research. Int. J. Hum. Comput. Stud. **64**(2), 79–102 (2006). https://doi.org/10.1016/j.ijhcs.2005.06.002
11. Iso, W.: 9241-11. Ergonomic requirements for office work with visual display terminals (VDTs). Int. Organ. Stand. **45**(9), 22 (1998)
12. Jankowski, N., Schönijahn, L., Salchow, C., Ivanova, E., Wahl, M.: User-centred design as an important component of technological development. In: Current Directions in Biomedical Engineering, vol. 3, pp. 69–73. Walter de Gruyter GmbH (2017). https://doi.org/10.1515/cdbme-2017-0015
13. Lattimer, B.Y., et al.: Use of unmanned aerial systems in outdoor firefighting (2023). https://doi.org/10.1007/s10694-023-01437-0
14. Lee, M., Billinghurst, M.: A wizard of Oz study for an AR multimodal interface. Tech. rep. (2008)
15. Lewis, J.R.: The system usability scale: past, present, and future. Int. J. Hum Comput Interact. **34**, 577–590 (2018). https://doi.org/10.1080/10447318.2018.1455307
16. Maulsby, D., Greenberg, S., Mander, R.: I!WRCHI'93 24-29 April1993 Prototyping an Intelligent Agent through Wizard of Oz. Tech. rep
17. Mcconville, A., Tzoumas, G., Salinas, L.R., Munera, M., Hauert, S.: Adoption of UAV swarm technology: survey and opinions of firefighters. In: Proceedings of IEEE Workshop on Advanced Robotics and its Social Impacts, ARSO, pp. 228–234. IEEE Computer Society (2024). https://doi.org/10.1109/ARSO60199.2024.10557806

18. Nafiz, M., Khan, H., Neustaedter, C.: Exploring drones to assist firefighters during emergencies. Tech. rep. (2019). http://hdi.famnit.upr.si
19. Richardson, D., et al.: Global increase in wildfire potential from compound fire weather and drought. NPJ Climate and Atmos. Sci. **5**(1) (2022). https://doi.org/10.1038/s41612-022-00248-4
20. Saffre, F., Hildmann, H., Karvonen, H., Lind, T.: Monitoring and cordoning wildfires with an autonomous swarm of unmanned aerial vehicles. Drones **6**(10) (2022). https://doi.org/10.3390/drones6100301
21. Scholtz, J., Gaithersburg, J.Y., Drury, J.L., Yanco, H.A.: Proceedings of the 2004 IEEE Inbrnational Conhnnce on RoboUss (LAutomatlon New Orleans. LA Aprll2W4 Evaluation of Human-Robot Interaction Awareness in Search and Rescue. Technical report (2004)
22. Shore, L., Power, V., de Eyto, A., O'Sullivan, L.W.: Technology acceptance and user-centred design of assistive exoskeletons for older adults: a commentary (2018). https://doi.org/10.3390/robotics7010003
23. Tzoumas, G., et al.: Wildfire detection in large-scale environments using force-based control for swarms of UAVs. Swarm Intell. **17**(1-2), 89–115 (2023). https://doi.org/10.1007/s11721-022-00218-9
24. Tzoumas, G., Salinas, L., Mcconville, A., Richardson, T., Hauert, S.: Extinguishing wildfires in large scale scenarios using swarms of UAVs. In: International Conference on Swarm Intelligence: ANTS, pp. 71–83 (2024)
25. Windracers Ltd: Drones - Windracers autonomous drones
26. Yao, J., et al.: Sub-daily exposure to fine particulate matter and ambulance dispatches during wildfire seasons: a case-crossover study in British Columbia, Canada. Environ. Health Perspectives **128**(6), 1–10 (2020). https://doi.org/10.1289/EHP5792

When Small Differences Matter: How Small Differences Create Leaders in Flocking Swarms

Yara Khaluf[(✉)] [iD]

Computational Intelligence Group/Department of Computer Science,
Vrije Universiteit Amsterdam, Amsterdam, The Netherlands
y.khaluf@vu.nl

Abstract. We study whether leadership can arise in collectives of agents that follow identical interaction rules but differ slightly in perceptual or kinematic traits. Using a continuous-time flocking model with controlled micro-heterogeneity, we measure directional influence through a lagged-correlation network metric. Fully homogeneous groups show uniformly low influence, whereas even a small elite subset produces stronger leaders. Moderate heterogeneity amplifies leadership, while excessive heterogeneity reduces it. These results show that minimal parametric differences alone can generate emergent leaders in decentralized swarms.

1 Introduction

Collective systems often exhibit coordinated motion without centralized control, yet directional influence and leader–follower structures frequently emerge even among nominally identical individuals [2,3,5,7,9]. Understanding how such influence arises from local interactions remains a central question in collective intelligence. Leadership can therefore appear without explicit hierarchy, raising the question of whether symmetry alone can give rise to persistent directional influence. In swarm robotics, leadership directly affects responsiveness, stability, and resilience. While many studies introduce explicit leader roles or heterogeneous control policies, it remains unclear whether leadership can emerge spontaneously among agents that follow identical interaction rules.

Recent work has shown that heterogeneity in sensing, control rules, or error profiles can improve swarm performance, adaptability, and robustness [1,4,6,8,10]. For example, individuality in physical robot swarms has been shown to arise from persistent differences in sensing and actuation, sometimes improving task outcomes [6]. Other studies demonstrate that mixing agents with different behavioral rules or decision strategies can enhance adaptability and resilience in dynamic environments [8,10]. Similarly, heterogeneous foraging swarms and systems with diverse error profiles can outperform homogeneous teams by enabling specialization or improved task partitioning [1,4]. However, most of these studies rely on explicit role assignment or algorithmic diversity,

R. Groß et al. (Eds.): ANTS 2026, LNCS 16515, pp. 465–472, 2026.
https://doi.org/10.1007/978-3-032-26123-6_42

and do not address whether minimal, unintended micro-heterogeneity alone can generate leadership.

In this study, we isolate whether small, persistent differences in perception, speed, or reaction delay are sufficient to break symmetry and produce measurable leadership. Using a continuous-time flocking model with controlled micro-heterogeneity, we quantify directional influence through a lagged-correlation network metric. We show that even a small elite subset produces stronger and more unequal leadership patterns, while excessive heterogeneity reduces this effect. Unlike prior work on designed or rule-level heterogeneity, our findings demonstrate that infinitesimal parametric differences alone can give rise to emergent leaders in decentralized collectives.

2   Model

We study how structured individual differences in perception, responsiveness, and locomotor capacity influence emergent leadership in coordinated motion. To this end, we implement a continuous-time, discrete-space flocking model in which all agents follow the same interaction principles, but differ systematically in their perceptual radii, visual anisotropy, reaction delay, preferred speed, and sensitivity to global directional cues.

Each agent i moves in a two-dimensional toroidal domain of width $W = 1400$ and height $H = 1000$ units. Its state is given by position $x_i(t) \in \mathbb{R}^2$, velocity $v_i(t)$, and acceleration $a_i(t)$, updated at a fixed timestep $\Delta t = 1/60\,\mathrm{s}$. Agents are initialized with random headings and speeds drawn from $[1, v_{\mathrm{max},i}]$. Motion follows standard self-propelled dynamics:

$$v_i(t + \Delta t) = \mathrm{clip}(v_i(t) + a_i(t), v_{\mathrm{max},i}), \quad x_i(t + \Delta t) = x_i(t) + v_i(t + \Delta t),$$

with periodic boundary conditions.

At each time step, each agent computes a steering vector s_i combining the three standard Reynolds components. Neighbors are defined by rule-specific radii and individual fields of view. The three components (see Fig. 1) are:

1. **Alignment**, which steers the agent toward the mean heading of its visible neighbors,

$$s_i^{ali} = \left(\frac{1}{|N_i^A|} \sum_{j \in N_i^A} v_j \right)^* - v_i,$$

   where $(\cdot)^*$ denotes rescaling to $v_{\mathrm{max},i}$ and N_i^A uses the alignment radius.
2. **Cohesion**, which drives the agent toward the local centre of mass,

$$s_i^{coh} = (c_i - x_i)^* - v_i, \quad c_i = \frac{1}{|N_i^C|} \sum_{j \in N_i^C} x_j.$$

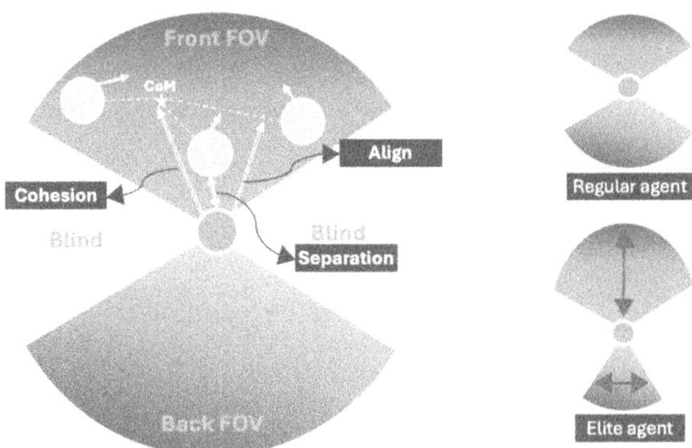

Fig. 1. The perception fields of regular and elite agents. The focal agent (purple) senses neighbors differently depending on whether they lie within its front field of view (FOV) or back FOV. Neighbors contribute to alignment, cohesion, and separation. All regions outside front/back FOV sectors constitute blind areas.

3. **Separation**, which prevents collisions,

$$s_i^{sep} = \frac{1}{|N_i^S|} \sum_{j \in N_i^S} \frac{x_i - x_j}{\|x_i - x_j\|} - v_i.$$

The total intended steering force is

$$s_i = w_{ali} s_i^{ali} + w_{coh} s_i^{coh} + w_{sep} s_i^{sep},$$

and is clipped to a maximum magnitude $f_{\max} = 0.05$.

Neighborhood membership depends on individual perceptual differences. Each agent has rule-specific radii (R_i^A, R_i^C, R_i^S) and an asymmetric field of view defined by a frontal half-angle ϕ_i^{front} and a rear half-angle ϕ_i^{back}, applied by checking whether the relative bearing of neighbor j lies within the appropriate cone. Elites possess expanded radii and a pronounced frontal bias, whereas non-elites have reduced radii and nearly symmetric views.

Agents differ in responsiveness. Each agent stores a queue of length τ_i containing its most recent steering vectors and applies the delayed vector $s_i(t - \tau_i)$ rather than the instantaneous one. Agents also differ in their maximum speeds $v_{\max,i}$.

To examine the system's sensitivity to directional information, we periodically impose global heading perturbations. Every $T = 5\,\mathrm{s}$, the mean group heading $\bar{\theta}(t)$ is computed and shifted to a new target direction

$$\theta^* = \bar{\theta}(t) \pm \delta, \quad \delta = 10°.$$

A unit steering cue $u^* = (\cos\theta^*, \sin\theta^*)$ is then applied to each agent for a fixed duration $\Delta t_{nudge} = 1\,\mathrm{s}$. However, each agent i experiences this cue only after an individual-specific delay δ_i^{nudge}. The additional steering applied to agent i is

$$a_i^{nudge}(t) = \begin{cases} gu^*, & t \in [t_{nudge} + \delta_i^{nudge}, \ t_{nudge} + \delta_i^{nudge} + \Delta t_{nudge}] \\ 0, & \text{otherwise}, \end{cases}$$

with a small gain $g = 0.05$. Elites typically have smaller δ_i^{nudge} and τ_i, allowing them to react earlier.

2.1 Leadership Metric

In this study, we use a network–based metric derived from the heading dynamics to define leaders. For each run, we record at discrete times

$$t_k = k\Delta t, \quad k = 0, \ldots, T - 1,$$

the position $x_i(t_k)$ and heading $\theta_i(t_k)$ of each agent $i \in \{1, \ldots, N\}$. From the headings we construct wrapped heading increments

$$\Delta\theta_i(k) = \mathrm{wrap}\big(\theta_i(t_{k+1}) - \theta_i(t_k)\big), \quad k = 0, \ldots, T - 2, \tag{1}$$

where $\mathrm{wrap}(\cdot)$ maps angles to $[-\pi, \pi]$. These increments encode each agent's turning dynamics and form the basis of the influence estimate.

Pairwise Directional Influence Matrix. For each ordered pair of distinct agents (i, j), we quantify how well past turning of i predicts future turning of j via time–lagged Pearson correlations. Let L be the maximum lag in time steps, corresponding to a maximum lag of $1\,\mathrm{s}$ (i.e. $L = \lfloor 1\,\mathrm{s}/\Delta t \rfloor$). For each lag $\ell \in \{1, \ldots, L\}$ we compute

$$C_{i \to j}(\ell) = \mathrm{corr}\big(\Delta\theta_i(k), \Delta\theta_j(k + \ell)\big), \tag{2}$$

where the correlation is computed over all valid time indices.

The directed influence from i to j is then defined as the strongest positive lagged correlation,

$$I_{ij} = \max\Big(0, \max_{\ell \in \{1, \ldots, L\}} C_{i \to j}(\ell)\Big), \quad i \neq j, \tag{3}$$

and $I_{ii} = 0$ by definition. Collecting all entries yields a directed weighted influence matrix

$$I = \begin{bmatrix} I_{11} & \cdots & I_{1N} \\ \vdots & \ddots & \vdots \\ I_{N1} & \cdots & I_{NN} \end{bmatrix} \in \mathbb{R}^{N \times N}, \tag{4}$$

interpreted as a data–driven leadership network.

Outgoing Influence Strength (per–agent leadership). Given the influence matrix I for a run, the outgoing influence strength of agent i is defined as

$$s_i^{out} = \sum_{j=1}^{N} I_{ij},$$

(5)

i.e. the total predictive influence that i exerts on all other agents. Large values of s_i^{out} indicate that the turning of agent i systematically precedes that of others, and we interpret it as a continuous leadership score.

3 Results and Discussion

We simulate flocking in a 1400×1000 unit periodic environment with $N = 50$ agents governed by alignment, cohesion, and separation. Each run lasts $30\,\text{s}$ and is repeated across 20 random seeds. A homogeneous baseline condition (**H0**$_{\text{IDENTICAL}}$) was used to characterise the leadership structure of a perfectly symmetric flock in which all agents share identical motion parameters, perception field of view (270°), reaction delay, preferred speed, and nudge-responsiveness. The heterogeneous condition (**H1**$_{\text{PERCEPTION\_HET}}$) introduces a small elite subset of agents (2% of the population) endowed with slightly different perceptual and behavioral capabilities. Elites possess a wider and more asymmetric forward field of view (back-FOV reduction factor 0.1), larger perception radius, faster reaction time, and increased preferred speed (1.5× baseline). These asymmetries allow leadership to emerge through natural interactions rather than imposed hierarchy.

We employ the outgoing influence measure defined in Sect. 2.1 both at the condition level—to compare how different heterogeneity configurations reshape the global distribution of leadership—and in one-parameter sensitivity analyses.

Condition-Level Analysis. In the condition-level comparison between homogeneous (**H0**$_{\text{IDENTICAL}}$) and heterogeneous (**H1**$_{\text{PERCEPTION\_HET}}$) groups, we use two summaries of outgoing influence: **(i) Agent-level distributions:** pooling all s_i^{out} across agents and seeds. This reveals whether leadership is evenly shared or concentrated in a few individuals, and how this distribution changes between H0 and H1. **(ii) Run-level strongest leader:** for each run, the maximum outgoing influence

$$s_{max}^{out} = \max_i s_i^{out}.$$

In Fig. 3(a,b), perceptual heterogeneity produces consistently stronger and more uneven influence patterns in the flock. In Fig. 3(a), which shows the distribution of outgoing influence across all agents pooled by condition, the heterogeneous-perception group exhibits a clear upward shift in median influence together with a broader spread, indicating that individuals both exert more influence on average and display greater variability. In contrast, the identical-perception group maintains lower and more tightly clustered values, reflecting a more uniform influence structure. In Fig. 3(b), which summarizes each run by

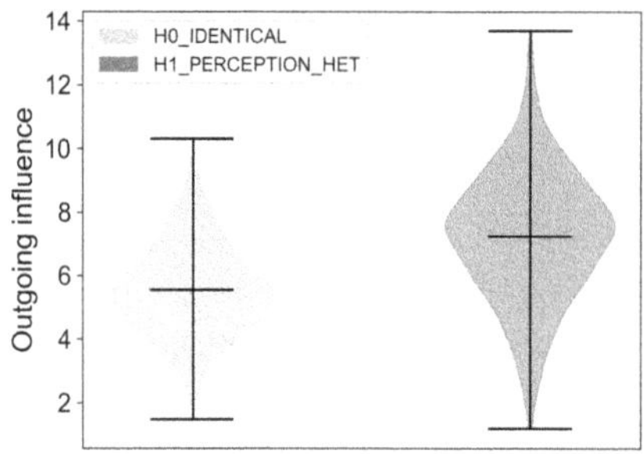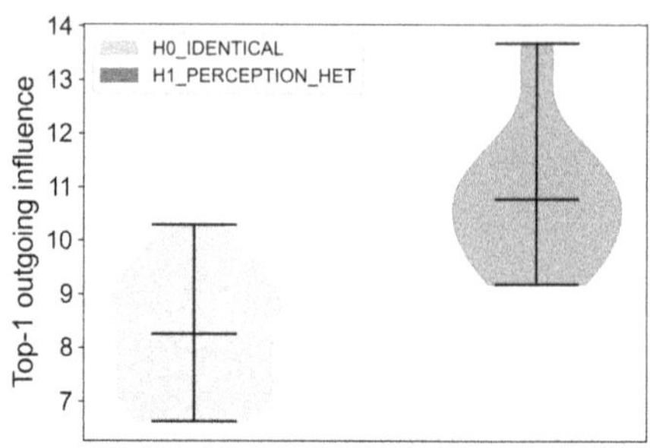

Fig. 2. Outgoing influence under identical and heterogeneous perception. (a) Distributions are lower and more uniform under identical perception, and higher with greater variability under heterogeneity. (b) Top-1 influence per run is consistently higher under heterogeneity.

its single most influential agent, the maximum outgoing influence per run is systematically higher under perceptual heterogeneity, with several runs producing exceptionally dominant individuals.

One-Parameter Sensitivity Analysis. Having established the condition-level differences, we next isolate the contribution of individual behavioral traits through targeted one-parameter sweeps. Four parameters were varied independently: (i) elite fraction (0.01–0.20); (ii) elite speed factor (1.0–1.8×); (iii) backward field-of-view reduction factor; (iv) perception-radius gain.

For each parameter setting and seed, we compute s_{max}^{out} and report the mean and standard deviation across seeds. The resulting curves in Fig. 2 quantify how the strength of the most influential agent changes as heterogeneity is increased. Across all configurations, even small trait differences consistently elevate top-1 influence above the homogeneous baseline. Figure 3(a) shows that keeping the elite group small is essential: when only a few elites are introduced, the flock exhibits a sharp increase in top-1 outgoing influence, but this advantage diminishes once too many elites are present. Larger elite fractions introduce competing high-influence individuals, weakening overall leadership coherence.

In contrast, when the elite fraction is fixed at 0.02, increasing the elite speed factor (Fig. 3(b)) produces a clear monotonic rise in leadership strength. Faster elites are better able to position themselves advantageously, move ahead of the group, and maintain directional control. Figure 3(c) shows that increasing the elites' backward sensing produces an immediate rise in top-1 influence, after which the values stabilize at a plateau, suggesting that elites can maintain influence chains without losing track of followers. Finally, Fig. 3(d) shows that increasing the perception radius allows elites to detect and interact with neighbors at larger distances, raising leadership strength consistently above baseline.

Across all experiments, even minimal heterogeneity fundamentally reshapes the distribution and magnitude of leadership. The homogeneous baseline exhibits low and tightly bounded outgoing influence, reflecting a symmetric system in which directional changes are shared relatively evenly across agents.

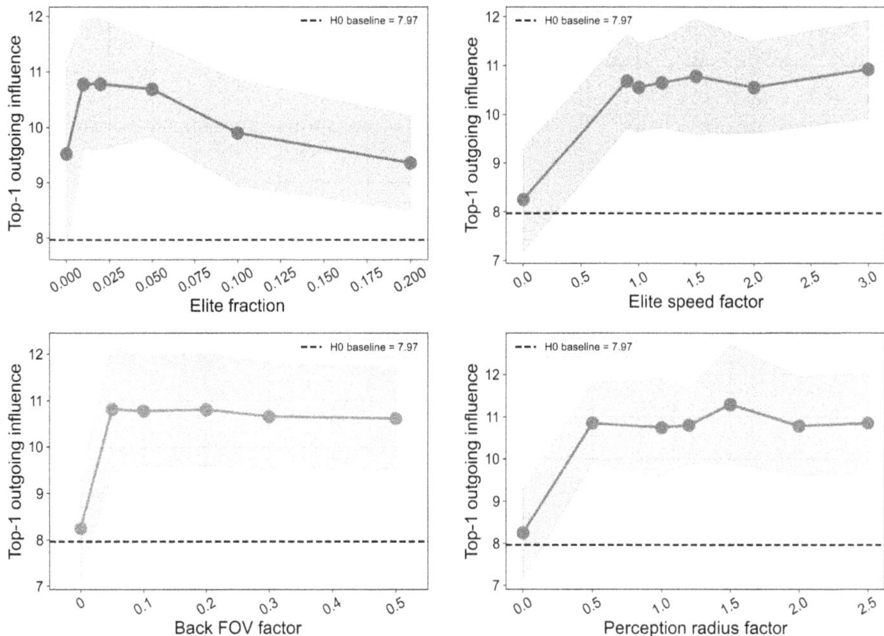

Fig. 3. Top-1 outgoing influence for four heterogeneity factors. Shaded regions show between-seed variability; dashed line marks the homogeneous baseline (H0).

The moment heterogeneity is introduced, this symmetry is broken. For every parameter sweep, the first non-zero heterogeneity value produces a sharp rise in leadership strength, demonstrating that only a minimal deviation from uniformity is required for strong leaders to emerge. This consistent effect across distinct mechanisms indicates that leadership arises generically from symmetry breaking in the interaction network rather than from any specific behavioral parameter. However, the relationship is not monotonic. In all four sweeps, leadership peaks at relatively low levels of heterogeneity before stabilizing or declining at more extreme values. Increasing heterogeneity beyond moderate levels appears to introduce competing influential individuals or reduce the decisiveness of directional updates. This suggests an optimal regime where a small minority of distinct agents most effectively shape collective motion.

4 Conclusions

This study shows that leadership in decentralized swarms can emerge from small deviations from homogeneity. Minimal perceptual or kinematic advantages in a minority of agents produce stable leader–follower structures without explicit hierarchy. Across heterogeneous conditions, the distribution of outgoing influence becomes heavy-tailed, indicating frequent highly influential individuals. Parameter sweeps show that moderate heterogeneity strengthens leadership, whereas excessive asymmetry reduces its effect. Our results show how small agent-level differences scale into group-level influence patterns.

Disclosure of Interests. The authors have no competing interests to declare.

References

1. Buchanan, E., Alden, K., Pomfret, A., Timmis, J., Tyrrell, A.M.: A study of error diversity in robotic swarms for task partitioning in foraging tasks. Front. Robot. AI **9**, 904341 (2023)
2. Couzin, I.D., et al.: Effective leadership and decision-making in animal groups. Nature (2005)
3. Hamann, H., Valentini, G., Khaluf, Y., Dorigo, M.: Derivation of a micro-macro link for collective decision-making systems: Uncover network features based on drift measurements. In: International conference on parallel problem solving from nature, pp. 181–190. Springer (2014)
4. Kaminka, G.A., Douchan, Y.: Heterogeneous foraging swarms can be better. Front. Robot. AI **11**, 1426282 (2025)
5. Khaluf, Y., Rausch, I., Simoens, P.: The impact of interaction models on the coherence of collective decision-making: a case study with simulated locusts. In: International Conference on Swarm Intelligence, pp. 252–263. Springer (2018)
6. Raoufi, M., Romanczuk, P., Hamann, H.: Individuality in swarm robots with the case study of kilobots: Noise, bug, or feature? In: Artificial Life Conference Proceedings 35, vol. 2023, p. 35. MIT Press One Rogers Street, Cambridge, MA 02142-1209, USA journals-info ... (2023)
7. Rausch, I., Reina, A., Simoens, P., Khaluf, Y.: Coherent collective behaviour emerging from decentralised balancing of social feedback and noise. Swarm Intell. 321–345 (2019). https://doi.org/10.1007/s11721-019-00173-y
8. Reina, A., Njougouo, T., Tuci, E., Carletti, T.: Speed-accuracy trade-offs in best-of-n collective decision making through heterogeneous mean-field modeling. Phys. Rev. E **109**(5), 054307 (2024)
9. Reynolds, C.W.: Flocks, herds and schools: a distributed behavioral model. Computer Graphics (1987)
10. Zakir, R., Salahshour, M., Dorigo, M., Reina, A.: Heterogeneity can enhance the adaptivity of robot swarms to dynamic environments. In: International Conference on Swarm Intelligence, pp. 112–126. Springer (2024)

Extended Abstracts

A Gaussian Bounded Confidence Model for Resisting Misinformation in Swarm Robotics

Yuxuan Yuan[(✉)], Paul O'Dowd, and Jonathan Lawry

School of Engineering Mathematics and Technology, University of Bristol, Bristol, UK

yuxuan.yuan@bristol.ac.uk, paul.odowd@bristol.ac.uk, J.Lawry@bristol.ac.uk

Swarm robotic systems are vulnerable to persistent misinformation from obstinate agents (zealots), particularly under sensor noise and limited interaction ranges. Bounded confidence models (BCMs), such as HK and DW [1, 2], provide a classical framework for opinion dynamics but typically rely on fixed confidence thresholds and constant update step sizes. Recent variants introduce adaptive interaction bounds [3, 4, 6], yet do not explicitly address persistent misinformation combined with sensor bias in physical swarm robotic systems.

We propose a Gaussian Bounded Confidence Model (G-BCM) that replaces fixed thresholds with a smooth trust kernel, enabling continuous influence weighting. Neighbour information and environmental evidence are fused through Bayesian weighting, and an integrated bias correction mechanism compensates for systematic sensor offsets.

We replace static thresholds with a Gaussian trust kernel

$$K(x, y) = \exp\left(-\frac{(x - y)^2}{2\sigma^2}\right),$$

(1)

and compute neighbour influence via the trust weight

$$k = \frac{P_A(x|y)P_A(y)}{P_A(x|y)P_A(y) + P_A(x|\neg y)P_A(\neg y)}.$$

(2)

Here $P_A(x|y)$ denotes the likelihood that agent A considers its own belief x correct under the hypothesis that neighbour belief y is true. Under the binary hypothesis space $\{y, \neg y\}$, where y and $\neg y$ are mutually exclusive and exhaustive, the complementary relations $P_A(x|\neg y) = 1 - P_A(x|y)$ and $P_A(\neg y) = 1 - P_A(y)$ follow directly. Beliefs update as $x_{\text{new}} = \frac{x + k\,y}{1 + k}$, and evidence is fused analogously with bias correction $e_A \leftarrow e_A + k(y - e_A)$.

In simulation (10 normal agents + 1 zealot fixed at 0.1; evidence 0.7), G-BCM consistently converges to the evidence within 10 runs. DW fails for multiple threshold settings and typically converges more slowly when it succeeds (Fig. 1).

Physical experiments with eleven Pololu 3Pi+ robots used ambient light as evidence, and employed a custom IR communication board (Swarm-B2) and the 3Pi+ Arduino support library for inter-robot communication [5]. Real sensor bias increased initial dispersion, including values near the zealot (0.1). With

R. Groß et al. (Eds.): ANTS 2026, LNCS 16515, pp. 475–476, 2026.
https://doi.org/10.1007/978-3-032-26123-6

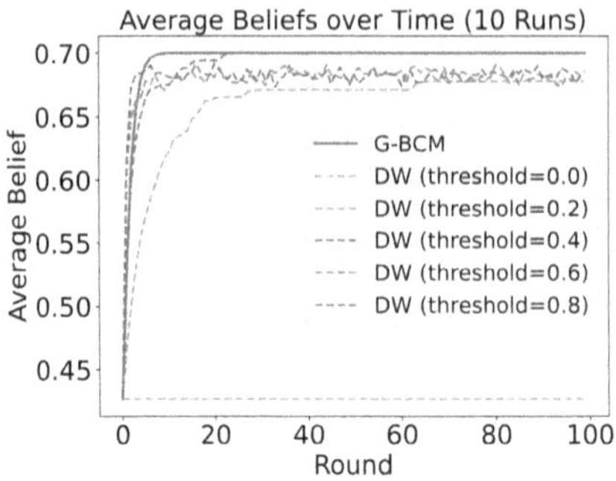
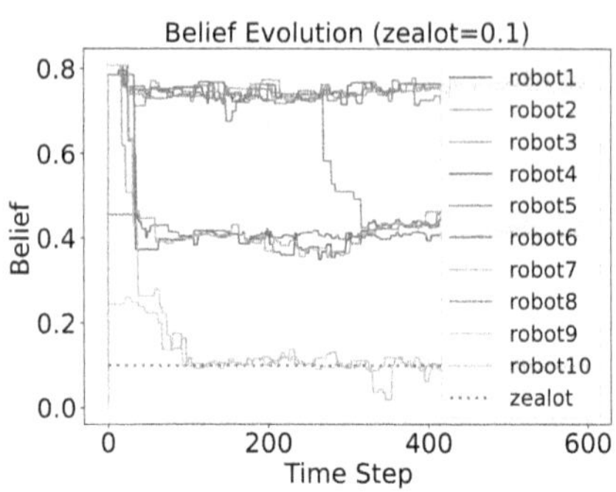
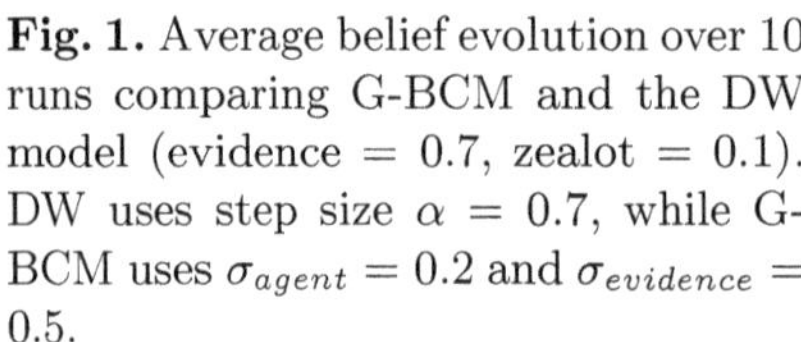

Fig. 1. Average belief evolution over 10 runs comparing G-BCM and the DW model (evidence = 0.7, zealot = 0.1). DW uses step size $\alpha = 0.7$, while G-BCM uses $\sigma_{agent} = 0.2$ and $\sigma_{evidence} = 0.5$.

Fig. 2. Belief evolution of 11 robots under zealot value 0.1. Bias correction reduces systematic offsets while bounded-confidence dynamics yield stable multi-polar convergence.

small σ_{agent}, G-BCM formed stable multi-polar clusters (Fig. 2). Bias correction reduces inter-robot offsets, enlarges communication bounds while maintaining resistance to the zealot.

Overall, G-BCM improves robustness to misinformation and sensor bias in both simulation and physical swarms. Future work will investigate adaptive tuning of σ_{agent}, systematic variation of zealot proportion, and improved physical calibration to further reduce multi-polar fragmentation while preserving robustness to persistent misinformation.

Disclosure of Interests. The authors have no competing interests to declare.

References

1. Deffuant, G., Neau, D., Amblard, F., Weisbuch, G.: Mixing beliefs among interacting agents. Adv. Complex Syst. **3**, 87–98 (01 2000). https://doi.org/10.1142/S0219525900000078
2. Hegselmann, R., Krause, U.: Opinion dynamics and bounded confidence: models, analysis and simulation. J. Artif. Soc. Soc. Simul. **5**(3) (2002)
3. Kan, U., Feng, M., Porter, M.A.: An adaptive bounded-confidence model of opinion dynamics on networks (2022). https://arxiv.org/abs/2112.05856
4. Li, G.J., Luo, J., Porter, M.A.: Bounded-confidence models of opinion dynamics with adaptive confidence bounds (2024). https://arxiv.org/abs/2303.07563
5. O'Dowd, P.: Swarm-B2: IR communication board for Pololu 3Pi+ robots (2023). https://github.com/paulodowd/Swarm-B2
6. Vasca, F., Bernardo, C., Iervolino, R.: Practical consensus in bounded confidence opinion dynamics. Automatica **129**, 109683 (2021). https://doi.org/10.1016/j.automatica.2021.109683

Cooperative Energy-Replenishment in Robot Swarms with Optimal Performance and Efficiency

Julian Rau[1]([envelope])[iD], Mohamed S. Talamali[2][iD], Genki Miyauchi[2][iD],
Usama Ali[1][iD], Mengyao Liu[3][iD], Danny Hughes[3][iD], Thomas Watteyne,
and Roderich Groß[1,2][iD]

[1] Department of Computer Science, Technical University of Darmstadt, Darmstadt,
Germany
`julian.rau@tu-darmstadt.de`
[2] School of Electrical and Electronic Engineering, University of Sheffield, Sheffield,
UK
[3] DistriNet, KU Leuven, Leuven, Belgium

Many real-world applications, like warehouse logistics and agriculture, benefit from large groups of robots that operate over extended periods of time. This necessitates strategies that determine how and when robots should replenish their energy, enabling long-term operation. We developed and validated an analytical model for a cooperative energy-replenishment strategy for robot swarms and show how it can support the system design and configuration.

We consider a rectangular environment divided into *charge* and *work* regions, and a *commute* region separating the two. The system comprises of two types of robots: n_w *workers* and n_c *chargers* with finite energy capacities $q_w^{\max}$ and $q_c^{\max}$, respectively. Workers can work, rest, charge, move, or receive energy, whereas chargers can move, rest, charge, or transfer energy. Workers may only work in the work region, and all robots may only charge in the charge region. Any robot requires at least $\Delta_{\mathrm{commute}}$ time to travel between work and charge regions. All robots consume a baseline of $\nu_{\min}$ energy per unit time, in addition to action-dependent consumptions ν_{move}, ν_{work}, or ν_{transfer}. Charging yields a net energy gain of $\nu_{\mathrm{charge}} - \nu_{\min}$. During energy transfer, a fraction $\xi \in (0,1]$ of energy is successfully received by the worker, while the charger provides $\frac{1}{\xi}\nu_{\mathrm{transfer}}$ per unit time to each nearby worker that participates in the transfer. We assume $\nu_{\min} \ll \min(\nu_{\mathrm{charge}}, \nu_{\mathrm{move}}, \nu_{\mathrm{work}}, \nu_{\mathrm{transfer}})$. Initially, all robots are in the work region; workers begin working while chargers commute to the charge region.

The individual strategy (IS) [3] relies only on workers that commute to the charge region once below a certain energy level, charge, and commute back to the work region to work (refer to [3] for the analytical model). The cooperative strategy (CS) allows a charger to simultaneously transfer energy to $\zeta \in \mathbb{N}$ workers. Each worker starts with energy $q_w^{\mathrm{charged}} \le q_w^{\max}$, works, then rests while awaiting a charger, and then receives energy from the charger. Each charger begins with sufficient energy to commute and rest, travels to the charge region, rests and charges to $q_c^{\mathrm{charged}} \le q_c^{\max}$, and then returns to the work region. Upon arrival, it transfers energy to ζ workers. Worker and charger operations are synchronized

R. Groß et al. (Eds.): ANTS 2026, LNCS 16515, pp. 477–478, 2026.
https://doi.org/10.1007/978-3-032-26123-6

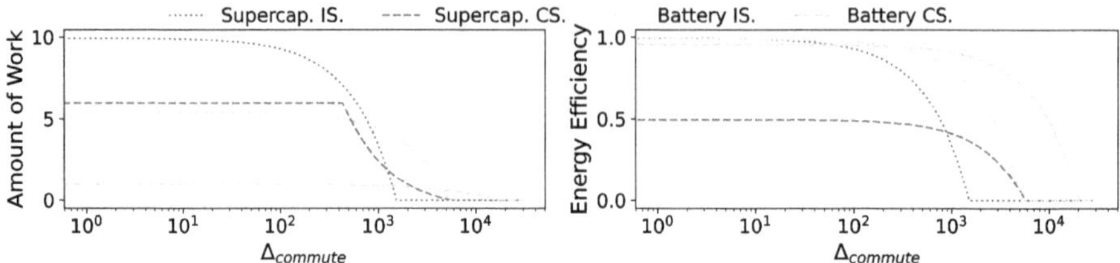

Fig. 1. Amount of work and energy efficiency achieved by a charger with four times the capacity of a worker supplying six workers depending on the commuting time Δ_{commute}.

so that their energy transfer durations coincide. The analytical model for CS calculates all durations (work, rest, charge, transfer) and the charge levels q_w^{charged} and q_c^{charged} and is omitted due to length. Both IS and CS aim to maximize the amount of work performed. The CS-model was validated with physics-based simulations using a similar setup to the one in [3].

We compare IS and CS using supercapacitors ($q_{\text{cap,max}}^{\text{w}} = 3060$, $\nu_{\text{cap,charge}} = 191.25/\text{s}$, $\xi_{\text{cap}} = 0.5$ [2]) and lithium-ion batteries ($q_{\text{bat,max}}^{\text{w}} = 10800$, $\nu_{\text{bat,charge}} = 1.2/\text{s}$ [1], $\xi_{\text{bat}} = 0.99$ [4]) with $\nu_{\text{transfer}} = \nu_{\text{charge}}$, $\nu_{\text{min}} = 0.005/\text{s}$ and $\nu_{\text{work}} = \nu_{\text{move}} = 1/\text{s}$ for both. Work and energy efficiency of all combinations of energy-storage and strategy are shown in Fig. 1 for varying commuting time Δ_{commute}. CS, using a charger with four times the capacity of a worker and supplying six workers, is compared to IS using ten workers. For small Δ_{commute}, IS performs best, whereas for larger Δ_{commute}, CS dominates as a single commuting charger is more efficient than five commuting workers. Supercapacitors favor short commutes due to fast charging, whereas batteries achieve higher energy efficiency from larger capacity and lower transfer losses. Hence, the model provides guidance for selecting a suitable system design and configuration given the operational mission parameters.

Acknowledgments. This work was co-funded by EU Horizon Europe Framework Programme OpenSwarm (grant 101093046); BMBF (Robotics Institute Germany; grant 16ME1001); LOEWE center emergenCITY [LOEWE/1/12/519/03/05.001(0016)/72].

Disclosure of Interests. The authors have no competing interests to declare.

References

1. GCtronic: e-puck2 (2025). https://www.gctronic.com/doc/index.php/e-puck2. Accessed 03 Nov 2025
2. Liu, M., et al.: CapBot: enabling battery-free swarm robotics. In: 2025 IEEE International Conference on Robotics and Automation (ICRA), pp. 570–576. IEEE (2025)
3. Miyauchi, G., Talamali, M.S., Groß, R.: A comparative study of energy replenishment strategies for robot swarms. In: Swarm Intelligence. Lecture Notes in Computer Science, vol. 14987, pp. 3–15. Springer, Cham (2024)
4. Şahin, M.E., Blaabjerg, F., Sangwongwanich, A.: a comprehensive review on supercapacitor applications and developments. Energies **15**(3) (2022)

Development of an Integrated Swarm Robotics Platform with Real-Time Human-Based Guidance

Rugved Upaddhye[iD], Akshat Singh[iD], Swadhin Agrawal[iD],
and P. B. Sujit[(✉)][iD]

Department of Electrical Engineering and Computer Science, Indian Institute of
Science Education and Research, Bhopal, India
`sujit@iiserb.ac.in`

Self-emergent behaviors have inspired the development of robot swarms. However, human-in-the-loop can significantly enhance their utility in unpredictable scenarios [2]. The immersive experience and free operator mobility in Virtual Reality (VR) is well suited for remote operations [1, 4]. Existing platforms [4] limit human-swarm interactions to high-level task assignments, preventing operators from collaborating effectively. Moreover, quantitative metrics of fitness for training and evaluating operators' remained overlooked. To address this, we present an integrated VR-based hybrid swarm robotics platform that supports operator training and enables them to remotely operate a robot swarm.

Consider a hybrid team $D = \{d_i \mid d_i \in (D^r \cup D^v)\}$, where $D^r = \{d_i^r, i = 1 \ldots, m^r\}$ is the set of physical, and $D^v = \{d_i^v, i = 1 \ldots, m^v\}$ is the set of virtual drones (for source of virtual potential fields and scalability during training). The virtual world consists of D^v, "digital twin" of the arena ($3.5\text{m} \times 3\text{m} \times 3\text{m}$), and the clones of real robots, denoted by d^c. As a proof of concept, the operator's objective is to navigate D from the start to a goal region by teleoperating a leader, denoted by $d_l \in D$ (using HTC Vive Pro 2). The operator selects a leader, while the rest become followers, denoted by d_f. The followers flock based on repulsion and attraction ranges as per the physicomimetic model [3]. The platform architecture (see Fig. 1a) consists of two synchronized components: the Hardware/ROS side and the Software/Unity side. The Crazyswarm2 package (ROS2) handles low-level controls of the real agents. The TCP endpoint facilitates bidirectional messaging; position estimates derived from the lighthouse tracking system, fused with IMU data via an extended Kalman filter, and published to the clones d_i^c. The velocity commands from the flocking model, and the operators (roll (R), pitch (P), yaw (Y), and thrust (T)) commands, transformed to linear and angular velocity in the body frame, are transmitted to D.

We performed three tests, Expt. 1: validation of VR control pipeline, Expt. 2: validation of flocking model, and Expt. 3: Operator navigating a swarm ($2\ d^r$ and $1\ d^v$), and report quantitative errors to depict the platforms' effectiveness in training operators. As shown in Fig. 1c, the Expt. 3, (see Figs. 1b,1d,1e) shows that the leader tracked operators' commands, and the swarm maintained a triangle formation (equilibrium of model [3]). The error in actual to model tra-

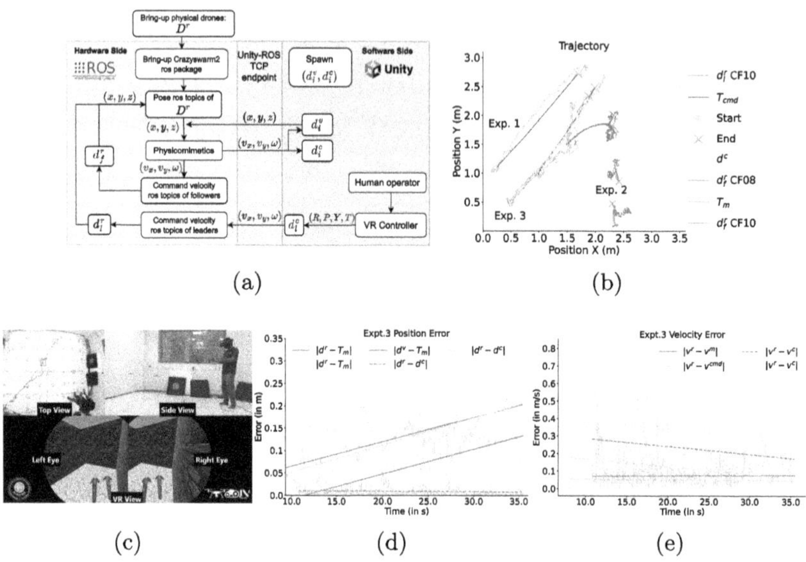

(a)   (b)

(c)   (d)   (e)

Fig. 1. Overview of, (a) The platform architecture. (b) UAVs Trajectory in Expt. 1, 2, and 3. (c) Snapshot of Expt. 3. (d-e) Errors with respect to the model and the clones.

jectories is below 0.2 m. The error in actual to commanded velocities is constant ($< 10\,\mathrm{cm/s} < 2$ UAV size, can vary among user and external disturbances).

In conclusion, we validated the feasibility of persistent manipulation of hybrid swarms using VR and demonstrated that the platform can serve as a practical, transferable testbed for operator training and for remotely deploying robot swarms. Future directions include (i) an operator interface, (ii) on-the-fly behavioral parameter tuning, and (iii) scaling to larger outdoor swarms.

Acknowledgments. This work has been partially supported by IISER Bhopal, MeitY PUSHPAK project, & ZuKo Fellowship 2024–2025 (S.A), Uni. Konstanz.

Disclosure of Interests. The authors have no competing interests to declare.

References

1. Dorigo, M., Theraulaz, G., Trianni, V.: Swarm robotics: past, present, and future [Point of View]. Proc. IEEE **109**(7), 1152–1165 (2021). https://doi.org/10.1109/JPROC.2021.3072740
2. Kolling, A., Walker, P., Chakraborty, N., Sycara, K., Lewis, M.: Human interaction with robot swarms: a survey. IEEE Trans. Hum. Mach. Syst. **46**(1), 9–26 (2016). https://doi.org/10.1109/THMS.2015.2480801

3. Spears, W.M., Spears, D.F., Heil, R., Kerr, W., Hettiarachchi, S.: An overview of physicomimetics. In: Şahin, E., Spears, W.M. (eds.) SR 2004. LNCS, vol. 3342, pp. 84–97. Springer, Heidelberg (2005). https://doi.org/10.1007/978-3-540-30552-1_8
4. Zheng, C., Jarecki, A., Lee, K.: Integrated system architecture with mixed-reality user interface for virtual-physical hybrid swarm simulations. Sci. Rep. **13**(1), 14761 (2023)

Environmental Perception in a Swarm of Conversational Agents

Absera Yihunie[1], Lilly Schwarzenbach[2], Hanan Salam[1], and Eliseo Ferrante[1,2](✉)

[1] Department of Computer Science, New York University Abu Dhabi, Abu Dhabi, United Arab Emirates
ef2698@nyu.edu
[2] Department of Computer Science, Vrije Universiteit Amsterdam, Amsterdam, The Netherlands

Collective perception, the process whereby multiple agents integrate partial local observations into a shared understanding of their environment, remains a core challenge in swarm robotics. Many traditional swarms struggle to construct rich, descriptive understanding of their environment due to their cognitive simplicity and local perception [2]. This limitation stems from their reliance on simple, non-semantic message passing signals for coordination, which constrains their ability to process high-level environmental elements [1]. Overcoming this challenge requires new mechanisms for interpreting and exchanging information in conceptually meaningful ways, an ability that is essential for complex perception tasks [1]. In this work, we integrate Large Language Models (LLMs) within the control loop to achieve this cognitive capability [3].

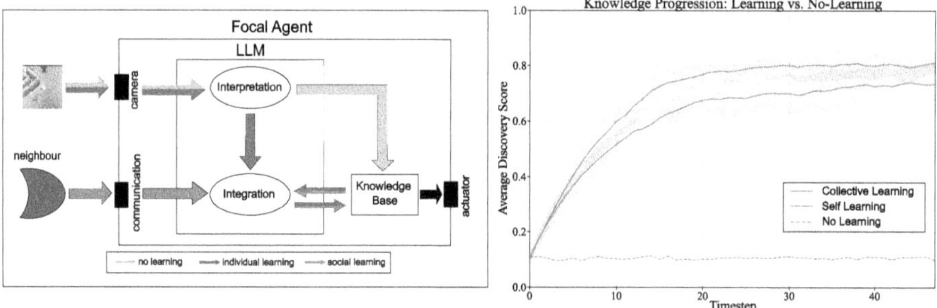

We propose a framework for collective environmental perception that integrates LLM-powered agents into a self-organized swarm. Each agent moves through the environment and converts its local visual input into a natural language description. A process termed "Integration" enables agents to exchange their textual environmental descriptions, or "Knowledge Bases", peer-to-peer, and use the LLM's summarization capacity to fuse these disparate, partial reports into a coherent, shared world model [4].

We consider three separate conditions: 1) no learning without integration of new information, 2) individual learning with integration of information from direct observations into the existing Knowledge Base, and 3) collective learning where input from neighbors is integrated into the existing Knowledge Base.

We propose a novel evaluation metric, the "Discovery Score," inspired by BERTScore [5]. The Discovery Score metric evaluates an agent's Knowledge Base (T_s) by comparing it against the ground truth. The ground truth consists of a summary produced by an LLM (identical to those used in the agents) whose input is the image of the entire environment.

$$\text{Score}(S, G) = \frac{1}{|G|} \sum_{g_i \in G} \mathbb{I}\left(\max_{s_j \in S} \text{cosine\_sim}(g_i, s_j) > \tau \right)$$

where $\mathbb{I}$ is the indicator function. This score, ranging from 0 to 1, represents the percentage of total facts that the agent has successfully recorded in its log.

The results show that without any learning, the agents cannot form an understanding of the entire environment, as the knowledge of the agent does not increase over time. In the individual learning condition, the agents discover a large part of the environment but they discover less than if collective learning is also enabled (p-value = 0.000074). This demonstrates that the process integrating socially transmitted information is highly effective, enabling the swarm's collective understanding to become demonstrably greater than the simple sum of its parts. Other agents may have observed elements that the agent has never encountered and thus transmit information that would elude the agent otherwise.

We have demonstrated that a decentralized swarm of LLM-powered agents can collectively build a rich, semantic map of an unknown environment. The results indicate that our framework provides a promising direction in collective perception. Subsequent work should explore this framework in more complex environments and investigate its efficacy in tasks other than random exploration.

Acknowledgments. This work is supported in part by the NYUAD Center for Artificial Intelligence and Robotics (CAIR), funded by Tamkeen under the NYUAD Research Institute Award CG010, and by the NYUAD Center for Interdisciplinary Data Science & AI (CIDSAI), funded by Tamkeen under the NYUAD Research Institute Award CG016.

Disclosure of Interests. The authors have no competing interests to declare.

References

1. Cambier, N., Miletitch, R., Frémont, V., Dorigo, M., Ferrante, E., Trianni, V.: Language evolution in swarm robotics: a perspective. Front. Robot. AI **7**, 12 (2020)
2. Hamann, H.: Swarm Robotics: A Formal Approach. Springer, Cham (2018). https://doi.org/10.1007/978-3-319-74528-2
3. Strobel, V., Dorigo, M., Fritz, M.: LLM2Swarm: robot swarms that responsively reason, plan, and collaborate through LLMs. arXiv:2410.11387 (2024)
4. Wan, F., Huang, X., Cai, D., Quan, X., Bi, W., Shi, S.: Knowledge fusion of large language models (2024)
5. Zhang, T., Kishore, V., Wu, F., Weinberger, K.Q., Artzi, Y.: BERTScore: Evaluating Text Generation with BERT (2020)

Experimentally Validated Distributional Modelling and Control for Passive Swarm Robots

Seth Lim[1], Yuanbo Nie[1(✉)], Mohamed S. Talamali[1], Roderich Groß[1,2], and Visakan Kadirkamanathan[1]

[1] School of Electrical and Electronic Engineering, The University of Sheffield, Sheffield, UK
{jhlim2,y.nie,m.s.talamali,r.gross,visakan}@sheffield.ac.uk
[2] Department of Computer Science, Technical University of Darmstadt, Darmstadt, Germany

Deploying large-scale passive robot swarms requires a scalable and robust control framework, without the complexity of individualized commands. A popular choice is the advection-diffusion equation, where the dynamical states, representing the swarm distribution, are driven by a control policy as the advection term. Recent work [3] defines the policy as an external environmental control field, numerically obtained using finite element discretisation. Instead, we construct a reduced-order model by parametrising the state distribution and control fields with Gaussian basis functions. By applying Galerkin projection, a finite-dimensional, closed-form representation of the swarm dynamics can be obtained. This representation reduces the problem dimension and also allows the environmental control field to be sparse.

We model the swarm's collective behaviour as a density distribution on the spatial domain $s = [s_x, s_y]^\top$, evolving under a time-varying control field. Such an infinite-dimensional problem is parametrised by approximating the probability density function (PDF) $p(s, t)$ and the control field $F(s, t)$ with a finite number of basis functions $\Phi(s)$ and $\Psi(s)$, respectively:

$$p(s, t) :- \Phi(s)^\top x(t) \quad \text{and} \quad F(s, t) :- \Psi(s)^\top u(t).$$

The infinite-dimensional dynamics, based on the advection-diffusion model [1], is projected onto the finite set of basis functions via Galerkin approximation, yielding a compact finite-dimensional model with states x and inputs u [1]. The passive robot swarm is actuated solely by the locally sensed gradient information of the control field $F(s, t)$, reconstructed from u. This field induces motion of the individual robot velocity to be proportional to $-\nabla F(s, t)$.

This control framework enables the development of optimization-based control to yield time-varying control fields as solutions to an optimal control problem (OCP) to minimise the differences between the current states x_0 and the desired final states x_d, which represent the desired swarm distribution:

$$\min_{x(\cdot), u(\cdot)} \int_{t_0}^{t_f} (x_d - x(t))^\top Q (x_d - x(t)) + u(t)^\top R u(t) \, dt,$$

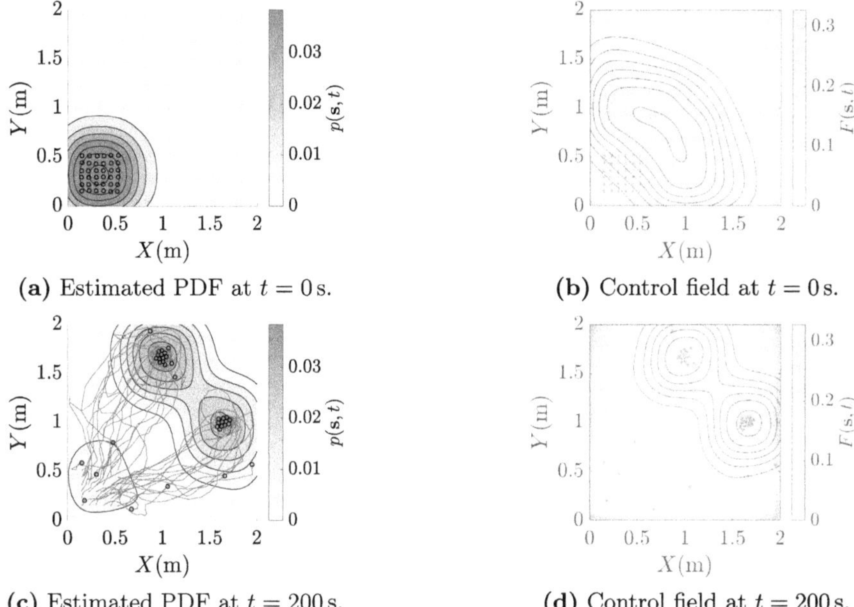

(a) Estimated PDF at $t = 0\,$s.

(b) Control field at $t = 0\,$s.

(c) Estimated PDF at $t = 200\,$s.

(d) Control field at $t = 200\,$s.

Fig. 1. Evolution of 36 physical Kilobots' locations and trajectory histories, overlaid with the estimated PDF and the OCP solution of the control field.

subject to the reduced-order advection-diffusion dynamics, the state constraint $x(t) \in [0,1]$, and the input constraint $u(t) \in [0,1]$. Matrices Q, R manage the trade-off between minimising the tracking error and penalizing control effort.

This proposed framework was experimentally validated using a swarm of 36 Kilobots operating in a $2\,$m by $2\,$m arena [2], as shown in Fig. 1. The objective was for Kilobots to reach one of two target areas centred at $(1, 1.666)$ and $(1.666, 1)$. Despite significant mismatches in system dynamics and unreliable motion of Kilobots, the proposed modelling and control framework robustly achieves distributional control objectives, with more than 72% of the Kilobots reached the target regions in multiple independent experiments.

In conclusion, experimental evidence demonstrates that reduced-order distributional models based on Galerkin approximations can enable efficient and scalable control of passive robot swarms.

Disclosure of Interests. The authors have no competing interests to declare.

References

1. Lim, S.J.: Distributional modelling and control of large-scale passive swarm robots. Ph.D. thesis, University of Sheffield (2024)
2. Reina, A., Cope, A.J., Nikolaidis, E., Marshall, J.A., Sabo, C.: ARK: augmented reality for kilobots. IEEE Robot. Autom. Lett. **2**(3), 1755–1761 (2017)
3. Sinigaglia, C., Manzoni, A., Braghin, F., Berman, S.: Robust optimal density control of robotic swarms. Automatica **176**, 112218 (2025)

Fission–Fusion Processes for Regulation of Group Size and Number in Multi-Agent Systems

Tianfu Zhang[1(✉)], Suet Lee[1,2], and Heiko Hamann[1,2]

[1] Department of Computer and Information Science, University of Konstanz,
Konstanz, Germany
tianfu.zhang@uni-konstanz.de, suet.lee@uni-konstanz.de,
heiko.hamann@uni-konstanz.de
[2] Centre for the Advanced Study of Collective Behaviour, University of Konstanz,
Konstanz, Germany

Multi-agent systems often require the formation of subgroups of varying sizes to solve their assigned task in dynamic environments. Inspired by fission−fusion processes [1], we propose a decentralized controller that enables agents to autonomously regulate group membership (Fig. 1). We also propose an algorithm for precisely estimating group size based on gossiping, which relies on an information diffusion process. While the diffused content (component-wise minima extrema propagation [2]) is an engineering choice for precision, we have adapted this approach for swarms: we changed it from a static estimation tool into a time-continuous, sliding-window sensing mechanism. This allows agents to dynamically track group size G_E online.

Our controller's probabilistic decision-making process is based on the subjective group-size preference G^* as the desired group size. The controller's minimal behavior is a following behavior, constrained by a follow probability P and a follow range r. Our controller implements four state transitions: random walk, fusion, fission, and stay. By executing finite state transitions, it enables the agent to switch between groups. We use each potential target agent's group size G_T as reference information. Before deciding whether to follow a given potential target, we compare G_T with G^*; if $G_T \geq G^*$, we abandon that target. Based on how frequently this comparison is performed during the decision-making process, we have designed three communication sub-modes with different information requirements and message complexities: positional signaling (no target agent's size information or comparison), group-size signaling with one-shot decision (a single comparison), and group-size signaling with continuous decision (repeated comparisons over time). When an agent's group size is smaller than its desired size, it waits for a time T that is linearly proportional to the current group size.

We simulate $N = 42$ robots in a $20\ m \times 20\ m$ arena using ARGoS [3] (see Fig. 1). The system is tasked to form three groups of size 14 each. Initially, many groups form; subsequently, they dissolve, and larger groups emerge. As shown in the group-size evolution plot, the fourth-largest group gradually declines and eventually disappears as agents continuously regroup. After about 100 s, the system stabilizes into three groups, each reaching the desired size of 14. We present

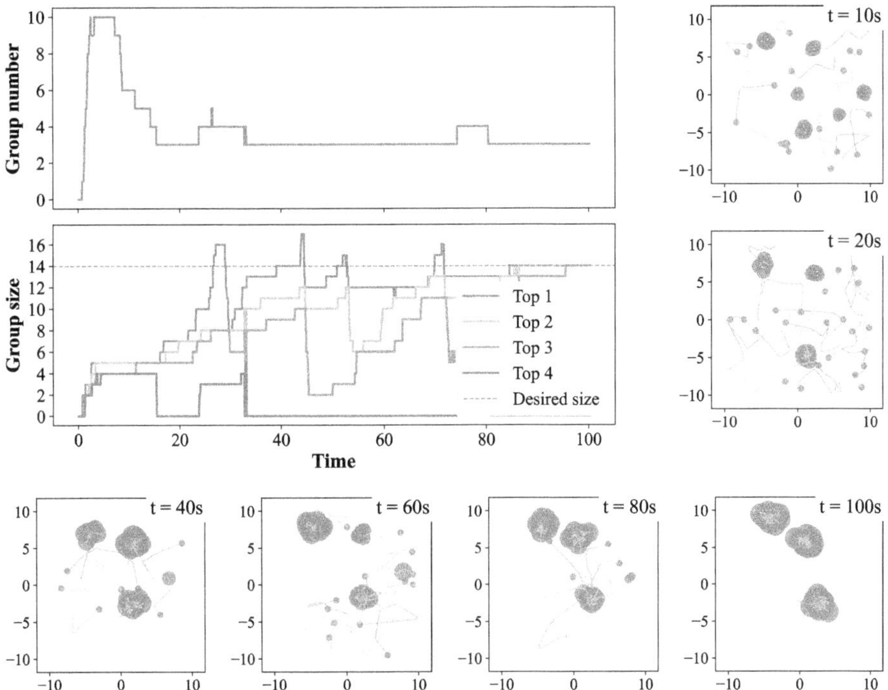

Fig. 1. Swarm behavior evolution in the 20 m × 20 m ARGoS simulation with $N = 42$ robots. (a) Size and number of groups over time. (b) Spatial distribution and group evolution over time. Blue dots represent agents, with dot size giving each agent's group size estimate.

snapshots showing agent trajectories. Agents are initially dispersed. They gradually aggregate and decide based on group sizes, leading to multiple fission/fusion events. The system converges to the desired configuration.

Disclosure of Interests. The authors have no competing interests to declare.

References

1. Aureli, F., et al.: Fission-fusion dynamics: new research frameworks. Curr. Anthropol. **49**(4), 627–654 (2008)
2. Baquero, C., Almeida, P.S., Menezes, R., Jesus, P.: Extrema propagation: fast distributed estimation of sums and network sizes. IEEE Trans. Parallel Distrib. Syst. **23**(4), 668–675 (2011)
3. Pinciroli, C., et al.: Argos: a modular, parallel, multi-engine simulator for multi-robot systems. Swarm Intell. **6**(4), 271–295 (2012)

Grid-Based Complete Resource Foraging for Robot Swarms

Arturo Gonzalez[iD] and Qi Lu[✉][iD]

Department of Computer Science, The University of Texas Rio Grande Valley,
Edinburg, TX, USA
qi.lu@utrgv.edu

The foraging task involves searching for resources (e.g., minerals or survivors) collectively in a large, unknown arena and delivering them to a specified location. Existing work demonstrates that resource intake rates are efficient when the density of resources is high [1, 4]. The results in [2] indicate that swarms foraging with the Central Place Foraging Algorithm (CPFA) [3] spend between 63% and 75% of their time collecting the last 12% resources. A complete collection of resources is crucial in various real-world applications. We proposed the grid-based complete foraging algorithm (GCFA) to improve the performance of the complete resource collection.

We assume that each robot maintains a local FIFO queue with a maximum capacity of 20 locations. It adds a location to the queue every 25 s to capture a general snapshot of its path when searching. Robots can not communicate directly. When a robot returns to the central collection zone, it shares this data with the server and accesses the shared data in the server. When robots leave the central server, they make decisions on their own. We create a $n \times n$ grid for the search arena based on the size of the arena and the memory capacity of the server. Robots deliver resources and share visited locations with the central server when they return to the server. Each cell has a counter (weight) (see Fig. 1a). If a visited location is in a cell, the counter increases by one. Therefore, the server does not need to remember all reported locations. 2) When a robot returns to the center, the server identifies a block 3×3 of cells with the minimum cumulative count of visits. To ensure complete local coverage, the robot picks a random location in each and visits these 9 cells in a fixed counter-clockwise search order (see Fig. 1c). When the robot reaches a random location in each cell, it runs a spiral search. If it completes the search of all 9 cells and has not found a resource, it performs a correlated random walk.

Figure 2 visualizes the foraging performance with different distributions of resources and numbers of resources. It shows that the CPFA takes longer to complete the foraging task. The GCFA has a more linear relationship between resource count and collection time. The GCFA significantly outperforms the CPFA with high exploration requirements. Furthermore, GCFA can alleviate exponential growth in time in the last 20% of resources, increasing efficiency by over 48% during this final collection phase. Robustness evaluation also confirmed that the benefits of our grid-based approach increase with arena size.

The running time to select a region for an uninformed search is $O(n^2)$, where n is the number of cells. Specifically, sorting cells by visit count requires $O(n^2)$

R. Groß et al. (Eds.): ANTS 2026, LNCS 16515, pp. 488–489, 2026.
https://doi.org/10.1007/978-3-032-26123-6

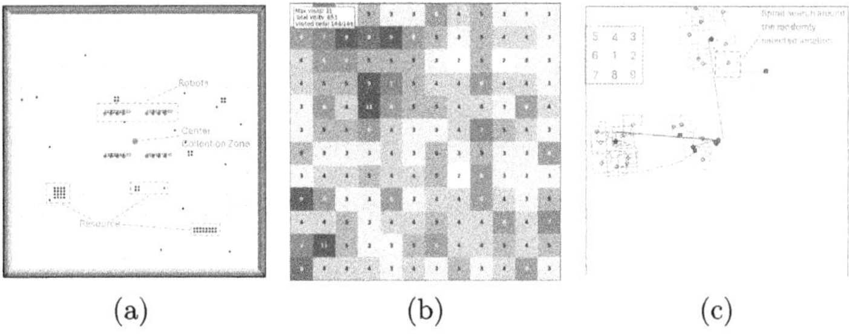

(a)   (b)   (c)

Fig. 1. (a) The ARGoS simulation; (b) The counts of visits in each cell for the 12×12 meter arena; (c) The search pattern in selected regions

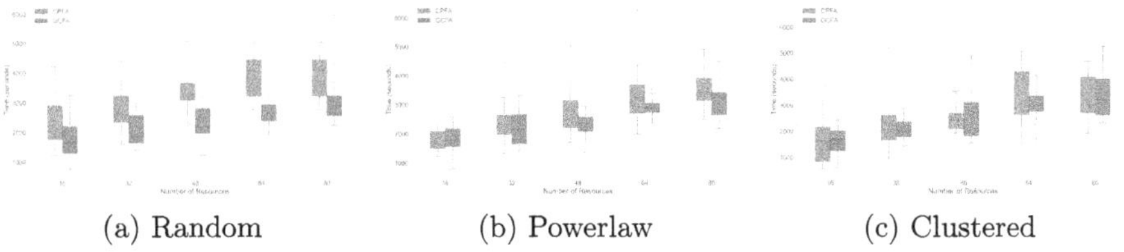

(a) Random   (b) Powerlaw   (c) Clustered

Fig. 2. The time to complete the collection in three resource distributions

time, which dominates the overall computation. The number of cells, therefore, affects both the foraging performance and the running time. A larger n results in smaller cell sizes and a greater number of unvisited cells, which can improve the foraging efficiency. However, increasing n also leads to a higher computational cost. The findings will benefit other stochastic search strategies for robots with limited resources and capabilities.

Disclosure of Interests. The authors have no competing interests to declare.

References

1. Fricke, G.M., Joshua, P.H., Antonio, D.G., Linh, T.T., Melanie, E.M.: A distributed deterministic spiral search algorithm for swarms. In: 2016 IEEE/RSJ International Conference on Intelligent Robots and Systems (IROS), pp. 4430–4436 (2016)
2. Hecker, J.P., Carmichael, J.C., Moses, M.E.: Exploiting clusters for complete resource collection in biologically-inspired robot swarms. In: 2015 IEEE/RSJ International Conference on Intelligent Robots and Systems (IROS), pp. 434–440 (2015)
3. Hecker, J.P., Moses, M.E.: Beyond pheromones: evolving error-tolerant, flexible, and scalable ant-inspired robot swarms. Swarm Intell. **9**(1), 43–70 (2015). https://doi. org/10.1007/s11721-015-0104-z
4. Lu, Q., Hecker, J.P., Moses, M.E.: The MPFA: a multiple-place foraging algorithm for biologically-inspired robot swarms. In: 2016 IEEE/RSJ International Conference on Intelligent Robots and Systems (IROS), pp. 3815–3821 (2016)

Knowledge Distillation for Developing Versatile Controllers of Robotic Swarms

Asad Razzaq[1] and Toshiyuki Yasuda[2]($\boxtimes$)

[1] Faculty of Engineering, Kyoto University of Advanced Science, Kyoto, Japan
asad9731@gmail.com
[2] Faculty of Engineering, University of Toyama, Toyama, Japan
yasuda@eng.u-toyama.ac.jp

Swarm robotic systems (SRS) are systems that utilize multiple relatively simple autonomous robots to generate emergent collective behavior from the interactions between individual robots [3]. One method for constructing the control system in SRS is evolutionary robotics (ER) [1]. Most existing research that employs the ER approach in SRS focuses on simple environments and does not address environments with multiple task types.

To overcome this specialization gap and enhance controller versatility, this study proposes a transfer learning framework based on knowledge distillation (KD). KD is a technique conventionally used in deep learning to transfer generalized knowledge from a large, complex teacher model to a smaller, more efficient student model [2]. In our adaptation, we prepare the same number of teacher models as the number of subtasks performed by the SRS, with each teacher model trained on one subtask. All the information from these teacher models is integrated into a single student model. Additionally, we aim to reduce performance disparities by adjusting the data volume according to the learning difficulty of each task. We define the data increase ratio $R_i = P \times \frac{A_{\max}}{A_i}$ based on the accuracy of the i-th teacher model, A_i $(i = 1, \ldots, N_{\text{Task}})$, where N_{Task} is the number of tasks, $A^i_{\max}$ is the accuracy of the i-th model with the highest accuracy, and P is the ratio coefficient,

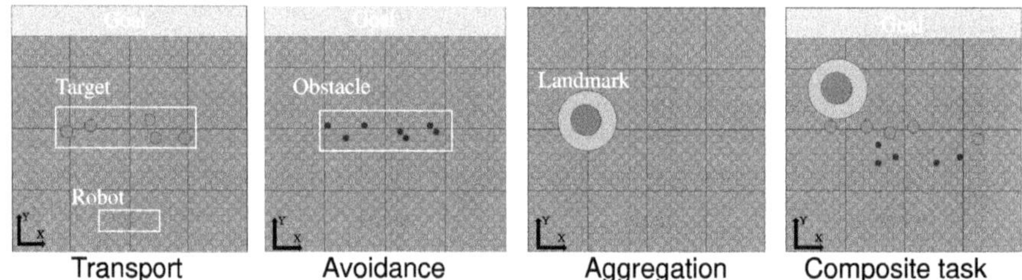

Transport   Avoidance   Aggregation   Composite task

Fig. 1. Experimental environments for individual and composite tasks

In our simulated experiments, three types of tasks: transport, avoidance, and aggregation, as well as a composite task that includes all of them in a 40-meter square field, as shown in Fig. 1, are performed. The robot is equipped with a

R. Groß et al. (Eds.): ANTS 2026, LNCS 16515, pp. 490–491, 2026.
https://doi.org/10.1007/978-3-032-26123-6

Table 1. Teacher model accuracy and increase rate R.

Model	Accuracy	$P = 0.5$	$P = 1.0$	$P = 2.0$
Transport-teacher	0.195	1.35	2.70	5.40
Avoidance-teacher	$0.527\ (= A^{\mathrm{Avoid}}_{\max})$	1	1	1
Aggregation-teacher	0.230	1.15	2.30	4.60

camera and a distance sensor, both mounted on the front. The camera has a range of $4\,\mathrm{m}$ and provides an image with a resolution of 64×64 pixels. The field of view of the camera is $60°$, and objects in the camera's view are identified based on their color. In addition to the camera, the robot also has a distance sensor with a detection range of $4\,\mathrm{m}$. The robot moves using a differential drive system with left and right driving wheels, allowing for precise control of its movement. The robot has a controller represented by an artificial neural network (ANN). The input layer of the ANN receives inputs from the camera sensor and 2 inputs representing the relative angle from the robot's initial position. The hidden layer has neurons and features a recurrent connection configuration, including recurrent connections for all nodes. The output layer outputs the target rotational speeds of the left and right motors.

The fitness of the teacher and student models is evaluated. The teacher model is trained for each specific task by using evolution strategies algorithm, while the ER model is created under the same experimental settings as the teacher model for the composite task. The student model integrates the teacher model using KD. Table 1 shows that the learning accuracy was highest for the avoidance teacher model, followed by the aggregation teacher model, and then the transportteacher model. The accuracies of the student models for $P = 0.0, 0.5, 1.0, 2.0$ are 0.807, 0.812, 0.827, 0.836, respectively. The task performance depends on the task executed. For example, the fitness in the avoidance task was highest for the student model with $P = 2.0$, followed by the avoidance teacher model, the aggregation teacher model, and the student models with $P = 1.0$ and 0.5, in descending order.

Acknowledgments. This work was supported by JSPS KAKENHI Grant Number 25K15286.

Disclosure of Interests. The authors have no competing interests to declare.

References

1. Floreano, D., Husbands, P., Nolfi, S.: Evolutionary robotics. In: Siciliano, B., Khatib, O. (eds.)Springer Handbook of Robotics, pp. 1423–1451. Springer, Heidelberg (2008). https://doi.org/10.1007/978-3-540-30301-5_62
2. Hinton, G.E., Vinyals, O., Dean, J.: Distilling the knowledge in a neural network. CoRR **abs/1503.02531** (2015). https://arxiv.org/abs/1503.02531
3. Şahin, E.: Swarm robotics: from sources of inspiration to domains of application. In: Şahin, E., Spears, W.M. (eds.) SR 2004 LNCS, vol. 3342, pp. 10–20. Springer, Heidelberg (2005). https://doi.org/10.1007/978-3-540-30552-1_2

MagBotSim: Physics-Based Simulation and Reinforcement Learning Environments for Magnetic Robotics

Lara Bergmann[1]([✉])[iD], Cedric Grothues[1][iD], and Klaus Neumann[1,2][iD]

[1] CITEC, Bielefeld University, Bielefeld, Germany
{lara.bergmann,cedric.grothues,klaus.neumann}@uni-bielefeld.de
[2] Fraunhofer IOSB-INA, Lemgo, Germany

Magnetic levitation (MagLev) is about to revolutionize in-machine material flow and individualized product transport in manufacturing systems due to additional degrees of freedom (DoF), high configurability, and flexibility. These MagLev systems consist of two basic components, as shown in Fig. 1. Firstly, dynamically actuated shuttles, so-called *movers*, consist of a complex permanent magnet structure based on Halbach arrays [2]. Secondly, static motor modules, so-called *tiles*, enable coil-induced emission of electromagnetic fields that interact with the mover's field. During operation, the movers hover above the tiles and can be controlled in six dimensions. MagLev systems can contain a large number of independently actuated movers that dynamically rebalance production capacity. Beyond their capabilities for dynamic transportation, these systems possess the inherent yet unexploited potential to perform manipulation. By merging the fields of transportation and manipulation into a coordinated swarm of magnetic robots (MagBots), we enable manufacturing systems to achieve significantly higher efficiency, adaptability, and compactness. Therefore, MagLev systems are a special kind of robot, and we introduce the more general term *Magnetic Robotics*.

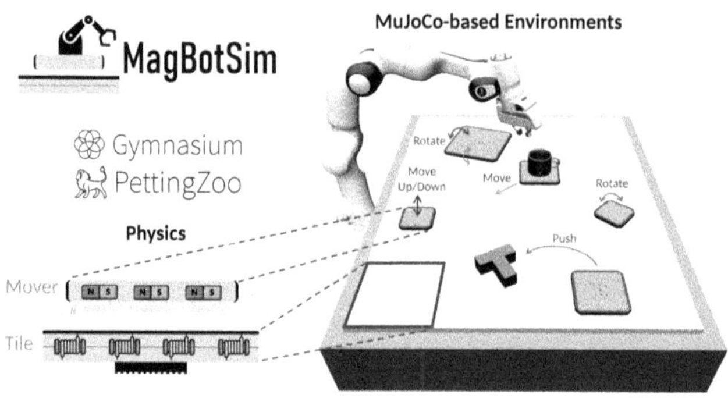

Fig. 1. Schematic overview of the proposed MagBotSim library, a physics-based simulation for *Magnetic Robotics* that includes reinforcement learning environments.

Developing motion planning algorithms for *Magnetic Robotics* requires a physics-based simulation, as MagLev systems are scalable and reconfigurable, and can be modeled as coordinated multi-agent systems. Simulations can help to shift computational load into the offline phase, reducing computation time during motion. Additionally, simulations are typically employed to accelerate training and evaluation of reinforcement learning (RL) agents. Existing proprietary simulations focus on system-specific control rather than algorithm development, leaving a gap for system-agnostic, RL-compatible tools. In this paper, we present *MagBotSim* (*Magnetic Robotics Simulation*), a physics-based simulation and RL environments for motion planning and object manipulation with MagLev systems. MagBotSim is based on MuJoCo [5], supports transfer of learned policies to real systems, runs on a laptop CPU, and includes benchmarks to compare motion planning approaches. Although MagBotSim can also be used without RL API, it is compatible with common single-agent (Gymnasium [6]) and multi-agent (PettingZoo [4]) RL APIs, as well as RL libraries, e.g. StableBaselines3 [3] or TorchRL [1]. Furthermore, MagBotSim can be installed via PIP, includes tutorials and example environments, and provides utilities, such as mover impedance control. Thus, MagBotSim is a unique starting point for the development, application, and evaluation of intelligent motion planning and manipulation capabilities that transform Magnetic Levitation to *Magnetic Robotics*. MagBotSim's documentation, videos, and code are available at: https://ubi-coro.github.io/MagBotSim/

Disclosure of Interests. The authors have no competing interests to declare.

References

1. Bou, A., et al.: TorchRL: a data-driven decision-making library for PyTorch (2023). https://doi.org/10.48550/ARXIV.2306.00577
2. Lu, X., Usman, I.U.R.: 6D direct-drive technology for planar motion stages. CIRP Annal. **61**(1), 359–362 (2012). https://doi.org/10.1016/j.cirp.2012.03.145
3. Raffin, A., Hill, A., Gleave, A., Kanervisto, A., Ernestus, M., Dormann, N.: StableBaselines3: reliable reinforcement learning implementations. J. Mach. Learn. Res. **22**(268), 1–8 (2021)
4. Terry, J., et al.: PettingZoo: gym for multi-agent reinforcement learning. In: Advances in Neural Information Processing Systems. vol. 34, pp. 15032–15043. Curran Associates, Inc. (2021)
5. Todorov, E., Erez, T., Tassa, Y.: MuJoCo: A physics engine for model-based control. In: Proceedings of the IEEE/RSJ International Conference on Intelligent Robots and Systems (IROS), pp. 5026–5033. IEEE (2012). https://doi.org/10.1109/IROS.2012.6386109
6. Towers, M., et al.: Gymnasium: a standard interface for reinforcement learning environments (2024). https://doi.org/10.48550/ARXIV.2407.17032

Minimizing Uncertainty as a Principle for Task Allocation in Robot Swarms

Yannick Wesseloh[1], Paolo Leopardi[1,2], Jonas Kuckling[1,2,3],
and Heiko Hamann[1,2(✉)]

[1] University of Konstanz, Konstanz, Germany
Heiko.Hamann@uni-konstanz.de
[2] Center for the Advanced Study of Collective Behaviour, University of Konstanz,
Konstanz, Germany
[3] Zukunftskolleg, University of Konstanz, Konstanz, Germany

As swarms are deployed in increasingly unstructured and dynamic environments, uncertainty becomes a central design challenge: sensing is noisy, communication is intermittent, and local decisions must remain robust under incomplete information. Recent research has shown that focusing too much on swarm performance can result in fragile systems. Instead, we should push for robustness by declaring uncertainty minimization a design objective.

In this work, we study how minimizing uncertainty can increase robustness in a variant of a sequentially interdependent task allocation scenario [1]. We consider a foraging task that consists of two subtasks: harvesting and storing. The subtasks are spatially adjacent and sequentially interdependent. Located between the two subtasks is the *task interface*, where robots from both subtasks can exchange items. The robot swarm is expected to maximize the number of stored objects by optimally allocating robots to both subtasks. Robots are allowed to switch subtasks within the task interface, but task switching incurs a performance cost of c_s, implemented as a waiting time.

We extend the original scenario [1] by introducing a probabilistic harvesting time and two harvesting strategies. Harvesters can choose a safe harvesting strategy ψ_s, that results in reliable harvesting times (normal distribution with $\mu = 50$, $\sigma = 5$), or a risky harvesting strategy ψ_r (multi-modal distribution with $\mu_1 = 20$, $\mu_2 = 100$, $\mu_3 = 200$), that promises faster harvesting times ($\mu_{\psi_r} = 41\text{s} < 50\text{s} = \mu_{\psi_h}$) but poses the risk of rarely experiencing much longer harvesting times ($\sigma_{\psi_r} = 47.95 > 5 = \sigma_{\psi_h}$). Robots can switch their harvesting strategy at no cost after having finished harvesting an object at the source.

We consider the *time-minimizing* (TM; robots switch based on mean completion time) and the *uncertainty-minimizing* (UM; robots switch based on standard deviation of completion time) approach. Robots calculate their *switching probability* by a sigmoid function using their respective difference in believes δ. To assess the quality of alternative harvesting strategies, harvester broadcast their experienced harvesting times. For task switching, robots can assess the alternative task by estimating completion times based on their own waiting times at the task interface. We simulate the experiments using the ARGoS simulator [3] and a swarm of 12 foot-bot robots [2]. More details and source code on GitHub: https://github.com/StudentWorkCPS/foraging-task-allocation.git.

We see that robots with either method quickly approach an optimal subtask allocation. UM employs mostly safe harvesters, as expected. In contrast, TM has a median allocation of safe harvesters that stabilizes with slightly more risky than safe harvesters. Robots exhibit a higher subtask-switching rate at the beginning of the experiment, when the allocation is most unbalanced. Once the allocation is more balanced, δ decreases, and robots switch tasks less frequently.

In terms of strategy switches, we see significant differences between the two methods. UM has a higher rate of strategy switches early in the experiment, but this rate decreases to zero over the course of the experiment, and most robots choose the safe harvesting strategy. TM has a constant rate of strategy switches throughout the whole experiment. Risky harvesters occasionally experience longer-than-expected waiting times, causing them to switch to the safe strategy and revert back due to the lower mean waiting time.

Finally, we compare the performance of UM and TM. Both approaches perform similarly (medians: 299.5 for TM and 298.0 for UM). The performance spread of TM is wider, indicating greater variance in performance. Due to the initial adaptation phase, both approaches perform worse than the experimentally determined maximum performance $P_{max_N} = 365$. Our results show that both the uncertainty-minimizing and time-minimizing approaches are effective, achieve similar performance, and rapidly drive the swarm toward a near-optimal task allocation. However, the uncertainty-minimizing swarm achieves a more stable allocation and reduces unnecessary strategy switches, making it a better choice for scenarios where a more conservative swarm behavior is expected.

Acknowledgments. PL, JK, and HH acknowledge support from DFG through Germany's Excellence Strategy-EXC 2117-422037984 and Centre for the Advanced Study of Collective Behaviour (CASCB), University of Konstanz, Konstanz, Germany. JK acknowledges support from the Zukunftskolleg and the Carl-Zeiss-Foundation.

Disclosure of Interests. The authors have no competing interests to declare.

References

1. Brutschy, A., Pini, G., Pinciroli, C., Birattari, M., Dorigo, M.: Self-organized task allocation to sequentially interdependent tasks in swarm robotics. Auton. Agent. Multi-Agent Syst. **28**(1), 101–125 (2014). https://doi.org/10.1007/s10458-012-9212-y
2. Dorigo, M., et al.: Swarmanoid: a novel concept for the study of heterogeneous robotic swarms. IEEE Robot. Autom. Mag. (2012). https://doi.org/10.1109/MRA.2013.2252996
3. Pinciroli, C., et al.: ARGoS: a modular, parallel, multi-engine simulator for multi-robot systems. Swarm Intel. (2012). https://doi.org/10.1007/s11721-012-0072-5

SonoRo: A Swarm Robotics Platform to Study Acoustically-Driven Collective Behaviour

Alberto Doimo[1,2,3]($\boxtimes$) (iD), Heiko Hamann[2,4] (iD), Andreagiovanni Reina[2,3,4] (iD), and Thejasvi Beleyur[1,2,3] (iD)

[1] Active Sensing Collectives Lab, Department of Biology, University of Konstanz, Konstanz, Germany
[2] Centre for the Advanced Study of Collective Behaviour, University of Konstanz, Konstanz, Germany
[3] Department of Collective Behaviour, Max Planck Institute of Animal Behavior, Konstanz, Germany
[4] Department of Computer and Information Science, University of Konstanz, Konstanz, Germany
{alberto.doimo,heiko.hamann,andreagiovanni.reina,
thejasvi.beleyur}@uni-konstanz.de

Acoustic signals play a significant role in swarm coordination among animals, enabling individuals to interact and organise collectively. Many acoustically mediated animal collectives (bat swarms, bird flocks, frog and insect choruses) are naturally tolerant, and even robust, to temporal and spectral overlap [2]. In contrast, mobile robotics has mainly relied on specialised hardware such as cameras or radio transceivers that are simultaneously computationally and data intensive.

The SonoRo swarm robotics platform is focussed on developing sound-based coordination without the need for explicit spectral or temporal partitioning and investigates how agents can interpret the complex sounds in groups to show collective behaviour. We designed and implemented SonoRo by combining off-the-shelf, low-cost hardware components and open-source lightweight software, suitable for onboard applications on small, mobile robots. We use the Thymio II robot as a mobile base equipped with a Raspberry Pi 4B, an array of microphones, and a speaker. This setup allows compatibility with Python and enables SonoRo to interact with other agents by alternating the emission of a chirp with a listening phase. During the listening phase, the robot records the incoming audio, which is used to calculate the Direction of Arrival (DoA) using the Delay-And-Sum algorithm. The DoA algorithm returns an egocentric distribution of the sound source directions over the azimuth.

We showcase SonoRo's basic capabilities in environmental awareness, neighbour detection, and spatial target localisation through experiments in four distinct scenarios: collision avoidance with static sound sources, goal finding in a static environment, multirobot aggregation, and multirobot dispersion. Results are discussed in Fig. 1. Videos of all experiments are available at [3]. Our results with three robots demonstrate reliable collective behaviours in aggregation and dispersion tasks, indicating that SonoRo is a promising platform

R. Groß et al. (Eds.): ANTS 2026, LNCS 16515, pp. 496–497, 2026.
https://doi.org/10.1007/978-3-032-26123-6

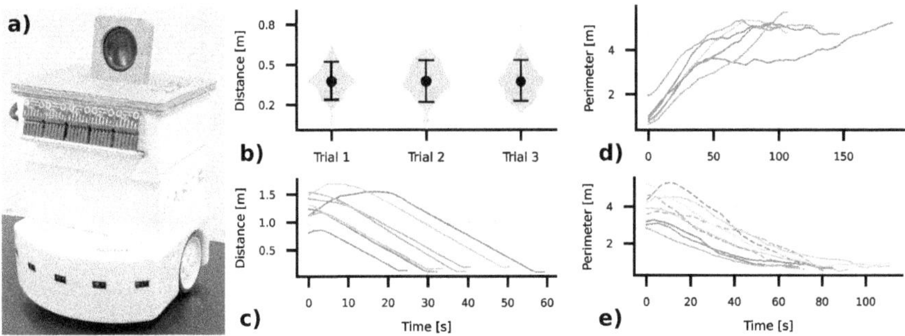

Fig. 1. (a) The SonoRo robot. (b) Results from a single SonoRo performing sound obstacle avoidance. The violin plots quantify performance as the distance to the nearest loudspeaker, showing with the mean value as a black dot and the 10th and 90th percentiles as whiskers. (c) Results from a single SonoRo reaching a loudspeaker goal are shown as the distance between the centre of the robot and the loudspeaker. (d-e) Results from three robots dispersing (panel d) and aggregating (panel e) in space are shown as the perimeter of the convex polygon connecting the three robots.

for swarm robotics research. Unlike other previous sound-based approaches to swarm robotics [1, 4], our novel contribution lies in demonstrating attraction and repulsion using acoustic signals without any form of temporal or spectral partitioning. The robustness to temporal overlap caused by the homogeneous nature of the swarm is a novel feature that allows on-the-fly scaling of group size. Our study indicates that acoustic signalling provides a fast and low-cost coordination modality for robot swarms, particularly useful in challenging conditions such as GPS-denied, low-light, or visually cluttered environments.

Acknowledgments. We acknowledge funding from the Carl-Zeiss-Stiftung, the Deutsche Forschungsgemeinschaft (DFG) under Germany's Excellence Strategy – EXC 2117-422037984, and the DFG's Walter Benjamin program - 502056951.

Disclosure of Interests. The authors have no competing interests to declare.

References

1. Basiri, M., Schill, F., Lima, P., Floreano, D.: On-board relative bearing estimation for teams of drones using sound. IEEE Robot. Autom. Lett. **1**(2), 820–827 (2016)
2. Bee, M.A., Micheyl, C.: The cocktail party problem: what is it? How can it be solved? And why should animal behaviorists study it? J. Comp. Psychol. **122**(3), 235–251 (2008)
3. Doimo, A.: SonoRo: a swarm robotics platform to study acoustically driven collectives behaviour (2025). https://doi.org/10.5281/zenodo.17664282
4. Tsunoda, Y., Nghia, L.T., Sueoka, Y., Osuka, K.: Experimental analysis of shepherding-type robot navigation utilizing sound-obstacle-interaction. J. Robot. Mechatron. **35**(4), 957–968 (2023)

Swarm Vs. Swarm Behaviour via Multi-Objective Multi-Agent Reinforcement Learning

Sune S. Nielsen[1]($\boxtimes$), Negin Mohammadi[1], Tanaz Ghahremani[1], and Grégoire Danoy[1,2]

[1] SnT, University of Luxembourg, Luxembourg, Luxembourg
sune.nielsen@uni.lu, negin.mohammadi.001@student.uni.lu,
tanaz.ghahremani.001@student.uni.lu
[2] FSTM/DCS, University of Luxembourg, Esch-sur-Alzette, Luxembourg
gregoire.danoy@uni.lu

Efficiently training large swarms of AI agents under multiple, often conflicting objectives remains a central and increasingly significant challenge in swarm intelligence. Even when user preferences are known a priori, translating them into scalarisation weights is non-trivial, as the impact of weights on the resulting policy and trade-offs is difficult to predict. Therefore, multi-objective reinforcement learning (RL) algorithms typically approximate a diverse set of Pareto-optimal policies, enabling informed preference-driven selection a posteriori. In this work, we introduce a GPU accelerated multi-objective multi-agent RL (MOMARL) [2]) framework that achieves a posteriori MO preference interpolation while relying on a single trained policy. Agents are trained on Boids [3] inspired interaction rules and are organised into two teams, with the ability to distinguish between teammates and adversaries. This design supports large-scale swarm-versus-swarm [1] scenarios, such as pursuitevasion games, and enables the systematic study of competitive and cooperative multi-objective behaviours.

In RL, agents learn through trial-and-error interactions with an environment by optimising a policy to maximise cumulative rewards. The environment is modelled as a partially observable Markov Decision Process (MDP) $\mathcal{M}_{POMDP} = (\mathcal{S}, \mathcal{A}, T, R, \mathcal{O}, Z)$. Here $\mathcal{S}$ and $\mathcal{O}$ describe the global state space and observation state space while $\mathcal{A}$ is the agent action space. The functions T, R and Z define state transition, reward and partial observation in a given state. In our setting, states are agent positions and movement directions, while observations are local directions of other agents.

We extend the well known Proximal Policy Optimization (PPO) [4] algorithm to evaluate an agent action a_t^i as $\pi_\theta(a_t^i|(o_t^i, w_t^i))$ by appending objective preference w_t^i to observations o_t^i of agents. The preferences are adjusted during training, and a replay buffer is used to retain diverse high-quality behaviours and associated trade-offs. Figure 1(a) shows correlations between preference weights and resulting objectives ranging from 0.32 to 0.78, demonstrating effective preference conditioning. Figure 1(b) shows reactions to a sudden switch in retreat and intercept roles. Experiments on HPC [5] with a Xeon Gold 6132 CPU @

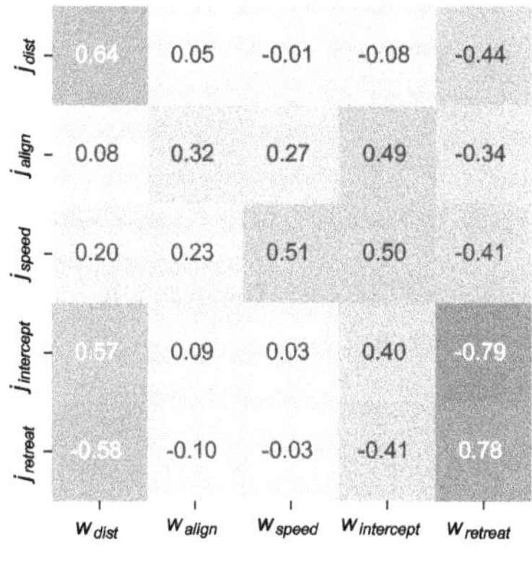

(a) MO preference response

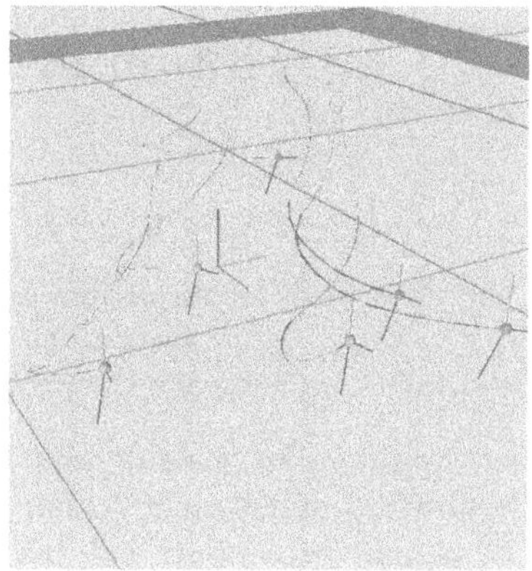

(b) 20 steps after switching

Fig. 1. Agent response to change in multi-objective preference weights.

2.6 GHz and NVIDIA Tesla V100 SXM2 GPU achieve over 218 steps/s for policy inference and swarm simulation combined.

In summary we have introduced a multi-agent framework for learning multi-objective behaviour in a swarm vs. swarm scenario. Our work shows that 1) a single policy can accommodate and interpolate between multiple, potentially conflicting objectives 2) a replay buffer is essential for learning and retaining all objectives and their trade-offs, and 3) our scalable GPU vectorised environment allows fast training and simulation of large swarms in real time.

Disclosure of Interests. The authors have no competing interests to declare.

References

1. Brust, M.R., Danoy, G., Stolfi, D.H., Bouvry, P.: Swarm-based counter UAV defense system. Discov. Internet Things **1**(1), 2 (2021)
2. Rădulescu, R., Mannion, P., Roijers, D.M., Nowé, A.: Multi-objective multi-agent decision making: a utility-based analysis and survey. Auton. Agent. Multi-Agent Syst. **34**(1), 10 (2020)
3. Reynolds, C.W.: Flocks, herds and schools: a distributed behavioral model. In: Proceedings of the 14th Annual Conference on Computer Graphics and Interactive Techniques, pp. 25–34 (1987)
4. Schulman, J., Wolski, F., Dhariwal, P., Radford, A., Klimov, O.: Proximal policy optimization algorithms (2017). https://arxiv.org/abs/1707.06347
5. Varrette, S., Cartiaux, H., Peter, S., Kieffer, E., Valette, T., Olloh, A.: Management of an academic HPC & research computing facility: The ULHPC experience 2.0. In: Proceedings of the 2022 6th High Performance Computing and Cluster Technologies Conference, pp. 14–24 (2022)

Trust and Perception of Robot Swarm Motion in Remote Contexts

Yue Cao[1], Razanne Abu-Aisheh[1(✉)], Shyamli Suneesh[2], and Sabine Hauert[1]

[1] Bristol Robotics Laboratory, University of Bristol, Bristol, UK
`razanne.abu-aisheh@bristol.ac.uk`
[2] School of Computing and Communications, Lancaster University, Lancaster, UK

Robot swarms offer scalable and adaptable solutions for various applications. Yet real-world deployment remains limited, partly due to gaps in understanding of human perception and trust. In our prior in-person study [1], participants physically interacted with a swarm cloakroom exhibiting two motion styles and reported similar trust levels across both. However, each participant experienced only one motion type in person with researchers present, leaving open how perceptions might differ when observing swarms remotely or comparing motion patterns directly. To address this, we conducted a video-based within-subjects study where online participants viewed recordings from the previous cloakroom study [1]. The videos featured three DOTS [2] robots performing identical deposit, storage, and retrieval tasks with either structured (grid-like) or organic (reactive) motion. Videos were matched for content, timing, and visuals, differing only in motion style as shown in Fig. 1. Order was randomised, and participants were unaware of the manipulation. After each video, participants completed the Trust in Automation (TiA) questionnaire [3] and provided open-ended feedback. Ethical approval was granted (Ref. 17590), and all participants gave informed consent.

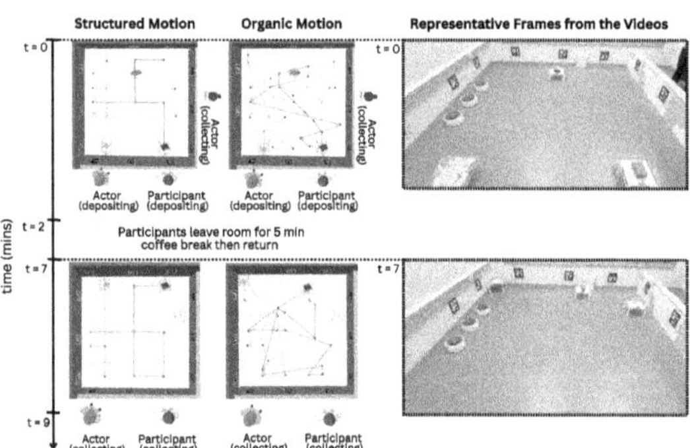

Fig. 1. Study design comparing structured and organic swarm motion. Coloured lines show robot trajectories. Representative frames of starting positions shown.

Y. Cao and R. Abu-Aisheh—These authors contributed equally to this work as co-first authors.

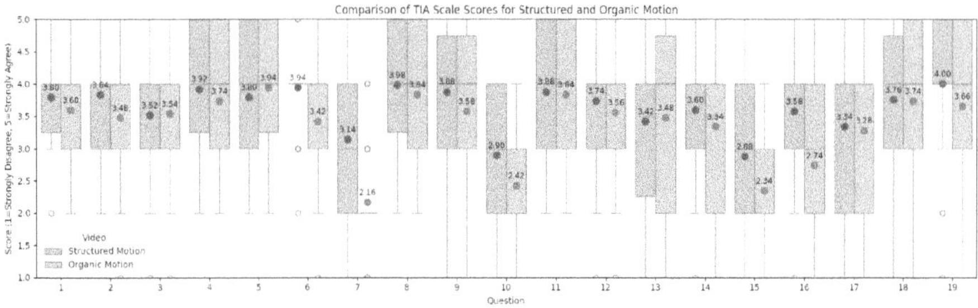

Fig. 2. Comparison of Trust in Automation (TiA) scores across motion styles. Box-plots indicate the median, interquartile range, and extremes on a 5-point Likert scale (1 = Strongly Disagree, 5 = Strongly Agree). TiA Questions: [1/6/10/13/15/19: reliability/competence, 2/7/11/16: understanding/predictability, 3/17: familiarity, 4/8: intention of developers, 5/12/18: propensity to trust, 9/14: trust in automation]

We analysed 49 valid responses (ages 19–57, mean $\approx$ 27) from a technically experienced, geographically diverse sample. TiA scores differed by motion type, with **Structured Motion** rated higher than Organic Motion (Fig. 2). Paired tests showed a modest but significant increase in overall trust for Structured Motion ($p = 0.03$, $d = 0.32$), driven by stronger effects on **predictability** ($d = 1.10$) and **failure perception** ($d = 0.73$). Familiarity and trust in developers did not differ, indicating motion primarily influenced system predictability. Open-ended responses tied trust to smooth, predictable, goal-directed motion. Structured Motion was seen as clear, reliable, and easy to follow, promoting comfort and confidence, while Organic Motion felt less predictable. Overall, across both in-person and remote settings, trust scores in the swarm were high for both motion styles; however, in the remote setting structured motion elicited significantly higher trust.

Disclosure of Interests. The authors have no competing interests to declare.

References

1. Abu-Aisheh, R., et al.: Towards understanding the impact of swarm motion on human trust. In: 2025 34th IEEE International Conference on Robot and Human Interactive Communication (RO-MAN), pp. 2260–2265. IEEE (2025)
2. Jones, S., Milner, E., Sooriyabandara, M., Hauert, S.: Dots: an open testbed for industrial swarm robotic solutions. arXiv preprint arXiv:2203.13809 (2022)
3. Körber, M.: Theoretical considerations and development of a questionnaire to measure trust in automation. In: Bagnara, S., Tartaglia, R., Albolino, S., Alexander, T., Fujita, Y. (eds.) IEA 2018. AISC, vol. 823, pp. 13–30. Springer, Cham (2019). https://doi.org/10.1007/978-3-319-96074-6_2

Author Index